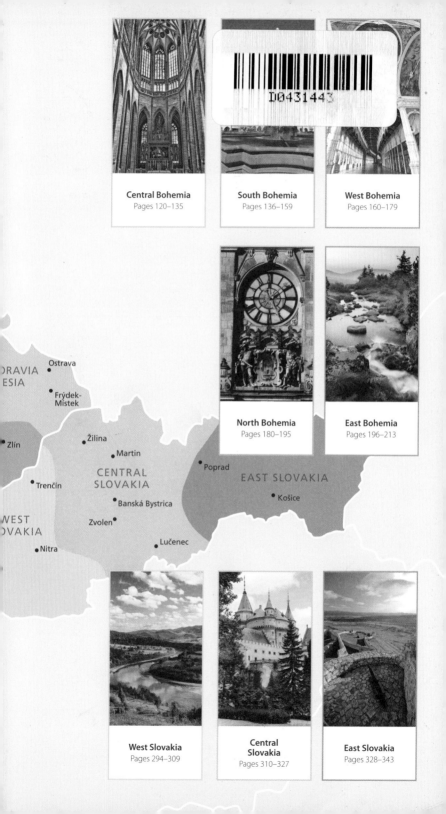

D0431443

MORAVIA
SILESIA

Ostrava
Frýdek-Místek
Zlín
Žilina
Martin
Trenčín
CENTRAL SLOVAKIA
Banská Bystrica
Zvolen
WEST SLOVAKIA
Nitra
Lučenec
Poprad
EAST SLOVAKIA
Košice

EYEWITNESS TRAVEL

CZECH & SLOVAK REPUBLICS

EYEWITNESS TRAVEL

CZECH & SLOVAK REPUBLICS

LONDON, NEW YORK,
MELBOURNE, MUNICH AND DELHI
www.dk.com

Produced by Wiedzę i Życie
Art Editor Paweł Pasternak
Consultant Jan Bosnovič
Graphic Design Paweł Kamiński
DTP Elżbieta Dudzińska
Maps Magdalena Polak

Contributors
Marek Pernal, Tomasz Darmochwał, Marek Rumiński,
Jakub Sito, Barbara Sudnik-Wójcikowska

Photographers
Dorota i Mariusz Jarymowiczowie, Krzysztof Kur, Oldřich Karasek

Illustrators
Michał Burkiewicz, Dorota Jarymowicz, Paweł Marczak

Dorling Kindersley Limited
Translator Magda Hannay
Editors Jane Simmonds, Emily Hatchwell
Senior DTP Designer Jason Little
Production Controller Shane Higgins
Printed and bound in China

First published in Great Britain in 2006
by Dorling Kindersley Limited, 80 Strand, London WC2R 0RL, UK.

15 16 17 18 10 9 8 7 6 5 4 3 2 1

Reprinted with revisions 2009, 2011, 2013, 2015

Copyright © 2006, 2015 Dorling Kindersley Limited, London
A Penguin Random House Company

A CIP catalogue record is available from the British Library.

ISBN 978-1-4093-7142-7

Floors are referred to throughout in accordance with British usage; ie the "First Floor"
is the floor above ground level.

MIX
Paper from
responsible sources
FSC™ C018179
www.fsc.org

**The information in this
DK Eyewitness Travel Guide is checked regularly.**
Every effort has been made to ensure that this book is as up-to-date as possible
at the time of going to press. Some details, however, such as telephone numbers,
opening hours, prices, gallery hanging arrangements and travel information are
liable to change. The publishers cannot accept responsibility for any consequences
arising from the use of this book, nor for any material on third party websites, and
cannot guarantee that any website address in this book will be a suitable source of
travel information. We value the views and suggestions of our readers very highly.
Please write to: Publisher, DK Eyewitness Travel Guides, Dorling Kindersley,
80 Strand, London, WC2R 0RL, UK, or email: travelguides@dk.com.

Front cover main image: The beautiful Český Krumlov town in South Bohemia

◀ The majestic Oravský Castle in Slovakia at sunset

Contents

The impressive façade of St Vitus's Cathedral
in Prague, Czech Republic

Introducing the
Czech Republic

Stained-glass window in the Church of
St Maurice, Olomouc, Czech Republic

The town hall in České Budějovice, South Bohemia

Introducing Slovakia

Slovakia Region by Region

Travellers' Needs

Survival Guide

Interior of the Church of St James in Jičín, East Bohemia

Jindřichův Hradec Castle *(pp146–7)*

HOW TO USE THIS GUIDE

This guide helps you to get the most out of your visit to the Czech and Slovak Republics. The section at the start of each country entitled *Introducing* provides information about that country's geographic location, history and culture. The sections devoted to each capital

and the individual regions describe the major historic sights and tourist attractions, using maps, photographs and illustrations. Information on accommodation and restaurants can be found in *Travellers' Needs*. The *Survival Guide* provides many practical tips.

Prague and Bratislava Area by Area

The guide divides Prague into three areas described in individual sections. Sights outside the centre are dealt with in the *Further Afield* chapter. A chapter is devoted to Bratislava; it ends with the historic sights situated away from the town's centre.

Sights at a Glance lists the sights in an area by category, such as: Streets and Historic Buildings, Museums and Galleries, Places of Worship, Parks and Gardens.

1 Area Map
For easy reference, sights are numbered and located on an area map, as well as on the Prague Street Finder on *pp110–15*.

Colour-coded thumb tabs mark each area.

A locator map shows the area in relation to other parts of the city.

2 Street-by-Street Map
This gives a bird's-eye view of the key areas described in each chapter.

A suggested route for sightseeing is indicated by a red dotted line.

Stars indicate sights that no visitor should miss.

3 Detailed information
All the major sights are described individually. Practical information includes their addresses, telephone numbers, opening hours and whether they charge for admission. The key to the symbols is on the back flap.

1 **Introduction**
This section deals with the landscape, history and character of each region, explaining how it has changed over the centuries and describing its visitor attractions.

Region by Region

The guide divides the Czech Republic outside Prague into seven regions, each given a separate chapter. Slovakia is split into three regions outside Bratislava. The most interesting cities, towns, and other places to visit are numbered on a *Regional Map* at the start of each chapter.

2 **Regional Map**
This map shows the main road network and the overall topography of the region. All the best sights to visit are numbered and there is also information concerning transport.

Story boxes highlight related topics.

Each region of either country can easily be found by its colour coding, shown on the front flap of the book.

3 **Detailed information**
All major cities, towns and tourist attractions are described individually. They are listed in order, following the numbering on the Regional Map. Each entry contains detailed information on important sights.

The Visitors' Checklist gives the practical information you need when planning your visit.

4 **Major Sights**
At least two pages are devoted to each major sight. Historic buildings are dissected to reveal their interiors. Interesting towns or their centres have maps with the principal sights marked on them.

INTRODUCING THE CZECH REPUBLIC

DISCOVERING THE CZECH REPUBLIC

The following itineraries have been designed to take in as many of the Czech Republic's highlights as possible, while keeping long-distance travel manageable. First comes a three-day tour of Prague; an enduringly romantic city packed with historical monuments and cultural diversions. This itinerary can be enjoyed individually or combined with the itinerary that follows; a two-week tour that takes you right through the Czech Republic. Combining natural wonders such as the Krkonoše hills with historic towns, hilltop castles, landscaped parks and culturally vibrant cities, it provides a taste of pretty much everything this varied country has to offer. As a circular tour, it has more than one potential starting point; and it's relatively simple to dip in and out of the tour depending on your interests.

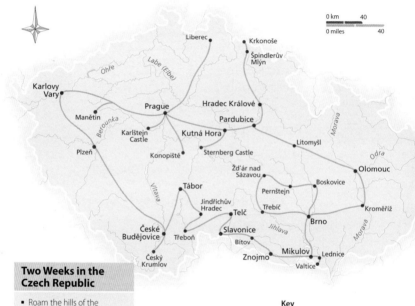

Two Weeks in the Czech Republic

- Roam the hills of the **Krkonoše**, exploring rocky outcrops, deep forests and dramatic waterfalls.

- Indulge in the Czech Republic's famous lager beer at the historic brewing city of **Plzeň**.

- Wander the cobbled alleys of **Český Krumlov**, one of Europe's most evocative medieval towns.

- Enjoy a relaxing city break in **Olomouc**, Moravia's laid-back Baroque pearl.

- Marvel at the neatly arranged skulls and bones on display in the famous ossuary of **Kutná Hora**.

Key

━━ Two weeks in the Czech Republic

Kutná Hora Ossuary
The vast display of bones and skulls in the ossuary at Kutná Hora was created in 1870

◄ The highly decorated façade of the Neo-Renaissance Town Hall in Prachatice, South Bohemia

Three Days in Prague

Prague is home to a unique blend of magical urban skylines and Baroque, Gothic and Art Nouveau architecture. The city centre can be covered on foot and for the sights a bit further away, the tram or metro can be used.

- **Arriving** Ruzyně is 10 km (6 miles) north of the centre and connected by regular bus. The Central Station, to the east of the city centre, is served by express trains from several western European capitals.

Distinct Gothic steeples of the Church of Our Lady before Týn

Day 1
Morning Enter Prague's **Staré Město** *(pp74–5)*, or Old Town, via the landmark **Powder Gate** *(p75)*, proceeding down the famous **Celetná Street** *(p78)* to the multi-steepled **Church of Our Lady before Týn** *(p78)*. Allow time to take in the array of Baroque façades in the **Old Town Square** *(p74)*, before climbing the **Old Town Hall Tower** *(p77)* for great views. Join the crowds on the hour at the Old Town Hall's **Astronomical Clock** *(p77)*, when a mechanical parade of figures accompanies the chimes.

The Gothic Powder Gate at the entrance of the Old Town

Afternoon Follow Pařížská Street north from the square into the heart of Josefov, Prague's former Jewish quarter. Visit the beautifully preserved **Old-New Synagogue** *(pp80–81)* before taking a stroll through the evocative **Old Jewish Cemetery** *(pp82–3)*. Feast on the glorious collection of Czech medieval art at the riverside **Convent of St Agnes** *(p79)* before returning south towards the **Old Town** *(pp74–5)* along bustling Revoluční. Admire the pre-World War I architecture of the **Municipal House** *(pp86–7)* as you walk back to your original starting point, the **Powder Gate** *(p75)*.

Day 2
Morning Cross the statue-studded **Charles Bridge** *(pp70–71)* to the Malá Strana Quarter, before ascending the picturesque **Nerudova Street** *(p65)* to the Hradčany castle district. Take time to visit the Renaissance interiors of **Schwarzenberg Palace** *(p65)* before entering the **Prague Castle** *(pp56–7)* complex, passing through the first two courtyards to reach the splendid gothic **St Vitus's Cathedral** *(pp60–61)*. From here, continue past **St George's Basilica** *(p58)* to the quaint alley of **Golden Lane** *(p59)*, before strolling through the castle's South Gardens.

Afternoon Just west of the castle, the National Gallery's Old Master collections at the **Sternberg Palace** *(pp62–3)* deserve an hour or two of your time. Follow this with visits to the Loreto Chapel and **Strahov Monastery** *(p65)* before descending back towards Malá Strana quarter. Take a look inside the Baroque **Church of St Nicholas** *(pp66-7)* before wandering around the historic streets surrounding **Little Quarter Square** *(pp68–9)*. Round things off with a drink or meal in one of Malá Strana's many pub-restaurants.

Day 3
Morning Spend time in busy **Wenceslas Square** *(p92)*, with a few moments at the monument to anti-Soviet martyr Jan Palach. The **National Museum** *(pp92–3)*, spread over two buildings at the top of the square, could occupy the rest of the morning. Or, explore Prague's Art Nouveau heritage with a visit to the **Mucha Museum** *(p93)* and the opulently decorated **Main Railway Station** *(p93)*.

Afternoon Enjoy a ride on Prague's smooth metro system by taking line C to the exhibition grounds of **Trade Fair Palace** *(pp104–5)*, or Veletržní Palác, home to an engrossing collection of modern and contemporary art. If you have energy for one more sight, then choose between a tour of the Baroque **Troja Palace** *(pp106–7;* take a bus from Veletržní Palác), or the stunning views on offer at the soaring Žižkov TV Tower (use the metro line A).

> **To extend your trip...**
> The magnificent **Karlštejn Castle** *(pp134–5)* and **Konopiště** *(p133)* can be clubbed into a day-trip.

Two Weeks in the Czech Republic

- **Arriving** This tour takes the form of a circle that starts and finishes in Prague, whose airport and railway station have a high number of international connections. However, you can also join the circuit at **Brno**, which boasts a handful of international flight connections; or **Plzeň**, which has good railway links with Western Europe.

- **Transport** The Czech railway and bus networks will get you to the main overnight destinations mentioned in this tour. However, to reach some of the smaller towns and attractions mentioned as potential stop-offs, you will need a car.

Day 1 & 2
Pick any of the days from the detailed 3-day itinerary provided on p11.

Day 3
The magnificent Gothic **Karlštejn Castle** (pp134–5), built for the Holy Roman Emperor Charles IV, is the one day-trip destination from Prague you really should not miss. It will probably take a day to tour the state rooms and roam the grounds of this restored royal residence and treasury. Make an early start, however, and you may also be able to fit in a visit to the

Sculpture of the Holy Trinity in Peace Square, Jindřichův Hradec

nearby Gothic castle of **Konopiště** (p133), once home to the ill-fated heir to the Habsburg throne, Archduke Franz Ferdinand. It is famous for its amazing collection of weapons and hunting trophies.

> **To extend your trip…**
> Spend a day hiking in the arrestingly beautiful hill country of **České Švýcarsko** (pp190–91), or Czech Switzerland, stopping by at **Liberec** town (pp184–7).

Day 4
Travel west from the capital to the elegant resort town of **Karlovy Vary** (pp176–7), celebrated for its mineral springs, glassware and *belle époque* architecture. On the way

there, consider a detour to the Baroque, sculpture-filled **Manětín** (p175), which looks like an open-air gallery.

Day 5
A morning drive from **Karlovy Vary** (pp176–7) to **Plzeň** (pp164–7) leaves you with a whole afternoon and evening to cover the main economic and cultural centre of Western Bohemia. Plzeň has much to offer visitors, but its Gothic **Cathedral of St Bartholomew** (pp166–7) is the most spectacular of a significant cluster of historic buildings. The rich variety of pubs clearly reflects the city's status as the birthplace of Pilsner beer.

Day 6
Travel southeast via **České Budějovice** (pp140–41), with its huge market square edged by ancient buildings, towards the historical town of **Český Krumlov** (pp154–7). The Gothic-Baroque centre of this river-encircled, UNESCO-protected town invites long, aimless wandering; while the **Egon Schiele Centrum** (p165) is something of a must-see for all art fans.

Day 7
To get the best of South Bohemia's historic towns you should undertake a looping tour that takes in **Tábor** (pp144–5), with its maze of medieval alleys, and **Jindřichův Hradec** (pp146–7), site of a monumental castle. Finish up and spend the night at **Třeboň** (p148), a well-preserved Renaissance town surrounded by fish ponds, and home to many fine fish restaurants.

Day 8
Heading east from **Třeboň** (p148), the market towns of the Bohemian-Moravian border are among the most picturesque in the Czech Republic. Stop off in **Telč** (p237) for lunch and enjoy the stunning main square before staying overnight in **Slavonice** (p148), another quaint town characterized by arcaded medieval buildings.

View of the imposing Karlštejn Castle

For practical information on travelling around the Czech Republic, see pp410–11

Day 9

Journey east through the rolling hills of Moravia via the dramatically perched **Bítov Castle** (p238) to one of Moravia's oldest towns, **Znojmo** (p240). Spend a couple of hours looking around the castle and exploring the Old Town. Continue to **Mikulov** (p240), a picture-postcard pretty town at the heart of the Moravian wine-growing region offering plenty of accommodation. Consider spending all or part of the afternoon touring the beautiful, UNESCO-listed landscaped park, **Lednicko-Valtický areál** (p240), just east of Mikulov.

Day 10

A short drive from **Mikulov** (p240) takes you to the second largest city of the Czech Republic, **Brno** (pp230–33). The best part of a day can be spent exploring South Moravia's vibrant, student-filled capital with its numerous museums and a buoyant theatre scene. Devote plenty of time at **Špilberk** (pp232–3), the hilltop fortress housing several museum displays. The church-filled Old Town below the castle is well worth a stroll; while the Mies van der Rohe-designed **Villa Tugendhat** (p231) is an essential stop-off for architecture buffs.

Exterior of the Špilberk Castle, Brno

> ### To extend your trip…
>
> **Brno** (pp230–33) is the ideal base from which to undertake a day tour of small-town Moravia, taking in delightful **Třebíč** (p237), with its historic Jewish quarter; the pilgrimage church at **Žd'ár nad Sázavou** (p236); **Pernštejn** and its castle-museum (p236); and the hill-town of **Boskovice** (p234–5).

Day 11

The road north of **Brno** (pp230–33) passes through **Kroměříž** (pp242–3), a pretty provincial town whose UNESCO-protected **Archbishops' Palace** (p242) and ornamental gardens is one of Moravia's most popular tourist draws. From here, it's a short drive to the university city of **Olomouc** (pp218–21); filled with Baroque churches, absorbing museums and good restaurants, it fully deserves an overnight stay.

Day 12

Travel west from **Olomouc** (pp218–21) to the East Bohemian capital and one of the most beautiful towns of Bohemia, **Hradec Králové** (pp200–3). Wander through the streets, enjoying the mix of Baroque and modernist architecture. Consider stopping off en route at **Litomyšl** (p204), with its

Detail of the Holy Trinity column in Olomouc

charming clutch of palaces and museums, or **Pardubice** (pp206–7), home to the East Bohemian Museum, the Pardubice Castle and a handsome market square.

Day 13

Head north from **Hradec Králové** (pp200–3) towards the smooth green hills of the **Krkonoše** (pp210–11) on the Czech-Polish border. The Krkonoše National Park has a network of hiking trails, chair-lifts, ski runs and snowboarding facilities, making it an ideal destination both in summer and winter. If you have your own transport, a range of scenic spots such as the **Mumlov Waterfall** (p210) and the **Mount Sněžka** (p211) cable car can be fitted into a day's tour. Otherwise, the resort town of **Špindlerův Mlýn** (p211) is a good base for local hikes.

Day 14

Return to Prague via the historic silver-mining town of **Kutná Hora** (pp124–5). You will need at least half a day to visit both the spectacular Gothic **St Barbara's Cathedral** (p124) and the extraordinary ossuary in the suburb of Sedlec. If you have any energy left for more sightseeing, the sprawling **Sternberg Castle** (p133), located on a high cliff above the Sázava river valley just to the southwest, makes for the perfect mid-afternoon stop-off.

Putting the Czech Republic on the Map

The Czech Republic lies at the heart of Central Europe, sharing borders with Germany, Poland and Austria, as well as Slovakia. Comprising the regions of Bohemia in the west and Moravia in the east, the country covers an area of 78,865 sq km (30,499 sq miles), of which some 80 per cent is made up of mountains and highlands; the highest peak is Sněžka (1,602 m/5,256 ft), in the Krkonoše Mountains of East Bohemia. The Czech Republic has around 10.3 million inhabitants, more than 1 million of whom live in the capital, Prague.

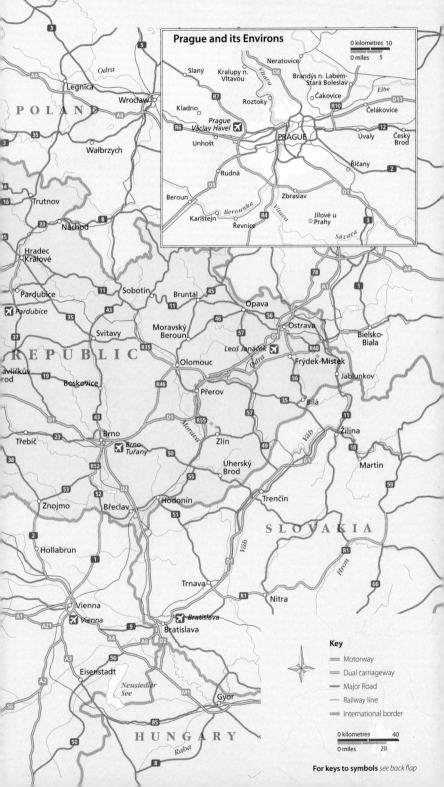

Prague and its Environs

0 kilometres 10
0 miles 5

Slaný
Kralupy n. Vltavou
Brandýs n. Labem-
Staré Boleslav
Neratovice
Roztoky
Čakovice
Čelákovice
Kladno
Prague
Václav Havel
PRAGUE
Úvaly
Český
Brod
Unhošť
Říčany
Rudná
Beroun
Zbraslav
Jílové u
Prahy
Karlštejn
Řevnice
Berounka
Vltava
Sázava

Legnica
Odra
Wrocław
P O L A N D
Wałbrzych
Trutnov
Náchod
Hradec
Králové
Pardubice
Pardubice
Svitavy
R E P U B L I C
Boskovice
avlíčkův
rod
Třebíč
Brno
*Brno-
Tuřany*
Znojmo
Břeclav
Hollabrun
Sobotín
Bruntál
Moravský
Beroun
Olomouc
Přerov
Morava
Zlín
Uherský
Brod
Hodonín
Váh
Opava
Ostrava
Odra
Frýdek-Místek
Bílá
Leoš Janáček
Trenčín
Bielsko-
Biała
Jablunkov
Žilina
Martin
S L O V A K I A
Trnava
Nitra
Hron
Vienna
Vienna
Bratislava
Bratislava
Eisenstadt
*Neusiedler
See*
Győr
Raba
H U N G A R Y
Elbe

Key

═══ Motorway
─── Dual carriageway
─── Major Road
─── Railway line
▬▬▬ International border

0 kilometres 40
0 miles 20

For keys to symbols *see back flap*

A PORTRAIT OF THE CZECH REPUBLIC

The Czech Republic has blossomed into a vibrant and fascinating place to visit in the post-Communist era. Bohemia and Moravia, neglected under the Communists, now delight visitors with their picturesque towns and cities, well-preserved palaces and castles, and magnificent scenery.

Situated in the centre of Europe, the Bohemian Basin was for centuries a crossroads of trading routes and a place where different religious and national traditions came into close contact. This cultural diversity has produced a rich historical heritage, which survives in remarkable condition: the Czech Republic escaped serious damage during the two World Wars, though the decimation of the Jewish community and the expulsion of German-speakers after 1945 had a devastating effect on Czech society. Wherever you go in the country, you will find well-preserved historic buildings and medieval districts, and many attractive towns and villages.

Since the Velvet Revolution of 1989, the Czech Republic has experienced a rapid process of change. While those who lived under Soviet domination have found this economic and social upheaval hard to accept, the younger generations have embraced the change. The speed with which the country is shaking off the aura of its Communist past is astounding. Soviet-style architecture cannot be wiped out overnight, but many cities are now lively cultural and commercial centres. None more so than Prague, which, as well as being a major tourist destination, is carving out a role for itself, both political and cultural, in the European Union.

The pace of change in rural areas has been much slower. Here, the people tend to be more inward-looking and are the most sceptical about the country's membership of the EU, ratified in 2004. While 77 per cent of Czechs voted in favour, only just over half of the population voted. There is widespread concern that EU membership will bring rocketing prices and erode the country's vibrant folk culture. This culture is most visible in the country's numerous folk festivals, its music and its art and architecture.

The view from the terrace of the café in Střekov Castle, North Bohemia

◀ One of the many narrow, meandering cobbled streets of Prague

Tradition of Democracy

The Czechs are very proud of their traditional commitment to democratic values. This means, on the one hand, opposition to any signs of autocracy, and, on the other, a deep-seated belief in the indisputable nature of laws as decreed by the majority. Rules and regulations are respected by Czech society much more than in other European countries. The Czech people's high regard for law and order means that it is rare to encounter any violence while in the country. The widely proclaimed egalitarianism seems rather at odds, however, with the Czech penchant for titles and ranks – a result perhaps of the society's bourgeois roots and the centuries-long rule by Austrian bureaucracy.

Český Krumlov festival, a typical folk celebration

Social Heritage

In a country where almost every town and village has an historic castle or chateau, the people's awareness of their history is strong – although this doesn't hold true in areas of the Czech Republic where the chain of local traditions has been broken: by the murder or deportation of entire Jewish communities by the Nazis during World War II, for example, or by the expulsion of German-speakers after the war.

Allegory of Science by Antonín Břenek

The vagaries of history also help explain the fact that the Czechs are the most secular society in Europe. Closed and empty churches bear witness to the anticlerical feelings of a nation for whom the Catholic Habsburg monarchy was, for centuries, the symbol of national repression.

Socially, Czech atheism means that the often divisive issues of divorce, abortion and childbirth outside marriage raise relatively few eyebrows.

Public Versus Private

For the Czech people, spending time with family and friends is of paramount importance. Weekends in the country are popular,

Czechs demonstrating during the Velvet Revolution of 1989

The historic Park Colonnade in the spa town of Karlovy Vary

but the most important venues for socializing are restaurants, pubs and bars. Here, it is easy to strike up a conversation with local people. Visitors shouldn't hesitate to ask if they can join a group of friends at a communal table; indeed, this is common practice. Czechs are well-educated, and are often well-informed about foreign events and politics. It is rare, however, to be invited into a Czech home, which is regarded as a person's oasis of privacy.

The dualism of Czech society is also reflected in its language. The literary version of Czech (spisovná čeština), used in public life, exists side by side with the colloquial version (hovorová čeština), which has a different grammar; the latter is used on private occasions by all social groups.

The dramatic changes experienced in the last decade or so have not entirely removed the Czech penchant for retrospection and a nostalgic cult of old things. An attachment to favourite clothes, places and customs occasionally takes on unusual forms. Nowhere else in Europe will you see so many long-haired men who appear to have been transported straight from the 1960s and 70s.

The Czech Republic Abroad

Most Czechs are deeply patriotic and, by extension, are proud of their country's reputation abroad. The Czech Republic's prestige has undoubtedly been strengthened by the playwright turned politician Václav Havel, admired worldwide for his relentless defence of democracy and civil rights. A major role in the promotion of Czech culture abroad has also been played by a group of prominent authors and artists, including the writers Milan Kundera and Bohumil Hrabal and film director Miloš Forman.

The historic heart of Český Krumlov

Landscape and Wildlife

The Czech Republic's western region of Bohemia is basically
a high plateau surrounded by modest mountains, while
Moravia is a largely lowland region with just a handful of
mountains. A depression called the Moravian Gate (Moravská
brána), which separates these regions from the Carpathian
mountains to the east, played a major role in shaping the
diversity of Central Europe's wildlife. It provided a north-south
migration route for many species of plants and animals.
The ease of migration, the diversity of climates and soils, plus
the varied topography have all contributed to the region's
biodiversity. For a visitor, the only problem is the mountainous
and wooded terrain, which makes wildlife-spotting tricky.

Stalactite in the Punkva Caves in the
Moravian Karst

Mountains

Most of the mountains in the Czech Republic
are lower than 800 m (2,625 ft). The highest are
the aptly named Krkonoše (Giant) Mountains
in East Bohemia, and it is only here that sub-
alpine and alpine flora can be found. The other
mountain ranges include the Šumava, an
unpopulated wilderness in South Bohemia,
and the White Carpathians (Bílé Karpaty) in
South Moravia.

Highlands

Much of the country is made up of the so-
called Bohemian-Moravian Highlands plateau
(Českomoravská Vysočina), which consists of
schist and granite and is furrowed by the valleys
of the Vltava and Morava, the Czech Republic's
two main rivers, and their tributaries. Its upper
sections are covered in forest, while the lower
parts are where crops such as rye are cultivated
and cattle are bred.

Plants

The land in the Czech Republic is less
intensively used than in many other
European countries. The country's diversity
of trees, plants and flowers is shown by
the fact that it has the same number of
plant species as neighbouring Poland, a
country four times the size. These include
relatively large numbers of endemic
plants. It is of concern, however, that in
a listing of rare and endangered plant
species in the Czech and Slovak Republics,
more than 80 species are singled out as
being on the verge of extinction.

Meadows catch
the eye in the late
spring and summer
with their fantastic
variety of colourful
flower species.

The number of rose species
growing in the Czech Republic
is estimated at over 100. Look
out for these on the fringes
of woodland and in small
deciduous thickets.

Fauna

The Czech Republic is home to many animals common to Central Europe, though their survival is threatened by industrial development, intensive agriculture and tourism. The most numerous larger mammals are the wild boar, suslik, fox, hare, roe deer and badger.

The suslik, or ground squirrel, is related to the marmot and chipmunk. It lives underground in colonies, usually in meadows.

The gyrfalcon, a bird of prey found primarily in mountain areas, is the world's largest falcon.

The otter, a predatory mammal, inhabits the shores of reservoirs and feeds on fish, frogs and crayfish.

Agricultural Land

Some 40 per cent of the Czech Republic is cultivated land. Besides cereals and root crops, a particular feature of the Czech agricultural landscape are the fields of rape, flax, hops and sunflowers. Vineyards are a common sight in some areas, primarily in Moravia, where they grow on south-facing hillsides. Most livestock farming is concentrated around towns.

Rivers and Lakes

Bohemia's high plateau is drained by the Labe river (known as the Elbe in Germany), along with its tributary the Vltava, the republic's longest river at 430 km (267 miles). Moravia's principal river is the Morava, which joins the Danube at Bratislava; the scenery along one of its tributaries, the Dyje, is particularly beautiful. The Czech Republic has only a few natural lakes but many artificial reservoirs.

The hop plant (whose dried flowers are used in the brewing of beer) is endemic in the Czech Republic, often seen in damp woodlands and thickets, or along riverbanks.

The kingcup, with its showy golden-yellow flowers, appears in early spring; it favours damp habitats, such as meadows and the banks of streams and ponds.

The peach-leaved bellflower is a beautiful species which grows primarily in oak or hornbeam forests; it flowers in early summer.

Religious Architecture

The two most momentous periods in the development of Czech religious architecture were the medieval and Baroque eras. The peak of these two architectural heydays were, respectively, the second half of the 14th century and the 18th century (the Late-Baroque era). In between, vicious religious wars in the 15th and 17th centuries seriously affected new architectural development, and also caused brutal damage to many medieval churches.

Basilica of St Procopius in Třebíč, an example of Czech Baroque architecture

Romanesque Architecture

The oldest churches in the Czech Republic date from the 9th century. The styles developed during this period culminated in the flowering of Romanesque architecture in the 11th to 13th centuries. Romanesque churches fell into three main categories: rotundas, simple hall churches and triple-aisle basilicas with apses. Sadly, few of these buildings, which were often quite opulent with rich architectural details, have survived intact.

St George's Basilica in Prague *(see p58)*, begun in the 10th century, was altered often and even partially rebuilt. However, it remains the best-preserved Romanesque basilica in the Czech Republic.

The Rotunda of St Catherine in Znojmo *(see p240)* is one of Moravia's few Romanesque churches to have escaped alteration.

Gothic Architecture

From the time Emperor Charles IV chose Prague as his capital in the 14th century, the Czech Lands became one of Europe's most prominent focal areas for the arts. The style in vogue here was known as the "Parler" style, its name derived from that of the prominent German architect Peter Parler and his sons. Its distinctive features include light and airy interiors decorated with intricately carved details.

The Church of St Bartholomew in Kolín *(see p126)*, which shares many features with St Vitus's Cathedral in Prague, is a prime example of the Parler style.

St Bartholomew's Cathedral in Plzeň *(see pp166–7)*, built from the 13th to 16th centuries, has massive columns supporting classic Gothic vaulting above the nave.

The church in Zlatá Koruna *(see p158)*, attached to the Cistercian monastery, dates from the mid-14th century and was worked on by Peter Parler.

Baroque Architecture

The Baroque period was the last great phase in Czech religious architecture. Following the destruction of the Thirty Years' War, a massive rebuilding campaign was launched in Bohemia. In the 17th century, the architects of the new style were mainly from Italy, but they were later superseded by more local builders, mainly Germans and Austrians with a few Czechs. Most talented among

them were the Bavarian Christoph Ignaz Dientzenhofer and his son Kilian. They helped to develop the new internal layout of churches, based on interlocking geometrical figures. This spatial sophistication was accompanied by opulent furnishings, stuccowork and frescoes. Often executed by top sculptors and painters, the exuberance of the decoration reached a peak in the Late-Baroque era.

The Church of St Nicholas in Malá Strana, in Prague *(see pp66–7)*, the work of Christoph and Kilian Ignaz Dientzenhofer, is one of the most innovative churches of the time in Europe, with its flowing lines and flamboyant colours. The floorplan of the nave consists of a series of interlocking ellipses.

The Church of St Mary Magdalene in Karlovy Vary *(see p176)*, designed by Kilian Ignaz Dientzenhofer, was built in the 1730s. Inside are the original fine sculptures and a beautiful main altarpiece.

The hospital-church complex in Kuks *(see p212)* was designed by Italian-born G B Alliprandi in 1707–10. In front of the hospital is a terrace with sculptures by Tyrolean sculptor, Matthias Braun.

The 19th and 20th Centuries

The 19th century did not see the flowering of any distinct architectural style; the buildings erected during this period drew on earlier styles, often mixing them together. In the 20th century, more effort was made to search for new architectural expression. Czech architects adopted the geometric forms of Cubism, and the austere Functionalist style was much in vogue between the World Wars, most visible now in Prague and the Moravian capital of Brno.

The Church of the Most Sacred Heart in Vinohrady, Prague, built in 1928–32, was so shockingly modern in its day that it was almost Post-Modern. It was the work of the Slovenian architect, Josip Plečnik.

The Church of St Wenceslas in Prague-Vršovice was designed in 1929 by the Czech architect Josef Gočár, a leading exponent of the avant-garde. The concrete structure, dominated by a tall bell tower, is denuded of decoration.

Czech Music

The Czech Republic has a rich, largely home-grown musical heritage. Psalms written as long ago as the 13th century used the Czech language. It was nationalism which, centuries later, inspired Bedřich Smetana and Antonín Dvořák, the most famous of the unusually large number of composers to emanate from this small country.

Jan Kubelík, famous Czech violinist, in around 1908

Religious Music of the Hussite Period

The earliest surviving pieces of Czech music include choral elements of the Christian liturgy, interwoven with native folk melodies. The oldest known composition is the 10th–11th-century psalm *Hospodine Pomiluj ny* ("Lord have mercy on us").

During the 15th century, the reformist Hussite movement began to oppose the Latin singing that was the norm in Czech churches; this in turn inspired the growth of Czech religious songs. Hussite works were published in hymn books both at home and in neighbouring countries, including Germany. The subsequent development of music in the Czech Lands occurred during the Renaissance period, when artistic life centred around the imperial court and palaces of the nobility.

After the Defeat at the White Mountain

After the defeat of the Czechs in 1620 at the Battle of the White Mountain, increased repression by the Habsburgs forced many musicians to leave the Czech Lands. Meanwhile, the imperial court, which moved to Vienna, ceased to sponsor Czech composers. Among the few musicians who worked during the 1700s, the most prominent positions went to the church music composers Jan Jakub Ryba and František Brixi.

Mozart in Prague

Mozart visited Prague for the first time in 1787, and fell in love with the city. He returned here to write *Don Giovanni*, which he dedicated to "the good people of Prague". The citizens of Prague were entranced by Mozart; opera was already a popular form of entertainment, and was open to everyone rather than just the wealthy classes.

Smetana and the Era of National Rebirth

Music played an important role in shaping the Czech national identity.

The first composer whose works espoused the aspirations of his countrymen was Bedřich Smetana (1824–84), who was active in the 1848 revolution and, later, the national revival movement. While his music was rooted in German Romanticism, it took its themes primarily from the legends and history of his homeland. Smetana also borrowed elements from Czech folklore. Most popular among his large volume of work is his cycle of six symphonic poems known collectively as *Má Vlast* ("My Country"), written in 1874–9 and whose melodious theme is one of the signatures of Czech music, and his comic opera *The Bartered Bride* (1866), his most famous work internationally.

Antonín Dvořák

When Smetana died, he handed the baton to Antonín Dvořák (1841–1904), with whom he had worked at the National Theatre. Dvořák's first musical experience had been playing the violin in his village band. From these humble

Piano recital given by Bedřich Smetana for his friends

beginnings, Dvořák became the source of inspiration for a new generation of Czech musicians and, much later, the most renowned Czech composer in the world.

At heart a peasant, Dvořák was naturally drawn to the folk music tradition of his homeland. He combined this with foreign influences, from Wagner to American folk music. The latter influenced his most famous work, the Ninth Symphony, subtitled *From the New World*. This was written during his stint as director of the New York's conservatory from 1892–5.

Poster advertising a Janáček opera

The Turn of the 20th Century

Among the large group of composers who worked during the late 19th and early 20th century, a prominent place is occupied by Zdeněk Fibich (1850–1900), a pupil of Smetana. Considered, along with his teacher and Dvořák, as one of the fathers of Czech music, Fibich showed little interest in folk music or in patriotic themes; instead, his works were inspired by the music of Berlioz, Schumann and Liszt. His *Poem* is his most famous composition.

Despite being a contemporary of Fibich, Leoš Janáček (1854–1928), born in North Moravia, was a much more modern composer. He resisted the lure of Prague, instead devoting many years of his life to researching the folklore of Bohemia, Moravia and Slovakia. He wrote down numerous native folk songs, investigated the intonation of the spoken language, and

Dvořák's viola, from the Michna Palace

even notated the sounds made by animals and objects; he gave the name "speech tunes" to these sounds. While taking his inspiration from the very traditional life and art of country people, Leoš Janáček's music was definitely avant-garde. As a result, his music was not given the recognition that it deserved at the outset. His *Glagolitic Mass* (1926), for which he achieved renown internationally, was composed at the very end of his life.

Two other musicians worth a mention are Josef Suk (1874–1935), the pupil and son-in-law of Dvořák, and violinist Jan Kubelík (1880–1940). While Kubelík achieved fame for his virtuoso technique and interpretation, he was also a composer. The great German composer and conductor Gustav Mahler (1860–1911) was born in a village near Humpolec in southeast Bohemia. He spent a significant part of his life in Olomouc and Prague. Another famous name in the Czech Republic is Emma Destinnová, Emmy Destinn in Czech (1878–1930). A soprano, she performed with Enrico Caruso at New

York's Metropolitan Opera. Her portrait is still used on 2,000-crown Czech banknotes.

Choirs and Dechovky

In the 19th century, choirs and amateur wind instrument orchestras known as *dechovky* started to play a significant role in the musical life of Bohemia and Moravia. One such choir, the famous Hlahol ensemble from Prague, founded in 1860, became an important element in the shaping of the Czech national culture. *Dechovky* remain a typical and widely popular form of music-making.

Singer Karel Kryl during one of his live performances

Music and the Drive for Democracy

Music stagnated during the Communist era: jazz, for example, a hugely popular genre, was proclaimed decadent. Yet music also played a role in the ideological conflict. In 1976, the punk band, the "Plastic People of the Universe", was put on trial for "crimes against the state". This helped ignite the process that led to the creation of the Charter 77 manifesto. Also famous for their resistance to the regime are the singers Karel Kryl and Jaromír Hutka, who, until 1989, were banned from performing.

Art and Decorative Arts

Proof of the wealth of artistic life and traditions in the Czech Republic is shown by its magnificent works of painting and sculpture and a wide range of decorative arts. Artists that made a lasting contribution to the arts in Europe range from the 14th-century painter Master Theodoric and the great sculptor of the Baroque era, Matthias Bernhard Braun, to Alfons Mucha, the undisputed master of the Czech Art Nouveau style. Czech artists and sculptors have always enjoyed great respect in their country, and their works of art are, to this day, the pride of numerous museums, galleries and public places.

The Krumlov Madonna (c.1390), the work of an anonymous artist, is one of the best-known examples of the so-called "Beautiful Style" in Czech Gothic sculpture.

Master Theodoric, court painter to Emperor Charles IV and one of the greatest Bohemian artists of the 14th century, painted this *St Elizabeth*, which can be seen at Karlštejn Castle.

Pose symbolizing dancing

The voluptuous gown shows a masterful portrayal of movement.

Jan Kupecký (1667–1740), who spent most of his life outside his native Bohemia, was a highly regarded portrait painter who pioneered a trend for realism in Late-Baroque painting. This *Self-Portrait* (1711) is his most famous work.

Ferdinand Maxmilian Brokof and Matthias Bernhard Braun, the two most famous sculptors of the Czech Baroque, were responsible for 12 of the statues on the Charles Bridge in Prague.

Přemysl and Libuše, one of the four group sculptures by Josef Václav Myslbek (1848–1922) now standing in Vyšehrad, once decorated the Palacký Bridge in Prague. The most famous work of the artist is the equestrian statue of St Wenceslas in the capital's Wenceslas Square.

Intricate floral decoration

Max Švabinský (1873–1962) was not only a painter but also a hugely talented graphic artist. He designed, among other things, postage stamps and banknotes.

Soft, flowing lines typical of Art Nouveau

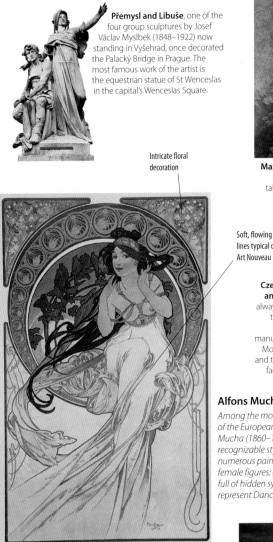

Czech glass, crystal and porcelain were always highly regarded throughout Europe. The most famous manufacturers included Moser of Karlovy Vary and the Dubí porcelain factory near Teplice.

Alfons Mucha

Among the most outstanding exponents of the European Art Nouveau, Alfons Mucha (1860–1939) developed an instantly recognizable style. Typical subjects of his numerous paintings and posters were female figures: graceful, enigmatic and full of hidden symbols. Those shown here represent Dance and Music.

This Baroque cupboard was built of walnut and oak by František Maximilián Kaňka (1674–1766) in c.1740. It is now in the library inside the Clementinum *(see p84)* in Prague.

Toyen (1902–80) was a founding member of the Czech Surrealist movement in the 1930s. Marie Čermínová took on the cryptic pseudonym Toyen in order to disguise her gender.

Czech Literature and Film

The first concerted effort to write in Czech rather than in Latin came in the 14th century, when the work of reformist preachers prepared the way for the writings of Jan Hus. From then on, literature flourished in Bohemia, halted only temporarily by the Thirty Years' War. Writers and, more recently, film makers, have played an important role in the nation's history (Václav Havel, a playwright, even became president), and in its search for a cultural identity.

Ninth-century *Book of Gospels*, the oldest in Strahov's library

Early Czech Literature

The dawn of literature in the Czech language is linked with the Slavic writings associated with the 9th-century missionary work of St Cyril and St Methodius. In the 13th century, religious literature, usually chronicles and the lives of the saints, was still in Latin but started to be accompanied by text written in Czech.

The 14th century saw more concerted efforts to write in the Czech language, in lyrical poetry as well as secular and religious prose. Reformist preachers adopted Czech as their preferred language, and it was the trail-blazing reformer, Jan Hus (1369–1415), who made perhaps the most significant contribution to the development of the Czech language of the day. He codified the rules of orthography and extended the readership of the national literature to include the bourgeoisie.

The Humanist Period

The use of the vernacular spread during the 16th and 17th centuries, boosted by the humanist movement and the boom in printing. The crowning glory of this age was the publication of the Kralice Bible (1579–94), a Protestant translation of the Bible in Czech. With the Thirty Years' War, however, came repression. Czech, the language of the reformists, all but died out as a written form, and became little more than a peasant dialect. But Czech was still used by exiles abroad. The most famous exiled writer was Jan Ámos Komenský (1592–1670), also known as Comenius. He won recognition in many fields of science, but became truly famous all over Europe for his ground-breaking ideas on education.

The Literature of National Revival

The counter-reformation, and the Germanization process that accompanied it, prevented any revival of a national Czech literature in the early 1700s, but by the end of the 18th century, the more liberal approach of Joseph II gave Czech scholars the chance to revive their language. A leading role in this campaign was played by Josef Dobrovský (1753–1829), who codified the Czech literary language. Among other leading writers active in the movement of national revival was Karel Hynek Mácha, one of the greatest ever Czech poets. The second half of the 19th century heralded the arrival of realist literature represented by the great Jan Neruda (1834–91), a poet of world renown and also the author of some fine short stories. His *Tales of the Little Quarter* (1878), set in Prague, is a marvellous portrayal of life in the city.

Jan Ámos Komenský

Literature Between the Wars

In the period between the two World Wars, Czech writers did not follow a single path.

The Kralice Bible, the first Czech translation of the Bible

Jaroslav Hašek (1883–1923) wrote *The Good Soldier Švejk*, an hilarious novel that pokes fun at the Habsburg empire. Instantly popular, its hero became a symbol of the Czech nation.

Another prominent figure was Karel Čapek (1890–1938), famous primarily for his plays. These included *R.U.R.* (Rossum's Universal Robots), written in 1921 and the source from which the word "robot" entered the English language. In this and other works, such as his novel *The War with the Newts* (1936), Čapek combines his interest in ordinary life with his love of science fiction.

Franz Kafka (1883–1924), a German-speaking Jew, did not write in Czech, but spent his entire life in Prague and was part of a thriving German-Jewish literary circle. His bleak works were banned during the Communist era.

Repression and Literary Resurgence

Accompanying the political upheaval of 1948 came curbs on freedom of expression. "Socialist realism" became the only style acceptable to the authorities.

The period of "thaw" in the 1960s, which peaked in 1968 during the Prague Spring, inspired a literary resurgence. Writers such as Josef Škvorecký (1924–2012) and Milan Kundera (b.1929) penned their first great works during this period. Škvorecký, an ironic chronicler of life during and after World War II, is as famous in his homeland as Kundera. Communist oppression is a common theme in Kundera's often erotic books. A great storyteller, he was influenced by the revered Bohumil Hrabal (1914–97), famously scornful of war in his novella *Closely Observed Trains* (1965).

Russian intervention in 1968 forced many writers to go underground. Some of them decided to emigrate,

Scene from Jiří Menzel's film *Closely Observed Trains*

including Kundera, who shot to international fame with the publication of his novel *The Unbearable Lightness of Being* (1984). With the Velvet Revolution came a new era, in which literary life could flourish and young writers could work unrestrained.

Theatre

Czech theatre, which has a long and worthy tradition, hit a peak in the 1950s and '60s with the emergence of many small theatres. One such was the Theatre on the Balustrade, which staged Václav Havel's first play in 1963. Havel tackled the issue of life under totalitarianism and was typical of the Czech theatrical community in his determination to fight repression. Since 1989, the theatre has faced other enemies, such as funding crises, but it is still a potent cultural force.

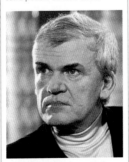
Milan Kundera, world-famous Czech writer working in Paris

Czech Cinema

Czech cinema earned a reputation as far back as the 1930s, mainly thanks to the work of Martin Frič and Karel Zeman. After 1945, film makers struggled to express themselves in the repressive Communist era; it is not by chance that the most avant-garde works of the period were animated films.

The more liberal 1960s saw the golden age of Czech cinema, although the Soviet invasion of 1968 brought this renaissance to a rapid end. This success was associated with the work of a group of young film makers, who created the style known as the "New Wave". In their films, they tackled moral and historical judgments of World War II as well as contemporary moral and social issues. One of the young film makers was Miloš Forman, who fled the country after 1968 and later achieved international fame as director of films such as *One Flew Over the Cuckoo's Nest* and *Amadeus*. Other great movies made in this period were *A Report on the Party and the Guests* by Jan Němec, and *Closely Observed Trains* by Jiří Menzel.

Czech cinema's greatest success in recent years was *Kolja (Kolya)*, directed by Jan Svěrák, which won an Oscar for best foreign film in 1997.

THE CZECH REPUBLIC THROUGH THE YEAR

The Czech Republic is a very popular destination in the summer, when Prague and the other main places of interest get unbearably crowded. It is much better to come in late spring or early autumn. While Prague and large towns can still offer plenty of entertainment in winter, castles and palaces in many smaller places tend to be closed from early November to late March. Anyone who loves stunning scenery or outdoor activities, on the other hand, can have a great time even then. While large-scale religious festivals don't really exist in the Czech Republic, there are many festivals at which you can see the country's folk traditions in action, admire local crafts and taste traditional cuisine. Throughout the country, throughout the year, there are famous music, film and theatre festivals.

Concert in St Vitus's Cathedral during Prague Spring Festival

Spring

Many people say that spring arrives earlier in the Bohemian Basin, encircled as it is by mountains, than in neighbouring countries. Whatever the case, the scenery in spring is gorgeous, with fruit trees in blossom along the roadsides.

After the winter break, castles and palaces start to open their gates (some may open only at weekends in March and April); it is still easy to find a hotel room, car parking space or a table at a restaurant.

March
The Easter Festival of Sacred Music, *(Mar/Apr)*, Brno. This is held in the magnificent setting of the Cathedral of St Peter and St Paul.
Prague Photo Festival *(late Mar–early Apr)*. The biggest photographic festival in the country held at a variety of locations across Prague.

April
Witch-burning *(30 Apr)*. A Czech version of Halloween, celebrated all over the country. Old brooms are burned and bonfires are lit, all to ward off evil spirits.

Blooming spring flowers in South Bohemia

May
Anniversary of the Prague Uprising *(5 May)*. The anniversary of the 1945 anti-Nazi uprising is marked by the laying of flowers at the commemorative plaques of those who died.
Prague Spring International Music Festival *(early May–early Jun)*. A feast for lovers of classical music, with a busy schedule of concerts, ballet and opera. The festival traditionally begins with a performance of Smetana's *Má vlast* (My Country).
Prague Marathon *(early May)*. An annual event since 1995, the marathon route runs through the city's historic centre.
"Without Frontiers" (Bez Hranic) Theatre Festival *(late May)*, Český Těšín, North Moravia. Performances by some of the top theatre groups from the Czech Republic, Slovakia and Poland.
Prague–Prčice March *(late May)*. Thousands of people walk from the city centre to Prčice (southwest of Prague) to celebrate the arrival of spring.

Summer

In summer, Prague is truly besieged, but even here, there are peaceful parks and quiet museums and churches. While the capital's streets are buzzing well into the night, smaller towns go to sleep much earlier.

Average daily hours of sunshine

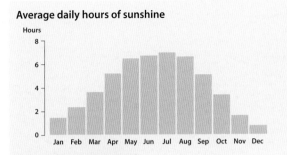

Hours

Sunshine
The greatest number of sunny days occurs between May and August. The fewest occur from November to January, during the winter months, when the hours of daylight are shorter. When the snow falls, of course, everything sparkles in the clear sunlight.

Boy in traditional costume at Strážnice folk festival

The majority of folklore events and cultural festivals are staged in the summer.

June
Prague Writers' Festival (early Jun). This event brings together writers from all over the world to take part in lectures and workshops.
Concentus Moravia: International Music Festival (all month). Classical concerts featuring international artistes take place in the churches and castles of Moravia's 13 historic towns.
Smetanova Litomyšl: International Opera Festival (Jun/Jul), Litomyšl, East Bohemia. The Czech Republic's biggest outdoor music festival, in Bedřich, Smetana's birthplace. Works by Smetana and other composers are performed.

Five-Petalled Rose Festival (mid-Jun), Český Krumlov, South Bohemia. On the weekend nearest the summer solstice, people dress up in medieval gear and have a great time.
International Folk Festival (last week in Jun), Strážnice, South Moravia. One of the biggest events of its type in Europe.

July
International Film Festival (early Jul), Karlovy Vary, West Bohemia. Launched in 1946, this festival is one of Europe's top film events, along with those held in Cannes, Berlin and Venice.
International Music Festival (mid-Jun–late Jul), Janáčkovy Hukvaldy, North Moravia. Devoted to the works of the world-famous composer, Leoš Janáček, who was born here.

Crystal Globe award, Karlovy Vary Film Festival

International Music Festival (mid-Jun–late Jul), Český Krumlov, South Bohemia. Staged mostly in the castle. Organ recitals are held in the monastery church here and in churches in neighbouring towns.

August
Chopin Festival (mid-Aug), Mariánské Lázně, West Bohemia. The great Polish composer visited this famous resort on several occasions and it now has a festival in his honour. In every odd-numbered year, there is a piano competition for budding young pianists (held in early Aug).
International Bagpipe Festival (end Aug), Strakonice, South Bohemia. An annual event, staged in the town's castle, this is one of the Czech Republic's biggest international folk festivals.

The Five-Petalled Rose Festival, held in June in Český Krumlov

Average monthly rainfall

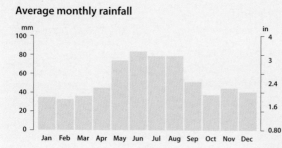

Rainfall
The heaviest rainfall occurs during the summer months in the Czech Republic's mountainous areas. Other, low-lying regions receive much less precipitation. Winter snowfalls can be reasonably heavy.

Autumn

Autumn is generally long and mild, and the weather is normally pleasant until early November. The new cultural season begins with theatres, concert halls and opera houses reopening after the summer break. Grape harvest festivals are held in wine-making districts, such as Moravia.

Poster promoting Brno's September tuba competition

Forests all over the country are invaded by armies of mushroom-pickers, since gathering fungi is the favourite autumn activity of many Czechs.

September

Dance Bohemia *(early Sep)*, Prague. Global festival open to amateur dance folklore ensembles from all over the world.

International Tuba Competition *(3rd week in Sep)*, Brno, South Moravia. Part of Brno's International Music Festival, with year-round events.

International Theatre Festival *(2nd half of Sep)*, Plzeň, West Bohemia. Theatre groups from all over Europe perform.

Organ Festival, Olomouc, North Moravia. Works by Czech and foreign composers

Performers in costume, Prague Autumn music festival

are performed on the organs of Olomouc's Church of St Maurice *(see p218)*.

October

The Great Pardubice Steeplechase *(2nd Sun)*, Pardubice, east of Prague. This famous horse race, first held in 1874 and run on Pardubice steeplechase course, is one of the most difficult of its kind in Europe.

Day of the Republic *(28 Oct)*. Despite the splitting up of Czechoslovakia in 1993, the anniversary of the founding of the independent republic in 1918 remains a public holiday.

November

Battle for Freedom and Democracy Day *(17 Nov)*. The anniversary of the Velvet Revolution is celebrated all over the country. In Prague, leading Czech politicians lay wreaths at the monument of St Wenceslas in Wenceslas Square.

Autumn view of St Vitus's Cathedral in Prague

Average monthly temperature

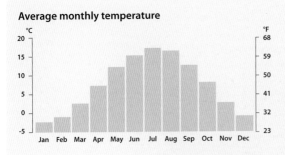

Temperature
Summer is generally warm, with the average temperature approaching 20°C (68°F); the coolest regions are, of course, the mountains. Winters tend to be harsh, with the temperature often dropping below zero in December, January and February.

Winter

The snowy landscapes of the Czech Republic in winter are stunning, and the Czechs make the most of the snow and ice. Ice hockey is played on frozen ponds throughout the country, and cross-country skiing is another popular activity. Tourist centres in the Krkonoše (Bohemia's highest mountains) stage international sports events, including the prestigious ski-jumping and ski-flying tournaments in Harrachov, and the downhill skiing events in Špindlerův Mlýn. The roads are kept in excellent condition, but driving conditions can be hazardous in the mountains.

Prague fares less well in the winter. On foggy days, which are not uncommon, temperatures can drop as low as -5°C (23°F).

December

Christmas and New Year season. Throughout December, countless markets sell all kinds of Christmas merchandise, from tree decorations to svařák (hot wine); just before Christmas Eve, they also sell live carp, the traditional Christmas delicacy. The arrival of the New Year is celebrated with huge and boisterous street parties. Prague experiences a real invasion of visitors at this time, and it is difficult to find a room in a hotel or a pension; restaurants and pubs are busy, too.

Winter scenery in the Krkonoše (Giant Mountains)

Swimming competitions in the Vltava (26 Dec). Hundreds of swimmers gather on the banks of the Vltava river in Prague to swim in temperatures not much above freezing point 0°C (32°F).

January

New Year's Day and Foundation of the Czech Republic (1 Jan). Public holiday.

One of the many traditional Christmas stalls lining the streets in December

February

St Matthew's Fair (late Feb–early Apr), Prague. Known in Czech as Matějská pouť, this is essentially a giant funfair. It is held at Výstaviště fairground in Holešovice.

Public Holidays in the Czech Republic

New Year's Day and Foundation of the Czech Republic (1 Jan)

Easter Monday

Labour Day (1 May)

VE Day (8 May)

St Cyril and St Methodius Day (5 Jul)

Anniversary of Jan Hus's death (6 Jul)

Czech State Day (28 Sep)

Czechoslovak Independence Day (28 Oct)

Battle for Freedom and Democracy Day (17 Nov)

Christmas Eve (24 Dec)

Christmas Day (25 Dec)

St Stephen's Day (26 Dec)

THE HISTORY OF THE CZECH REPUBLIC

From the middle ages until the 17th century, the Czech Lands played a significant role in European history. Defeat at the start of the Thirty Years' War, however, marked the beginning of three centuries of domination by the Habsburgs. The joint state of Czechoslovakia, founded after World War I, came to an end in 1993.

The Latin name of Bohemia derives from the Boii, one of the two Celtic tribes who, from the 3rd century BC, settled in the territories of the present-day Czech Republic. Towards the end of the 1st century BC, the Celts were dislodged by two Germanic tribes, the Quadi and the Marcomanni. They inflicted several defeats on the Romans who, as a result, decided not to extend their empire beyond the Danube. In the end, it was tribes from the east who displaced the Germanic tribes in the 5th and 6th centuries. In the 7th century, Bohemia and Moravia were briefly part of a vast Slav state ruled by the Frankish merchant, Prince Samo.

The Great Moravian Empire

The early 9th century saw the rise of the Moravians. They forged an alliance with the Slavs of Bohemia, and thus the Great Moravian Empire was born. At its peak, in around 885, the empire included Bohemia, Moravia, Silesia and parts of modern Slovakia, Germany and Poland. In response to German ambitions in the region, the second Moravian emperor invited Byzantine missionaries to spread Christianity in the Slavic language. The two monks, the so-called Apostles to the Slavs, were later canonized as St Cyril and St Methodius.

The Přemyslid Dynasty

Following the fall of the Moravian empire, brought about by a Magyar invasion in 906, a new political centre emerged in Bohemia under the Přemyslid princes. One of the dynasty's early rulers, Prince (St) Wenceslas, improved his state's relations with Germany but was murdered by his brother Boleslav in 935. Under Boleslav, Bohemia became part of the Holy Roman Empire. In 973, a bishopric (subordinate to the archbishopric of Mainz) was founded in Prague. The murder of Bishop Adalbert, who became the first Czech-born Bishop of Prague in 983, stunned Christian Europe *(see p103)*.

In 1085, Prince Vratislav II received from Holy Roman Emperor Henry IV the (non-hereditary) title of king. He thus became the first crowned ruler of Bohemia.

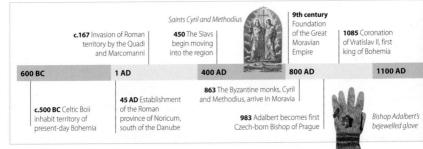

c.167 Invasion of Roman territory by the Quadi and Marcomanni

Saints Cyril and Methodius

450 The Slavs begin moving into the region

9th century Foundation of the Great Moravian Empire

1085 Coronation of Vratislav II, first king of Bohemia

| 600 BC | 1 AD | 400 AD | 800 AD | 1100 AD |

c.500 BC Celtic Boii inhabit territory of present-day Bohemia

45 AD Establishment of the Roman province of Noricum, south of the Danube

863 The Byzantine monks, Cyril and Methodius, arrive in Moravia

983 Adalbert becomes first Czech-born Bishop of Prague

Bishop Adalbert's bejewelled glove

◀ *St Wenceslas and St Vitus* by Bartholomaeus Spränger, c.1600

Sicilian Golden Bull

In exchange for supporting Frederick II of Sicily in his endeavours to secure the Holy Roman Emperor's throne, in 1212 Přemysl king Otakar I received the Golden Bull of Sicily. This edict established the right of succession to the Bohemian crown. Bohemian rulers were also made electors of the emperor.

The Golden Bull, stating the Bohemian crown heredity

The 13th century saw a rapid increase in both the political and economic power of Bohemia. Many towns, including České Budějovice and Hodonín, were founded during this period. The discovery of silver in Kutná Hora and Jihlava helped transform the Bohemian court into one of Europe's richest. Actively encouraged by the Přemyslids, vast numbers of Germans came to settle in Bohemia. They even founded entirely new towns.

Bohemia became the most powerful state within the Empire. During 1254–69, its territory expanded to include parts of what is now Austria. The endeavours of Přemysl Otakar II to win the throne of Germany and the imperial crown met with opposition from the imperial princes, however. The Bohemian king's death at the Battle of the Moravian Field (Marchfeld), in 1278, put an end to the ambitious monarch's plans.

A period of chaos followed the death of Přemysl Otakar II. The early death of Václav II was followed by the murder of his heirless son, Václav III, in 1306. This marked the end of the Přemyslid dynasty.

The Luxemburg Dynasty

By cleverly choosing a member of the Přemyslid family as his wife, John of Luxemburg found himself in a position to secure the Bohemian throne. While John rarely visited Bohemia, his son Charles IV, crowned Holy Roman Emperor in 1355, had much closer links with his kingdom. Charles IV's reign as King of Bohemia (1346–78) is often described as Bohemia's "Golden Age", a period of great economic and cultural growth. Prague, which became the imperial capital, acquired the first university north of the Alps, a new royal palace and a stone bridge across the Vltava river; work started on St Vitus's Cathedral,

Miniature of Přemsylid king Václav II

Přemysl king Otakar II lying dead on the Moravian Field

1278 Přemysl Otakar II killed in the Battle of the Moravian Field

1283 Václav II ascends the throne

1200

1250

1300

1212 Otakar I receives the Sicilian Golden Bull.

The seal used by Emperor Charles IV (14th century)

1306 Přemyslid dynasty ends with death of Václav III

Charles IV, with a cross from the French Dauphin

and the city became the seat of an archbishop. The network of roads and navigable stretches of rivers grew rapidly; weaving, as well as the cultivation of cereals, hops and grapes flourished; the mining of silver, gold, iron and tin all increased. There was success abroad, too; through his four marriages, Charles IV extended his kingdom north into parts of Poland and Germany. In short, Charles presided over a period of great prosperity and relative peace.

St Wenceslas' crown, worn by Charles IV

Charles IV's son, Václav IV (1361–1419), failed to continue his father's success. Hoping to exploit the weakness of the Church at a time of increasing crisis for the Papacy, he engaged in a dispute with the arch-bishop of Prague and some sections of the nobility. The consequences of this conflict, including Václav IV's own imprisonment and the weakening of the king's position, coincided with the effects of an outbreak of bubonic plague which, in 1380, ravaged certain parts of Europe.

Early Hussite Movement

In the late 14th century, the notion that the source of the social crisis lay in the Church's departure from the teaching of the Gospels began to gain support. One of the advocates of this view was a peasant-born preacher, Jan Hus (1371–1415). He became the main ideologue of the reformation movement, which demanded the curtailing of the Church's influence over state affairs. When, following the Council of Constance in 1415, Hus was burned at the stake as a heretic, unrest spread throughout the country. It reached boiling point in 1419, when several Catholic councillors were thrown out of Prague's New Town Hall's window, in the first "Prague defenestration" *(see p98)*.

Jan Hus teaching in Prague's Chapel of Bethlehem

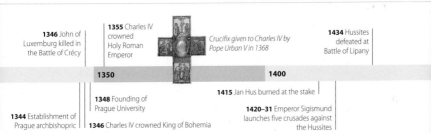

1346 John of Luxemburg killed in the Battle of Crécy

1355 Charles IV crowned Holy Roman Emperor

Crucifix given to Charles IV by Pope Urban V in 1368

1434 Hussites defeated at Battle of Lipany

1350

1400

1344 Establishment of Prague archbishopric

1348 Founding of Prague University

1346 Charles IV crowned King of Bohemia

1415 Jan Hus burned at the stake

1420–31 Emperor Sigismund launches five crusades against the Hussites

The Hussites

In the 15th century, the followers of Jan Hus became a major fighting force. They achieved great successes against the Emperor's crusades, due largely to the skill of their leader, Jan Žižka. The Hussites split into the radical Táborites and the moderate "Utraquists" (from *sub utraque specie*, symbolizing the wish to celebrate Mass with both bread and wine). While the former were finally beaten at Lipany in 1434, the Utraquists recognized papal supremacy in return for consent for the Czech language to be used in church. The Utraquists were active until the Battle of the White Mountain in 1620.

Burning of Jerome of Prague
Jerome of Prague, the Czech theologian and supporter of Jan Hus and John Wycliffe, was burned at the stake in 1416. He was condemned for heresy by the Council of Constance.

The Czech Nobility's Letter of Protest
Several hundred seals of the Bohemian nobility were affixed to a letter protesting the execution of Jan Hus in 1415.

Gilded monstrance, carried by a priest.

Jan Žižka was a brilliant commander and a key strategist of the Hussite army.

God's Warriors
The early 16th-century Codex of Jena illustrated the Hussites' victories. Here, the Hussites, who included artisans, urban merchants and minor nobility, are shown singing their hymn. They are led by their blind leader, Jan Žižka.

Sigismund of Luxemburg
Boosted by papal support, Emperor Sigismund (1368–1437) launched five crusades against the Hussites. They all ended in failure.

Satan Disguised as the Pope
This type of lurid image, satirizing the corrupt Church and the excessively free lifestyle of priests, was painted on placards and carried through the streets.

Hussite Victory (1420)

In the Battle of Vitkov, the Hussites, led by Jan Žižka, won a victory over the Catholic army of Emperor Sigismund.

The chalice was an important symbol for the Hussites, who demanded the right to take wine at Mass.

Farm implements were used as makeshift weapons by the peasants.

The peasant army marched behind Jan Žižka.

Reformer Jan Hus

Jan Hus was one of the most important religious thinkers of his day. His objections to the Catholic Church's corrupt practices and opulent lifestyle were shared by many Czechs – peasants and nobles alike. His reformist preaching in Prague earned him a huge following and was noticed by the Papacy, which excommunicated him. In 1414, Hus decided to defend his teaching at the Council of Constance. Even though he had received a guarantee of safe conduct from Emperor Sigismund, Hus was imprisoned and burned at the stake in 1415.

Jan Hus at the stake Wearing the hat of shame given to heretics, Hus became a martyr of the Czech people.

Hussite Shield

Wooden shields like this one bearing the arms of Prague were used to fill any gaps in the tight formations of military wagons.

George of Poděbrady

In 1458, Czech nobles elected a Utraquist – George of Poděbrady – as king. The first and last Hussite king, he reigned until 1471.

Táborite Wagon

Hussite armies struck terror in the whole of Europe. They employed new methods of combat, including the use of reinforced battle wagons.

Illuminated manuscript of sacred music from Kutná Hora (1471)

George of Poděbrady

The end of the Hussite wars in 1434 and the dying out of the Luxemburg dynasty were followed by nine years of interregnum, which ended in 1458, when the Czech nobility elected as their king George of Poděbrady (1458–71), a moderate Hussite, who also enjoyed the approval of the Czech Catholics.

The new king of Bohemia, who represented the reforming spirit and preached religious tolerance, was initially accepted by a number of European monarchs. In 1462, George put forward a plan to establish a League of Christian Monarchs to resist the Turkish expansion. This visionary proposal did not, however, meet with approval and the king's position was worsened by the hostile attitude of Rome. In 1466, Pope Paul II excommunicated George and called for a crusade against the "Czech heretics". The ensuing war ended only with the death of King George, in 1471.

The Jagiellonian Dynasty

In compliance with the late monarch's wishes, the Czech nobility chose as their new king the Polish Prince Vladislav Jagiello (1471–1516), who, in 1490, also ascended the throne of Hungary and moved his capital to Buda (today's Budapest). The king's absence was exploited by the Bohemian nobility to strengthen their own political and economic power. The fortunes of families such as the Rosenbergs and Pernsteins grew; they founded new towns and supported agriculture and trade.

A treaty concluded at Kutná Hora between Catholics and Utraquists in 1485 laid the foundation for religious peace that lasted more than half a century. Ideas of humanism percolated into the Czech Lands, and local architects created Late-Gothic masterpieces such as Prague Castle's Vladislav Hall (1502).

In 1526, Vladislav's successor, Louis Jagiello, was killed fighting the Turks at the

Late 15th-century view of Malá Strana in Prague

1458 George of Poděbrady elected to the Bohemian throne

Vladislav Jagiello

1471 Coronation of Vladislav Jagiello, king of Bohemia

1526–64 Reign of Ferdinand I

1450   1475   1500   1525

1466 Paul II anounces a crusade against Bohemia

1490 Vladislav II becomes king of Hungary

1526 Louis Jagiello killed at the Battle of Mohács

Rudolph II and the Danish astronomer Tycho Brahe

Battle of Mohács. He left no heir, so based on the political treaty concluded in 1515 between Vladislav and Maximilian I, the throne passed into the hands of the Austrian Habsburgs.

The Habsburgs

Ferdinand I (1526–64), the first representative of the Habsburg dynasty, tried to centralize the monarch's power, which met with violent opposition among the Bohemian Estates (essentially the nobility). Tension increased when attempts were made to re-establish the Catholic faith, which eventually eased when an Act of Tolerance, giving the various Christian denominations equal rights, was signed in 1609 by Rudolph II (1576–1611). This emperor, who made Prague his capital and was a great lover of the arts, presided over Bohemia's second Golden Age. Sadly, intensifying pressure from the clergy,

combined with the Emperor's deepening mental illness, forced Rudolph to abdicate in favour of his brother Matthias.

The Thirty Years' War

Rudolph II's Act of Tolerance failed to put an end to the conflict between the Catholic monarch and the non-Catholic Bohemian Estates. In 1618, representatives of the latter threw two of the emperor's envoys out of the windows of Prague Castle. This second "Prague defenestration" signalled an open anti-Habsburg rebellion and marked the beginning of the Thirty Years' War (1618–48), which was to engulf much of Europe.

In 1620, the army of the rebellious Bohemian Estates was crushed by the forces of Emperor Ferdinand II at the Battle of the White Mountain (Bílá Hora), near Prague. The collapse of the insurgence was followed by severe repression in Bohemia: 27 leaders of the anti-Habsburg opposition were executed in Prague's Old Town Square. Around 75 per cent of the land belonging to the Bohemian nobility was confiscated; thousands of families had to leave the country; and dissenters were forced to convert to Catholicism.

Defeat of the Czechs at the Battle of the White Mountain, 1620

Charter for manglers and dyers

1550

1556 Arrival of Jesuits in the Czech Lands

1575 Maximilian II confirms religious freedom in Czech Lands

1575

1576–1611 Reign of Rudolph II

A ten-ducat coin of Rudolph II

1600

1618 "Prague defenestration". Outbreak of the Thirty Years' War

1620 Czech defeat at the Battle of the White Mountain

1609 Emperor's edict confirming religious freedom and privileges of the Estates

1621 Execution of 27 leaders of the uprising in Prague

1625

1634 Killing of Albrecht von Wallenstein

1648 Peace of Westphalia ends the Thirty Years' War

Maria Theresa and Joseph II

The Thirty Years' War, which ended in 1648 with the Peace of Westphalia, reduced Bohemia's international stature and caused both devastation and depopulation. The war also elevated the position of Catholic noble families, who arrived mostly from abroad and were granted the confiscated estates of Bohemian landowners. Many of the latter went into exile.

With the Czech Lands now firmly under Catholic control, a period of intense Counter-Reformation activity followed, spearheaded by the Jesuits. As a result of the campaign, the majority of the population converted to Catholicism. A major role in the shaping of the religious consciousness was played by Baroque art. During this period, some outstanding works were created by architects Carlo Lurago, Giovanni Santini, and Christoph and Kilian Ignaz Dientzenhofer; sculptors Ferdinand Brokof and Matthias Braun; and painters Karel Škréta and Petr Brandl. The immigrant Catholic nobility built themselves grand palaces.

Following the war, the legal position of the Czech Crown within the empire changed. The Habsburgs were given hereditary rights to the throne and the German language was made legally equal to Czech. The most important national issues were now being decided by the central administration in Vienna.

Emperor Joseph II, the enlightened despot

Empress Maria Theresa with her children

When Maria Theresa (1740–80) inherited the Habsburg crown, she introduced the principles of the Enlightenment in the empire. Her most notable act was to expel the Jesuits. Her son Joseph II (1780–90) felt an even stronger need for change. He abolished serfdom and even granted certain Christian denominations equal rights. Bohemia's Jews, in particular, felt the benefits of this new freedom of worship.

Meeting of Napoleon and Franz II after the Battle of Austerlitz (1805)

1648 Peace of Westphalia signed

1711–40 Reign of Charles VI

1781 The Edict of Tolerance allows some freedom of worship

1780–90 Reign of Joseph II

| 1650 | 1675 | 1700 | 1725 | 1750 | 17 |

1657–1705 Reign of Leopold I

1676–8 Vyšehrad fortifications reinforced with new bastions

Baroque goblet made of Czech glass (1730)

1740–80 Reign of Maria Theresa

However, Joseph II, often described as an "enlightened despot", was not very popular. In his drive to unify his vast empire, he made German the official language and centralized power in Austria. The ruthless enforcement of his reforms and the Germanization of the Czech Lands bred dissatisfaction.

Joseph's successor, Franz II, was a conservative who largely swept aside his predecessors' reforms. His most memorable act was to sign a peace treaty with Napoleon following the latter's victory at the Battle of Austerlitz in 1805 *(see p234)*.

The Road to National Revival

In response to the unification policies of the Habsburgs, the early 1800s saw the emergence of a new but uncoordinated movement to rebuild Czech culture. The fight to restore the position of the Czech language became the key element of the revival programme. New plays and literary works were written in Czech. A vital role in this revival was played by Josef Dobrovský, who wrote a history of the Czech language and literature *(see p28)*.

Barricades by the Charles Bridge in Prague, June 1848

Franz Joseph I, a staunch supporter of absolute monarchy

The Springtime of Nations

In the mid-19th century, the Czech Lands, like many other European countries, became a scene of revolutionary struggle against absolute monarchy. The demands included political autonomy and the granting of civic rights, including freedom of speech, assembly, press and religion. In June 1848, an uprising in Prague was quashed by the imperial army. Franz Joseph I, who became emperor that same year, continued the policy of absolute monarchy but could not prevent the decline of the Habsburg Empire. Following the defeat of Austria by Prussia in 1866, the so-called Dual Monarchy of Austria-Hungary was established, creating two independent states under one ruler. This decision was a disappointment to Czech politicians, who failed to win the same rights for the Czech Lands as those enjoyed by Hungary. The disgruntled Czechs turned their energies to economic activities. New companies (such as Škoda) were established, and new theatres and national museums were built. Increasing importance was attached to the standards of education.

1792–1835 Reign of Franz II	**1814–15** Congress of Vienna	**1848** The Prague Uprising	**1867** Founding of the Austro-Hungarian Empire	**1883** Birth of writer Franz Kafka in Prague
1800	**1825**	**1850**	**1875**	**1900**
1792–1814 Wars with France	**1834–9** First volumes of Josef Jungmann's Czech-German dictionary	**1848** Franz Joseph I succeeds to the throne	**1868–83** Building of the National Theatre in Prague	*Franz Kafka*

The Czech National Revival

The 19th century saw the rapid growth of Czech culture and the shaping of a modern national consciousness. Playing a vital role in this process were musicians, artists and writers, including the composers Bedřich Smetana and Antonín Dvořák, the painter Mikoláš Aleš, sculptor Josef Myslbek and novelist Antonín Jirásek, whose works inspired a huge popular response. The Czech language became the basic tool in the process of shaping the national identity. Theatres and museums sprang up all over the country, emphasizing the importance of Czech culture in the nation's life.

Antonín Dvořák
The conductor and composer Antonín Dvořák (1841–1904) was a major exponent of Czech national music *(see pp24–5).*

The National Theatre in Prague
When the theatre, one of the symbols of the Czech national revival, burned down in 1881, people from all walks of life contributed money towards its rebuilding. The picture illustrates the ceremonial laying of the cornerstone.

Coat of arms of Prague's Old Town

Smetana's Libuše
Written for the opening of the National Theatre in 1881, this opera drew on legendary Czech history.

Old Town Clock Tower Calendar

In 1866, the revolving dial on Prague's famous landmark was replaced by a new one made by celebrated artist Josef Mánes. Individual months are symbolized by scenes from peasant life, corresponding with the signs of the zodiac painted on medallions.

Expo 95 Poster
Vojtěch Hynais designed this Art Nouveau poster for the ethnographic exhibition of 1895. It reflects the new appreciation of regional traditions.

Where to See the National Revival

Many fine buildings were built during this period in Prague and other major cities; they include the National Museum in Prague and Brno's Mahenovo Theatre. Among the best examples of Art Nouveau are Prague's Municipal House (see pp86–7), with murals by Alfons Mucha, and the Modern Art Gallery building in Hradec Králové, designed by Osvald Polívka (see p201). Prague's Rudolfinum (see p84) and the National Theatre (see pp96–7) both have glorious interiors by great artists of the day.

Portrait of a Woman
A young woman dressed in traditional costume poses for a portrait in a Litomyšl studio, in c.1860–70.

National Museum, Prague
Symbol of the Czech National Revival, with a glass dome, this Neo-Renaissance building was finished in 1890 (see pp92–3).

Mahenovo Theatre, Brno
Built in 1882, this building has Corinthian columns and a lavish gilt interior.

Municipal House in Prague
The Art Nouveau interior is adorned with allegories of civic virtues by Alfons Mucha.

October

Scorpio

Symbols of the months and signs of the zodiac revolve around the centre.

The First Automobile in Prague, 1898
Prague businessman, Klubal, takes a ride around Prague Castle in the first motor car to be seen in the capital.

Assassination of Archduke Ferdinand, 1914

The First World War

Few Czechs (or Slovaks) had the appetite to fight for the empire during World War I, and it was during the war that the idea of a joint Czech and Slovak state independent of Austria arose. Its main champion was Tomáš Masaryk, a professor at Prague University. In 1916, together with Edvard Beneš, he created the Czechoslovak National Council, based in Paris, which was later recognized by the Allies as the representative of the future Czechoslovakia. In May 1918, in Pittsburgh, USA, representatives of Czech and Slovak émigré organizations signed an agreement that provided for the creation of a joint Czechoslovak state after the war.

The political endeavours were supported by the military efforts of Czechs and Slovaks fighting on the side of the Allies. Czechoslovak legions fought in Italy, France and Russia. Back at home, where there had been growing anti-Habsburg dissent, the Czechoslovak National Council became the supreme political authority. On 28 October 1918, as the Austro-Hungarian Empire collapsed, the independent Czechoslovak Republic was declared in Prague. Tomáš Masaryk was its first president.

Czechoslovakia

Thanks to the industry established under the Habsburgs, Czechoslovakia flourished economically. However, the ethnic situation was much more problematic. The new state had a diverse population made up of some 6 million Czechs, 2 million Slovaks, and 3 million Germans, as well as communities of ethnic minorities including Ukrainians and Hungarians. While the Czechs were generally content with their new situation, the other ethnic groups were much less satisfied with their lot.

It was thanks to the skills of Tomáš Masaryk that Czechoslovakia became such a progressive and staunchly democratic nation. The new Czechoslovak constitution ensured that there was, at least for the moment, peaceful coexistence among the ethnic minorities by ensuring that any area

Signing of the Pittsburgh Agreement, in 1918

Woman wearing Czech national costume

1918 Pittsburgh Agreement

1920–21 Formation of the Small Entente, an alliance between Czechoslovakia, Romania and Yugoslavia

1910   1915   1920   1925

1914 Assassination of Archduke Franz Ferdinand in Sarajevo. Outbreak of World War I

1916 Czechoslovak National Council created in Paris

1918 Founding of the Czechoslovak Republic. Tomáš Masaryk becomes president

Poster for 10th Sokol Rally, aimed at promoting sport

with an ethnic community exceeding 20 per cent of the population would be officially bilingual. This relative calm disappeared in the 1930s. On top of the economically devastating Wall Street Crash of 1929 came political instability; this coincided with the growing threat posed by the Third Reich. Hitler's rise to power in 1933 helped to activate the disgruntled German minority living in northern Bohemia and Moravia (the Sudetenland). They found a voice in the Sudeten German Party (SdP), a far-right group with direct links with the Nazis. The retirement in 1935 of President Masaryk, to be replaced by Edvard Beneš, couldn't have come at a worse time.

The Munich Treaty

Following the Nazi annexation of Austria in March 1938, Czechoslovakia became Hitler's next target. Later that year, he demanded the Sudetenland. In a bid to avoid war, President Beneš agreed that the heads of France (Daladier) and Great Britain (Chamberlain) should negotiate with Hitler and Mussolini to settle the dispute. In September 1938, the four powers signed the notorious Munich Agreement, which handed Sudetenland to the Nazis. Czechoslovakia lost 5 million inhabitants and a vast chunk of its land. President Beneš resigned and left the country.

The nation carved out by the Munich Agreement survived only for another six months. In March 1939, Hitler forced the

WIR DANKEN UNSERM FÜHRER

Poster showing the area of the Protectorate

ineffectual Emil Hácha (Beneš's successor) to agree to make Bohemia and Moravia a German Protectorate. Nazi troops marched into Bohemia.

Repression against the population, while not as brutal as that seen in Poland, intensified after 1941, when Reinhard Heydrich was appointed Reich protector. A concentration camp was established in Terezín for the Jews brought from Germany, Austria, Holland and Denmark, as well as from the Protectorate. In 1942, Heydrich was assassinated by Czech paratroopers trained in England.

German troops entering Prague in March 1939

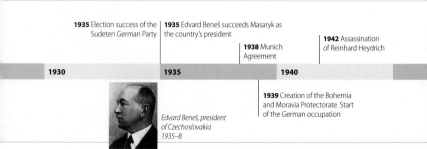

1935 Election success of the Sudeten German Party

1935 Edvard Beneš succeeds Masaryk as the country's president

1938 Munich Agreement

1942 Assassination of Reinhard Heydrich

1930

1935

1940

Edvard Beneš, president of Czechoslovakia 1935–8

1939 Creation of the Bohemia and Moravia Protectorate. Start of the German occupation

Celebrating Gottwald's new government, 1948

"Victorious February"

On 5 May 1945, in the closing days of World War II, there was an armed uprising in Prague against the Nazis. Four days later, the city was liberated by the Red Army. Beneš returned to the country as its president. The reprisals against Czech German-speakers were inevitable. Thousands died and more than 2 million were forcibly expelled (or fled).

The years immediately after the war were marked by the rapid rise of the Communist Party (KSČ). It was the party with the most votes at the 1946 election, its leader, Klement Gottwald, became prime minister and several Party members joined the cabinet. While the Communists had great popular support, there was growing dismay among the non-Communist members of the cabinet. In February 1948, 12 of them resigned, hoping thereby to bring an end to Gottwald's premiership; in the event, he managed to orchestrate a Communist coup, without the military assistance that Stalin had offered. Failing in health, Beneš resigned. This so-called "Victorious February" opened an era of Stalinization, bringing with it nationalization, collectivization and massive industrialization. There was also repression and persecution. Farmers opposed to the collectivization of the land were sent to work in the mines or to prison; clergymen were sent to concentration camps. Many people opted to emigrate.

The "Prague Spring"

In the 1960s, a reform movement within the Communist Party took shape. It demanded a liberalization of the Stalinist approach to economics, politics and individual free-doms. After failed attempts to win over and then repress the reformers, in January 1968, President Novotný was forced from office. The new First Secretary, Alexander Dubček, declared his wish to build "a socialism with a human face". The subsequent democratic reforms, which met with an enthusiastic reception,

Funeral of Czech student Jan Palach, in 1969

Citizens of Prague queuing for food in 1965

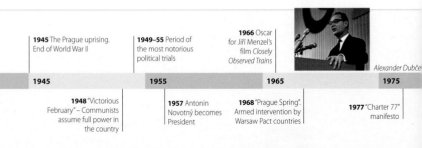

1945 The Prague uprising. End of World War II

1949–55 Period of the most notorious political trials

1966 Oscar for Jiří Menzel's film *Closely Observed Trains*

Alexander Dubče

| 1945 | 1955 | 1965 | 1975 |

1948 "Victorious February" – Communists assume full power in the country

1957 Antonin Novotný becomes President

1968 "Prague Spring". Armed intervention by Warsaw Pact countries

1977 "Charter 77" manifesto

embraced all aspects of social and political life. It all came to an abrupt end on 21 August 1968, when, on Soviet orders, troops from the Warsaw Pact nations invaded Czechoslovakia. Dubček and other reformers were sent to Moscow, and people protested in the streets. Among the few who died was a student Jan Palach, who set fire to himself in Wenceslas Square.

An invading Russian tank after the "Prague Spring" of 1968

The suppression of the "Prague Spring" returned orthodox Communists to power. Dubček was replaced by Gustáv Husák, a man totally subservient to the Soviet Union. During the next 21 years of "normalization", totalitarian rule was re-established and all dissent quashed. Many intellectuals fled abroad.

In 1977, a group of politicians and intellectuals, including the playwright Václav Havel, signed a document demanding basic human rights. This so-called Charter 77 became a rallying point for all dissidents.

The Velvet Revolution

In the autumn of 1989, the wave of democratic changes that was sweeping across Europe reached Czechoslovakia. In response to a mass demonstration in the capital, Václav Havel and Alexander Dubček appeared on a balcony in Wenceslas Square on 22 November. Their call

Crowds in Wenceslas Square in Prague: the Velvet Revolution

for a general strike was enough to cause the downfall of the Communist regime. A hastily formed new political party, the Civic Forum, embarked upon negotiations with the outgoing government. On 29 December 1989, Václav Havel became president.

The Velvet Divorce

Without the strong, centralizing authority of the Communists, the historical tensions between Prague and Slovakia reappeared. The Civic Forum split into two (the centre-left Civic Movement and the right-wing Civic Democratic Party), and the 1992 general elections brought to power parties intent on breaking up the joint state. On 1 January 1993, the Czech Republic was established. Václav Havel remained its president for two terms of office, until 2003. He was replaced by Václav Klaus. In 1999, the Czech Republic became a member of NATO and in 2004, joined the European Union.

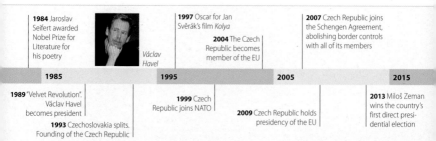

1984 Jaroslav Seifert awarded Nobel Prize for Literature for his poetry

1997 Oscar for Jan Svěrák's film *Kolya*

2004 The Czech Republic becomes member of the EU

2007 Czech Republic joins the Schengen Agreement, abolishing border controls with all of its members

Václav Havel

1985	1995	2005	2015

1989 "Velvet Revolution". Václav Havel becomes president

1993 Czechoslovakia splits. Founding of the Czech Republic

1999 Czech Republic joins NATO

2009 Czech Republic holds presidency of the EU

2013 Miloš Zeman wins the country's first direct presidential election

PRAGUE AREA BY AREA

Prague at a Glance

Most major historic sites in Prague are found in the city centre within the three districts marked on the map. From Staré Město (Old Town) and Josefov (Jewish Quarter), it is only a short distance to Charles Bridge and, beyond, Malá Strana (Little Quarter), from where a steep uphill climb ends at Prague Castle and Hradčany.

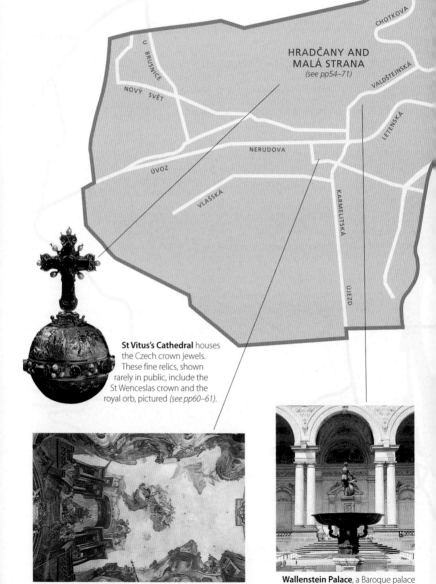

CHOTKOVA

HRADČANY AND
MALÁ STRANA
(see pp54–71)

VALDŠTEJNSKÁ

U BRUSNICE

NOVÝ SVĚT

LETENSKÁ

NERUDOVA

ÚVOZ

KARMELITSKÁ

VLAŠSKÁ

ÚJEZD

St Vitus's Cathedral houses the Czech crown jewels. These fine relics, shown rarely in public, include the St Wenceslas crown and the royal orb, pictured *(see pp60–61).*

The Church of St Nicholas, in the centre of Malá Strana, is perhaps the most magnificent of the many fine examples of Baroque architecture in Prague *(see pp66–7).*

Wallenstein Palace, a Baroque palace built in the 1620s for Count Albrecht von Wallenstein, was intended to outshine Prague Castle *(see p68).*

◀ Picturesque view of Prague as seen from Petřín Hill

Maisel Synagogue was built in 1590–92 and paid for by Mordechai Maisel, then mayor of the Jewish Quarter. It houses one of the world's most magnificent collections of Judaica *(see p81).*

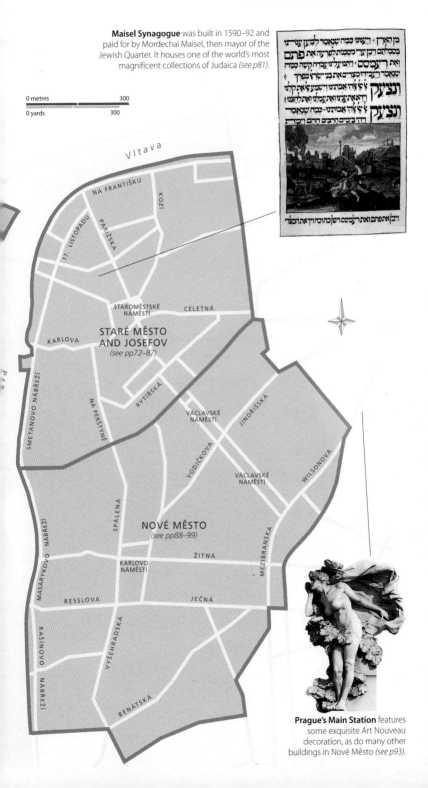

```
0 metres        300
0 yards         300
```

Vltava

NA FRANTIŠKU

KOŽÍ

17. LISTOPADU

PAŘÍŽSKÁ

STAROMĚSTSKÉ NÁMĚSTÍ

CELETNÁ

KARLOVA

STARÉ MĚSTO AND JOSEFOV
(see pp72–87)

NA PERŠTÝNĚ

RYTÍŘSKÁ

SMETANOVO NÁBŘEŽÍ

VÁCLAVSKÉ NÁMĚSTÍ

JINDŘIŠSKÁ

VODIČKOVA

VÁCLAVSKÉ NÁMĚSTÍ

WILSONOVA

SPÁLENÁ

NOVÉ MĚSTO
(see pp88–99)

MEZIBRÁNSKÁ

MASARYKOVO NÁBŘEŽÍ

KARLOVO NÁMĚSTÍ

ŽITNÁ

RESSLOVA

JEČNÁ

RAŠÍNOVO NÁBŘEŽÍ

VYŠEHRADSKÁ

BENÁTSKÁ

Prague's Main Station features some exquisite Art Nouveau decoration, as do many other buildings in Nové Město *(see p93).*

HRADČANY AND MALÁ STRANA

The history of Prague began with the Castle, founded in the 9th century high above the Vltava river. Among the buildings enclosed within the castle walls were three churches and a monastery. In around 1320, a settlement called Hradčany was founded in part of the outer bailey. The castle complex has undergone numerous reconstructions. Malá Strana ("little quarter") occupies the slopes beneath Prague Castle and has changed little since the 1700s. Its maze of streets abounds in lavishly decorated Baroque palaces and churches. Once the realm of nobles, Malá Strana is now home to artists and musicians.

Sights at a Glance

Churches, Monasteries and Monuments

- ❷ St Vitus's Cathedral pp60–61
- ❸ Old Royal Palace
- ❹ St George's Basilica
- ❻ Belvedere
- ❿ Loreto
- ⑪ Černín Palace
- ⑫ Strahov Monastery
- ⑬ Schwarzenberg Palace
- ⑮ Church of St Nicholas pp66–7
- ⑯ Wallenstein Palace
- ⑰ Church of St Thomas
- ⑳ Church of Our Lady beneath the Chain
- ㉑ Church of Our Lady Victorious
- ㉓ Charles Bridge pp70–71

Museums and Galleries

- ❶ Prague Castle Picture Gallery
- ❽ Sternberg Palace pp62–3

Historic Streets, Squares and Parks

- ❺ Golden Lane
- ❼ Royal Garden
- ❾ Hradčanské Square
- ⑭ Nerudova Street
- ⑱ Little Quarter Square
- ⑲ Palace Gardens
- ㉒ Petřín Hill

See also Street Finder maps 1 & 2

0 metres 400
0 yards 400

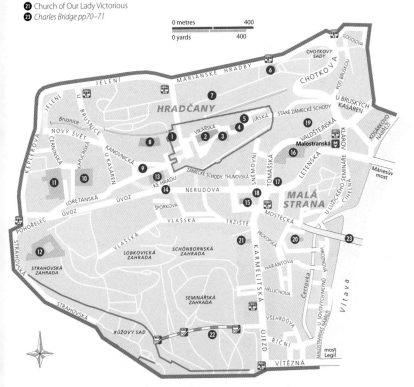

◀ Beautiful red-tiled buildings with the Church of St Nicholas towering above the rooftops

For map symbols see back flap

Street-by-Street: Prague Castle

Despite periodic fires and invasions, Prague Castle has retained churches, chapels, halls and towers from every period of its history, from the Gothic splendour of St Vitus's Cathedral to the Renaissance additions of Rudolf II, the last Habsburg to use the castle as his principal residence. The courtyards date from 1753–75, when the whole area was rebuilt in Late Baroque and Neo-Classical styles. The castle became the seat of the Czechoslovak president in 1918, and the current president of the Czech Republic has an office here.

② ★ St Vitus's Cathedral
This relief decorates St Vitus's Golden Portal.

The Powder Tower, used in the past for storing gunpowder and as a bell foundry, is now a museum.

To Royal Garden

President's office

① Prague Castle Picture Gallery
Renaissance and Baroque paintings hang in the restored stables of the castle.

Second courtyard

Matthias Gate (1614)

First courtyard

To Castle Square

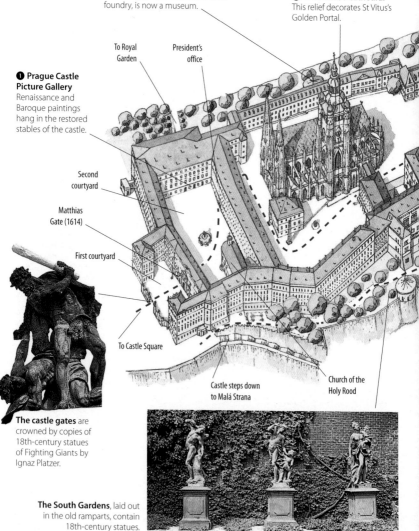

Castle steps down to Malá Strana

Church of the Holy Rood

The castle gates are crowned by copies of 18th-century statues of Fighting Giants by Ignaz Platzer.

The South Gardens, laid out in the old ramparts, contain 18th-century statues.

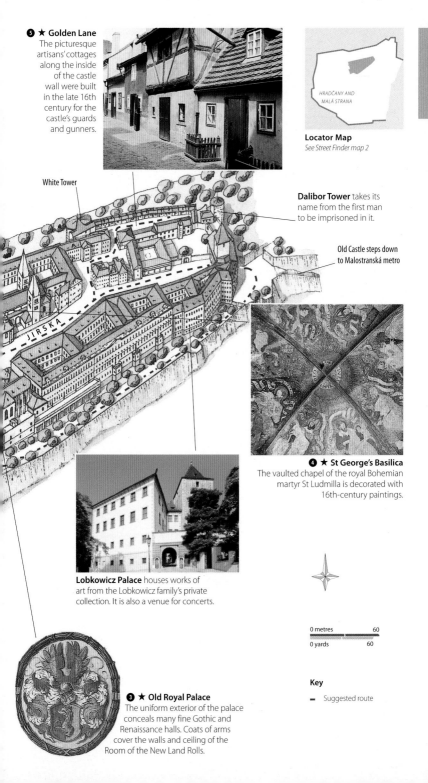

⑤ ★ Golden Lane
The picturesque artisans' cottages along the inside of the castle wall were built in the late 16th century for the castle's guards and gunners.

Locator Map
See Street Finder map 2

HRADČANY AND
MALÁ STRANA

White Tower

Dalibor Tower takes its name from the first man to be imprisoned in it.

Old Castle steps down to Malostranská metro

JIŘSKÁ

❹ ★ St George's Basilica
The vaulted chapel of the royal Bohemian martyr St Ludmilla is decorated with 16th-century paintings.

Lobkowicz Palace houses works of art from the Lobkowicz family's private collection. It is also a venue for concerts.

| 0 metres | 60 |
| 0 yards | 60 |

Key

— Suggested route

❸ ★ Old Royal Palace
The uniform exterior of the palace conceals many fine Gothic and Renaissance halls. Coats of arms cover the walls and ceiling of the Room of the New Land Rolls.

Titan's *The Toilet of a Young Lady* in Prague Castle Picture Gallery

❶ Prague Castle Picture Gallery
Obrazárna Pražského Hradu

Prague Castle, second courtyard. **Map** 2 D2. **Tel** 224 373 531. Ⓜ Malostranská, Hradčanská. 🚋 22. **Open** 9am–6pm daily (to 4pm in winter). 🅿 ♿ Ⓦ **kulturanahrade.cz**

The gallery was created in 1965 to display, among other works, what remains of the great art collection of Rudolph II, Bohemia's own Renaissance king *(see p41)*. Though many works were looted in 1648 by the occupying Swedish army, some fine paintings remain, including works by Hans von Aachen and Bartolomeus Spranger.

Paintings from the 16th–18th centuries make up the bulk of the gallery's collection; highlights include Titian's *The Toilet of a Young Lady* and Rubens' *The Assembly of the Olympic Gods*. Master Theodoric, Paolo Veronese, Tintoretto and the Czech Baroque artists Jan Kupecký and Petr Brandl are among other painters represented. The sculptures include a copy of a bust of Rudolph II by Adriaen de Vries.

You can see the remains of the castle's first church, the 9th-century Church of Our Lady, believed to have been built by Prince Bořivoj, the first Přemyslid prince to be baptized a Christian.

❷ St Vitus's Cathedral
See pp60–61.

❸ Old Royal Palace
Starý Královský Palác

Prague Castle, third courtyard. **Map** 2 D2. **Tel** 224 373 102. Ⓜ Malostranská, Hradčanská. 🚋 22. **Open** Apr–Oct: 10am–5pm daily; Nov–Mar: 10am–4pm daily. 🅿 ♿ ♿ Ⓦ **hrad.cz**

The vast complex of the Old Royal Palace consists of several layers. The first palace on the site, remains of which are still visible in the basement, was built by Soběslav I in around 1135. Two further palaces were built above the original, in the 13th and 14th centuries, followed by the Gothic Vladislav Hall, designed by Benedikt Ried for King Vladislav Jagiellon in the 1490s. This vast and opulent hall is the highlight of the palace. It has superb rib vaulting and is lit by large windows that heralded the advent of the Renaissance in Bohemia. The room was used not only for state functions, but also for jousting. The architect's unusual staircase design, with gently sloping steps, allowed knights to enter the hall without having to dismount from their horses.

The adjacent Ludvík Wing was, in 1618, the scene of the famous defenestration which led to the outbreak of the Thirty Years' War. All Saints' Church, behind the Vladislav Hall, was built by Peter Parler but was badly damaged in the great fire of 1541. The same fire

The Riders' Staircase, Vladislav Hall in the Royal Palace

destroyed Ried's Diet Hall, but this was rebuilt so its intricate Late Gothic vault can still be enjoyed.

❹ St George's Basilica and Convent
Bazilika a Klášter Sv. Jiří

Jiřské náměstí. **Map** 2 E2. **Tel** 224 371 111. Ⓜ Malostranská, Hradčanská. 🚋 22 to Pražský hrad (Prague Castle). **Open** 10am–5pm. 🅿 ♿ ♿

The building of St George's Church began before 920, during the reign of Prince Vratislav, making it the oldest remaining part of Prague Castle. The church's two distinct light-coloured stone towers date from after the 1142 fire. The wonderful, austere interior contains the 10th-century tomb of Vratislav I, found opposite the presbytery. Also buried in the church are Prince Boleslav II, who died in 992, and Princess Ludmilla (grandmother of St Wenceslas), who was murdered in 921 and is revered as the first Bohemian saint; her 14th-century tombstone is located in the Gothic side chapel. The south portal of the church features a 16th-century relief depicting St George and the dragon.

Today, the basilica provides an atmospheric setting for classical concerts.

The adjacent former Benedictine nunnery is the oldest convent building in Bohemia. It was founded in 973 by Princess Mlada, sister of Boleslav II. Throughout the Middle Ages, the convent, together with St George's Basilica, formed the heart of the castle complex. Many times rebuilt, the convent and its religious functions finally ceased to operate in 1782.

The convent building was formerly home to a collection of the National Gallery's 19th-century Czech art. However, it is now closed and there are presently no plans for any future exhibitions.

❺ Golden Lane
Zlatá Ulička

Map 2 E2. 🚇 Malostranská, Hradčanská. 🚋 22. 🔲

Named after the goldsmiths who lived here in the 17th century, this short, narrow street is one of the prettiest in Prague. One side of the lane is lined with tiny, brightly painted houses which were built right into the arches of the castle walls. They were constructed in the late 16th century for Rudolph II's 24 castle guards. A century later, the goldsmiths moved in and modified the buildings. However, by the 19th century, the area had degenerated into a slum and was populated by Prague's poor and the criminal community. In the 1950s, all the remaining tenants were moved and the area restored to something like its original state. Most of the houses were converted into shops selling books, Bohemian glass and a variety of other souvenirs for visitors, who now flock to this narrow lane.

Golden Lane has been home to some well-known writers, including Franz Kafka *(see pp28–9)*, who stayed at No. 22 with his sister for a few months in 1916–17.

Despite the street's name, Rudolph II's alchemists never produced gold here. Their labs were in Vikářská, the lane between St Vitus's and the Powder Tower (Mihulka).

One of the tiny, colourful houses in Golden Lane

❻ Belvedere
Belvedér

Prague Castle, Royal Garden.
Map 2 E1. 🚇 Malostranská, Hradčanská. 🚋 22 to Královský Letohrádek. **Open** 10am–6pm Tue–Sun during exhibitions only. 🔲 ♿

Built in the 16th century by Ferdinand I for his beloved wife Anne, the Belvedere is the popular name for Queen Anne's Palace (Letohrádek královny Anny), one of the finest Italian Renaissance buildings north of the Alps. An arcaded summer-house with Ionic columns, it is topped by a roof shaped like an inverted ship's hull clad in blue-green copper. The main architect, Paolo della Stella, also designed the reliefs inside the arcade. In the garden is the Singing Fountain, so-called for its musical sound.

Detail from the bronze Singing Fountain in the Belvedere gardens

Spring flowers in Prague Castle's Royal Garden

❼ Royal Garden
Královská Zahrada

Prague Castle, U Prašného mostu.
Map 2 D2. 🚇 Malostranská, Hradčanská. 🚋 22. **Open** May–Oct: 10am–6pm daily (to 7pm May & Sep, to 9pm Jun–Aug). ♿ 🌐 **hrad.cz**

Of the gardens around Prague Castle, the Royal Garden, on the north side, is the most important historically. It was laid out for Ferdinand I in 1534, and became famous for its rare and exotic plants. Some fine examples of 16th-century garden architecture have survived, notably the Belvedere and the Ball Game Hall (Míčovna). The latter is covered in much-restored but still beautiful Renaissance *sgraffito*.

The garden is a beautiful place for a stroll, especially in spring when thousands of tulips bloom in its immaculate beds. This is where tulips (originally from Turkey) were first acclimatized to the North European climate.

Paradise Garden

The South Gardens below Prague Castle were developed in stages, the oldest part being the Paradise Garden, first laid out in 1559. In the 1920s, as part of President Masaryk's plan to revamp the castle, Josip Plečnik, a Slovenian architect, redesigned the gardens. He was responsible for the spiralling Bull Staircase, which leads from the Paradise Garden up to Prague Castle.

Plečnik's ingenious Bull Staircase

❷ St Vitus's Cathedral
Chrám Sv. Víta

Work began on the city's most distinctive landmark in 1344. Peter Parler was largely responsible for the grandiose Gothic design, though the building was not finally completed for another 600 years. The cathedral contains the tomb of "Good King" Wenceslas, some fine works of art, among them an exquisite Alfons Mucha window.

Chancel
The chancel, first built by Parler and repaired in Neo-Gothic style is remarkable for its vault, counter-pointed by the intricacy of the webbed tracery.

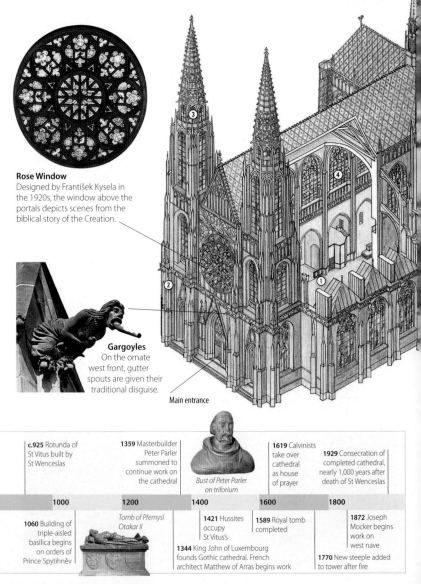

Rose Window
Designed by František Kysela in the 1920s, the window above the portals depicts scenes from the biblical story of the Creation.

Gargoyles
On the ornate west front, gutter spouts are given their traditional disguise.

Main entrance

c.925 Rotunda of St Vitus built by St Wenceslas

1359 Masterbuilder Peter Parler summoned to continue work on the cathedral

Bust of Peter Parler on triforium

1619 Calvinists take over cathedral as house of prayer

1929 Consecration of completed cathedral, nearly 1,000 years after death of St Wenceslas

1000	1200	1400	1600	1800

1060 Building of triple-aisled basilica begins on orders of Prince Spytihněv

Tomb of Přemysl Otakar II

1421 Hussites occupy St Vitus's

1589 Royal tomb completed

1872 Joseph Mocker begins work on west nave

1344 King John of Luxembourg founds Gothic cathedral. French architect Matthew of Arras begins work

1770 New steeple added to tower after fire

★ Flying Buttresses
The slender buttresses that surround the exterior of the nave and chancel, supporting the vaulted interior, are richly decorated like the rest of the cathedral.

VISITORS' CHECKLIST

Practical Information
Prague Castle, third courtyard.
Map 2 D2.
Cathedral: **Open** 9am–4pm
Mon–Sat (to 5pm Apr–Oct),
noon–4pm Sun (to 6pm Apr–
Oct). ✝ Mass 7am Mon–Sat,
8am, 9:30am, 11am Sun. ♿

Transport
Ⓜ Hradčanská, Malostranská.
🚊 22 to Pražský hrad
(Prague Castle).

★ Chapel of St Wenceslas
This opulent, jewel-studded chapel, home to the saint's tomb, is the highlight of a visit to St Vitus's. This bronze ring hangs on the chapel's north portal.

★ Golden Portal
Until the 19th century, this was the main cathedral entrance, and it is still used on special occasions. Above it is a mosaic of *The Last Judgment* by 14th-century Venetian craftsmen.

Gothic Vaulting
The skills of architect Peter Parler are never more clearly seen than in the delicate fans of ribbing that support the three Gothic arches of the Golden Portal.

KEY

① **Nave**

② **West front**

③ **Twin west spires**

④ **Triforium**

⑤ **The Renaissance bell tower** is capped with a Baroque "helmet".

⑥ **Chancel**

⑦ **To Old Royal Palace** *(see p58)*

⑧ **The tomb of St Wenceslas** is connected to an altar, decorated with semi-precious stones.

❽ Sternberg Palace

Šternberský Palác

Built between 1697 and 1707 for Count Wenceslas Adalbert, the palace was named after Franz Josef Sternberg, who founded the Society of Patriotic Friends of the Arts in Bohemia in 1796. Fellow noblemen would lend sculptures and pictures to the society, which had its headquarters here in the early 1800s. Today, it houses the National Gallery's superb collection of European art by various Old Masters.

The Lamentation of Christ
The frozen, sculptural figures make this one of the finest paintings by Lorenzo Monaco (1408).

First floor

Cardinal Cesi's Garden in Rome
Henrick van Cleve's painting (1548) provides a valuable image of a Renaissance collection of antiquities. The garden was later destroyed.

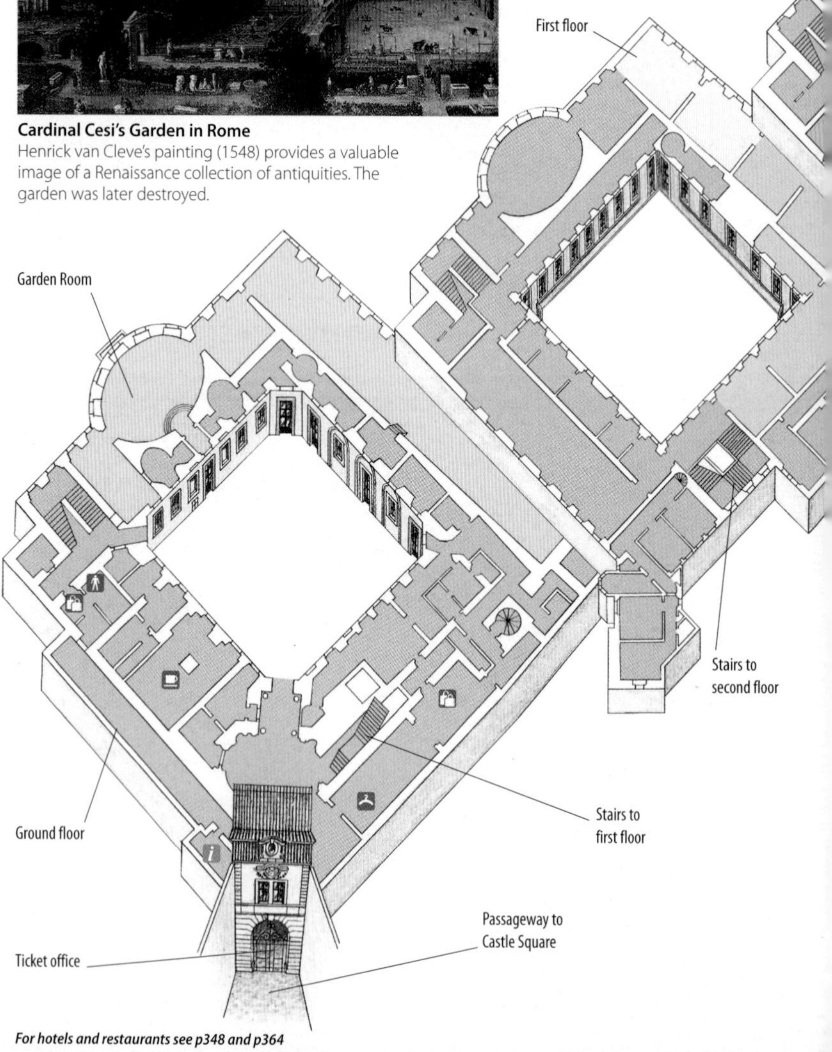

Garden Room

Stairs to second floor

Ground floor

Stairs to first floor

Passageway to Castle Square

Ticket office

★ Scholar in his Study
In this painting from 1634, Rembrandt used keenly observed detail to convey wisdom in the face of the old scholar.

VISITORS' CHECKLIST

Practical Information
Hradčanské náměstí 15.
Map 1 C2.
Tel 233 090 570.
Open 10am–6pm Tue–Sun (last guided tour at 5pm).
🖼 🚻 📷
W **ngprague.cz**

Transport
Ⓜ Hradčanská, Malostranská.
🚊 22 to Pražský hrad (Prague Castle) or to Brusnice.

Chinese Cabinet

Eden (1618)
Roelandt Savery studied the animals in the menagerie of Emperor Rudolph II. He liked to include them in his biblical and mythological works.

Second floor

Stairs down to other floors and exit

★ Head of Christ
Painted by El Greco in the 1590s, this portrait emphasizes the humanity of Christ. At the same time, the curious square halo gives the painting the qualities of an ancient icon.

Gallery Guide

The gallery is arranged on three floors around the central courtyard of the palace. The ground floor, reached from the courtyard, houses German and Austrian art from the 15th to 19th centuries. The stairs to the collections on the upper floors are beyond the ticket office at the main entrance.

Key

- German and Austrian Art 1400–1800
- Flemish and Dutch Art 1400–1600
- Italian Art 1400–1500
- Roman Art
- Flemish and Dutch Art 1600–1800
- French Art 1600–1800
- Icons, Classical and Ancient Art
- Venice 1700–1800 and Goya
- Spanish Art 1600–1800
- Naples and Venice 1600–1700
- Italian Art 1500–1600
- Non-exhibition space

For keys to symbols *see back flap*

★ The Martyrdom of St Thomas
This magnificent work is by Peter Paul Rubens, the foremost Flemish Baroque painter of the 17th century.

⁹ Hradčanské Square

Hradčanské Náměstí

Map 2 D3. 🚇 Malostranská, Hradčanská. 🚊 22.

The vast square in front of Prague Castle was once the home of workshops and artisans' houses, but after the fire of 1541, they were replaced by a series of imposing palaces. These were built by Czech and foreign nobles, eager to live close to the court of the Habsburgs. On the south side, the huge 16th-century Schwarzenberg Palace (Schwarzenberský palác; *see p65*) is one of the most beautiful Renaissance buildings in Prague, with graceful attics and magnificent *sgraffito* that gives the impression that the façade is clad in Italian-style diamond-point stonework.

The broad, western end of the square is taken up by the Thun-Hohenstein Palace (Thun-Hohenšteinský palác), a more austere affair built in 1689–91. Its roof is crowned with statues by F M Brokoff.

On the north side of the square, between the castle and Sternberg Palace, is the Archbishop's Palace (Arcibiskupský palác), a 16th-century building boasting a fancy Rococo façade in pink and white that was added in the 1760s.

The Renaissance Martinic Palace (Martinický palác), at the corner of Castle Square and Kanovnická Street, has *sgraffito* depicting scenes from the Bible and mythology.

The square also has a high terrace that affords a famous view embracing virtually the entire city of Prague.

The Loreto's entrance, with statues of St Joseph and St John the Baptist

¹⁰ Loreto

Loretánské náměstí 7, Hradčany. **Map** 1 C3. **Tel** 220 516 740. 🚊 22 to Pohořelec. **Open** Apr–Oct: 9am–12:15pm & 1–5pm daily; Nov–Mar: 9:30am–12:15pm & 1–4pm daily. 📷 📹 🎵 6pm Sun. 🌐 **loreta.cz**

The religious complex of Prague's Loreto, occupying virtually the entire west side of Loretánské náměstí, was built in 1629, shortly after the victory of the Catholic forces in the Battle of the White Mountain. Its founder was Kateřina of Lobkowicz, a Czech aristocrat who was eager to promote the legend of the Santa Casa – the "holy house" in Nazareth in which Archangel Gabriel told Mary about the future birth of Jesus, and which, in 1295, was miraculously transported to the Italian town of Loreto. Replicas of the house were erected all over Bohemia and Moravia, the grandest of which lies at the heart of

Capital on Černín Palace

Prague's Loreto complex. In it, stuccoes and statues show characters from the Old Testament and scenes from the life of the Virgin Mary. The Santa Casa is enclosed by lavishly decorated 17th-century cloisters, which meet on one side at the Baroque Church of the Nativity.

The Loreto's treasury has many valuable liturgical vessels, among which the collection of monstrances (for displaying the host) is particularly precious: one dazzling monstrance is encrusted with no fewer than 6,222 diamonds.

Every hour, an unusual concert is played by 27 bells in the Loreto's Baroque tower.

¹¹ Černín Palace

Černínský Palác

Loretánské náměstí 5. **Map** 1 B3. 🚊 22. **Closed** to the public. 🌐 **mzv.cz**

Begun in 1669 for Count Černín of Chudenice, the Imperial Ambassador to Venice, the Černín Palace was Prague's first truly Baroque building, though later changes do not make this obvious. Its 150-m (490-ft) long façade, with a row of vast Corinthian half-columns, towers over the small, grassy square that lies between it and the Loreto.

The huge building suffered as a result of its prominent position on one of Prague's highest hills. It was looted by the French in 1742 and badly damaged in the Prussian bombardment of the city in 1757. In 1851, the now-impoverished Černín family sold the palace to the state and it became a barracks. Following the creation of Czechoslovakia in 1918, the palace was restored to its original design and became the Ministry of Foreign Affairs. Thirty years later, a few days after the Communist coup, the Foreign Minister Jan Masaryk, the popular son of Czechoslovakia's first President,

Schwarzenberg Palace, with its *sgraffito* decoration, in Castle Square

Tomáš Masaryk, died as the result of a fall from a top-floor window of the palace. He was the only non-Communist in the new government. No one really knows whether he was pushed or jumped, but he is still widely mourned.

⓬ Strahov Monastery
Strahovský Klášter

Královská Kanonie Premonstrátů na Strahově, Strahovské nádvoří 1/132, Strahovská. **Map** 1 B4. **Tel** 233 107 730. 🚋 22 to Pohořelec. **Open** 9am–noon & 1–5pm daily. Theological Hall, Philosophical Hall, Church of Our Lady, Picture Gallery: **Open** 10–11:30am & noon–5pm daily. **Closed** Easter Sun, 24 & 25 Dec. 🖼 🏛 🚫
🌐 **strahovskyklaster.cz**

When it was founded by Vladislav II in 1140, to serve an austere religious order, the Premonstratensians, Strahov rivalled Prague Castle in size. Burnt down in the 13th century, then rebuilt, Strahov acquired its present magnificent, Baroque form in the 18th century. In 1783, during the reign of Joseph II, the monastery managed to escape dissolution by cleverly declaring itself an educational establishment, citing its vast library. The monks were finally driven out of Strahov in 1950 by the Communists. Now, following the Velvet Revolution, the monastery has resumed its original function, and monks can sometimes be seen going about their daily business.

The abbey courtyard is entered via a Baroque gateway sporting a statue of St Norbert, the founder of the Premonstratensian Order. The nearby 17th-century Church of St Roch now houses one of Prague's finest art galleries. The main monastery church is the vast Church of Our Lady, whose façade features expressive statues by Johan Anton Quitainer. The lovingly restored Baroque interior dazzles with its opulence. Besides the magnificent altars and furnishings, including the pulpits, particularly striking

Philosophical Hall, Strahov Monastery

are the impressive frescoes covering the ceiling and the walls above the arcades.

Inside the monastery itself, the two Baroque libraries are among the most beautiful in Europe. The first of these, the Philosophical Hall (Filosofický sál), was built expressly to house the books (and splendid bookcases) from Louca monastery, in Moravia, dissolved by Joseph II. The breathtaking vault is decorated with a 1782 fresco depicting mankind's *Quest for Truth*. The second, the Theological Hall (Teologický sál), dates from the 16th century and is equally impressive with its beautiful frescoes filling the stucco frames, and superb furnishings, including a number of 17th-century astronomical globes.

⓭ Schwarzenberg Palace
Schwarzenberský Palác

Hradčanské náměstí 2. **Map** 2 D3. 🚋 22 to Pražský hrad. **Open** 10am–6pm Tue–Sun. ♿

Schwarzenberg Palace is one of the most beautiful and well-preserved Renaissance palaces in Prague, recognizable by the rich black and white *sgraffito* decorations on its walls.

The palace stands on the site of three former buildings which were destroyed by a great fire in 1541. The ruins were bought

by Jan Popel of Lobkowicz, one of the wealthiest noblemen in Bohemia. The majority of the palace was built in 1567, with the western wing completed several years later.

Today, the palace belongs to the National Gallery and exhibits sculptures and paintings dating from around 1580. These include depictions of famous mythological scenes, including *The Judgement of Paris* by Peter Paul Rubens and *The Escape of Aeneid* by Raffaello Sanzio.

⓮ Nerudova Street
Nerudova Ulice

Map 2 D3. Ⓜ Malostranská. 🚋 12, 20, 22. 🚌 292 to Malostranskénáměstí.

A picturesque narrow street leading up to Prague Castle, Nerudova is named after the poet and journalist Jan Neruda, who wrote many short stories set in this part of Prague. From 1845 to 1857, he lived in the house called At the Two Suns (No. 47). Bustling, noisy and crowded during the day, Nerudova Street becomes deserted at night.

Until the introduction of house numbers in 1770, the city's dwellings were distinguished by signs. Nerudova Street's houses have a splendid selection of these; they often indicate a profession or particular interest of the former occupants.

Look out in particular for the Red Eagle (No. 6), the Three Fiddles (No. 12), the Golden Horseshoe (No. 34), the Green Lobster (No. 43) and the White Swan (No. 49), as well as the Old Pharmacy Museum at No. 32.

There are also a number of grand Baroque buildings, most of which have now become embassies. Among them are the Thun-Hohenstein Palace (No. 20), and Morzin Palace (No. 5).

⓯ Church of St Nicholas
Kostel Sv. Mikuláše

The Church of St Nicholas divides and dominates the two sections of Malostranské náměstí (Little Quarter Square). Building began in 1704, and the last touches were put to the glorious frescoed nave in 1761. It is recognized as the masterpiece of father-and-son architects Christoph and Kilian Ignaz Dientzenhofer, Prague's greatest exponents of High Baroque, though neither lived to see the church's completion. The statues, frescoes and paintings inside are by leading Baroque artists, and include a fine Passion Cycle (1673) by Karel Škréta. Renovation in the 1950s dealt with the damage caused by 200 years of leaky cladding.

Altar Paintings
The side chapels hold many works of art. This painting of St Michael is by Francesco Solimena.

★ Pulpit
Dating from 1765, the ornate pulpit is by Richard and Peter Prachner. It is lavishly adorned with golden cherubs.

Baroque Organ
A fresco of St Cecilia watches over the superb organ, built in 1746 by Tomáš Schwarz. There were originally three Schwarz organs here.

Façade
St Paul, by John Frederick Kohl, is one of the statues that grace the curving façade. It was completed in 1710 by Christoph Dientzenhofer, who was influenced by Italian architects Borromini and Guarini.

★ Dome Fresco
Franz Palko's fresco, *The Celebration of the Holy Trinity* (1753–4), fills the 70-m (230-ft) high dome.

KEY

① **Chapel of St Catherine**

② **Chapel of St Anne**

③ **Entrance from west side of Little Quarter Square**

④ **The dome** was completed by Kilian Ignaz Dientzenhofer in 1751, shortly before his death.

⑤ **The belfry**, added in 1751–6, was the last part to be built. Visitors can climb up it to admire the view.

⑥ **The High Altar** is surmounted by a copper statue of St Nicholas by Ignaz Platzer. Below it is the painting of St Joseph by Johann Lukas Kracker, who also painted the nave fresco.

★ Statues of the Eastern Church Fathers
The statues of the four great teachers by Ignaz Platzer stand at the base of the four columns supporting the dome. Pictured here is St Cyril.

The Dientzenhofer Family

Christoph Dientzenhofer (1655–1722) came from a family of Bavarian master builders. His son Kilian Ignaz (1689–1751) was born in Prague and educated at the Jesuit Clementinum *(see pp84–5)*. They were responsible for the greatest treasures of Jesuit-influenced Prague Baroque architecture. The Church of St Nicholas, their last work, was completed by Kilian's son-in-law, Anselmo Lurago.

Kilian Ignaz Dientzenhofer

The magnificent main hall of Wallenstein Palace

⓰ Wallenstein Palace and Garden

Valdštejnský Palác

Valdštejnské náměstí 4. **Map** 2 E3.
Ⓜ Malostranská. **Tel** 257 075 707.
🚊 12, 18, 20, 22. Palace: **Open** 10am–
5pm Sat & Sun (advance booking
required). ✉ ♿ from Valdštejnská.
Garden: **Open** Apr–Oct: 10am–6pm
daily (to 7pm Jun–Sep). ♿ from
Valdštejnské náměstí.
🖥 🌐 **senat.cz**

The first large secular building
of the Baroque era in Prague,
the palace stands as a
monument to the fatal
ambition of imperial military
commander Albrecht von
Wallenstein (1583–1634). His
string of victories over the
Protestants in the Thirty Years'
War *(see p41)* made him vital
to Emperor Ferdinand II.
Already showered with titles,
Wallenstein soon started to
covet the crown of Bohemia.
When he dared to negotiate
independently with the
enemy, he was assassinated
on the emperor's orders.
    Wallenstein spent only
12 months in the palace that
he had built in 1620–30.
Intended to overshadow even
Prague Castle, the palace was
designed by Andrea Spezza
who, like most of the artists who
helped decorate the building,
were Italians. The superb main
hall has a ceiling fresco of
Wallenstein himself portrayed
as Mars, the god of war, riding
in a triumphal chariot. Today,
the palace is home to the

Czech Senate. The gardens
are laid out as they were
when Wallenstein dined in
the huge garden pavilion
that looks out over a fountain
and rows of bronze statues.

⓱ Church of St Thomas

Kostel Sv. Tomáš

Josefská 8. **Map** 2 E3. **Tel** 257 530 556.
Ⓜ Malostranská. 🚊 12, 20, 22.
Open 11:30am–1pm & 4–6pm Mon–
Sat. ✝ 12:15pm Mon–Sat, 9:30am,
12:30pm Sun; English: 6pm Sat, 11am
Sun. ✉ ♿ 🌐 **augustiniani.cz**

Founded by Wenceslas II
in 1285 as the monastery
church of the Augustinians,
the original Gothic church
was completed in 1379. During

Glass coffin with relics of St Justus,
in St Thomas's Church

the Hussite period, this was
one of the few churches to
remain Catholic, and, as a
result, it suffered serious
damage. Further misfortune
arrived in 1723, when the
church was struck by lightning.
Kilian Ignaz Dientzenhofer was
called in to rebuild it. The
shape of the original church
was preserved, but, apart from
the spire, the church today
retains little of its Gothic origins.
    Frescoes adorn the dome
and the curving ceiling in the
nave, while above the altar
are copies of paintings of
St Thomas and St Augustine
by Rubens. The English-speaking
community of Prague meets
in this church.

The Baroque Church of St Nicholas in Little
Quarter Square

⓲ Little Quarter Square

Malostranské Náměstí

Map 2 E3. Ⓜ Malostranská.
🚊 12, 20, 22.

This sloping square, busy with
trams and people stopping for
a drink or bite to eat, has been
the centre of activity in Malá
Strana since its foundation in
1257. It began as a marketplace
in the outer bailey of Prague
Castle. Most of the houses
here have a medieval core,
but all were rebuilt during
the Renaissance and
Baroque periods.
    The square is dominated by
the Church of St Nicholas *(see
pp66–7)*, opposite which is the
vast Neo-Classical façade of
Lichtenstein Palace. Other

important buildings include Malá Strana's Town Hall, with its fine Renaissance façade, and Sternberg Palace, built on the site of the outbreak of the 1541 fire, which destroyed most of the district.

⑲ Palace Gardens below Prague Castle

Palacove Zahrady Pod Pražkým Hradem

Valdštejnská 14. **Map** 2 F2. ⓜ Malostranská. 🚋 12, 18, 20, 22. **Open** Apr–Oct: 10am–6pm daily (to 7pm May–Sep).

When, in the 1500s, nobles started building palaces on the slopes below Prague Castle, they also laid out formal gardens based on Italian Renaissance models. Redone in the 18th century, when Baroque statuary and fountains were added, some of the gardens now form a public park. As well as offering superb views of the city, the gardens are full of interest. The Kolowrat-Černín Garden is undoubtedly the finest, with its highly decorated pavilion and assortment of staircases, balustrades and loggias, as well as fountains, pools and Classical statuary.

⑳ Church of Our Lady beneath the Chain

Kostel Panny Marie Pod Řetězem

Lázeňská. **Map** 2 F4. ⓜ Malostranská. **Tel** 257 530 876. 🚋 12, 20, 22. **Open** for concerts & services. ✝ 5pm Wed, 10am Sun.

This church, the oldest in Malá Strana, was founded in the 12th century. King Vladislav II presented it to the Knights of St John, the order later known as the Knights of Malta. It stood in the centre of the Knights' heavily fortified monastery guarding the approach to the old Judith Bridge. The church's name refers to the chain used in the Middle Ages to close the monastery gatehouse. In the 14th century, the original

Detail from the Church of Our Lady beneath the Chain

Romanesque church was demolished. What can be seen today dates largely from a Baroque facelift performed in 1640 by Karel Škréta.

The painting on the high altar shows the Virgin Mary and John the Baptist coming to the aid of the Knights of Malta in the famous naval victory over the Turks at Lepanto in 1571.

㉑ Church of Our Lady Victorious

Kostel Panny Marie Vítězné

Karmelitská. **Map** 2 E4. **Tel** 257 533 646. 🚋 12, 20, 22. **Open** 8:30am–7pm Mon–Sat, 8:30am–8pm Sun. ✝ 5pm Thu (Czech), 5pm Sat (Spanish), noon (English), 5pm (French), 6pm (Italian) Sun.

Built in the early 17th century by German Lutherans, the church was given to the Carmelites by the Catholic

authorities after the Battle of the White Mountain. They rebuilt the church and renamed it after the victory.

The building is of little interest, but the church attracts many visitors who come to see the Pražské Jezulátko, better known by its Italian name, *il Bambino di Praga* – a wax effigy of the infant Jesus in a glass case in the south aisle. This figure has a record of miracle cures and is one of the most revered images in the Catholic world. It was presented to the Carmelites by one of the Lobkowicz family's Spanish brides in 1628. The figure has a vast number of clothes, some of which are in the museum.

㉒ Petřín Hill

Petřínské Sady

Map 2 D5. 🚋 6, 9, 12, 20, 22, 23, then take funicular railway from Újezd.

Petřín Hill, to the west of Malá Strana, is the highest of Prague's nine hills, and an area of greenery much loved by local citizens.

A path winds up the slopes of Petřín, offering fine views of Prague, but it is also fun to take the funicular from Újezd. Once at the top, there are many paths to explore and several attractions, including a mini version of the Eiffel Tower (Rozhledna), built in 1891, which can be climbed, and a mini-Gothic castle (Bludiště), containing a hall of distorting mirrors which is hugely popular with children.

Albrecht von Wallenstein

Albrecht von Wallenstein (Valdštein) was born in Bohemia in 1583. He studied in Italy and later converted to Catholicism and joined the army of Rudolph II. He rose to lead the Imperial armies in Europe, and during the Thirty Years' War, he scored numerous victories over the Protestants. In 1630, he negotiated secretly with the Protestants and then joined them. For this, he was killed in 1634 by mercenaries acting on the orders of the Emperor Ferdinand.

Wallenstein, politician and commander

⊗ Charles Bridge

Karlův Most

Prague's most familiar monument was built by Peter Parler for Charles IV in 1357, and replaced the ruined Judith Bridge; it was the only bridge across the Vltava until 1741. Due to wear and tear, many of the statues that witness the constant parade of people across the bridge are copies.

Malá Strana

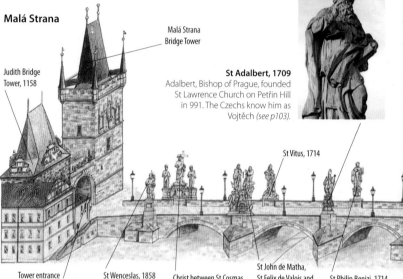

Malá Strana
Bridge Tower

Judith Bridge
Tower, 1158

St Adalbert, 1709
Adalbert, Bishop of Prague, founded St Lawrence Church on Petřin Hill in 991. The Czechs know him as Vojtěch *(see p103)*.

St Vitus, 1714

Tower entrance

St Wenceslas, 1858

Christ between St Cosmas and St Damian, 1709

St John de Matha, St Felix de Valois and the Blessed Ivan, 1714

St Philip Benizi, 1714

Staré Město

St Francis Xavier
The Jesuit missionary is supported by Moorish and Oriental converts. The sculptor Brokof is seated on the saint's left.

Thirty Years' War
In the last hours of this war, Staré Město was saved from the Swedish army. The truce was signed in the middle of the bridge in 1648.

St Norbert, St Wenceslas and St Sigismund, 1853

St Christopher, 1857

St Anne, 1707

St Francis Borgia, 1710

St John the Baptist, 1857

St Cyril and St Methodius, 1938

St Joseph, 1854

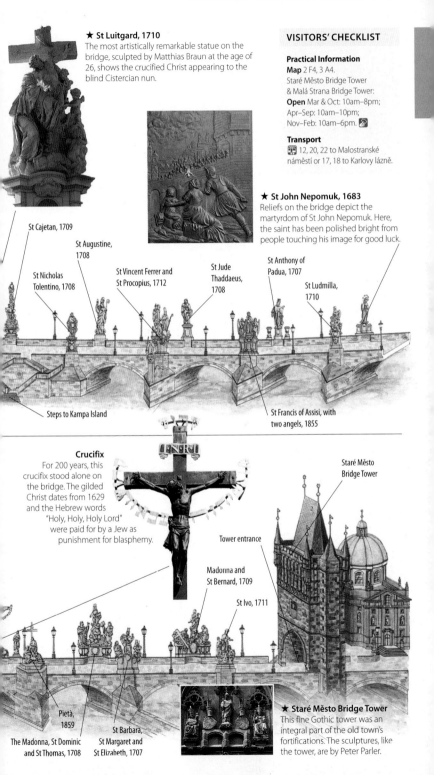

★ St Luitgard, 1710
The most artistically remarkable statue on the bridge, sculpted by Matthias Braun at the age of 26, shows the crucified Christ appearing to the blind Cistercian nun.

VISITORS' CHECKLIST

Practical Information
Map 2 F4, 3 A4.
Staré Město Bridge Tower
& Malá Strana Bridge Tower:
Open Mar & Oct: 10am–8pm;
Apr–Sep: 10am–10pm;
Nov–Feb: 10am–6pm.

Transport
12, 20, 22 to Malostranské
náměstí or 17, 18 to Karlovy lázně.

★ St John Nepomuk, 1683
Reliefs on the bridge depict the martyrdom of St John Nepomuk. Here, the saint has been polished bright from people touching his image for good luck.

St Cajetan, 1709

St Augustine, 1708

St Nicholas Tolentino, 1708

St Vincent Ferrer and St Procopius, 1712

St Jude Thaddaeus, 1708

St Anthony of Padua, 1707

St Ludmilla, 1710

Steps to Kampa Island

St Francis of Assisi, with two angels, 1855

Crucifix
For 200 years, this crucifix stood alone on the bridge. The gilded Christ dates from 1629 and the Hebrew words "Holy, Holy, Holy Lord" were paid for by a Jew as punishment for blasphemy.

Staré Město Bridge Tower

Tower entrance

Madonna and St Bernard, 1709

St Ivo, 1711

Pietà, 1859

The Madonna, St Dominic and St Thomas, 1708

St Barbara, St Margaret and St Elizabeth, 1707

★ Staré Město Bridge Tower
This fine Gothic tower was an integral part of the old town's fortifications. The sculptures, like the tower, are by Peter Parler.

STARÉ MĚSTO AND JOSEFOV

In the 11th century, the settlements built around Prague Castle spilled over onto the right bank of the Vltava. Thus Staré Město, the Old Town, was created. With time, houses and churches built around the market square developed into an irregular network of streets, many of them surviving to this day. In the Middle Ages, this area was home to two distinct Jewish communities, Ashkenazi and Sephardi Jews. These groups gradually merged and became confined to a ghetto. The discrimination they suffered was partially relaxed in 1784, by Joseph II, and the Jewish Quarter was named Josefov in his honour. The ghetto area was razed in the 1890s, but the Town Hall and some synagogues were saved.

Sights at a Glance

Churches and Synagogues
3 Church of Our Lady before Týn
4 Church of St James
6 Spanish Synagogue
7 *Old-New Synagogue pp80–81*
9 Maisel Synagogue
11 Pinkas Synagogue
17 Church of St Giles

Historic Buildings
1 *Old Town Hall pp76–7*
8 Jewish Town Hall
14 Clementinum
19 Municipal House

Museums and Galleries
5 Convent of St Agnes
12 Museum of Decorative Arts
16 Smetana Museum

Historic Streets
2 Celetná Street
15 Charles Street

Theatres and Concert Halls
13 Rudolfinum
18 Estates Theatre

Cemeteries
10 *Old Jewish Cemetery pp82–3*

See also Street Finder
maps 3 & 4

◀ View over the rooftops of Staré Město

For map symbols *see back flap*

Street by Street: Staré Město

Free of traffic and ringed with historic buildings, Prague's Old Town Square (Staroměstské náměstí) ranks among the finest public spaces in any city. Nearby streets, including Celetná, are also pedestrianized. In summer, café tables spill out onto the cobbles, and although the area draws visitors in droves, the unique atmosphere has not yet been destroyed. Prague's colourful history comes to life in the buildings around the square.

❸ **Church of Our Lady before Týn** has spectacular Gothic steeples that have become the Old Town's most distinctive landmark.

Kinský Palace (palác Kinských), by Kilian Ignaz Dientzenhofer, has a stucco façade crowned with statues of the four elements.

The Church of St Nicholas has an imposing façade which dominates one corner of Old Town Square.

Old Town Square is depicted in this late 19th-century watercolour by Václav Jansa, which shows how little Staroměstské náměstí has changed in more than 100 years.

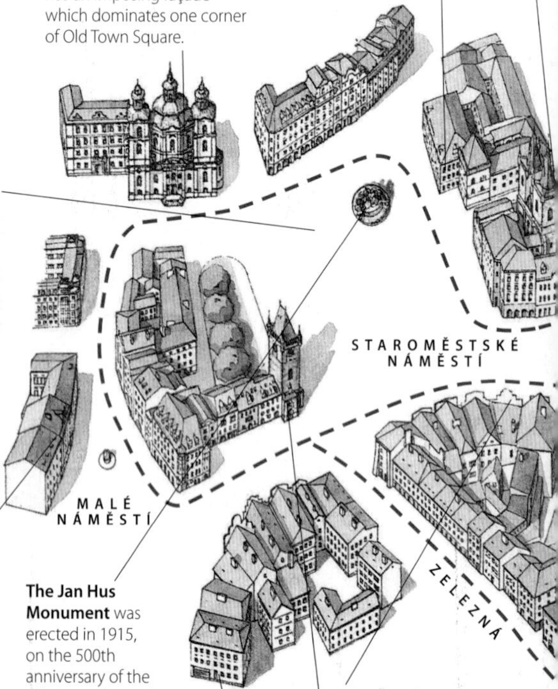

STAROMĚSTSKÉ NÁMĚSTÍ

MALÉ NÁMĚSTÍ

ŽELEZNÁ

The Jan Hus Monument was erected in 1915, on the 500th anniversary of the religious reformer's burning at the stake as a heretic. To the Czechs, he is a hero.

The Štorch House has painted decoration based on designs by Mikoláš Aleš showing St Wenceslas on horseback.

The House at the Two Golden Bears has a carved Renaissance portal which is the finest of its kind in Prague.

U Rotta, now Hotel Rott, is a former ironmonger's shop, decorated with colourful paintings by the 19th-century artist Mikoláš Aleš.

❶ ★ **Old Town Hall**
The town hall's famous astronomical clock draws a crowd of visitors every hour.

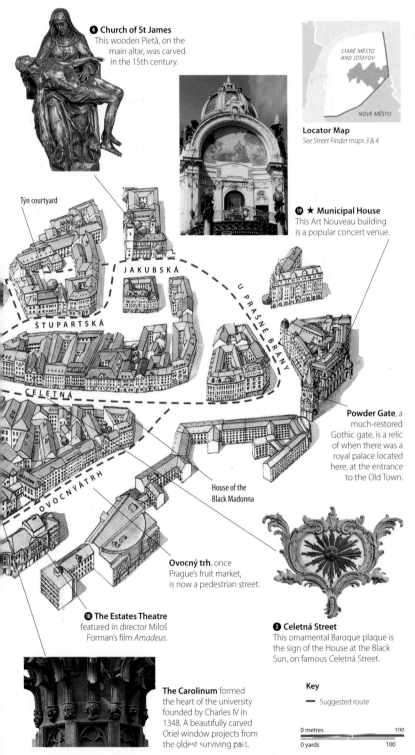

❹ Church of St James
This wooden Pietà, on the main altar, was carved in the 15th century.

Locator Map
See Street Finder maps 3 & 4

STARÉ MĚSTO AND JOSEFOV

NOVÉ MĚSTO

Týn courtyard

JAKUBSKÁ

❿ ★ Municipal House
This Art Nouveau building is a popular concert venue.

ŠTUPARTSKÁ

U PRAŠNÉ BRÁNY

CELETNÁ

Powder Gate, a much-restored Gothic gate, is a relic of when there was a royal palace located here, at the entrance to the Old Town.

House of the Black Madonna

OVOCNÝ TRH

Ovocný trh, once Prague's fruit market, is now a pedestrian street.

⓮ The Estates Theatre
featured in director Miloš Forman's film *Amadeus*.

❷ Celetná Street
This ornamental Baroque plaque is the sign of the House at the Black Sun, on famous Celetná Street.

The Carolinum formed the heart of the university founded by Charles IV in 1348. A beautifully carved Oriel window projects from the oldest surviving part.

Key

— Suggested route

0 metres   100
0 yards   100

❶ Old Town Hall
Staroměstská Radnice

One of the most striking buildings in Prague, the Old Town Hall was established in 1338 by King John of Luxemburg. Over the centuries, several nearby houses were knocked together as the Town Hall expanded, and it now consists of a row of colourful Gothic and Renaissance buildings; most of these have been restored after damage inflicted by the Nazis in 1945. The 69-m (228-ft) tower offers a great view.

Old Council Hall
This 19th-century engraving features the well-preserved 15th-century ceiling.

Old Town Coat of Arms
Above the inscription, "Prague, Head of the Kingdom", is the coat of arms of the Old Town, which was adopted in 1784 for the whole city.

Executions in the Old Town Square

A bronze tablet below the Old Town Hall chapel records the names of the 27 Protestant leaders executed here by order of Emperor Ferdinand II on 21 June 1621. This was the result of the humiliating defeat at the Battle of the White Mountain, which also led to the emigration of Protestants unwilling to give up their faith, a Counter-Reformation drive by the Catholic Church and a campaign of Germanization.

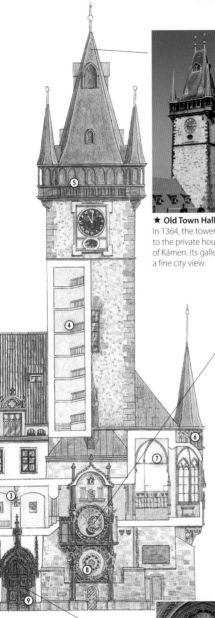

VISITORS' CHECKLIST

Practical Information
Staroměstské náměstí 1.
Map 3 B3. **Tel** 236 002 629.
Halls: **Open** 9am–6pm daily
(from 11am Mon).
Tower: **Open** 9am–10pm daily
(from 11am Mon). 🧩 ♿ 🅿
w prazskeveze.cz
w staro mestskaradnice
praha.cz

Transport
Ⓜ Staroměstská, Můstek.
🚊 17, 18.

★ **Old Town Hall Tower**
In 1364, the tower was added
to the private house of Wolflin
of Kámen. Its gallery provides
a fine city view.

★ **Astronomical Clock**
Mechanical figures perform above the zodiac
signs in the upper section; the lower section
is a calendar.

KEY

① **Temporary art exhibitions**

② **Tourist information and
entrance to Tower**

③ **The house of Wolflin of
Kámen** was purchased by the
authorities in 1338.

④ **Steps to gallery**

⑤ **Viewing gallery**

⑥ **The Oriel Chapel's** original
stained-glass windows were
destroyed in the last days of World
War II, but were replaced in 1987.

⑦ **Ornate ceiling of the
Oriel Chapel**

⑧ **Calendar**

⑨ **Entrance hall decorated
with mosaics**

Gothic Door
This late Gothic main entrance to the
Town Hall and Tower was carved by
Matthias Rejsek. The entrance hall is
filled with wall mosaics after designs
by the Czech painter Mikoláš Aleš.

❷ Celetná Street
Celetná Ulice

Map 3 C3. 🚇 Náměstí Republiky, Můstek. House of the Black Madonna: **Tel** 224 211 746. **Open** 10am–6pm Tue–Sun. 🐾 ♿ 📱

One of the oldest streets in Prague, Celetná follows an old trading route from eastern Bohemia. Its name comes from the plaited bread rolls that were first baked here in the Middle Ages. It gained prestige in the 14th century as a section of the so-called Royal Route, which linked the Royal Court (on the site of the Municipal House) and Prague Castle via Old Town Square; it was used during coronation processions.

Most of the houses along Celetná Street date from the Middle Ages. The foundations of Romanesque and Gothic buildings can be seen in some of the cellars, but most of the houses with their picturesque signs are the result of Baroque remodellings.

At No. 34, the House of the Black Madonna (Dům U Černé Matky Boží) is a splendid example of Cubist architecture. The building was designed by Josef Gočár in 1911 and is home to the historic Grand Café Orient, the only surviving Cubist café in the world. (Note that the distinctive polychrome figure of the Madonna with Child comes from an earlier house that stood on this site.) The building also holds temporary exhibitions and there is a Cubist gallery on the ground floor.

The 1759 Pachts' Palace, across the street, has a balcony that rests on the shoulders of four miners and soldiers sculpted by Ignaz Platzer. The most impressive example of Baroque architecture is Hrzánský Palace (No. 558), whose façade features busts, gargoyles and stuccoes, as well as a portal with caryatids. Used for state dinners, the palace has been visited by numerous heads of state.

House of the Black Madonna

The towering nave of the Church of Our Lady before Týn

❸ Church of Our Lady before Týn
Kostel Matky Boží Před Týnem

Staroměstské náměstí 14. **Map** 3 C3. **Tel** 222 318 186. 🚇 Staroměstská, Můstek. **Open** 10am–1pm & 3–5pm Tue–Sat, 10:30am–noon Sun. ✝ 6pm Tue–Thu, 8am Sat, 9:30am & 9pm Sun. 📷

Dominating the Old Town Square are the magnificent multiple steeples of this historic church. The present Gothic building was started in 1365 and soon became associated with the reform movement in Bohemia. From the early 15th century until 1620, Týn was the main Hussite church in Prague. It was taken over by the Jesuits in the 17th century, and it was they who were responsible for the Baroque renovation inside, which jars with the Gothic style of the original church.

On the northern side is a beautiful entrance portal (1390) decorated with scenes of Christ's passion. The dark interior has notable features, including Gothic sculptures of *Calvary*, a pewter font (1414) and a 15th-century Gothic pulpit. The Danish astronomer Tycho Brahe (1546–1601) is buried here.

❹ Church of St James
Kostel Sv. Jakuba

Malá Štupartská. **Map** 3 C3. **Tel** 224 828 816. 🚇 Můstek, Náměstí Republiky. **Open** 9:30am–noon & 2–4pm Tue–Sat (to 3:30pm Fri), 2–4pm Sun. ✝ 8:30am, 10:30am Sun.

This attractive Baroque church was originally the Gothic presbytery of a Minorite monastery. The order (a branch of the Franciscans) was invited to Prague by King Wenceslas I in 1232. The Baroque reconstruction occurred after a fire in 1689, allegedly started by agents of Louis XIV. More than 20 side altars were added, decorated with works by painters such as Jan Jiří Heinsch and Petr Brandl.

The tomb of Count Vratislav of Mitrovice (1714–16), designed by Johann Bernhard Fischer von Erlach and with sculptures by Brokof, is the most beautiful Baroque tomb in Bohemia. The count is said to have been accidentally buried alive: his corpse was later found sitting

Baroque organ loft in the Church of St James

For hotels and restaurants see pp348–9 and pp364–6

up in the tomb. There is an equally macabre tale surrounding a 400-year old mummified forearm to be found hanging on the right of the entrance. The story goes that when a thief tried to steal the jewels from the Madonna on the high altar, the Virgin grabbed his arm and held on so tightly that it had to be cut off.

The acoustics in the nave are excellent and concerts are often held here. The splendid organ dates from 1702.

Panel (c.1370) showing a kneeling Charles IV, in St Agnes's Convent

❺ Convent of St Agnes
Klášter Sv. Anežky České

U Milosrdných 17. **Map** 3 C2. **Tel** 224 810 628. Ⓜ Náměstí Republiky, Staroměstská. 🚊 17 to Law Faculty (Právnická fakulta), 5, 8, 14 to Dlouhá třída. 🚌 207 to Nemocnice na Františku. **Open** 10am–6pm Tue–Sun. 🚫 🚭 🚹 Ⓦ ngprague.cz

The convent of the Poor Clares was founded by Princess Agnes, sister of King Wenceslas I, in 1234, and was one of the first Gothic buildings in Bohemia. It functioned as a convent until 1782, when the Order was dissolved by Joseph II.

Following painstaking restoration, the premises now

house a magnificent collection of medieval art belonging to the National Gallery in Prague. Among its most precious exhibits are works by two outstanding Czech artists of the 14th century: the so-called Master of the Vyšší Brod Altar, who adorned a monastic altarpiece with exquisite scenes from the life of Christ, and Master Theodoric. The latter's splendid series of panels for the chapel of Karlštejn Castle are the unmissable works in the gallery. Other works worth seeing include the moving *Crucifixion* from Prague's Na Slovanech Monastery, 14th-century panels by the Master of Třeboň, and an anonymous sculpture of the Madonna and Child, much influenced by the famous Krumlov *Madonna*.

The early 16th century is represented by works by the Master of Litoměřice; these include the Holy Trinity triptych and the *Visitation of the Virgin Mary*.

❻ Spanish Synagogue
Španělská Synagóga

Vězeňská 1. **Map** 3 B2. **Tel** 221 711 511. Ⓜ Staroměstská. 🚊 17, 18. 🚌 207 to Nemocnice na Františku. **Open** Apr–Oct: 9am–6pm Sun–Fri; Nov–Mar: 9am–4:30pm Sun–Fri. 🚫 🚹 Ⓦ jewishmuseum.cz

Prague's first synagogue, known as the Old School (Stará škola), once stood on this site. In the 11th century, the Old School was the centre of the Sephardic Jewish community, who lived strictly apart from the Ashkenazi Jews, who were concentrated around the Old-New Synagogue.

The present Moorish building dates from the second half of the 19th century. The ornate exterior gives way to an even more fantastically decorative and gilded interior. The rich stucco decorations are

Ten Commandments motif on the Spanish Synagogue façade

reminiscent of the Alhambra in Spain, hence the name. Once closed to the public, the Spanish Synagogue is now home to a permanent exhibition dedicated to the history of the Jews of Bohemia.

❼ Old-New Synagogue
See pp80–81.

❽ Jewish Town Hall
Židovská Radnice

Maiselova 18. **Map** 3 B3. Ⓜ Staroměstská. 🚊 17, 18. 🚌 207. **Closed** to the public.

The core of this attractive blue and white building is the original Jewish Town Hall, built in 1570–77 by the hugely rich mayor, Mordechai Maisel. In 1763, it acquired its flowery late Baroque image; further alterations were made in the early 20th century.

On the roof stands a small wooden clock tower with a distinctive green steeple. On one of the gables, there is another clock. This one has Hebrew figures and, because Hebrew reads from right to left, hands that turn in an anti-clockwise direction.

Façade and clock tower of the Jewish Town Hall

❼ Old-New Synagogue
Staronová Synagóga

Built around 1270, this is the oldest synagogue in Europe and one of the earliest Gothic buildings in Prague. The synagogue has survived fires, the slum clearances of the 19th century and many Jewish pogroms. Residents of the Jewish Quarter have often had to seek refuge within its walls and today it is still the religious centre for Prague's Jews. It was originally called the New Synagogue until another synagogue (later destroyed) was built nearby.

Right-hand Nave
The glow from the chandeliers provides light for worshippers who sit in the seats lining the walls.

★ Jewish Standard
The historic banner of Prague's Jews is decorated with a star of David and, within it, the hat that had to be worn by Jews in the 14th century.

★ Five-Rib Vaulting
Two massive octagonal pillars inside the hall support the five-rib vaults: one rib was added to the traditional four ribs.

Entrance in Červená Street

Entrance Portal
The tympanum above the door in the south vestibule is decorated with bunches of grapes and vine leaves.

East Façade
The east and the west façades possess an austerity that is in strong contrast with the Gothic interior.

★ Rabbi Löw's Chair
A star of David marks the chair of the Chief Rabbi, placed where Rabbi Löw once sat. A 16th-century scholar, he was Prague's most revered Jewish sage *(see p82)*.

The Ark
This is the holiest place in the synagogue as it holds the sacred scrolls of the *Torah* (the first five books of the Bible) and of the books of the Prophets.

VISITORS' CHECKLIST

Practical Information
Pařížská & Červená 2.
Map 3 B2. **Tel** 224 800 812.
Open 9:30am–6pm Sun–Thu
(to 5pm Nov–Mar).
Closed Jewish hols. 🎫 📷
⭐ 7:30am Mon–Fri, 9am Sat.
🅦 synagogue.cz

Transport
Ⓜ Staroměstská. 🚊 17, 18 to Staroměstská, 17 to Právnická fakulta (Law Faculty).

KEY

① **The cantor's platform** (or *bima*) is surrounded by a wrought-iron Gothic grille.

② **Candlestick holder**

③ **These windows** formed part of the 18th-century extensions built to allow women a view of the service.

④ **Stepped brick gable (14th century)**

⑤ **The tympanum** above the Ark is decorated with 13th-century leaf carvings.

⑥ **The interior** is dim since the small windows do not allow much light in.

❾ Maisel Synagogue
Maiselova Synagóga

Maiselova 10. **Map** 3 B3. **Tel** 222 749 211. Ⓜ Staroměstská. 🚊 207.
Open Apr–Oct: 9am–6pm Sun–Fri; Nov–Mar: 9am–4.30pm Sun–Fri.
Closed Jewish hols. 🎫 📷 ♿
🅦 jewishmuseum.cz

When it was first built, in the late 16th century, this was a private house of prayer for use by mayor Mordechai Maisel and his family. It was also the most richly decorated synagogue in the city. Maisel, who made a fortune lending money to Rudolph II, funded the extensive Renaissance reconstruction of the ghetto.

The original building was a victim of the fire that also devastated the Jewish Town in 1689, and a new synagogue was built in its place. Its present Gothic aspect dates from the early 20th century.

The synagogue now houses a superb collection of Jewish silver and other metalwork dating from Renaissance times. It includes early examples of items used in the Jewish service, such as Torah crowns and finials, used to decorate the rollers which hold the text of the Torah (the five books of Moses), shields (hung on the mantle draped over the Torah) and pointers (used by readers to follow the text).

By a tragic irony, most of these treasures were brought to Prague by the Nazis from synagogues all over Bohemia and Moravia.

18th-century silver Torah crown in the Maisel Synagogue

❿ Old Jewish Cemetery
Starý Židovský Hřbitov

This remarkable site was, for over 300 years, the only burial ground permitted to Jews. Founded in 1478, it was slightly enlarged over the years but still basically corresponds to its medieval size. Due to the lack of space, people had to be buried on top of each other, up to 12 layers deep. Today, you can see over 12,000 gravestones crammed into the tiny area, but an estimated 100,000 people are thought to have been buried here. The last burial was in 1787.

View across the cemetery towards the western wall of the Klausen Synagogue

David Gans' Tombstone
The tomb of the writer and astronomer (1541–1613) is adorned with the symbols of his name – a star of David and a goose (*Gans* in German).

Rabbi David Oppenheim (1664–1736) The chief rabbi of Prague owned the largest collection of Hebrew manuscripts and prints in the city.

Main entrance

Rabbi Löw and the Golem

The 16th-century scholar and philosopher Rabbi Löw was thought to possess magical powers. It is claimed that he created a figure, the Golem, from clay and then brought it to life. When his creature went berserk, the rabbi is said to have hidden it in the Old-New Synagogue (*see pp80–81*).

★ **14th-century Tombstones** Embedded in the wall are fragments of Gothic tombstones brought here from an older Jewish cemetery in Staré Město.

Prague Burial Society
Founded in 1564, the group carried out ritual burials and performed charitable work. In this 18th-century painting, members of the society wash their hands after leaving the cemetery.

VISITORS' CHECKLIST

Practical Information
Široká 3. **Map** 3 B3.
Jewish Museum: **Tel** 222 749 464 (bookings). **Open** Apr–Oct: 9am–6pm Sun–Fri; Nov–Mar: 9am–4:30pm Sun–Fri (last adm 30 mins before closing). 🅦 jewishmuseum.cz

Transport
Staroměstská. 17, 18. 207.

★ Tombstone of Rabbi Löw
The most visited tomb in the cemetery is that of Rabbi Löw (1520–1609). Visitors place a pebble on the grave as a mark of respect.

Tombstone of Hendela Bassevi
The highly decorated tomb (1628) was built in honour of the beautiful wife of Prague's first Jewish nobleman.

KEY

① **Klausen Synagogue**

② **The Nephele Mound** was where infants who died under a year old were buried.

③ **The gravestone of Moses Beck**

④ **Rabbi Kara Tomb (1439),** the oldest in the cemetery

⑤ **The Pinkas Synagogue** is the second-oldest in Prague (see p84).

⑥ **Jewish printers,** Mordechai Zemach (d.1592) and his son Bezalel (d.1589), are buried under this square gravestone.

⑦ **The Museum of Decorative Arts** (see p84)

⑧ **The Neo-Romanesque Ceremonial Hall**

⑨ **Mordechai Maisel** (1528–1601) was Mayor of Prague's Jewish Town and a philanthropist (see p81).

Understanding the Gravestones

From the late 16th century onwards, tombstones in the Jewish cemetery were decorated with symbols denoting the background, family name or profession of the deceased.

Blessing hands: Cohen family

A pair of scissors: tailor

A stag: Hirsch or Zvi family

Grapes: blessing or abundance

Stage of the Dvořák Hall in the Rudolfinum

⓫ Pinkas Synagogue

Pinkasova Synagóga

Široká 3. **Map** 3 B3. **Tel** 222 326 660. 🚇 Staroměstská. 🚊 17, 18. 🚌 207. **Open** Apr–Oct: 9am–6pm Sun–Fri; Nov–Mar: 9am–4:30pm. 🖼 🖾 🔊 Ⓦ jewishmuseum.cz

The synagogue was founded in 1479 by Rabbi Pinkas and enlarged in 1535 by his great-nephew Aaron Meshulam Horowitz. It has been rebuilt many times since. Excavations have turned up fascinating relics of life in the medieval ghetto, including a *mikva*, or ritual bath. The core of the present building is a hall with Gothic vaulting. The gallery for women was added in the early 17th century.

The synagogue now serves as a memorial to all the Jewish Czechoslovak citizens who were imprisoned in Terezín concentration camp *(see pp192–3)* and later deported to various Nazi extermination camps. The names of the 77,297 who did not return are inscribed on the synagogue walls. There is also a display of haunting children's drawings from Terezín camp.

⓬ Museum of Decorative Arts

Uměleckoprůmyslové Muzeum

17. listopadu 2. **Map** 3 B3. **Tel** 251 093 111. 🚇 Staroměstská. 🚊 17, 18. 🚌 207. **Open** 10am–6pm Wed–Sun (to 7pm Tue). 🖼 🖾 🔊 🔊 Ⓦ upm.cz

The museum's collection of glass is one of the largest in the world, but space constraints mean that only a fraction of it is ever on

Stained-glass window from inside the Museum of Decorative Arts

display. Pride of place goes to the Bohemian glass, of which there are many fine Baroque and 19th- and 20th-century pieces. Other exhibits include Meissen porcelain, Gobelin tapestries, costume, textiles, photographs and furniture.

⓭ Rudolfinum

Alšovo nábřeží 12. **Map** 3 A3. 🚇 Staroměstská. 🚊 17, 18. 🚌 207. Philharmonic: **Tel** 227 059 205/227 059 309. **Open** 10am–6pm Tue–Sun (to 8pm Thu). 🖾 🔊 🔊 Ⓦ galerierudolfinum.cz

Now the home of the Czech Philharmonic Orchestra, the Rudolfinum is one of the most impressive landmarks on the Old Town bank of the Vltava. Many of the major concerts of the Prague Spring music festival are held here. The most impressive of the various concert halls is the sumptuous Dvořák Hall, one of the finest creations of 19th-century Czech architecture.

The Rudolfinum itself is a superb example of Czech Neo-Renaissance style. The curving balustrade is adorned with statues of distinguished Czech, Austrian and German composers and artists.

Between 1918 and 1939, the Rudolfinum was the seat of the Czechoslovak parliament.

⓮ Clementinum

Klementinum

Křižovnická 190, Karlova 1, Mariánské náměstí 5. **Map** 3 A4. **Tel** 222 220 879. 🚇 Staroměstská. 🚊 17, 18. Baroque Library, Astronomical Tower and Chapel of Mirrors: **Open** Apr–Oct: 10am–7pm; Nov–Mar: 10am–6pm. 🖾 🔊 🔊 🔊 Ⓦ klementinum.com

In 1556, emperor Ferdinand I invited the Jesuits to Prague to undo the work of the Hussites and help bring the Czechs back into the Catholic fold. They took over the former Dominican monastery and, over two centuries, made it the largest complex of buildings in the city after Prague Castle. They built the

Church of St Saviour (1593–1714), adorned with large statues of the Apostles by Jan Bendl (1659).

The most brutal expansion involved the demolition of 30 houses after the Jesuits were given control of the university. The sumptuous Baroque library (Barokní sál), with a splendid *trompe l'oeil* ceiling, dates from 1727. The lovely Chapel of Mirrors (Zrcadlová kaple), and the Astronomical Tower (Astronomická věž), offering great views, also date from the 18th century. In 1773, when the pope dissolved their Order, the Jesuits left Prague. The Clementinum eventually became the National Library.

Former Jesuit Church of St Saviour in the Clementinum

⑮ Charles Street
Karlova Ulice

Map 3 A4. Ⓜ Staroměstská.

Dating back to the 12th century, this narrow, winding street was part of the Royal Route, along which coronation processions passed on the way to Prague Castle. Many original Gothic and Renaissance houses remain, most converted into shops to attract tourists.

A café in the House at the Golden Snake (No. 18) was established in 1714 by an Armenian, Deodatus Damajan, who handed out slanderous pamphlets from here. It is now a restaurant. At No. 3, At the Golden Well has a magnificent

Baroque façade and stucco reliefs of saints including St Roch and St Sebastian, who are believed to offer protection against plagues.

A 19th-century sign on the House at the Golden Snake, Charles Street

⑯ Smetana Museum
Muzeum Bedřicha Smetany

Novotného lávka 1. **Map** 3 A4. **Tel** 222 220 082. Ⓜ Staroměstská. 🚋 17, 18. **Open** 10am–5pm Wed–Mon. 🌐 **nm.cz**

On a spit of land beside the Vltava, a former Neo-Renaissance waterworks has been turned into a memorial to Bedřich Smetana (1824–84), the father of Czech music. The one-room museum contains documents, letters, scores and musical instruments from the composer's life and work. Visitors can listen to extracts from some of Smetana's key works by waving an electronic baton at music stands.

Smetana was an ardent patriot and his music helped inspire the Czech national revival. Deaf towards the end of his life, he never heard his cycle of symphonic poems, *Má Vlast* (My Country), being performed. The opera, *The Bartered Bride*, brought him the greatest renown abroad.

⑰ Church of St Giles
Kostel Sv. Jiljí

Husova 8. **Map** 3 B4. **Tel** 224 220 235. Ⓜ Národní třída. 🚋 6, 9, 17, 18, 22. **Open** timings vary, call ahead for details. ✝ 7am & 6:30pm Mon–Fri, 6:30pm Sat, 9:30am, noon, 6:30pm Sun.

Despite a beautiful Gothic portal on the south side, the inside of this church is essentially Baroque. Founded in 1371, it became a Hussite church in 1420. Following the Protestant defeat in 1620, Ferdinand II gave the church to the Dominicans, who built on a huge friary. The monks were booted out under the Communists, but they have since been able to return.

The vaults of the church are decorated with frescoes by the painter Václav Vavřinec Reiner, who is buried in the nave. The main fresco, a glorification of the Dominicans, shows St Dominic and his friars helping the pope defend the Catholic Church from non-believers.

Sgraffito façade of the Smetana Museum

The Estates Theatre, once the most important theatre in Prague

⑱ Estates Theatre

Stavovské Divadlo

Ovocný trh 1. **Map** 3 C4. Ⓜ Můstek. **Open** for guided tours – call 224 902 231. Ⓖ Ⓦ **narodni-divadlo.cz**

Built in 1783 by the German-speaking Count Nostitz Rieneck, the theatre is one of the finest examples of Classical elegance in Prague. Its white, gold and blue auditorium resembles a luxury chocolate box. While performances were given in Czech or Italian occasionally, until 1920 the main language used on stage was German.

The theatre is renowned for its premieres of operas by Mozart. On 29 October 1787, the public was treated to the world premiere of *Don Giovanni*, with Mozart himself conducting from the piano. Acknowledging the connection between Mozart and the theatre, the interior was used by Miloš Forman in his famous Oscar-winning film *Amadeus* (1984).

In 1834, *Fidlovačka*, a comic opera by Josef Kajetán Tyl, was performed here for the first time. One of its songs, *Kde domov můj?* (Where is My Home?), later became the Czech national anthem. More than a century later, in the spirit of the national revival, the theatre was renamed after Tyl, though it has since reverted to its original name.

The Carolinum, opposite, is the core of Prague University founded by Charles IV. In the 15th and 16th centuries, the university led the movement to reform the church. It was later taken over by the Jesuits.

⑲ Municipal House
Obecní Dům

Prague's most prominent Art Nouveau building was built in 1905–11 on the site of a former royal palace. It includes Prague's top concert venue, as well as other smaller halls, a restaurant and café. The flamboyant and exciting interior, decorated with works by leading Czech artists, including Alfons Mucha, is well worth savouring. The guided tour is excellent and also good value.

★ **Mosaic by Karel Špillar**
The façade includes a vast semicircular mosaic depicting *Homage to Prague*, by Karel Špillar.

Glass Dome
The imposing glass dome, a local landmark, towers above Hollar's Hall, a circular room next to the exhibition rooms.

★ **Mayor's Salon**
This splendid room has furniture by J Krejčuk and murals depicting Czech heroes by Mucha.

Main Hall
Lifts in the main hall have beautiful Art Nouveau details and ornaments.

★ Smetana Hall
The auditorium seating 1,500 is occasionally used as a ballroom. The box to the left of the stage is reserved for the President of the Republic, the one to the right for the Mayor.

VISITORS' CHECKLIST

Practical Information
Náměstí Republiky 5.
Map 4 D3.
Tel 222 002 101.
Gallery: **Open** for guided visits only: 10am–7pm daily. 📷 by arrangement. ♿ 📱 ✏ 📷
W obecnidum.cz

Transport
Ⓜ Náměstí Republiky.
🚊 5, 8, 24, 26.

Decorative Detail
This delightful detail by Alfons Mucha is found in the Mayor's Salon.

Side Portal
Here, the carved decoration is in perfect harmony with the architecture.

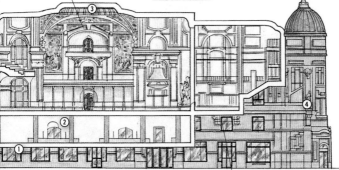

KEY

① **Shops**

② **The wing** facing U Obecního Domu Street includes four dining rooms with original panelling, mirrors and clocks.

③ **Magnificent glass dome**

④ **Figures** seen on all sides of the building are by Czech artists who combined Classical and historic symbols with modern motifs.

Decorative Elements
Lavish stucco decoration covers all sides of the Municipal House; seen here are floral motifs, typical of the Art Nouveau style (see p99).

NOVÉ MĚSTO

The new town, or Nové Město, founded in 1348 by Charles IV, was planned around three central market squares: the Horse Market (Wenceslas Square), the Cattle Market (Charles Square) and the Hay Market (Senovážné Square). Twice as large as the Old Town, the district was inhabited mainly by merchants and craftsmen. In the late 1800s, a large section of the New Town was demolished and completely redeveloped, giving it the appearance it has today.

There are many historic sites and attractions in Nové Město. Wenceslas Square, a wide boulevard housing restaurants, hotels and shops, is surrounded by fine buildings and is busy day and night. For some peace and quiet, head for the park in Charles Square.

Sights at a Glance

Churches
2 Church of Our Lady of the Snows
8 Church of St Stephen
10 Emauzy Slavonic Monastery
15 Church of St Ursula
18 Cathedral of St Cyril and St Methodius

Theatres
5 State Opera
14 National Theatre pp96–7

Historic Squares, Buildings and Gardens
1 Wenceslas Square
3 Franciscan Garden
7 Main Station
11 Faust House
12 Charles Square

13 Dancing House
16 U Fleků
17 New Town Hall

Museums and Galleries
4 National Museum
6 Mucha Museum
9 Dvořák Museum

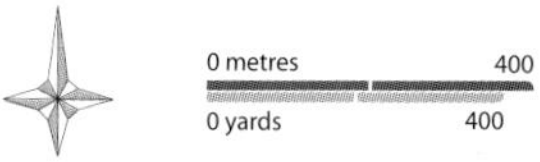

0 metres		400
0 yards		400

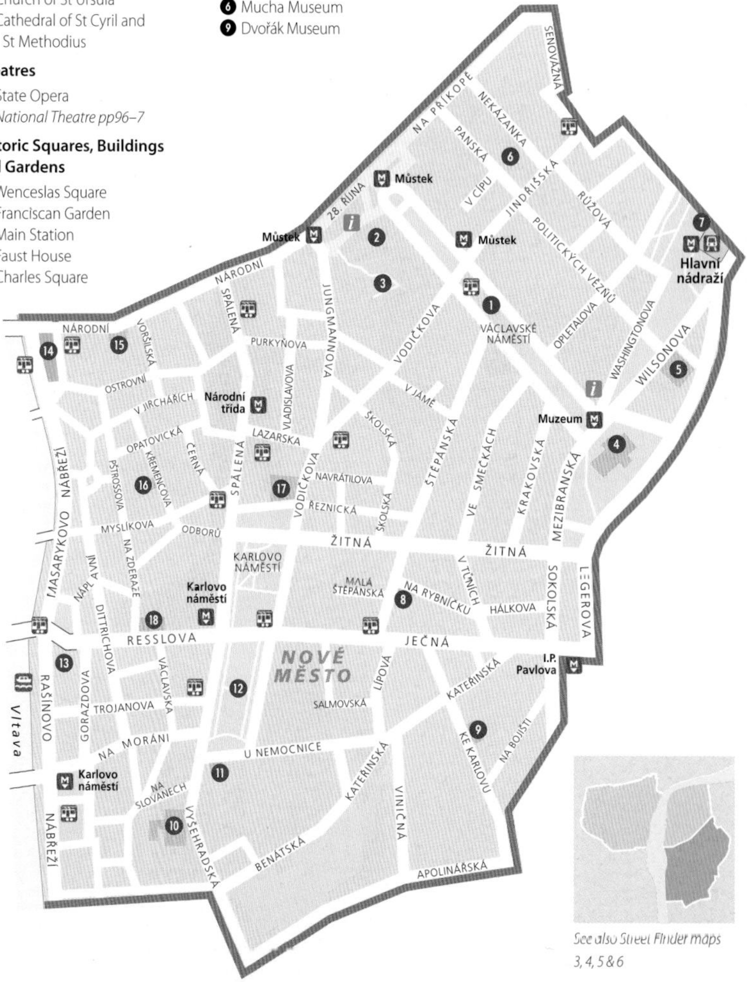

See also Street Finder maps 3, 4, 5 & 6

◀ The vast and elegant interior of the National Museum

For map symbols see back flap

Street-by-Street: Around Wenceslas Square

Hotels and restaurants occupy many of the buildings around Wenceslas Square, though it remains an important commercial centre. As you walk along, look up at the buildings, most of which date from the beginning of the 20th century, when the square was redeveloped. There are some fine examples of the Czech decorative styles used during that period. Many blocks have dark, covered arcades leading to shops, theatres and cinemas.

Koruna Palace (1914) is an ornate block of shops and offices. Its corner turret is topped with a crown *(koruna)*.

NA PŘÍKOPĚ

U Pinkasů, housed in a building with Gothic, Renaissance and Baroque features, started serving Pilsner Urquell in 1843.

Můstek

❷ **Church of Our Lady of the Snows**
The towering Gothic building is only part of a vast church planned during the 14th century.

Můstek

Můstek

Jungmann Square is named after Josef Jungmann (1773–1847), an influential linguist and lexicographer, and there is a statue of him in the middle. The Adria Palace (1925) used to be the Laterna Magika Theatre *(see p96)*, which was where Václav Havel's Civic Forum worked in the early days of the 1989 Velvet Revolution.

Lucerna Palace

❸ **Franciscan Garden**
A small park, which features this striking fountain, is laid out in an old monastery garden.

VODIČKOVA

0 metres 100
0 yards 100

Wiehl House was completed in 1896. The five-storey building is in striking Neo-Renaissance style, with a loggia and colourful *sgraffito*. Mikoláš Aleš designed some of the Art Nouveau figures.

❶ ★ Wenceslas Square
The square is named after the patron saint of Bohemia, St Wenceslas, a Přemyslid prince who was murdered by his brother Boleslav. The dominant features of the square are the bronze equestrian statue of St Wenceslas (1912) and the National Museum behind it.

Locator Map
See Street Finder maps 3, 4 & 6

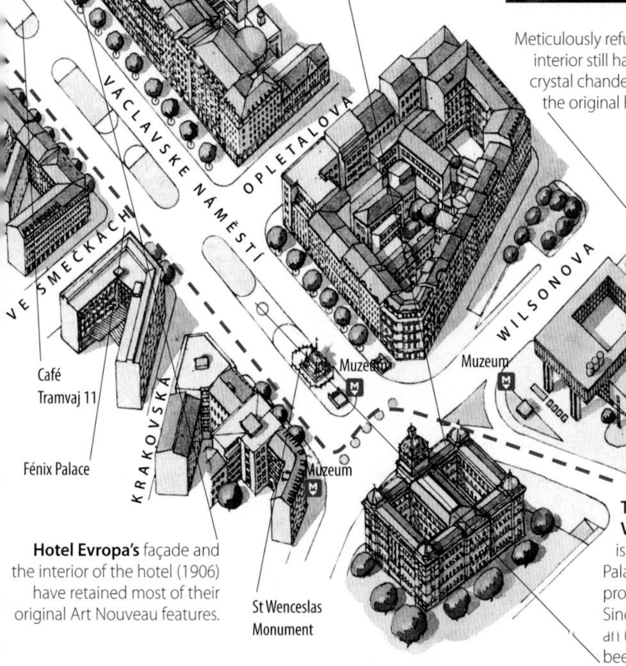

The Assicurazioni Generali Building
was where Franz Kafka worked as an insurance clerk for ten months in 1906–7.

❹ ★ National Museum
The grand building with its monumental staircase was completed in 1890 as a symbol of national prestige.

❺ ★ State Opera
Meticulously refurbished in the 1980s, the interior still has the luxurious red plush, crystal chandeliers and gilded stucco of the original late-19th-century theatre.

Key
— Suggested route

VÁCLAVSKÉ NÁMĚSTÍ

OPLETALOVA

WILSONOVA

VE SMEČKÁCH

KRAKOVSKÁ

Café Tramvaj 11

Fénix Palace

Muzeum

Muzeum

Muzeum

Hotel Evropa's façade and the interior of the hotel (1906) have retained most of their original Art Nouveau features.

St Wenceslas Monument

The Monument to the Victims of Communism
is on the spot where Jan Palach killed himself in protest against the regime. Since the Velvet Revolution, an unofficial shrine has been maintained here.

Wenceslas Monument in Wenceslas Square

❶ Wenceslas Square

Václavské Náměstí

Map 3 C5. 🚇 Můstek, Muzeum.
🚊 3, 9, 14, 24.

The square has witnessed many key events in recent Czech history. It was here that the student Jan Palach burnt himself to death in 1969, and in November 1989, a protest rally in the square against police brutality led to the Velvet Revolution and the overthrow of Communism.

Wenceslas "Square" is something of a misnomer, for it is some 750 m (2,460 ft) long and only 60 m (196 ft) wide. Originally a horse market, today it is lined with hotels, restaurants, clubs and shops, reflecting the seamier side of global consumerism.

The huge equestrian statue of St Wenceslas in front of the National Museum was erected in 1912. Cast in bronze, it is the work of Josef Myslbek, the leading Czech sculptor of the late 19th century. At the foot of the pedestal, there are several other statues of Czech patron saints. A memorial near the statue commemorates the victims of the former regime. Walking down the square from

the monument, there are several buildings of interest. To the left, down a passage, is Lucerna Palace, built in the early 20th century by Václav Havel, grandfather of the former Czech president. It is now a shopping and entertainment complex. The cinema is worth a visit to see its Art Nouveau furnishings.

On the opposite side of the square, at No. 29, stands the lavishly decorated Art Nouveau Grand Hotel Evropa, built in 1903–6. This is a wonderfully preserved reminder of the golden age of hotels. Its magnificent façade is crowned with gilded nymphs, while inside the original bars, the mirrors, panelling and light fittings have survived virtually intact.

❷ Church of Our Lady of the Snows

Kostel Panny Marie Sněžné

Jungmannovo náměstí 18. **Map** 3 C5. **Tel** 222 246 243. 🚇 Můstek. **Open** 9am–6pm daily. 🕇 7am, 8am, 6pm Mon–Fri; 8am, 6pm Sat; 9am, 10:15am, 11:30am, 6pm Sun. ♿
🌐 **pms.ofm.cz**

Charles IV founded this church in 1347 to mark his coronation. The name refers to a 4th-century miracle in Rome, when the Virgin Mary appeared to the pope in a dream telling him to build a church on the spot where snow fell in August. Charles's church was supposed to

Views of the Church of Our Lady of the Snows

have been over 100 m (330 ft) long, but was never completed. The towering building we see today was just the presbytery of the projected church.

In 1603, the Franciscans restored the building, and the intricate net vaulting of the ceiling dates from this period. Most of the interior decoration is Baroque. Note the splendid three-tiered altar, crowded with statues of saints.

❸ Franciscan Garden

Františkánská Zahrada

Passages of Jungmannovo náměstí, Vodičkova & Václavské náměstí. **Map** 3 C5. 🚇 Můstek. **Open** Apr–Sep: 7am–10pm daily; Sep–Oct: 7am–8pm daily; Nov– Mar: 8am–7pm daily. ♿

The physic garden of a Franciscan monastery, the area was opened to the public in 1950 as an oasis close to Wenceslas Square. By the entrance is a Gothic portal leading to the U františkánů cellar restaurant. In the 1980s, some beds were replanted with herbs of the kinds cultivated by the Franciscans in the 17th century.

❹ National Museum

Národní Muzeum

Václavské náměstí 68. **Map** 6 E1. **Tel** 224 497 111. 🚇 Muzeum. **Open** 10am–6pm daily. 📷 for a fee. 🌐 **nm.cz**

The Neo-Renaissance building at one end of Wenceslas Square houses the National Museum. Designed by Josef Schulz as a triumphal affirmation of the Czech national revival, the museum was completed in 1890. The entrance is reached by a ramp flanked by allegorical statues: seated by the door are History and Nature; in front is a fountain with an allegorical figure symbolizing the Czech nation and the Czech rivers. If you look closely at the façade you can pick out pockmarks left by shells from Warsaw Pact tanks during the invasion of Prague in 1968. Unmissable overhead is a gilt-framed glass cupola.

Inside, the monumental staircase lit by grand brass candelabras leads to the Pantheon, a dome-topped hall. This contains statues and busts of the most prominent figures in Czech political, intellectual and artistic life. The vast room with windows overlooking Wenceslas Square has four huge paintings by Václav Brožík and František Ženíšek and Vojtěch Hynais.

While the marbled decoration is impressive, it overwhelms the museum's displays devoted mainly to mineralogy (including one of Europe's largest collections of rocks), archaeology, anthropology, numismatics and natural history.

Façade of the State Opera, formerly the New German Theatre

The magnificent gilded interior of the State Opera

❺ State Opera

Státní Opera Praha

Wilsonova 4. **Map** 4 E5. **Tel** 224 227 266 (box office). 🚇 Muzeum. **Open** for performances only. 🌐 opera.cz

The first theatre built here, the New Town Theatre, was pulled down in 1885 to make way for

the present building. This was originally known as the New German Theatre, built to rival the Czech National Theatre *(see pp96–7)*. By attracting top-quality conductors and musical directors, including Mahler, the theatre gained a reputation for staging some of the best German operas outside Germany; this is due partly to the excellent acoustics. Nowadays, the opera house stages both traditional and modern works.

A Neo-Classical frieze decorates the pediment above the loggia at the front of the theatre. Inside, original paintings in the auditorium and on the curtain have been preserved. In 1945, the theatre became the city's principal opera house.

❻ Mucha Museum

Muchovo Muzeum

Panská 7. **Map** 4 D4. **Tel** 224 216 415. 🚇 Můstek, Náměstí Republiky. 🚊 3, 9, 14, 24, 26. **Open** 10am–6pm daily. 🅿 🖳 ♿ 🌐 mucha.cz

The 18th-century Kaunicky Palace is home to the first museum dedicated to Alfons Mucha, the Czech master of Art Nouveau *(see p27)*. The exhibits include paintings, drawings, sketchbooks and photographs (some taken by Mucha) as well as personal memorabilia. Special attention is paid to the artist's time in Paris. The documentary film is also well

worth seeing. The central courtyard is given over to a café in the summer.

❼ Main Station

Hlavní Nádraží

Wilsonova 8. **Map** 4 E5. 🚇 Hlavní nádraží.

Prague's main railway station, designed by Josef Fanta and constructed in 1901–9, is one of the finest examples of Czech Art Nouveau architecture. The vast structure is magnificently decorated, with the walls and ceilings covered with allegorical figures, animals and floral motifs. The turrets of the two towers that flank the building's central section rest on the shoulders of giant Atlantes. Even before the building was completed, the nudity of these youths caused heated controversy between the local moralists and the sculptor – Stanislav Sucharda.

The main station façade, hiding an equally impressive interior

❽ Church of St Stephen

Kostel Sv. Štěpána

Štěpánská. **Map** 5 C2. 🚊 4, 10, 16, 22. **Open** only for services. ✝ 11am Sun. ♿

Founded by Charles IV in 1351 as the parish church of the upper Nové Město, St Stephen's was finished in 1401 with the completion of the multi-spired steeple. In the late 17th century, the Branberg Chapel was added; it is now home to the tomb of the prolific Baroque sculptor Matthias Braun. Most of the subsequent Baroque additions were removed when the church was scrupulously re-Gothicized in the 1870s. There are some fine Baroque paintings, however, including a picture of St John Nepomuk by Jan Jiří Heinsch to the left of the pulpit. But the church's greatest treasure is a stunning Gothic panel painting of the Madonna, known as *Our Lady of St Stephen's*, which dates from 1472.

View of the Gothic pulpit in the Church of St Stephen

❾ Dvořák Museum

Muzeum Antonína Dvořáka

Ke Karlovu 20. **Map** 6 D2. **Tel** 224 918 013. 🚇 IP Pavlova. 🚌 291. **Open** 10am–5pm Tue–Sun and for concerts. 🅿 ♿ 🌐 nm.cz

One of the most enchanting secular buildings of the Prague Baroque, this red and ochre villa now houses the Dvořák Museum. On display are Dvořák scores,

The Michna Summer Palace, home of the Dvořák Museum

as well as photographs and memorabilia of the 19th-century Czech composer, including his piano, viola and desk.

The building, designed by the great Baroque architect Kilian Ignaz Dientzenhofer, has an elegant tiered mansard roof. It was built in 1720 for the Michnas of Vacínov and was originally known as the Michna Summer Palace.

In the 19th century, the villa and garden fell into decay, but both have been heavily restored. The garden statues and vases, from the workshop of Matthias Braun, date from about 1735. Inside, the ceiling and walls of the large room on the first floor, often used for recitals, are decorated with 18th-century frescoes.

❿ Emauzy Slavonic Monastery

Klášter Na Slovanech

Vyšehradská 49. **Map** 5 B3. **Tel** 224 917 662. 🚇 Karlovo náměstí. 🚊 3, 4, 7, 10, 16, 17, 18, 24. Monastery church: **Open** Jun–Sep: 11am–5pm Mon–Sat; Oct–May: 11am–5pm Mon–Fri. Cloisters: **Open** by appt. ✝ 10am daily. 🅿 ♿ 🌐 emauzy.cz

Both the monastery and its church were almost destroyed in an American air raid in 1945;

it was one of the few historic buildings in the city to be damaged during World War II. When the church was reconstructed, it was given two concrete spires, which form an incongruous part of the city's skyline.

The monastery was founded in 1347 by Croatian Benedictines, whose services were held in the Old Slavonic language, hence its name "Na Slovanech". In the course of Prague's tumultuous religious history, the monastery has since changed hands many times. In 1446, a Hussite order was

The vaulted cloisters in the Slavonic Monastery

formed here, then in 1635 the building was acquired by Spanish Benedictines. In the 18th century, the complex was given a thorough Baroque treatment, but then in 1880 it was taken over by German Benedictines, who decided to rebuild virtually everything in Neo-Gothic style.

The complex, also known as the Emmaus Monastery, is now functioning again since the return of monks exiled under Communism. Some historically important 14th-century wall paintings are preserved in the cloisters, though many were damaged in World War II.

The beautiful Baroque façade of Faust House

⓫ Faust House
Faustův Dům

Karlovo náměstí 40, 41. **Map** 5 B3. Ⓜ Karlovo náměstí. 🚊 3, 4, 6, 10, 14, 16, 18, 22, 24. **Closed** to the public.

This ornate Baroque mansion is the object of one of Prague's most enduring legends: namely, that this house, whose origins can be traced to the 12th century, was once the home of the notorious Dr Faustus.

In the 16th century, an English alchemist-cum-con man Edward Kelly lived here. However, it was the experiments of alchemist Count Ferdinand Mladota of Solopysky, who owned the house in the 1700s, which gave rise to its association with the legend of Faust.

⓬ Charles Square
Karlovo Náměstí

Map 5 B2. Ⓜ Karlovo náměstí. 🚊 3, 4, 6, 10, 16, 18, 22, 24.

The southern part of Nové Město resounds to the rattle of trams, as many routes converge in this part of the city. The public garden in Charles Square, laid out in the mid-19th century, offers a peaceful and welcome retreat, though its trees do make it hard to enjoy broad vistas within the square. The statues in the park are of various figures from Czech history.

Prague's largest square – it is almost twice the size of Wenceslas Square – was laid out when Charles IV was establishing Nové Město in 1348. Built at its centre was a wooden tower, where the coronation jewels were put on display once a year. Some time later, the tower was replaced by a chapel. It was from here, in 1437, that the famous document informing the Czechs about the concessions granted to the Hussites by the pope and the council in Basle was read out for the first time.

Until the 19th century, Charles Square was used mainly as a cattle market, and for selling firewood, coal and other goods. On its north side is the New Town Hall *(see p98)*, while on the south side is the magnificent church of St Ignatius. Built by Carlo Lurago in the 1660s, this is a prime example of Baroque Jesuit architecture, intended to symbolize the strength and the power of the faith. The façade is topped by a statue of the church's patron saint, St Ignatius of Loyola, framed by a radiant sunburst. The Church's rules allowed only Christ and the Virgin Mary to be represented in this fashion, but the Jesuits succeeded in obtaining an exemption from the pope for their Prague

Detail from a house in Charles Square

church. Inside, the profusion of gilts is truly dazzling.

To the right of St Ignatius stands the rather featureless former Jesuit college, also designed by Carlo Lurago. It is now a teaching hospital that is attached to Charles University, which makes use of several buildings in and around this square.

Façade of the Dancing House, nicknamed "Fred and Ginger"

⓭ Dancing House
Tančící Dům

Rašínovo nábřeží 80. **Map** 5 A2. **Tel** 221 984 160. Ⓜ Karlovo náměstí. 🚊 3, 4, 6, 10, 14, 16, 17, 18, 22, 24. 🚌 176. Restaurant: **Open** noon– 11:30pm daily. ✉ Ⓦ **tancici-dum.cz**

On the banks of the Vltava, west of Charles Square, is an extraordinary building affectionately named the "Dancing House". Its other popular name – "Fred and Ginger" – alludes to the fact that its silhouette brings to mind the famous American dancing pair, Fred Astaire and Ginger Rogers. The glass and concrete structure which, in fact, is two buildings with different façades and of different heights, is the 1996 work of Californian architect Frank Gehry and his associate Vlado Milunič. It was awarded a special prize by *Time*, the American magazine, for blending modern architecture with an older, historical environment. The French restaurant on the top floor, Céleste, offers great views of the city.

⓮ National Theatre
Národní Divadlo

This gold-crested theatre is a cherished symbol of the Czech cultural revival. Work on the original Neo-Renaissance building, designed by Josef Zítek and funded largely by voluntary contributions, began in 1868. After the devastating fire of 1881 (see opposite), however, Josef Schulz was given the job of rebuilding it; all the best Czech artists of the day contributed to the new theatre's superb decoration. In the 1970s and 80s, the theatre was restored and the New Stage (Nová Scena) was built by Karel Prager.

The theatre from Slovanský ostrov (island)

★ Auditorium
The elaborate ceiling, painted by František Ženíšek, is adorned with allegorical figures representing the arts.

KEY

① **The five arcades** of the loggia are decorated with lunette paintings by Josef Tulka, entitled *Five Songs*.

② **The New Stage auditorium**

③ **The Laterna Magika**, where shows combine film, theatre, dance and light.

④ **A bronze three-horse chariot**, designed by Bohuslav Schnirch, carries the Goddess of Victory.

⑤ **The roof**, sky-blue and covered with stars, is said to represent the sky – the summit that all artists should aim for.

★ Lobby Ceiling
This ceiling fresco is the final part of a triptych painted by František Ženíšek in 1878, depicting the *Golden Age of Czech Art*.

★ **Stage Curtain**
This sumptuous red and gold stage curtain, showing the origin of the theatre, is the work of Vojtěch Hynais.

VISITORS' CHECKLIST

Practical Information
Národní 2, Nové Město.
Map 3 A5.
Auditorium: **Tel** 224 901 448.
Open daily for performances.
(224 902 231 for bookings).
w narodni-divadlo.cz

Transport
Národní třída. 17, 18, 22 to Národní divadlo.

Façade Decoration
This standing figure on the attic of the western façade is one of the many figures representing the Arts sculpted by Antonín Wagner in 1883.

Fire in the National Theatre

On 12 August 1881, just days before the official opening, the National Theatre was completely gutted by fire. It was thought to have been started by metalworkers on the roof. Just six weeks later, enough money had been collected to rebuild the theatre. It was finally opened two years late in 1883 with a performance of Smetana's opera *Libuše (see p44).*

The President's Box
The former royal box, lined in red velvet, is decorated with paintings of famous historical figures from Czech history by Václav Brožík.

Renaissance painted ceiling in the New Town Hall

tower was added in the mid-15th century and contains an 18th-century chapel. In the 16th century, an arcaded courtyard was added.

After the four towns of Prague were coalesced in 1784, the Town Hall ceased to be the seat of the municipal administration and became a courthouse and prison. It is now used for cultural and social events.

❺ Church of St Ursula
Kostel Sv. Voršily

Národní 8. **Map** 3 A5. **Tel** 224 930 511. 🚇 Národní třída. 🚊 6, 9, 17, 18, 22. 🕇 5pm Sat; 11am, 5pm Sun. **Open** daily. 📷

The delightful Baroque church of St Ursula was built as part of an Ursuline convent founded in 1672. The original sculptures still decorate the façade, and in front of the church stands a group of statues featuring St John Nepomuk with angels (1740), the work of Ignaz Platzer the Elder.

The light airy interior has a frescoed, stuccoed ceiling, beautiful Baroque furnishings, and on the various altars, there are lively Baroque paintings. The main altar has one of St Ursula.

The adjoining convent was returned to the Ursuline order in 1989 and is now a Catholic school. To the right of the church lies the entrance to the Institute of Endocrinology.

❻ U Fleků

Křemencova 11. **Map** 5 B1. 🚇 Národní třída, Karlovo náměstí. 🚊 6, 9, 18, 22. **Tel** 224 934 019. **Open** 10am–11pm daily. 🌐 **ufleku.cz**

A short walk south from the Church of St Ursula is one of the city's most famous (and also most touristy) beer halls, U Fleků. Records have it that beer has been brewed here since 1459. The owners have kept up the tradition of brewing: the current

brewery, the smallest in the capital, produces and serves special strong, dark beer, sold exclusively on the premises.

❼ New Town Hall
Novoměstská Radnice

Karlovo náměstí 23. **Map** 5 B1. 🚇 Karlovo náměstí. 🚊 3, 4, 6, 10, 14, 16, 18, 22, 24. **Tel** 224 948 229. Tower: **Open** Apr–Oct: 10am–6pm Tue–Sun. 🌐 **nrpraha.cz**

In 1960, a statue of Hussite preacher Jan Želivský was unveiled at the New Town Hall. It commemorates the first and bloodiest of Prague's defenestrations. On 30 July 1419, Želivský led a crowd of demonstrators to the Town Hall to demand the release of some prisoners. When they were refused, they stormed the building and threw the Catholic councillors they found inside out of the windows. Those who survived the fall were finished off with pikes in the street. The Town Hall already existed in the 14th century; the Gothic

Façade of the Baroque Church of St Ursula

❽ Cathedral of St Cyril and St Methodius
Katedrála Sv. Cyrila a Metoděje

Resslova 9. **Map** 5 B2. **Tel** 224 920 686. 🚇 Karlovo náměstí. 🚊 3, 4, 6, 10, 14, 16, 18, 22, 24. Museum: **Open** 9am–5pm Tue–Sun (Nov–Mar: Tue–Sat). Church: **Open** 8–9:30am Sat, 9am–noon Sun. 🕇 9:30am Sun, 8am Tue & Sat. 📷 📷 ♿

This Baroque church, with a pilastered façade and a small central tower, was built in the 1730s. It was dedicated to St Charles Borromeo and served as the church of a community of retired priests, but was closed in 1783. In the 1930s, the church was restored and given to the Czechoslovak Orthodox Church. It was rededicated to St Cyril and St Methodius, the 9th-century Greek monks who brought Christianity to the Czechs and who are often referred to as the "Apostles to the Slavs" *(see p35)*.

In 1942, the parachutists who had assassinated Reinhard Heydrich, the Nazi governor of Czechoslovakia, hid in the crypt along with members of the Czech Resistance. Surrounded by German troops, they took their own lives rather than surrender. Bullet holes made by the German machine guns during the siege can still be seen below the memorial plaque on the outer wall of the crypt, which now houses a museum.

For hotels and restaurants see p349 and pp366–7

Art Nouveau in Prague

The decorative style known as Art Nouveau originated in Paris in the 1890s. Its influence quickly spread internationally as most of the major European cities quickly responded to its graceful, flowing forms. In Prague, as in the rest of central Europe, the movement was known as the Secession. It reached its height in the first decade of the 20th century but died out during World War I, when the style seemed frivolous and even decadent. There is a wealth of Art Nouveau in Prague, mainly in Josefov and Nové Město, with the style perhaps at its most expressive in the decorative and applied arts: artists adorned every type of object – from doorknobs to lamps and vases – with plant-like forms in imitation of the natural world from which they drew their inspiration.

Architecture

Architecturally, the new style was a deliberate attempt to break with the 19th-century tradition of monumental buildings. In Art Nouveau, the important feature was ornament, either painted or sculpted, often in the form of a female figure, applied to a fairly plain surface. This technique was ideally suited to wrought iron and glass, which were both light and strong and became popular materials. The style created buildings of lasting beauty in Prague.

Hotel Meran, 1904
This grand Art Nouveau building is notable for its fine detailing both inside and out.

Ornate pilasters

Decorative statues

Brass and wrought-iron balustrade

One of the many examples of Art Nouveau decoration in Prague's Main Station *(see p93)*

Alfons Mucha

Many painters, sculptors and graphic artists were influenced by Art Nouveau. One of the style's most successful exponents was Alfons Mucha (1860–1939). He is celebrated chiefly for his posters, yet he also designed stained glass, furniture, jewellery, even postage stamps (see p93).

Poster for Sokol Movement
This beautiful colour lithograph by Mucha, for the Sokol gymnastic movement, dates from 1912.

Iridescent green vase made of Bohemian glass

FURTHER AFIELD

Visitors to Prague, finding the historic centre so full of sights, often ignore the suburbs. It is true that once visitors venture away from the centre, language can become a problem. However, it is well worth the effort, both to escape the crowds and also to realize that Prague is a living city as well as a picturesque time capsule. The majority of the museums and other attractions are easily reached by Metro, tram, bus or even on foot. The sights of particular interest include the Mozart Museum; the Trade

Fair Palace, with its superb modern art collection; the former monastery at Zbraslav, now a repository for some impressive Asian art and artifacts; the Břevnov Monastery, co-founded by St Adalbert; Vyšehrad, the rocky seat of the Přemyslid princes; Žižkov, site of a famous Hussite victory and of a giant monument that towers over Prague; Bílá Hora (White Mountain), which remains the symbol of national calamity; and the Troja Palace, a splendid 17th-century villa with a French garden.

Sights at a Glance

Museums and Galleries

① Mozart Museum
④ *Trade Fair Palace pp104–5*
⑧ Villa Müller

Monastery

⑥ Břevnov Monastery

Historic Districts

② Vyšehrad
③ Žižkov

Historic Sites

⑦ White Mountain and Star Hunting Lodge

Historic Building

⑤ *Troja Palace pp106–7*

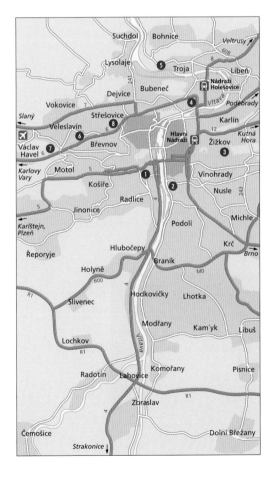

Key

▨ Central Prague
▬▬ Major road
═══ Minor road

◀ Sculptures adorn the garden staircase of the 17th-century Troja Palace

For keys to symbols *see back flap*

❶ Mozart Museum
Bertramka

Mozartova 169. **Tel** 257 317 465.
🚇 Anděl. 🚊 6, 9, 10, 16.
Open 10am–5pm daily. 🚻 ♿ 🖵

Though slightly off the beaten track, in a busy, traffic-ridden district, the museum is well signposted. The Czech people's reverence for Mozart means that the composer is treated more like a Czech than an Austrian citizen.

Bertramka is a 17th-century farmhouse, enlarged in the following century into a comfortable suburban villa in walled grounds. Mozart and his wife Constanze stayed here as the guests of the composer František Dušek and his wife Josefina in 1787, when Mozart was working on *Don Giovanni*. He composed the overture to the opera in the garden pavilion just a few hours before its premiere at the Nostitz Theatre, now the Estates Theatre *(see p86)*.

The house has a small exhibition devoted to Mozart, including his most valuable documents, letters and musical mementoes. Among the most unique objects on display are a lock of his hair and two keyboards on which he performed in Prague. In summer, recitals celebrating his work take place on the terrace.

Bertramka, the villa now housing the Mozart Museum

❷ Vyšehrad

Map 5 B5. 🚇 Vyšehrad. 🚊 3, 7, 17 to Výtoň; 7, 18, 24 to Albertov.
🌐 **praha-vysehrad.cz**

According to legend, Vyšehrad was the original seat of the Přemyslid family, and it was from here that Princess Libuše, the mythical mother of Prague, saw the future glory of her city. Research has proved that as early as the 10th century, the wooded outcrop above the Vltava river, south of Nové Město, was the site of a fortified settlement. Vyšehrad ("The Castle on the Heights") later rose to the rank of a royal residence, though its privileged status was soon overshadowed by Prague Castle, on the opposite side of the river.

The fortress is entered from the south via two gates: the Tábor Gate (17th century) and the slightly later Leopold Gate. The oldest remaining structure on the hill is the 11th-century Rotunda of St Martin, the oldest complete Romanesque building in the capital, albeit greatly restored.

The mighty walls on top of the crag give a magnificent view of the river and town of Vyšehrad. The hillside park below contains some interesting sculptures of Czech legendary heroes, including Libuše and her ploughman spouse, Přemysl (after whom the early Bohemian kings were named). The most imposing building in Vyšehrad is the vast,

Portal of St Peter and Paul Church, Vyšehrad

Neo-Gothic church of St Peter and St Paul (sv. Petra a Pavla). Nearby is Vyšehrad Cemetery, conceived by the National Revival movement and founded in 1869 as the burial ground for the greatest contributors to Czech cultural life. Buried here are composers Antonín Dvořák and Bedřich Smetana, poet Jan Neruda, and artists Alfons Mucha and Mikoláš Aleš.

Equestrian statue of Jan Žižka

❸ Žižkov

🚇 Jiřího z Poděbrad, Flóra. 🚊 9, 11.
🚌 133, 175. National Memorial: **Tel** 222 781 676. TV Tower: **Tel** 210 320 081.
Open 8am–midnight daily. 🚻 ♿
🌐 **towerpark.cz**

This area was the scene of an historic battle in 1420, in which a tiny force of Hussites defeated an army of several thousand Crusaders. In 1877, the area around Vítkov was renamed Žižkov in honour of the leader of the Hussites, Jan Žižka; in 1950, a 9-m (30-ft) high bronze statue of Žižka on horseback was erected on the hill. It stands in front of the vast National Monument (1927–32), built as a symbol of the Czech struggle for independence and later used as a mausoleum for early Communist leaders.

The ugly, futuristic Žižkov TV Tower, reaching over 216 m (709 ft) high, was built in the 1980s. There are fine views over the city from its eighth-floor viewing platform.

❹ Trade Fair Palace

See pp104–5.

❺ Troja Palace

See pp106–7.

Břevnov Monastery, designed largely by the Dientzenhofers

❻ Břevnov Monastery

Břevnovský Klášter

Markétská 28. **Tel** 220 406 111. 🚋 22, 25. 🅿 🕐 10am, 2pm, 4pm Sat & Sun; by appt Mon–Fri – call 220 406 270. 🌐 **W** brevnov.cz

From the surrounding suburban housing, you would never guess that Břevnov is one of the oldest inhabited parts of Prague. A flourishing community grew up here around the Benedictine abbey founded in 993 by Prince Boleslav II and Bishop Adalbert (Vojtěch) – Bohemia's first monastery. An ancient well called Vojtěška marks the spot where the prince and bishop are said to have met and decided to found the monastery.

Saint Adalbert

Adalbert, born in Bohemia as Vojtěch, became Bishop of Prague in 982. Dismayed by the heathen behaviour of its people, however, he resigned. He ended up at the court of Prince Boleslav in Poland, from where, in 997, he set out on a mission to convert the Prussians. They welcomed Adalbert by murdering him. Boleslav brought the martyr's body back and buried it in Gniezno cathedral in Poland. Canonized in 999, St Adalbert became the patron saint of Poland.

The Martyrdom of St Adalbert

The gateway, courtyard and most of the present monastery buildings are by the great Baroque architects Christoph and Kilian Ignaz Dientzenhofer *(see p67)*: the monastery church of St Margaret (sv. Markéty) is Christoph's work. Essentially a substantial reworking of the original 10th-century church, it is based on a floorplan of overlapping ovals, as ingenious as any of Bernini's churches in Rome. For four decades, the Ministry of the Interior used St Margaret's as storage space. Also of interest is the abbey's meeting hall, or Theresian Hall, with a painted ceiling dating from 1727.

❼ White Mountain and Star Hunting Lodge

Bílá Hora/Letohrádek Hvězda

🚋 22 (White Mountain), 1, 2, 18 (Star Hunting Lodge). White Mountain: **Open** 24 hrs daily. Star Hunting Lodge: **Tel** 220 612 230. **Open** Apr–Oct: 10am–5pm Tue–Sun (to 6pm May–Sep). 🅿 🌐

The Battle of the White Mountain, the decisive first battle of the Thirty Years' War fought on 8 November 1620, affected the two main communities of Prague in different ways. For the Protestants, it was a disaster that led to 300 years of Habsburg domination; for the Catholic supporters of the Habsburgs, it was a triumph, so they erected a memorial chapel on the hill. In the early 1700s, this was converted into the Church of Our Lady Victorious and decorated by leading Baroque artists.

In the 16th century, the woodland around the White Mountain battle site had been a royal game park. The Star Hunting Lodge (Letohrádek Hvězda), completed in 1556, survives today. This fascinating building has a six-pointed star design – *hvězda* means star. In 1950, it became a museum dedicated to the writer of historical novels Alois Jirásek (1851–1930), and the painter Mikoláš Aleš (1852–1913).

Also on site is a small exhibition on the history of the building, along with exhibits on the Battle of the White Mountain. There are also temporary exhibitions on Czech culture.

The 16th-century Star Hunting Lodge, close to Bílá Hora

❾ Trade Fair Palace
Veletržní Palác

The National Gallery in Prague opened its collection of 20th- and 21st-century art in 1995, housed in a reconstruction of a former Trade Fair building of 1928. Since 2000, it has also housed a 19th-century collection. Its vast, skylit spaces make an ideal backdrop for the paintings, which range from French 19th-century art and superb examples of Impressionism and Post-Impressionism, to works by Munch, Klimt, Picasso and Miró, as well as a splendid collection of Czech modern art. The collection is subject to rearrangement so the placement of artworks may change.

Grand Meal (1951–5)
Mikuláš Medek's works range from post-war Surrealism to 1960s Abstraction.

Fourth Floor

Third Floor

Cubist Bust (1913–14)
Otto Gutfreund was one of the first artists to apply the principles of Cubism to sculpture, and this work marks his move towards abstract art.

Cleopatra (1942–57)
This painting by Jan Zrzavý, a major representative of Czech modern art, took the artist 45 years to complete and is his best-known piece.

St Sebastian (1912)
This self-portrait by Bohumil Kubišta takes its inspiration from the martyrdom of St Sebastian, who was persecuted by being bound to a tree and shot with arrows.

Pomona (1910)
Aristide Maillol was a pupil of Rodin. This work is part of an exceptional collection of bronzes.

Key to Floorplan

- ☐ Czech Art 1900–1930
- ☐ 19th- and 20th-century French Art
- ☐ Czech Art 1930–present day
- ☐ 20th-century Foreign Art
- ☐ Temporary exhibition space
- ☐ Non-exhibition space

For hotels and restaurants see p350 and pp367–8

★ **Big Dialog** (1966)
Karel Nepraš's sculpture, made from industrial scrap metal held together with wires, was painted red to poke fun at the Communist regime.

VISITORS' CHECKLIST

Practical Information

Veletržní Palác, Dukelských hrdinů 47.**Tel** 22 43 01 111.
Open 10am–6pm Tue–Sun (last adm 30 mins before closing).
W ngprague.cz

Transport

Ⓜ Vltavská. 🚊 12, 17, 24 to Veletržní; 1, 8, 25, 26 to Strossmayerovo náměstí.

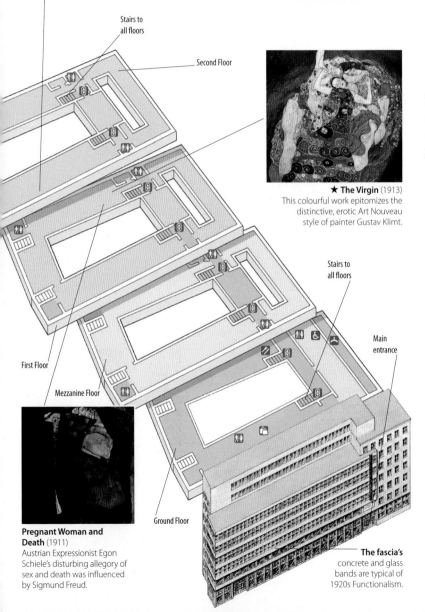

Stairs to all floors

Second Floor

★ **The Virgin** (1913)
This colourful work epitomizes the distinctive, erotic Art Nouveau style of painter Gustav Klimt.

Stairs to all floors

Main entrance

First Floor

Mezzanine Floor

Pregnant Woman and Death (1911)
Austrian Expressionist Egon Schiele's disturbing allegory of sex and death was influenced by Sigmund Freud.

Ground Floor

The fascia's concrete and glass bands are typical of 1920s Functionalism.

❺ Troja Palace
Trojský Zámek

One of Prague's most striking summer palaces, Troja was built in the late 1600s by Jean-Baptiste Mathey for Count Sternberg, member of a leading Bohemian aristocratic family. Lying at the foot of the Vltava Heights, the palace was modelled on a Classical Italian villa, while its garden was laid out in formal French style. The superb interior is full of extravagant frescoes expressing the Sternbergs' loyalty to the Habsburg dynasty. Troja houses a good collection of 19th-century art.

★ Grand Hall Fresco
The frescoes in the Grand Hall depict the story of the first Habsburg Emperor, Rudolph I, and the victories of Leopold I over Christianity's arch-enemy, the Ottoman Empire.

Defeat of the Turks
This turbaned figure, tumbling from the Grand Hall ceiling, symbolizes Leopold I's triumph over the Turks.

★ Garden Staircase
The two sons of Mother Earth which adorn the oval-shaped staircase (1685–1703) are part of a group of sculptures by Johann Georg Heermann and his nephew Paul, showing the struggle of the Olympian Gods with the Titans.

Personification of Justice
Abraham Godyn's image of Justice gazes from the lower east wall of the Grand Hall.

VISITORS' CHECKLIST

Practical Information
U Trojského zámku 1, Prague 7.
Tel 283 851 614.
Open Apr–Oct: 10am–6pm Tue–Sun (from 1pm Fri).
Closed Nov–Apr. 🚫 ✉ 🖥 ♿
W ghmp.cz

Transport
🚌 112 from Holešovice metro station.

❽ Villa Müller
Müllerova Vila

Nad Hradním vodojemem 14.
Tel 224 312 012. 🚇 Hradčanská, then 🚊 1, 2, 18 to Ořechovka.
Open Apr–Oct: 9am–5pm Tue, Thu, Sat & Sun; Nov–Mar: 10am–4pm Tue, Thu, Sat & Sun. 🚫 📷 Apr–Oct: 9am, 11am, 1pm, 3pm & 5pm; Nov–Mar: 10am, noon, 2pm & 4pm. ♿
W mullerovavila.cz

Characterized by a severe, white concrete façade, asymmetric windows and a flat roof, the Villa Müller was designed by Modernist architect Adolf Loos and built in 1928–30 by construction entrepreneur František Müller for himself and his wife Milada. Loos used his innovative spatial theory known as "Raumplan" in the design of both the outside and the inside of the building, so that all the spaces look and feel interconnected. The roof terrace at the top of the house provides a "framed" view of Prague cathedral in the distance.

In contrast to the building's functional exterior, the interiors combine traditional furnishings with vibrant use of marble, wood and silk. The villa fell into disrepair during the 1950s, and in 1995, ownership passed to the city of Prague. A programme of restoration took place between 1997 and 2000, when it was opened to the public as a National Cultural Monument.

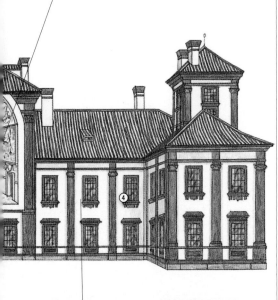

★ Chinese Rooms
Several rooms feature 18th-century murals of Chinese scenes. This room makes a perfect backdrop for a ceramics display.

KEY

① Statues of sons of Mother Earth

② Statue of Olympian God

③ Belvedere turret

④ Stucco decoration

Modernist Villa Müller, as seen from the garden

PRAGUE STREET FINDER

The map references given for all the sights described in the Prague chapter, and also for the hotels and restaurants listed in Travellers' Needs *(see pp348–50 and 364–8)* refer to the street maps in this section. The key map (right) shows the area of Prague covered by the Street Finder. This map includes sightseeing areas, as well as districts for hotels and restaurants.

In keeping with Czech maps, none of the street names on the Street Finder has the Czech word for street, *ulice*, included (though you may see it on the city's street signs). Churches, buildings, museums and monuments are marked on the Street Finder with their English and Czech names.

Key to Street Finder

- Major sight
- Place of interest
- Other building
- Metro station
- Train station
- Bus station
- Tram stop
- Funicular railway
- Riverboat boarding point
- Tourist information office
- Hospital with emergency unit
- Police station
- Church
- Synagogue
- Railway line
- City wall
- Pedestrian street

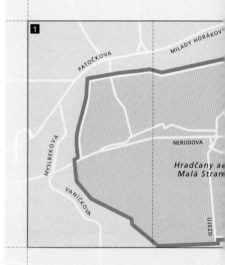

Scale of Map Pages

0 metres   200

0 yards   200

1:8,400

Looking across Charles Bridge towards Prague Castle

Aerial view of the Baroque Church of St Nicholas in Old Town Square

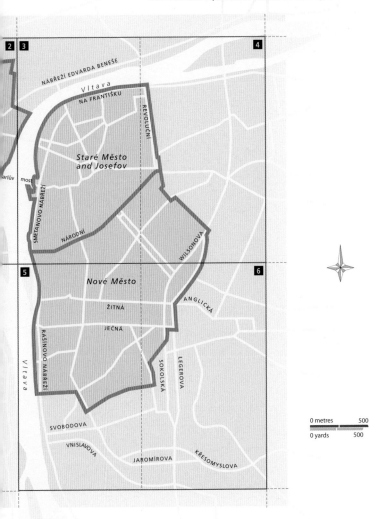

2 3 4

NÁBŘEŽÍ EDVARDA BENEŠE

V l t a v a
NA FRANTIŠKU

REVOLUČNÍ

**Staré Město
and Josefov**

arlův most

SMETANOVO NÁBŘEŽÍ

NÁRODNÍ

WILSONOVA

5 6

Nové Město

ŽITNÁ

ANGLICKÁ

JEČNÁ

RAŠÍNOVO NÁBŘEŽÍ

V l t a v a

SOKOLSKÁ

LEGEROVA

SVOBODOVA

VNISLAVOVA

JAROMÍROVA

KŘESOMYSLOVA

| 0 metres | 500 |
| 0 yards | 500 |

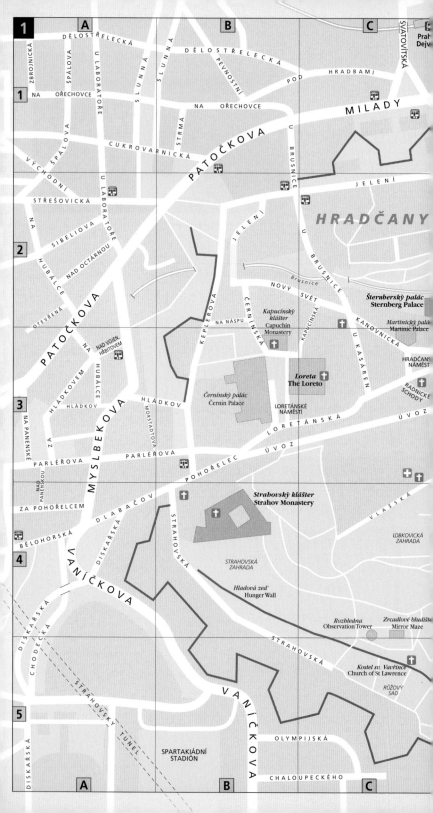

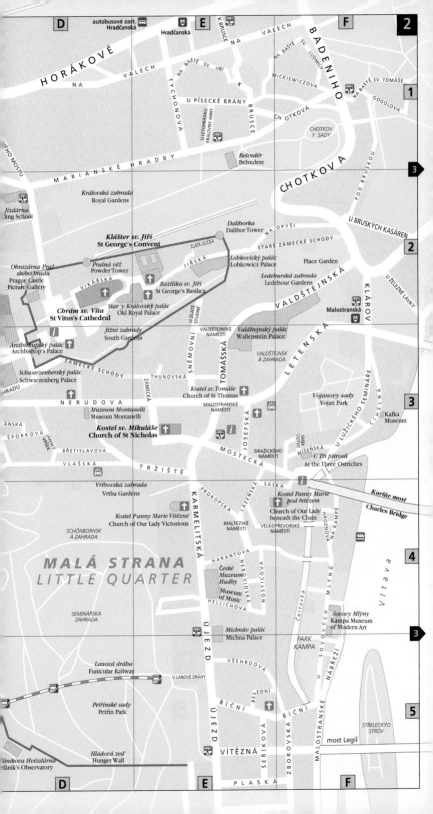

3

A   B   C

Letenské sady
Letná Park

1

BENEŠE

EDVARDA

2

NÁBŘEŽÍ

U PLOVÁRNY

KOSÁRKOVO NÁBŘEŽÍ

Rásnovka

FRANTIŠKU

MALÁ KLÁŠTERSKÁ

KLÁŠTERSKÁ

Klášter sv. Anežky České
Convent of St Agnes's

NÁMĚSTÍ CURIEOVÝCH

EL. KRASNOHORSKÉ

Kostel sv. Šimona a Judy
Church of St Simon and St Jude

U MILOSRDNÝCH

DUŠNÍ

KOZÍ

HAŠTALSKÉ NÁMĚSTÍ

VĚZEŇSKÁ

DVOŘÁ

ANEŽSKÁ

RÁSNOVKA

ZA HAŠTALEM

Vltava

DVOŘÁKOVO NÁBŘEŽÍ

BŘEHOVÁ

17. LISTOPADU

PAŘÍŽSKÁ

Čechův most

Kubistické domy
Cubist Houses

BÍLKOVA

U STARÉHO

JOSEFOV
JEWISH QUARTER

HAŠTALSKÁ

Kostel sv. Haš...
Church of St Cast...

2

NA REJDIŠTI

U STARÉHO HŘBITOVA

U STARÉ ŠKOLY

Staronová synagóga
Old-New Synagogue

Klausová synagóga
Klausen Synagogue

ČERVENÁ

MAISELOVA

Vysoká synagóga
High Synagogue

Kostel sv. Ducha
Church of the
Holy Ghost

Španělská synagóga
Spanish Synagogue

DLOUHÁ

MASNÁ

Uměleckoprůmyslové muzeum
Museum of Decorative Arts

Mánesův most

Rudolfinum

Starý židovský hřbitov
Old Jewish Cemetery

Židovská radnice
Jewish Town Hall

KOSTEČNÁ

SALVÁTORSKÁ

MASNÁ

MALÁ ŠTUPARTSKÁ

Kostel sv. Jakuba
Church of James

JAKUBSK

NÁMĚSTÍ JANA PALACHA

Pinkasova synagóga
Pinkas Synagogue

ŠIRO KÁ

VALENTINSKÁ

Maiselova synagóga
Maisel Synagogue

JÁCHYMOVA

MAISELOVA

PAŘÍŽSKÁ

Pomník Jana Husa
Jan Hus
Monument

DLOUHÁ

TÝNSKÁ ULIČKA

Palác Golz-Kinských
Golz-Kinský
Palace

TÝNSKÁ

3

ALŠOVO NÁBŘEŽÍ

KŘIŽOVNICKÁ

VELESLAVÍNOVA

KAPROVA

ŽATECKÁ

Staroměstská

Kostel sv. Mikuláše
Church of St Nicholas

STAROMĚSTSKÉ NÁMĚSTÍ

Kostel Panny Marie před Týnem
Church of Our
Lady before Týn

ŠTUPARTSKÁ

CELETNÁ

PLATNÉŘSKÁ

MARIÁNSKÉ NÁMĚSTÍ

LINHARTSKÁ

U RADNICE

Staroměstská radnice
Old Town Hall

OVOCNÝ TRH

Kostel sv. Františka
Church of St. Francis

Karlův most

KŘIŽOVNICKÉ NÁMĚSTÍ

Klementinum
Clementinum

SEMINÁŘSKÁ

HUSOVA

KARLOVA

MALÉ NÁMĚSTÍ

MELANTRICHOVA

Clam-Gallasův palác
Clam-Gallas Palace

ŽELEZNÁ

KAMZÍKOVA

KOŽNÁ

Karolinum
Carolinum

Stavovské divadlo
Estates Theatre

HAVÍŘSKÁ

4

Muzeum Bedřicha Smetany
Smetana
Museum

NOVOTNÉHO LÁVKA

ANENSKÁ

STŘÍBRNÁ

LILIOVÁ

JALOVCOVA

JILSKÁ

HLAV SOVA

Dům U Dvou zlatých medvědů
House at the Two
Golden Bears

MICHALSKÁ

HAVELSKÁ

V KOTCÍCH

RYTÍŘSKÁ

Kostel sv. Havla
Church of St Gall

NA MŮSTKU

PROVAZNICKÁ

Národní Muzeum
Museum
Communi...

NA PŘÍKOPĚ

Kostel sv. Jiljí
Church of St Giles

U ZÁBRADLÍ

ANENSKÉ NÁMĚSTÍ

ŘETĚZOVÁ

ZLATÁ

VEJVODOVA

Betlémská kaple
Bethlehem Chapel

SKOŘEPKA

UHELNÝ TRH

Můstek

2

NÁPRSTKOVA

KAROLÍNY

BORŠOV

BETLÉMSKÉ NÁMĚSTÍ

DOBŘEJSKÝCH

Náprstkovo muzeum
Náprstek Museum

STARÉ MĚSTO
OLD TOWN

PERLOVA

28. ŘÍJNA

VÁCLAVSKÉ NÁMĚSTÍ

SMETANOVO NÁBŘEŽÍ

SVĚTLÍKOVA

BETLÉMSKÁ

DIVADELNÍ

KONVIKTSKÁ

NA PERŠTÝNĚ

BARTOLOMĚJSKÁ

MARTINSKÁ

Kostel sv. Martina ve zdi
Church of
St Martin in the Wall

Můstek

JUNGMANNOVO NÁMĚSTÍ

Kostel Panny Marie Sněžné
Church of Our Lady of the Snows

Františkánská zahrada
Franciscan Garden

5

KROČÍNOVA

SVĚTLÉ

KAROLÍNY SVĚTLÉ

NÁRODNÍ

ŠPÁLENÁ

CHARVÁTOVA

JUNGMANNOVA

PALACKÉHO

most Legií

NÁRODNÍ

Národní divadlo
National Theatre

Kostel sv. Voršily
Church of St Ursula

VORŠILSKÁ

OSTROVNÍ

MIKULANDSKÁ

PURKYŇOVA

VLADISLAVOVA

VODIČKOVA

Národní třída

A   B   C

5

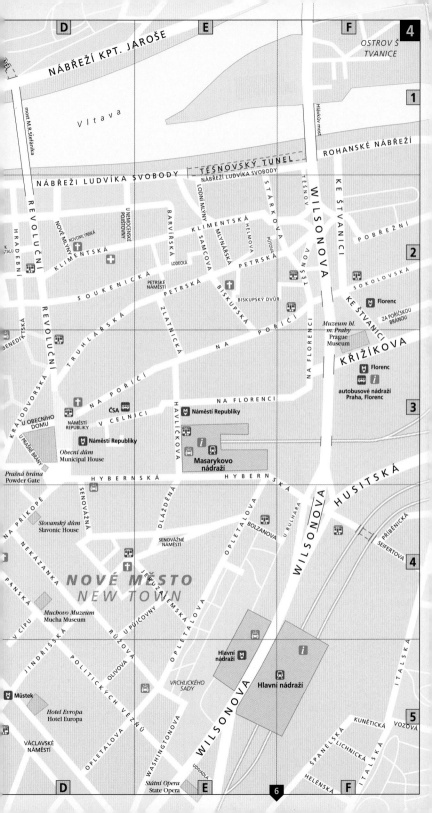

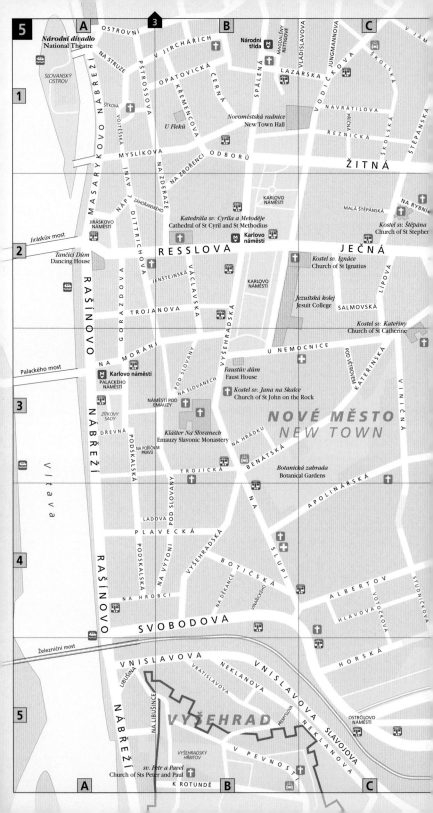

CZECH REPUBLIC REGION BY REGION

The Czech Republic at a Glance

The Czech Republic is a country with over 70 per cent of its land occupied by uplands full of rolling hills and sweeping valleys. It comprises three historic regions. Bohemia, the largest, has a central basin surrounded by ranges of mountains and hills. To the east, it borders Moravia, a paradise for lovers of good wine, which stretches eastwards to the border with Slovakia. The third and smallest region, Silesia, is a highland area to the north, bordering Poland.

České Švýcarsko, an area of extraordinary sandstone formations, is best symbolized by Pravčická brána – the largest natural rock bridge in Central Europe *(see pp190–91)*.

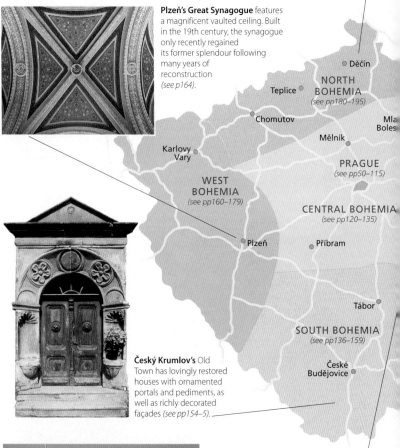

Plzeň's Great Synagogue features a magnificent vaulted ceiling. Built in the 19th century, the synagogue only recently regained its former splendour following many years of reconstruction *(see p164)*.

Děčín

NORTH BOHEMIA
(see pp180–195)

Teplice

Chomutov

Mělník

Mla Boles

Karlovy Vary

PRAGUE
(see pp50–115)

WEST BOHEMIA
(see pp160–179)

CENTRAL BOHEMIA
(see pp120–135)

Plzeň

Příbram

Tábor

SOUTH BOHEMIA
(see pp136–159)

České Budějovice

Český Krumlov's Old Town has lovingly restored houses with ornamented portals and pediments, as well as richly decorated façades *(see pp154–5)*.

St James's Church, Kutná Hora is the oldest church in a town that is famous for its silver mining and its vast St Barbara's Cathedral. St James's has only one tower – the second was never built as there were fears that it might collapse due to the instability of the ground, which had been disturbed by mining operations *(see pp124–5)*.

◀ The colourful rooftops in Old Town, Prague

Častolovice Palace, returned in 1989 to Franziska Diana Sternberg-Phipps, is among the best-preserved castles in East Bohemia. Now its historic interiors serve as an exclusive hotel and a museum *(see p213)*.

Bouzov Castle, formerly the property of the Order of Teutonic Knights, was given its Neo-Gothic form in the late 19th and early 20th centuries. Now it is a favourite setting for films whose action takes place in the Middle Ages *(see pp222–3)*.

erec

Trutnov

Hradec Králové

olín

EAST BOHEMIA
(see pp196–213)

Jeseník

Svitavy

NORTH MORAVIA AND SILESIA
(see pp214–225)

Ostrava

Olomouc

Jihlava

Brno

Zlín

SOUTH MORAVIA
(see pp226–243)

Znojmo

Břeclav

0 kilometres   50

0 miles   25

The village of Křtiny is home to an important Baroque church. Also in the village is a Baroque residence that was converted in the first half of the 19th century by František Xavier of Dietrichstein into a small castle, where this coat of arms can be seen *(see p234)*.

CENTRAL BOHEMIA

The region surrounding Prague offers the combined attractions of an extraordinary landscape with its magnificent rock formations furrowed by river canyons, as well as a wealth of historic towns and spectacular castles. Situated relatively close to the city, these sights provide visitors and locals alike with superb opportunities for exploration.

From the 6th century AD, Central Bohemia (Střední Čechy) saw the arrival of numerous Slav tribes, who built settlements and fortresses here. In the 10th century, the Czechs emerged as the dominant people in the region. The first duke in the Přemyslid dynasty, which held sway in Bohemia from the 9th century, was a Christian, and many ecclesiastical remains in Central Bohemia testify to the importance of this new influence. Nowhere else in the country are there so many examples of Romanesque and Early Gothic stone architecture. At Sázava Monastery, founded in the 11th century, the Old Slavonic liturgy continues to be celebrated in the tradition of the missionaries St Cyril and St Methodius *(see p35)*.

Nearly every town in Central Bohemia has an historic town centre. The old silver-mining town of Kutná Hora has over 300 excellently preserved buildings from the Middle Ages and the Baroque eras.

In a region of many castles, the most famous is undoubtedly Karlštejn – an imposing Gothic fortress built by Emperor Charles IV to house the crown jewels and religious relics. More recent history is reflected at Konopiště Castle, owned by the Archduke Franz Ferdinand. Many of the castles are set on craggy hilltops, and some of the more beautiful rock formations of the area can be seen at Český Kras, not far from Karlštejn. This fertile region also has a wine-growing area around the historic town of Mělník.

The formal Baroque façade of Dobříš Palace

◀ Lofty interior of the Gothic-style St Barbara's Cathedral, Kutná Hora

Exploring Central Bohemia

For those on a short visit to the Czech Republic, the central part of the Bohemian Basin provides an excellent cross-section of all the attractions that this beautiful country has to offer. Within an hour's journey, or certainly a day trip, from Prague are a variety of spectacular castles. Karlštejn, with its turrets and towers and immaculate interiors, is one of the most-visited places in the country; it has some interesting walking trails nearby. Other, less-visited, castles, such as Křivoklát and Kokořín, offer quieter opportunities for exploration. The town of Kutná Hora, with its atmospheric old centre and Gothic Cathedral of St Barbara, is also hugely popular. Superb Renaissance buildings can be seen in Nelahozeves, and Dobříš Palace is a Baroque treasure.

Schwarzenberg coat of arms made of bones, Sedlec ossuary, Kutná Hora

Key

- ▬▬ Motorway
- ▬▬ Dual carriageway
- ▬▬ Main road
- ▬▬ Minor road
- ▬▬ Main railway
- ▬▬ Minor railway
- ▬▬ Regional border

Svata Horá Church above the mining town of Příbram

Getting Around

The capital provides a convenient starting point for exploring the sights of Central Bohemia. The local transport network is well developed and reliable. Railway lines offer regular services north through Mělník and Mladá Boleslav, east through Kolín and Kutná Hora, south via Konopiště and west to Karlštejn and Křivoklát. Buses from Prague and between towns also serve the region well.

Entrance to the grounds of Sázava Monastery

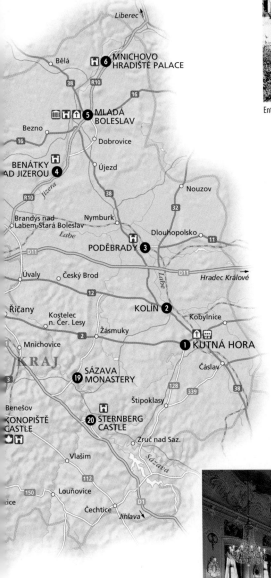

Sights at a Glance

1. Kutná Hora pp124–5
2. Kolín
3. Poděbrady
4. Benátky nad Jizerou
5. Mladá Boleslav
6. Mnichovo Hradiště Palace
7. Kokořín Castle
8. Mělník
9. Veltrusy Chateau
10. Nelahozeves
11. Lány
12. Křivoklát Castle
13. Točník Castle
14. Český Kras
15. Karlštejn Castle pp134–5
16. Dobříš Palace
17. Příbram
18. Konopiště Castle
19. Sázava Monastery
20. Sternberg Castle

The imposing Hall of Mirrors in Dobříš Palace

For keys to symbols see back flap

❶ Kutná Hora

A rich source of silver from the 13th to the 18th centuries, Kutná Hora (Kuttenberg) was the second most important town in Bohemia, after Prague. Its wealth funded many beautiful buildings, including St Barbara's Cathedral; the Italian Court (Vlašský Dvůr), which housed the royal mint and later the town hall; the 14th-century Gothic Church of St James (sv. Jakub); and the 15th-century Stone House (Kamenný Dům). Since 1995, the historic centre of Kutná Hora has been on the UNESCO Cultural Heritage List. Three km (2 miles) northeast of the centre is the suburb of Sedlec, home to an extraordinary ossuary where bones accumulated over centuries were put together by carver František Rint in 1870 to form crosses, a coat of arms and even a chandelier.

Cathedral's Front Façade
In 1388, Peter Parler planned this five-aisled building, with three tented spires. The last architectural additions were in the late 19th century.

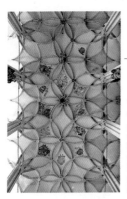

★ Vault
The central nave with its magnificent geometric vaulted ceiling was designed in the early 16th century by Benedikt Ried. It incorporates coats of arms from local craft guilds.

Organ
The Baroque organ case dating from 1740–60 hides a much newer mechanism installed in the early 20th century by the local organmaker Jan Tuček.

St Barbara's Cathedral

Dedicated to the patron saint of miners, St Barbara's Cathedral (sv. Barbora) is one of Europe's most spectacular Gothic churches. Both interior and exterior are richly ornamented, and the huge windows ensure it is filled with light. Many of the side chapels are decorated with interesting frescoes, some of which depict miners at work and men striking coins in the mint, reflecting the sources of the town's wealth.

Pulpit
The pulpit dating from 1655 is decorated with four stone reliefs produced in 1566 by Master Leopold, depicting the four Evangelists.

VISITORS' CHECKLIST

Practical Information
Road map D2.
🏙 21,000. 🛈 Palackého náměstí 377. **Tel** 327 512 378.
Cathedral: **Open** Nov–Mar: 10am–6pm daily; Apr–Oct: 9am–6pm daily. 🚫
Ossuary: **Open** daily. 🚫
🆆 kutnahora.cz

Transport
🚊 🚌 from Prague.

Oak Stalls
The late 15th-century stalls, originally designed for St Vitus's Cathedral in Prague, feature Gothic spired canopies and carved balustrades.

Stained-glass Window
The Art Nouveau stained-glass windows designed by František Urban were added in the early 20th century.

★ High Altar
The central scene of the Neo-Gothic high altar (1901–5), a replica of the original, depicts the Last Supper.

Balustrade
The stone balustrade of the presbytery includes the initials of King Vladislav Jagiello ("W") and his son Ludwig ("L").

Sgraffito in the courtyard of the castle in Benátky nad Jizerou

❷ Kolín

Road map D2. 30,000. from Prague. from Prague. *i* Na Hradbách 157. **Tel** 321 712 021.

Founded in the 13th century by German colonists, the town of Kolín centres around the **Charles Square** (Karlovo náměstí). On the western side of the square is the **town hall** (radnice), originally Gothic, and rebuilt in the 19th century in the Neo-Renaissance style.

Kolín's dominant feature is its Early Gothic **Church of St Bartholomew** (sv. Bartoloměj), begun in 1261. The choir of this triple-aisled basilica is by Peter Parler – builder of St Vitus's Cathedral in Prague. In the **Regional Museum**, an exhibition details the battle fought nearby on 18 June 1757 during the Seven Years' War between Britain and France.

Arms of Kolín on its town hall

Regional Museum
Brandlova 27. **Tel** 321 722 988. **Open** 9am–5pm Tue–Fri, 10am–5pm Sat & Sun.

❸ Poděbrady

Road map D2. 14,100. from Prague. from Prague. *i* Jiřího náměstí 1/1. **Tel** 325 511 946.

Strategically located on the Labe (Elbe) river on the trade route linking Prague with East Bohemia, Silesia and Poland, Poděbrady was built in the mid-12th century. George of Poděbrady (Jiří z Poděbrad) was elected the King of Bohemia in 1458.

The town's oldest historic sight is **Poděbrady Castle**. Begun in the second half of the 13th century and altered many times since, it is not particularly attractive architecturally, but its magnificent location on the riverbank and its Gothic tower topped by a Baroque cupola – the town's symbol – make it worth visiting. The castle chapel with its traces of medieval frescoes houses an exhibition on King George.

In 1905, the town's life changed when a German dowser, von

View of the historic Poděbrady Castle, on the Labe

Bülow, discovered a local source of mineral water and Poděbrady became famous as a spa. Its waters still draw many visitors.

Poděbrady Castle
Tel 325 612 640. **Open** Tue–Sun. polabskemuzeum.cz

❹ Benátky nad Jizerou

Road map D1. 7,400. from Prague. *i* Castle Zámek 50. **Tel** 326 316 102.

With a name that translates as Venice (Benátky) on the Jizera, this town was founded in the mid-13th century, on the flood-prone River Jizera. Its main historic sight is the **Castle**, built in 1526–7. A striking element of its decor is the 16th-century Renaissance *sgraffito* on the courtyard façade. In 1599, Emperor Rudolph II bought the estate and allowed the castle to be used by his court astronomer and alchemist Tycho Brahe, who built a small observatory and laboratory here, where he produced an elixir against plague. It was also here that Brahe met with another stargazer, Johannes Kepler, in 1600. The castle acquired its Baroque form in the 18th century.

Benátky nad Jizerou Castle
Tel 326 316 682. **Open** May–Oct: 9am–5pm.

❺ Mladá Boleslav

Road map D1. 👥 45,500.
🚉 2 km (1 mile). 🚌 from Prague.
ℹ Železná 107. **Tel** 326 109 405.
🌐 mladoboleslavsko.eu

Famed as the home of Škoda cars, Mladá Boleslav (Jungblunzau) is dominated by a vast **Castle**, now the home of the local museum. It stands on the site of a former Přemyslid stronghold, established here in the late 10th century. The present heavy silhouette is the result of its mid-18th-century conversion into army barracks. Traces of the Renaissance style can still be glimpsed in the arcaded courtyard.

More interesting is the permanent archaeological exhibition in the Gothic Temple Palace in the town square, with its display of local finds. The Protestant **Church of Bohemian Unitas Fratrum** (Unity of Bohemian Brethren) at 123 Českobratrské Náměstí, dating from 1544–54, now an art gallery, is a reminder of the town's former prominence as a centre of Reformation in the 16th century.

In the northern district of town is the interesting **Škoda Museum** with its exhibition of motorcycles and cars that have been produced here since the early 20th century.

🏰 **Mladá Boleslav Castle**
Tel 326 325 616. **Open** 9am–noon & 1–5pm daily (to 4pm Oct–Apr). 🎫

🏛 **Škoda Museum**
V Klementa 294. **Tel** 326 831 134.
Open daily. 🎫 🌐 skoda-auto.com

❻ Mnichovo Hradiště Palace

Road map D1. 🚉 from Prague.
🚌 from Prague. **Tel** 326 773 098.
Open Jan–Mar: by appt; Apr & Oct: 8:45am–3pm Sat, Sun & public hols; May–Sep: 8:45am–4pm Tue–Sun.
🎫 ♿ 🌐 mnichovo-hradiste.cz

This Renaissance palace, built in about 1606 by Václav Budovec of Budov, is in the industrial town of Mnichovo Hradiště (Münchengrätz). Following the Battle of the White Mountain in 1620 (see p41), its owner – one of

The castle in Mladá Boleslav, now a museum

the leaders of the anti-Habsburg insurrection – was beheaded and his confiscated estate passed to Count Albrecht von Wallenstein. Mnichovo Hradiště remained in the Wallenstein family until the mid-20th century.

The present Baroque form of the palace is due to extensive rebuilding at the turn of the 17th and 18th centuries. The opulent interiors are furnished with Baroque and Rococo furniture. The ceiling in the main hall of the palace has a particularly striking fresco.

The court theatre, which opened in 1833, is unusual in that it still has many of its original costumes and stage settings. The palace Chapel of St Anne is Albrecht von Wallenstein's final resting place. After his murder in 1634, his body was taken to the monastery at Valdice, near his centre of power in Jičín (see p209). It was moved here in 1785 near to the body of his first wife.

A sculpture from Kokořín Castle

❼ Kokořín Castle

Road map C1. 🚌 from Mělník.
Tel 315 695 064. **Open** Apr & Oct: 9am–4pm Sat & Sun; May–Sep: 9am–4pm Tue–Sun (to 5pm Jun–Aug); Nov–Mar: by appt only.
🎫 📷 🌐 hrad-kokorin.cz

In a region of forests and sandstone rocks lies Kokořín Castle, notable for its spectacular 38-m (125-ft) tall tower, which offers a sweeping panorama. Built in the 14th century, the castle suffered severe damage in the 15th century during the Hussite Wars and was later abandoned. The Špaček family restored it in the early 20th century. Its ruins inspired many 19th-century painters and poets, including the Czech Romantic poet Karel Hynek Mácha (1810–36). The understated castle rooms house exhibits relating to its history.

Škoda

The bicycle and motorcycle manufacturers Laurin and Klement made their first motor car in Mladá Boleslav in 1905. Named Voiturette, it had a 1-litre, 7-HP engine and cruising speed of 45 km/h (28 mph). They continued to develop and improve on their models, and, in a quest for the means to expand, they merged with the existing Škoda company in the 1920s. This highly successful company became synonymous with the Czech motor industry. Since 1991, Škoda Auto has belonged to the Volkswagen Group of Companies.

A 1937 Škoda Rapid II

The fountain in Mělník's market square

❽ Mělník

Road map C1. 👥 19,500. 🚃
🚌 from Prague. 🛈 Legionářů 51.
Tel 315 627 503. 🌐 **melnik.cz**

Perched high on an escarpment, surrounded by vineyards, Mělník lies at the confluence of the two biggest Czech rivers, the Labe (Elbe) and the Vltava. The town centres on its market square (Náměstí Míru), dominated by the Renaissance town hall (radnice) with its clock tower. The Baroque arcaded houses around the square have vast cellars that were used for storing wine. The town has been a wine-producing centre since the 14th century, and the square's fountain commemorates that heritage.

The Gothic **Church of St Peter and St Paul** (sv. Petr a Pavel) is a conspicuous structure, with its tall onion-domed tower. Inside, a beautiful vault and an interesting ossuary can be viewed.

The Lobkowicz family **Castle** is a vast edifice adjacent to the church, its walls covered with some of the oldest *sgraffito* in Bohemia, dating from 1533. Inside is an impressive array of Czech Baroque art including works by Jan Kupecký *(see p26)*, Karel Škréta and Petr Brandl. The paintings are hung in well-restored castle rooms, including the grand bedchamber and the study of the Chancellor George Christian. The castle's vast 14th-century three-level wine cellars occupy over 1,500 sq m (16,000 sq ft). Here you can see lavishly decorated old wine casks, and also sample some of the wines produced in Mělník.

🏰 **Mělník Castle**
Svatováclavská 19. **Tel** 317 070 154.
Open daily. 🎫 🚫
🌐 **lobkowicz-melnik.cz**

❾ Veltrusy Chateau

Road map C1. 4 km (2 miles) N of Kralupy nad Vltavou. 🚃
🚌 from Prague. **Tel** 315 781 146.
Open Apr: 8:30am–5pm Sat & Sun; May–Oct: 8:30am–5pm Tue–Sun (to 7pm Jun–Aug). 🎫 🚫
🌐 **zamek-veltrusy.cz**

Built during the first half of the 18th century by the Chotek family, the château was designed by František Kaňka. Its floor plan is in the shape of a cross, with a domed rotunda. Inside are Baroque and Empire-style decorations and furnishings, including inlaid Dutch furniture, Chinese, Japanese and Viennese porcelain and Dutch decorated earthenware.

The château's vast English-style park, established in 1764–85, is one of the best preserved in Europe, and

Sgraffito decoration on the castle in Nelahozeves

occupies nearly 300 ha (750 acres). Its creator, Rihard van der Schott, took advantage of the watery conditions on the banks of this stretch of the Vltava river. Numerous pavilions in Classical and Romantic styles were built from 1792 to 1830 amid meadows, ponds and canals. Attractions include the Doric Pavilion; the Pavilion of the Friends of Villages and Gardens; the Egyptian Cabinet; a bridge with a sphinx inspired by Napoleon's Egypt expedition; the Empire-style Pavilion of Maria Theresa and the Neo-Gothic Red Mill.

In 2002, Veltrusy was flooded and major damage was caused; the majority of the park is now fully restored, while the castle's reconstruction is ongoing.

Pavilion of the Friends of Villages and Gardens in Veltrusy Park

❿ Nelahozeves

Road map C1. 👥 1,200. 🚃
🚌 from Prague. 🌐 **nelahozeves.cz**

The village of Nelahozeves is the birthplace of the composer Antonín Dvořák *(see pp24–5)*. Today, the building where he was born, opposite the church, is a small **museum**.

Nelahozeves has a huge Renaissance **Castle**, which since 1623 has belonged to the Lobkowicz family. In 1950, the estate was nationalized by the Communists, but in 1992, it was returned to the family. The courtyard façades are decorated with beautiful *sgraffito*. Inside are original wooden coffered ceilings with stucco decorations. The **Roudnice Lobkowicz**

Collection includes paintings by Rubens, Breughel and Veronese, as well as porcelain and furniture. There are also music archives and a library. An exhibition, entitled *Private Spaces*, explores the life of the Lobkowicz family.

Dvořák's Birthplace
Tel 315 785 099. **Open** 9:30am–noon & 1–5pm Wed–Fri; also open 1st & 3rd weekends of the month.
w nm.cz

Castle and Roudnice Lobkowicz Collection
Tel 315 709 154. **Open** Apr–Oct: 9am–5pm Tue–Sun.
w lobkowicz.cz

⓫ Lány

Road map C2. 1,600. from Prague to Stochov (2 km/1 mile). **Tel** 313 502 041.

In 1929, Slovenian architect Josip Plečnik remodelled the Renaissance **Palace** in the village of Lány into the summer residence of the president of the Czech Republic. Its first occupant was Tomáš Garrigue Masaryk (*see p46*), the first democratically elected President, and a highly popular figure, who was buried in the village cemetery in 1937. The palace is not open, but it is worth exploring its beautiful **park**. The former Baroque granary now houses the **Tomáš G Masaryk Museum** of the former president's life.

Lány Park
Open Apr–Oct: Wed, Thu, Sat, Sun.

Tomáš G Masaryk Museum
Tel 313 511 209. **Open** daily (call ahead for hours). **Closed** Mon.

The vast Royal Hall in Křivoklát Castle

⓬ Křivoklát Castle

Road map C2. 13 km (8 miles) SE of Rakovník. from Prague. **Tel** 313 558 440. **Open** Jan–Mar: 10am–3pm Sat; Apr & Oct: 10am–4pm Tue–Sun; May: 10am–5pm Tue–Sun; Jun–Sep: 9am–5pm Tue–Sun (to 6pm Jul & Aug); Nov & Dec: 10am–3pm Sat & Sun. **w** krivoklat.cz

Built in the mid-13th century by Přemysl Otakar II, Křivoklát (Pürglitz) was the childhood home of Emperor Charles IV. From 1493 to 1522, it was remodelled by King Vladislav Jagiello and his son Ludwig. Lying in a beautiful area of woodland, the castle is dominated by its 42-m (130-ft) cylindrical Great Tower. This adjoins the red roofs and spires of the three-wing palace and chapel. The most beautiful interior is that of the Royal Hall with its star-spangled vault, the second-largest room of its type in Bohemia, after the Vladislav Hall in Prague Castle.

Relief from Křivoklát Castle

⓭ Točník Castle

Road map C2. 15 km (9 miles) SW of Beroun. from Prague via Beroun or Zdice. **Tel** 311 533 202. **Open** Mar & Oct: 10am–4pm Sat, Sun & hols; Apr & Sep: 10am–5pm Tue–Sun; May: 10am–6pm Tue–Sun; Jul & Aug: 9am–6pm Tue–Sun. **w** tocnik.com

Točník was one of the last castles to be built in Bohemia during the Middle Ages, commissioned in about 1394 by Wenceslas IV as a new royal residence following the fire which destroyed the nearby Žebrak Castle. In the 16th century, Točník was remodelled in Renaissance style. After the Thirty Years' War, it was abandoned. Now, although partly ruined, it still provides a rare example in Bohemia of the monumental architecture of the turn of the 14th and 15th centuries. The mighty, five-storey edifice of the royal palace can be seen from afar. Its Renaissance gate dates from 1524.

The red roofs of the village of Lány at sunset

The Velká Amerika gorge, Český Kras

⓮ Český Kras

Road map C2. 🚌 to Beroun.

The land around Karlštejn and along the banks of the Berounka river, southwest of Prague, known as the Český Kras, or Bohemian Karst, is the largest karst region in Bohemia, made up of picturesque limestone formations. At over 800 m (2,600 ft) long, the **Koněpruské Caves**, 5 km (3 miles) south of Beroun, are the largest cave system in the republic open to visitors.

Between the towns of Mořina and Kozulupy, about 5 km (3 miles) north of Karlštejn, is one of the most extraordinary sights of the Český Kras. The disused and now flooded quarry known as **Velká Amerika** (Great America) has provided dramatic settings for numerous Western films.

Along the road that links Loděnice with Srbsko is the village of **Sv. Jan pod Skalou** (St John under the Rock). Set in a ravine, at the foot of a mighty crag, is the Baroque Church of the Nativity of St John the Baptist (Narození Jana Křtitele), built by Carlo Lurago in 1657. From inside the church, there is access to three travertine caves – the site of a cult of St Ivan, a 9th-century hermit.

🪨 **Koněpruské Caves**
Tel 311 622 405. **Open** Apr–Oct: daily.
📷 🎧 🌐 **jeskyne.cesky-kras.cz**

⓯ Karlštejn Castle

See pp134–5.

⓰ Dobříš Palace

Road map C2. 23 km (14 miles) SW of Prague. 🚌 from Prague. **Tel** 318 521 240. **Open** Jun–Sep: 8am–5:30pm daily; Oct–May: 8am–4:30pm daily. 📷 🎧
🌐 **zamekdobris.cz**

This Rococo palace was built in 1745–65. The owner of the estate, Jindřich Pavel Mansfeld, commissioned French architect Jules de Cotte and Italian interior designer G N Servadoni to prepare the design. The palace remained in the hands of the Colloredo-Mansfeld family until 1942, when it was confiscated by the Nazi authorities and turned into a residence for the German Reich Protector. Nationalized by the Communists, it was returned to its former owners after 1989. Now it charms visitors with its restored interiors, which are furnished in a combination of late Baroque, Rococo and Neo-Classical styles.

The French garden, one of the most beautiful in the Czech Republic, is set out on five levels and features a huge cascading fountain.

⓱ Příbram

Road map C2. 🏔 34,000. 🚆
🚌 from Prague. **Tel** 318 402 211.

Founded in the 13th century, the town of Příbam (Pribrans) was famous for its mines, which over the centuries yielded some 3.6 million tons of silver, as well as lead and antimony. In the country's biggest **Mining Museum** (Hornické muzeum), in the district of Březové Hory, in the disused mine of Ševčínský důl, visitors can take a ride on an underground train along a 300-m (1,000-ft) section of the mine, at a depth of 1,600 m (5,250 ft). The mine's ornate early 19th-century pithead has been listed as a UNESCO World Industrial Heritage Site.

On top of a hill above the town is **Svatá Hora** (Holy Mountain), the Marian Sanctuary, once the biggest and most famous pilgrimage site in the entire Austro- Hungarian Empire. Built by Carlo Lurago in 1658–75 on the site of an earlier Gothic church, the early Baroque complex has a church with vivid frescoes depicting the Sanctuary's history.

🏛 **Mining Museum**
Tel 318 626 307. **Open** Nov–Mar: Tue–Fri; Apr–Oct: Tue–Sun.

The palace in Dobříš from the gardens

◀ The monumental Točník Castle, overlooking undulating green fields

Underground exhibition
Open Apr–Oct: as museum.

🔼 **Church of Svatá Hora**
Tel 318 429 930. **Open** daily.

Hunting trophies in the corridors of Konopiště Castle

⑱ Konopiště Castle

Road map C2. 2 km (1 mile) W of Benešov. 🚆 🚌 to Benešov. **Tel** 317 721 366. **Open** Apr, May & Sep: 10am–noon & 1–4pm Tue–Sun; Jun–Aug: 10am–5pm Tue–Sun; Oct & Nov: 10am–3pm Sat & Sun. 3 routes. 🖥 **zamek-konopiste.cz**

One of the most popular tourist sites in the Czech Republic, Konopiště Castle belonged to the heir to the Austrian throne, Franz Ferdinand. The Gothic castle has richly furnished apartments, a collection of late Gothic paintings in the chapel, and a gallery of the Archduke's artifacts relating to the cult of St George. It also houses a famous collection of the weapons of Franz Ferdinand, including items produced by the best armourer and gunsmith workshops in Europe. But many visitors are particularly amazed by the Crown Prince's collection of about 300,000 hunting trophies: countless antlers and stuffed animals line the corridors and numerous rooms of the castle. Three tour routes explore the different collections.

The huge park of 225 ha (555 acres) contains a terraced garden, many statues, a deer park, a lake and a superb rose garden.

⑲ Sázava Monastery

Road map D2. 18 km (11 miles) SE of Benešov. 🚆 🚌 from Prague. **Tel** 327 321 177. **Open** Apr & Oct: 10am–5pm Sat, Sun & public hols (by appt Tue–Fri); May & Sep: 10am–5pm Tue–Sun; Jun–Aug: 10am–6pm Tue–Sun. 🖥 **klaster-sazava.cz**

Founded in 1032, this Benedictine monastery has remained a centre of the Slavonic liturgy, and to this day, every Sunday an Old Slavonic liturgy mass is celebrated here. A new church was started in 1315, but only the tower and a wall of one of the naves, with high Gothic windows, were completed; these remain today. The original frescoes in the church date from the time of Charles IV and include unusual images of the life of the Virgin Mary.

Archduke Franz Ferdinand

The Austrian Archduke Franz Ferdinand bought Konopiště in 1887. For the Archduke, criticized by the Habsburg Court for marrying a Bohemian noblewoman Sophie Chotek, the castle was a refuge from the hostilities of Viennese society. Franz Ferdinand lived in his Bohemian home until his death alongside his wife at the hands of an assassin in Sarajevo – the event that led to the outbreak of World War I in 1914.

---

⑳ Sternberg Castle

Road map D2. Český Šternberk. 🚆 🚌 from Prague to Český Šternberk zastávka. **Tel** 317 855 101. **Open** Apr & Oct: 9am–5pm Sat, Sun & public hols; May–Sep: 9am–5pm Tue–Sun (Jun–Aug: to 6pm); last adm 45 mins before closing. All year: groups of 10 and over by appt daily. 🖥 **hradceskysternberk.cz**

The sprawling edifice on top of a high cliff above the Sázava river valley is a truly impressive sight. The early Gothic castle erected on this site in the mid-13th century by the Sternberg (Šternberk) family was captured and destroyed by the army of King George of Poděbrady in 1467. At the turn of the 15th and 16th centuries, the owners restored the demolished walls and extended the fortifications. The 17th-century Baroque interiors contain some striking Italian stucco work, especially in the Knights' Hall. Some of the rooms house displays of engravings and historic weapons.

View of Sternberg Castle above the Sázava river

⓯ Karlštejn Castle

This imposing Gothic castle is one of the most frequently visited historic sites in the Czech Republic. It was built for the Holy Roman Emperor Charles IV in 1348 as a royal residence and a treasury where imperial insignia and crown jewels as well as documents, works of art and holy relics were stored. In the 16th century, Karlštejn (Karlstein) was remodelled in Renaissance style. The castle owes its present form to the restoration work carried out in the 19th century, mainly by Josef Mocker, who returned the building to its original appearance. At that time, the castle was given its ridge roofs as a typical feature of medieval architecture.

★ Holy Cross Chapel
The walls of the Holy Cross chapel are hung with a unique collection of 129 portraits of saints and monarchs – works of Master Theodoric, court painter to Charles IV.

Voršilka Tower Gate
The Voršilka Tower was once the castle's main entrance. Now the entrance is via the gate below the Tower, and along the former moat.

The Well Tower
The Well Tower is situated at the lowest point of the castle complex. Inside is an old wooden treadwheel for hauling water, operated by two people.

★ St Mary's Tower
One of the paintings in the church of St Mary depicts Charles IV receiving two thorns from the crown of Jesus from the French Dauphin, Charles.

VISITORS' CHECKLIST

Practical Information
Road map C2.
Tel 311 681 617.
Open Mar–Oct: 9am–3pm
Tue–Sun (to 5:30pm May,
Jun & Sep; to 6:30pm Jul & Aug).
Chapel: **Closed** Nov–May.
2 routes (reservation
compulsory for route II).
W hradkarlstejn.cz

Transport
from Prague (30-min walk
from stn to Karlštejn).

St Catherine's Chapel
Used as a place of meditation by Charles IV, this tiny chapel has walls that are richly decorated with paintings and semi-precious stones.

Madonna Statue
The 14th-century marble statue of the Madonna, in the royal bedchamber, belonged to King Charles IV.

KEY

① **Grand Tower**

② **The first floor of the Grand Tower** features two rooms, which in the 19th century were turned into a museum with a collection of pictures depicting Karlštejn and other castles.

③ **The Imperial Palace's** first floor was used by courtiers; the second by the Emperor himself for private and official functions.

Vassals' Hall of the Imperial Palace
A striking feature of the Vassals' Hall is the late Gothic altarpiece from St Palmatius's Church in the village of Budňany at the foot of Karlštejn Castle.

SOUTH BOHEMIA

Wooded hills and spreading meadows characterize much of South Bohemia, while in the flatter, central area around Třeboň, hundreds of glittering medieval fish ponds, still used for raising carp, can be seen. The backbone of the region is the Vltava river. This rises in the Šumava Mountains to the southwest, a remarkably unspoilt area of dense forests and tiny villages.

In the 13th century, several fortified towns were established in South Bohemia (Jižní Čechy), with the aim of defending the king's rule. The foremost of them, České Budějovice, is now the region's capital and source of Budvar, the famous local beer.

The deciding influence on the life of South Bohemia in the Middle Ages was often exerted by two powerful aristocratic families – the Rožmberks (Rosenbergs) and the lords of Hradec. Both built numerous castles and fortified towns, known as "Rose Towns" after the red rose of the Rožmberks and the black rose of the Hradec. Český Krumlov, owned by the Rožmberk family, is the region's top tourist destination for the picture-postcard perfection of its old town and its fascinating castle,

but many other historic towns, such as Jindřichův Hradec and Třeboň are equally rich in well-preserved buildings.

South Bohemia played a prominent role in the history of the Hussite movement. Tábor became the main centre of the more radical faction of the religious reformers who strongly opposed the 15th-century social conditions.

In the 17th century, the Bavarian Schwarzenberg family achieved great power in the region. It is to them that the fortress in Hluboká nad Vltavou, the most frequently visited castle in this part of the country, owes its fairy-tale Neo-Gothic form. One of the most magnificent collections of Late Gothic art is found here in the Aleš South Bohemian Gallery.

Panoramic view over the red-tiled rooftops of Český Krumlov, South Bohemia

◄ The ornate Samson fountain at the town square in České Budějovice

Exploring South Bohemia

The historic sights of South Bohemia, its magnificent scenery and its opportunities for hiking and canoeing satisfy a wide range of interests. The architectural variety is astonishing as well-preserved grand squares and churches jostle for attention with the traditional architecture of Holašovice. Individual buildings stand out: the fairy-tale castle in Hluboká, for example, with its bristling turrets, and the vast, soaring cooling towers of the Temelín power station. In the southern part of the region, along the border with Austria, runs the Šumava mountain range. It is worth making time to explore the Vltava river and its villages, not forgetting to sample the local beers in any of the many Bohemian beer halls.

Coat of arms above the entrance to Hluboká Castle

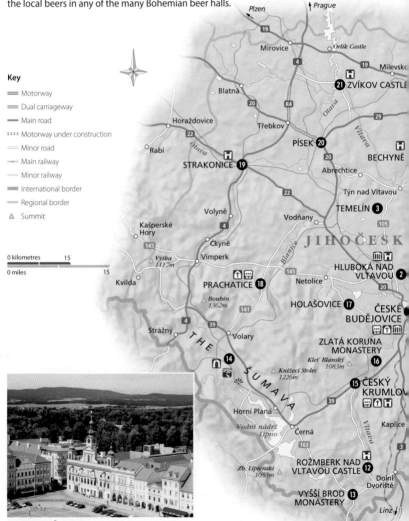

Key

━━━ Motorway

━━━ Dual carriageway

━━━ Main road

┅┅┅ Motorway under construction

═══ Minor road

⊶⊶ Main railway

──── Minor railway

━━━ International border

━━━ Regional border

△ Summit

0 kilometres 15

0 miles 15

The town hall in České Budějovice

For hotels and restaurants see p351 and pp369–70

Sights at a Glance

Getting Around

The main transport artery of the region is the north–south main road 3 (international E55 route) linking Prague with Linz in Austria. The capital of South Bohemia – České Budějovice – is linked by a network of local buses with all the neighbouring towns. Buses provide fast and relatively frequent access to most parts of the region. Trains serve much of the region, even mountainous areas, although routes may take a little planning. Check the frequency of buses and trains during weekends and public holidays.

The frescoed Grand Hall at Bechyně Castle

❶ České Budějovice

Founded by Přemysl Otakar II in 1265, the town of České Budějovice (Budweis) fast became the stronghold of the king's power in South Bohemia. As early as the 13th and 14th centuries, it had two magnificent churches and mighty town walls. Spared by the Thirty Years' War, it was subsequently destroyed by the great fire of 1641. Today, the capital of South Bohemia is an important industrial centre, not least for its internationally renowned Budvar Brewery.

Náměstí Přemysla Otakara II – one of Europe's largest squares

Exploring the Town

The town's well-preserved historic centre lies on a peninsula created at the confluence of the rivers Vltava, Malše and Mlýnská stoka. It has maintained its original layout with a central square and surrounding streets in a grid pattern. Most sights are within this compact central area.

🏛 Náměstí Přemysla Otakara II

Coat of arms on the town hall

The town square bears the name of the town's founder. Measuring 133 x 133 m (436 x 436 ft), the huge square is surrounded by arcaded houses built mostly during the Middle Ages, and now – after numerous alterations by their German owners – with Renaissance and Baroque façades. At the square's centre stands the Baroque Samson's Fountain, built in 1727, with a sculpture of Samson and the lion. It was produced by Josef Dietrich, and for a while it was the only source of water for the town's population. Look out for cobblestones laid in 1934 in a distinctive pattern of large squares.

🏛 Town Hall

Náměstí Přemysla Otakara II. **Tel** 386 801 401. **Open Tours:** Jul & Aug: 10am, 2pm, 4pm Mon–Fri; 10am, 2pm Sat, Sun; May, Jun & Sep: 2pm daily.

The southwest corner of the town square is occupied by a Baroque, white and blue town hall (radnice) with three towers, built by Antonio Martinelli in 1727–30 to replace a Renaissance building. Allegorical statues of Providence, Justice, Wisdom and Honesty stand on the roof. On top of the tallest tower is a statue of the Czech lion, and on the left side is the medieval

The elaborate three-towered façade of the town hall

standard ell measure (the "forearm") used when measuring cloth. The Debating Hall features *The Judgement of Solomon* (1730) by Jan Adam Schöpf.

🏛 Dominican Monastery and Church of the Sacrifice of the Virgin

Piaristické náměstí.
Open 10am–5pm daily.

Built at the same time as the founding of České Budějovice, and altered by Peter Parler in the 14th century, is this interesting former monastery.

Inside the church (Kostel Obětování Panny Marie), cross-rib vaulting can be seen. The furnishing is mostly Neo-Gothic, but there is also a spectacular Rococo pulpit dating from 1759, and 17th-century organs. The large stone amphibian seen on the side wall by the church entrance, is a reminder of the local legend about the creature, who was guarding the treasure supposedly hidden on the site, and tried to prevent the start of the church building. The Gothic cloister also has two original tracery windows that are lovely examples of medieval stonemasonry work.

🏛 Butchers' Market

Krajinská 13.
The Renaissance butchers' market (Masné krámy) now houses a restaurant. On its top are three stone masks, and the year of building: 1531.

🏛 Black Tower

U Černé věže. **Tel** 386 352 508.
Open Apr–Jun, Sep & Oct: 10am–6pm Tue–Sun; Jul & Aug: 10am–6pm daily.

Standing next to St Nicholas's Cathedral is the Gothic-Renaissance Black Tower (Černa věž) dating from 1577, formerly serving as a belfry and the town's observation tower. In 1723, two bells were placed in the belfry; in 1995, a third bell was added – Budvar – presented to the town by the nearby brewery. The reward for climbing the 225 winding stairs to the top at a height of 72 m (236 ft), is the magnificent panorama.

Entrance to the Baroque-style St Nicholas's Cathedral

🔼 St Nicholas's Cathedral
U Černé věže.

On a small plot at the north-eastern corner of the town square is St Nicholas's Cathedral (Chrám sv. Mikuláše). This triple-aisled edifice started as a church in the 13th century. The original Gothic building burned down in 1641 and was rebuilt a few years later in the Baroque style. Inside, take a look at the pulpit and an interesting 1740 painting *Death of the Virgin Mary* in the south chapel; also at the main altarpiece by Leopold Huber (1791).

🏛 South Bohemia Museum
Dukelská 1. **Tel** 391 001 531.
Open 9am–5pm Tue–Sun.
w muzeumcb.cz

Established in 1887, this museum (Jihočeské muzeum) is the oldest of its kind in South Bohemia. It houses a natural science collection, regional exhibits and 16th–18th-century art.

🗼 Železná Panna
Zátkovo nábřeží.

This tower, erected in the 14th century, was used as a prison and torture chamber. Its name translates as "Iron Maiden" after the instrument of torture (and death) used here whose shape resembled a woman.

Painting from a house (No. 140) close to Železná Panna

VISITORS' CHECKLIST

Practical Information
Road map C3.
🚇 93,900. ℹ️ Náměstí Přemysla Otakara II 2. **Tel** 386 801 413.
🎭 City Hall Summer (Festival of Music and Theatre): Jul–Aug.
w visitceskebudejovice.cz

Transport
🚉 Nádražní 119/4.
🚌 Nádražní 1759.

🏛 Motorcycle Museum
Piaristické náměstí. **Tel** 723 247 104.
Open Apr–Oct: 10am–6pm Tue–Sun.

The motorcycle museum (Motocyclové muzeum) in the former Salt House has well-preserved old Czech machines and some Harley-Davidsons.

Environs
North of the centre is the famous, state-owned **Budvar Brewery**, where beer has been made since the 19th century; visits can be arranged.

🍺 Budvar Brewery
Karolíny Světlé 4. **Tel** 387 705 347.
Open Mar–Dec: 9am–5pm daily; Jan–Feb: 9am–5pm Tue–Sat. 🎫 📷
w visitbudvar.cz

Česke Budějovice Town Centre

① Náměstí Přemysla Otakara II
② Town Hall
③ Dominican Monastery and Church of the Sacrifice of the Virgin
④ Butchers' Market
⑤ Black Tower
⑥ St Nicholas's Cathedral
⑦ South Bohemia Museum
⑧ Železná Panna
⑨ Motorcycle Museum

For keys to symbols *see back flap*

Sumptuously furnished Tapestry Room in Hluboká Castle

❷ Hluboká nad Vltavou

Road map C3. ⛰ 5,000. ⬛ from České Budějovice or Prague. ℹ Zborovská 80. **Tel** 387 966 164. ⬜ **hluboka.cz**

Hluboká village is known for its **Castle**, regarded by many as Bohemia's most beautiful aristocratic residence. Built in the 13th century by Wenceslas I, the Gothic castle was remodelled in the 16th century in Renaissance style; then under the ownership of the Schwarzenbergs in the 18th century in Baroque style; and from 1839 to 1871 in English Neo-Gothic style. It has 11 towers and over 120 rooms filled with furniture and paintings.

In the castle's former riding school is the **Aleš South Bohemian Gallery** (Alšova jihočeská galerie), a collection of 57 Flemish tapestries and Bohemian medieval art. The *Adoration of Infant Jesus* by the Master of Třeboň (1380) is a highlight.

🏰 **Hluboká Castle**
Tel 387 843 911. **Open** Jul & Aug: daily; Sep–Jun: Tue–Sun. 🈲 🅲
⬜ **zamek-hluboka.eu**

Aleš South Bohemian Gallery
Open daily. ⬜ **ajg.cz**

Environs
In the Baroque **Ohrada Hunting Lodge**, just south of Hluboká, is a hunting, fishing and forestry museum, filled with hunting trophies.

🏛 **Ohrada Hunting Lodge**
Tel 387 965 340. **Open** daily.

❸ Temelín

Road map C3. ⬛ from České Budějovice. ⬛ from České Budějovice or Prague. **Tel** 381 102 639. **Open** Jul & Aug: 9am–5:30pm daily; Sep–Jun: 9am–4pm daily (appt recommended). ⬜ **cez.cz**

The atomic power station in Temelín was started under the Communists in 1983, using Soviet technology, and completed in the 1990s using US and European technology. Designed to provide up to 20 per cent of the Czech Republic's electricity, it finally opened in 2000. Prior to that, it became famous for the protests it provoked in the Czech Republic and other European countries, particularly Austria, whose border is a mere 50 km (30 miles) away. Critics of the project point out that from the time of its commissioning in 2000, there have been frequent failures. A stop at the station's visitor centre provides information on the functioning of Temelín, but much more impressive is the close-up view of its 150-m (500-ft) high cooling towers.

The massive towers of Temelín nuclear power station

Environs

In **Albrechtice**, 5 km (3 miles) north of Temelín, by the Baroque Church of St Peter and St Paul, is an unusual cemetery. In 1841–54, 108 small shrines were built here, each painted in a naive style to record events in the life of the deceased.

❹ Bechyně

Road map C3. ⛰ 5,500. ⬛ from Tábor. ⬛ from České Budějovice or Prague. ℹ Náměstí TG Masaryka 5. **Tel** 381 213 822. ⬜ **mestobechyne.cz**

The most beautiful view of this picturesque spa resort is from the Rainbow (Duha) bridge, 50 m (160 ft) above the Lužnice river. The train ride from Tábor takes you over this bridge. Bechyně's spring waters attract those seeking treatment for rheumatism and metabolic disorders.

The **Castle** is the town's oldest sight. A 12th-century Gothic fortress given a Renaissance makeover four centuries later, it now houses an exhibition of its history. In the former synagogue near the main square is the **Firefighters' Museum** (Hasičské muzeum), with several old fire engines on display.

Coat of arms, Bechyně Castle

🏰 **Bechyně Castle**
Tel 381 213 143. **Open** Jun & Sep: Sat & Sun; Jul–Aug: Tue–Sun. 🈲

🏛 **Firefighters' Museum**
Tel 602 840 275. **Open** May: Thu–Sun; Jun–Aug: Tue–Sun.

Environs
Týn nad Vltavou, 11 km (7 miles) south of Bechyně, has a market square with many Renaissance houses, the most prominent of them being the town hall with its arcades and richly ornamented Rococo façade. In the Baroque palace, which dates back to 1699, is an interesting regional museum.

▥ Týn nad Vltavou Museum
Náměstí Míru 1. **Tel** 385 772 303.
Open Mar, Apr, Oct & Nov: Mon–Fri;
May: daily; Sep & Dec: Sun–Fri; Jun–
Aug: Tue–Sun. **w** tnv.cz

❺ Tábor

See pp144–5.

❻ Pelhřimov

Road map D2. ⛰ 16,500. 🚃
🚌 from Prague. 🛈 Masarykovo
náměstí 10. **Tel** 565 326 924.
📷 Festival of Records and
Curious Performances: mid-Jun.
w pelhrimovsko.cz

The charming town of
Pelhřimov has a medieval
pedigree. It retains its defence
walls with two tower gates,
and the Gothic **Church
of St Bartholomew**
(sv. Bartoloměj). The town
square has houses with
Renaissance and Baroque
façades and pediments. No. 13,
originally Baroque, is particularly
striking: Pavel Janák gave it a
Cubist façade in 1913–15.

An attraction of Pelhřimov
is its Festival of Records and
Curious Performances, held in
mid-June for those who want
to earn a place in the *Guinness
Book of World Records*. Some of
these extraordinary feats are
documented in the **Museum
of Records** (Muzeum rekordů
a kuriozit) in one of the town's
Gothic gates. Those taller than
205 cm (80 in), and adults
shorter than 145 cm (57 in) or
measuring more than 135 cm
(53 in) around the waist, are
admitted free of charge.

▥ Museum of Records
Tel 565 321 327. **Open** 9am–5pm
daily. 📷

Environs
A **Motorcycle Museum** is
housed in a 14th-century
castle in the tiny village of
Kámen (meaning "rock"), which
lies 15 km (9 miles) west of
Pelhřimov. There are numerous
exhibits from the National
Technical Museum in Prague,
including an 1898 Laurin and
Klement motorcycle.

Baroque gable on a house in Pelhřimov

In **Žirovnice**, 20 km (12 miles)
south of Pelhřimov, is a
Renaissance **Castle** featuring
historic interiors and a museum
of wickerwork and button-
making – products for which
the town became famous in the
19th century. **Počátky**, situated
nearby, is a small town with
a Baroque church and a
picturesque market square.

▥ Motorcycle Museum
Tel 565 323 184. **Open** Apr & Oct: Sat,
Sun & holidays; May–Sep: Tue–Sun.

🏠 Žirovnice Castle
Tel 565 494 095. **Open** Apr–Oct: daily.

The Gothic Červená Lhota Castle
across the lake

❼ Červená Lhota Castle

Road map D3. 🚃 8 km (5 miles)
Kardašova Řečice. **Tel** 384 384 228.
Open Apr & Oct: 9:30am–5pm Sat, Sun
& public hols; May–Sep: 9:30am–5pm
Tue–Sun (Jun–Aug: to 6pm). 📷 📷

Enjoying an exceptionally
scenic location amid forests,
the Červená Lhota Castle is
on an island at the centre

of a small lake. The
original Gothic castle
was remodelled in
the 16th century into a
Renaissance residence
named Nova Lhota. In
the early 17th century,
the island was linked
with the mainland by
a stone bridge and the
castle roof was covered
with red tiles, which
subsequently gave it
its name (*červená*
means "red"). The
German composer Karl Ditters
von Dittersdorf lived here until
his death in 1799.

In 1945, the castle was taken
out of private hands by the
state and turned first into a
children's hospital and later into
a cultural establishment open
to visitors. Displayed inside
are furnishings representing
periods from the Renaissance
to Biedermeier in the mid-19th
century, as well as porcelain
and tapestries. The castle is
surrounded by a park, where
there is also a castle chapel.
In summer, it is possible to hire
a boat to go on the lake, and
to take a ride in a horse and
carriage around the grounds.

Environs
Pluhův Žďár, 2 km (1 mile)
south of Červená Lhota, is
a 14th-century fortress
transformed in the 18th century
into a Baroque residence. The
last owners of the palace before
World War II were the president
Edvard Beneš and his brother
Vojta. The family descendants,
who regained possession of
the castle in 1992, are happy
to admit visitors.

Soběslav, 11 km (7 miles) to
the west, is famous with Czech
visitors for its 16th- century love
story involving one of the most
powerful Bohemian lords, Peter
Vok of Rožmberk, and a miller's
daughter Zuzana Vojířova.
It now delights visitors with
its picturesque town square
flanked by historic houses,
and two fine Gothic churches:
St Vitus (sv. Víta) and Our Lady
(Panny Marie). Both are worth
visiting for their magnificent
arched ceilings.

❺ Tábor

A military camp established in 1420 by Hussite refugees from Prague grew into the town of Tábor, named after the mountain where Christ's Transfiguration took place. Radical Hussite reformers *(see pp38–9)* became known as Táborites, and fought battles throughout Bohemia, but were finally defeated in 1434. Today, the lively Old Town retains its maze-like narrow streets and alleyways. It lies between the town walls, the Lužnice river and Jordán lake, a short walk west of the new town.

Church of the Transfiguration
This image of Christ is from the beautiful Baroque pulpit of this Neo-Gothic church. There is also an unusual vault over the presbytery. Its tall bell tower offers a panorama of the town.

★ Town Hall
On the main square, Žižkovo náměstí, is the Town Hall (1440–51). Inside, the Grand Hall features superb net vaulting. The Hussite Museum (Husitské muzeum) now occupies the building.

ŽIŽKOVO NÁMĚSTÍ

A stroll along Klokotská takes you to Bechyňska brána (gate) and tower – the only one left.

Key

— Suggested route

★ Škoch House
This gable of Škochův dům is one of the finest examples of Gothic-Renaissance architecture in Bohemia. The gables of houses facing the main square are astonishingly varied.

Ctibor House

One of the town's most interesting houses (Ctiborův dům), this is a magnificent example of the late Gothic, built in 1532. Its gable with tracery decorations crowns the cream-white façade.

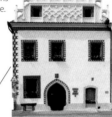

VISITORS' CHECKLIST

Practical Information
Road map C2. 🚗 35,200.
ℹ️ Žižkovo náměstí 2.
Tel 381 486 230. 🌐 taborcz.eu
🎭 Hussite Festival: Sep.
Hussite Museum: Náměstí
Mikuláše z Husi 44. **Tel** 381 252
242. 🌐 husitskemuzeum.cz

Transport
🚆 🚌 U Bechyňské dráhy.

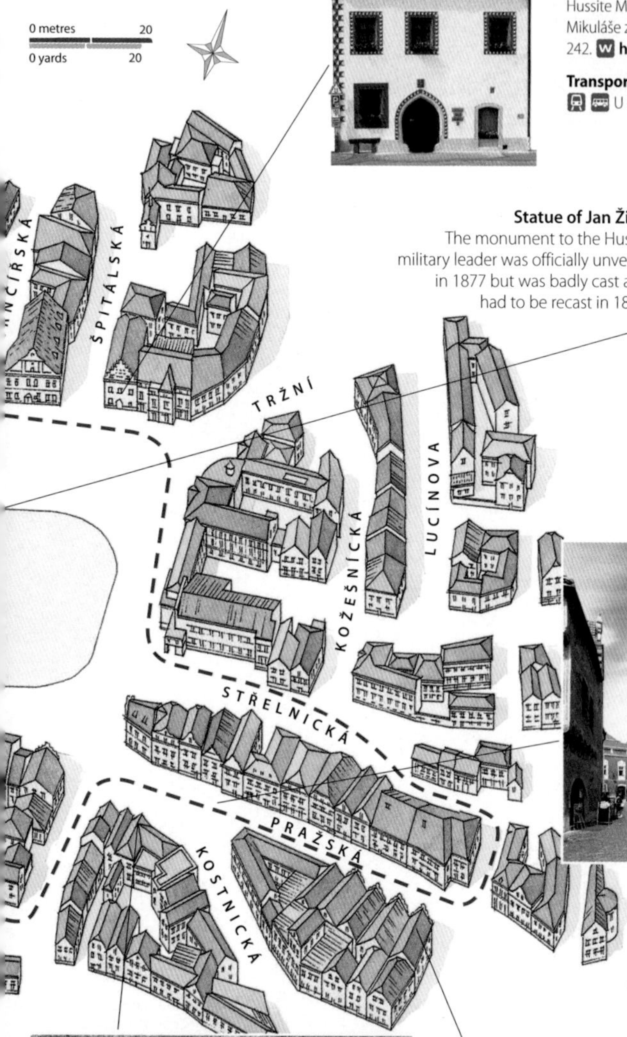

0 metres 20
0 yards 20

Statue of Jan Žižka

The monument to the Hussite military leader was officially unveiled in 1877 but was badly cast and had to be recast in 1884.

ŠPITÁLSKÁ

NČÍŘSKÁ

TRŽNÍ

LUČNOVA

KOŽEŠNICKÁ

STŘELNICKÁ

PRAŽSKÁ

KOSTNICKÁ

★ Ulice Pražská

The extraordinary Renaissance houses flanking the street that runs from the south-east corner of the main square were built after the Great Fire of 1532.

The 1603 house at No. 210 – a very fine Flemish Renaissance building – has an intricate gable decorated with figurative and floral *sgraffito*.

Stark House

The façade of Starkův dům (No. 157), dating from 1526, is decorated with lavish 1570 *sgraffito* inspired by nature and history.

❽ Jindřichův Hradec

One of the most beautiful towns in South Bohemia, situated among medieval fish ponds, Jindřichův Hradec (Neuhaus) lies slightly off the main tourist track. It was founded in the 13th century by the lords of Hradec. The Old Town, a peaceful, interesting area, centres on the main square (náměstí Míru), lined with vividly coloured houses, many of which were rebuilt after a fire in 1801. Northwest of the square are cobbled alleys leading to the Church of the Assumption of the Virgin Mary (Nanebevzetí Panny Marie), with a tower offering excellent views. To the west of the Old Town is the huge castle.

★ Rondel
The interior of this 1592 music pavilion is decorated with the family tree tracing the descent of Adam II of Hradec from the biblical Adam.

Adam II's Bedchamber
The spread on the Baroque bed is decorated with symbols of the marriage of Adam II and Katherine de Montfort.

Černín's Dining Room
The dining room houses a valuable dining service made of "habanska majolica", collected during the 17th century.

Jindřichův Hradec Castle
Beside the Vajgar fish pond lies this 13th-century castle, once the main residence of the lords of Hradec. Originally a Gothic building, it was made into a Renaissance palace by Italian architects in the late 16th century. Antonio Cometa added the three-tiered courtyard arcades at this time.

The Spanish Wing
The vast state room of the Renaissance Spanish Wing was built to a design by Baldassare Maggi. Its grand furnishings include this 16th-century wardrobe.

VISITORS' CHECKLIST

Practical Information
Map D3.
🏛 22,000.
ℹ Panská 136. **Tel** 384 363 546.
Castle: **Tel** 384 321 279.
Open Apr–Oct: Tue–Sun.
📷 📹 3 tour routes.
🌐 jh.cz

Transport
🚉 🚌 from Prague or České Budějovice.

The Red Tower Kitchen
The kitchen with its open hearth and four corner chimneys projecting above the roof of the tower was built around 1500 and is still in use. This is the best-preserved kitchen of its type in the Czech Republic, and includes the original equipment.

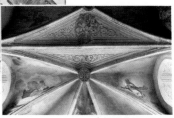

★ **Holy Spirit Chapel**
The chapel frescoes uncovered during reconstruction works in about 1727 depict scenes from the life of Christ and other biblical motifs.

KEY

① **Prince Adam's palace** was designed by Baldassare Maggi in 1561.

② **The Black Tower**, 32-m (104-ft) high, dates from the early 13th century. It was used as a prison.

The Royal Hall
The paintings hung in the vaulted hall are portraits of the former rulers of Bohemia.

⑨ Slavonice

Road map D3. 🏰 2,700. 🚊 from Telč. 🚌 from Prague. 🛈 Náměstí Míru 476. **Tel** 384 493 320.
🌐 **slavonice-mesto.cz**

Slavonice (Zlabings), situated next to the Austrian border, is a pleasant, sleepy little town with a street layout preserved unchanged since the 13th century.

An exceptional number of its Gothic and Renaissance houses feature decorative *sgraffito* and opulent gables. The houses at Nos. 25 and 46 Dolní náměstí are particularly stunning with their beautiful ground-floor vaulted ceilings; also worth a visit is the house at No. 517 Horní náměstí, whose first-floor rooms are decorated with 16th-century wall paintings depicting scenes from the Apocalypse.

There are also two Gothic-Renaissance town gates and two Gothic churches. The **Church of the Assumption of the Virgin Mary** (Nanebevzetí Panny Marie) has some valuable frescoes; the **Church of St John the Baptist** (sv. Jana Křtitele) features an interesting vault above the presbytery.

Environs
The imposing ruins of **Landštejn Castle** lie 9 km (6 miles) east of Slavonice. It was built in the early 13th century, modelled on German or Austrian

Beautiful façade of a *Sgraffito*-decorated house in Slavonice

fortresses. The ground floor of one of its mighty square towers is occupied by a chapel.

🏰 Landštejn Castle
Tel 384 498 580. **Open** Apr & Oct: Sat & Sun; May–Sep: Tue–Sun. 🎨

Renaissance arcades in the inner courtyard of the Castle in Třeboň

⑩ Třeboň

Road map D3. 🏰 8,800. 🚊 🚌 1 km (0.5 miles). 🛈 Masarykovo náměstí 103. **Tel** 384 721 193.
🌐 **mesto-trebon.cz**

Situated among hills and fish ponds, Třeboň (Wittingau) has a tiny medieval centre dominated by a huge castle; it is also a spa town. It was founded in the 12th century, and the Rožmberk family took over during the 14th century. During their rule, it reached the peak of its glory, with exceptionally fast economic development. The Rožmberks funded the development of local fish ponds into more formal fish farming, a system of 6,000 ponds that remain productive today.

The main square, Masarykovo náměstí, is lined with Renaissance and Baroque houses; in the square stand a Renaissance ten-sided fountain and a 1781 Marian column. The Renaissance town hall has a façade with three semi- circular arcades and a 31-m (100-ft) high tower added in the 17th century. To the east, the square ends with a 1527 gate (Hradecká

brána). The **Church of St Giles** (sv. Jiljí) on Husova has an unusual twin-aisled interior.

The town's huge Renaissance **Castle** was built in the first half of the 16th century on the site of a Gothic fortress. Inside, visitors can view the Renaissance Rožmberk apartments and the 19th-century living quarters of the last owners – the Schwarzenbergs, who owned many estates throughout South Bohemia.

🏰 Třeboň Castle
Tel 384 721 193. **Open** Apr–Oct: Tue–Sun. 🎨 🌐 **zamek-trebon.eu**

Environs
On the opposite side of the Svět pond from Třeboň stands the vast **Schwarzenberg Mausoleum** (Schwarzenberská hrobka). This three-storey edifice with its monumental stairs and lofty tower was built in Neo-Gothic style in 1877. It is the resting place of 27 members of the Schwarzenberg family.

🚌 Schwarzenberg Mausoleum
Open Apr–Oct: Tue–Sun.

⑪ Nové Hrady

Road map D3. 🏰 2,600. 🚊 5 km (3 miles). 🛈 Náměstí Republiky 46. **Tel** 386 362 195. 🌐 **novehrady.cz**

Coat of arms from Nové Hrady

To the east of the town square stands the **Church of St Peter and St Paul** (sv. Petr a Pavel), which has a magnificent presbytery vault and monumental Baroque furnishings dating from the late 17th century. Nearby is the Empire-style palace built in 1801–10 for the Buquoy family.

The 13th-century **Castle** was built to guard the trading route between Bohemia and Austria. Damaged, first during Hussite wars and again by a gunpowder explosion in 1537 and then the earthquake of 1605, it was given its present Baroque form in the 18th century. The entrance to the castle leads over a bridge

Entrance to the 13th-century Nové Hrady Castle

that spans the deep brick-lined moat, the largest moat in the Czech Republic.

🏠 Nové Hrady Castle
Tel 386 362 135. **Open** Apr–Jun & Sep: Mon–Sun; Jul & Aug: daily. 🔳 🖼

Environs
Žumberk, 6 km (4 miles) west of Nové Hrady, is worth a short detour for its late 15th-century Gothic fortress and the unusual four-aisle church built in 1455 and featuring a lovely vault resting on six slender columns.

⑫ Rožmberk nad Vltavou Castle

Road map C3. 🚗 4 km (2 miles). **Tel** 380 749 838. **Open** Tue–Sun (timings vary, call ahead or check website for details). 🔳 🖼
🌐 hrad-rozmberk.eu

The 13th-century fortified estate of the powerful Rožmberk family towers on a hilltop above the tiny village at its base. The Rožmberks used it as a base for running their estates in the region from the 13th to the 17th century. It consists of the Upper Castle, the only remains of which are now the Jacobean Tower, closed to visitors; and the Lower Castle, originally Gothic and in the 16th century remodelled in the Renaissance style. In 1840–57, the then owners, the Buquoy family, renovated the castle, giving it its English Neo-Gothic features.

Inside the castle are displayed collections of precious glass, paintings, weapons, porcelain and furniture, and there is also a marvellous frescoed Banquet Hall.

Environs
On the border with Austria 8 km (5 miles) to the east is the small town of **Dolní Dvořiště**. The church of St Giles (sv. Jiljí) here is the prime example of the South Bohemian Gothic style, featuring magnificent net-vaulting over the presbytery and all the aisles.

To the north, west and south of Dolní Dvořiště, there are remains of the horse-drawn train lines that once linked České Budějovice with Linz. Built in 1825–31, it was the first railway of its kind in Continental Europe. The total route was 131 km (81 miles) long, and the journey took 14 hours. The most numerous fragments of the railway (embankments, pillars, bridges) can be seen near the village of Suchodol, 2 km (1 mile) to the north of Dolní Dvořiště.

⑬ Vyšší Brod Monastery

Road map C3. 🚗 from České Budějovice. 🚌 from Český Krumlov. **Tel** 380 746 674. **Open** May–Sep: 9:30am–4:30pm Mon–Sat. 🔳
🖼 Postal Museum: **Open** Apr–Oct: 9am–5pm Tue–Sun; Nov–Mar: by appt. 🔳

In the mid-13th century, the Rožmberk family founded a Cistercian monastery here. The completion of the entire complex took the whole of the next century, when Peter Parler was invited to help with its construction. The damage inflicted by the Hussite army in 1422 was soon repaired due to the monastery's effective fortifications.

During the 17th and 18th centuries, new Baroque buildings were added to the older parts of the church. The Communists closed the monastery in 1950, imprisoning the monks. Since the 1990s, it has undergone major renovation work.

The most beautiful room is the Chapter House dating from 1285–1300, its vaulted ceiling supported by a single column. Also very impressive is the Rococo library, entered by a hidden door, decorated with frescoes and topped with a ceiling adorned with gold leaf. It houses 70,000 volumes. Inside the Church of the Assumption of the Virgin Mary (Nanebevzetí Panny Marie), the aisles and the church sacristy have beautiful Gothic vaults. The main altarpiece dates from 1644–6.

The works of art found in the monastery are of the highest quality; they include the *Crucifixion* by the Master of Vyšší Brod, which was returned to the Cistercians by the National Museum in Prague.

The outer buildings of the monastery now house a Postal Museum (Poštovní muzeum) devoted to the history of mail delivery in the Czech Republic since 1526, including uniforms and post coaches.

Entrance to the 13th-century Cistercian Monastery in Vyšší Brod

⓮ A Tour of the Šumava

The Šumava mountains form a natural border between the Czech Republic, Germany and Austria. This is the largest forested area in Central Europe at 120 km (75 miles) long and up to 45 km (28 miles) wide. The unspoilt Boubín Virgin Forest has been a reserve since 1858. Nearby, some of the densest woodland makes up the Šumava National Park *(see also p168)*. The whole area, preserved in part due to a period during the Cold War when it was closed off, was made a UNESCO biosphere reserve in 1990. The Šumava offers superb trekking, canoeing and cycling.

⑨ Velhartice
The castle at Velhartice, now a ruin, was built in the late 13th and early 14th century. The four-span stone bridge was erected in about 1430 *(see also p168).*

⑧ Rabí
The Czech Republic's largest medieval fortress, Rabí is made up of Gothic ruins dominated by a square tower that offers a great viewpoint *(see also p159).*

⑦ Srní
The pretty village of Srní has a couple of pleasant places to stay. The village, surrounded by forests and meadows, makes a good base for trekking, mountain biking and, in winter, skiing.

0 kilometres   10
0 miles   10

Key

▬ Tour route

▬ Other scenic routes

= Other roads

–··– International border

⑥ Kvilda
The highest altitude parish in the Czech Republic (1,065 m/ 3,495 ft above sea level), Kvilda is a quiet winter sports centre in an area of peat bogs.

Klatovy

Strakonice

22
187
⑨
670 m
(2198 ft)
8
149
Otava
171
Sušice
971 m
(3186 ft)
149
902 m
(2959 ft)
171
170
Stra
Otava
⑦
Kašperské Hory
1317 m
(4321 ft)
175
4
(2.
169
Vimperk
145
1117 m
(3665 ft)
Šumava National Park
⑥
168
Boubín Virgin Forest
167
1302 m
(4272 ft)
1314 m
(4311 ft)
1362 m
(4469 ft)
12
(41
167
4
39
4
Passau
Vltava

⑤ Volary
The town of Volary has some 20 original wooden houses, built by Tyrol farmers who settled here in the 16th century. It is also a gateway to Boubín. A single-track train service links Volary with České Budějovice.

Tips for Drivers
Length: 190 km (118 miles). Many side roads do not allow cars. There are six bus routes that provide transport in the region.
Stopping-off points: Hotels, pensions and hostels are in many towns; camp sites are numerous.

④ Schwarzenberg Canal
Close to the hamlet of Jeleni vrchy is a 429-m (1,407-ft) long underground tunnel, a fragment of the 1789 Schwarzenberg Canal linking the Vltava with the Danube.

③ Lake Lipno
The man-made water reservoir, Lipno, built in 1950–59, is often referred to as the "South Bohemian Sea". Ferries cross regularly, and it offers excellent facilities for sport and recreation, attracting many local visitors.

② Rožmberk nad Vltavou
The castle, perched high above the Vltava river valley, was the home of the Rožmberks – one of the most powerful Bohemian families (see also p149).

Písek

Prachatice

141

1008 m
(3307 ft)

953 m
(3127 ft)

143

České
Budějovice

166

① Klet'
Blanský les

Český Krumlov

39

3

656 m
(2152 ft)

39

1226 m
(4022 ft)

**Horní
Planá**

744 m
(2441 ft)

918 m
(3012 ft)

Kaplice

39

Vltava

162

160

④

Lake
Lipno

3

163

②

984 m
(3228 ft)

791 m
(2595 ft)

813 m
(2667 ft)

163

1053 m
(3455 ft)

935 m
(3067 ft)

Vyšší Brod

Linz

① Klet' Mountain
This mountain is the highest peak (1,083 m/ 3,553 ft) in the Blanský forest area. On top is a stone observation tower, the oldest in the Czech Republic, built in 1825. There is a chairlift to the top, and in fine weather it offers views of the Alps.

Linz

The sprawling countryside of South Bohemia ▶

⑮ Český Krumlov

An astonishingly beautiful and well-preserved small medieval town, Český Krumlov (Krumau) is one of the most visited in the Czech Republic. Founded in the 13th century, it belonged to the Rožmberk dynasty from 1302 to 1602. The family crest of a five-petalled red rose is one of the most often seen motifs in Český Krumlov. The Eggenbergs held sway for 100 years, then the Schwarzenbergs took over from 1719 to 1947. In 1992, it was added to the UNESCO World Cultural Heritage List.

Exploring the town

The historic town centre is situated on the rocky banks of the sharply meandering Vltava. The Inner Town (Vnitřní Město), with its market square, town hall and St Vitus's Church, is located on the right bank, in an area enclosed on three sides by water. The left side meander features the castle and the village called Latrán. The town centre is a pedestrian zone.

Coat of arms on the town hall

🏛 Náměstí Svornosti

The most imposing building in the market square, náměstí Svornosti, is the town hall. Occupying a corner site on the north side, it was created in the mid-16th century by combining two Gothic houses. The Marian plague column at the centre of the square was erected in 1716 as a thanksgiving for sparing the town from the Black Death in 1682. Matthäus Jäckel, a Prague sculptor, placed a statue of the Madonna at the top, and at the foot of the column, in

one of the niches, a figure of St Roch, the saint invoked for protection against plague.

🏛 Egon Schiele Centrum

Široká 71. **Tel** 380 704 011.
Open 10am–6pm Tue–Sun.
🅿 🏠 🔲 ♿
W **schieleartcentrum.cz**

A former brewery not far from the market square now houses a gallery devoted to Austrian artist Egon Schiele (1890–1918), who lived in Český Krumlov in 1911. On display are watercolours and drawings, including several famous male and female nudes, which in Schiele's day caused a scandal. He was driven out of the town for employing young local girls to pose for him. There are also other temporary exhibitions of contemporary works.

🏛 Church of St Vitus

St Vitus's Church (sv. Víta) provides a visual counterbalance to the lofty tower of the castle. Dating from the early 15th century, and built on the site of an earlier church, this triple-aisled Gothic edifice features one of the oldest examples of net vaulting in Europe. The

sanctuary by the north wall of the presbytery is a splendid example of stonemasonry dating from about 1500. The Early Baroque high altar, made in 1673–83, has paintings depicting St Vitus and the coronation of the Virgin Mary. The Late Gothic porch has an unusual vault in the shape of octagonal stars.

Gothic wall paintings dating from 1430 can be seen on the north wall of the side aisle (*The Crucifixion, St Veronica, St Elizabeth with a beggar, Mary Magdalene, St Katherine* and *St Bartholomew*). The church once housed the famous *Krumlov Madonna* of 1393, regarded by many as the finest example of the International Gothic style, now kept in the Art History Museum, Vienna. Its 15th-century replica can be seen in the National Gallery, Prague.

The imposing nave of the Church of St Vitus

🏛 Ulice Horní

Regional Museum 380 711 674.
Open 9am–noon & 12:30–5pm Tue–Sun. W **muzeumck.cz**

Horní street, off the market square, was once terminated by a town gate, demolished in 1839. At No. 159 is the Chaplaincy (Kaplanka) dating from 1514–20, with a Gothic gable and Renaissance window jambs. At No. 155 is the former Prelature built in the 14th century and remodelled several times since. Adjoining it is the former Jesuit College (No. 154), designed by Baldassare Maggi and now a hotel. At No. 152, the **Regional Museum** includes a scale model of the town in 1800.

Part of the façade of the former Jesuit College in Ulice Horní

For hotels and restaurants see p351 and pp369–70

The arcaded bridge linking Krumlov Castle with its Theatre

🔲 Latrán

The old quarter of Latrán was once a village inhabited by craftsmen and merchants, who provided services for the castle. It is linked to the Inner Town by a bridge over the Vltava. Still remaining is a complex of late Gothic and Baroque buildings including the Minorite monastery, the **Convent of the Poor Clares** and a church. The entire complex was linked with the castle by a covered walkway running over Latrán. Close by is the Renaissance **Budějovice gate**, the only one left of the original eight town gates.

🏰 Krumlov Castle

Zámek 59. **Tel** 380 704 721. **Open** Apr–Oct: 9am–5pm Tue–Sun (Jun–Aug: to 6pm). 🎫 🎫 2 routes. 📷

Perched high up on a rock, the castle is the second only to Prague Castle in terms of its size. The oldest part of this sprawling complex is Dolní Hrad, also known as Hrádek, with a tall, cylindrical tower painted in colourful designs, built in 1580.

The castle has a total of 300 rooms. The most beautiful are the stately Rožmberk Rooms with wooden vaults and Renaissance wall frescoes, completed in 1576 under the patronage of Vilém Rožmberk. Particularly unusual is the Hall of Masks, which is vividly decorated with some extraordinary *trompe l'oeil* paintings depicting carnival scenes.

A spectacular 17th-century tiered bridge (Plášťovy most),

VISITORS' CHECKLIST

Practical Information
Road map C3.
🚉 13,600. 🅘 Náměstí Svornosti 2. **Tel** 380 704 622.
🎭 Five-Petalled Rose Celebration: mid-Jun; International Music Festival: mid-Jul–Aug.
🌐 ckrumlov.info

Transport
🚌 1 km (0.5 mile) N of Krumlov Castle. 🚌

complete with statues, links the Upper Castle with its Theatre.

🎭 Castle Theatre
See pp156–7.

Entrance to the Minorite Monastery in Latrán

Český Krumlov Town Centre

① Náměstí Svornosti
② Egon Schiele Centrum
③ Church of St Vitus
④ Ulice Horní
⑤ Latrán
⑥ Krumlov Castle
⑦ Castle Theatre

For keys to symbols *see back flap*

Český Krumlov: Castle Theatre

The Baroque theatre (Zámecké divadlo) in Krumlov Castle is virtually unique in that its interior, furnishings, stage settings, costumes and stage machinery are so numerous and so well preserved. It was rebuilt on the site of a previous theatre in 1766 to a commission by Prince Josef Adam Schwarzenberg. The scene-shifting machinery was constructed by Lorenz Makh from Vienna. Following a 30-year refurbishment in the 20th century, the theatre offers a fascinating glimpse of 18th-century theatrical life.

★ Painted Ceiling
The ceiling mural above the auditorium and wall paintings were by Viennese artists Leo Märkl and Hans Wetschel.

Costumes
The theatre wardrobes house 540 original costumes for men, women and children.

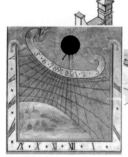

Sundial
A sundial adorns the Renaissance House, which, since the building of the new theatre, now houses wardrobes, laundries and stables.

KEY

① **A theatre building** was built in 1682 by Prince Johann Christian Eggenberg, under the supervision of the Italian builders G A de Maggi and G M Spinetti.

② **Remains** of the Late Gothic fortified walls of the castle.

③ **Plášťový most (bridge)**, linking the theatre with the castle, was built in 1691.

Wind Machine
The sound of wind was simulated by turning a revolving drum, loosely covered with a linen cloth.

For hotels and restaurants see p351 and pp369–70

Stage Scenery

Among the surviving scenery are 13 complete typical stage sets including 11 backcloths, 40 ceilings, 100 props, 50 machines for creating special effects and 250 wings.

VISITORS' CHECKLIST

Practical Information
Český Krumlov Castle, fifth courtyard. Theatre: **Tel** 380 704 721. **Fax** 380 704 710.
Open May–Oct: 10am–4pm (every hour, last adm 3pm) Tue–Sun. 🅿 🅲 (compulsory).
W **zamek-ceskykrumlov.eu**

Transport
🚃 1 km (0.5 mile) N of Krumlov Castle. 🚌

★ Stage

This setting represents a military camp; other preserved sets include a forest, a town, a prison, a garden, a harbour, a cathedral and a colonnaded hall.

Auditorium

Rising wooden benches are provided for the audience, and the centre of the circle has a comfortable royal box. The auditorium would have been lit by chandeliers with oil lamps.

Scene-shifting Machinery

A sophisticated system of ropes and pulleys, which still works well, allowed for fast shifting of the wings. The same device or a similar one controlled the lifting and lowering of the backcloth, the ceiling and the curtain.

⑯ Zlatá Koruna Monastery

Road map C3. 🚌 from Prague or České Budějovice. **Tel** 380 743 126. **Open** Apr–Oct: 9am–5pm Tue–Sun (Apr, May, Sep & Oct: to 4pm). 🎨 📷
Ⓦ **klaster-zlatakoruna.eu**

Founded in 1263 by Přemysl Otakar II, this Cistercian monastery has at its centre a courtyard surrounded by cloisters. Adjoining is the Church of the Assumption with a pentagonal presbytery dating from about 1500. The main altarpiece is a magnificent example of monumental Rococo architecture.

The Chapterhouse, built in 1280–1300, features vaulting supported by two Gothic columns. The Chapel of the Guardian Angels, at the southern end of the monastery grounds, is a beautiful two-storey church from the late 13th century, featuring the original rib vaulting on both levels. Another building houses a **Museum of South Bohemian Literature** (Památník písemnictví jižních Čech).

Intricate vaulting in the Chapterhouse at Zlatá Koruna Monastery

⑰ Holašovice

Road map C3. 15 km (9 miles) W of České Budějovice. 🏔 335. 🚌 from České Budějovice. 387 982 145.

This picturesque village contains a splendidly pre-served set of early 19th-century historic buildings grouped around a central fish pond, which is used jointly by all the inhabitants. Nowhere else is such a collection of buildings found in its original setting. The stone buildings – including both homes and farmsteads as well as a pub – represent the architectural style known as Folk Baroque, found only in this part of Bohemia, and are characterized by colourful façades with white stucco ornamentation. The gables differ from house to house. Most of them face the central square and pond, and have an entrance gate leading to a yard. Larger homesteads have brick granaries resembling small fortresses.

Providing an enchanting glimpse of traditional rural life, this tiny village was declared a UNESCO World Cultural and Natural Heritage Site in 1998. Holašovice was the setting for the 1932 film version of *The Bartered Bride* by Bedřich Smetana.

⑱ Prachatice

Road map C3. 🏔 11,400. 🚉 from České Budějovice. 🚌 from Prague. 🛈 Velké náměstí 1. **Tel** 388 607 574. 🎭 Gold Trail Festival: Jun.

The town's tiny centre is surrounded by a ring of defensive walls, with a mighty entrance gate. It was a key point along the salt trade route into Bohemia. The lovingly restored town square (Velké náměstí) has a 17th-century **Old Town Hall** (Stará radnice), its façade decorated with *sgraffito*. Many buildings are covered with *sgraffito;* No. 31 has the finest, of the Last Supper (1563). The **Church of St James** (sv. Jakuba) has magnificent net vaulting.

Folk Baroque buildings overlooking the fish pond in the village of Holašovice

⓳ Strakonice

Road map C3. 🏘 23,100. 🚃 from Plzeň. 🚌 from Prague. 🛈 Velké náměstí 2. **Tel** 383 700 700. 🎵 International Bagpipe Festival: mid-Aug. 🌐 **strakonice.eu**

In the 19th century, Strakonice was a textile manufacturing town and centre of the woollen industry. It became most famous for making fezzes. At one point, nearly 5 million a year were being exported to Turkey, India, Arabia and Egypt. Also made here are Czech bagpipes *(dudy)*; the International Bagpipe Festival every August attracts large numbers of bagpipe enthusiasts.

Situated at the con-fluence of the Otava and Volyňka rivers, Strakonice has a 13th-century **Castle**, one of the oldest stone buildings in the Czech Republic. Until 1694, this was the headquarters of the Knights of St John in Bohemia. The castle still features original Gothic details, which can also be seen in the cloisters and porch of the adjacent **Church of St Procopius** (sv. Prokop). The **Regional Museum** in the castle has displays of fezzes, bagpipes and motorcycles (also made in the town).

In the town itself, the main square (Velké náměstí) has a couple of beautifully decorated buildings: the town hall (radnice) and a savings bank.

🏰 **Strakonice Castle and Regional Museum**
Tel 383 700 111. **Open** May, Sep & Oct: 9am–4pm Tue–Sun; Jun, Jul & Aug: 9am–5pm daily. 🎨 🎫
🌐 **hradstrakonice.cz**

Environs
About 20 km (12 miles) west of Strakonice, **Rabí** fortress *(see also p150)*, built in the early 14th century, became a target of Hussite army attacks in 1420. After a long siege, it was captured by the troops of Jan Žižka *(see pp38–9)*, who is thought to have been blinded in one eye here.

⓴ Písek

Road map C3. 🏘 30,000. 🚃 from Tábor. 🚌 from Prague. 🛈 Velké náměstí 113. **Tel** 387 999 999.
🌐 **icpisek.cz**

Statue of St Barbara in the Regional Museum

On the Otava river, Písek was at the centre of a gold-panning region and is named after the sand from which gold is separated. Přemysl Otakar II founded the town in the 13th century. Its main draw today, the medieval bridge, survives from that time, making it older than Prague's Charles Bridge *(see pp70–71)*. It has several statues of saints, including St John Nepomuk. The fascinating **Prácheňské Museum**, in the former royal castle, has an exhibition on the town's history, including 20th-century upheavals, and the region's natural environment.

🏛 **Prácheňské Museum**
Velké náměstí 114. **Tel** 382 201 111.
Open Mar–Dec: Tue–Sun. 🎨

㉑ Zvíkov Castle

Road map C2. 🚌 from Písek to Zvíkovské Podhradí 43, 1.5 km (1 mile). **Tel** 382 285 676. **Open** Apr & Oct: 9:30am–3:30pm Sat & Sun; Jun–Aug: 9am–5pm Tue–Sun; May & Sep: 9:30am–4pm Tue–Sun. 🎨
🌐 **hrad-zvikov.eu**

Originally built on the Vltava river, Zvíkov now overlooks the artificial lake that has resulted from the Orlík dam downstream. Zvíkov was built in the reign of Přemysl Otakar II in the mid-13th century, and during the Thirty Years' War, it became the final stronghold of the Protestant army in South Bohemia. The oldest part of the castle is its mighty keep. The royal palace has an interesting chapel of St Wenceslas with lovely medieval frescoes.

Environs
The Neo-Gothic **Orlík Palace**, 14 km (9 miles) north of Zvíkov, belongs to the Schwarzenberg family, and its historic interiors illustrate this prominent family's history.

🏰 **Orlík Palace**
Tel 382 275 101. **Open** Apr–Oct: Tue–Sun. 🌐 **zamekorlik.cz**

Gothic entrance gate to the Zvíkov Castle, built in the 13th century

St John Nepomuk

Jan of Pomuk, known as John Nepomuk, was from 1389 the vicar-general of the Prague Archbishopric. In 1393, on the orders of Wenceslas IV, he was imprisoned, tortured and then drowned in the Vltava. Later sources claim that he was murdered for refusing to reveal the secret of the queen's confession. Canonized in 1729, John Nepomuk became a phenomenon of the Baroque period. Because he is regarded as the patron saint of good reputation and bridges, and guardian against floods, countless statues of the saint were placed by bridges. His was the first statue on Prague's Charles Bridge *(see p71)*.

WEST BOHEMIA

This border region, strongly affected by its proximity to German neighbours, attracts visitors for its natural beauty, its spa resorts, and, not least, its excellent beer. Fortresses on the frontiers of the former Přemyslid state are reminders of its distant past; its more recent past can be seen in the areas from which, after World War II, many Germans were expelled, leaving traces of their long presence.

Some of the most interesting historic sites of West Bohemia (Západní Čechy) include the structures that were built to defend the Kingdom of Bohemia; they include the castles of Přimda, Velhartice and Švihov, as well as a number of smaller fortresses scattered along the foothills of the Šumava mountains.

Several magnificent monasteries, including Kladruby, Plasy and Teplá, are truly outstanding sights. Founded in the Middle Ages, these Gothic centres of monastic life were remodelled during the Baroque era and now provide excellent examples of the art that was intended to serve the ideas of Counter-Reformation.

The famous spa resorts of Karlovy Vary (Karlsbad), Mariánské Lázně (Marienbad) and Františkovy Lázně (Franzensbad) played a significant role in European history. Their habitués were the rich and influential from the worlds of politics and culture, including Goethe, Gogol, Chopin, Wagner, Russian Emperor Peter the Great, British King Edward VII and Austrian Emperor Franz Josef I.

Yet the attractions of West Bohemia are not limited to historic relics. Its capital, Plzeň, is a flourishing industrial centre, the home of Pilsner beer. The town of Domažlice near the German border retains aspects of Slav folk culture. The region also offers intriguing natural phenomena at Soos – a strange landscape of small mud geysers – and the beautiful Černé and Čertovo lakes near the Šumava mountains.

Façade of the sanatorium (Bath V) overlooking Smetana Park in Karlovy Vary

◀ Painted ceiling of the Colonnade in Mariánské Lázně

Exploring West Bohemia

The region's capital and its biggest town, Plzeň, is an
interesting place to visit and gives a flavour of the region.
It is also the home of the world-renowned beer *(see p169)*.
The main tourist attractions of West
Bohemia are its spa resorts of Karlovy
Vary and Mariánské Lázně. Monasteries
are another highlight *(see pp178–9)*, and
there are numerous small picturesque
towns. The large forested areas of Český
and Slavkovský les form a backdrop to
a number of the towns and offer many
kilometres of hiking and cycling trails,
and, in winter, excellent skiing facilities.

The monumental columns of the Mill Spring Colonnade in Karlovy Vary

Sights at a Glance

0 kilometres 10

0 miles 10

Coat of arms from the palace in Lázně Kynžvart

View of the monastery buildings in Plasy

Key

--- Motorway
--- Dual carriageway
--- Main road
--- Minor road
--- Main railway
--- Minor railway
--- International border
--- Regional border

One of the Baroque sculptures
of saints and apostles at
the palace in Manětín

Getting Around

West Bohemia is crosscut by one of the country's
main transport arteries – the D5 motorway
(international E50 route), linking Prague with the
German city of Nuremberg. Plzeň has good road
and rail links with many towns of the region, and
buses and trains run between most towns, but
always check the frequency of weekend services.
Severe weather can hamper winter travel.

For keys to symbols *see back flap*

❶ Plzeň

The large and bustling capital of West Bohemia, Plzeň (Pilsen) has two main industries that contribute to its vibrant atmosphere. It is mainly associated with beer, producing Pilsner Urquell (Plzeňský Prazdroj) in the brewery founded here in 1842 *(see p169)*. Since the late 19th century, a large Škoda factory in the city has made armaments as well as cars. The city was established in 1295 by Wenceslas II, at the crossroads of the main trading routes between Bohemia, Bavaria and Saxony.

View of the Plague Column on Náměstí Republiky

Exploring the City

The majority of Plzeň's historic sites are found on the left bank of the Radbuza river. The historic centre, laid out in a grid pattern, is surrounded by Plzeňske sady – a green belt created on the site of the old town walls in the 19th century. On the opposite eastern side of the Radbuza is Pilsner Urquell brewery, the Prazdroj.

🏛 Náměstí Republiky

Náměstí Republiky is one of the largest market squares in the Czech Republic, measuring 139 x 193 m (456 x 633 ft). Standing at its centre is the Church of St Bartholomew. The square is fringed by a number of beautifully decorated houses, with the best-preserved along the south side. Particularly striking are the Red Heart

A statue on Cisařský dům

House (U červeného srdce), built in 1894 and sporting magnificent *sgraffito* by Czech painter Mikuláš Aleš, of two mounted knights in full tournament gear; and the Baroque Bishoprie building (Biskupství) on the west side. A market is held in the square during festivals.

🏛 Cathedral of St Bartholomew
See pp166–7.

🏛 Town Hall
Náměstí Republiky. **Open** 8am–6pm daily.

The Renaissance town hall (stará radnice), one of the loveliest buildings of its kind in Bohemia, was designed by Italian architect Giovanni de Statio. This four-storey edifice with its magnificent gables was built in 1554–9. The interesting *sgraffito* decorations on the façade are the work of J Koul, produced during 1907–12. Standing in front of the town hall is a Plague Column, erected in 1681 in thanksgiving for the fact that the plague epidemic suffered at that time was only mild.

🏛 Císařský dům
Náměstí Republiky 41.

An imposing Renaissance edifice to the left of the town hall, dating from 1606, twice played host to Emperor Rudolph II. Now it houses the tourist information office. The next door Pechlátovský dům was created by combining two smaller, Renaissance buildings and adding a Neo-Classical façade.

❇ Great Synagogue
Sady Pětatřicátníků 11. **Tel** 377 235 749. **Open** Apr–Oct: 10am–6pm Sun–Fri. **Closed** Jewish religious festivals.

The Great Synagogue (Velká synagoga) is the world's third-largest Jewish sacred building, after the Jerusalem and Budapest synagogues. It was built in the 1890s, funded by voluntary donations from the Plzeň Jewish community. Its architect, Rudolf Štech, designed it in a romantic "Moorish-Romanesque" style. It could accommodate 2,000 worshippers, and in addition, the high balcony, intended for women, could take up to 800. Following World War II the building and its furnishings, including the unique organ located above the Torah, suffered gradual deterioration. In 1998 the synagogue was reopened after careful restoration.

Twin towers with onion domes of the Great Synagogue

🎭 Tyl Theatre
Smetanovy sady 16. **Tel** 378 038 070. 🌐 djkt-plzen.cz

Plzeň's theatre (Divadlo J K Tyla) is named after Josef Kajetan Tyl, Czech playwright and novelist, and a champion of national culture in the 19th century. This striking Neo-Classical-style building was erected in 1902 and, just like the National Theatre in Prague, its design was intended to symbolize and reinforce Czech patriotism. The figures on the façade are

Frescoes, dating around 1460, in the Franciscan Monastery Chapel

allegories of Opera and Drama. The beautiful stage curtain was painted by Augustin Nějmece.

🏛 Franciscan Monastery and Church of the Assumption
Františkánská.

The early Gothic monastery is one of the town's oldest buildings. Off the lovely cloisters is the 13th-century Chapel of St Barbara, with a stellar vault supported by a single column; the chapel is decorated with frescoes from about 1460. The monastery's Church of the Assumption has a main altarpiece painting of the Annunciation, a copy of Rubens' work. The Gothic Madonna, below the painting, is from the late 14th century.

🏛 West Bohemian Museum
Kopeckého sady 2. **Tel** 378 370 111.
Open 10am–6pm Tue–Sun. 🖼
W zcm.cz

This large museum (Západočeské muzeum) is a Neo-Baroque building with an Art Nouveau interior dating from 1898. Take time to look at the reliefs on the staircase and the Art Nouveau library furnishings. Exhibits include Charles IV's armoury, and a beautiful glass and porcelain collection in the vast, stately Jubilee Hall.

🏛 Brewing Museum
Veleslavínova 6. **Tel** 377 235 574.
Open Apr–Sep: 10am–6pm daily;
Oct–Mar: 10am–5pm daily.
W prazdrojvisit.cz

Appropriately housed in an old malt house, this museum (Pivovarské muzeum) traces the history of brewing in Plzeň, with a fascinating range of beer-related exhibits.

🍺 Pilsner Urquell Brewery
U Prazdroje 7. **Tel** 377 062 888.
Open Apr–Sep: 8am–6pm; Oct–Mar: 8am–5pm. 🖼 🎫
W prazdrojvisit.cz

The opulent brewery (pívovar) building, with its imposing Empire-style gate, is a 1917 work of architect H Zapala. The attractions here – besides tasting Plzeňský Prazdroj

VISITORS' CHECKLIST

Practical Information
Road map C2.
🗺 170,000. ℹ Náměstí Republiky 41. **Tel** 378 035 330.
Open 9am–7pm daily (to 6pm Oct–May).
🍺 Beer Festival: early Oct.
🎭 During festivals.
W pilsen.eu

Transport
🚌 1 km (0.5 mile) SE of centre.
🚉 1 km (0.5 mile) W of centre.

(Pilsner Urquell) beer – include the chance to explore its 10-km (6-mile) long cellars, used from 1838 until 1930 to store the fermenting brew (*see p169*).

Neo-Baroque façade of the West Bohemian Museum

Plzeň City Centre

1. Náměstí Republiky
2. Cathedral of St Bartholomew
3. Town Hall
4. Císařský dům
5. Great Synagogue
6. Tyl Theatre
7. Franciscan Monastery and Church of the Assumption
8. West Bohemian Museum
9. Brewing Museum
10. Pilsner Urquell Brewery

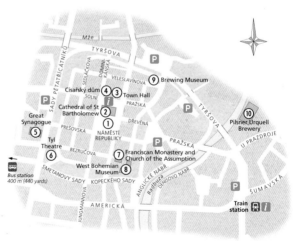

| 0 metres | 200 |
| 0 yards | 200 |

Cathedral of St Bartholomew

The Gothic Cathedral of St Bartholomew (Chrám sv. Bartoloměje) dominates Plzeň market square from its position in the centre. Its 102-m (335-ft) spire – the tallest in Bohemia – can be seen from all over the city, and was used in the 19th century by the imperial land surveyors in laying out transport routes around Plzeň. Construction of the church continued from the late 13th century until 1480. The Sternberg Chapel, adjoining the south wall of the presbytery, is an early 16th-century addition, featuring an unusual keystone at the centre of the vault, and Renaissance paintings.

★ Cathedral Tower
Originally the cathedral had two towers. One collapsed when struck by lightning in 1525.

Sculptures in the Cathedral
The church houses a large number of sculptures, including the figures of St Barbara, St Katherine and St Wenceslas seen on the pillars of the main nave.

Stained-Glass Windows
The magnificent elongated stained-glass windows in the aisles and the presbytery, which provide the entire church interior with beautiful light, were fitted in the early 20th century.

KEY

① **Main door**

② **The tower** has a balcony at the top, which is open to the public.

③ **This small tower** is over the main nave.

④ **The presbytery** was given its present form in around 1360.

Pulpit
The Gothic pulpit of sandstone, as well as the magnificent traceried canopy above it, date from the same period as the rood arch figures, and were made in about 1360.

VISITORS' CHECKLIST

Practical Information
Náměstí Republiky.
Tel 377 236 753.
W katedralaplzen.org
Open 10am–4pm Wed–Sat
(to Fri Nov–Mar).
Tower: **Open** 10am–6pm daily.

★ Plzeň Madonna
The statue of the Virgin Mary dating from about 1390, set at the centre of the main altarpiece, is an outstanding example of the International Gothic style.

Pendant Boss, Sternberg Chapel
In the vault of the chapel, this unusual hanging keystone is a unique late Gothic detail.

★ Sternberg Chapel
The Sternberg family founded this chapel in the early 16th century. It has a beautiful altar (right) and marvellous Renaisssance paintings.

Entrance

Rood Arch
Standing on the beam of the rood arch are figures in a Calvary scene. The crucifix was made in the 1470s by the Bohemian Master of Plzeň.

❷ Švihov Castle

Road map B2. 🚉 🚌 from Prague or Plzeň. **Tel** 376 393 378. **Open** Apr & Oct: 10am–3pm Sat, Sun & public hols; May, Jun & Sep: 10am–4pm Tue–Sun & public hols; Jul & Aug: 9:30am–5:30pm Tue–Sun. 🎦 🎫 2 routes. 🌐 **hradsvihov.cz**

This beautifully preserved Gothic castle, surrounded by water and meadows, has been the fairytale backdrop for numerous films. Built in 1480, it is a relatively recent castle for Bohemia. Following the Thirty Years' War, it was condemned to demolition by Ferdinand III, but its then owners – the Czernín family – avoided carrying out the orders. The entire estate now includes two palaces, a tower, and the defence walls with four bastions. The grand hall of the south castle has a lovely coffered ceiling. The 1515 wall painting in the castle chapel, *Saint George Slaying the Dragon*, includes Švihov in the background.

Side tower of Švihov Castle rising above the moat

❸ Klatovy

Road map B2. 👥 22,600. 🚉 🚌 from Prague or Plzeň. 🛈 Náměstí Míru 63. **Tel** 376 347 240. 🌐 **klatovy.cz**

One of the richest towns in Bohemia in the 15th century, Klatovy was founded by Přemysl Otakar II. In the 19th century, Klatovy achieved international fame for its carnations, grown from seeds brought from Nancy in 1813.

The town's dominant feature is the Renaissance **Black Tower**

Black Tower, town hall and Jesuit church in Klatovy

(Černá věž), a lofty stone structure in the southwest corner of the town square (náměstí Míru).

Close by is the Baroque **Jesuit Church** (Jezuitský kostel), the work of Giovanni Orsi and Carlo Lurago, built in 1655–75. It was renovated in 1717 by Karl Dientzenhofer, who is credited with designing its magnificent doorway. The interior includes valuable Baroque furnishings, furniture pieces and vivid *trompe l'oeil* paintings. The fascinating **catacombs** beneath the church contain scores of mummified monks. The **Baroque Apothecary** on the west of the square has its original 17th-century interior lined with bottles and jars of intriguing ingredients. It was a working pharmacy until the 1960s.

🏛 **Catacombs**
Tel 376 320 160. **Open** Apr–Oct: 9am–6pm daily; Nov–Mar: 11am–4pm Mon–Fri, 9am–5pm Sat & Sun.

🏛 **Baroque Apothecary**
Open May–Oct: Tue–Sun.

❹ Velhartice Castle

Road map B3. 🚉 🚌 from Klatovy, Plzeň. **Tel** 376 583 315. **Open** Apr & Oct: 10am–4pm Sat & Sun; May, Jun & Sep: 10am–5pm Tue–Sun; Jul & Aug: 10am–6pm Tue–Sun. 🌐 **hradvelhartice.cz**

Between the towns of Klatovy and Sušice, the castle was built between 1290 and 1310. Now in ruins, it once consisted of two palace buildings connected by a huge four-span stone bridge – the only one of its kind in Bohemia (*see also p150*). In the 18th century, a Renaissance palace was built next to the old one. The castle's most famous owner was Bušek of Velhartice, a secretary to Charles IV.

❺ Černé Lake

Road map B3. 🚉 from Plzeň to Železná Ruda.

By the German border, at the northwest tip of the Šumava (*see pp150–51*), lies a beautiful glacial lake known as Black (Černé) Lake. Čertovo (Devil's) Lake is nearby. They are within the National Park area, near the towns of Špičák and Železná Ruda, and can be reached by walking from Špičák station. Black Lake is the largest, the deepest (over 40 m/130 ft) and the lowest-lying lake on the Bohemian side of the Šumava. Its name is believed by some to derive from the reflection in its water of the dark forest wall; others attribute it to the dark silt on the bottom; others put it down to the water's high acidity, which prevents most organisms from populating it.

The serene glacial waters of Černé Lake

Pilsner Urquell

Pilsner beer, produced in Plzeň since 1842, is prized for its outstanding clarity, golden colour and transparency. The beer-making tradition in Plzeň goes back to the times of Wenceslas II, who granted 260 of the town's citizens a licence to produce this golden liquid. Its quality was poor, however, until the Plzeň brewery was established on the banks of the Radbuza in 1842 after a dozen or so independent breweries were amalgamated. Purpose-built, the brewery *(see p165)* was erected on sandy soil, which made it easy to build tunnels and cellars. Word of the new beer, Pilsner Urquell, quickly spread around Europe, and it was widely imitated. "Pilsner" soon became the generic name for beer produced by similar methods.

The information centre, the starting point for a visit, is in a modernized section of the old brewery.

Cellars and tunnels of the brewery, some 10 km (6 miles) long, are open to the public. Here, visitors can see how the beer is produced and stored using traditional methods.

In the vast information centre, visitors can view the unique equipment and procedures of beer-making which are not used elsewhere in Europe.

The label on the bottles containing the original beer includes at its centre a picture of the entrance gate.

The wooden casks containing beer are stored for three months in the maze of long tunnels that were manually dug under the brewery.

In the past, the beer was matured at low temperatures, in oak or beech barrels sealed inside with resin.

The brewery entrance gate, in the shape of a triumphal arch, was erected in 1892, the 50th anniversary of the first golden Pilsner being produced.

❻ Domažlice

Road map B2. 🗺 11,000. 🚉
🚌 from Plzeň. 🛈 Náměstí Míru 51.
Tel 379 725 852. 🎭 Chod Folk
Festival: Aug. 🌐 **idomazlice.cz**

This town, situated on an old trading route, has a long, narrow town square (náměstí Míru), lined by gabled houses. Dominating the square is the leaning **tower** of the Gothic Church of the Nativity of the Virgin Mary (Děkanský kostel Narození Panny Marie). At 56 m (184 ft) tall, it offers a magnificent panorama from its top. Inside the church are Baroque frescoes.

The **Castle**, southwest of the square, was once a fortified Gothic building. All that remains is the cylindrical tower and some 18th-century buildings, now housing the **Chod Museum** (Muzeum Chodska), which traces the town's history. Domažlice was the base of the Chods, a Slav group who guarded the border region.

There is more on the Chods in the **Jindřich Jindřich Museum** outside the old town. Jindřich Jindřich was a composer and collector of Chod folk items. The display recreates a Chod cottage interior.

🏛 Chod Castle and Museum
Tel 379 776 009. **Open** Apr–Oct: daily; Nov–Mar: Mon–Fri. 📷

🏛 Jindřich Jindřich Museum
Náměstí svobody 67. **Tel** 379 722 974.
Closed for renovation; call ahead for details.

The altar in the Holy Trinity Chapel at Horšovský Týn Castle

A gabled house in the town square in Domažlice

❼ Horšovský Týn

Road map B2. 🗺 5,000. 🚌 from Prague or Plzeň. 🛈 5 Května 50.
Tel 379 415 151.

The bishops of Prague used to own this town, which has a square (náměstí Republiky) of Baroque houses with lovely Gothic doorways. In 1258, Bishop Jan III of Dražice built a fortified Gothic **Castle** here. All that remains is the west wing and the chapel in the south tower. This features beautiful cross-vaulting supported by slender columns, an early Gothic doorway and Renaissance wall paintings. In the 16th century, the castle was transformed into a Renaissance palace surrounded by a park. Inside is an interesting exhibition on the life of the nobility over the last 400 years.

🏛 Horšovský Týn Castle
Tel 379 423 111. **Open** Apr & Oct: Sat, Sun & public hols; May–Sep: Tue–Sun; 26–31 Dec: daily. 📷 📷 4 routes.

❽ Stříbro

Road map B2. 🗺 8,000. 🚌 🚉 from Prague, Plzeň. 🛈 374 627 247.

The name Stříbro means "silver", after the silver mines that existed here from as early as the 12th century. The town centre is partly flanked by 14th-century walls. Within a tower that

forms part of the walls on Plzeňská is a winery.

The late Gothic **Church of All Saints** (Všech svatých) has Baroque frescoes. The 1543 **town hall** (radnice) has a façade with *sgraffito* gables. The former **Minorite Monastery**, dissolved during the reforms of Joseph II, has an exhibition on the history of silver- and lead-mining.

🏛 Minorite Monastery Municipal Museum
Tel 374 622 214. **Open** 9am–4pm Tue–Fri, 9am–3pm Sat (Oct–May: closed Sat). 📷

Environs

About 6 km (4 miles) southeast of Stříbro, near the village of Kladruby, is **Kladruby Monastery and Church** *(see also pp178–9)*. The 12th-century Benedictine monastery was founded by Vladislav I, remodelled by Kilian Ignaz Dientzenhofer, and includes Baroque sculptures by Matthias Braun. The monastery church of the Assumption of the Virgin Mary (kostel Nanebevzetí Panny Marie) was the lifetime achievement of Giovanni Santini, beautifully combining Gothic and Baroque outside and in.

A figure from Stříbro winery

🏛 Kladruby Monastery
Tel 374 631 773. **Open** Jan–Mar & Nov, Dec: by appt; Apr & Oct: Sat & Sun; May–Sep: Tue–Sun. 📷 📷 2 routes. ♿

❾ Přimda Castle

Road map B2. 🚌 from Bor.
Tel 374 631 773.

By the motorway to the Czech–German border crossing in Rozvadov are the ruins of Přimda – the oldest stone castle in Bohemia. Built in Romanesque style in the 12th century, it was for four centuries one of the strongholds guarding the west of the kingdom. Now its most imposing part is its keep, whose lower section, with its 4-m (13-ft) thick wall, was once used as a prison.

⑩ Mariánské Lázně

Road map B2. 🏛 15,000. 🚆
🚌 from Prague. 🛈 Hlavní 47.
Tel 354 622 474. 🎿 Chopin
Festival: Aug. 🌐 **marianskelazne.cz**

Although the therapeutic powers of the local springs were recognized from the 16th century, it was only in the second half of the 19th century that Mariánské Lázně (formerly Marienbad) became a European spa resort. Its guests at that time included Chopin, Mark Twain, Goethe, Freud, Kafka and British King Edward VII.

Today, Mariánské Lázně has a much quieter ambience, very different from the cosmopolitan bustle of Karlovy Vary *(see pp176–7)*, and is open to all. Visitors have at their disposal about 40 cold mineral water springs that are strongly saturated with natural carbon dioxide. The mountain air remains refreshing, and there are plenty of walks here.

The town has some fine historic buildings spectacularly set on the wooded slopes. The most prominent is the Neo-Baroque spa **colonnade** (kolonáda) built in 1889 of cast iron. At one end of this is the **Cross spring** (Křížový pramen) in an 1818 Empire-style pavilion. Behind the colonnade is the octagonal Neo-Byzantine **Church of the Assumption of the Virgin Mary** (Nanebevzetí Panny Marie). The **Town Museum** (Městské muzeum), in the house once inhabited by Goethe, traces the spa's history. There is a small **Fryderyk Chopin Monument** in the building in which the composer stayed.

🏛 **Town Museum**
Goethovo Náměstí 11. **Tel** 354 622 740. **Open** Mar–Dec: 9:30am–5:30pm Tue–Sun.

🏛 **Fryderyk Chopin Monument**
Hlavní 47. **Tel** 354 595 267.
Open Apr–Oct: Tue, Thu & Sun. 🎭

Fresco on the colonnade in Mariánské Lázně

⑪ Lázně Kynžvart

Road map B2. 🏛 1,600. 🚆 🚌 from Prague, Plzeň, Cheb, Mariánské Lázně.
Tel 354 691 221. 🌐 **laznekynzvart.cz**

Nestling in dense woodland, the small town of Lázně Kynžvart (Königswart) competed with Mariánské Lázně in the 19th century in terms of fame.

It is now a children's spa. The town's best-known historic site is the **Palace** of Klemens von Metternich – the creator of the Holy Alliance and from 1821 the all-powerful Chancellor of Austria. This Neo-Classical residence, built in 1820–33 by Viennese architect Pietro Nobile, houses a large assortment of furniture, paintings, sculpture, porcelain and other objects from Metternich's own collection. The park is one of the most beautiful English-style gardens in Bohemia.

Perched on top of a wooded hill are the Gothic ruins of Kynžvart **Castle**, which up to the Thirty Years' War still served as a strategic defence structure. The **New Baths**, in the promenade of the spa centre, occupy a Neo-Gothic building built in 1863.

🏠 **Kynžvart Palace**
Tel 354 691 269. **Open** Feb, Mar, Nov & Dec: by appt; Apr & Oct: Sat, Sun & public hols; May–Sep: Tue–Sun. 🎭
🎭 🌐 **kynzvart.cz**

⑫ Cheb

Road map B2. 🏛 33,500. 🚆
🚌 from Prague, Karlovy Vary, Mariánské Lázně. 🛈 Jateční 2.
Tel 354 440 302. 🌐 **mestocheb.cz**

Only 10 km (6 miles) from the border with Germany, Cheb (Eger) is one of Bohemia's oldest towns. From the late 19th century on, there was resistance here to Czech nationalism, as well as anti-Semitic feeling. The town was incorporated into the Third Reich in 1938; after the war, most of its German population was forcibly removed.

At the centre is the funnel-shaped market square (náměstí krále Jiřího z Poděbrad), with colourful 17th-century houses. The Špalíček, at its lower, narrow end, consists of 11 medieval half-timbered German-Jewish merchant houses. Also on the square is the **Cheb Museum** (Chebské Muzeum) in the house where Albrecht von Wallenstein was murdered *(see p69)*.

The 13th-century **Church of St Nicholas** (sv. Mikuláše) was given its Baroque features by Balthazar Neumann, a Cheb native. The **Castle** is Cheb's oldest site, built after 1167. Its ruins include the Black Tower (Černá věž), and a beautiful Romanesque chapel.

🏛 **Cheb Museum**
Tel 739 322 499. **Open** Tue–Sun.
🌐 **muzeumcheb.cz**

🏠 **Cheb Castle**
Tel 602 169 298. **Open** Apr–Oct: Tue–Sun; Nov–Mar: Sat & Sun. 🎭

View of the Church of St Nicholas and the roofs of the old town in Cheb

⑬ Františkovy Lázně

Road map B2. 🗺 6,500. 🚆
🚌 from Prague, Cheb. 🛈 Kollárova
180/7, Národní 19. **Tel** 354 201 170.
w flinfo.cz

The spa town of Františkovy
Lázně (Franzensbad) was
established in 1793, by the
decree of Emperor Franz I.
The local spa waters and mud
baths became famous for their
effectiveness in the treatment
of heart, urinary tract, gynaecol-
ogical and rheumatic conditions.
The streets are in a compact grid
layout around the main street,
Národní, and the buildings are
Neo-Classical. The town has
successfully resisted any industrial development and remains
an oasis of greenery and calm.

The symbol of Františkovy
Lázně is the statue of František,
a naked boy with a fish. One
small highly polished part of
the statue attests to the popular
belief that stroking it assists
conception. Amid the gardens,
cafés and Neo-Classical
buildings is a rotunda over the
Františkův pramen, a pavilion
over the **Glauber springs**
(Glauberovy prameny), an
1882 **music pavilion**, and
the 1820 **Church of the Holy
Cross** (Povýšeni sv. Kříže).

Environs
Seeberg Castle, 5 km (3 miles)
northwest of the town, is a
former Romanesque fortress
with lavishly furnished
19th-century interiors.

🏰 **Seeberg Castle**
Tel 354 595 081.
Open Mar–Nov: daily. 📷

The rotunda of Františkův pramen

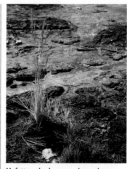

Mofettes, also known as bog volcanoes,
in the Soos Nature Reserve

⑭ Soos Nature Reserve

Road map B1. 6 km (4 miles) NE
of Cheb. **Tel** 354 542 033. **Open** Mar
& Nov: 10am–4:30pm; Apr:
9am–4:30pm; May & Jun: 9am–
5:30pm; Jul & Aug: 9am–
6:30pm; Sep: 9am–5:30pm;
Oct: 9am–4:30pm. 📷

The Soos nature
reserve is a
marshy area of
extraordinary
hot springs, quite
exceptional in this
part of Europe,
and testifying to
relatively recent
volcanic activity.
Established in 1964,
the reserve covers
an area of 2 sq km
(three-quarters of a square
mile). A special 1,200-m
(4,000-ft) wooden trail gives
visitors a chance to gaze at
the lunar landscape full of
bubbling gaseous springs
called mofettes (or bog
volcanoes), as well as some rare
salt-loving plants (halophytes).
The footpath leads along
the bottom of a dried lake
with a yellow and white
crust of crystallized salt.
The local **museum** has
an interesting exhibition
devoted to the region's
natural history, the
Soos hot springs and
the Earth's geological
history; also on display
are numerous stuffed
animals. Tickets to the
reserve include admission
to the museum.

⑮ Chlum sv. Máří

Road map B1. 10 km (6 miles) E
of Cheb (near Kynšperk nad Ohří).
🚌 from Sokolov. **Tel** 352 682 091.

Chlum sv. Máří is one of
the most famous sites of the
Marian cult in Bohemia.
The church that formerly stood
on this site was plundered in
the 15th century by the Hussite
army, and demolished in 1620
by the local Protestant nobility.
Built on its ruins in the late
17th century by Christoph
Dientzenhofer is the present
imposing triple-aisled church.
The Chapel of Mercy, which also
serves as the church vestibule,
features a late 13th-century
Gothic statue of the Virgin
Mary, famous for its miracles.
The church has exceptionally
lavish furnishings. All of the
vaulted ceilings, including
that of the dome, are
covered with
17th-century
paintings by
Johann Jakob
Steinfels. The aisle
around the church
(the ambulatory),
with its colonnade
opening onto the
courtyard, and the
corner chapels, are
by Giovanni Santini.

Statue of the Virgin Mary,
Chlum sv. Máří

⑯ Loket

Road map B1. 🗺 3,200. 🚌 from
Prague, Karlovy Vary. 🛈 T G Masaryka
12. **Tel** 352 684 123. 🎭 Loket
Summer Cultural Festival: late Jul.
w loket.cz

The tiny town of Loket (Elbogen)
lies in a rocky crook of the Ohře
River; its Czech and German
names both mean "elbow".
The town, which just like Český
Krumlov is washed around on
three sides by running waters,
is an exceptionally scenic
medieval settlement. Since
the early 19th century, it has
been renowned for its fine
porcelain. The picturesque
market square (náměstí T G
Masaryka) sports a plague
column and numerous
interesting Gothic houses. It
also features a graceful early

Houses and town hall in Loket market square

Baroque **town hall** (radnice) built in 1682–96. It was thoroughly restored in 1989.

The Gothic **castle** has well-preserved towers, gates, walls and keeps. In 1319, John of Luxembourg used it to imprison his wife Eliška of the Přemysl family, and their three-year-old son, Wenceslas, later Emperor Charles IV.

The town was frequently visited by Goethe who in 1823, in the house called **Bílý kůň** on the main square, now a hotel (see p352), met for the last time with the great love of his declining years, Ulrika von Levetzow. At that time, he was 74 years old; she was 19. She refused his marriage proposal and died unmarried at the age of 93.

🏠 **Loket Castle**
Tel 352 684 648. **Open** daily. ▨
Ⓦ hradloket.cz

Environs

In Bečov nad Teplou, 10 km (6 miles) southeast of Loket, is a **Castle** and **Palace** complex, a unique example of combining a medieval fortress with a Baroque residence. This majestic structure stands perched on a high rock above the Tepla river valley. Its oldest, Gothic section, dating from the first half of the 14th century, has never been modified and remains in its original state.

At the foot of the medieval castle, its successive owners have made their own mark on the castle, building a Renaissance residence in the 16th century, and an octagonal, domed Baroque palace with a tower two centuries later. The state rooms and the large library have survived particularly well.

Displayed in the palace chapel is one of the most precious ecclesiastical objects in Europe – the Romanesque reliquary of St Maurus, made in the Benedictine monastery in Florennes, in present-day Belgium. It was brought to Bohemia in the 19th century, by the then owner of Bečov – Alfred de Beaufort. Before the end of World War II, the Beauforts, who collaborated with the Germans, left their home in a hurry, burying the reliquary, which is encrusted with gold, silver and precious stones, under the chapel floor. Following long years of searching, it was found in 1985.

🏠 **Bečov Castle and Palace**
Tel 353 999 394. **Open** Jan, Feb & Dec: by appt; Apr & Oct: Sat, Sun; May–Sep: Tue–Sun. ▨ 🔲 2 routes.
Ⓦ zamek-becov.cz

⓱ Karlovy Vary

See pp176–7.

The castle in Bečov nad Teplou

⓲ Manětín

Road map B2. 🔼 1,300. 🚌 from Prague, Plzeň. **Tel** 373 392 161.

The earliest records of Manětín date from 1169, when King Vladislav II donated it to the Knights of St John of Prague. It now has a large collection of Baroque sculpture, resembling a vast open-air gallery.

Manětín Palace occupies one entire side of the long market square. Built after 1712 to a design by Giovanni Santini, it features an interesting staircase decorated with allegories of the four elements. The interiors and surroundings have been decorated with 18th-century sculptures produced by local artists Josef Herscher and Štěpán Boroviec. Their figures of the saints and apostles stand on the terrace before the palace's north façade, by the main routes towards Plzeň, Nečtin and Rabštejn and on many further sites around the town. Among the sculptures are an image of the Holy Trinity, and figures of St John Nepomuk, St Florentius, St Anne, St Joseph, St Sebastian, St Donatus, and the Archangel Michael.

Works by Herscher and Boroviec can also be found in the **Church of St John the Baptist**, linked with the palace by a covered corridor, and in the Baroque **Church of St Barbara**. There are also fine paintings by Petr Brandl – the *Baptism of Christ* in the first, and the *Death of St Isidore* and the *Killing of St Wenceslas* in the second church.

🏠 **Manětín Palace**
Tel 373 392 283. **Open** May–Sep: 10am–4pm Tue–Sun; Apr & Oct: 10am–4pm Sat & Sun. ▨ 🔲
Ⓦ zamek-manetin.cz

⑰ Karlovy Vary

World-famous for its mineral springs, the town of Karlovy Vary (Karlsbad) was founded by Charles IV in the mid-14th century. Legend has it that he discovered it when one of his dogs fell into a hot spring (*vary* means "hot spring") when out hunting. Since the 18th century, the rich and famous have flocked here to take the waters. The town is also known for its china – the first porcelain factory opened in the early 19th century – and for Moser glassware.

Wooden Market Colonnade and castle tower

Exploring the town
The spa district of Karlovy Vary starts in T G Masaryka Street, which runs into Zahradní; the spas continue south along the banks of the Teplá river, in the valley flanked on both sides by wooded slopes. The two streets that follow the river, lined with pleasant 19th- and 20th-century houses, are linked by numerous road- and foot-bridges. All the mineral springs are also found along the river, as well as the historic colonnades and the majority of interesting architectural sights.

🏛 Imperial Baths
Mariánskolázeňská 2.
The imposing Imperial Baths or Kaiserbad (Lázně I), looking more like a theatre than a medical establishment, was once the most opulent building in Karlovy Vary. Built in 1892–5, they feature a magnificent Neo-Renaissance façade and Art Nouveau decorations, inside and out.

🏛 Karlovy Vary Museum
Nová Louka 23. **Tel** 353 226 252.
Open 9am–noon & 1–5pm Wed–Sun. 📷
The museum, established in 1853, has collections relating to the region's history and its natural environment; also on display are glass and porcelain items and handicrafts. Besides permanent displays, there are also topical exhibitions organized throughout the year.

🎭 Karlovy Vary Theatre
Divadelní náměstí 21.
Tel 353 225 621.
The Karlovy Vary Theatre (Městské divadlo), built in 1884–6, is the work of Viennese architects Ferdinand Fellner and Hermann Helmer, who designed many theatre buildings all over Europe. It is worth stepping inside to see the magnificent interior decor, which includes paintings by Gustav Klimt, his brother Ernst, and Franz Matsche. A collective work of all three artists is the curtain, on which they painted their joint self-portrait. The theatre hosts a varied cultural program with musical events and theatrical productions.

⛪ Church of St Mary Magdalene
Kostelní náměstí. **Tel** 353 223 668.
Dating from 1732, and among the best work of Kilian Ignaz Dientzenhofer, this church (sv. Máří Magdalény) is one of the finest examples of Baroque architecture in Bohemia.

Detail above Karlovy Vary Theatre entrance

The single-aisled church with an oval floor plan has an impressively spacious interior with fine decor. The high altar features an image of Mary Magdalene from 1752. It is flanked by Jakob Eberle's 1759 sculptures of St Augustine, St Jerome, St Peter and St Paul. It is also worth taking a closer look at the lavishly decorated side altars, the dome and the magnificent galleries high up. The wavy façade with two towers features a splendid semi-circular stairway.

🏛 Market Colonnade
Tržiště.
This lovely white wooden colonnade, Tržni kolonáda, designed in Swiss style by Ferdinand Fellner and Hermann Helmer, was built in 1883–4 on the site of a former town hall, which was demolished in 1879. It contains two springs. In 1991–2, it underwent a thorough reconstruction, although it has kept its original appearance.

Bohemia's Spa Resorts

Clustered in the western part of the country, spa resorts (lázně) began to emerge and flourish in the 18th century. Crowds of patients and prominent figures of the day visited spas, initially to take medicinal baths, and later to drink spring waters in truly exclusive company and opulent surroundings. During the Communist era, spa cures were open to all who needed them, and spa treatments remain popular in the Czech Republic today. The spa towns also still attract numerous German, Austrian and Russian visitors, and over the past decades, many have been restored to their former glory.

Karlovy Vary in 1891

Columns of the Mill Colonnade

🏛 Mill Colonnade
Mlýnské nabřeží.
Built in 1871–81 by Josef Zítek, creator of the National Theatre in Prague *(see pp96–7)*, the Mill Colonnade (Mlýnská kolonáda) is the largest of the resort's colonnades, and one of its most opulent. The Neo-Renaissance gallery, 132 m (430 ft) long and 13 m (43 ft) wide, has a coffered ceiling resting on 124 columns with Corinthian capitals. Inside are five springs, with a water temperature exceeding 50°C (120°F). Statues at each end represent the twelve months of the year.

🏛 Park Colonnade
Dvořákovy sady.
On the west bank of the Teplá, right at the centre of town, stands Sadová Kolonáda – a beautiful painted wrought-iron structure made of columns decorated with sculptures, terminating in two pavilions.

The colonnade was designed by Ferdinand Fellner and Hermann Helmer in 1880–81. It stands in the Dvořákovy sady gardens.

🏛 Church of St Peter and St Paul
Krále Jiřího. **Open** 10am–5pm daily.
This church (sv. Petr a Pavel) with its five gilded domes,

Gilded domes of the Church of St Peter and St Paul

built in 1893–7 by G Wiedermann, is among the world's largest Russian Orthodox churches. It was built for the Russian aristocracy, who in the 19th century flocked to Karlovy Vary in great numbers.

🌿 Diana Viewpoint
Funicular. **Open** 9am–5pm daily (to 6pm Apr, May & Oct; to 7pm Jun–Sep).

Behind the town's top hotel, the Grand Hotel Pupp *(see p351)*, at the southern end of Stará Louka, is the lower station of the funicular, which runs to the top of the Hill of Friendship. Built in 1912, the funicular rises 167 m (550 ft), covering a distance of 435 m (1,425 ft). At the top is the Diana viewpoint, providing a great view over the resort.

Karlovy Vary Town Centre

① Imperial Baths
② Karlovy Vary Museum
③ Karlovy Vary Theatre
④ Church of St Mary Magdalene
⑤ Market Colonnade
⑥ Mill Colonnade
⑦ Park Colonnade
⑧ Church of St Peter and St Paul
⑨ Diana Viewpoint

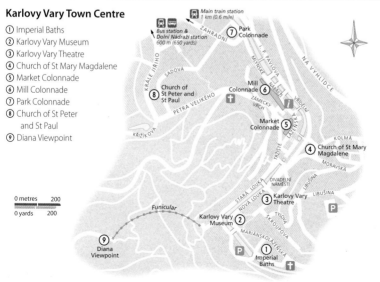

0 metres 200
0 yards 200

For keys to symbols *see back flap*

West Bohemian Monasteries

In the Middle Ages, West Bohemia experienced the emergence of numerous centres of monastic life. The most prominent were the abbeys: the Benedictine in Kladruby *(see p170)*, the Cistercian in Plasy and the Premonstratensian in Teplá. In the Baroque era, the medieval buildings were converted by the leading architects of the day into vast church and monastery complexes, with opulent interior decor and furnishings.

The Cistercian Monastery in Plasy, about 20 km (12 miles) north of Plzeň, was founded in 1144–5, by Vladislav II. Giovanni Santini and the French-born architect Jean-Baptiste Mathey gave it its present Baroque appearance.

The lantern above the cupola of Kladruby Church, which gives it its distinctive silhouette, was designed by Giovanni Santini in 1716–18. Topped with a golden crown, it filters a beautiful light into the building.

Inside Kladruby Church, the nave is 85 m (280 ft) long, the longest in Bohemia. The interior was designed by Santini, including the highly decorative vaulting. The tomb of the monastery's founder, Vladislav I, is at the front of the church, to the left.

The lavishly decorated façade of the church dates from 1726, which is confirmed by the date in the porch of the main entrance. The statue of the Madonna with a halo, seen on top of the façade in a niche above the tall window, dates from 1716.

The Premonstratensian Monastery, Teplá, 15 km (9 miles) east of Mariánské Lázně, was founded in 1193. The spectacular Neo-Baroque Monastery library was added in the 1900s and houses about 100,000 volumes.

The Teplá Monastery Church of the Annunciation of the Virgin Mary is a beautiful Romanesque building, part of the original 12th-century monastery complex. Much of the rest of the complex was built in Baroque style in 1689–1721 by K I Dientzenhofer.

The mosaic seen above the beautiful portal of the Romanesque-Gothic Church of the Annunciation, in Teplá, depicts the Virgin Mary and Child.

Kladruby Monastery

This Benedictine monastery, founded in 1114 by Vladislav I, became a major centre of Přemyslid power. Early in the 18th century, St Mary's, the original church, was remodelled by Giovanni Santini in Baroque style with some obvious Gothic elements. It is considered to be the greatest achievement of this brilliant Czech-born architect. In 1785, the monastery was closed and rebuilt as a chateau to designs by K I Dientzenhofer (see p67).

The new building was designed by K I Dientzenhofer as a chateau.

Mariánsky Týnec has belonged to the Cistercians from nearby Plasy Monastery since 1230. Giovanni Santini was responsible for numerous Baroque additions in the first half of the 18th century.

NORTH BOHEMIA

One of the most prosperous and industrial parts of the country for many centuries, divided in two by the Labe (Elbe), North Bohemia is a diverse and rewarding region to explore. The attractive main city of Liberec offers a good taste of Czech culture, while slightly off the beaten track are a surprising number of castles and atmospheric old towns.

The wealth of North Bohemia (Severní Čechy) was based principally on the region's natural resources. Iron ore and coal were mined here from the Middle Ages. During the past few centuries, the production of fine porcelain has played a significant role in its economy. Unfortunately, the intensive exploitation of raw materials, especially strip-mining for lignite (brown coal), and industrial overdevelopment have ravaged the region's landscape. Since 1989, much has been done to reduce pollution and limit the ecological damage, but even now the dominant features of much of North Bohemia are factory chimneys and areas of lunar landscape left by mining works.

While the region has shared much of its history and culture with Bohemia, a considerable section of its population has been German. Many surviving relics of Gothic architecture bear witness to the mingling of Czech and Saxon cultures. In 1938, a large part of North Bohemia, dominated by Germans, was incorporated into the Third Reich, who set up Terezín as a concentration camp. The forcible expulsion of all local Germans after World War II left many towns and villages deserted. These have since been resettled, but some border areas remain underpopulated. Roma (Gypsies) live in many areas, and tension exists between them and the local Czechs.

Tucked away in the region are some remarkably well-preserved or lovingly restored castles, towns and monasteries. The weird geological formations of České Švýcarsko ("Czech Switzerland") attract many visitors interested in outdoor activities.

River Elbe cutting through the beautiful natural surroundings of České Švýcarsko

◄ The clock and ornate details on the façade of the Liberec Town Hall

Exploring North Bohemia

The jewels of North Bohemian architecture – Litoměřice, Louny, Žatec, Kadaň and Úštěk – must be included in the itinerary of any visitor exploring this part of the country. Their amazingly well-preserved old towns are truly impressive, although to restore individual buildings to their former glory still requires a great deal of work and money. The region's main city, Liberec, is a thriving centre, with some excellent art collections. The extraordinary rock formations are the main feature of České Švýcarsko, where the Labe (Elbe) has cut a narrow gorge on its way through the Czech Republic to Germany.

Palace in Teplice

Ústí nad Labem

Statue of Jan Hus in Louny town square

0 kilometres   15

0 miles   15

For hotels and restaurants see p352 and pp371–2

Getting Around

The easiest way of getting to North Bohemia from Prague is along D8 motorway (the international E55 route), which links the Czech capital with Dresden. The wide expressway R10 goes to Turnov, and then through R35 to Liberec. The main transport route cutting across the entire region, from Liberec all the way to Chomutov, is the popular and often congested road 13. Buses and trains provide reasonable coverage of North Bohemia but are less frequent during weekends and holiday periods.

Interior staircase, Liberec Town Hall

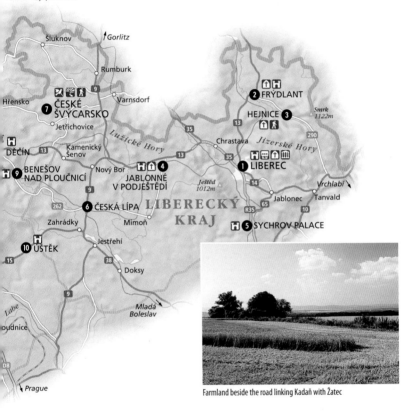

Farmland beside the road linking Kadaň with Žatec

Key

═══ Motorway

═══ Dual carriageway

─── Main road

═══ Minor road

╍╍╍ Motorway under construction

──── Main railway

─── Minor railway

▬▬▬ International border

▬▬▬ Regional border

△ Summit

Sights at a Glance

For keys to symbols *see back flap*

❶ Liberec

As early as the 16th century, Liberec (Reichenberg) was a major weaving centre. With the 19th-century industrial revolution, large textile factories and metalwork plants brought true prosperity to the city. Between the two World Wars, Liberec was the main political centre of the Czech Germans; under German occupation, it was made the capital of Sudetenland. After the war, it regained its position as North Bohemia's main city, while also becoming a tourist centre.

Lavishly decorated façade of F X Šaldy Theatre

Exploring the city

Liberec is rich in historic buildings, similar to many Czech towns, but also has equally interesting, modern buildings, which can be seen between the main square and Sokolovské náměstí. Sights outside this area include the Oblastní Gallery, and a little further east from the centre, the Severočeské Museum.

🔲 Náměstí Dr E Beneše

Liberec's main square, and the entire town, are dominated by the Neo-Renaissance town hall (see pp186–7). In front of the town hall is a fountain by Franz Metzner dating from 1927. By the steps of the town hall is a modest monument to those who died fighting in 1968 after the Warsaw Pact invasion.

The houses around the square are not as uniformly well preserved as in many other old towns, and mostly date from the 19th and 20th centuries, but a few fine buildings survive. The square is named after Edvard Beneš, the president of Czechoslovakia during World War II.

🔲 Town Hall (Radnice)

See pp186–7.

🎭 F X Šaldy Theatre

Náměstí Dr E Beneše 22. **Tel** 485 101 523. **Open** 10am–6pm (until 7pm on performance days) Mon–Fri.

At the rear of the town hall is the F X Šaldy Theatre (Divadlo F X Šaldy), designed in 1883 by the Viennese architects Ferdinand Fellner and Hermann Helmer. Its ornate façade has an allegory of Art holding a torch, and a figure of Apollo surrounded by dolphins. Inside, take a look at the curtain painted by Gustav Klimt.

Façade of an early 19th-century building in Sokolovské náměstí

🔲 Sokolovské Náměstí

This square includes some houses with highly ornate façades, but its main sight is the Church of St Anthony (sv. Antonína). This triple-aisled edifice has a 70-m (230-ft) tall tower. Built in 1579–87 and remodelled in the 19th century in Neo-Gothic style, it is the town's oldest brick building. Its interior is dominated by a 10-m (33-ft) high altarpiece with figures of the patron saints of Bohemia.

🔲 Wallenstein Houses

Větrná.

Just off Sokolovské náměstí, in narrow Větrná street, are some of the oldest and most interesting buildings in Liberec: the Wallenstein Houses (Valdštejnské domky). The three buildings of timber-frame construction and with street-facing gables date from 1678–81. They were once inhabited by cloth-makers, and one was an inn.

One of the three half-timbered Wallenstein Houses

⬆ Church of the Holy Cross

Malé Náměstí. **Tel** 485 108 506.

This Baroque church (sv. Kříže) with a cross-shape floorplan was built by Johann Josef Kunz in 1753–61 on the site of an older church that stood on a former plague cemetery. Its richly fitted interior includes a statue of the Virgin Mary holding the dead body of Christ, which dates from 1506. The beautiful Plague Column (1719) standing behind the church came from the workshop of Matthias Braun.

Liberec Castle – one of the town's early brick buildings

VISITORS' CHECKLIST

Practical Information
Road map D1.
🗺 105,000.
ℹ Náměstí Dr E Beneše 23.
Tel 485 101 709.
W visitliberec.eu

Transport
🚉 Nákladní 495.
🚌 Vaňurova 885.

🏛 Liberec Castle
U tiskárny. **Closed** to visitors.
The original Renaissance palace dating from 1583–7 was remodelled several times. It has a Renaissance chapel with a lovely coffered ceiling, and beautifully carved wooden oratory supported by five columns. There are plans to turn the castle into a showcase for local crystalware.

🖼 Regional Gallery
Masarykova 723/14. **Tel** 485 106 325. **Open** 10am–6pm Tue–Sun.
♿ W ogl.cz
One of the finest galleries in the Czech Republic, since early 2014 this has been housed in the municipal spa building of Liberec. Much of the art collection was donated to the town in 1904 by the Liebig family; it now includes works by 16th–18th century Dutch and Flemish artists, 19th-century French landscapists and

many superb modern paintings, drawings and sculptures by Czech artists. There is also a collection of 19th-century German and Austrian painting.

🏛 North Bohemian Museum
Masarykova 11. **Tel** 485 246 111.
Open 9am–5pm Tue–Sun. ♿
W muzeumlb.cz
This eclectic museum is housed in a Neo-Renaissance

Dvorek v Benátkách by August Pettenkofen, Regional Gallery

building erected in 1897–8. The large, varied collection includes glass, ceramics, porcelain, textiles, furniture, clocks and jewellery, much of it locally produced. There are also photography, archaeology and history exhibitions. Particularly valuable is its extraordinary collection of mechanical music instruments.

Environs
A further walk eastwards along the tree-lined Masarykova leads to the **Botanical Gardens** and the **Zoo**, the oldest (1904) in Bohemia. To the southwest of the centre is one of Liberec's landmarks, **Ještěd** peak. On the 1012-m (3,320-ft) summit, reached by cable car, is a 1960s tower, part of a hotel, which offers superb views.

Liberec Town Centre

① Náměstí Dr E Beneše
② Town Hall
③ F X Šaldy Theatre
④ Sokolovské Náměstí
⑤ Wallenstein Houses
⑥ Church of the Holy Cross
⑦ Liberec Castle
⑧ Regional Gallery

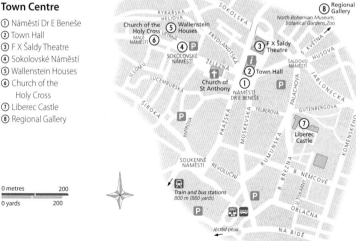

0 metres 200
0 yards 200

Liberec Town Hall

A majestic edifice, the town hall (radnice) was built in the German Neo-Renaissance style in 1888–93 to a design by Viennese architect Franz Neumann. The size and ornamentation were intended to highlight the status and wealth of the town, which in the late 19th century was one of the main industrial centres of the Austro-Hungarian Empire. The councillors and townsfolk were undoubtedly flattered by the fact that the silhouette of the new building was strongly reminiscent of Vienna's town hall.

★ Main Façade
The symmetrical façade sports a 65-m (210-ft) tower; in 2005, a knight with a banner was placed at the top.

Staircase Ceiling
The painting by A Groll on the ceiling of the main staircase depicts a female figure symbolizing Liberec and the god of trade, Mercury.

★ Staircase
The main staircase to the first-floor state rooms emphasized the town's wealth with its use of marble and its sheer size.

Entrance Hall
Marble stairs, illuminated by stained-glass windows donated by the guild of bakers, lead from the hall to the first-floor rooms.

Above the main entrance is the date of completion, and a relief by Theodore Friedel.

Stained-Glass Window in the Debating Chamber
The Debating Chamber, used for official functions and as a concert hall, is lavishly decorated with wood. Its six stained-glass windows were the pride of Liberec's glass industry. They depict allegories of Art, Science, Trade, Craft and Administration.

VISITORS' CHECKLIST

Practical Information
Náměstí Dr E Beneše 1.
Tel 485 101 709.
Open Jun–Sep: 9am–3pm Mon–Fri, 9–11am Sat; Oct–May: 9am–3pm Thu (visits booked via Liberec info centre – see p185).
 by appt.
 liberec.cz
w visitliberec.eu

Transport
San Marco.

Drawing Room
A large stained-glass window in the Drawing Room shows Liberec's old town hall, demolished in 1893.

Mayoral Offices
The second-floor drawing room is a part of the office of the town's mayor; it is used to hold official meetings.

Side Entrance
Two ornate columns (right) flank the entrance on the side of the building.

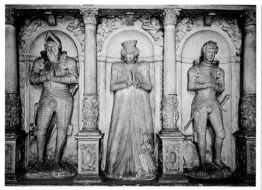

Tomb of Frederick I, his wife and son, Church of the Holy Cross, Frýdlant

❷ Frýdlant

Road map D1. 🏘 7,500. 🚉
🚌 from Liberec. 🛈 Náměstí T G
Masaryka 37. **Tel** 482 464 013.

The small town of Frýdlant
(Friedland) is dominated by
its vast, sprawling castle.
Frýdlant Castle reputedly
inspired Franz Kafka as the
setting for his famous novel
The Castle. An earlier Gothic
fortress was extended in the
16th century by an Italian
architect, Marco Spazzio di
Lancio, commissioned by
the von Redern family who
owned the castle from 1558.
Following the Battle of the
White Mountain in 1620, this
opulent residence became
the property of the powerful
Albrecht von Wallenstein, who
assumed the title of Duke of
Frýdlant. The Swedes, who
occupied the castle at the
end of the Thirty Years' War,
strengthened its defence walls
and built fortified barbicans.

The castle was opened to
the public as early as 1801.
Now it is possible to view
its magnificently restored
interiors, including the Knights'
Hall, Portraits Hall and Trophies
Room. Inside are many
valuable pieces of furniture,
tapestries, porcelain, ceramics,
chandeliers, suits of armour
and uniforms. The collection
of paintings is outstanding,
with works by Karel Škréta,
Václav Vavřinec Reiner and
others. The castle museum
has an exhibition on the
Thirty Years' War.

The beautiful **Church of the
Holy Cross** (sv. Kříž), built by
Italian architects in the mid-16th
century, has a lavishly decorated
interior and a monumental
mausoleum (1610) to the von
Redern family.

🏛 **Frýdlant Castle**
Tel 482 312 130. **Open** Apr–Oct:
9:30am–4:30pm Tue–Sun (to 3:30pm
Apr & Oct). 🎫 🎫 2 routes.
🌐 zamek–frydlant.cz

❸ Hejnice

Road map D1. 7 km (4 miles) SE of
Frýdlant. 🏘 2,800. 🚌 from Liberec.
🛈 Klášterní 87. **Tel** 482 322 276.

Hejnice is a small, pleasant town
with a spa. Visitors come mainly
for its **Church of the Visitation
of the Blessed Virgin Mary**
(Navštívení Panny Marie), one
of the Czech Republic's major
pilgrimage centres. On this site,
according to tradition, the Virgin
Mary has bestowed miraculous
graces and favours since the

13th century. The earlier stone
Gothic church was replaced
by a magnificent Baroque one
in 1729, able to accommodate
7,000 worshippers.

The main altarpiece has a
14th-century Gothic Madonna.
During the Reformation, when
the district was ruled by the
Protestant Redern family,
the church was closed, and the
statue transferred to Frýdlant
Castle. When the statue survived
a fire in the castle in 1615,
this was taken as a sign that
it should be returned, and it
was soon afterwards.

🏛 **Church of the Visitation
of the Blessed Virgin Mary**
Tel 482 360 211. **Open** daily. 🕐 4pm
Tue–Sun, 9am Sun. 🌐 mcdo.cz

Environs
Hejnice is the best starting
point for forays into **Jizerské
mountains**, an extension of
the Krkonoše massif. A well-
signposted hiking route (about
30 km/18 miles long) leads
from Hejnice to the top of Smrk
(1,122 m/ 3,680 ft), with a view
over the peat moor Na Čihadle.

❹ Jablonné v Podještědí

Road map D1. 🏘 3,800. 🚉
🚌 from Liberec. 🛈 Náměstí
Míru 23. **Tel** 487 829 960.

One of the oldest towns in
Bohemia, Jablonné (Gabel)
was founded in 1240. Activity
centres around the main square
(náměstí Míru), where cafés
overlook the **Basilica of
St Lawrence and St Zdislava**

View of the pilgrimage church in Hejnice

(sv. Vavřince a Zdislavy). This Baroque edifice with its lofty dome was built in 1699. In the Baroque crypt below the high altar is the tomb of St Zdislava, who lived in the 13th century, the wife of the local lord of Lemberk (see below). In 1995, she was canonized. The façade includes Baroque statues of saints, including St Zdislava and St Lawrence.

🏛 **Basilica of St Lawrence and St Zdislava**
Tel 487 762 105. **Open** May–Sep: Tue–Sun; Apr & Oct: Sat & Sun.
W zdislava.cz

Environs
About 2 km (1 mile) northeast of the village is **Lemberk Castle**, St Zdislava's home, which has interesting displays on her life.

The Basilica of St Lawrence and St Zdislava in Jablonné v Podještědí

❺ Sychrov Palace

Road map D1. 🚌 from Liberec.
Tel 482 416 011. **Open** Jan–Mar: 10am–2pm daily; Apr, Sep & Oct: 9am–3:30pm daily; May–Aug: 9am–4:30pm daily; Nov & Dec: 10am–2pm daily. 🐾 🎫
W zamek-sychrov.cz

The palace stands in the romantic valley of the Mohelka river. An earlier Baroque building was remodelled in the 19th century in Neo-Classical, and later in Neo-Gothic style. From 1820 to 1945, the palace belonged to the aristocratic French Rohan family, who assembled a large collection of art here. Now the Rohan Gallery has a superb collection of French portrait paintings, unrivalled outside France. Antonín Dvořák came several times to Sychrov to rest between 1877 and 1880. The palace is surrounded by a large English-style garden with many exotic trees. Here, concerts are held over the summer months.

❻ Česká Lípa

Road map C1. 🚶 37,500. 🚉 from Děčín, Liberec. 🚌 from Prague. 🛈 Náměstí T G Masaryka 2. **Tel** 487 881 105. **W** mucl.cz

In the 15th century, Česká Lípa (Böhmisch Leipa) was one of the major centres of the Hussite movement. Later, in the 19th century, it gained a reputation as a dynamic centre of the textile industry, producing popular printed fabrics. Today, Česká Lípa is an industrial town with some interesting architectural sights.

The main square is lined with attractive houses. All that remains of the former Renaissance castle is the lovely decorated 1583 **Red House** (Červený dům), with a magnificent loggia running along its first floor. The **Church of the Holy Cross** (sv. Kříž) was founded in 1381 and bears evidence of later remodelling. The **Regional Museum** has a small collection of local historic materials. It is housed in the former Augustinian monastery, founded in 1627 by Albrecht von Wallenstein.

🏛 **Regional Museum**
Tel 487 824 145. **Open** Mar, Apr & Oct–Dec: Wed–Sun; May–Sep: Tue–Sun. 🐾 **W** muzeumcl.cz

❼ České Švýcarsko

See pp190–91.

Baroque castle in Děčín, built in the 13th century

❽ Děčín

Road map C1. 🚶 50,600. 🚉 🚌 from Prague. 🛈 Karla Čapka 1441/3. **Tel** 412 532 227.
W mmdecin.cz

Lying on the Labe (Elbe), Děčín (Tetschen) is made up of the more industrial Podmokly on the left bank, and the older Děčín on the right. In Děčín, the **Church of the Holy Cross** (sv. Kříž) is an ornate Baroque building from the late 17th century. The town square has a 1906 Art Nouveau fountain. The **castle** is a royal fortress built in the 13th century and adapted in the 17th and 18th centuries. Entrance is via Dlouhá jízda, a steep, narrow alley built in the 1670s. The castle has a superb rose garden.

🏛 **Děčín Castle**
Tel 412 518 905. **Open** daily. 🐾 🎫 3 routes. **W** zamekdecin.cz

Houses in the main square in Česká Lípa

❼ České Švýcarsko

An extraordinary area of natural beauty, České Švýcarsko is a landscape of forests and fantastically shaped sandstone rocks, criss-crossed by gorges and ravines. This region was attracting tourists as early as the 19th century, when the Romantic poets first dubbed it the "Czech Switzerland" (it is also referred to as "Bohemian Switzerland"). The National Park established over this area, in 2000, continues to attract many visitors, mainly from Germany.

Pravčická brána
This is the largest natural rock bridge in Central Europe, at 26 m (85 ft) long, 7–8 m (25 ft) wide, and rising to a height of 16 m (52 ft).

Falcon's Nest
This small castle (1881), by the Pravčická brána, belonged to the Clary-Aldringen family. It now houses a restaurant and the National Park Museum.

From Mezní Louka, a red hiking trail leads to the stone bridge of Pravčická brána, 6.5 km (4 miles) away. From here, you can continue on the same trail to Hřensko, a further 2.5 km (2 miles).

Labe (Elbe)
62
Hřensko
↓
Děčín

Mezni Louka

Mezná

Kamenice

Kamenická Stráň

0 km   1
0 miles 1

Tichá Souteska
Known as the "quiet gorge", this section of Kamenice Gorge stretches for 960 m (3,150 ft).

Kamenice Gorge
This narrow gorge runs between vertical walls of rocks, 50–150 m (165–500 ft) high. Boat trips go up- or downstream. The footpath along its banks was built in the 19th century by Italian workers.

For hotels and restaurants see p352 and pp371–2

Wildlife in the National Park
České Švýcarsko used to be rich in animal species. Although the animal diversity is not as great as it once was, the Park remains a haven for wildlife, including European beaver, river otter, lynx, which settled here in the 1930s, and the Alpine chamois, introduced in 1907.

VISITORS' CHECKLIST

Practical Information
Road map C1.
Hřensko 82. **Tel** 412 554 286.
National Park Museum:
Falcon's Nest.
Open Apr–Oct: 10am–6pm daily;
Nov–Mar: 10am–4pm Fri–Sun.
W pbrana.cz

Transport
from Děčín.

Sokolí vrch
486 m
(1594 ft)

Doubice

Tourist Trails
The entire area of the Park has a network of clearly signposted hiking and cycling trails.

Ostroh
484 m
(1588 ft)

štejn

á Lípa   **Jetřichovice**

Rynartice

Šaunštejn
The high rock platform, which once was the site of the small Šaunštejn Castle, known also as Robbers' castle (Loupežnický hradek), can now be reached only by a series of vertical stepladders.

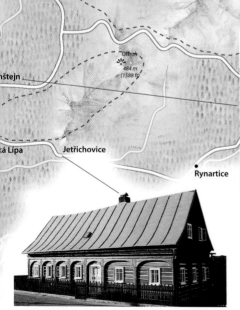

Jetřichovice
This scenic village, whose timber houses now provide beds for the many walkers, makes a good base for forays into the rocky Jetřichovické range.

Key

= Road

--- Hiking trail

≈ River

For keys to symbols *see back flap*

❾ Benešov nad Ploučnicí

Road map C1. 🅰 4,000. 🚉
🚌 from Děčín. 🛈 Náměstí Míru 1.
Tel 412 589 811.

Two 16th-century castles are the pride of Benešov, an attractive town centred on its main square. The 15th-century **Church of the Nativity of the Virgin Mary** (Narození Panny Marie) has a 16th-century sandstone pulpit. There is also a fine Renaissance town hall. The castles are in the Saxon Renaissance style, rare in Bohemia. Both adjoin the 15th-century city walls. The **Upper Castle**, built in the 16th century, is the oldest mansion in the town and holds several events in summers The **Lower Castle** has some interesting interiors.

🏰 **Benešov Castles**
Tel 412 586 575. **Open** Apr & Oct: Wed–Sun; May–Sep: Tue–Sun. 🖼
w zamek-benesov.cz

❿ Úštěk

Road map C1. 🅰 2,700. 🚉 🚌 from Litoměřice. 🛈 Mírové náměstí 47. **Tel** 416 795 368. **w** mesto-ustek.cz

The picturesque buildings of Úštěk have provided locations for numerous films. This sleepy

town lies on a narrow rocky ridge, its former Gothic castle in ruins, but retaining a pleasant inner courtyard. The mightiest part of the town's fortifications is Pikartská věž, with 2-m (6-ft) thick walls, now housing the local **art gallery**.

The narrow town square features several Gothic houses with street-facing gables. The **Church of St Peter and St Paul** (sv. Petr a Pavel) has an altarpiece by Karel Škréta. Unique to the town are the birds' houses (ptačí domky), wooden homes perched on a rocky ledge. They were inhabited by Jewish families and then in the 19th century by Italians who worked on the construction of the railway.

🏛 **Gallery U Brány**
Tel 416 731 643. **Open** daily.

Gable of the town hall in Benešov

⓫ Litoměřice

Road map C1. 🅰 24,400. 🚉
🚌 from Prague. 🛈 Mírové náměstí 16/8a. **Tel** 416 916 440.
w litomerice-info.cz

Beautiful Litoměřice was founded in the 13th century. The zenith of its glory was in the mid-15th century, when it was among the largest towns in Bohemia. Following the Thirty Years' War, in 1655, it became the seat of a new diocese, the main centre for reintroducing Catholicism to North Bohemia.

The Renaissance **town hall** (radnice) in the main square (Mírové náměstí) has Gothic arcades. Nearby is the 1537 **House at the Chalice** (Dům u Kalicha), with a goblet-shaped roof finial – symbol of the Hussites. In several other old buildings on the square is the superb collection of religious paintings in the **Diocesan Museum and**

Gallery (Galerie & Muzeum litoměřické diecéze). Near the square, in the **North Bohemian Art Gallery** (Severočeská galerie výtvarného umění) are Bohemian Gothic altar paintings by the Master of Litoměřice.

During the late 17th and early 18th centuries, the architect Ottavio Broggio changed many of the town's buildings. His father Giulio remodelled **St Stephen's Cathedral** (sv. Štěpána), a vast basilica just west of the town centre.

🏛 **Regional Museum**
Dlouhá 173. **Tel** 416 731 339.
Open Tue–Sun. 🖼

🏛 **Diocesan Museum & Gallery**
Mírové náměstí 16/24. **Tel** 416 732 382. **Open** Tue–Sun.

🏛 **North Bohemian Art Gallery**
Michalská 7. **Tel** 416 732 382.
Open Tue–Sun. 🖼 **w** galerie-ltm.cz

Detail of a wall-painting in the House at the Chalice, Litoměřice

⓬ Terezín

Road map C1. 🅰 3,100. 🚌 from Prague, Litoměřice. 🛈 Náměstí ČSA 179. **Tel** 416 782 227. **w** terezin.cz

In 1780, Joseph II began the construction of a fortified garrison to stop the potential advance of an enemy coming from the direction of Dresden. The fortress, called Terezín (Theresienstadt) in honour of the Emperor's mother, Maria Theresa, took 11 years to build. The resulting structure consists of the octagonal **Main Fortress** (Hlavní pevnost) and the rectangular **Small Fortress** (Malá pevnost). A system of corridors, 29 km (18 miles) long, runs under the town.

Picturesque houses in Úštěk town square

Fountain in Lázeňský Sad, the spa park in Teplice

Within the Main Fortress is Terezín town centre. From the second half of the 19th century, the Small Fortress was used as a jail for political prisoners; Serb student Gavrilo Princip, the assassin of Archduke Franz Ferdinand, was kept here until his death. In 1940, the Small Fortress became a prison and, later, a concentration camp within the Protectorate of Bohemia and Moravia. In the autumn of 1941, the Germans transformed the Main Fortress into a ghetto for the Jews, who were brought here from all over Europe, and subsequently dispatched to death camps.

The **Ghetto Museum** inside the main fortress uses artifacts, photographs and videos to give a detailed and shocking picture of ghetto life. This continues in the **Magdeburg Barracks** where the cramped conditions are reconstructed. Exhibits also cover the ghetto's rich cultural life.

🏛 **Small Fortress**
Komenského 154. **Tel** 608 726 950.
Open daily. 📷

🏛 **Ghetto Museum and Magdeburg Barracks**
Principova Alej 304. **Tel** 416 782 577.
Open daily. 📷

🔴 Ústí nad Labem

Road map C1. 🏙 95,000. 🚊
🚌 from Prague. 👁 Mírové náměstí 1.
Tel 475 271 700. 🅦 usti-nl.cz

A major river port on the Labe (Elbe), Ústí nad Labem (Aussig) is an industrial and trade centre. The 14th-century **Cathedral Church of the Assumption of the Virgin Mary** (Nanebevzetí Panny Marie) has a lovely late Gothic altarpiece dating from

1498. Its tower, following the Allies' bombing of Ústí in the final stages of World War II, was pushed out of plumb by nearly 2 m (6 ft). A fine example of modern engineering and architecture is the **Mariánsky Bridge** over the Labe (Elbe), opened in 1998 – an unusual suspended structure that is supported by a single pylon.

Environs
A couple of kilometres from the town centre are the ruins of **Střekov Castle**, perched on a steep rock above the Labe. In 1842, they inspired Wagner to compose his *Tannhäuser*. In the Krásne Březno district, near

Interior of the church of the Assumption in Ústí nad Labem

the castle, stands the Gothic-Renaissance **Church of St Florian**, built in 1597–1603 and featuring a magnificent Renaissance main altarpiece, the work of Master T Lindner of Freiberg, dating from 1605; there is also a lovely vault.

🏛 **Střekov Castle**
Tel 475 530 682. **Open** Apr–Oct:
Tue–Sun. 🅦 hrad-strekov.cz

🔴 Teplice

Road map C1. 🏙 50,700. 🚊
🚌 from Prague. 👁 Benešovo nam 840. **Tel** 417 510 666. 🅦 teplice.cz

Teplice is the oldest health resort in Bohemia. The curative effects of local spring waters were recognized as far back as the 15th century, but hydro-therapy was only developed in the 19th century. In 1879, the spa waters stopped flowing for a while after a nearby mining disaster.

Much of the old town centre was destroyed by the Communists, but the **palace**, built in 1585–1634, survives, and was later rebuilt in Baroque and Neo-Classical styles. In the palace chapel it is worth taking a closer look at the Renaissance altarpiece now used as a tombstone – a fine 1420 work by an Italian master. The palace also houses the **Regional Museum**. St John's church (sv. Jan) in the town square has rich Baroque paintings inside.

🏛 **Regional Museum**
Zámecké Náměstí 14. **Tel** 417 537 869.
Open Tue–Sun. 📷

The Terezín Ghetto

Terezín ghetto was intended to keep in isolation Jews brought here from all parts of occupied Europe. The conditions were, ostensibly, shown as adequate for survival, and an International Red Cross delegation was persuaded twice that the ghetto was a self-governing Jewish "town". In fact, at least 35,000 perished in the ghetto, and over 100,000 prisoners passed through on their way to near-certain death in concentration camps.

Part of the Jewish cemetery in Terezín

The impressive Duchcov Palace – a blend of Baroque and Neo-Classical architecture

⓭ Osek Monastery

Road map C1. 🚊 🚌 from Teplice.
Tel 417 822 138. **Open** May–Sep:
9am–5pm Tue–Sun (from 10am Sun);
Oct–Apr: 9am–4pm Tue–Sun.
📷 🅦 osek.cz

The main attraction of Osek
(Ossegg) is its Cistercian
monastery founded in
1196. The interior of
the monastery church
overflows with lavish
Baroque furnishings
and ornaments,
added as part of the
17th-century revival of
Catholicism in
Bohemia. Ottavio
Broggio made the
exterior alterations.
The spectacular
wall and ceiling
stucco is by
Giacomo Corbellini.

Sculpture of St Matthew,
Osek monastery church

The adjacent monastery has
an early Gothic chapterhouse;
its ceiling is supported by
two columns with magnificent
capitals. At its centre stands an
exceptionally lovely, UNESCO-
listed Romanesque lectern,
made of stone, supported on
two intertwined posts. The
inner courtyard is surrounded
by cloisters, which are linked
with the church by a pre-1240
Romanesque portal.

⓰ Duchcov Palace

Road map C1. 🚊 🚌 from Prague,
Most. **Tel** 417 835 301. **Open** Apr &
Oct: 10am–4pm Sat, Sun & hols;
May–Sep: 10am–5pm Tue–Sun
(Jun–Aug: to 6pm). 📷 📷 3 routes.

The imposing Baroque palace
of the Wallenstein family was

where Giacomo Casanova
spent the final years of his
life (see box, opposite). The
north wing, a former bedroom
and study, houses a few of
his mementos.

The guests entertained by
the Wallensteins here
included Haydn, Mozart,
Goethe and Schiller. The
family had the palace
remodelled in the
early 19th century
in Neo-Classical
style. The ceiling
of the large ballroom
was painted by Václav
Vavřinec Reiner. The
main courtyard and the
stairway to the English-style
garden is decorated
with sculptures by
Matthias Braun.

⓱ Louny

Road map C1. 🚹 18,700. 🚌 from
Prague. 🅸 Pražská 95. **Tel** 415 621
102. 🅦 mulouny.cz

The town of Louny (Laun) was
founded in the 13th century
by Přemysl Otakar II, on the old
trading route that led to Saxony.

Much was destroyed by a fire
in 1517. Standing to this day
are fragments of its original
defensive walls and one
imposing 16th-century gate –
Žatecká brána – sporting the
town's emblem.

A treasured survivor is its Late
Gothic **Church of St Nicholas**
(sv. Mikuláš), built in 1520–38
by Benedikt Ried, on the ruins
of a church. The building's
conspicuous roof, in the shape
of three tents, resembles that
of St Barbara's Cathedral in
Kutná Hora (see pp124–5). The
walls are supported on all sides
by tall buttresses. The south
vestibule with its "donkey back"
portal features exceptionally
intricate net vaulting. Inside,
take a look at the Baroque high
altarpiece dating from the
early 18th century, the twin
side altars and the late Gothic
pulpit from 1540.

The **town hall** was built at
the end of the 19th century to
replace an earlier 14th-century
building. Also built in the 19th
century is the **synagogue**.

🏛 **Church of St Nicholas**
Open Tue–Sun. 📷 for tower only.

The lavishly decorated façade of the town hall in Louny

⓲ Žatec

Road map C1. ⛰ 19,200. 🚌 from
Prague, Louny. ℹ Náměstí
Svobody 1. **Tel** 415 736 156.
🌐 **mesto-zatec.cz**

Žatec's pride is not limited to
its excellent locally grown hops,
used for Pilsner Urquell and
other beers worldwide. Žatec
(Saaz) also has a well-preserved
old town, with many interesting
buildings. Particularly striking
are the numerous Gothic,
Renaissance and Baroque
houses with their original
doorways, gates and arcades.
One of the loveliest is the
Hošt'alkov House, from around
1500. The town's oldest church
is the **Church of the Assumption
of the Virgin Mary**, originally
Romanesque, remodelled in
the Baroque period, and in the
19th century, reconstructed in
the Gothic style.

Oriel of a house in the main square
(No. 184) in Kadaň

⓳ Kadaň

Road map B1. ⛰ 18,100. 🚉
🚌 from Prague, Klášterec. ℹ Jana
Švermy 7. **Tel** 474 319 550.

Despite the fact that most of
the town burned down in 1811,
Kadaň (Kaaden) is still one of
the best-preserved historic cities
in Bohemia, and the beautiful
surroundings make the town
a lively and interesting place
to visit.

The medieval town is almost
fully encircled by defensive
walls, accessed by a number
of gates. A small Gothic gate
is reached via the narrow

Giacomo Casanova

The notorious Venetian adventurer
and seducer arrived in Duchcov in
1785 and took on the position of
palace librarian. He was also hired
to entertain the castle's owners
– members of the Wallenstein
family. In Duchcov, Casanova
wrote most of his *Memoirs*. He
died in 1798 and was buried in the
cemetery of the nearby Church of
St Barbara, although the exact location
of his grave is not known.

Portrait of Giacomo Casanova

Hangman's Lane (Katová ulička)
leading from the south side
of the main square; until the
17th century, the only person
entitled to use the gate was the
town's hangman. Kadan's **town
hall** (radnice) dates from the
early 14th century; its tower is
54 m (177 ft) high. The **Church
of the Fourteen Holy Martyrs**
(Čtrnáct svatých Pomocníků),
an ornate Late Gothic building,
contains the marble sarco-
phagus of John of Lobkowicz,
which dates from 1517, by
the north wall of the presbytery.

Perched on top of a rock
above the Ohře river is a
former royal **castle** dating from
the 13th century, which is now
a private home and closed to
the public.

⓴ Klášterec nad
Ohří

Road map B1. ⛰ 15,200. 🚉 🚌 from
Prague. ℹ Náměstí E Beneše 86.
Tel 474 359 687. 🌐 **klasterec.cz**

Following the Battle of the
White Mountain in 1620,
Klášterec nad Ohří (Klösterle-
an-der-Eger) fell into the hands

of the Thun family. They built
their Renaissance **palace** a
short distance from the
village. Over the centuries,
the original palace has undergone many changes, some
made by the Italian architects
Rossi de Luca and Carlo
Lurago, who designed the
adjacent church of the Holy
Trinity. In 1856, the palace
was remodelled into a
fashionable Romantic edifice
by changing the shape of
the façades, raising the roofs
and towers, and adding
decorative elements in the
spirit of Neo-Gothic. The
palace has retained this form.
The interiors now house an
impressive collection of
Czech porcelain.

The adjacent English park
is beautifully laid out, with
rare species of trees, sculptures by Jan Brokof and the
beautiful tomb of the Thun-
Hohenstein family displaying
their family tree in the form
of a porcelain relief.

🏛 **Palace and Park**
Tel 474 375 436. **Open** Apr–Sep:
Mon–Sun; Oct–Mar: Tue–Sat. 🎟 📷

The palace in Klášterec nad Ohří

EAST BOHEMIA

Scenery is the star attraction in much of East Bohemia, an area of exceptional diversity. The flat, somewhat monotonous landscape around Hradec Králové and Pardubice forms a marked contrast with the dramatic scenery to the north in the Krkonoše mountain range, which draws visitors in summer and winter alike to Sněžka, the highest peak in the Czech Republic.

The capital of East Bohemia (Východní Čechy), Hradec Králové, is a town that has passed through many stages of development – from Slav settlement, through medieval stronghold and Baroque fortress, to showcase for spectacular Modernist architecture in the 1920s. The region's other large towns – Pardubice, with its famous steeplechase course, and Litomyšl, with its imposing Renaissance palace and its links with the Czech national composer, Bedřich Smetana – are also beautiful and interesting places to explore.

The Krkonoše and Orlické mountain ranges form the northern border of the region and the country. They attract many visitors keen on skiing and hiking. Within the Krkonoše range, the Krkonoše National Park and its flora are strictly protected. The

region near Turnov and Jičín includes Český ráj (the "Bohemian Paradise"), a land full of castle ruins and extraordinary geological formations, exceptionally rich in precious minerals.

Central and eastern parts of East Bohemia are characterized by the extensive, flat plain around the River Labe (Elbe). The towns in this region suffered badly in the Thirty Years' War *(see p41)*, and their prosperity declined. This resulted in recolonization and Germanization, but also in the development of Baroque art and architecture. East Bohemia has many fine works by Kilian Ignaz Dientzenhofer, Giovanni Santini and Matthias Braun. A special place among the historic buildings of the region must be given to the castle and church complex in Kuks – a unique structure born on a whim of Count Špork.

Hydroelectric power station on the Labe (Elbe), in Hradec Králové

◀ A tranquil stream at the Krkonoše National Park

Exploring East Bohemia

The geological formations of East Bohemia, such as Český ráj and the Adršpach and Teplice Rocks, are among the most beautiful in Central Europe. Aside from these, the most interesting sight in the northern part is Jičín, formerly the centre of the vast estate of Albrecht von Wallenstein. Nearby, the Krkonoše mountains attract walkers and skiers. In the centre of the region are the two major cities of Hradec Králové and Pardubice. Further south, the Renaissance town of Litomyšl is a must for any visitor.

Cathedral of the Holy Ghost, Hradec Králové

Sights at a Glance

Terrace and steps linking Nové Město nad Metují Palace and gardens

Getting Around

The main transport artery of the region is the D11 motorway leading from Prague to Hradec Králové, the region's largest city. The second largest city, Pardubice, lies on the main railway linking Prague with Moravia and Slovakia. From both cities, roads and railway lines radiate out to all parts of the region. Buses are reasonably efficient throughout East Bohemia. Trips to more remote places are possible on public transport, but need more advance planning.

Key

- ▦▦ Motorway
- ▦▦ Dual carriageway
- ▬ Main road
- ▦▦ Minor road
- ▬ Scenic route
- ▦▦ Main railway
- ▬ Minor railway
- ▦▦ International border
- ▦▦ Regional border
- △ Summit

Part of the 17th-century arcaded market square in Jičín

For keys to symbols *see back flap*

❶ Hradec Králové

The capital of East Bohemia, at the confluence of the Labe (Elbe) and Orlice rivers, Hradec Králové (Königgrätz) is one of the most beautiful cities in Bohemia. It first appears in historic records as early as 1225 and later became an important Hussite and then Counter-Reformation centre. In the 20th century the town acquired a new face when architects Jan Kotěra and Josef Gočár built many Modernist structures outside the medieval centre on the east and west banks of the Labe.

Town Hall and White Tower in Velké náměstí

Exploring the Town

The oldest part of the town, with historic buildings clustered around the two medieval squares, occupies high ground between the two rivers *(see also pp202–3)*. The New Town, built in 1920–30, starts on the east, and continues on the west bank of the Labe.

🏛 Velké náměstí

One of the most opulent buildings in the former market square is the old town hall (radnice). This Gothic edifice, erected before 1418, was remodelled in the late 16th century in the Renaissance style. At that time, it was used as the town prison. In 1786, it acquired two clock towers.

On the south side of the square stands the Bishop's Palace, one of the town's finest Baroque buildings. Its designer was Giovanni Santini, who also designed its magnificent entrance portal. Adjacent is the charming, small-scale Baroque Špulak House (Dům U Špuláků). It was remodelled in 1750 by

Relief from the house opposite the cathedral

F Kermer. The 20-m (66-ft) column was erected in 1717 in thanksgiving for sparing the town from the plague of the previous year. The monument is probably by sculptor and architect G B Bullo. Adjoining the square to the northeast is the smaller medieval square Malé náměstí.

🏛 Cathedral of the Holy Ghost

The magnificent brick Gothic Cathedral of the Holy Ghost (Katedrála sv. Ducha), founded in 1307, is evidence of the town's wealth in the early 14th century. In 1424, the church was the temporary burial site of Jan Žižka, leader of the Hussite movement. Striking features of its plain interior are the Late Gothic, 15th-century high altar, and in the south aisle, the Baroque altarpiece with a painting of St Anthony, by Petr Brandl. The pewter baptismal font, dating from 1406, is one of the oldest in Bohemia.

🏛 White Tower

Franušova 1. **Tel** 495 512 542.
Open Apr–Sep: 9am–noon & 1–5pm daily.

The 72-m (235-ft) tall Renaissance belfry next to the cathedral was erected in 1589. The white stone used as the building material gave the structure its name White Tower (Bílá věž), though the stone is now grey. The bell inside, nicknamed "Augustin", is Bohemia's second-largest. Do not be misled by the replacement clock that was fitted in the White Tower in 1829: the small hand points to the minutes, and the large one to the hours!

🏛 Church of the Assumption of the Virgin Mary

The church (Nanebevzetí Panny Marie) was built for the Jesuit Order by Carlo Lurago in the mid-17th century. One hundred years later, the church burned down and only the chapel of St Ignatius Loyola, with its wall paintings and a picture by Petr Brandl of the glorification of the saint, was spared. The present façade, graced with two towers, dates from 1857. The former

Interior of the Church of the Assumption of the Virgin Mary

Entrance hall of the five-storey Modern Art Gallery

Jesuit College, the long building to the right of the church, dates from 1671–1710.

🏛 Modern Art Gallery

Velké náměstí 139/140. **Tel** 495 514 893. **Closed** until spring 2016. 🖼 ♿ **W** galeriehk.cz

The striking five-storey Art Nouveau building of the Modern Art Gallery (Galerie moderního umění) was designed in 1912 by Osvald Polívka. Inside is a superb and extensive collection of works by the finest Czech artists of the 19th and 20th centuries, including Jan Zrzavý, Jan Preisler, Josef Váchal, Václav Špála, Josef Čapek and Jiří Kolář.

✡ Former Synagogue

Československé armády.
This distinctive building has a magnificent dome overlaid with sheet copper. It was built in 1904–5 to a design by Václav Weinzettel, in the Art Nouveau style, with some Oriental elements. Apart from the prayer hall, it also included the domestic quarters of the rabbi, the shammash and the caretaker; there was also a meeting room and space for the archives. The building served the Jewish community until World War II. After 1960, it was acquired and renovated by the Hradec Králové Research Library, and it remains a library today.

🏛 Museum of Eastern Bohemia

Eliščino nábřeží 465. **Tel** 495 512 391. **Open** 9am–5pm Tue–Sun. 🖼 ♿ **W** muzeumhk.cz

The monumental building of Museum of Eastern Bohemia (Museum východních Čech) is one of the prime examples of Bohemian Modernism. It was built in 1909–12 to a

View of river Labe from the Pražský Bridge

VISITORS' CHECKLIST

Practical Information
Road map D2.
🗺 94,200. ℹ Velké náměstí 165. **Tel** 495 580 492.
Open 8am–noon & 1–5pm daily. Oct–May: closed Sat & Sun.
🎭 Folklore Festival: early Jun; International Jazz Festival: Oct.
W ic-hk.cz

Transport
🚃 🚌 1 km (0.5 mile) W of Old Town.

design by Jan Kotěra. Inside, through the doorway flanked by gigantic statues, are some interesting exhibits, in particular a scale model of the town from 1865, complete with all of its fortifications.

🌉 Pražský Bridge

The Pražský Bridge was designed in 1910 by Jan Kotěra. The 60-m (200-ft) long structure replaced the oldest bridge in Hradec Králové, dating from 1796. In 1910–12, Kotěra added four pavilions to house shops; he also gave it distinctive lighting and masts with the town's emblem. The bridge leads into the section of the new town over the river built by Modernist Josef Gočár.

Hradec Králové Town Centre

① Velké Náměstí
② Cathedral of the Holy Ghost
③ White Tower
④ Church of the Assumption of the Virgin Mary
⑤ Modern Art Gallery
⑥ Former Synagogue
⑦ Museum of Eastern Bohemia
⑧ Pražský Bridge

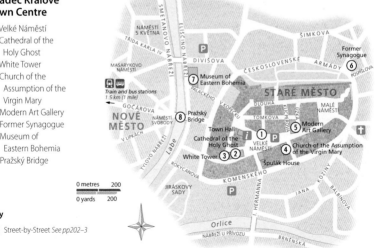

0 metres 200
0 yards 200

Key

▨ Street-by-Street See pp202–3

For keys to symbols see back flap

Street-by-Street: Hradec Králové Old Town

The historic sights of the Old Town are clustered around its former market square, Velké náměstí, and the adjoining, smaller Malé náměstí. Charming streets lined with beautiful houses are juxtaposed with the opulent edifices of museums, churches, theatres and palaces. Make a point of going down the narrow street that runs behind the White Tower to see the restored historic houses, and then ascend the tower to gain a bird's-eye view of the Old Town stretching beneath.

★ Town Hall
The façade of this three-storey building is decorated with the national emblem of the former Czechoslovakia.

St Clement Chapel
Squeezed between the Town Hall and the White Tower is the Baroque St Clement Chapel (1716). It would be easy to miss it, were it not for its golden crown glittering in the sunlight, visible from any point in the main square.

The White Tower is the work of Burian Vlach, in 1574–89. It offers a superb view of the town from the top.

Plague Column

ROKITANSKÉHO

K. TOMANA

★ Cathedral of the Holy Ghost
This Gothic brick church founded in 1307 has slender stained-glass windows and a magnificent high altar.

"Bono publico"
This Empire-style covered staircase with three cupolas was built in 1810 on the site of the Fisherman's Gate, which once formed part of the town's fortifications.

Key

— Suggested route

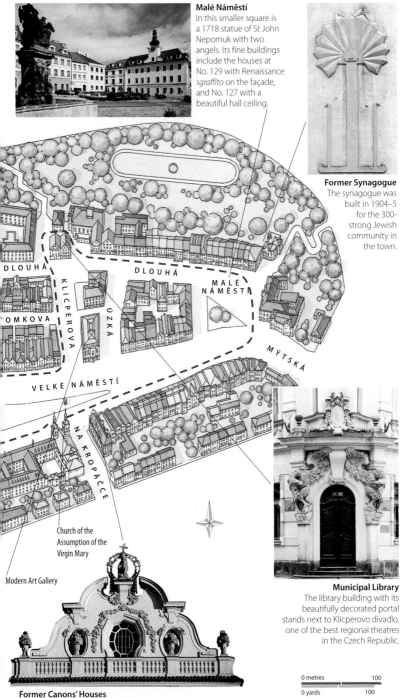

Malé Náměstí
In this smaller square is a 1718 statue of St John Nepomuk with two angels. Its fine buildings include the houses at No. 129 with Renaissance *sgraffito* on the façade, and No. 127 with a beautiful hall ceiling.

Former Synagogue
The synagogue was built in 1904–5 for the 300-strong Jewish community in the town.

DLOUHÁ

KLICPEROVA

DLOUHÁ

MALÉ NÁMĚSTÍ

OMKOVA

ÚZKÁ

MÝTSKÁ

VELKÉ NÁMĚSTÍ

NA KROPÁČCE

Church of the Assumption of the Virgin Mary

Modern Art Gallery

Municipal Library
The library building with its beautifully decorated portal stands next to Klicperovo divadlo, one of the best regional theatres in the Czech Republic.

Former Canons' Houses
Seen along the south side of the square are former canons' houses – lovely Renaissance buildings with eye-catching gables.

| 0 metres | 100 |
| 0 yards | 100 |

Architectural decorations on the façade of the Knights' House, Litomyšl

❷ Litomyšl

Road map E2. 🏛 10,400. 🚌 from Prague. 🚌 from Prague, Hradec Králové. ℹ️ Smetanovo náměstí 72. **Tel** 461 612 161. 🎭 International Opera Festival: late Jun. 🌐 litomysl.cz

One of Bohemia's oldest historic towns, Litomyšl (Leitomischl) is small but dynamic, dominated by its fine Renaissance palace, and its associations with composer Bedřich Smetana (see p24). The town was established over 1,000 years ago on the trading route that linked Bohemia with Moravia. In the 11th century, Prince Břetislav II founded a Benedictine monastery here. The settlement that sprang up nearby was accorded municipal status in 1259 by Přemysl Otakar II; in 1344, the town became the seat of the second bishopric in Bohemia, after Prague. Captured by Hussites in the 15th century, it became a centre of the Bohemian Brethren community.

In 1567, the town fell into the hands of Vratislav of Pernštejn, Chancellor of the Bohemian Kingdom, who built a magnificent Renaissance palace, the main seat of his family. **Pernštejn Palace** is to the northeast of the main square (Smetanovo náměstí). Built in 1568–81, it was included in 1999 on the UNESCO World Cultural Heritage List. The finial-topped building features two courtyards. The main one, square-shaped, is flanked on three sides by three-storey arcades. The fourth wall is lavishly decorated with *sgraffito*. The external *sgraffito* is regarded as the most beautiful of its kind in the former Austro-Hungarian Empire.

Inside the palace, highlights among the many rooms with historic furnishings include the Battle Hall and the Great Dining Hall. Particularly striking is the late 18th-century theatre, one of the oldest and best-preserved in Europe. Smetana made his debut as a pianist in this theatre.

Opposite the palace is the birthplace of Bedřich Smetana, now the **Smetana Museum**. The building used to belong to the brewery as Smetana's father was a brewer. One of the town's attractions is the annual International Opera Festival in June, which brings together many outstanding opera performers.

Amid the lavishly decorated arcaded Baroque houses in the long, thin **main square** is the **Knights' House** (Dům U Rytířů), with magnificent Renaissance façade decorations including vivid knights, merchants and creatures. It now houses an art gallery. Close to the palace stands the early Baroque **Church of the Finding of the Holy Cross** (Nalezení sv. Kříže), built in 1730 by Giovanni Alliprandi. Its façade is winged by two obliquely positioned towers, while the richly decorated interior is dominated by larger-than-life figures of the four Evangelists. The originally Gothic **Church of the Exaltation of the Holy Cross** (Šantovo náměstí) has an interesting semi-circular entrance portal dating from 1605, flanked by Tuscan columns.

🏛 **Pernštejn Palace**
Tel 461 615 067. **Open** Apr & Oct: Sat & Sun, public hols; May–Sep: Tue–Sun. 🌐 zamek-litomysl.cz

🏛 **Smetana Museum**
Zámecký Pivovar. **Tel** 461 615 287. **Open** Apr & Oct: Sat, Sun & public hols; May–Sep: Tue–Sun. 🌐 rml.cz

❸ Nové Hrady Palace

Road map E2. 🚌 from Litomyšl, Chrudim. **Tel** 469 325 353. **Open** May–Sep: 10am–4pm daily; Apr, Oct: 10am–4pm Sat, Sun. 🌐 🔲

Bohemia's most beautiful Rococo palace is in the small town of Nové Hrady. Commissioned by Count

The majestic Nové Hrady Palace viewed from its English-style gardens

Façades of Baroque houses in Havlíčkův Brod

Jean Antonín Harbuval de Chamaré, it was built in 1774–7 by a Tyrolean architect Josef Jäger, in the style of a French summer residence. The sloping site was used to set off the stately character of the building: it has often been called the "Bohemian Versailles".

The salmon-pink palace consists of the central building with two wings embracing a raised courtyard, which forms a terrace above the lower floor of the entrance section. All of it is completed by an imposing three-part gate dating from 1782. Palace interiors feature original Rococo furnishings. The main hall on the first floor has some interesting Rococo stuccoes. The adjoining English-style park features Baroque Stations of the Cross, dating from 1767.

❹ Havlíčkův Brod

Road map D2. 23,700. from Prague. 569 497 357.
mic.muhb.cz

Scenically located on the banks of River Sázava, Havlíčkův Brod was until 1945 known as Německý Brod ("German Ford"). The town's current name comes from the name of Karel Havlíček-Borovský – a poet and a prominent member of the Czech patriotic movement, who studied and worked here in the 19th century.

The historic centre is focused on the quadrangular **market square** (Havlíčkovo náměstí) surrounded by Baroque houses with lavishly decorated façades. Rising above their roofs is the massive tower of the 13th-century **Church of the Assumption of the Virgin Mary** (Nanebevzetí Panny Marie) with a high altar, with four levels of angels and saints; there are also some interesting side altars. The tower houses one of Bohemia's biggest bells, "Vilém", dating from 1300.

At the square's centre is a Marian column decorated with figures of saints Andrew, Florian, John Nepomuk and Wenceslas. Nearby is a stone fountain in the shape of the Greek sea god Triton.

❺ Lipnice nad Sázavou

Road map D2. 660. from Havlíčkův Brod. **Tel** 569 486 139.

This village is where the novelist Jaroslav Hašek lived from 1921 until his death in 1923. He is now buried in the local cemetery. It was in Lipnice that he wrote the second, third and fourth (unfinished) volumes of his comic masterpiece, *The Good Soldier Švejk*.

Statue of Jaroslav Hašek in Lipnice nad Sázavou

The twin-towered silhouette of **Lipnice Castle** dominates the landscape. This mighty Gothic edifice was built in the early 14th century as a fortress guarding the trade route from Havlíčkův Brod to Humpolec. The main body of the castle and the tower date from this period. After a fire in 1869, it fell into ruin. The 14th-century chapel is decorated with fine frescoes.

Lipnice Castle
Tel 569 486 189. **Open** Apr, Sep & Oct: Sat, Sun & public hols; May–Aug: Tue–Sun. **hrad-lipnice.eu**

❻ Ledeč nad Sázavou

Road map D2. 5,600. from Prague. Husovo náměstí 60. **Tel** 569 721 471.
ledecns.cz

Perched on a high escarpment on the right bank of the Sázava is the 12th-century **Ledeč Castle**. The ground floor houses a **Regional Museum**, with ethnographic exhibits and old weaponry. One of the rooms has a unique *sgraffito* decoration on its ceiling. The town itself, on the left bank of the river, is dominated by the **Church of St Peter and St Paul** (sv. Petr a Pavel) in the square. Originally Gothic, the church was remodelled in Baroque style. The town has some interesting reminders of the Jewish community, who were forcibly removed from here in 1942; they include an early 18th-century **synagogue** and a **Jewish cemetery** established in 1601, one of the oldest in Bohemia, with many Baroque tombstones.

Ledeč Castle (museum)
Tel 731 612 457. **Open** Apr–Sep: Tue–Sun.

Hall housing an exhibition of sculpture in Lipnice Castle

❼ Žleby Castle

Road map D2. 🚇 🚌 from Čáslav.
Tel 327 398 121. **Open** Apr & Oct: 9am–
4pm Sat, Sun & public hols; May–Sep:
9am–4pm Tue–Sun (to 5pm Jul & Aug).
🅿 📷 3 routes. 🆆 **zamek-zleby.cz**

This fairytale castle has
undergone dramatic changes
over the centuries. In the 13th
century, Žleby Castle was a
Gothic defensive fortress. In the
16th century, it was remodelled
in Renaissance style, and in
the 19th century, its owners,
the Auersperg family, gave it a
romantic Neo-Gothic look. The
castle sports a massive tower
with a pointed roof, and an
entrance portal decorated with
an unusual relief of a bison. The
Auersperg family fled at the end
of World War II, leaving behind
the contents of their home.

On the courtyard's ground
and first floors are Renaissance
and Baroque arcades, partially
glazed with lovely stained-glass
windows produced in Germany
and Switzerland. Palace rooms
were decorated extravagantly
in the 1840s. The palace chapel,
built in 1853–8, has unusually
lavish furnishings including
Renaissance figures of St John
the Evangelist and St John the
Baptist, made of terracotta in
the Florence workshop of
Giovanni della Robbia. In the
adjacent game park are herds
of white stags.

Environs
About 6 km (4 miles) to the
northwest is the town of **Čáslav**,

Bison relief above the entrance to
Žleby Castle

which has a rectangular square
with a Baroque town hall, and
houses in a variety of styles,
from Gothic to Empire. The
Late Gothic Church of St Peter
and St Paul (sv. Petr a Pavel)
has a 13th-century presbytery
supported by two vast buttresses, and fine portals in the
west and south walls.

❽ Slatiňany Palace

Road map D2. 🚇 🚌 from Pardubice.
Tel 469 681 112. **Open** Apr & Oct:
10am–3pm Sat, Sun & public hols;
May–Sep: 10am–4pm Tue–Sun. 🅿 📷

A place of interest for all horse
lovers, Slatiňany Palace was
built in the 16th century in
Renaissance style. At the turn of
the 18th and 19th centuries, it
was remodelled in Neo-Gothic
style. In 1947, it became home
to an equestrian museum,
unique in Europe. It has nearly
2,100 exhibits associated with
horse breeding. There are also
paintings, prints, sculptures,
porcelain and tapestries
devoted to the subject of
horses; and a collection of
saddles and harnesses. In the
large English-style palace park
are paddocks used for horses
bred at the local stud farm.

Environs
The main reason to visit
Chrudim, 6 km (4 miles)
northwest of Slatiňany, is its
fascinating Puppet Museum
(Muzeum loutkářských kultur).
It started with the collection of
Jan Malík, a Czech pedagogue
and historian, of puppets
worldwide. The town hosts
a Puppet Festival in July. The

Flower-filled courtyard of Slatiňany Palace

museum is in the town's most
beautiful Renaissance structure –
the Mydlářovský dům – with a
two-storey arcaded façade and
a slender tower resembling a
minaret. Nearby, on the main
square, is the Gothic Church
of the Assumption of the Virgin
Mary (Nanebevzetí Panny
Marie). Also in the square is
an imposing Plague Column.

🏛 **Puppet Museum**
Břetislavova 74. **Tel** 469 620 310.
Open daily. 🅿 🆆 **puppets.cz**

The highly ornate ceiling in
Pardubice Castle

❾ Pardubice

Road map D2. 🔺 90,600. 🚇 from
Prague. 🛈 Nám Republiky 1.
Tel 466 768 390. 🆆 **ipardubice.cz**

A large centre of industry,
commerce and administration,
Pardubice (Pardubitz) has a
pedigree going back to the
14th century. Following great
fires in 1507 and 1538, the
town was rebuilt in the form
that has survived to the present

day. As well as its architecture, Pardubice is known for the production of the explosive Semtex in a factory in its suburb of Semtim.

To fans of horse-racing, Pardubice is known for the Velká Pardubická – a steeplechase race held annually since 1874. The course of 6,900 m (over 4 miles) includes 31 jumps. The most difficult of them – the notorious Taxis – was the cause of so many injuries to horses and riders that it was redesigned in 2012. The Velká Pardubická is regarded as more gruelling than the Grand National, run at Aintree, even though it is not quite as long.

As in so many Bohemian towns, **Pardubice Castle** dominates, and was once the favourite residence of Emperor Ferdinand I and his court. Now it houses the **Museum of East Bohemia** with some eye-catching frescoes in the Renaissance Knights' Halls.

The town has about 100 Gothic and Renaissance houses. They surround the **market square** (Pernštýnské náměstí). Particularly striking is Jonah's House (Dům U Jonáše) at No. 50, with a relief depicting the Prophet being spat out by the whale. The Neo-Renaissance town hall, dating from 1894, sports at the top, between two towers, a copper figure of a knight – the town's guardian.

In the town's modern square (náměstí Republiky) is the **Church of St Bartholomew** (sv. Bartoloměj), a Gothic edifice with a slender spire at the centre of the roof. It contains a fine Renaissance tombstone of Vojtěch of Pernštejn, and a monumental sculpture depicting Calvary, dating from 1736. Also in the

Pardubice market square with the Plague Column and town hall

square is the boldly Art Nouveau **Municipal Theatre** (Mětské divadlo).

🏠 Pardubice Castle and Museum of East Bohemia

Tel 466 799 240. **Open** 10am–6pm Tue–Sun. 🖼 🖼 **vcm.cz**

Environs

On a large spreading plain 5 km (3 miles) south of Pardubice is an 8-m (26-ft) high solitary hill, **Kunětická Hora**. The castle on its top is the dominant feature of the district. Built in the 15th century by the Hussites, it was captured by the Swedes in the Thirty Years' War. In the early 20th century, reconstruction works started, which are still going on. In good weather, the 35-m (115-ft) tower affords a view of the distant Krkonoše. A castle houses a small museum of its history.

🏠 Kunětická Hora Castle

Tel 466 415 428. **Open** Apr & Oct: Sat, Sun & public hols; May–Sep: Tue–Sun. 🖼

❿ Hrádek u Nechanic Palace

Road map D1. 🚌 from Hradec Králové. **Tel** 495 441 244. **Open** Apr & Oct: 9am–4pm Sat, Sun & public hols; May–Sep: 9am–5pm Tue–Sun. 🖼 🖼
🌐 **hradekunechanic.cz**

The palace in Hrádek u Nechanic is one of the finest Romantic buildings in Bohemia. Commissioned by Count František Arnošt Harrach, this grand Neo-Gothic English-style residence, complete with crenellations, was built in 1839–57. The lengthy building works were supervised by the Viennese architect Karl Fischer.

Particularly attractive rooms are the Golden Hall, with lovely panelled ceilings and an impressive fireplace; also the Knights' Hall, which is decorated with laboriously worked, ostentatious wood-carvings along the lower sections of the walls and around the doors. Much of the furniture was imported from Germany and Austria in the 19th century.

Around the palace are sweeping, landscaped gardens and a golf course.

The romantic, Neo-Gothic Hrádek u Nechanic Palace

Karlova Koruna Palace at Chlumec nad Cidlinou

⓫ Chlumec nad Cidlinou

Road map D2. 🗻 5,500. 🚉 🚌 from Hradec Králové. 🛈 Kozelkova 26. **Tel** 495 484 121.

The riverside town of Chlumec nad Cidlinou is known for the **Karlova Koruna Palace**. Designed by Giovanni Santini, it was built in 1721–3. The owner, Count František Kinský, named it "Charles's Crown" in honour of Emperor Charles VI, who stayed here in 1723, following his coronation as King of Bohemia. The palace has an unusual central cylindrical section and three radiating wings. Inside are paintings and memorabilia of the Kinský family, who after 1989 regained ownership of the palace from the Czech government. The Chapel of the Annunciation (1740) is also by Santini.

🏠 **Karlova Koruna Palace**
Tel 495 484 519. **Open** Apr–Jun, Sep & Oct: Sat, Sun & public hols; Jul & Aug: daily. 📷 🆆 **kinskycastles.com**

⓬ Jičín

Road map D1. 🗻 16,700. 🚉 🚌 from Prague. 🛈 Valdštejnovo náměstí 1. **Tel** 493 534 390. 🎭 Fairytale Festival: Sep. 🆆 **jicin.org**

Jičín (Gitschin) borders the Český ráj nature reserve and makes an ideal place to stay while exploring the surrounding countryside. Jičín reached the peak of its glory during the Thirty Years' War, when the supreme commander of the Imperial Army, Albrecht von Wallenstein, made it the centre of his vast Duchy of Friedland. Here, this most powerful Bohemian warlord built his residence, minted his own money and dreamt of founding a university. All these plans collapsed after the assassination of Wallenstein in Cheb, in 1634 *(see p171)*; yet the town has retained many mementoes of the ambitious duke.

A silent witness to his unfulfilled plans is the town's

⓭ Tour of Český ráj

Český ráj, or "Bohemian Paradise", is the oldest protected nature reserve in the Czech Republic. The scenic landscape is full of extraordinary geological formations: "rock towns", "gates" and high-rise "towers" popular with climbers. There are also a number of medieval castles and an extensive network of walking trails. Jičín and Turnov make good bases for exploring.

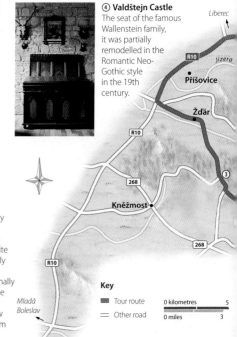

④ **Valdštejn Castle**
The seat of the famous Wallenstein family, it was partially remodelled in the Romantic Neo-Gothic style in the 19th century.

Liberec

Přišovice

Žďár

Kněžmost

③ **Kost Castle**
This 14th-century fortress is dominated by a 32-m (105-ft) high White Tower, with nearly 4-m (13-ft) thick walls. Used originally as the final refuge of the castle's defenders, it now houses a museum of torture.

Mladá Boleslav

Prague

Key

▓▓ Tour route

═ Other road

0 kilometres   5

0 miles   3

square, built by Wallenstein and now named after him – Valdštejnovo náměstí. It is surrounded on all sides by superb and well-preserved 17th-century arcaded houses. Standing at the southeast corner of the square is the former ducal castle, now housing a **Regional Museum**. The most interesting of its historic interiors is the Conference Hall where Tsar Alexander I of Russia, King Frederick William III of Prussia and Emperor Francis I of Austria formed the Holy Alliance against Napoleon in 1813. The **Jesuit Church of St James the Great** (sv. Jakuba Většího) beside the castle is of Baroque design, and dates from 1627. Just to the west of the main square is the 14th-century **Church of St Ignatius** (sv. Ignáce).

The town's tallest building is the 16th-century quadrangular

Coat of arms at Jičín Castle

Valdice Gate (Valdická brána). At 52 m (170 ft) high, its tower affords a lovely view of the town from the top. Close to Valdice Gate is **Rumcajs's Cobbler House**, which consists of a craft workshop, playroom for children, a herb garden and a small shop with local souvenirs.

Environs
Wallenstein ordered the planting of an avenue of over 1,200 lime trees in two straight lines over 2 km (1 mile) long, leading from Jičín to his 1630 park pavilion, known as **Libosad**. This is now a quiet, somewhat overgrown spot.

Near Libosad is the town of **Valdice** (Walditz), with its 17th-century Baroque Carthusian monastery.

The monastery was turned into a prison by the Habsburgs, used later by the Communists to house political prisoners, and it still serves as a top-security prison, one of the harshest in Bohemia.

Regional Museum
Tel 493 532 204. **Open** Tue–Sun.

Valdice Gate
Open Apr: Sat & Sun; May–Sep: daily.

Interior of the Church of St James, Jičín

⑥ **Trosky**
The imposing castle, built in the late 14th century on two adjacent rock summits, is one of the symbols of the Bohemian Paradise.

⑤ **Hrubá Skalá Castle**
This Renaissance castle surrounded by an English-style park is the starting point for a 4-km (2-mile) trek through the rock town of Hruboskalské.

Tips for Drivers

Tour length: 50 km (31 miles).
Stopping-off points: The best accommodation and choice of eating places can be found in nearby Jičín. On the tour route, the Hrubá Skalá Castle is now a hotel with bars and restaurants.

① **Prachovské skály**
Prachovské skály reserve is a huge rock town featuring sandstone rocks scattered amid trees, and several breathtaking viewpoints.

② **Sobotka**
The Baroque hunting lodge, Humprecht, near Sobotka, was named after its eccentric owner, Count Humprecht Černín.

Žehrovka

Jičín

⑭ Krkonoše

The Krkonoše range (Riesengebirge) stretches along the Polish-Czech border for about 35 km (22 miles). Krkonoše means "Giant Mountains". On the Polish side, the mountains slope more steeply, while on the south side they open out into numerous valleys. The Krkonoše National Park (KRNAP) opened in 1963, an area of 385 sq km (150 sq miles) within the range, and provides a habitat for many indigenous species of plants. Particular care is taken of the local spruce forests, which in the past have suffered greatly due to environmental pollution. A network of clearly marked hiking trails, plus hundreds of chairlifts and ski runs, as well as snowboarding facilities, make this an excellent holiday region, winter or summer.

Spirit of Krkonoše
Legend tells of a wicked and – later – a benign spirit of Krkonoše, called Rýbrcoul.

Jelenia Góra

Prague

Lobe (Elbe)

1294 m (4245 ft)

1509 m (4951 ft)

Harrachov

1022 m (3353 ft)

1210 m (3970 ft)

1435 m (4708 ft)

1235 m (4052 ft)

Horní Mísečky

Špindl

910 m (2985 ft)

Rokytnice nad Jizerou

1218 m (3996 ft)

Jizerka

295

Jablonec nad Jizerou

1038 m (3405 ft)

Vítkovice

Benecko

Strážr

Jizerka

Křižlice

Poniklá

Mrklov

Lobe (Elbe)

Víchová nad Jizerou

Vrch

Semily

Valteřice

Jičín

Ceramic Altar, Harrachov
The glassworks established here in the 18th century made the local products famous worldwide. In the Church of St Wenceslas, glass and ceramics are used to decorate its interior.

Mumlov Waterfall
This 8-m (26-ft) high waterfall on the Mumlava river is an attractive destination for a walk along the trail from the nearby ski resort of Harrachov.

Vrchlabí
This small town in the foothills of the mountains has a Renaissance castle, many times remodelled; its owners included Albrecht von Wallenstein.

Studnični hora
This is the third-highest peak in Bohemia; its eastern and southern slopes are notorious for their frequent avalanches. Snow here may reach 14 m (46 ft) deep.

Rich Plantlife
The varied environment, including mountain forests, meadows, glacial basins, sub-Arctic peat moors and ridge fells, supports many rare plants.

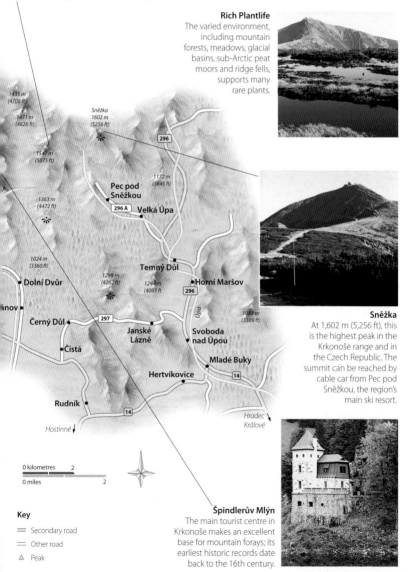

Sněžka
At 1,602 m (5,256 ft), this is the highest peak in the Krkonoše range and in the Czech Republic. The summit can be reached by cable car from Pec pod Sněžkou, the region's main ski resort.

Špindlerův Mlýn
The main tourist centre in Krkonoše makes an excellent base for mountain forays; its earliest historic records date back to the 16th century.

Key
= Secondary road
= Other road
△ Peak

0 kilometres 2
0 miles 2

For keys to symbols *see back flap*

Tiger, an inmate at Dvůr Králové Zoo

⓯ Dvůr Králové

Road map D1. 🏔 16,100. 🚌
🚌 from Hradec Králové, Prague.

The local zoo is what makes this town such a popular destination. It is one of the largest in Europe, and special care is lavished on African animals, including zebras, giraffes, white rhinos and a huge herd of antelopes. The star attraction is the evening safari – a ride on a special bus over the site where the animals roam free.

Founded in the 13th century, the town itself has several fine historic buildings and an arcaded main square. The **Church of St John the Baptist** (sv. Jana Křtitele) has a 64-m (210-ft) tower. The Renaissance town hall is decorated with *sgraffito*.

🔀 Dvůr Králové Zoo
Tel 499 329 515. **Open** 9am–4pm daily (to 6pm in summers; evening safaris May–Sep). 🚐 **w** zoodk.cz

⓰ Kuks

Road map D1. 🚌 🚍 from Hradec Králové, Prague. Historic hospital complex: **Tel** 499 692 161. **Open** Apr & Oct: 9am–5pm Sat, Sun & public hols; May–Sep: 9am–5pm Tue–Sun. 🚐 🎫 3 routes. ♿ **w** hospital-kuks.cz

The history of the founding, the growth and the sudden decline of Kuks is quite extraordinary. The spa resort, of European fame, was built in 1694–1724 by Count František Antonín Špork and visited by Europe's elite, including J S Bach. In 1740, just two years after Špork's death, it was partially swept away by the rising waters of the Labe

(Elbe) in the course of one night. Now the remaining evidence of the town's former glory is its magnificent hospital and the Holy Trinity Church, both the work of Giovanni Alliprandi. On the hospital terrace are figures depicting the *Virtues* and *Vices*; apart from the figure of *Fraud*, they were all produced by Matthias Braun in 1715–18.

Environs
In a forest about 5 km (3 miles) away it is worth taking a look at Betlém (Bethlehem) – a gallery of scenes and figures representing the Nativity. These were carved by Matthias Braun directly into the rocks, again at the behest of Špork.

Statues symbolizing the *Virtues*, on Kuks hospital terrace

⓱ Adršpach-Teplice Rocks

Road map E1. 15 km (9 miles) E of Trutnov. 🚌 from Trutnov. 🚍
ℹ Dolní Adršpach 26. **Tel** 491 586 012. **w** skalyadrspach.cz

The two rock towns at Adršpach and Teplice (Adršpašsko-teplické skály) are fascinating sandstone formations, the region's finest. The Adršpach rock town can be explored on a marked trail that takes in some of the most spectacular rock formations. The path leads to Adršpach lake, and on to the Teplice rock town. The area attracts hikers and rock climbers and can be busy in high season.

⓲ Náchod

Road map E1. 🏔 20,800. 🚌
🚍 from Prague. ℹ Masarykovo náměstí 74. **Tel** 491 426 060.
w mestonachod.cz

On the major trade route from Bohemia to Poland, Náchod was founded in the 13th century. Above the town is a Gothic **Castle**, subject to Renaissance and later Baroque remodelling. The castle was owned by Ottavio Piccolomini, an officer serving with Albrecht von Wallenstein. Piccolomini was given the castle as a reward by Emperor Ferdinand II for his part in the murder of his commander.

The Gothic **Church of St Lawrence** (sv. Vavřinec) in the town square (náměstí T G Masaryka) has a rare 15th-century pewter baptismal font. The two onion-domed towers, nicknamed Adam and Eve, are 40 m (130 ft) tall. The Neo-Renaissance **town hall** (radnice) is decorated with *sgraffito* designed in 1909 by Mikoláš Aleš. **U Beránka Hotel** has an Art Nouveau interior and theatre auditorium.

Embedded in the pavement of Karlovo náměstí is a horse-shoe, reputedly lost by King Frederick's horse in 1618 as he escaped through Náchod to Silesia after his defeat at the Battle of the White Mountain.

🏰 Náchod Castle
Tel 491 426 201. **Open** Apr & Oct: Sat, Sun & public hols; May–Sep: Tue–Sun. 🚐 3 routes. **w** zamek-nachod.cz

Art Nouveau panels on a house façade in Náchod market square

⑲ Nové Město nad Metují

Road map E1. 🏛 9,800. 🚃 from Prague, Náchod. 🛈 Husovo náměstí 1225. **Tel** 491 472 119.
Ⓦ **novemestonm.cz**

Set in a beautiful location in the crook of a river, Nové Město (Neustadt) is surrounded on three sides by water. Its charming Renaissance **market square** (Husovo náměstí) has arcaded houses with joint gables decorated with finials. This uniform design of an entire frontage of a square is unique in Europe. The unusual **Castle**, in a corner of the square, was originally Gothic, and owes its present form to restoration carried out during 1909–15. The castle interiors provide a unique aesthetic experience: its Renaissance furnishings stand side by side with Art Nouveau and Cubist furniture. There are 1654 Baroque stuccoes by Giovanni Bianco, and 20th-century works by Czech artists Josef Myslbek and Max Švabinský among others. The corner tower, called Máselnice, or the "butter churn" after its domed shape, affords a magnificent view. Matthias Braun created the Baroque sculptures by the bridge over the castle moat.

🏰 Nové Město Castle
Tel 491 470 523. **Open** check website for opening hours. 🖼 🎫
Ⓦ **zameknm.cz**

⑳ Josefov

Road map D1. 🏛 12,000. 🚃 to Jaroměř, 1 km (0.5 mile) N of Josefov.

One of the prime historic sites of 18th-century military architecture, Josefov (Josefstadt) is a vast fortress town, erected in the reign of Joseph II. Ironically, it never played any military role. Its extensive system of underground corridors, 45 km (28 miles) long, runs on two, and in some places, on three levels. The 5-km (3-mile) long section of prisons is open to the public, who have to carry candles to light the darkness.

🏰 Fortifications
Tel 491 812 343. **Open** Apr, Sep & Oct: Sat & Sun; May–Aug: Tue–Sun. 🖼 🎫

Statue of Emperor Joseph II, in Josefov

㉑ Opočno

Road map E1. 🏛 3,200. 🚃 from Hradec Králové, Prague. **Tel** 494 668 111.

The beautiful and well-preserved **Opočno Castle** is perched dramatically above its small town. It was built for the Colloredo family, on the site of an earlier Gothic fortress, in 1562–7. The only remaining part of the original structure is the cylindrical tower. The unusual courtyard, with three-storey arcades on three sides, opens out into a park on the once-enclosed fourth side. Inside is an impressive collection of arms and armour. There is also a gallery with works of Italian, Bohemian and Dutch masters, and a library of over 12,000 volumes.

In Kupka square (Kupkovo náměstí) is the **Church of the Nativity** (Narození Páně), which has a splendid Baroque *Way of the Cross* in the ambulatory. There are a number of beautiful houses, including the Baroque house at No. 14. In Trčka square (Trčkovo náměstí), there are Renaissance houses at Nos. 9 and 13.

🏰 Opočno Castle
Tel 494 668 216. **Open** May–Sep: Tue–Sun; Apr & Oct: Sat, Sun & public hols. 🖼 🎫 Ⓦ **zamek-opocno.cz**

㉒ Častolovice Palace

Road map E2. 8 km (5 miles) SW of Rychnov nad Kněžnou. 🚃 🚃 from Prague. **Tel** 494 323 646. **Open** mid-Apr–Sep: 9am–6pm Tue–Sun. 🖼 🎫
Ⓦ **zamek-castolovice.cz**

Originally a Renaissance building, Častolovice Palace was remodelled in the late 19th and early 20th centuries in Neo-Gothic and Neo-Renaissance styles. Its opulent interiors have been arranged with a great deal of expertise by the current owner of the palace – Franziska Diana Sternberg-Phipps, who regained the estate after 1989.

The most impressive room is the Knights' Hall (Rytířský sál), hung with portraits of the Sternbergs, and featuring a ceiling with images from the Old Testament. The dining room ceiling is painted with the biblical story of Tobias; and in two other rooms the coffers include illustrations from Ovid's *Metamorphoses*.

The palace courtyard features magnificent colourful paintings from about 1600, depicting figures of emperors and battle scenes, and a Baroque fountain. There is a pleasant, landscaped English-style park around the palace.

The arcaded courtyard of Opočno Castle

Exploring North Moravia and Silesia

The best point from which to start exploring this region is the historic town of Olomouc, to which it is worth allocating at least a few days. From here on, heading north for the Jeseníky mountains, it is possible to see the impressive Bouzov and Sternberg castles and visit the subterranean world of the Javoříčské Caves.

Further east are the Beskydy mountains, with their wooden churches and traditional wooden buildings, offering walking opportunities and a break from the industrial landscapes elsewhere in the region.

Priessnitz Park in Jeseník, named after the founder of the nearby spa

Sights at a Glance

1. Olomouc pp218–21
2. Plumlov Palace
3. Náměšť na Hané Palace
4. Javoříčské Caves
5. Bouzov Castle
6. Jeseník
7. Šternberk Castle
8. Opava
9. Hradec nad Moravicí Castle
10. Ostrava
11. Příbor
12. Nový Jičín
13. Hranice
14. Lipník nad Bečvou
15. Rožnov pod Radhoštěm

Coach from Náměšť na Hané Palace

Key

- ▬ Motorway
- ▪▪▪▪ Motorway under construction
- ▬ Dual carriageway
- ▬ Main road
- ▪▪▪▪ Dual carriageway under construction
- ═══ Minor road
- ▬ Scenic route
- ▪▪▪▪ Main railway
- ── Minor railway
- ▬ International border
- ▬ Regional border
- △ Summit

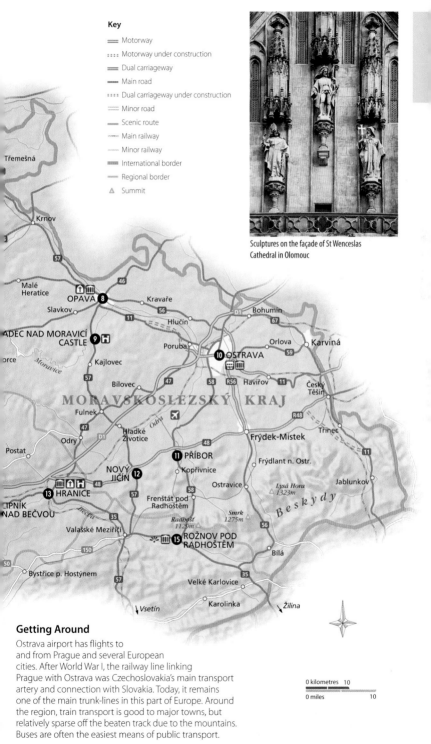

Sculptures on the façade of St Wenceslas Cathedral in Olomouc

Getting Around

Ostrava airport has flights to and from Prague and several European cities. After World War I, the railway line linking Prague with Ostrava was Czechoslovakia's main transport artery and connection with Slovakia. Today, it remains one of the main trunk-lines in this part of Europe. Around the region, train transport is good to major towns, but relatively sparse off the beaten track due to the mountains. Buses are often the easiest means of public transport.

0 kilometres   10
0 miles   10

For keys to symbols *see back flap*

❶ Olomouc

According to legend, Olomouc (Olmütz), one of Moravia's oldest towns, was founded by Julius Caesar. In fact it did not come into existence until the 7th century, when it was a major centre. In 1063, it was made a bishopric and in 1187, the capital of Moravia. Its university was founded in 1573. From 1655, the town became a military stronghold. Today, it is a prosperous and vibrant university city off the main tourist trail, retaining its beautiful religious buildings.

Detail from the stained-glass window in St Maurice Church

Exploring the town

The fine historic town centre is second only to Prague's old town in terms of size. Its oldest part centres on the main square of Horní náměstí (see also pp220–21), and is surrounded by a ring of parks and the remains of the medieval town walls. This part of the city is fascinating to explore for its lively atmosphere as well as its architecture.

⬆ Church of St Maurice

8. Května. **Tel** 585 223 179. **Open** 7am–6pm daily. 📷

This huge 15th-century edifice with two asymmetrical towers resembles a medieval fortress. The church (sv. Mořice) has an unusual architectural detail of an external staircase enclosed within a round cage. The interior is impressive with beautiful stained-glass windows and a vast 1505 wall painting. The church organ made by

Silesian organ maker Michael Engler in 1745 is the largest in Central Europe.

🚏 Horní náměstí

The main square has at its centre the 13th-century town hall (radnice), which was greatly extended in the 15th century, when it acquired its astronomical clock (see p221), beautifully vaulted Gothic Debating Hall and the chapel dedicated to St Jerome.

The huge Holy Trinity Column (sousoší Nejsvětější Trojice) in front of the town hall is on the UNESCO World Cultural Heritage List. This example of European Baroque sculpture was erected in 1716–17. Its three tiers are peopled with historic figures and saints.

Standing in the market square are three out of the total number of seven of Olomouc's fountains. The largest of them, made in 1725 by Jan J Schauberger, is the Caesar Fountain, sporting an equestrian statue of the legendary founder of the town. The other two are the Arion Fountain and the Hercules Fountain on which the hero is depicted holding a white eagle – the town symbol.

Top of the Holy Trinity Column

⬆ Church of St Michael

Žerotínovo náměstí. **Tel** 603 282 975. **Open** 10am–noon & 2:30–3:30pm Wed, 2:30–3:30pm Fri. 📷

The Dominicans, who arrived in Olomouc in about 1240, soon began to build their monastery and Church of St Michael (sv. Michala) on the town's most elevated site. In the 14th and 15th centuries, it was destroyed by fire, and in the 17th, it suffered damage from the Thirty Years' War. It was rebuilt in 1673–99 in Baroque style. The architect, Giovanni Pietro Tencalla, designed the first three-domed edifice in Moravia. Most of the furnishings date from the Baroque period, including organs by Josef Sturmer and Augustine Thomasberger. In 1829, the main façade of the building was decorated with statues of the Virgin Mary and the Saviour, produced in the 18th century by Ondřej Zahner; they are fine examples of Baroque in Olomouc.

⬆ St Jan Sarkander Chapel

Na Hradě. **Tel** 603 282 975.

This chapel (sv. Jana Sarkandera) is a Neo-Baroque building designed by E Sochor in 1909–12. It was erected on the site of the town prison, and an old torture chamber still runs beneath it.

Sculptures in the cloisters of the Church of St Michael

⬆ Church of Our Lady of the Snows

Denisova. **Open** 10am–5pm daily. 📷

Built in 1712–22 by Olomouc Jesuits, this church (Panny Marie Sněžné) served until 1778 as the university church. Features of its wavy façade are the monumental portal including four columns, a balustraded balcony and a

Sculptures on the dome of St Jan Sarkander Chapel

cartouche with the letters JHS, designed by Václav Bender. The interior includes some interesting Baroque paintings. In 2005, a bronze altar with a marble top, by the famous Czech sculptor Otmar Oliva, was fitted in the church.

🏛 Olomouc Art Museum

Denisova 47. **Tel** 585 514 111. **Open** 10am–6pm Tue–Sun. 🅿 ♿
w olmuart.cz

The historic town art gallery (Muzeum umění) is superbly modernized. It has a range of paintings by Italian artists from the 14th century onwards, plus an excellent collection of 20th-century Czech works.

✝ St Wenceslas Cathedral

Václavské náměstí. **Tel** 731 402 036. **Open** daily.

Not many traces remain of the Romanesque church that was built on this site in 1107. The present church (sv. Václav) owes its shape to the initiative of Archbishop Bedřich Fürstenberg, who ordered its reconstruction to be carried out in 1883–92, in Neo-Gothic style.

✝ Přemyslid Palace

Václavské náměstí. **Tel** 585 514 174. **Open** Apr–Sep: 10am–6pm Tue–Sun. Museum: Tue–Sun. 🅿 ♿
w olmuart.cz

One of Olomouc's most picturesque buildings is the

Decorative motifs on the pillars inside St Wenceslas Cathedral

VISITORS' CHECKLIST

Practical Information
Road map E2.
🅰 100,000.
ℹ Horní náměstí. **Tel** 585 513 385. **Open** 9am–7pm daily.
w tourism.olomouc.eu

Transport
🚆 2 km (1 mile) E of centre (Jeremenkova). **Tel** 584 722 175.
🚌 Sladkovského 41. **Tel** 585 313 848 (ext. 292).

Romanesque palace beside St Wenceslas Cathedral. It was built after 1126 by Bishop Jindřich Zdík. In its day, this was one of the most magnificent works of residential architecture in Europe. The bishop's rooms with their beautifully carved Romanesque windows and columns have no equal in the Czech Republic. The Olomouc Archdiocesan Museum opened here in 2006 and includes some fine paintings collected by bishops of Olomouc. There is also the Mozarteum concert hall.

Town Centre

① Church of St Maurice
② Horní náměstí
③ Church of St Michael
④ St Jan Sarkander Chapel
⑤ Church of Our Lady of the Snows
⑥ Olomouc Art Museum
⑦ St Wenceslas Cathedral
⑧ Přemyslid Palace

Key

▨ Street-by-Street *See pp220–21*

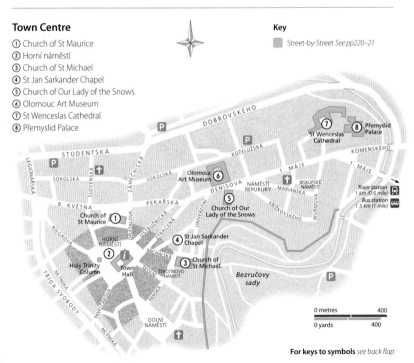

| 0 metres | 400 |
| 0 yards | 400 |

For keys to symbols *see back flap*

Street-by-Street: Horní náměstí

Olomouc's cobbled main square is famous, above all, for its grand Town Hall, and the remarkable highly decorated Holy Trinity Column. Equally impressive are its three fountains: the Caesar Fountain of 1725, the 1687 Hercules Fountain, and the newest – the 2002 Arion Fountain. The square is a popular meeting place, especially around the Holy Trinity Column, and its many sidestreets offer pleasant and interesting places to explore.

Edelmann Palace
One of the most opulent buildings in the square is the Renaissance palace dating from 1572–86, built for the wealthy local merchant Václav Edelmann.

Hercules fountain

28. ŘÍJNA

R. TEGROVA

HORNÍ NÁMĚSTÍ

PAVELČÁKO

★ Holy Trinity Column
The massive Baroque column is crowned by figures representing the Holy Trinity. Below is the Archangel Michael with his fiery sword.

★ Town Hall
The magnificent external staircase built in 1591 is decorated with heraldic emblems. The slender tower, which dominates the entire building, affords a lovely view over the market and the surrounding streets.

Arion Fountain
The work of Ivan Theimer and a Tuscan artist, Angela Chiantelli, this fountain depicting the ancient poet Arion was produced in 2002 to a design created by the Olomouc councillors 350 years ago.

Coat of Arms, Town Hall
The shield of Olomouc was placed next to the town hall's stairs in 1591. It features the Moravian chequered eagle.

Chapel Oriel
In 1488, the remodelled chapel of the town hall was given a lavishly decorated oriel, unique in the Czech Republic.

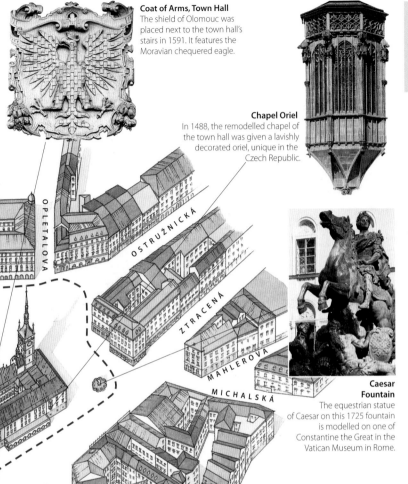

Caesar Fountain
The equestrian statue of Caesar on this 1725 fountain is modelled on one of Constantine the Great in the Vatican Museum in Rome.

Key

— Suggested route

Town Hall Clock

The first clock was placed in the Gothic niche on the north wall of the town hall in the early 15th century. The mechanism displaying astronomical data was added in 1573. After damage in World War II, it was remodelled so that wooden figures of proletarians replaced those of saints. A mosaic added at the same time also shows workers.

The clock by Master Hanuš with its new figures and mosaic

0 metres   100
0 yards   100

Plumlov Palace beside Plumlov Reservoir

❷ Plumlov Palace

Road map E2. 7 km (4 miles) W of Prostějov. 🚌 from Prostějov, Olomouc. **Tel** 773 444 500. **Open** Apr & Oct: 1–6pm Sat, Sun & public hols; May, Sep: 10am–6pm; Jun–Aug: 10am–6pm Tue–Sun. 🎨

An astonishing sight, Plumlov Palace is a tall, three-storey structure (there are two further, intermediate storeys inside), which is also unusually flat. The entire façade is lavishly decorated with columns, cornices, stuccoes and balustrades.

The palace's unusual shape is due to its history. The 17th-century prince-bishop Karl Eusebius of Liechtenstein, Lord of Valtice, designed a huge four-wing palace that was to be the most beautiful residence in Moravia. Unfortunately, his son, Jan Adam, saddled by his father with the responsibility of accomplishing the task, was unable to meet the financial demands associated with the project. The family became embroiled in arguments about financial affairs and consequently, by the end of the century, only one wing was completed and roofed. This now serves as a small museum and a venue for a variety of cultural events.

❸ Náměšť na Hané Palace

Road map E2. 13 km (8 miles) W of Olomouc. 🚉 🚌 from Prostějov, Olomouc. **Tel** 585 952 184. **Open** Apr, Oct: 9am–4pm Sat & Sun; May–Sep: 9am–5pm Tue–Sun. 🎨

The palace, with its mansard roof typical of late 18th-century French architecture, was built in 1760–63 by Ferdinand Bonaventura Harrach. Its two ground-floor wings surround a courtyard that ends with a gate leading to the palace garden. Laid out in the shape of a perfect circle, the garden is crisscrossed by four avenues of lime trees leading to the four points of the compass.

Riches of the interior include the Red and the Gold Parlours with Rococo, Classical and Empire furnishings; there is also an extensive library. Large collections of Meissen porcelain and the stately coaches are housed in the ground-floor wings, from the collection of the Olomouc Archbishopric.

The palace Chapel of the Holy Trinity took an extraordinarily long time to be completed; the building works started in 1672 and ended 50 years later. In 1834, it was remodelled in the Empire style.

❹ Javoříčské Caves

Road map E2. 4 km (2 miles) S of Bouzov. 🚌 from Bouzov. **Tel** 585 345 451. **Open** Jan–Mar & Nov: 10am–1pm Mon–Fri; Apr & Oct: 9am–3pm Tue–Sun; May–Sep: 9am–5pm Tue–Sun. 🎨 📷

The maze of limestone caves (jeskyně) discovered here in 1938 stretches for over 3 km (2 miles). Part of the subterranean complex, nearly 800 m (2,600 ft) long, is open to the public. Its chambers, some of which are more than 10 m (33 ft) high, feature extraordinary stalactite formations.

Stalactite formations inside the Cave of Giants in Javoříčské Caves

❺ Bouzov Castle

Road map E2. 🚉 12 km (7 miles) Mohelnice. **Tel** 585 346 202. **Open** Apr & Oct: 9am–4pm Sat & Sun; May–Sep: 9am–5pm Tue–Sun (to 6pm Jun–Aug). 🎨 📷

Founded in the 14th century, Bouzov Castle (Busau) was

Interior of the palace in Náměšť na Hané

probably the birthplace of George of Poděbrady, the future king of Bohemia. In 1696, Bouzov became the property of the Teutonic Knights. It gradually fell into disrepair until the end of the 19th century, when the Order's Grand Master, Archduke Eugene Habsburg, commissioned Georg von Hauberisser to remodel the structure in the Romantic spirit. As a result, Bouzov acquired the form of a huge Gothic fortress complete with towers and turrets.

In 1939, the castle became the headquarters of a Nazi SS unit. After the war, it was taken over by the Czech state authorities, and now, impeccably maintained, it is among the Czech Republic's most popular historic sites.

Its interiors, decorated with paintings and sculptures, include the luxurious apartments of the Grand Master; the Column Hall; Royal Quarters and Guest Rooms; Chapel and Armoury; castle kitchens and fortress defence system.

❻ Jeseník

Road map E2. 🔼 11,900. 🚍 🚌 from Olomouc. 🚶 Palackého 2. **Tel** 776 773 503.

One of the towns in the Jeseníky peaks, away from the industry of the lower-lying parts of Moravia, Jeseník (Freiwaldau) has a castle known as the Water Fortress for its now-dry moat. It withstood a siege by the Swedes in 1641. The fortress was given its present shape in the mid-18th century. It now houses the **Regional Museum**. Perched above the town, on a hillside, is the small spa resort of **Lázně Jeseník**, founded by Vinzenz Priessnitz, who advocated cold-water therapy. It was at the height of its fame in the 19th century.

🏛 **Regional Museum**
Tel 584 401 070. **Open** 9am–5pm Tue–Sun (Feb, Jul & Aug: daily). 🚫

Arcaded cloister in the courtyard of Šternberk Castle

❼ Šternberk Castle

Road map E2. 🚍 🚌 from Olomouc. **Tel** 585 012 935. **Open** Apr & Oct: 10am–5pm Sat, Sun & public hols; May–Sep: 10am–5pm Tue–Sun (to 6pm Jun–Aug). 🚫 📷 2 routes. 🌐 **hrad-sternberk.cz**

The oldest surviving part of the castle, the cylindrical tower, dates from the second half of the 13th century. The remaining buildings of this medieval structure took a lot of battering during the 15th-century Hussite wars, and in the course of the Thirty Years' War, in 1618–48. In the 19th century, Jan II of Liechtenstein rebuilt the decaying castle in Neo-Gothic style. Now it is home to the Liechtenstein collection, which includes furniture, paintings, sculptures and fireplaces. The second floor has an interesting exhibition of furnishings brought from Northern Moravian castles, which after 1945 were closed to the public.

Relief image of Priessnitz, in Jeseník

❽ Opava

Road map F2. 🔼 58,600. 🚍 🚌 from Prague. 🚶 Horní náměstí 67. **Tel** 553 756 143. 🌐 **infocentrum.opava.cz**

The capital of Austrian Silesia following the Austro-Prussian war of 1742, Opava (Troppau) started life as an important trading centre. Its most interesting historic sites include the vast 14th-century brick **Church of the Assumption of the Virgin Mary** (Nanebevzetí Panny Marie), a splendid example of Silesian Gothic. Masaryk Street (Masarykova třída) is a handsome street that includes the 18th-century palaces of the Sobek and Blücher families.

The oldest museum in the Czech Republic, founded in 1814, is the **Silesian Municipal Museum** (Slezské zemské Museum). Its opulent building was erected in 1893–5 to a design by Viennese architects Scheinringer and Kachler. It has history, ethnography and natural history displays. Its other division, in Hlučín-Darkovičky, includes Czech fortifications erected in the late 1930s – a rare example of well-preserved military technology of that time.

🏛 **Silesian Municipal Museum**
Komenského 10. **Tel** 553 622 999. **Open** 9am–7pm daily. 🚫

Altar in the Church of the Assumption in Opava

Courtyard view of the red castle in Hradec nad Moravicí

❾ Hradec nad Moravicí Castle

Road map F2. 🚉 from Opava, Přerov.
📧 **Tel** 553 783 444. **Open** Apr &
Oct: 10am–4pm Sat & Sun; May–Sep:
10am–6pm Tue–Sun. 🎫 📷 2 routes.
🌐 **zamek-hradec.cz**

As early as the 9th century,
a Slav settlement stood here.
The fortress, built in the 11th
century, kept watch over the
Polish-Czech borderland.
Following consecutive
reconstructions, including
late 16th-century Renaissance
works and late 18th- to early
19th-century Neo-Classical
remodelling, the castle acquired
its present Romantic Neo-
Gothic form in 1860–67. Its
owners, the ducal family of
Lichnovský of Voštice, turned
it into a centre of culture and
music. Now, the lovingly
restored interiors exhibit
paintings, porcelain and
mementoes associated with
visits from Beethoven, Liszt
and Paganini.

❿ Ostrava

Road map F2. 🚶 302,500.
🚉 Nádražní 196. 🚌 Vitkovická 2.
ℹ️ Jurečkova 1935/12. **Tel** 596 123
913. 🌐 **ostrava.cz**

The third-largest city in the
Czech Republic, Ostrava
(Ostrau) expanded rapidly
from 1763 onwards, when rich
coal deposits were discovered
nearby. The development
of mines, steelworks and
construction and chemical
plants turned Ostrava and its
environs into an industrial

district and pollution was a
huge problem. However,
Ostrava lost its heavy industrial
appearance when coal-mining
in the city came to an end in
1994. Over time, museums
have been established where
mines once stood.

The centre has been
declared a historic zone.
Masarykovo náměstí, the main
square, has one of the city's
oldest buildings: the 17th-
century **Old Town Hall** (Stará
radnice). Some of Ostrava's
finest buildings date from
the 1920s. They include
the former **Anglo-Czech
Bank** designed by Josef
Gočár; the Constructivist
Arts Centre (Dům umění),
now the **Gallery of
Arts and Crafts**
(Galerie výtvarného umění),
and the **New Town Hall**,
north of the old centre.
In Petřkovice suburb
is a vast open-air
**Landek Park –
Mining Museum**
(Hornické muzeum), where
visitors can see an old mine.

Fountain in Příbor
market square

🏛 Gallery of Arts and Crafts
Jurečkova 9. **Tel** 596 112 566.
Open 10am–6pm Tue–Sun.
🎫 🌐 **gvuostrava.cz**

🏛 Landek Park – Mining Museum
Pod Landekem 64. **Tel** 596 131 804.
Open 9am–6pm daily (except Nov–
Mar: Mon). 🌐 **landekpark.cz**

⓫ Příbor

Road map F2. 🚶 8,800.
🚉 Ostrava. 🚌 Olomouc, Ostrava.
ℹ️ Náměstí Sigmunda Freuda 19.
Tel 556 455 442. 🌐 **pribor.eu**

The birthplace of Sigmund
Freud, Příbor (Freiberg)
is in the foothills of the
Beskydy. Its market square
(náměstí Sigmunda Freuda)
is surrounded by
Renaissance houses
with Baroque façades. At
its centre is a 1713 statue
of the Virgin Mary. Příbor
is dominated by the
tower of the **Church
of St Mary** (sv. Marie),
which has a Gothic
statue of the Madonna dating
from 1400. The former 1694

Houses in Poštovna, near Masarykovo náměstí in Ostrava

Piarist college houses the **Příbor Museum** with some Freud mementoes.

🏛 **Příbor Museum**
Lidická 50. **Tel** 556 725 191. **Open** Tue, Thu & Sun. 🖼 **W** muzeumnj.cz

⑫ Nový Jičín

Road map F2. 🔼 24,000. 🚌 from Olomouc. ℹ️ Masarykovo nám 45/29. **Tel** 556 711 888. **W** novyjicin.cz

The old part of Nový Jičín (Neutitschein) has maintained its original square layout dating from the Middle Ages. The striking house of Mayor Ondřej Řepa, dating from 1563 and known as the **Old Post Office** (stará pošta), features a two-storey arcaded loggia. The "White Angel", continuously used as a pharmacy since 1716, has a 1790 Neo-Rococo façade.

In a Gothic former castle is the fascinating **Nový Jičín Museum** with its remarkable collection of hats, as well as history and art exhibitions.

🏛 **Nový Jičín Museum**
Tel 556 701 156. **Open** Tue–Sun. 🖼 **W** muzeumnj.cz

⑬ Hranice

Road map F2. 🔼 18,900. 🚌 from Ostrava, Přerov. ℹ️ Pernštejnské nám 1. **Tel** 581 607 479.

In Hranice, there is a late-Renaissance **castle**, a four-wing structure with an arcaded courtyard. The most opulent building in the market square is the Baroque **Church of St John the Baptist** (sv. Jana Křtitele) dating from 1763. At one corner of the square stands the Neo-Gothic town hall, built in the first half of the 16th century. Several nearby houses have interesting Renaissance façades. The **Municipal Museum** also lies on the main square; it contains local history exhibits.

🏛 **Municipal Museum**
Masarykovo náměstí 71. **Tel** 581 601 160. **Open** Tue–Sun. 🖼

The castle housing the Nový Jičín Museum

⑭ Lipník nad Bečvou

Road map F2. 🔼 8,400. 🚉 🚌 from Přerov. ℹ️ Náměstí T G Masaryka 13. **Tel** 581 773 763.

The town's historic core centres on its L-shaped market square, lined with Renaissance and Baroque houses. Its most eye-catching buildings are the **Town Hall** (radnice), and the 1609 bell tower. The **Church of St Jacob** (sv. Jakub) has a unique Renaissance tower. Another place of interest is the Late-Gothic former **synagogue**.

Environs
Helfštýn, 4 km (2 miles) southeast of Lipník, is the largest of the Moravian castles. This 14th-century Gothic edifice was several times extended. The drive to the castle complex leads through five gates and across four courtyards. The last features ruins of a late-Renaissance palace, whose basement houses an interesting historical exhibition.

Emblem of Hranice at the Municipal Museum

⑮ Rožnov pod Radhoštěm

Road map F2. 🔼 17,200. 🚉 🚌 from Valašské, Meziříčí. ℹ️ Masarykovo náměstí 131. **Tel** 571 652 444.

To the south of Radhošť mountain lies a small town (its name means Rožnov under

Radhošť') that is immensely popular for its **Wallachian Open-Air Museum** (Valašské muzeum v přírodě). This consists of three open-air exhibitions (or skansen) of beautiful traditional wooden buildings of the Wallachs of the Beskydy region. The Wallachs were sheep farmers who lived in Moravia and parts of Slovakia. The skansen, established in 1925, aim to preserve and illuminate their culture and way of life with examples from the 17th to the 20th centuries.

From the museum, it is possible to walk up **Radhošť** mountain, which at 1,129 m (3,700 ft) above sea level, provides extraordinary views of the surrounding peaks and villages. On its top stands a Byzantine-style wooden chapel of St Cyril and St Methodius, dating from 1898.

🏛 **Wallachian Open-Air Museum**
Palackého 147. **Tel** 571 757 111. **Open** daily (some areas May–Sep only). **Closed** Mon. 🖼 📷 **W** vmp.cz

Portal of the Church of St Jacob in Lipník nad Bečvou

SOUTH MORAVIA

The wealth of historic remains in this region would enthral most visitors. Around virtually every corner you are likely to come across lovely towns and villages or imposing monasteries, castles and palaces. The stunning Renaissance town of Telč, the archbishop's residence in Kroměřiž, Villa Tugendhat in Brno, the church in Žd'ár nad Sázavou, and the Lednicko-Valtický park and palace complex are all UNESCO World Heritage sites.

South Moravia (Jižní Morava), once a frontier region of the Roman Empire, was the cradle of the first state set up by the Slavs, who arrived in the region from Eastern Europe. The so-called Great Moravian Empire *(see p35)* lasted from 830 until the early 10th century, when Magyars made incursions into Moravian territory. In the subsequent centuries, South Moravia was the scene of some of the most momentous events in the history of the Czech Lands.

The capital of the region (and of the whole of Moravia) is Brno. This university town, the second largest in the Czech Republic, is often neglected by visitors, but it has a pleasant and compact historic centre as well as a modernist landmark, Mies van der Rohe's Villa Tugendhat. Elsewhere in the region, there are architectural treasures from most periods: Znojmo's magnificent Romanesque rotunda; the splendid Gothic castle of Pernštejn; the Renaissance gem of Telč; and the Baroque castle in Valtice. Besides the buildings that testify to Moravia's strong links with Catholicism, there are also many sights associated with the history of the region's Jewish population, including those in Boskovice, Mikulov and Třebíč.

While South Moravia's hills and forests are similar to Bohemia's, the southern part of the region is flatter and more open. Home to fertile vineyards, it has a long tradition of winemaking. Around Mikulov and other southern towns, it is worth visiting the historic cellars, and tasting the highly respected wines.

Fountain in front of the elegant arcades in Kroměřiž gardens

◄ The 18th-century column of Virgin Mary at the Town Square in Telč

Exploring South Moravia

Brno is the most convenient place to begin a visit. As well as
having some attractions of its own, the city is also within easy
reach of other places of interest, such as Pernštejn Castle and
the breathtaking caves of the Moravský kras. South of Brno,
much of the land was once owned by the Liechtenstein family,
who built many of the churches and castles here, including
Lednice and Vranov. The neglected hilly region in the
west is home to the idyllic town of Telč, while in
the eastern reaches beats the heart
of Moravia's folk culture.

Oriel of a house in Telč's main square

Getting Around

Brno lies at the junction of major transport routes. The D1
motorway cuts through the centre of the region linking
Prague to Brno, and continuing to Silesia and Ostrava. The
D2 heads south from Brno towards Bratislava and Slovakia.
Running through the eastern part of the region, through
Otrokovice and Břeclav, is the main railway line linking Warsaw
with Vienna, via Bratislava, but generally, the train network in
South Moravia is not as good as in Bohemia.

For hotels and restaurants see p353 and pp374–5

Sights at a Glance

Statue of the Three Graces in the palace gardens at Valtice

Key

▬▬▬ Motorway

▭▭▭ Dual carriageway

▬▬▬ Main road

▬ ▬ ▬ Dual carriageway under construction

▭▭▭ Minor road

▬▬▬ Main railway

──── Minor railway

▬▬▬ International border

▬▬▬ Regional border

Lednice castle gardens, in the Lednicko-Valticky areál

For keys to symbols *see back flap*

● Brno

Now the second-largest city in the Czech Republic, Brno (Brünn) occupies the site of what, in the 9th century, was the main settlement in the Great Moravian Empire. The city that you see today first developed at the foot of Petrov Hill, where the Přemyslids built a castle in the 11th century. In 1641, the walled town became the new capital of Moravia but didn't develop significantly until the 19th century. World War II devastated the city and, despite being totally rebuilt, Brno has never quite regained its former lustre. Even so, thanks to its buoyant theatre life and numerous museums, Brno has become a major cultural centre.

View of the St Peter and St Paul Cathedral

Exploring the Town

Brno's Old Town, with the city's main historic sites and museums, is focused around two squares: Zelný trh and náměstí Svobody. Two major landmarks outside the Old Town are the twin-towered cathedral atop Petrov Hill, and **Špilberk fortress**, to the west (see pp232–3). The other sites of interest are Villa Tugendhat and the Augustinian Monastery.

⛪ Cathedral of St Peter and St Paul

Petrov Hill. **Tel** 543 235 031.
Open 8:15am–6:30pm daily.
✝ 7:30am daily; 9am, 10:30am Sun; 7:30am Sat (in Latin).

The cathedral (katedrála sv. Petra a Pavla), with its soaring towers visible from afar, stands on what was, in the 11th and 12th centuries, the probable site of Brno's first castle. Originally Romanesque, the church acquired a Gothic appearance in the 1200s. Subsequent alterations obliterated its original shape. It was restored to its Gothic form in the late 1800s. Of most interest inside is the church crypt. There are great views from the tower.

⛪ Church of the Holy Cross

Kapucínské náměstí 5. Crypt: **Tel** 539 002 163. **Open** 9am–noon & 2–4pm Tue–Sat (also May–Sep: Mon), 11–11:45am & 2–4:30pm Sun.

The austere façade of the Church of the Holy Cross (kostel sv. Kříže), near the foot of Petrov Hill, is typical of other Capuchin churches elsewhere in Europe. The macabre attraction here is the mummified monks in the crypt.

🏛 Zelný trh

This square (literally "cabbage market") has served as a vegetable market since the Middle Ages, and has even kept its original, sloping shape. Its main adornment, the Parnassus Fountain, is Brno's finest piece of sculpture. Made to a design by Fischer von Erlach in the 1690s, it combines the best traits of Baroque naturalism, *trompe l'oeil* and theatrics. Among the rather motley group of buildings around Zlený trh is the home of the Reduta theatre. This is the oldest theatre

building in Brno. The Dietrichstein Palace (Dietrichsteinský palác), at the square's southern end, has a fine entrance portal (1700) and is home to the **Moravian Museum**, devoted to Brno's early history.

Sculptures by Anton Pilgram on the Old Town Hall's doorway

🏛 Old Town Hall

Radnická 8. **Tel** 542 427 150.
Open Apr–Sep: 9:30am–6pm daily.

Just off Zelný trh, the Old Town Hall (Stará radnice) is the oldest secular building in Brno, dating from 1240. In 1510, a doorway was cut into the tower on Radnická and framed by a superb Gothic portal. This work by Anton Pilgram is decorated at the lower level with figures of knights and, above, with figures of the town's aldermen. At the centre is the allegorical figure of Blind Justice. A pinnacle above the statue is deliberately twisted, said to be Pilgram's revenge for being underpaid for his work. The main tourist office is here, and there are views from the tower.

🏛 New Town Hall

Dominikánské náměstí 1.
The "New" Town Hall (Nová radnice), the seat of the city council, dates mainly from the 1700s. It was built inside a former Dominican monastery; the Dominican **St Michael's Church** stands nearby. Gothic cloisters survive inside the town hall. The first courtyard is skirted by Renaissance buildings and has a lovely sundial (1728).

Eighteenth-century sculpture outside St Michael's Church

🏛 Náměstí Svobody

Brno's main square buzzes with life, its many restaurants and cafés being popular meeting places. The chief landmark is the Baroque **plague column**, while the architecture around the square spans 400 years. Its finest buildings include the Schwartz House (Schwarzův palác), with an ornate 16th-century façade decorated with *sgraffito,* and the House of the Four Mamlases (Dům u čtyř mamlasů) (1928), whose four comical Atlas figures strain to support the building.

🏛 Moravian Gallery

Husova 18, Husova 14 Moravské náměstí 1a & Jana Nečase 2. **Tel** 532 169 111. **Open** 10am–6pm Wed & Fri–Sun, 10am–7pm Thu. 🖼

The Moravská galerie is spread over four premises.

The most spectacular among these is the Jurkovič House located at Jana Nečase 2. Built in Brno around the beginning of the 20th century, the building is a splendid example of Art Nouveau architecture.

🏛 Villa Tugendhat

Černopolni 45. 🚃 9, 11. **Tel** 515 511 015. **Open** 10am–6pm Tue–Sun; reservation required. 🖼 📷 W
tugendhat.eu

Designed in the spirit of Functionalism, Villa Tugendhat was built by well-known German architect, Ludwig Mies van der Rohe in 1929–30. By covering a steel frame with glass, van der Rohe achieved a superb effect of linked space both inside and outside the building. Fortunately,

alterations made by the Communists did not manage to ruin the building.

🏛 Augustinian Monastery

Mendlovo náměstí 1. **Tel** 543 424 010. Mendel's Museum: **Open** 10am–6pm Tue–Sun (to 5pm Nov–Mar). 🖼 ♿ W **opatbrno.cz**

This monastery (Augustiniánský klášter) has a fine Gothic church, but it is famous above all as the place where renowned scientist Gregor Mendel (1822–84) discovered and formulated his theory of genetics. The monk's contribution to modern biology was acknowl-edged only after his death. A **museum** dedicated to his work is in the monastery's west wing.

Brno's náměstí Svobody, with its Baroque plague column (1680)

Brno City Centre

① Cathedral of St Peter and St Paul
② Church of the Holy Cross
③ Zelný trh
④ Old Town Hall
⑤ New Town Hall
⑥ Náměstí Svobody
⑦ Moravian Gallery

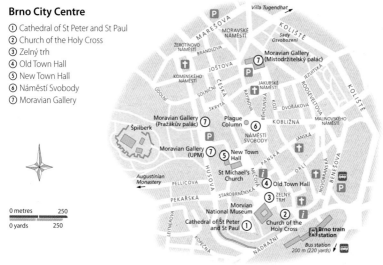

0 metres 250
0 yards 250

For keys to symbols *see back flap*

Brno: Špilberk

A hilltop castle was built on this site by a Moravian margrave, the future Přemysl Otakar II, in the 13th century, but Špilberk gained the status of a true royal residence only 400 years later, when it was transformed into a mighty Baroque fortress. After the Napoleonic wars, the castle became a prison and gained a reputation as one of the harshest symbols of Habsburg repression. Špilberk was also used as a prison by the Nazis. Displays inside relate to Brno and the castle. Concerts and plays are staged here in summer.

Coat of Arms
The coat of arms with a twin-headed eagle and an imperial crown is a reminder that Špilberk was one of the main fortresses defending the mighty Habsburg Empire.

"From Castle to Fortress"
The rooms devoted to the history of Špilberk also have an excavated area showing some of the citadel's earliest foundations.

"Brno at Špilberk"
This extensive exhibition seeks to bring to life the history of Brno, from its earliest records in 1091 to the end of World War II.

"From Renaissance to Modernism"
This permanent exhibition displays works by painters and sculptors associated with Brno, from the mid-16th century to 1945.

Baroque Pharmacy
From the mid-18th until the early 20th century, the pharmacy belonged to a convent in Brno. Its historic furnishings include hundreds of jars, instruments and the original cupboards.

VISITORS' CHECKLIST

Practical Information
Špilberk. **Tel** 542 123 611.
Open 9am–5pm Tue–Sun
(to 6pm Jul–Sep). Baroque
Pharmacy: May–Sep: 10am–
6pm Tue–Sun. Casements:
10am–5pm Tue–Sun (to 6pm
Jul–Sep). 🗺 🖳 **spilberk.cz**

Transport
✈ 🚃 Hlavní nádraží. 🚌 Zvonařka.

Tower
The tower at the northeast corner of the castle provides an excellent viewpoint overlooking the entire Špilberk area. It is also used for staging exhibitions.

★ Dungeons
This maze of dark, dank subterranean corridors was transformed, in the reign of Emperor Joseph II, into a series of unbelievably gruesome prison cells, particularly those in the north wing.

★ Chapel
Little remains of the original Gothic castle. The Gothic look of the eastern wing, and of the chapel, dates from controversial reconstruction work carried out in the 1990s.

The façade and ornamental lake of the Baroque chateau in Slavkov u Brna

❷ Slavkov u Brna

Road map E3. 🏔 6,300. 🚍 🚌
ℹ Palackého 1/126. **Tel** 513 034 156.
🆆 slavkov.cz

The plains between Brno and Slavkov (Austerlitz) were, in 1805, the site of the great battle in which Napoleon defeated the Austrians and Russians *(see box)*. Before the battle, Emperor Francis II and Tsar Alexander I stayed at the Baroque **Slavkov Chateau** (zámek Slavkov), which Napoleon chose as his base following his victory.

The vast building, with its squat central dome, has some beautifully preserved rooms. The finest is the Ancestors' Hall (Sál předků) with its stucco decoration. It was here that Napoleon and the defeated Emperor and Tsar signed their peace treaty. In the museum is a model of the battlefield.

🏰 **Slavkov Chateau**
Palackeho náměstí 1. **Tel** 544 227 548.
Open Apr–May, Sep–Nov: Tue– Sun;
Jun–Aug: daily. 🅿 🅲
🆆 zamek-slavkov.cz

❸ Křtiny

Road map E3. 🏔 770. 🚌
Tel 516 439 109.

Hidden amid forests and rocks northeast of Brno is Křtiny. Home to a castle, the village is more famous for its **Church of Our Lady**, one of the crowning achievements of Moravian Baroque architecture.

Designed by the superb Baroque architect, Giovanni Santini, this large pilgrimage

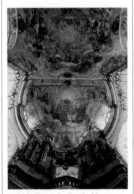

Vaulted ceiling in the Church of Our Lady, Křtiny

church was built between 1712 and 1750. Inside, the nave has a definite Byzantine feel, with its frescoed domes in garish colours illuminated by light from numerous windows. The high altar itself, crowned with a baldachin, is a riot of colour. Here can be found the venerated 15th-century statue of Our Lady.

The interior is decorated with works by leading artists of the Czech Baroque. The wall paintings (1747) are by Johann J Etgens, and the Way of the Cross stations by the Jesuit painter, Ignaz Raab.

🏰 **Church of Our Lady**
Křtiny. **Tel** 516 439 189.

❹ Boskovice

Road map E2. 🏔 11,400. 🚍 🚌
ℹ Masarykovo náměstí 1. **Tel** 516
488 677. 🆆 boskovice.cz

The town of Boskovice, 48 km (30 miles) north of Brno, is one of the most beautiful in the region with two impressive historic sights.

The first is the ruined 13th-century **Boskovice Castle** (hrad Boskovice), which was obtained by the Dietrichstein family in the 17th century but abandoned by them in the 18th. The vast structure, one of the biggest of its kind in Moravia, still has its original defensive walls, complete with a gate and a tower.

Nearby is the magnificent **Boskovice Chateau** (palác Boskovice), built from 1819–26 by the Dietrichsteins. With its clean architectural lines, it is the finest example of the Empire style

Gate and walls of the impressive castle ruins in Boskovice

The Battle of Austerlitz

On 2 December 1805, Napoleon's 75,000-strong forces crushed the 90,000-strong combined Russian and Austrian armies near the town of Slavkov. The battle claimed the lives of some 33,000 Russian and Austrian troops, and about 7,000 French. The Monument of Peace (Mohyla míru), a soaring Art Nouveau pyramid, was erected on the battlefield, 8 km (5 miles) southwest of Slavkov, in 1912. The fields around are scattered with crosses.

The Monument of Peace

SOUTH MORAVIA | 235

in Moravia. Of particular interest inside are the main hall, library and Neo-Classical furnishings. There is also an exhibition illustrating the everyday life of the Czech nobility in the 19th century.

Boskovice, once home to a large Jewish community, has one of the best preserved former Jewish ghettoes in the country, encompassing some 80 buildings. These include the richly decorated Grand Synagogue (see p239) on Taplova Street. The large Jewish cemetery, established in the 17th century, is now overgrown with trees.

🏛 Boskovice Castle
Tel 516 452 043. **Open** Apr & Oct: Sat & Sun; May, Jun & Sep: Tue–Sun; Jul & Aug: daily. 🏛

🏛 Boskovice Chateau
Tel 516 452 241. **Open** May–Sep: Tue–Sun. **W** zamekboskovice.cz

Macocha Abyss, created by the collapse of a cave roof

⑤ Moravský kras

Road map E3. 🚌 to Blansko from Brno; from Blansko to Skalní Mlýn. 🛈 Skalní Mlýn. **Tel** 516 413 575. ♿ Some caves accessible: phone for information. **W** caves.cz

The limestone karst region of the Moravský kras covers an area of some 85 sq km (33 sq miles) north of Brno, and is hollowed out by a vast system of caves. Four caves are open to the public, three of which can be reached on foot from Skalní Mlýn (5 km/3 miles from Blansko), home to the main Moravský kras information centre.

The first, the **Punkva Caves** (Punkevní jeskyně) are the largest in the whole region. On the one-hour tour, which

Moravia's Karst

In the Moravský kras, as in similar regions elsewhere, the karst formations are the result of the action of rainwater on limestone rock: over millions of years the water dissolves the rock, creating cracks which are then eroded by the constant flow. Great cave systems and deep gorges often result. Limestone-rich water dripping through the porous roofs of the caves often creates stalactites and stalagmites. Moravia's karst is famous for its rivers that repeatedly vanish and re-emerge. The word "karst" comes from the German name of the limestone plateau near Trieste.

Stalactites and stalagmites in the Punkva cave

includes a boat ride along the Punkva underground river, visitors can expect to see some fantastic stalactites and stalagmites, and to gaze in wonder up the 1,387-m (4,550-ft) Macocha Abyss (propast Macocha). To be sure of a place on this very popular cave tour, book ahead in the high season. It is also possible to visit the rim of the abyss separately.

The second, **Kateřinská Cave**, is the region's largest single cavern, measuring 100 m (328 ft) in length. The third, the **Balcarka Cave**, is small but has breathtakingly colourful stalactites and stalagmites. Evidence of prehistoric human dwellings has also been discovered here.

The caves are the big attraction but the scenery of the Moravský kras is worth seeing in its own right, with its densely wooded ravines. Visitors in need of a break

from the geological tour should stop off 5 km (3 miles) north of Blansko at Rájec-Jestřebí for a look at **Rájec nad Svitavou Chateau**, an unusual Moravian example of French Baroque built in the 1760s. Part of the attraction is the collection of 16th-century Dutch and Flemish paintings assembled by the Salm family, the original residents.

🏛 Punkva Cave
Tel 516 413 575. **Open** Jan–Oct: Tue–Sun (Apr–Sep: daily). 🏛 🎫 ♿

🏛 Kateřinská Cave
Tel 516 413 575. **Open** Mar, Apr & Oct–Dec: Tue–Sun; May–Sep: daily. 🏛 🎫 ♿

🏛 Balcarka Cave
Tel 516 413 575. **Open** Mar, Apr, Oct & Nov: Tue–Sun; May–Sep: daily. 🏛 🎫 ♿

🏛 Rájec nad Svitavou Chateau
Tel 516 432 013. **Open** Apr & Oct: Sat & Sun; May–Sep: Tue–Sun. **W** zamekrajec.cz

The French-style Rájec nad Svitavou Chateau, in the Moravský kras

❻ Pernštejn Castle

Road map E2. 🚌 🚐 Nedvědice,
2 km (1 mile) from Pernštejn. **Tel** 566
566 101. **Open** Apr & Oct: 9am–3pm
Sat, Sun & public hols; May–Sep: 9am–
4pm Tue–Sun (Jul & Aug: to 5pm). 🔲
🔲 W hrad-pernstejn.eu

The road that leads from the
village of Nedvědice, at the
foot of Pernštejn, gives an
unforgettable view of the sheer
walls, towers and turrets of the
Gothic castle. This, one of the
biggest and best-preserved
Gothic strongholds in the Czech
Republic, was damaged by fire
in 2005, but it is open to the
public once more.

Rebuilding work in the 15th
and 16th centuries turned the
medieval *hrad* into a fortress so
powerful that it withstood all
attempts by the Swedish army
to capture it during the Thirty
Years' War. The various sections
of the castle are linked by a
labyrinth of secret passages,
corridors and winding
staircases. The most interesting
rooms include the Knights' Hall
and the library. There are also
superb views to be had of the
surrounding hills and valleys.

The impressive Gothic Pernštejn Castle in Czech Republic

13th century, is named after the
church's Romanesque gateway
on the west front. Reminiscent
of French cathedral portals, it
is surprisingly ornate given the
traditional austerity of the
Cistercian Order.

🏛 **Porta Coeli Museum**
Tel 549 412 293. **Open** Tue–Sun. 🔲

❽ Žd'ár nad Sázavou

Road map D2. 🚹 23,000. 🚌 🚐
🚹 náměstí Republiky 24. **Tel** 566 625
808. W zdarns.cz

Located in the uplands of
the so-called Vysočina, this
industrial town is of little
interest in itself. The draw
here is the former Cistercian
monastery, 3 km (2 miles)
north. This is largely the
work of the visionary
Giovanni Santini, who
oversaw the Baroque
redesign of the Gothic
monastery in the early
1700s. The complex is
now known as **Žd'ár
Castle** (zámek Žd'ár)
and encompasses
various museums.
The Book Museum
(Muzeum Knihy) is
particularly good.

The most beautiful
and extraordinary sight,
however, is found on a
hilltop above the castle,
namely the **St John
Nepomuk Church**

Tišnov's Porta Coeli, showing its
Romanesque gateway

❼ Tišnov

Road map E3. 🚹 8,700. 🚌 🚐

If you drive from Brno to
Pernštejn, or take the train (a
lovely route), it is well worth
stopping off at Tišnov in order
to visit the Cistercian convent,
Porta Coeli ("Gate of Heaven"),
in the suburb of Předklášteří.
The nunnery, founded in the

(sv. Jan Nepomucký). Built in
1720, this is one of Santini's
most eccentric works and
is now part of the UNESCO
heritage list. Both its design and
decoration repeatedly allude to
the number five: the story goes
that when John Nepomuk had
his tongue cut out and was
thrown off the Charles Bridge
in Prague, five stars appeared
above his head. The church is in
the shape of a five-pointed star,
which is matched by the extraordinary, zigzagging cloisters. The
interior is full of images of the
saint, with repetitive use made
of the five stars.

🏛 **Žd'ár Castle and St John
Nepomuk Church**
Tel 566 629 152. **Open** Apr & Oct: Sat,
Sun & public hols; May–Sep: Tue–Sun;
Nov–Mar: groups only, by appt. 🔲
🔲 W zamekzdar.cz

Cloisters at St John Nepomuk Church

⑨ Jihlava

Road map D2. 🏔 51,300. 🚗 🚌
ℹ️ Masarykovo náměstí 96/2.
Tel 567 167 158. 🆆 jihlava.cz

In the Middle Ages, Jihlava (Iglau) grew from a small village into one of the richest towns in the Czech Lands: its fortunes were transformed by the discovery in the 13th century of nearby silver deposits. While the modern era has certainly left its mark, Jihlava retains a fine historic centre, still encircled by medieval defensive walls.

The cobbled main square, Masarykovo náměstí, is vast. While blighted by a hideous shopping complex, the square has scores of Renaissance and Baroque houses with fine façades, portals and finials. Running beneath the square is a maze of **catacombs** (katacomby), originally storage cellars, which extend for some 25 km (15 miles). The entrance is in the square, next door to the Baroque Church of St Ignatius (sv. Ignác).

It is worth having a stroll around the rest of the old town. Look out for the one remaining gateway in the old walls, brána Matky Boží.

🏛 Catacombs
Tel 567 167 887. **Open** Apr–Oct: daily for tours. 🅿️ 📷

⑩ Telč

Road map D3. 🏔 5,600. 🚗 🚌
ℹ️ náměstí Zachariáše z Hradce 10.
Tel 567 112 407. 🆆 telc.eu

This UNESCO-listed town is outstandingly beautiful. The turning point for Telč came in 1530, when a fire devastated the town. Lord Zachariáš, the governor of Moravia, brought in Italian master builders and architects to rebuild the castle. These craftsmen ended up rebuilding virtually all the houses in the Renaissance style, endowing the town with an architectural uniformity that has survived to this day. The main square, náměstí Zachariáše z Hradce, is arcaded and has a fine array of

Telč Chateau, a fine example of Renaissance architecture

pastel-coloured houses. At one end is **Telč Chateau** (zámek Telč), a magnificent Renaissance building. Inside, highlights are the rooms with superb coffered ceilings, such as the Knight's Chambers. It also has fine collections of arms and porcelain.

Modern Telč is separated from the old town by two fishponds which virtually surround the tiny historic centre.

🏛 Telč Chateau
Tel 567 243 943. **Open** Apr–Oct: Tue–Sun. 🅿️ 📷 🆆 zamek-telc.eu

⑪ Třebíč

Road map D3. 🏔 37,800. 🚗 🚌
ℹ️ Karlovo náměstí 47. **Tel** 568 847 070. 🆆 visittrebic.eu

Two reasons to visit this industrial town are the **Basilica of St Procopius** (Bazilika sv. Prokopa) and its historic Jewish quarter. The church once belonged to a monastery, founded by

the Přemyslids in 1101 and, in the 1600s, transformed into a castle. The 13th-century church was heavily restored in the Baroque period but retains its lovely Romanesque portal, adorned with floral and geometric patterns. Take a look at the beautiful rosette window in the apse and the unusual "dwarfs' gallery" running outside. The enormous crypt features 50 columns, each with a different capital.

The restored Jewish quarter in Třebíč, between the Jihlava river and Hrádek hill, is on UNESCO's World Heritage list. With many original buildings intact, it is still possible to feel something of the atmosphere of the old ghetto. Stroll along colourful Leopold Pokorný Street and look inside the richly frescoed Rear (New) Synagogue, or Zadní/Nová synagóga (see p239).

🏛 Basilica of St Procopius
Zámek 1. **Tel** 568 610 022. **Open** daily. 📷 📷 reservations preferred.

Stained-glass window in the Church of St Ignatius, Jihlava

⑫ Jaroměřice nad Rokytnou Chateau

Road map D3. 🚌 🚋 2 km (1 mile) away in Popovice. **Tel** 568 440 237. **Open** Apr & Oct: 9am–4pm Sat, Sun & public hols; May, Jun & Sep: 9am–5pm Tue–Sun; Jul–Aug: 9am–6pm Tue–Sun. 🚫 ✓ 3 routes. 🆆 zamek-jaromerice.cz

This small town, 14 km (9 miles) south of Třebíč, is dwarfed by the Baroque chateau (zámek Jaroměřice nad Rokytnou), one of the biggest palace complexes in Europe with a sprawling park. Essentially a reconstruction incorporating elements of older buildings, the work began in 1700 and was led by the famous Austrian Baroque architect, Jakob Prandtauer. It took 37 years to complete. The man who ordered the chateau's construction, Johann Adam von Questenburg, turned it into an influential centre for the arts.

Among the highlights of a tour are the two lavishly decorated halls, Taneční sál and Hlavní sál. Visitors can also see the library and theatre, as well as a large porcelain collection, or enjoy a stroll around the formal gardens. In the grounds is the monumental Church of St Margaret (sv. Markéty), with a magnificent dome decorated with elaborate frescoes.

⑬ Bítov

Road map D3. 🔼 500. 🚋 **Tel** 556 410 229.

Bítov village is set amid the densely wooded hills of the Podyjí National Park. Perched dramatically on a high crag above the Dyje river, 3 km (2 miles) from the village, is **Bítov Castle** (hrad Bítov), built in the 11th century to defend the Přemyslid kingdom's southern borders. The castle has kept its medieval character, despite

The colossal Baroque castle complex of Jaroměřice nad Rokytnou

much rebuilding work. The interior, mainly Neo-Gothic, has an armoury featuring more than 1,000 firearms dating from the 14th–19th centuries. More bizarrely, the castle has a collection of stuffed animals, including 50 stuffed dogs, all collected by the castle's last owner. Part of the enjoyment of visiting the fortress is the climb up from the village, as well as the great views.

Bítov itself has an unusual history. The medieval village was rebuilt in the 1930s, following the flooding of the original village during the creation of the Vranov reservoir. Visitors can see how the planners tried to recreate the layout of the old village, with a market square and a series of narrow streets.

Coat of arms above Bítov Castle gate

🏰 Bítov Castle
Tel 515 294 736. **Open** Apr & Oct: Sat, Sun & public hols; May–Sep: Tue–Sun. 🚫 ✓ 4 routes. 🆆 hradbitov.cz

Environs
In Uherčice, 6 km (4 miles) west of Bítov, is the Baroque **Uherčice Chateau** (zámek Uherčice). Built on the site of a late Gothic three-winged fortified house, it boasts some fine stucco decoration and a vast English-style park. The castle is open to the public only in summer months.

🏛 Uherčice Chateau
Tel 515 298 396. **Open** Jun: Sat & Sun; Jul–Aug: Tue–Sun. 🚫 🆆 zamek-uhercice.cz

⑭ Vranov nad Dyjí Chateau

Road map D3. 🚋 **Tel** 515 296 215. **Open** Apr & Oct: 9am–4pm Sat, Sun & public hols; May, Jun & Sep: 9am–5pm Tue–Sun; Jul–Aug: 9am–6pm Tue–Sun. Garden: by appt. 🚫 ✓ 3 routes.

The village of Vranov is overshadowed by its fairytale chateau (zámek Vranov nad Dyjí), which is dramatically sited on a cliff high above the Dyje river. First erected in the 13th century, the castle was rebuilt to a Baroque design by the illustrious Austrian architect, J B Fischer von Erlach, in the late 17th century.

The highlight inside is the Ancestors' Hall (Sál předků), with its great dome lavishly decorated with frescoes by Johann Michal Rottmayr. The extravagantly furnished and decorated interiors give an insight into aristocratic life at the start of the 19th century. The chapel is a delightful work by Fischer von Erlach.

Intricate ceramic artifact in Vranov nad Dyjí Chateau

Jewish Historic Sites

There were more than 136,000 Jews living in Bohemia, Moravia and Silesia in 1939. By the end of World War II, however, as a result of the Nazi extermination programme, there were just 15,000 left. The community, which for centuries was an essential part of Czech cultural life, left behind countless historic relics. Jewish communities built synagogues and other religious buildings; they founded schools and maintained large cemeteries. The best known historic sites associated with Czech Jews are found in Prague and Plzeň, but there are also many sites in South Moravia. The Jewish quarters in Boskovice, Mikulov and Třebíč, as well as others in Brno, Lipník nad Bečvou, Hranice and Holešov, now provide a valuable testimony to the part played by Jewish religion and culture in the history of the region.

The Renaissance New Synagogue in Třebíč dates from the early 17th century. Its interior includes some remarkable, strikingly colourful wall paintings.

The restored Jewish ghetto in Třebíč features two synagogues and a vast cemetery that contains 3,000 graves, dating from 1641 to the 1930s.

Boskovice's Grand Synagogue, built in 1698, features lavish Baroque decoration. Used as a storehouse under Communist rule, this fine building has been fully restored *(see p235)*.

Mikulov, which, from the 16th century, was the seat of Moravia's chief rabbi, has a vast overgrown cemetery, with beautifully carved headstones dating back to 1618.

Brno's hall of prayers, built in Neo-Renaissance style in 1900, stands at the entrance to Moravia's largest Jewish cemetery. It is the site of some 9,000 tombstones, many of them brought here from 17th- and 18th-century cemeteries.

Castle towering above the red rooftops of Mikulov

⑮ Znojmo

Road map D3. 🚆 34,100. 🚌 🚍
ℹ️ Obroková 10. **Tel** 515 222 552.

In a splendid spot above the Dyje river, Znojmo is one of Moravia's oldest towns, with a warren of small streets at its heart. The best of its historic sights is the Romanesque Rotunda of St Catherine (sv. Kateřiny), with some beautifully preserved frescoes and portraits of Přemyslid princes. The rotunda is inside **Znojmo Castle** (Znojemský hrad), a large part of which is now a brewery.

Znojmo's Gothic Cathedral of St Nicholas (sv. Mikuláš) has a charming Baroque pulpit in the shape of a vast globe.

🏰 **Znojmo Castle**
Přemyslovců 8. **Tel** 515 222 311.
Open Apr: 9am–5pm Sat & Sun; May–Sep: 9am–5pm Tue–Sun. 🎧
♿ limited access. 🅦 **znojmuz.cz**

⑯ Mikulov

Road map E3. 🚆 7,000. 🚌 🚍
ℹ️ Náměstí 1. **Tel** 519 510 855.
🅦 **mikulov.cz**

Built on a hillside close to the Austrian border east of Znojmo, Mikulov is picture-postcard pretty. The town is full of delightful streets, with some fine Renaissance and Baroque houses. **Mikulov Castle** (zámek Mikulov), 13th-century but much altered, was burned down by the retreating Germans in the final days of World War II and then

painstakingly rebuilt. It is worth visiting to see the fine vaults, for centuries used to store locally made wine.

West of the castle is the once thriving Jewish quarter, with an atmospheric, overgrown cemetery on Brněnská.

🏰 **Mikulov Castle**
Tel 519 309 019. **Open** Apr–Oct: Tue–Sun. 🎧

⑰ Lednicko-Valtický areál

Road map E3. 🚍 Valtice & Lednice.
🚌 to Valtice from Mikulov.
Valtice: ℹ️ Náměstí Svobody 4.
Tel 519 352 978. 🅦 **valtice.eu**
Lednice: ℹ️ Zámecké náměstí 68.
Tel 519 340 986. 🅦 **lednice.cz**

Near the Austrian border are Valtice and Lednice, two towns linked by the Lednicko-Valtický areál – a beautiful UNESCO-listed park scattered with follies such as temples, artificial ruins, arches and colonnades. Each town has a chateau built by the Liechtensteins, once one of the

Czech Lands' most powerful families. The two chateaus are linked by a 7-km (5-mile) avenue of lime trees.

Valtice Chateau (Valtický zámek) is a Baroque reworking of a Renaissance palace, designed by the leading architects of the early 18th century, among them J B Fischer von Erlach. Its state rooms are furnished with Baroque and Rococo flamboyance.

Lednice Chateau (zámek Lednice) is a Neo-Gothic fairytale creation dating from the mid-1800s, with heavily panelled and richly furnished interiors. The other big attraction of Lednice is the landscaped grounds, complete with lakes and a 60-m (196-ft) minaret, the tallest of its kind outside the Islamic world.

🏰 **Valtice Chateau**
Tel 519 352 423. **Open** Apr & Oct: Sat & Sun; May–Sep: Tue–Sun. 🎧 🎫
🅦 **zamek-valtice.cz**

🏰 **Lednice Chateau**
Tel 519 340 128. **Open** Apr & Oct: Sat & Sun; May–Sep: Tue–Sun. 🎧 🎫
🅦 **zamek-lednice.com**

Colonnade, one of the follies in the grounds of Valtice Chateau

⑱ Buchlovice Castle

Road map E3. 🚌 **Tel** 572 434 240.
Open Apr & Oct: 10am–5pm Sat,
Sun & public hols; May, Jun & Sep:
10am–5pm Tue–Sun; Jul & Aug:
10am–5:30pm Tue–Sun. 🅿 ♿
W zamek-buchlovice.cz

East of Brno on the fringes of
the Chřiby hills is this delightful
castle. Built in the 18th century
by the Italian architect D Martinelli
in the style of a country house,
it consists of two symmetrical
semi-circular buildings set
around a central octagon.
Inside are opulently furnished
rooms, while outside is a
magnificent Baroque garden,
with an impressive array of trees,
rhododendrons and fuchsias.

Velehrad's monastery church,
south Moravia

⑲ Velehrad Monastery

Road map F3. 🚌 **Tel** 571 110 538.
Open 8am–5pm daily. 🅿

Velehrad has one of the
Czech Republic's most popular
pilgrimage centres, in the form
of its Cistercian Monastery
(klášter Cisterciáků). Founded
in the 1200s, it commemorates
the work of saints Cyril and
Methodius *(see p35)*. The
present monastery buildings
are 18th-century Baroque,
though the church follows the
shape of the first Romanesque
building. There are some
exquisitely carved stalls and
a lapidarium, with remains of
the original church.

View of the 18th-century Buchlovice Castle from the garden

⑳ Kroměříž

See pp242–3.

㉑ Zlín

Road map F3. 🚶 76,000. 🚊 🚌
ℹ Náměstí Míru 12. **Tel** 577 630 222.
W zlin.eu

The history of this town is
inextricably linked with Tomáš
Bat'a, who founded a shoe
factory here in 1894. He invited
a group of architects to build
houses for his workers, and so
Functionalist buildings sprang
up here in the 1920s and 30s.
While Zlín has lost the utopian
feel of a planned city, it has a
unique atmosphere.

Zlín is the birthplace of the
playwright Tom Stoppard, who
fled the Nazis with his family
and settled in England.

㉒ Luhačovice

Road map F3. 🚶 5,300. 🚊 🚌
ℹ Masarykova 950. **Tel** 577 133 980.
W luhacovice.cz

Less grand than the spa towns
of west Bohemia, Luhačovice is
nonetheless Moravia's
largest spa town. The springs
of **Luhačovice Spa** are used
to treat digestive, metabolic
and respiratory disorders. For
most visitors, the main reason
to come here is to admire
the work of Dušan Jurkovič,
the Slovak architect who
brought his folk-inspired
Art Nouveau style to
Luhačovice in the early 20th
century. Most notable is the
Jurkovičův dům.

🏛 **Luhačovice Spa**
Lázeňské náměstí 436. **Tel** 577 682 330.
Open Mon–Fri. **W** spaluhacovice.cz

Luhačovice, an unpretentious spa town
with Art Nouveau villas

Moravia's Wine

The wine-making tradition in Moravia dates back to
the 13th century. The local climate favours the late
ripening of grapes, producing wines with a full, spicy
flavour. Most of the vineyards are given over to
white grape varieties. The best known are Veltlínské
zelené, with an aromatic honey flavour and Müller-
Thurgau, with a smooth, medium-sweet flavour
and low acidity. When travelling around, especially
near Mikulov, look out for the *sklepy*, or wine cellars,
where you can taste and buy wine. The region is a
hive of activity during the grape harvest.

White wine from a Moravian wine producer

⑳ Kroměříž

This is an appealing yet quite sleepy town, with some lovely and extensive gardens as well as fine architecture – many of the buildings in the heart of Kroměříž, still partially enclosed within the original walls, have survived the Communist period relatively unscathed. Hidden shops and galleries can be found in the arcades of the main square, Velké náměstí. The main attraction, just north of the square, is the magnificent, UNESCO-listed palace of the bishops of Olomouc, who had their seat here between the 12th and 19th centuries.

North Façade
The north front has a portico that doubles as a balcony. The formal garden below links up with the landscaped grounds.

Bedroom
The bedroom and the adjacent study form the Winter Quarters. The pseudo-Renaissance 19th-century furniture came from Venice.

The Vassals' Hall
The magnificent ceiling fresco (1759) in the hall (Mansky sál) is the work of Viennese artist F A Mauelbertsch. He was paid 12,300 ducats, an incredible sum at the time.

Main entrance

Throne Room
The throne and the baldachin were used by the Olomouc archbishops. Other furnishings here date from the late 18th century.

Archbishop's Palace

The vast Baroque palace (Arcibiskupský zámek) has some splendidly furnished rooms whose Rococo flourishes featured in Miloš Forman's film Amadeus. *It also houses the impressive art collection of the Liechtenstein family, a major influence in the town. This collection (the second largest in the republic) features some superb works of art, including* The Flaying of Marsyas, *a famous painting by Titian, and* King Charles I *and his wife Henrietta Maria by Van Dyck. Veronese and Cranach are among the other painters represented.*

★ Assembly Hall

The name of this superb Rococo room alludes to talks held here by the exiled Austrian Imperial Parliament in 1848–9, during which they drafted a new constitution. This became famous for its stated principle: "All the power within the state stems from the people."

★ Imperial Room

The portraits in this room include one of Franz Josef I, who was one of the many distinguished visitors to the palace. The emperor and Tsar Alexander III went hunting together here and their trophies can be seen in the Hunting Hall.

Staircase

Accessed via a fine staircase is the palace's art gallery (Zámecká obrazárna), which has an impressive collection of European paintings from the 16th and 17th centuries.

Library

The library rooms were laid out in 1694. Still in beautiful condition, they house 90,000 volumes dating from the 16th and 17th centuries.

KEY

① **Throne room**

② **North façade**

③ **The tower** soars 84 m (280 ft) above ground level.

INTRODUCING
SLOVAKIA

DISCOVERING SLOVAKIA

The following itineraries have been designed to pack as many of Slovakia's highlights as possible into a manageable space of time. First comes a two-day tour of the country's engrossing capital Bratislava, a city packed with historical monuments, cultural diversions and entertainment. This itinerary can be enjoyed individually or combined with the itinerary that follows; a two-week tour through the whole of Slovakia that packs a feast of historical sights and natural wonders

into an exhilarating fortnight. It begins with the vineyards and castles of western Slovakia, before proceeding to the deep valleys and high mountains that make up the middle of the country. The stunning alpine scenery of the High Tatras slowly gives way to the low hills and medieval trading towns of eastern Slovakia, where traditional lifestyles and folk culture still prevail. You can follow the tour in its entirety, or simply dip in and out and be inspired.

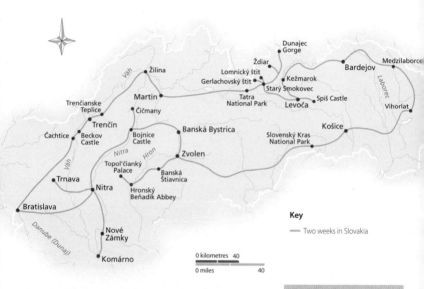

Key

═══ Two weeks in Slovakia

0 kilometres   40

0 miles   40

Tatras mountains
The snow covered peaks of the Tatras mountains during winter are a great draw for winter sports activities

◀ Picturesque rural landscape with lush green mountain slopes in Slovakia

Two Weeks in Slovakia

- Delve into Slovak history and vampire myth at **Čachtice Castle**.

- Get up close to the snow-capped majesty of the **Tatras mountains**, by cable car or on foot.

- Roam the windswept battlements of the once-mighty **Spiš Castle**.

- Relax in the cultured, elegant eastern city of **Košice**.

- Explore the numerous churches and palaces in the well-preserved Baroque town of **Trnava**.

Visitors in front of the Slovak National Theatre

Two Days in Bratislava

Slovakia's boisterous capital centres around an inviting warren of cobbled streets and small squares, much of which can be quickly explored on foot. A reliable bus and tram network will take you to suburban sights and outlying villages.

- **Arriving** Bratislava's airport is 12 km (7 miles) from the centre. Regular buses from the airport take 15 min to reach the centre. Vienna airport is less than 50 km (30 miles) and is linked to Bratislava by regular bus (40 min).

Day 1

Morning Enter Bratislava's pedestrianized, compact **Old Town** *(pp280–81)* via **Michael's Gate** *(p283)*, the only gate remaining from the medieval fortifications. Veering left along Zamočnická, you will reach the historic heart of the city. Spend some time admiring the statues, fountains and stuccoed façades of cute Baroque squares such as Františkánske námestie, Hlavné námestie, and Primacálne námestie. Consider pausing for morning coffee in one of the Old Town's numerous cafés. Next, get to grips with Bratislava's history and cultural heritage with a visit to the City Museum in the **Old Town Hall** *(p282)*, with its

beautifully-preserved set of Baroque interiors. Alternatively, admire the collection of old-master paintings of the City Gallery, housed in one of Bratislava's finest architectural relics, the Rococo-style **Mirbach Palace** *(p283)*.

Afternoon Head west from the **Old Town** *(pp280–81)* to **St Martin's Cathedral** *(pp284–5)*, celebrated for its rib-vaulted presbytery and Gothic winged altar of St Anne. Pass through the underpass beneath Staromestská to reach the Rococo **House at the Good Shepherd** *(p287)*, which houses the Museum of Clocks. It marks the start of the climb along picturesque Beblavého lane towards the strategically

The open air cafés lining the street near Michael's Gate

located **Bratislava Castle** *(p282)* on the banks of the Danube. The castle's hilltop position provides sweeping views of the city; while inside, the historic and ethnographic collections of the Slovak National Museum fully deserve a stay of an hour or two.

Day 2

Morning Broad, tree-lined Hviezdoslavovo namestie is a good place to start exploring the monuments of 19th-century Bratislava, notably the Neo-Renaissance **Slovak National Theatre** *(p286)*. A short walk from here is the imposing **Reduta** *(p286)*, built in an eclectic style combining Neo-Baroque, Rococo and Art Nouveau features. It is home to the Slovak Philharmonic and various concerts, theatre performances etc are staged here. Also close by is the riverside **Slovak National Gallery** *(p286)*, with its comprehensive collection of the nation's best paintings and sculptures ranging from the 13th century to Modern Slovak art. A stroll across the Danube-spanning **New Bridge** *(p287)* provides great views back towards the city; ascend the bridge's soaring single pylon by lift to enjoy the vistas on offer at the viewing tower. You can savour coffee or lunch in the panoramic café-restaurant at the top of the pylon.

Two Weeks in Slovakia

- **Arriving** Arrive and depart from Bratislava airport. Alternatively, join the circuit in the east by arriving and departing from Košice airport (see days 9 and 10).

- **Transport** The overnight destinations on this tour can be accessed using Slovakia's train and bus network, although a car is essential to access many of the recommended mid-day stop-offs, especially in rural areas.

Day 1 & 2
Pick any of the days from the detailed 3-day itinerary provided on p247.

Day 3 and 4: Bratislava to Trenčianske Teplice
The journey northeast along the Váh Valley is enjoyable scenic, with vineyard-cloaked hills and castle-topped crags visible on either side. Compelling stop-offs include the ruined castle of **Čachtice** (pp304–5), former home of 'Blood Countess' Elizabeth Báthory, and **Beckov Castle** (p305) with its dramatic clifftop location. You can spend the night in the relaxing spa resort of **Trenčianske Teplice** (p305), famous for its therapeutic mineral waters since the 14th century.

Historic main square, Námestie Majstra Pavla, Levoča

Spend the next morning looking around the town of **Žilina** (p326) with its striking arcaded market square before moving on to the mountain-shrouded historic town of **Martin** (p319), home to both the Slovak National Museum and the outdoor Slovak Village Museum with their vast collections of folk exhibits. Consider an overnight stay in one of the mountain resorts of the Low Tatras just outside Martin; places like Brezno and Demänovska Dolina boast several smart, contemporary resort hotels set in beautiful scenery.

Day 5: From the Low Tatras to the Tatra National Park
A short drive east of **Martin** (p319), you can see the spectacular alpine peaks of the Tatra National Park, ranged on the northern side of the Váh Valley. Base yourself at the historic spa resort of **Starý Smokovec** (p321), before preparing to spend the afternoon in the mountains. The cable car ride up the 2,632-metre (8,635-ft) **Lomnický štít** (p321) is one of the most popular local excursions.

Day 6: Exploring the Tatra National Park
There's a lot to explore in the Tatra National Park, with a particularly dense concentration of walking trails north and west of **Starý Smokovec** (p321), many offering lovely views of Slovakia's highest peak, **Gerlachovský štít** (p321). Otherwise, devote the day to the scenic rafting trip on the **Dunajec Gorge** (p321) just northeast of the National Park, calling in at the folkloric village of **Ždiar** (p321) on the way there or back.

Day 7: Spiš region
East of the Tatra National Park lies the evocative Spiš region, rich in historic towns and hilltop castles. **Levoča** (p338) with its Renaissance town-houses, arcaded **Town Hall** (pp338–9) and good local restaurants, is the obvious place to spend the night. It's also the ideal base from which to visit **Spiš Castle** (pp342–3), a vast semi-ruined fortress that occupies a panoramic hilltop site just to the east.

Day 8: Rural Northeast
Travelling from **Levoča** (p338) to the town of **Medzilaborce** (p336) will give you a good taste of Slovakia's rural northeast. Take a quick look at the market town of **Kežmarok** (p337) with its Byzantine-style Lutheran Church before proceeding to the regional centre of **Bardejov** (p337), where you should take time to stroll the market square and admire the craft and folk artifacts in the Šariš Museum. Try to arrive in Medzilaborce in time

Ruins of the Beckov Castle perched above the town

to visit the Warhol Family Museum of Modern Art honouring the Pittsburg-born pop artist whose parents emigrated from here in the 1920s.

Day 9: Medzilaborce to Košice

Travelling south from **Medzilaborce** (p336) towards regional capital **Košice** (pp332–5) takes you through a sparsely populated region of wooded Carpathian foothills and rolling fields. A slight detour eastwards will take you through the weird volcanic hills of the **Vihorlat** (p336), where the ascent of Sninský Crag will provide a challenge to hikers. The Zamplinská Širava reservoir on the south side of Vihorlat is the place to relax and take a swim in summer. From here, it's a straightforward drive across the eastern Slovak plain to **Košice** (pp332–5), where you could easily stay for a couple of nights.

Day 10: Košice

Spend the day exploring **Košice** (pp332–5), beginning with the main north-south street **Hlavná** (p332) and its parade of historic buildings and stately squares. Reserve most time for **St Elizabeth's Cathedral** (p332) with its Gothic main altar, and the **East Slovak Museum** (p333) with its spectacular hoard of gold coins. In the evening, return to **Hlavná** (p332) to enjoy the coloured lights and synchronized splashes of the **Singing Fountain** (p332).

Day 11: Around Košice

Use **Košice** (pp332–5) as your base to embark on a day tour of the **Slovenský Kras National Park** (pp340–41), a karst region celebrated for the spectacular show-caves of the **Jaskyňa Domica** (p340) and **Jasovská Jaskyňa** (p341). The former, with its subterranean boat ride, can easily take up half a day. Between the two caves, the **Zádielska Valley** (p341) takes the form of a limestone canyon, perfect for midday picnics and riverside walks.

Mountain lake at Štrbské Pleso, Tatra National Park

Day 12: To Banská Bystrica

Travelling west from **Košice** (pp332–5) takes you once again into mountain country, with the compellingly bleak heights of the Slovenské Rudoborie stretching on either side of the main road to the historic mining town of **Banská Bystrica** (pp314–15). Consider a stop-off en route in **Zvolen** (p318), site of a well-preserved castle. Try and arrive in Banska Bystrica early enough to visit the futuristic structure housing the **SNP Museum** (p315), devoted to the Slovak National Uprising of 1944.

> **To extend your trip…**
> Undertake a one-day tour of south-central Slovakia taking in the medieval mining town of **Banská Štiavnica** (p318), the **Hronský Beňadik Abbey** (p327), and the sumptuous interiors of **Topoľčianky Palace** (p327).

Day 13: Around Banská Bystrica

Nestling in the green foothills of the Mala Fatra mountains west of **Banská Bystrica** (pp314–5), romantic **Bojnice Castle** (pp324–5) contains a riot of Baroque and Neo-Gothic furnishings. It's the ideal journey-breaker en route to **Nitra** (p308), a fascinating Baroque town set beneath a walled castle and fortified cathedral. Depending on how early you set out, consider a detour from Bojnice to the folk-village of **Čičmany** (p326) and its restored wooden houses.

Day 14: Trnava

From **Nitra** (p308) it's a short hop to **Trnava** (pp300–3), a historic seat of Catholic learning that is filled with fine churches, convents and univer-sity buildings. The compact, park-ringed town centre is a delightful place to stroll. You can stay overnight at Trnava or return to nearby Bratislava, ready to board your flight home.

> **To extend your trip…**
> Head south from **Trnava** (pp300–3) to explore the Danube-plain towns of **Komárno** (p309) and **Nové Zámky** (p309), famous for their Hungarian-influenced, paprika-rich cuisine. Local speciality, halászlé (spicy fish stew) is served in almost all the area's restaurants.

Panoramic view of the Renaissance church in Žilina

Putting Slovakia on the Map

Located in the central part of Europe, Slovakia – more formally known as the Slovak Republic – is a landlocked country bordering Poland, Ukraine, Hungary, Austria and the Czech Republic. It covers an area of 49,036 sq km (18,930 sq miles) and its population is 5.43 million. The capital, Bratislava, with a population of 450,000, lies near the border with Austria, on the Danube. Other large centres include Košice and Prešov in the east, Žilina in the north, and Nitra near the capital. The Carpathian mountain range stretches across most of Slovakia's territory.

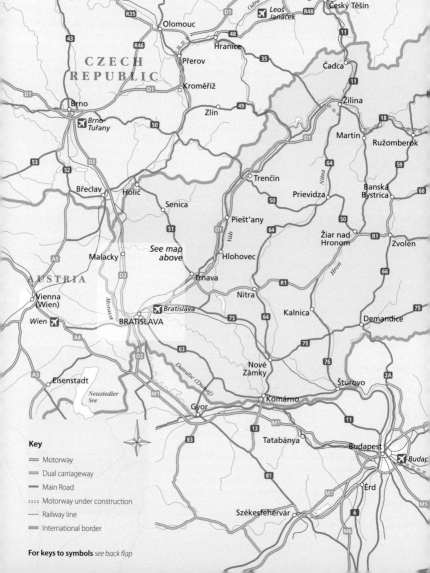

Key

— Motorway

— Dual carriageway

— Main Road

····· Motorway under construction

— Railway line

— International border

For keys to symbols see back flap

Apollo Bridge over Danube river in Bratislava

by the women. Pottery, basket work and other handmade products are still used in many homes for everyday purposes. Wooden folk buildings exist *in situ* and are also preserved in open-air museums to form traditional villages or skansen.

Ethnic Minorities

Of Slovakia's population of 5.4 million, over 85 per cent are Slovaks, according to official statistics. The most significant minorities are the Hungarians, found mainly in the south, Roma (Gypsies), Ukrainians, Czechs, Poles, and Ruthenians (Rusyns) in the east. Slovak-Hungarian relations are now friendly, but until recently, there were scars of the dramatic national conflict that arose in the second half of the 19th century. The situation of the Roma minority, the second-largest at about 350,000, is hard. In many regions, mainly in the east, large Roma communities live in great poverty, without any prospect of improving their lot.

Religious Life

Slovakia, as opposed to the secularized Czech Republic, is a country where religious life and traditions remain very strong. The majority of the population, nearly 70 per cent, declare themselves to be Roman Catholics, but there are sizeable groups attached to Protestant (7 per cent), Greek Orthodox and United Reformed (both 4 per cent) churches. Only 13 per cent of Slovaks regard themselves as atheists. Devotion to religious life is evident not only at times of religious feasts and colourful celebrations. Churches throughout the country, particularly in smaller towns and villages, fill up with the faithful during Sunday mass and other services.

Statue of St Cyril, by Jozef Bart

Independence

The 19th-century process of national rebirth strengthened the feeling of national identity among Slovaks and

Roma children in Svina

consolidated their aspirations to become an independent nation. The desire for autonomy within the Austro-Hungarian Empire and later Czechoslovakia, voiced by consecutive generations of politicians, had never been realized. Ironically, the first opportunity to achieve a semblance of independence arose within the puppet state created according to Hitler's wishes in 1939; the Slovak National Uprising against the Germans of 1944 is a key event in the national consciousness. The dream of independence came true only through the "Velvet Divorce", following the break-up of Czechoslovakia in January 1993. Slovakia became a member of the EU and NATO in 2004.

Chairlift station in Skalnaté pleso, the High Tatras

Slovakia's Diverse Attractions

An undeniable trump card of modern Slovakia is the wide range of attractions it offers to those interested in outdoor activities. Winter sports enthusiasts will appreciate the local skiing conditions – the best in Central Europe. Marked cycle routes of 3,500 km (2,175 miles) allow cyclists to undertake long-distance expeditions, while several thousand hiking trails lead through the most beautiful mountainous areas. Liptovská Mara and other artificial reservoirs offer good sailing and windsurfing; the waters of the Váh, Hron and Nitra rivers enable white water rafters to indulge their popular passion. Beautiful churches in styles ranging from the Romanesque to Art Nouveau are a feature of many towns and cities. In the Slovak landscape, numerous castles and ruined fortresses stand out. Those in lowland areas – such as Spiš Castle – have huge fortifications. Those in the mountains, such as Oravský, mostly cling, like eagles' nests, to the rocks. The abundance of castles testifies to the region's turbulent history, a history that makes an essential and vivid contribution to Slovakia's appeal.

Slovak Republic in the European Union

St Martin's Cathedral in Spišská Kapitula, East Slovakia

Landscape and Wildlife of Slovakia

Slovakia surprises visitors with its diversity of scenery and wealth of wildlife. Mountains and highlands constitute over 60 per cent of the country's area. Many of these mountainous areas have been given National Park status to protect the landscape and wildlife, but also to allow visitors access to these rewarding areas. Slovakia's mountain ranges form part of the huge Carpathian range. The Central Carpathians include Slovakia's highest mountain massif – the Tatras.

Dunajec river valley in the Pieniny National Park, Central and East Slovakia

Lowlands

The lowland areas are concentrated in the south of the country. In the southwest, dunes and forests growing on sandy soil dominate. The areas further to the east, including the Danube Lowland, where the Váh joins the Danube, and the East Slovakian Lowland, are intensely farmed. The most popular crops, besides cereals, include sugar beet, tobacco, hops, rape and sunflowers.

Water chestnuts were eaten in times of famine. They grow in ponds and old river beds, including in the valleys of the Danube and Latorica rivers. Today, they are becoming increasingly rare.

Sunflowers are widely cultivated throughout Slovakia. In the summer, when the crops flower, vast areas of the Danube Lowland and East Slovakian Lowland are covered with a yellow carpet.

The Karst Region

Slovenský kras, the Slovak Karst region, is a limestone plateau that occupies the southern part of the Slovenské Rudohorie mountains, close to the Hungarian border. The area has been shaped by surface and underground waters, as they cut their way through the limestone rock. The scenery here is extremely diverse in terms of karst formations, with ravines, funnels, and numerous caves containing stalactites and stalagmites.

Jasovská Jaskyňa, a cave with particularly lovely stalactites, is home to several species of bats.

Slovenský kras is the largest legally protected karst area in Central Europe. Brown bears and wolves roam here.

Dwarf irises, small perennial rhizomatous plants with purple, yellow, white or pinkish flowers, growing wild in the Slovak Karst and other areas, are now in serious danger of extinction.

Forests

It is estimated that forests cover over 30 per cent of Slovakia's territory. In the mountainous regions the forests are predominantly natural, with spruce, sycamore and beech; lower sections are covered with oak forests. Pine and mixed forests have colonized the poorer soils. Acid rain has affected Slovakia's forests, but not as severely as in the Czech Republic.

Turk's cap lilies grow wild in most areas, but are slightly more common in the Carpathians. The species is legally protected.

Virgin forests survive in some of the more inaccessible mountain regions of Slovakia, with trees up to 130 m (425 ft) tall.

Mountains

The most spectacular and highest of all the Slovak mountain ranges are the Tatras. Formed of granite and limestone, they support a wide variety of plant and animal life, including deer, foxes, boar and golden eagles. Particularly interesting are the alpine grasses, and the meadow vegetation found at lower levels.

Blue sow thistle grows in the forest belt and at sub-alpine levels; it has lovely purple-blue flowers, although white and pink varieties do occur. It often grows with the Austrian leopard's-bane in dense thickets.

The High Tatras are the only alpine group within the Carpathians and the smallest alpine range in Europe. They occupy 260 sq km (100 sq miles) and rise to over 2,500 m (8,200 ft); the highest peak – Gerlachovský štít is 2,654 m (8,707 ft) high. The range includes about 1,000 peaks.

Fauna

Slovak fauna is not as diverse as its flora but it does feature many interesting species. Along with the animals that inhabit lowlands, such as deer, fox and bear, there are also species typical of high mountain zones – chamois and marmot. Forested riverbanks are home to waterfowl such as cormorant, heron and crane. In the areas around the Danube, marshy meadows are home to the great bustard, now an endangered species.

The brown bear is the largest land predator in Slovakia. It is a good swimmer, and can climb steep slopes.

The lynx, a predator of the cat family, inhabits upper and lower forest zones; it is becoming increasingly rare.

The great bustard inhabits Central and Eastern Europe. It is the world's heaviest flying bird.

Slovak Architecture

From medieval times until the fall of the Habsburgs, Slovak architecture was linked with Hungarian culture. The south of the country also looked to Vienna for its inspiration, while the north tended to follow local traditions. Bratislava, which for a long time was the capital of the Hungarian kingdom, acquired many splendid residential buildings. For centuries the finest buildings in Slovakia were churches, particularly those of the Late-Gothic, and the opulent Baroque monasteries. The 19th and 20th centuries saw a rapid development of urban architecture.

The town hall in Bardejov, combining Gothic and Renaissance features

Middle Ages

The predominant architectural features of the early Middle Ages were fortified towns and castles. Small churches were built until the mid-14th century. Rapid growth of religious architecture – particularly in Bratislava and the Spiš region – took place during the 15th century. The spectacular Gothic churches in Levoča, Bardejov and Kremnica date from this period.

St Martin's Cathedral in Bratislava, built at the turn of the 14th and 15th centuries, is among the city's finest religious buildings *(see pp284–5)*.

St Elizabeth's Cathedral in Košice *(see pp332–5)* is a splendid example of Peter Parler's style, which emanated from Prague *(see p22)*.

Renaissance

Renaissance architecture concentrated mainly on secular buildings: castles, courts and palaces. It reached its apogee in the second half of the 16th and the early 17th century. The Italian styles, modified in Austria, south Germany, and Poland, acquired their specific local flavour in Slovakia. For instance, high roofs, ornate attics and plain undivided façades, with rustication at the corners, became its typical features.

Thurzo House in Levoča, although many times rebuilt, has kept some strong Renaissance elements, including the loggia, cloisters and buttresses *(see p338)*.

The town hall (radnica) in Levoča, originally Gothic, was turned into one of Slovakia's finest Renaissance builings in the early 17th century with arcades and a clock tower *(see pp338–9)*.

Baroque

Slovakia is particularly rich in Baroque architectural works, some of which are of international standing. Many were built in Bratislava, the coronation city of the Hungarian kings, in the 18th century. The royal status of the city attracted wealthy investors and prominent artists from Vienna, including G B Martinelli, A G Bibiena and G R Donner. At that time, many monasteries were built in southern and central Slovakia, particularly for the Franciscan and Jesuit orders.

The monastery church in Jasov (1750–66), with the opulence of its Late-Baroque architecture, was designed by Austrian architect Anton Pilgram. It draws on Italian-Austrian stylistic forms *(see p341)*.

The Summer Palace built for the Primate of Hungary, Franco Barkóczy, in Bratislava in 1761–5, was heavily influenced by Vienna's Baroque architectural forms.

19th and 20th Centuries

During the past two centuries, the development of Slovak architecture has gone hand-in-hand with Central European trends. The first half of the 19th century was dominated by Neo-Classical and Romantic styles, particularly in the flourishing sphere of residential architecture. The second half of that century was marked particularly by the development of urban architecture: apartment blocks and municipal buildings, designed in eclectic and historical styles. The early 20th century saw the arrival of splendid Art Nouveau and Modernist projects. Communist architecture blighted many towns, but since 1989, there has been extensive restoration of old town centres.

The English-style park that surrounds the Andrássys' residence in Betliar *(see p340)* is adorned with fountains, artificial ponds with cascades, grottoes and a variety of pavilions.

The Manor House in Dolná Krupá (1818–28), designed by Anton P Riegl, is a superb example of a Neo-Classical residence with a distinctive central columned portico and side breaks *(see p299)*.

The Slovak National Theatre in Bratislava *(see p286)* was built in Neo-Renaissance style during 1884–6 by Viennese architects Ferdinand Fellner and Hermann Helmer, who specialized in designing theatres and opera houses.

This detail from a house in Košice is typical of decorations used at the turn of the 19th and 20th centuries.

SLOVAKIA THROUGH THE YEAR

Although interesting at any time of the year, Slovakia is never swamped by waves of tourists. In winter, the snow-covered slopes attract skiers; spring is a time of magnificent flowers, particularly in the meadows; summer is the best time for exploring the country. Autumn attracts those who wish to taste Slovak wines – the pride of local producers. There is a full calendar of cultural events the whole year round, although they tend to be of a local character. Folk festivals, one of the country's main attractions, are especially popular among visitors. Slovakia is rich in religious traditions. Catholic feasts are celebrated throughout the country; Orthodox festivals are mainly observed in the eastern regions. Traditional pilgrimages to places of worship continue to attract large numbers of participants.

Braided willow twigs for an Easter folk ritual

Spring

Main festivals of the spring calendar are associated with Easter, when religious celebrations are accompanied by a variety of bucolic customs, such as egg painting, preparing decorated food baskets for blessing, or *šibačka* – an old fertility ritual involving mock-whipping girls with braided willow twigs.

Easter Easter festivities begin on "Green Thursday". Church bells are tied up to silence them, and their ringing is replaced by sounds of wooden rattles until "White Saturday". On Easter Sunday, churches fill with the faithful. On Easter Monday, water, which is believed to bring health and prosperity, is poured over women.

March
Swimming Competitions, Trnava, West Slovakia. The main international swimming event in Slovakia.
Bratislava City Marathon *(late Mar)*. A weekend of running, which includes shorter races for children.

April
Devin-Bratislava Run *(Apr)*. The capital's inhabitants welcome the arrival of spring by running the 12-km (7-mile) route from Devin. The run is regarded as one of the most important events of its kind in Europe.
Komárno Lehára *(late Apr)*, Komárno, West Slovakia. Singing competition held every two years in memory of the composer Franz Lehár, who was born here.
Flora Bratislava *(Apr–May)*. International flower fair on the banks of the Danube in Bratislava.
Festival duchov a strašidiel *(late Apr–early May)*, Bojnice, Central Slovakia. Festival of ghosts and spirits held in the castle: banquets, firework displays and theatrical performances.

May
Trenčín Musical Spring *(early May)*, Trenčín, West Slovakia. National and international musicians play at this annual classical festival.
Košice Music Spring International Festival *(whole of May)*, East Slovakia. Held since 1955.
International Dolls' Festival *(late May)*, Poprad, East Slovakia. Exhibitions of dolls in national costumes.
Festival of Ghosts and Monsters *(May)*, Bojnice Castle, West Slovakia. Spooky yet humorous festival.

Flowering spring meadows in the High Tatras

Average daily hours of sunshine

Sunshine
The largest number of sunny days in Slovakia occurs, naturally enough, in the summer, between June and August, although there is also fine weather in May and September. The cloudiest months are usually November, December and January.

Summer

Most folk festivals take place in the summer, when many regions, towns and villages present their local customs and cuisine. The largest events offer a chance to meet artists from many parts of the world.

Golden fields in the Small Carpathians in midsummer

June

Folk Festival (Jun), Myjava, West Slovakia.
Horehronské Dni, Heľpa (late Jun). Three-day folklore festival.
Dobrofest (mid-Jun), Trnava, West Slovakia. A festival organized in memory of Jan Dopjera, who founded the guitar-making firm, Dobro, in the United States.
ArtFilm Festival (second half of Jun), Trenčianske Teplice, West Slovakia. Week-long event with competitions for the best avant-garde and experimental productions.
Viva Musica! (Jun), Bratislava. International festival of classical, jazz and world music.

July

Folk Festival (early Jul), Detva, Central Slovakia.
Východná Folklore Festival (early Jul), Východná, north Slovakia.
Pilgrimage to Marian Sanctuary (1st Sat in Jul), Levoča, East Slovakia. The best-attended pilgrimage in Slovakia, with hundreds of thousands of Catholics, marking the start of many such pilgrimages in Slovakia.
International Handicraft Exhibition (mid-Jul), Kežmarok, East Slovakia.
International Folk Festival in Novohrad (27–31 Jul), Lučenec, Central Slovakia. A unique European-scale event, held at the same time on both sides of the Slovak-Hungarian border.
Jánošík Days (26–29 Jul), Terchová, Central Slovakia. The country's biggest folk festival celebrating the

Folk festival in Detva, Central Slovakia

highway robber, Juraj Jánošík (1688–1713), who robbed nobles and gave to the poor.

August

Kysucer Pilgrimage (15 Aug), Oščadnica near Žilina, Central Slovakia. Colourful, lively and often crowded religious festivities.
Kremnické Gagy (late Aug), Kremnica, Central Slovakia. Humour and satire festival, with top theatre, cabaret and musical performances.

Summer concert in the courtyard of the Old Town Hall, Bratislava

Average monthly rainfall

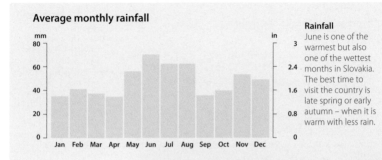

Rainfall
June is one of the warmest but also one of the wettest months in Slovakia. The best time to visit the country is late spring or early autumn – when it is warm with less rain.

Autumn

One of the most important events in the Slovak calendar is the September grape harvest festival – boisterous, jolly celebrations organized in all of the country's vine-growing areas. This is a unique opportunity to sample *burčiak* – a freshly fermented sweet grape juice, which is supposed both to purify the system and to rejuvenate the body, although overindulgence can give you a headache!

Full house at Bratislava Jazz Days festival

September

Coronation Celebrations *(early Sep)*, Bratislava. Actors dressed in historic costumes re-enact a royal coronation, and with great pomp and ceremony, march through the streets of the Old Town.

St Hubert's Day *(17 Sep)*, Svätý Anton, near Banská Štiavnica, Central Slovakia. Celebrations

Autumn at Gerlachovský štít, the Tatras

associated with hunting customs and traditions, combined with shooting competitions.

Radvanský jarmok *(Sep)*, Banská Bystrica, Central Slovakia. Colourful handicrafts market.

Biennale of Illustration *(first half Sep–end of Oct)*, Bratislava. Regular international exhibition of illustrations for books for children and young readers; takes place in odd-numbered years.

Bratislava Jazz Days *(3rd week in Sep–mid-Oct)*, Bratislava. International jazz festival, and one of the most important events of its kind in Central Europe. Participants include top jazz musicians and singers from all over the world.

October

International Jazz Festival *(early Oct)*, Košice, East Slovakia.

Ekotopfilm *(Oct)*, Bratislava and other cities. The world's biggest festival of environmental films.

November

Bratislava Music Festival *(Nov)*, Bratislava. The main Slovak festival of classical music.

Strážske Run *(2nd Sun in Nov)*, Strážske. This 6.6 km (4 mile) run through the city has been a local tradition since 1970. There is also a special 100 m run held, in which local children participate.

Festival of Greek-Catholic Choirs *(Nov)*, Prešov, East Slovakia.

Christmas Fair *(25 Nov– 23 Dec)*, Bratislava. One of Bratislava's most popular events. The town fills up with stalls selling handicrafts that make excellent Christmas presents.

Average monthly temperature

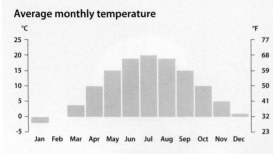

Temperature
Large variations in altitude cause the weather to vary between individual regions of Slovakia. The average summer temperature is about 20°C (68°F); at high altitudes, it does not exceed 15°C (59°F). Winters tend to be cold, with temperatures often dropping below freezing.

Winter

The early part of winter is dominated by Christmas and New Year celebrations. Epiphany marks the beginning of the carnival season, which continues until Ash Wednesday.

December
International Film Festival *(Dec)*, Bratislava. The annual festival for cinema lovers. Besides European films, it also includes works by independent producers.
Christmas *(24–26 Dec)*. On Christmas Eve morning, people put up the Christmas tree (usually a spruce) in their home. During traditional Christmas Eve supper, people break wafer bread spread with honey and nuts, or garlic. Honey symbolizes love; garlic health. The main dish is usually carp. In the evening, they also unwrap their presents.

New Year's Eve Ball *(31 Dec)*, Bratislava. Some 50,000 citizens of Bratislava and several thousand visitors meet in the town centre to participate in live concerts and an open-air disco. Fireworks and light displays on the banks of the Danube create an unforget-table atmosphere.

January
Epiphany *(6 Jan)*. In many villages and small towns, this is an opportunity to see boys sporting royal crowns, singing carols and collecting small donations.

February
Shrovetide is the traditional end of carnival season. Boisterous parties often last from Sunday until midnight on Tuesday before Ash

Cable car to Lomnický štít, the Tatras

Wednesday. The final carnival procession is the traditional "burial of the double bass", after which the music ceases for the entire period of Lent.
Gajdošské fašiangy *(last Sun before Ash Wed)*, Mala Lehota near Ždiar, Central Slovakia. International bagpipe-players' rally.

Public Holidays in Slovakia

Anniversary of the Independent Slovak Republic (1 Jan)
Epiphany (6 Jan)
Good Friday
Easter Monday
Labour Day (1 May)
VE Day (8 May)
St Cyril and St Methodius Day (5 Jul)
Anniversary of Slovak National Uprising (29 Aug)
Constitution Day (1 Sep)
Feast of St Mary, the Patron Saint of Slovakia (15 Sep)
All Saints' Day (1 Nov)
Struggle for Freedom and Democracy Day (17 Nov)
Christmas Eve (24 Dec)
Christmas Day (25 Dec)
Boxing Day (26 Dec)

Cinema foyer at the International Film Festival, Bratislava

St Stephen, founder of the Kingdom of Hungary

Mongol Invaders and German Settlers

Having been a highly disruptive force in central Europe, the Magyars settled down under St Stephen I (997–1038), the first King of Hungary. Initially, the Hungarians were reasonably just rulers, allowing the Slovaks to keep their own language and culture. The economy prospered, thanks largely to mining and trade. This progress was interrupted by a Mongol invasion in 1241–2, but the subsequent rebuilding of the devastated country initiated another period of prosperity. The country's rulers granted privileges to many towns, built many castles, and invited in large numbers of German settlers (a similar process was underway in the Czech Lands). The new arrivals brought with them new skills,

particularly useful in the field of mining. In the 14th century, the region of Banska Štiavnica and Kremnica yielded a quarter of Europe's silver and gold.

Turkish Expansion and the Arrival of the Habsburgs

Although Bohemia's Hussite armies disrupted the generally peaceful existence of its neighbour, the turning point in Slovakia's history was the Battle of Mohács (1526), in which the invading Turkish army crushed the forces of King Louis Jagiello, ruler of both Hungary and the Czech Lands. Louis died in battle leaving no heir, paving the way for Ferdinand I, a Habsburg, to become king *(see p40)*. With the Turks occupying most of the Hungarian plain, the only significant part of the Hungarian kingdom left in Ferdinand's hands was the territory of Slovakia, essentially Upper Hungary. In 1536, Bratislava (Pressburg) became capital of this much-reduced kingdom.

Lying between Christian Europe and the Muslim Turkish Empire, Slovakia was ravaged by raids and military campaigns.

The invasion of the Mongols in 1241

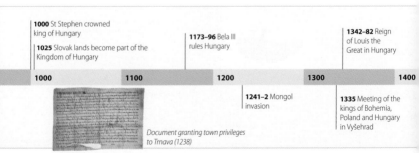

1000 St Stephen crowned king of Hungary

1025 Slovak lands become part of the Kingdom of Hungary

1173–96 Bela III rules Hungary

1342–82 Reign of Louis the Great in Hungary

| 1000 | 1100 | 1200 | 1300 | 1400 |

1241–2 Mongol invasion

1335 Meeting of the kings of Bohemia, Poland and Hungary in Vyšehrad

Document granting town privileges to Trnava (1238)

Two men working in a smithy, a 16th-century altarpiece in Rožnava

In 1663, the Turks invaded again, captured Nové Zámky, the mightiest castle in Hungary, and won more land. There was also home-grown trouble. In addition to the Reformation, to which the Habsburgs responded by bringing in the Jesuits, there was resistance by Hungarian nobles to the monarchy's centralist policies. This led to numerous acts of defiance, most famously in 1678 and 1703, led by Imre Thököly and Ferenz Rákoczi II respectively.

The Enlightenment and Slovak National Revival

The enlightenment reforms of Maria Theresa and her son Joseph II in the 18th century had a big impact in the empire (see p43). While German was made the official language, the role of national languages was also acknowledged. The codification of a Slovak vernacular became crucial to the forging of a national identity. The first codification of Slovakian

was by a Catholic priest called Anton Bernolák, in 1787, but it received little suppport. In the 1830s, a new generation of Slovaks, mostly anti-Magyar and pro-Czech, began to make themselves heard. The leading figure in this nationalist movement was Ľudovít Štúr, who helped codify a new literary language; this became the basis of modern Slovakian.

By 1848, revolutions had broken out all over Europe, including in Hungary. Štúr and his fellow activists demanded self-determination for Slovakia, but this was rejected by the leaders of the Hungarian revolution. The Slovak nationalists took a gamble by offering to support the Habsburgs in their fight against Hungarian insurgents. Their hope that the emperor would appreciate the loyalty and would look favourably on the request for Slovak independence proved futile.

After suppressing the 1848 revolution, Emperor Franz Joseph II restored absolute monarchy. All was not well in the empire, however, and in 1867, Hungary was granted autonomy by Austria under the so-called "Dual Monarchy".

1848 Revolution: detail of a painting by P M Bohúň

1526 Louis Jagiello killed at Mohács

1740–80 Reign of Maria Theresa

1780–1790 Reign of Joseph II

1683 Turks defeated at the Battle of Vienna

1787 First codification of Slovak language by Father Bernolák

1500 · 1600 · 1700 · 1800

1458–90 Reign of Matthias Corvinus

1536 Bratislava (Pressburg) becomes capital of the Kingdom of Hungary

1663 Turks capture Nové Zámky

1840s Ľudovít Štúr becomes leader of the Slovak nationalist movement

Ľudovít Štúr (1815–56)

Bratislava – City of Coronations

The modern capital of Slovakia, originally known as Pressburg, was first granted royal privileges in the 13th century. But it was the victory of the Turks at Mohács in 1526 that marked the start of great things for Bratislava. The town became capital of the much-reduced Kingdom of Hungary, and was made the coronation city of the Hungarian kings. For three centuries, the town hosted coronation ceremonies for 19 Hungarian monarchs, including Maria Theresa and Joseph I. Bratislava's heyday was in the 18th century during the reigns of Maria Theresa and Joseph II.

Crown of the Hungarian Kings
This crown is commonly believed to be that worn by King Stephen I, but its authenticity has long been questioned.

Maria Theresa, 1740–80
Empress Maria Theresa often took up residence at Bratislava Castle, and as a result numerous aristocrats from neighbouring Vienna chose to build palaces here.

The Primate's Palace
Built in 1778–81, this fine Neo-Classical palace became a favourite place to stay for many members of the Habsburg family. Leopold II was said to have stayed here in 1790 following his coronation as emperor.

The ceremony was attended by prominent state and Church dignitaries, including Jan Pálffy, governor of Hungary.

After the passing of the procession, the crowd scrambled to touch the cloth that lined the pavement.

The Wedderin Bell
The bell housed in St Martin's Cathedral rang to signal that a new monarch had ascended the throne of Hungary.

Bratislava – Centre of Culture
Bratislava's musical life flourished under Empress Maria Theresa. The imperial orchestra (with Joseph Haydn its leading composer) gave many concerts here, as did the six-year-old Mozart in 1762.

Bratislava Castle

Coronation of Leopold II
After his coronation ceremony on 15 November 1790, Leopold II knighted 33 noblemen in the Franciscan church.

The city walls, which the queen entered via Michael's Gate.

Maria Theresa is carried in the state coach to St Martin's Cathedral for the coronation ceremony.

Bratislava, 1741
This painting shows the coronation procession of Empress Maria Theresa on 25 June 1741. Modern visitors to Bratislava can walk the coronation route through the city (see p284).

Pressburg Peace
The Primate's Palace was the venue for the signing, on 26 December 1805, of the peace treaty between Napoleon and Franz II following the Battle of Austerlitz.

A village in East Slovakia before World War I

The Austro-Hungarian Era

The situation for Slovakia worsened drastically after the creation of the Austro-Hungarian monarchy in 1866. The Hungarian government, having a free hand in the shaping of internal policy, embarked on a process of ruthless Magyarization of non-Hungarian communities. The Slovak language was banned from schools, and the national cultural organization, Matica Slovenska, was abolished. Economically devastating was the handing over of vast swathes of land to Hungarian settlers. By the early 20th century, almost one-third of the Slovak population, driven by poverty and persecution, had fled abroad, mainly to the USA.

World War I

The lack of success in their attempts to win autonomy within the Hungarian state drove Slovak politicians to forge closer links with Czech activists, led by Tomáš Masaryk *(see p46)*. This cooperation intensified after the outbreak of World War I. In 1918, in Pittsburgh USA, representatives of Czech and Slovak emigré organizations signed an agreement providing for the creation of a joint state, in which Slovakia's autonomy would be guaranteed.

The First Czechoslovak Republic

With the Austro-Hungarian empire in tatters, the independent Czechoslovak Republic was declared in Prague on 28 October 1918. While the new state was composed of two countries with different histories, cultural traditions and ethnic compositions, President Masaryk and other leading politicians in Prague steadfastly promulgated the concept of a single country. The rejection of Slovakia's bid for autonomy caused disappointment among Slovakians. Ironically, autonomy came with the arrival of the Nazis.

The Slovak State, 1939–45

When Hitler took the Sudetenland, and with Czechoslovakia in crisis, the Slovaks seized their chance to declare independence. However, the new government,

Ribbentrop and the Slovak prime minister signing a pact in 1940

Stollwerck chocolate label

1867 Creation of the Austro-Hungarian monarchy

1896 German confectionery company, Stollwerck, opens a factory in Bratislava

1938 Parliament proclaims the Slovak Republic

1850   **1875**   **1900**   **1925**

1874–5 Slovak language banned in schools, and abolition of Matica Slovenska

1900 Tomáš Masaryk starts advocating closer cooperation between the Czechs and Slovaks

1918 Czechs and Slovaks sign, in Pittsburgh, a document proclaiming the creation of Czechoslovakia

headed by Jozef Tiso, became little more than a Nazi puppet state. Tiso banned opposition parties and deported thousands of Jews. Slovakia became the base of the Nazis' military industry and also actively supported the German army. Tiso's regime was popular since Slovakia was, for the first time, able to set up its own national institutions. But the support was not universal, and in August 1944, elements of the Slovak army, assisted by Communist partisans, launched the Slovak National Uprising. German troops quashed the revolt.

Soviet tanks on the streets of Bratislava in 1968

Reborn in 1945, the state of Czechoslovakia initially continued the pre-war democratic traditions of the First Republic. In 1948, however, it fell under the total control of the Communist Party (see p48). The era of Stalinist repression that followed affected both the democratic activists and the staunch Communists, who were often accused – like Gustáv Husák – of "Slovak nationalism".

The "Prague Spring"

In January 1968, reformists in the Communist Party reacted to the authorities' reluctance to adopt a more liberal course by taking control of the government. The democratic reforms of the so-called Prague Spring came to an abrupt end, however, on 21 August with an invasion by Warsaw Pact troops. The orthodox Communists returned to power and during the "normalization" process that followed, totalitarian rule was re-established and all dissent suppressed.

The Slovak Republic

After the "Velvet Revolution" of 1989, when the Communist government was overthrown (see p49), Czechoslovakia was finally in the hands of democrats. The country was not destined to remain a joint state, however, and on 1 January 1993, the sovereign Slovak Republic was proclaimed, headed by Michal Kováč. While democracy in the Slovak Republic has seemed extremely fragile at times, the position of the new state within the international community was confirmed when, in 2004, Slovakia joined NATO and the European Union.

President of Slovakia, Andrej Kiska

1944 Slovak National Uprising

1969 Alexander Dubček removed from office as First Secretary of the Communist Party

Slovak Constitution

ÚSTAVA SLOVENSKEJ REPUBLIKY

2005 Slovakia elected to a two-year term on the UN Security Council

2014 Andrej Kiska, entrepreneur and philanthropist, becomes president

| 1950 | 1975 | 2000 | 2025 |

1948 Communists take control of Czechoslovakia

1945 Liberation of Slovakia by the Red Army

1968 "Prague Spring"

1989 Velvet Revolution

1993 Creation of the Slovak Republic

2004 Slovakia joins NATO and becomes EU member

2007 Slovakia joins the Schengen agreement, abolishing border controls with all of its members

Slovakia at a Glance

This small Central European country displays a diverse topography. Although there are lowlands in the west of Slovakia, most of the territory is taken up by forest-clad mountains. The Small Carpathian mountains start just north of Bratislava. Central Slovakia is dominated by the Tatras range, which includes Slovakia's highest peak. In the east of the country is the Slovak Karst, which has huge limestone caves.

The Slovak Agricultural Museum, Nitra, is one of Slovakia's most interesting, full of historic implements for agriculture and wine-making, as well as displays illustrating folk and social history (see p308).

The Church of St Jacob in Trnava, built in 1640 on the site of a previous Early Gothic church, acquired some Baroque elements in 1712. The interior furnishings date from the 17th and 18th centuries (see pp300–1).

Žilina

Ružombero

Trenčín

CENTRAL SLOVAK
(see pp310–327)

Holič

Banská Bystrica

Piešťany

Zvolen

Trnava

BRATISLAVA
(see pp276–293)

Nitra

WEST SLOVAKIA
(see pp294–309)

Levice

Bratislava

Nové Zámky

Komárno

The Chapel of St John the Almsgiver was added to St Martin's Cathedral in Bratislava during the Baroque period; it holds the remains of the Saint (see pp284–5).

The altar of Our Lady of the Rosary, made by an Austrian Master in 1500–20, is one of many outstanding artifacts displayed inside Zvolen Castle (see p318).

◄ Aerial view of Bratislava, the capital of Slovakia

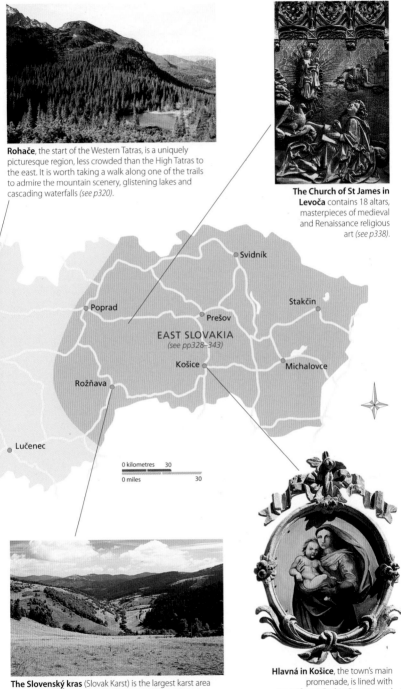

Rohače, the start of the Western Tatras, is a uniquely picturesque region, less crowded than the High Tatras to the east. It is worth taking a walk along one of the trails to admire the mountain scenery, glistening lakes and cascading waterfalls *(see p320)*.

The Church of St James in Levoča contains 18 altars, masterpieces of medieval and Renaissance religious art *(see p338)*.

Svidník

Poprad

Stakčin

Prešov

EAST SLOVAKIA
(see pp328–343)

Košice

Michalovce

Rožňava

Lučenec

0 kilometres   30

0 miles   30

The Slovenský kras (Slovak Karst) is the largest karst area in Europe, with exceptionally diverse wildlife, and glorious scenery. The beauty of the landscape and the many caves make this region highly attractive *(see pp340–1)*.

Hlavná in Košice, the town's main promenade, is lined with magnificent Gothic, Baroque and Neo-Classical buildings. This detail is from No. 37 *(see p332)*.

BRATISLAVA

The capital of Slovakia lies very near the country's south-western border. It straddles the River Danube (Dunaj) at the southern end of the Small Carpathian mountains. From here, it is a mere 2 km (1 mile) to the border with Austria, and only 10 km (6 miles) to the border with Hungary. In clear weather, both neighbouring countries can be seen from Bratislava Castle.

Bratislava has been the capital of Slovakia since 1993, when it became an independent state. It has always been a centre of the country's social and cultural life. It was known as Pressburg to German-speakers and as Pozsóny to Hungarian speakers.

A Celtic settlement in the 2nd century BC, it later became the base of a Roman garrison, and by the 10th century, one of the main centres of the Great Moravian Empire. In 1291, it was granted town privileges by the Hungarian King Andrew III and gradually strengthened its position within the Crown Lands of St Stephen. The city became particularly important after the capture of Buda by the Turks in 1541, when it was the capital of Hungary for nearly 200 years.

Pressburg reached the zenith of its glory during the reign of Maria Theresa when her beloved daughter Maria Kristina lived here with her husband. In the 19th century, it became the centre of the Slovak independence movement. The Grassalkovich Palace (now the presidential palace) is the setting for one of the great love stories of the 20th century. This is where the Austro-Hungarian crown prince Franz Ferdinand d'Este met his wife, Žofia Chotek. In 1914, the murder of the couple in Sarajevo started World War I. After the war and the creation of Czechoslovakia, the capital of the Slovak part of the country assumed the name of Bratislava. In 1939–45, as an ally of the Third Reich, Bratislava was spared destruction. Postwar development, however, destroyed the historic centre. Today, the old town of Bratislava has been lovingly restored.

Bratislava Castle with its lofty corner towers

◄ Detail of a sculpture at Bratislava Castle

Exploring Bratislava

The majority of historic sights in Bratislava can be found in the compact old town centre, on the left bank of the Danube. The landmark castle is on a hill to the west of the main road. The best point from which to view the city's layout is from the open-air observation decks of the restaurant UFO at the top of the New Bridge (Nový most) at a height of 80 m (262 ft). Outside of the centre, there are interesting villages and wine-growing areas, which are ideal for day trips.

Sights at a Glance

Churches

④ Franciscan Church
⑧ *St Martin's Cathedral*
　 pp284–5
⑮ Poor Clares Church

Buildings and Squares

① Bratislava Castle
② Old Town Hall
③ Primate's Palace
⑤ Michael's Gate
⑥ Mirbach Palace
⑦ Academia Istropolitana
⑨ Slovak National Theatre
⑩ Reduta
⑪ Slovak National Gallery
⑫ Pálffy Palace
⑬ House at the Good Shepherd
⑭ New Bridge
⑯ Námestie SNP
⑰ Grassalkovich Palace
⑱ Slavín Monument

Environs

⑲ St Andrew's Cemetery
⑳ Little Blue Church
㉑ Devín Castle
㉒ Rača
㉓ Rusovce
㉔ Svätý Jur
㉕ Pezinok
㉖ Modra
㉗ Červený Kameň
㉘ Stupava
㉙ Mariánka Shrine
㉚ Malacky
㉛ Veľké Leváre
㉜ Bernolákovo
㉝ Senec

VISITORS' CHECKLIST

Practical Information
Road map A6. 🚗 430,000.
ℹ️ Klobučnícka 2. **Tel** (02) 16186.
🌐 **bratislava.sk**

Transport
✈️ Štefanika, 9 km (6 miles) NE.
🚉 Hlavna stanica, Pražská,
1 km (0.5 mile) N. **Tel** (02) 18188.
🚌 Mlynske nivy.
🌐 **slovakrail.sk**

Getting Around

Central Bratislava is best seen on foot. The Old Town is very compact, and many of the major places to visit are grouped in and around it. For longer distances within the city and into its environs, there is a fast and efficient network of buses, trams and trolleybuses. These also run at intervals throughout the night, starting from Námestie SNP. From April to October, ferry and sightseeing boats run from Fajnorovo nábrežie. From May to October, Twin City Liner offers a connection with Vienna.

The main square and castle in Bratislava

| 0 metres | 200 |
| 0 yards | 200 |

Key

⬜ Sight

Pedestrian street

For keys to symbols *see back flap*

Street-by-Street: Old Town

The centre of Bratislava's historic Staré Město district consists of two interlinked squares: Hlavné námestie and Františkánske námestie. The first has the distinctive Old Town Hall. This square was also part of the coronation route of the Hungarian kings (*see p284*), now marked by golden crowns embedded in the pavement. The pride of Františkánske námestie, apart from its lovely trees, is the Marian Column erected in 1657. Both squares are popular meeting places, with many attractive cafés.

5 Michael's Gate
This is the only gate that remains from the medieval fortifications. In the 18th century, it was topped with a statue of the Archangel Michael.

6 Mirbach Palace
This Rococo palace, one of Bratislava's finest architectural relics, now houses the City Gallery.

This statue of Napoleon's soldier
is one of several life-sized figures in the Old Town, including a worker poking his head out of a round manhole and a paparazzo photographer aiming his lens from around a corner.

Marian column

ZAMOČNÍCKA

BIELA

FRANTIŠ KÁNSKE NÁMEST

SEDLÁRSKA

HLAVN NÁMEST

ZELENÁ

RYBÁ

In Hlavné námestie,
the main square of Bratislava and its former marketplace, is the 1572 Maximilian Fountain designed by Andreas Luttringer. On a tall plinth at the centre of the fountain is the figure of Roland, a knight who defended the townspeople's rights. The square has been beautifully renovated, and seasonal stalls add to its bustle and atmosphere.

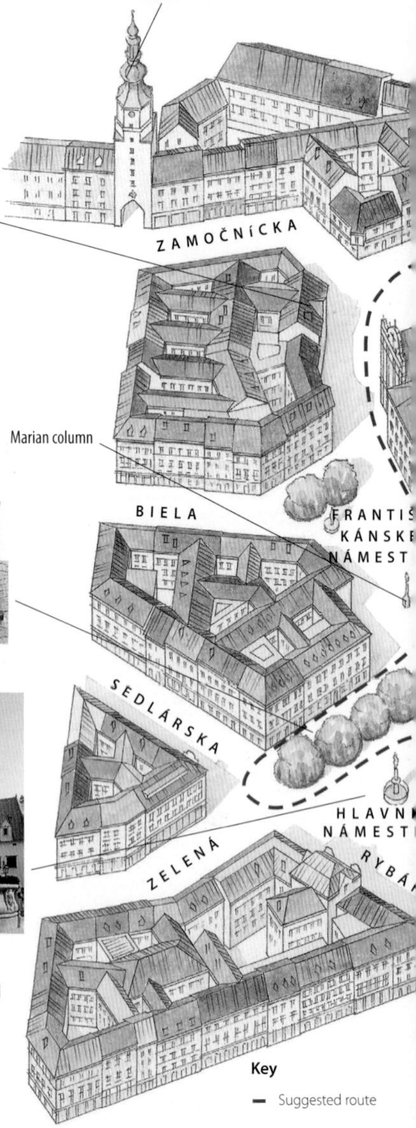

Key
 Suggested route

❹ ★ Franciscan Church
Bratislava's oldest religious building, this Gothic-style church was erected in the 13th century. Several times remodelled, it acquired its Baroque form in the 18th century.

Locator Map
See city map pp278–9

❸ ★ Primate's Palace
One of the city's finest Neo-Classical structures, this palace was built in 1778–81 by Melchior Hefele for the Archbishop Jozef Batthyány.

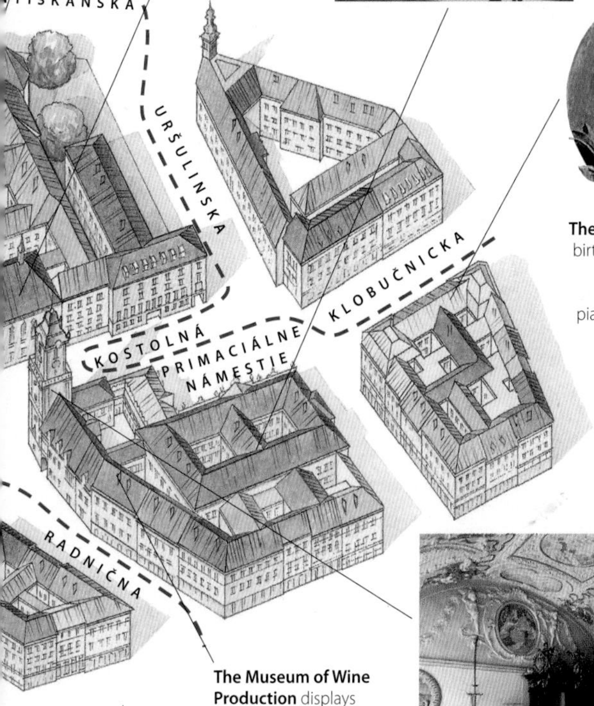

The Jesuit Church
(see p282) was built in 1636–8 by Protestants. Its greatest treasure is the Rococo pulpit by Ľudovít Gode.

The Museum of Music is in the birthplace of Johann Nepomuk Hummel (1778–1837), a celebrated composer and pianist. The Renaissance house in Klobučnicka has displays about his life and works, and the history of music in Bratislava.

T I Š K Á N S K A

U R Š U L I N S K A

K L O B U Č N I C K A

K O S T O L N Á

P R I M A C I Á L N E
N Á M E S T I E

R A D N I Č N A

The Museum of Wine Production displays a wooden wine barrel with writings on Napoleon's siege of Bratislava, dated 1808.

❷ Old Town Hall
The Stará radnica, many times remodelled and rebuilt since the 13th century, is now home to the City Museum.

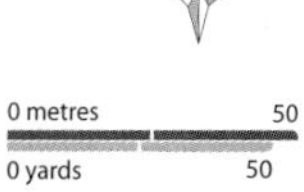

0 metres   50
0 yards   50

❶ Bratislava Castle

Bratislavský Hrad

Slovak National Museum: **Tel** (02) 20 48 31 11. **Open** 9am–5pm Tue–Fri, 10am–6pm Sat & Sun (last adm: 45 mins before closing).
W snm.sk

Bratislava Castle on the north embankment of the Danube

Perched forbiddingly on a large, rocky hill above the Danube, Bratislava's stronghold is first mentioned in 907. It was at a strategic location on the Danube, at the crossing of trade routes, including the ancient Amber Route. Fortified in the 11th and 12th centuries, the castle was rebuilt in Gothic style in the 15th century, and in 1552–60 remodelled into a Renaissance residence. In 1750–60, it was given beautiful Rococo furnishings. In 1811, the castle burnt down; it was rebuilt in the 1950s.

Today, visitors to the castle can enjoy magnificent views over the city and several exhibitions from the **Slovak National Museum**. Collections on permanent display include The National Historical Exhibition of Slovakia, Slovak Folk Culture, the History of Bratislava Castle and the Castle Picture Gallery. The reconstructed castle and all exhibitions held here are open to the public.

Bratislava's eclectic Old Town Hall in the main square

❷ Old Town Hall

Stará Radnica

City Museum: **Tel** (02) 32 18 13 12. **Open** 10am–5pm Tue–Fri, 11am–6pm Sat & Sun.
W muzeum.bratislava.sk

The charming Old Town Hall in Primaciálne námestie was created in the 15th century by combining a number of residential houses. At the turn of the 16th and 17th centuries, it was rebuilt in Renaissance style. In the 18th century, its much older corner tower was remodelled in Baroque style; this tower can be climbed for excellent views. Mounted on its lower section is a plaque marking the level of flood waters recorded in February 1850. Higher up, to the left of the Gothic window, is another historic relic – a cannonball embedded in the wall since the 1809 siege of Bratislava by Napoleon's army. It is worth taking a look at the unusual colourful roof covering of the building on the side of Primaciálne námestie.

The town hall houses the **City Museum** (Mestské múzeum). Displayed within its splendid vaulted interiors are exhibits associated with the history of Bratislava, including 17th–19th-century painted shooting targets.

Opposite the town hall stands the **Jesuit Church of the Holy Saviour**. It was built in 1636–8 for Bratislava's Protestant community, which explains its wide, plain façade with no tower. Its interesting Baroque furnishings include a fine Rococo pulpit.

❸ Primate's Palace

Primaciálny Palác

Primaciálne námestie 1. **Tel** (02) 59 35 63 94. **Open** 10am–5pm Tue–Sun.

The most beautiful palace in Bratislava was built during 1778–81 to a design by Melchior Hefele, for Jozef Batthyány, the primate of Hungary and archbishop of Esztergom. Its Neo-Classical pink-and-gold façade features a magnificent pediment that is crowned with the archbishop's coat of arms, topped with a giant-size cardinal's hat. The figures of angels on the façade hold the letters I and C, a reference to the motto in the cardinal's coat of arms – Iusticia (Justice) and Clementia (Mercy).

The palace, which is now the seat of the town's mayor, is partly open to the public. Its most opulent room is the Hall of Mirrors, where in 1805 the Peace Treaty of Pressburg was signed between Napoleon and Francis I, after the French victory at the Battle of Austerlitz. Other first-floor rooms are given to a branch of the Municipal Gallery with a modest collection of paintings and six unique English

The courtyard fountain at the Primate's Palace

tapestries dating from 1632, depicting the love story of Hero and Leander. The strikingly bright tapestries were discovered in a hidden compartment during building works in the early 20th century.

❹ Franciscan Church
Františkánský Kostol

Františkánske námestie.
Open 10:30am–5pm Mon–Fri.

The Franciscan Church behind an inconspicuous Baroque façade is the oldest religious building in Bratislava. Built in the 13th century, it was consecrated in 1297 in the presence of King Andrew II. Subsequent remodelling works obliterated its original Gothic form, but it is still possible to see the medieval rib vaulting above the presbytery. Particularly impressive is the two-tier 14th-century chapel of St John the Evangelist. During coronation pageants in Bratislava the church was used for knighting ceremonies, in which the new monarch appointed Knights of the Golden Spur.

The church's furnishings, mainly Baroque, date from the 17th and 18th centuries; an older, 15th-century Pietà in a side altar is a highlight.

❺ Michael's Gate
Michalská Brána

Michalská ulica 24. Museum of Weapons and Town Fortifications: **Tel** (02) 54 43 30 44. **Open** 10am–5pm Tue–Sun, 11am–6pm Sat & Sun. 🖼
🔲 **muzeum.bratislava.sk**

Built in the first half of the 14th century, Michael's Gate is the only surviving original gateway to the medieval city, and one of Bratislava's oldest buildings. In 1753–8, its Gothic tower was

Buildings of the Academia Istropolitana, site of a 15th-century university

Statue from the Franciscan Church

raised to the present 51 m (167 ft), by the addition of a Baroque cupola, and the statue of Archangel Michael was placed at the top. The tower houses the **Museum of Weapons and Town Fortifications** (Múzeum zbraní a mestského opevnenia). The viewing terrace affords a stunning panorama of the city and beyond. The small building next to the gate is Bratislava's oldest pharmacy – At the Red Lobster.

❻ Mirbach Palace
Mirbachov Palác

Františkánske námestie 11. City Gallery: **Tel** (02) 54 43 15 56. **Open** 11am–6pm Tue–Sun. 🔲 **gmb.sk**

The Rococo Mirbach Palace opposite the Franciscan Church has a beautiful façade with stuccoes and a triangular

Michael's Gate with its striking Baroque cupola

pediment. The building was erected in 1768–70 by a rich brewer, Martin Spech. Its subsequent owner, Count Karol Nyary, ordered his family crest to be placed in the tympanum. The last owner of the palace, Emil Mirbach, bequeathed the building to the town.

Now it is an art gallery, currently holding the main collection of Bratislava's **City Gallery** (Galéria mesta Bratislavy). Exhibits include examples of 17th- and 18th-century Baroque painting. Two of the first-floor halls have walls almost entirely covered with colourful 18th-century engravings set in wood panelling.

❼ Academia Istropolitana

Ventúrska 3.

The oldest university in present-day Slovakia, the Academia Istropolitana was founded by King Matthias Corvinus in 1465. It occupied two residential town houses belonging to Štefan Gmaitel. The university trained its students in three faculties. Following the death of King Matthias in 1490, the university closed down.

This building, with its stone entrance portal and oriel windows, is now a national cultural monument. Modernized in the 1960s, it houses the Bratislava Academy of Music; check with tourist information offices for times of occasional performances.

❽ St Martin's Cathedral
Dóm Sv. Martina

This Gothic edifice, with a wide nave flanked by two aisles, was built on the site of an earlier, 14th-century Romanesque church. Between 1563 and 1830, eleven Hungarian kings and eight queens were crowned here. It is possible to walk the former coronation route through the Old Town, starting from here, by following a series of golden crowns embedded in the pavement. In the late 19th century, the church was rebuilt in Neo-Gothic style by Jozef Lippert, and its interior was refurbished along more purist lines.

Structure of the Cathedral
Due to vibrations from heavy traffic on the nearby major road to the New Bridge (see p287), the cathedral is being damaged. It frequently undergoes repair work.

Presbytery
After completing the hall, the builders realized that the section by the altar was too small. They added a presbytery with a splendid net vault; the coat of arms on it is that of Matthias Corvinus.

★ Sculpture of St Martin
This dramatic sculpture, by Georg Raphael Donner (1734), was originally made for the main altar. St Martin is shown in Hungarian dress cutting his cloak to share with a beggar.

①

Chapel of St John the Almsgiver
In 1732, commissioned by Archbishop Esterházy, Georg Raphael Donner built the side chapel of St John the Almsgiver (sv. Ján Almužník), in which the saint's remains were laid to rest.

VISITORS' CHECKLIST

Practical Information
Rudnayovo námestie 1.
Tel (02) 54 43 13 59. **Open** Apr–Oct: 9–11:30am & 1–6pm Mon–Sat, 1:30–4pm Sun (Nov–Mar: times vary). 7:30am & noon Mon–Sat, 7:45am, 9am, 10:30am, noon & 5pm Sun.

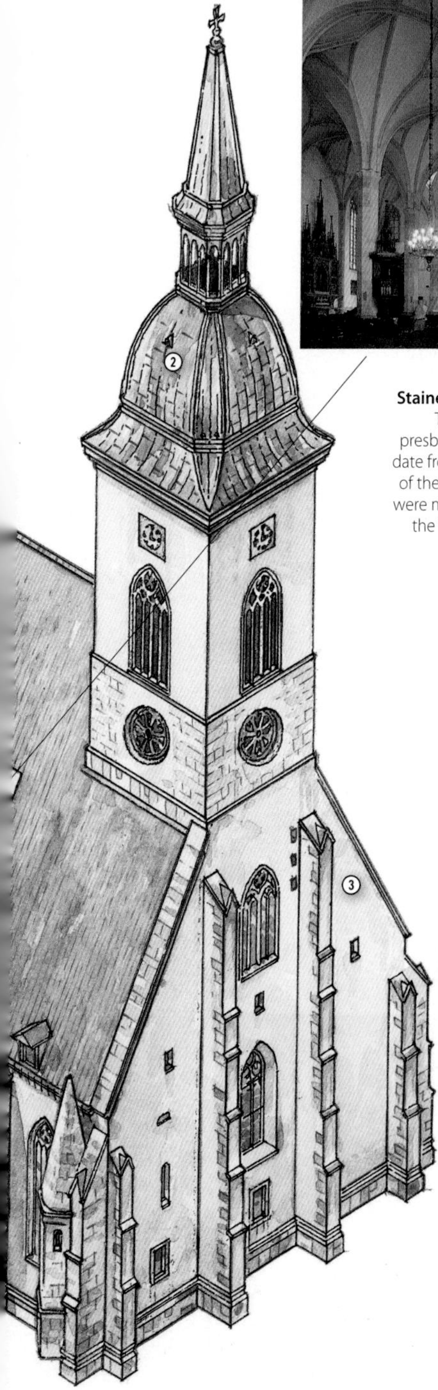

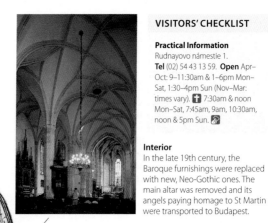

Interior
In the late 19th century, the Baroque furnishings were replaced with new, Neo-Gothic ones. The main altar was removed and its angels paying homage to St Martin were transported to Budapest.

Stained-Glass Windows
The windows in the presbytery and the aisles date from the second half of the 19th century; they were mostly produced by the Viennese company of K Geyling.

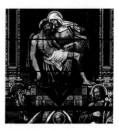

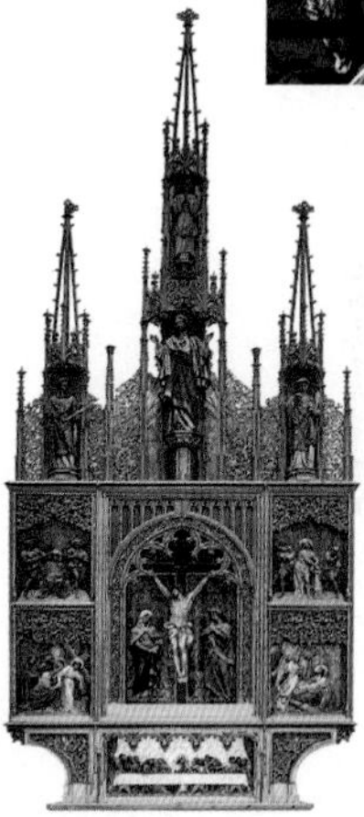

★ Altar of St Anne's Chapel
The central field of the ornate altarpiece in this chapel depicts the scene of the Crucifixion.

KEY

① **St Anne's Chapel**

② **The tower**, 85 m (280 ft) tall, is topped with a slender cupola, and includes a tiny copy of the Hungarian crown, a reminder that this was once the venue of royal coronations.

③ **The Canons' Chapel and the Chapel of the Czech queen Sophia** are adjacent to the sacristy under the tower.

④ **Main portal with Neo-Gothic vestibule**

Façade of the Neo-Renaissance Slovak National Theatre

❾ Slovak National Theatre

Slovenské Národné Divadlo

Hviezdoslavovo námestie 1.
Tel (02) 20 47 22 89. **W** snd.sk

This imposing Neo-Renaissance theatre on the east side of Hviezdoslavovo námestie was built in 1884–6. Its creators were two Viennese architects who specialized in theatres, Ferdinand Fellner and Hermann Helmer. The façade is decorated with busts including Goethe, Liszt and Shakespeare. At the centre of the tympanum is a sculptural group including the Muse of Comedy, Thalia. Opera and ballet performances are regularly staged here; the sumptuous interiors can only be seen by attending a performance. The bronze and marble fountain in front of the theatre, made in 1880 by V Tilgner, depicts the Trojan youth Ganymede flying on the back of Zeus, who has become an eagle.

In 2007, the National Theatre opened a second performance and exhibition venue at Pribinova 17, on the Danube's banks in Eurovea, showcasing additional productions.

❿ Reduta

Námestie Eugena Suchoňa 1.
Tel (02) 20 47 52 33. **Open** for concerts only. **W** filharmonia.sk

Close to the Slovak National Theatre is the imposing building of the Reduta, built in 1913–18 in an eclectic style that combines Neo-Baroque, Rococo and Art Nouveau features. It used to stage social and artistic events, symphony concerts and theatre performances. Today, the Reduta is the home of the Slovak Philharmonic, and it is the principal venue for the Bratislava Music Festival *(see p262)*. The part of the building on the side of Mostova houses a restaurant.

⓫ Slovak National Gallery

Slovenská Národná Galéria

Riečna 1. **Tel** (02) 20 47 61 11.
Open 10am–6pm Tue–Sun.
Closed 1 Jan, Easter Friday, 24, & 25 Dec. **W** sng.sk

Established in 1948, the National Gallery occupies a building that was created by combining the four-wing 18th-century Baroque naval barracks, designed by G Martinelli and F Hildebrandt, and, in the 1970s, V Dĕdeček's

house. In 1990, the gallery's collections were also placed in the neighbouring Neo-Renaissance Esterházy Palace. A long structure designed by I Feigler Jr and built in 1870–76, Esterházy Palace is reminiscent of an Italian Renaissance town palace.

The gallery boasts a number of magnificent works of art. The finest are the collections of 13th- and 14th-century Slovak art including altarpieces and statues from churches of the Spiš region in eastern Slovakia.

Modern Slovak art is also well represented, with models of buildings, photographs, ceramics, jewellery and posters, making an eclectic overview of the country's creative output over the last hundred years.

As well as Slovak artists, the collection also holds works by a number of foreign masters, including Caravaggio, Rubens, Manet and Picasso.

⓬ Pálffy Palace

Pálffyho Palác

Panska 19/21. City Gallery: **Tel** (02) 54 43 36 27. **Open** 11am–6pm Tue–Sun. **W** gmb.sk

The 1747 Baroque Pálffy Palace serves as another extension to Bratislava's **City Gallery** (Galéria mesta Bratislavy); the main collection is in the Mirbach Palace *(see p283)*. Its distinctive portal is decorated with images of war trophies, reminders of the fact that one of its first owners was Marshal Leopold Pálffy.

The Reduta, home of the Slovak Philharmonic

The Palace displays collections of Gothic panel painting, Central European painting, 19th-century sculpture and 20th-century Slovak painting and sculpture. It is this 20th-century section that holds the most interest, with its varied portrayals and interpretations of Slovak life.

⑬ House at the Good Shepherd

Dom U Dobrého Pastiera

Židovska 1. **Tel** (02) 54 41 19 40. Museum of Clocks: **Open** 10am–5pm Mon–Fri, 11am–6pm Sat & Sun.

One of the town's finest examples of Rococo architecture is the House at the Good Shepherd, named after the statue of the Good Shepherd on its corner. Built in 1760–65, it is now one of the few remaining original houses in the area at the foot of the castle. It is colloquially referred to as the "house like an iron", because of its tall flat wedge shape, dictated by the plot on which it was erected. It is believed to be the narrowest building in Europe, and there is only one room on each floor. It houses a **Museum of Clocks** (Múzeum hodín), a branch of the City Museum. The exhibits date from the 17th to the 20th centuries and are mostly the works of Bratislava's clockmakers.

⑭ New Bridge

Nový Most

Staromestská.

Also known as the bridge of the Slovak National Uprising (most SNP), this steel construction, which is suspended from one pylon on the south bank of the Danube (Dunaj), opened in 1972. At the top of the pylon is a restaurant, reached by a lift, which provides views of the city on the north bank, and of the vast housing

estates of Petržalka on the south. Built by the Communists, this estate houses around 150,000 of the city's inhabitants.

To build the New Bridge, and the major Staromestská highway that cuts through the city and over the bridge, a section of the old city was destroyed, including the former Jewish quarter at the foot of Bratislava Castle, just outside the old city walls.

⑮ Poor Clares Church

Klariský Kostol

Klariská ulica.

The former church and convent of St Clare stand near the 14th-century walls, which surrounded the city until the 18th century, when they were dismantled on the orders of Empress Maria Theresa. The remaining fragments are a meticulous reconstruction.

The 14th-century Gothic, single-nave church should, in line with the strict rules binding the mendicant and contemplative orders, be plain and have no ostentatious tower, only a small bell rung at times of prayer. This rule has been broken twice in Bratislava: the nearby Franciscan Church *(see p283)* and the Poor Clares Church were both given towers. The convent's fine church tower, dating from 1400 and richly decorated with sculptures,

Figure from the House at the Good Shepherd

is built on a rarely seen pentagonal ground-plan.

The convent itself was built after the great fire of 1590, in Renaissance style. From the second half of the 18th century until 1908, it housed the Law Academy and the Catholic Theological Seminary; one of its students

Richly decorated tower and spire of the Poor Clares Church

was the Hungarian composer Béla Bartók. It has been restored, and it now serves as a venue for exhibitions and, due to the church's excellent acoustics, concerts.

⑯ Námestie SNP

Námestie SNP.

The square of the Slovak National Uprising has been used for public gatherings for centuries. Celebrations that accompanied royal coronations were held here, and more recently it saw gatherings of activists in 1989 just before the fall of Communism.

Just off the square is the **Church and Monastery of the Brothers of Mercy** (kostol a kláštor milosrdných bratov). Here, the monks, who devoted themselves to caring for the sick, built a large complex of buildings outside the city walls. The early Baroque façade with its angular tower (1728) is clearly visible on many old drawings. The most interesting artifacts are the 18th-century altars and the tombstone of Ján Onell (1745). The still-functioning hospital played an important role during the plague that ravaged Europe in 1710–13.

National flags flying in front of Grassalkovich Palace

⑰ Grassalkovich Palace

Grassalkovičov Palác

Hodžovo námestie 1. Gardens: Štefánikova ulica. **Open** daily.

This Baroque palace, built in 1760 to a design by A Mayerhoffer, was originally the residence of Anton Grassalkovich, chairman of the Royal Hungarian Chamber, the Royal Crown's Guardian and one of the closest advisors to Empress Maria Theresa. In the early 20th century, Austro-Hungarian prince Franz Ferdinand met his future wife, a palace maid, here. Their deaths in Sarajevo in 1914 sparked the beginning of World War I. In 1939, it became the seat of Monsignor Jœsef Tiso, president of the Slovak Republic during World War II. It is still the residence of the President. In the late 18th century, the palace was surrounded by a French garden, which has been returned to its former glory and is open to the public.

⑱ Slavín Monument

Slavín.

The vast Soviet monument to the Red Army soldiers killed in battles with the Nazis around Bratislava in the closing stages of World War II stands on Slavín hill in the northwestern part of the city. The 40-m (130-ft) obelisk by Ján Svetlik is topped by a bronze figure by Alexander Trizulijak of a Red Army soldier holding a banner flapping in the wind. The

adjacent mausoleum is used as a venue for official celebrations. The monument is surrounded by a cemetery containing 6,845 war graves. The front terrace affords a fine prospect of Bratislava to the south and views of the distant Small Carpathian mountains to the north.

Monument to the Red Army soldiers on Slavín Hill

⑲ St Andrew's Cemetery

Ondrejský Cintorín

Entrance on Poľna. **Open** 7am–dusk daily.

The oldest and most interesting graveyard in Bratislava, St Andrew's Cemetery is a well-kept green oasis resembling a town park and is popular with the locals for a stroll.

Founded in 1784, it covers an area of 6 ha (15 acres) and entry to it is through St Andrew's Chapel, which was built by the architect I Feigler in 1861.

The cemetery is the resting place of several prominent citizens of Bratislava and Slovakia. Its avenues are lined with many tombs belonging to famous families. Among those buried here are sculptor Alois Rigele; Július Satinský, a famous Slovak actor, writer and comedian; and the Bratislavan Robinson Carl Jetting.

The cemetery has an exhibition of tomb monuments and details from memorials of the 19th and 20th centuries.

⑳ Little Blue Church

Modrý Kostolík

Bezručova ulica.

The unusual Art Nouveau Little Blue Church owes its name to its blue roof tiles and walls. Its designer, Ödön Lechner, was a Hungarian architect, one of the most famous creators of Art Nouveau in Budapest. The church was built in 1907–13 and dedicated to St Elizabeth (sv. Alžbeta) of Hungary, daughter of King Andrew II of the Arpad family, who was born in Bratislava Castle in 1207. Her portrait can be seen above the church's portal.

Figure of an angel, St Andrew's Cemetery

㉑ Devín Castle

8 km (5 miles) W of the centre of Bratislava. 🚌 29. 🚢 from Central Bratislava. **Tel** (02) 65 73 01 05. **Open** Oct–Apr: 10am–5pm Tue–Sun (May–Sep: to 7pm Sat & Sun). 🅿

At the point where the Morava river flows into the Danube stand the looming ruins of Devín Castle perched on a high rock. The rock was once the site of a Celtic settlement; later on, the Romans built their fortress here; and in the 9th century, Prince Rastislav, King of Great Moravia, chose it for his stronghold. It changed hands many times until in 1809 it was blown up by the French during the Napoleonic Wars.

In the 19th century, during the period of national rebirth, it became a prominent symbol in the shaping of Slovak national identity, promoted by the nationalist Ľudovít Štúr (*see p290*).

During the 1980s, the castle area, separated from Austria only by the Danube, was closed to the public. Now it is a favourite spot for a stroll for Bratislavans. It also features the remains of the Roman fortress and a museum of archaeological finds in a reconstructed fragment of the castle.

㉒ Rača

8 km (5 miles) NE of the centre of Bratislava. 🚶 21,000. 🚌 52, 55, 56, 59, 65, 515. 🚋 3, 5. 🍇 Grape Harvest: mid-Sep. 🅆 **raca.sk**

The small winemaking town of Rača has a history going back to Roman times. Its earliest written records, from 1245, mention a Roman settlement on the south-eastern slopes of the Small Carpathians. During the Middle Ages, the locally produced wine was regarded as the region's best, and exported to Silesia and Austria. In 1767, Empress Maria Theresa granted Rača's producers a licence to produce *terezianska frankovka*, so declaring the local red wine worthy of the imperial table.

The ruins of Devín Castle, high above the Danube

In order to protect their products against interference and fakes, Rača's winemakers marked their barrels by scorching special marks on them. Winemaking traditions are still a significant part of the local culture, and the annual grape harvest festivals, here and in Modra (*see p290*), attract many visitors.

㉓ Rusovce

9 km (6 miles) S of the centre of Bratislava. 🚶 1,700. 🚌 91, 191.

The remains of a Roman military camp called Gerulata were discovered in the suburban district of Rusovce in 1961. It had stood here from the 1st to the 4th centuries AD, and was one of the command posts that guarded the northern border of the Roman Empire along the Danube. Archaeological excavations unearthed fragments of fortifications, cult sites, tombstones and small everyday objects, many of which are displayed in the **Gerulata Museum**.

Another popular attraction is the 19th-century Neo-Gothic **Zichy Castle**. This houses part of the collection of the Slovak National Gallery, and is surrounded by a vast English-style park.

🏛 **Gerulata Museum**
Gerulatská 69. **Tel** (02) 62 85 93 32. **Open** Apr–Nov: 10am–5pm Tue–Sun. 🅿

🏰 **Zichy Castle**
Closed for renovation.

The fairytale Zichy Castle in Rusovce

Altar in the Church of St George, Svätý Jur

㉔ Svätý Jur

Road map A6. 14 km (9 miles) NE of the centre of Bratislava. 🚗 5,100. 🚌 🚆 **w** svatyjur.sk

A wine-producing centre, Svätý Jur lies in an extremely picturesque setting surrounded by vineyards with the remains of its ancient walls visible here and there. Its first records date from 1209, but this small town reached the peak of its prosperity in the 17th and 18th centuries, and most of its historic buildings date from that time. In the early 17th century, Emperor Rudolph II granted it town privileges, and in 1615, Matthias II conferred on it numerous further rights.

The town's highlight is the modest 13th-century **Church of St George** (sv. Juraj). Its Gothic interior contains many beautiful wall-paintings, stone epitaphs and a carved altarpiece depicting the church's patron saint fighting the dragon. The altarpiece was carved from white sandstone, in 1527, by Anton Pilgram.

Standing below the church is an early 17th-century Renaissance mansion that belonged to the Pálffy family, and is now the home of the new Academia Istropolitana (see p283). The nearby Baroque **Church of the Piarist Order** (Piaristický kláštor), with its steep roof, has the tallest clock tower in town.

㉕ Pezinok

Road map A6. 20 km (12 miles) NE of the centre of Bratislava. 🚗 22,700. 🚌 🚆 **i** M.R. Štefánika 1. **Tel** (033) 640 69 89. **w** pezinok.sk

Pezinok's winemaking tradition dates back to the late Middle Ages. The first vine growers were German settlers, who arrived in the 13th century. In 1615 Matthias II granted Pezinok the status of a free royal town and the town's walls were constructed. The **Old Town Hall** was built in the 17th century and rebuilt after a fire in Neo-Classical style. Kaviakov, the Renaissance house at No. 4 Štefanika, with its attractive oriel window and inner courtyard, houses the **Small Carpathian Museum** (Malokarpatské múzeum), devoted to local winemaking traditions and Pezinok's history. Hiking and skiing are popular in the nearby mountains.

🏛 **Small Carpathian Museum**
Tel (033) 641 20 57. **Open** Apr–Oct: Tue–Sun. **w** muzeumpezinok.sk

㉖ Modra

Road map A6. 30 km (19 miles) NE of the centre of Bratislava. 🚗 9,000. 🚆 **i** Štúrova 59. **Tel** (033) 647 23 12. 🍇 Grape Harvest: mid-Sep. **w** modra.sk

An annual highlight in Modra (Modern), sometimes called the "jewel" of the Small Carpathians, is the September grape harvest festival. The oldest of its five churches is the Catholic **Church of St John the Baptist** (sv. Ján Krstitel), from the beginning of the 14th century. Buried in its cemetery is one of the heroes of the Slovak national movement, Ľudovít Štúr (1815–56), whose life is illustrated by an exhibition in the local **Štúr Museum**, in the former town hall. His statue also dominates the main square. Modra is renowned for its majolica pottery (see p382).

🏛 **Štúr Museum**
Štúrova 84. **Tel** (033) 647 27 65. **Open** Tue–Sun. 🚗 **w** snm.sk

The 17th-century Upper Gate in Modra

㉗ Červený Kameň

Road map A6. 8 km (5 miles) N of Modra. 🚆 **Tel** (033) 690 58 03. **Open** Oct–Apr: 9:30am–3:30pm Tue–Sat; May–Sep: 9am–5pm daily. 🍇 Fencing Festival: May. 🚗 📷 ♿ 🅿 🎧 **w** hradcervenykamen.sk

One of the best-preserved Slovak castles, Červený

The Old Town Hall in Pezinok

Coats of arms from the well in the courtyard of Červený Kameň Castle

Kameň (Red Stone) owes its magnificent appearance to the fact that from 1580 until the end of World War II it remained in the hands of the wealthy Pálffy family. A mighty edifice with four corner towers, it was acquired in the 16th century by the German banking family, the Fuggers, on the site of a 13th-century fort. Anton Fugger, one of the richest men in 16th-century Europe, converted the fort into a Renaissance castle with huge cellars, 70 m (230 ft) long and 9 m (30 ft) high, which were used as a warehouse. After the Pálffy family took over, they converted it into a splendid Baroque residence. At the end of World War II, they fled the country.

The castle's magnificent interiors include many excellently preserved pieces of furniture, porcelain and historic furnishings. The eye-catching features of the octagonal castle chapel are its lavishly decorated walls and ceilings, and marble altars, while the castle pharmacy still has the original cabinets dating from 1752. An unusual feature of the castle is the 1656 *sala terrena*, a startling artificial grotto with *trompe l'oeil* paintings and stuccoes.

The castle also houses some interesting collections from the Slovak National Museum. There are historic weapons dating from the 15th to the 19th centuries. There is also a gallery of paintings with some fine family portraits of the Habsburgs, Pálffys and their courtiers. Many other exhibits illuminate the lives and living conditions of the aristocracy here and in other Slovak castles from Renaissance times until the 19th century.

Environs
Častá, about 1 km (half a mile) east of Červený Kameň, has been a centre of winemaking for several centuries. Its 15th-century Gothic **Church of St Imre** (sv. Emeryk) has some interesting medieval paintings, and in several private wine cellars in the town, you can taste the local wines.

㉘ Stupava

Road map A6. 🏔 9,300. 🚌 (02) 65 93 43 12. 👤 Agátová 16, Stupava. 🌐 **stupava.sk**

An important trading centre for several centuries, Stupava, then known as Ztumpa, is mentioned in the donation letter of the Hungarian King Bela IV as early as 1269. The local fairs were famous, and the town charged a three per cent tax on all goods sold, which contributed to its growing wealth.

The seat of the changing owners of Stupava was a modest-sized **Castle**, which in the second half of the 19th century was rebuilt in Romantic style, with some Rococo elements. Placed above the entrance is the Károlyi family crest. Unfortunately, the building burned down in 1947 and its subsequent reconstruction completely changed its appearance. The castle is surrounded by a lovely English-style garden with some rare species of trees.

The town's most notable religious building is the **Church of St Stephen** (sv. Štefana), the patron saint of Hungary. This Baroque edifice, erected on the site of a castle mentioned in 1271, was most recently remodelled in 1867. Close by is a Baroque chapel surrounded by a high wall with the Stations of the Cross.

Also of interest in Stupava are some well-preserved Baroque and Neo-Classical burghers' houses along Hlavná. The pillory, erected in 1766 for the punishment of minor offences, is still standing. The town's **Synagogue**, dating from 1803, is a square-shaped building with massive walls that give it a rather forbidding appearance. The synagogue is listed as a UNESCO World Architectural Heritage Site and holds social and cultural events occasionally. Inside, four huge pillars divide the vault into twelve segments. The ceiling and the walls still feature beautiful paintings in cobalt blue and dark red.

Figure from the Church of St Stephen, Stupava

Stupava has also been a well-known centre for ceramics, which is commemorated in the **Museum of Ferdiš Kostka**, a famous Slovak potter (1878–1951). It displays the original stone tiles, sculptures and vessels by Kostka with his decorations depicting the lives of the local inhabitants.

🏛 **Museum of Ferdiš Kostka**
F Kostku 26. **Tel** (02) 65 93 48 82. **Open** Tue–Sat (Sat to 1:30pm). 🌐 **muzeumpezinok.sk**

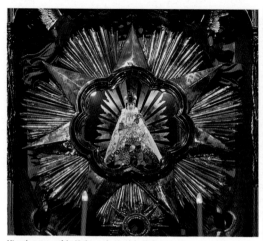

Miraculous statue of the Madonna, the Mariánka Shrine

㉙ Mariánka Shrine

Road map A6. 12 km (7 miles) NW of Bratislava. **Tel** (02) 65 93 52 26. **Open** daily. **w** marianka.sk

The charming sanctuary in Mariánka, a small town north-west of Bratislava, is the oldest site of the Marian cult in the territory of the former Hungarian Kingdom. The Gothic **Church of Our Lady** (Panny Márie), built in 1377, was founded by King Louis I of Hungary. Inside are five Baroque altars dating from 1717–35. The jewel of the church is the wooden statue of Our Lady, dating probably from the 13th century, made famous by numerous miracles. In the 17th century, during the wars with Turkey, the revered statue was hidden five times in the nearby Pajštún Castle (*see below*). The adjacent monastery is as old as the church. The building was given its present shape in 1711–14, when Cardinal Kristián August, Archbishop of Esztergom and Primate of Hungary, chose Mariánka – known at the time as Mariatál – for his summer residence.

Starting behind the church is a scenic footpath with thirteen Baroque Stations of the Cross. The path leads up to the site of a miraculous spring, which has a Baroque rotunda chapel built above it. Its founder, Count Jan Macholanyi, is depicted, with his family, in one of the ceiling paintings. Standing in front of the chapel are two Baroque statues by Georg Raphael Donner.

Environs

A popular but steep 90-minute walk from Mariánka via the town of Borinka leads to the remains of **Pajštún Castle**, once a magnificent Renaissance seat of the Pálffy family. The castle was unfortunately destroyed by a passing detachment of troops from Napoleon's army and today is just a pile of ruins. According to legend, the place is haunted by a knight on a charger, who each night jumps from the castle walls. The surrounding district offers several interesting and fairly difficult climbing trails.

Frontal view of Malacky Synagogue's twin-towered façade

㉚ Malacky

Road map A6. 17,770. Radlinskeho 1. **Tel** (034) 772 20 55. **w** malacky.sk

Belonging to the Balassy family, Malacky was granted town privileges in 1573. Its main attraction and a place of pilgrimage is the Baroque **Church of the Assumption of the Virgin Mary** (Nanebovzatia Panny Márie), built for the Franciscan order in 1653. Its "sacred stairs" are, according to tradition, a copy of those ascended by Christ as he entered the courtroom in Jerusalem, where he was sentenced to death. Pilgrims climb the ascending left-hand side of the staircase on their knees. Placed under every step are relics of saints. The right-hand side may be descended on foot. The entrance at the back of the church leads to the crypt, a resting place of members of the Pálffy family and several hundred Franciscan monks.

The **Synagogue**, built in 1886, sports a twin-towered façade, clearly inspired by Middle Eastern architecture.

Church of the Assumption of the Virgin Mary
Open Mon, Wed & Fri.

㉛ Vel'ké Leváre

Road map A6. 3,220.

Once a military base guarding the borders of the Hungarian Kingdom, this small town was first mentioned in historic records in 1378. It has houses, quite unique in Europe, built by the Anabaptists (locally known as Habans), members of a religious community who arrived here in 1588 from Swiss and South German territories. They exerted an enormous influence on the life of the local population and left behind a number of fine historic buildings. The **Haban Houses** (Hábanske domy) display distinctive design and are often painted blue. A display of Haban pottery can also be seen.

In 1981, Hábanský dvor (mansion) was declared a legally protected monument of folk architecture.

In the 16th century, the Kollonič family, who originated from Croatia, built a three-wing Baroque **Palace** here, surrounded by a sprawling English-style garden. Both palace and garden are closed to visitors.

In 1729–33, Cardinal Žigmund Kollonič, Archbishop of Vienna, erected an imposing twin-towered parish church. Its consecration date coincided with the 50th anniversary of the victory over the Turks at Vienna, in 1683.

The twin-towered parish church in Veľké Leváre

³² Bernolákovo

Road map A6. 🚹 4,500. 🚌 🚏
ℹ️ Hlavná 111. **Tel** (02) 45 99 39 11.

From the 13th century until 1948, Bernolákovo was known as Čeklí. It was renamed in honour of Anton Bernolák, author of the first book on Slovak grammar, who was the local priest here between 1787 and 1791.

The vast **Bernolákovo Palace** is regarded as the finest piece of secular Baroque architecture in Slovakia. It was built during 1714–22 for the Esterházy family, to a design by Johann Bernard Fischer von Erlach. The three wings surround its exquisite courtyard. Each of them sports a tower and is covered with a differently shaped roof. The entrance gate

The Baroque Bernolákovo Palace

is adorned with the Esterházy family crest and rich ornaments. The buildings stand surrounded by a sprawling French-style park with allegorical statues by Ľudovit Gode. It also features the Baroque Chapel of St Anna, dating from 1716.

Now the palace is a luxury hotel, part of the Bratislava Golf and Country Club. It has both a nine and an 18- hole golf course, the latter course being well-known throughout Europe.

³³ Senec

Road map A6. 🚹 14,700. 🚌 🚏
ℹ️ Námestie 1. Mája 4. **Tel** (02) 45 92 82 24. 🌐 senec.sk

The small town of Senec has been a major trading centre for many centuries and is now a gateway to the nearby Sunny Lakes resort. In Senec is one of the oldest relics of Renaissance architecture in Slovakia – the **Turkish House** (Turecký dom), which dates from 1560. The building, with its round corner turret and scalloped roof parapet, was built by Kristóf

Bat'an as the seat of the local administration. The building withstood attack by Turkish forces in 1663. It is now an upmarket restaurant.

While here, it is worth taking a look at the Gothic **Church of St Nicolas** (sv. Mikuláš) surrounded by walls, built in 1326 and subsequently remodelled in Baroque style. Inside are four fine Rococo altars. The market square features a 16th-century pillory, used until 1848, and a Plague Column dating from 1747. The most interesting of the surrounding buildings is the crumbling **Synagogue**, built in 1904 in Art Nouveau style with the use of floral motifs. In 1930, Jews constituted about 25 per cent of the town's population, but since World War II, they are a small community.

Two kilometres (1 mile) southeast of the town is the popular **Sunny Lakes** (Slnečné jazerá) resort built on the shores of two warm-water lakes, with hotels, camp sites, jetties, water slides and children's playgrounds.

The 1560 Turkish House in Senec

Exploring West Slovakia

Slovakia's western region offers a wide variety of visitor attractions. Those interested in history will find here remnants of every era, ranging from the region's earliest civilizations, in Dunajská Streda, to the numerous magnificent Gothic, Renaissance, Baroque and Neo-Classical buildings in Trnava, Nitra and Levice. Nature lovers can enjoy the endless hiking trails that crisscross the Small Carpathians, while visitors seeking to improve their health can take advantage of the famous thermal waters of the Piešt'any spa.

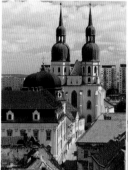

St Nicholas's Church in Trnava

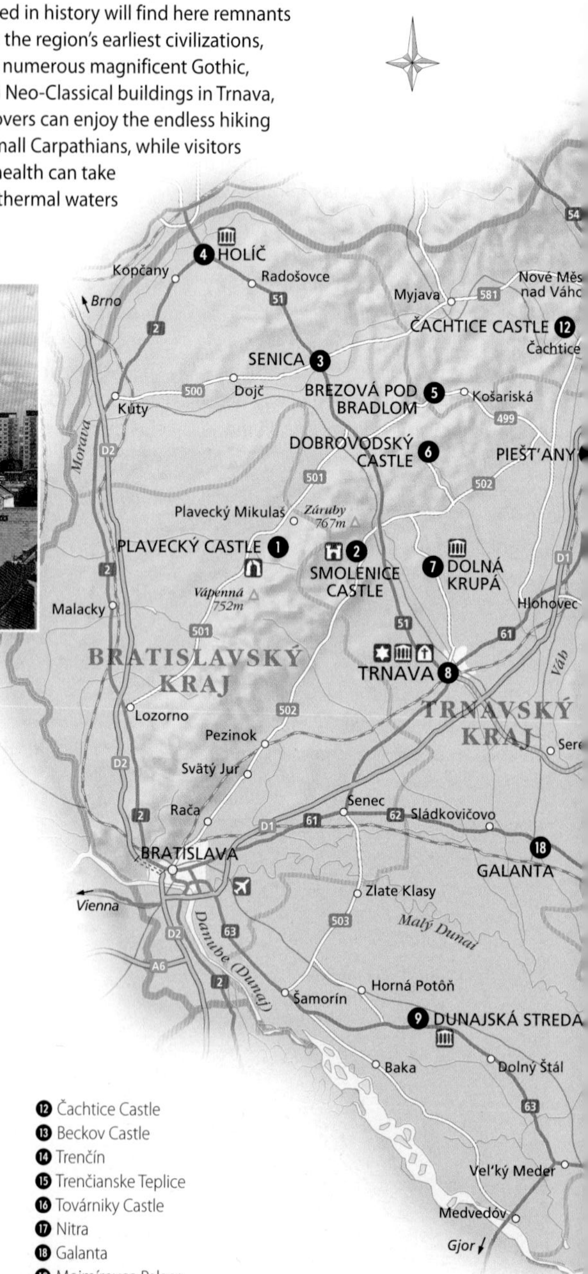

Key

- Motorway
- Dual carriageway
- Main road
- Minor road
- Scenic route
- Main railway
- Minor railway
- International border
- Regional border
- △ Summit

Sights at a Glance

1. Plavecký Castle
2. Smolenice Castle
3. Senica
4. Holíč
5. Brezová pod Bradlom
6. Dobrovodský Castle
7. Dolná Krupá
8. *Trnava pp300–3*
9. Dunajská Streda
10. Piešt'any
11. Topoľčiansky Castle
12. Čachtice Castle
13. Beckov Castle
14. Trenčín
15. Trenčianske Teplice
16. Továrniky Castle
17. Nitra
18. Galanta
19. Mojmírovce Palace
20. Nové Zámky
21. Komárno
22. Levice Castle

For hotels and restaurants see pp354–5 and pp378–9

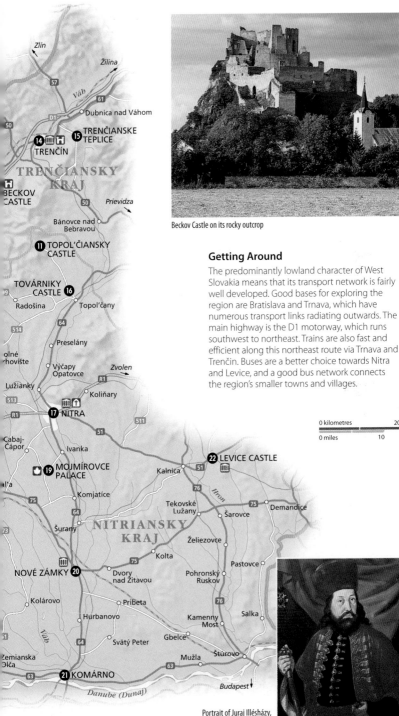

Beckov Castle on its rocky outcrop

Getting Around

The predominantly lowland character of West Slovakia means that its transport network is fairly well developed. Good bases for exploring the region are Bratislava and Trnava, which have numerous transport links radiating outwards. The main highway is the D1 motorway, which runs southwest to northeast. Trains are also fast and efficient along this northeast route via Trnava and Trenčín. Buses are a better choice towards Nitra and Levice, and a good bus network connects the region's smaller towns and villages.

0 kilometres 20
0 miles 10

Portrait of Juraj Illésházy, Trenčín Museum

For keys to symbols *see back flap*

Plavecký Castle ruins, in the Small Carpathian mountains

❶ Plavecký Castle

Road map B5. 35 km (22 miles) N of Senec. 🚌 to Plavecké Podhradie.

The lofty ruins of Plavecký Castle form a distinctive feature of the Small Carpathian mountains when viewed from the western side. The castle was built as a royal fortress guarding the border region in 1256–73. Many times remodelled since, it now bears traces of Gothic and Renaissance styles. From the 17th until the 20th century, it was the property of the Pálffy family. In the early 18th century, following Rákóczi's anti-Habsburg insurrection in 1703 (see p267), the castle was captured by the emperor's army. Since then, it has fallen into disrepair. In good weather, the ruins can be reached by a half-hour uphill walk from the village of Plavecké Podhradie.

❷ Smolenice Castle

Road map B5. 20 km (12 miles) NW of Trnava. 🚌 **Tel** (033) 535 48 90 (hotel reception). 🌐 **kcsmolenice.sav.sk**

In the foothills of the Small Carpathian mountains, Smolenice Castle towers above Smolenice village below. The castle was built in the 14th century as the final fortress defending the passes of this relatively low mountain range. The site, which initially belonged to the king and subsequently to a series of Hungarian families, fell into ruin in the 18th century and in the following century was destroyed by fire. In the early 20th century, its last owners –

the Pálffy family – rebuilt the structure in the Gothic style.

Now the castle is used by the Slovak Academy of Science, mainly as a hotel and conference venue, and some of its rooms have been opened to the public. Surrounded by an English-style garden and located in an exceptionally beautiful area, the castle has a romantic, fairy-tale silhouette.

Sculpture, Chapel of St Anna in Senica

❸ Senica

Road map B5. 44 km (27 miles) NW of Trnava. 🚹 20,000. 🚆 Železnična. 🚌 Hurbanova. 🚹 Nám. Oslobodenia 17. **Tel** (034) 651 64 59. **Open** 9am–5pm Mon–Fri. 🌐 **senica.sk**

As recently as the early 20th century, Senica was a sleepy little town populated mostly by craftspeople and farm workers. Historic records mention the fact that shoemakers formed the most numerous group of local tradespeople. Social and political changes turned it into a flourishing centre of trade and

industry, with a 20,000-strong population. The Gothic **Chapel of St Anna** (sv. Anna) is the oldest historic relic in Senica. The Castle now houses the **Záhorská Gallery** (Záhorská galéria), whose collection documents the art of the Slovak-Czech-German-Hungarian border region. The building, designed by Viennese architect Franz A Hillebrandt, features an opulent columned hall on the ground floor, which is now used for exhibitions. There is a **Catholic Church** dating from the first half of the 17th century and featuring an Early Baroque altarpiece.

The eastern part of the town has a fascinating **Jewish cemetery**, with original 18th and 19th century tombstones (masebbas).

🏛 **Záhorská Gallery**
Sadová 619/3. **Tel** (034) 651 29 37. **Open** Tue–Sun.
🌐 **muzeum.sk**

❹ Holíč

Road map A5. 80 km (50 miles) N of Bratislava. 🚹 11,400. 🚌 🚹 Bratislavská 6. **Tel** (034) 668 51 55.

Once an important border town, Holíč lies along the trading route that linked the two capital cities of Buda in Hungary and Prague in Bohemia. Duties levied on the transported goods provided a major source of revenue for the local authorities. The main historic sight in Holíč is its Baroque **Castle**. This four-storey edifice built on a "U"-shaped floorplan, and enclosed within

Entrance hall of Smolenice Castle

massive defensive walls and a moat, was once a Renaissance fortress built in the face of the Turkish threat. In the 18th century, Maria Theresa's husband, Francis Stephen of Lorraine, converted it into a Habsburg summer residence. Now it is a venue for cultural and folklore events, and houses the **Jaroslava Prílučíka Ethnographic Museum** (Mestské múzeum Jaroslava Prílučíka), the eclectic collection of one of the oldest inhabitants of Holíč.

🏛 **Jaroslava Prílučíka Ethnographic Museum**
Open Mon–Sat. 🖼

A house in Brezová pod Bradlom, west Slovakia

❺ Brezová pod Bradlom

Road map B5. 48 km (30 miles) N of Trnava. 🚌 Ⓦ **brezova.sk**

On top of Bradlom Hill, at 543 m (1,780 ft), stands the monumental tomb of General Milan Rastislav Štefánik (1880–1919), one of the founders of Czechoslovakia. The general, a close associate of Tomaš G Masaryk and Edvard Beneš, was killed in 1919 in an air crash near Bratislava, while returning to the country where he was due to assume the office of war minister in the newly formed government. The monument was built in 1927–8 to a design by Slovak architect Dušan Jurkovič. It is a vast structure of light grey stone. Steps lead up to the tomb, which has an obelisk at each corner. Brezová pod Bradlom also has Slovakia's only monument to Jan Hus (*see pp38–9*).

Environs
The family home of General Štefánik, in the village of

Košariská (4 km/2 miles from Brezová pod Bradlom), is an interesting **museum** devoted to his life.

🏛 **Štefánik Museum**
90615 Košariská. **Tel** (034) 624 26 26.
Open daily.

❻ Dobrovodský Castle

Road map B5. 30 km (19 miles) N of Trnava. 🚌

Standing on a wooded hill above the village of Dobrá Voda, Dobrovodský Castle belonged in the 14th century to the system of fortresses that guarded the road (no longer in existence) running along the ridge of the Small Carpathians. In the 16th century, it was so vast that access to the upper castle was via three separate entrances, each protected by its own defensive wall.

In the ensuing centuries, the importance of Dobrovodský Castle gradually diminished, and, following the 1762 fire that consumed the buildings, it was never rebuilt. Now the picturesque ruins are crumbling, although the remains of the two towers, the round turret, the entrance gate and the defensive walls are still very impressive.

❼ Dolná Krupá

Road map B5. 7 km (4 miles) NW of Trnava. 🚂 2,250. 🚌 from Trnava.

The Neo-Classical palace in Dolná Krupá was a stately

View from Dobrovodský Castle, a 14th-century fortress

home of the Brunswick family. This two-storey building with a columned portico was erected on earlier foundations in 1793–4.

The large English-style garden that stretches in front of the palace includes a small music pavilion, whose history is connected with the visits to Dolná Krupá by Ludwig van Beethoven who was friends with the Brunswick family. Tradition has it that it was here in 1801 that the composer wrote his famous *Moonlight Sonata*. The pavilion houses a small **Beethoven Museum** containing displays about his life and work.

🏛 **Beethoven Museum**
Tel (033) 557 72 71. **Open** daily.
🖼 ♿ Ⓦ **snm.sk**

Neo-Classical Brunswick Palace in Dolná Krupá

❽ Trnava

Trnava (Nagyszombat) was granted town privileges in 1238, making it one of Slovakia's oldest towns. In the 16th and 17th centuries, at the height of the Turkish threat, it was the seat of the Hungarian primate and the headquarters of the Church of Hungary. The town acquired numerous churches, convents and monasteries, becoming known as the "Slovak Rome". The first university in Hungary was founded here in 1635. Highlights for visitors are its religious buildings and relaxed ambience.

Baroque-styled St Joseph's column in St Nicholas's Square

Exploring Trnava

The historic town centre is enclosed within the old walls, which form an almost complete square. The main Holy Trinity Square is at its heart. Among the restored historic buildings in the Old Town are some modern structures erected in the postwar years. The main shopping street is the pedestrianized Hlavná.

🏛 St Nicholas's Square

This spindle-shaped square (námestie sv. Mikuláša) by the old city walls was in the Middle Ages the focus of the town. At its centre is the 1731 Baroque column of St Joseph, surrounded by chapter buildings including the **Archbishop's Palace**. The Palace was built by Pietro and Antonio Spazzi in 1562. During the 16th and 17th centuries, this imposing Renaissance edifice was the seat of the Hungarian primates whose residence in Esztergom had been appropriated by the Turks. The archbishops went back to

Esztergom in 1820, but a Slovak archbishopric was re-established here in 1990.

🏛 Cathedral of St Nicholas

The twin towers of the Cathedral of St Nicholas (sv. Mikuláša), with their distinctive bell-shape cupolas, are one of Trnava's chief landmarks. The church was built in 1380–1421. Its outside walls are supported by mighty buttresses, particularly imposing in the presbytery. The towers – initially of unequal size – were given their present shape after a fire in 1676. They are still not identical; a close look will reveal that the southern one is slightly narrower. Inside, the main attraction is the octagonal chapel of the Virgin Mary added in 1741 to the left aisle of the church. It contains the miraculous picture of the Trnava Madonna, which is particularly revered in Slovakia. The richly gilded Renaissance-Baroque main altarpiece dates from 1639. Built into the side walls

Interior of the Church of the Assumption of the Virgin Mary

of the chapels are a number of interesting Renaissance and Baroque tombstones.

🏛 Church of the Assumption of the Virgin Mary

The Order of the Poor Clares settled in Trnava during the Middle Ages. This church (Nanebovzatia Panny Márie) was built for the nuns in the 13th century as an aisleless Romanesque structure. Following a 17th-century fire, it was extended and remodelled in the Baroque style, which can be seen to this day. The original features of the interior include the early 18th-century high altar and three side altars.

🏛 Museum of West Slovakia

Muzejné námestie 3. **Tel** (033) 551 29 13. **Open** 8am–5pm Tue–Fri, 11am–5pm Sat & Sun. 🖼

One of the largest in West Slovakia, this interesting and varied museum (Západoslovenské múzeum) is housed in the 13th-century convent adjacent to the Church of the Assumption of the Virgin Mary. Following administrative restructuring of the empire's institutions carried out during the reign of Joseph II, the building became a military hospital, and then a warehouse. In 1954, it became a new museum with the aim of continuing Trnava's museum traditions. The collections, on two floors of the building, are

The twin towers of St Nicolas's Cathedral

highly diverse and include archaeological finds, an exhibition of religious art, ethnography and natural history displays and a unique collection of bells.

✪ Synagogue
Halenárska 2. **Tel** (033) 551 46 57. **Open** May–Sep: 10am–6pm Tue–Fri, 1–6pm Sat & Sun; Oct–Apr: 9am–5pm Tue–Fri, 1–6pm Sat & Sun. **w** snm.sk

The imposing edifice of Byzantine-Moorish style was built in the 19th century to a design by Viennese architect Jakub Gartner. Now it houses a centre of modern art and the Museum of Jewish Culture; it is also used as an exhibition and concert hall. In front of the

19th-century synagogue in Byzantine-Moorish style

synagogue is a black marble monument designed by Artur Szalatnai-Slatinský in memory of Trnava's Jews murdered in the Holocaust.

🏛 Music Museum
M S Trnavského 5. **Tel** (033) 551 25 56. **Open** 9am–5pm Tue–Fri, 11am–5pm Sat & Sun.

The Music Museum occupies Dom hudby, which used to be the home of one of Trnava's most famous citizens – the composer Mikulas Schneider Trnavský (1881–1958). It displays objects and mementos associated with the Slovak musician; it also serves as a concert venue.

🏛 Cathedral of St John the Baptist
See pp302–3.

🏛 Holy Trinity Square
The town's main square, Trojičné námestie, sports a lofty Municipal Tower dating from 1574, with a viewing gallery. Its cupola is crowned with a golden statue of Our Lady. There is also an 18th-century Plague Column. Close by is the 1831 **Municipal Theatre** (Trnavské

Holy Trinity statue, Holy Trinity Square

divadlo), the oldest theatre building in Slovakia. Just north of the square, the Holy Trinity Church (now known in Slovak as Jesuitský kostol) was built in the early 18th century by the Trinitarian monks. It has been used by the Jesuits since 1853. To the west of the square is the single-towered Church of St Jacob (sv. Jakub), built in 1640 and remodelled in a Baroque style in 1712.

🏛 Church of St Helen
Trnava's oldest church (sv. Helena), at the southern end of Hlavná, dates from the 14th century. Adjoining its north façade is the original tower with Gothic windows; seen above the portal are statues of the saints.

Trnava City Centre

① St Nicholas's Square
② Cathedral of St Nicholas
③ Church of the Assumption of the Virgin Mary
④ Museum of West Slovakia
⑤ Synagogue
⑥ Music Museum
⑦ Cathedral of St John the Baptist
⑧ Holy Trinity Square
⑨ Church of St Helen

0 metres 400
0 yards 400

For keys to symbols *see back flap*

Trnava: Cathedral of St John the Baptist

The first monumental Baroque structure in Slovakia and one of the country's largest religious buildings, the Cathedral of St John the Baptist (Katedrála sv. Jána Krstitela) was constructed in 1629–37. The building, intended as the church for the Jesuit-run university, was founded by Count Miklós Esterházy. The first mass was celebrated here by the Archbishop of Esztergom, Imrich Lósi. From 1777, when the university was moved to Buda, the church was used by war veterans; later on it became the local parish church. It has a richly ornamented Italianate interior.

Main Façade
The twin-towered façade, divided by protruding cornices, is decorated with statues of St Joachim, St Anna, St Elizabeth and St Zachary.

Main entrance

Main Portal
The Latin inscription above the entrance mentions Count Miklós Esterházy, the church's founder.

Interior
Walls, vault, arcades and windows are decorated with rich stucco ornamentation – figurative, floral and geometric – by Rossi, Tornini and Conti.

For hotels and restaurants see pp354–5 and pp377–8

St John's Pulpit
The Baroque pulpit is decorated with figures depicting the Fathers of the Church. It was built in 1640 by B Kniling and V Stadler.

★ The High Altar
This magnificent Baroque gilded wooden altarpiece (1640) depicts the scene of Christ's baptism.

Ornate Door
Above the richly carved wooden door leading to the sacristy is an ornate metal grille with gilded elements.

★ Vaulted Ceiling
The paintings on the arched vaulting of the presbytery ceiling depict scenes from the life of St John the Baptist.

KEY

① **Figures of the apostles** were placed in niches on the south side.

② **Pilasters** decorate the façade.

Distinctive modern buildings in Dunajská Streda town centre

⑨ Dunajská Streda

Road map B6. 45 km (28 miles) SE of Bratislava. 🚗 10,000. 🚌 🚈 ℹ️ Hlavná 50. **Tel** (031) 590 39 42. **Open** 9am–5pm Mon–Fri.

The town lies on Žitný ostrov, an island cut off from the main flow of the Danube by the Little Danube (Malý Dunaj). Archaeological discoveries here provide evidence of settlements in this area since the early Bronze Age and confirm the importance of the island under the Great Moravian Empire *(see p265)*. The earliest written records of the town date from the 12th century. Materials relating to the island's colonization can be seen in the **Regional Museum** (Žitnoostrovné múzeum) in Žltý kaštel, a pleasant Neo-Classical building erected in the 18th century.

The greatest attraction, however, is now the **town centre**, which in 1995–9 Imre Makovec returned to its former ambience by building a series of unusual white buildings with tiled roofs, decorated with arches, towers and wooden ornaments.

🏛️ **Regional Museum**
Múzejná 2. **Tel** (031) 552 24 02.
Open Tue–Sat. 🅿️ 🌐 **muzeum.sk**

⑩ Piešťany

Road map B5. 40 km (25 miles) S of Trenčín. 🚗 30,000. 🚌 🚈 W of town centre. ℹ️ Nálepkova 2. **Tel** (033) 774 33 55. **Open** 9am–5pm Mon–Fri. 🌐 **spapiestany.com**

A health resort that is famous all over Europe, Piešťany offers treatment for rheumatic and arthritic conditions. For many years, the town spa was owned by the Erdödy family, who in 1822 built the first spa. The town became a popular resort visited by Beethoven and Mucha, among others. The spa is located on the edge of the park, on the right bank of the Váh river, and on the spa island. Near the park is a pavilion, built in 1894 and now housing a concert hall and the **Spa Museum** (Balneologické múzeum). The **Columned Bridge** to the island is a fine example of 1930s Functionalist architecture.

🏛️ **Spa Museum**
Beethovenova 5. **Tel** (033) 772 28 75.
Open Tue–Sun.
🌐 **balneomuzeum.sk**

⑪ Topoľčiansky Castle

Road map B5. 56 km (35 miles) NE of Trnava. 🚈 to Podhradie.

On a high rocky ledge above the village of Podhradie are the scenic ruins of Topoľčiansky Castle, with a remarkable tower topped by a ridge roof. Originally a royal castle built in the mid-13th century, it became a stronghold of the Hussite army in 1431–4. In subsequent wars for control of Hungary, it was captured and burned down, and later on changed hands many times. Its last owners, the Stummer family, abandoned what was left of the castle in the mid-18th century and moved to a large castle in Tovarníký *(see p308)*.

Tower of Topoľčiansky Castle

⑫ Čachtice Castle

Road map B5. 15 km (9 miles) S of Beckov. 🚌 🚈 to Čachtice.

The conspicuous remnants of Čachtice Castle stand on a rocky hill (375 m/ 1,230 ft) between the towns of Čachtice and Višňové, offering a magnificent view of the surrounding area – the Small Carpathians and the Myjava Plateau. This fortified stronghold, whose construction was started in the first half of the 13th century, was part of the defence system that guarded the western border of the Hungarian Kingdom. Over the following centuries, the most famous person associated with Čachtice was the "Blood Countess" Elizabeth Báthory, wife of the district chief and Hungarian army captain, Ferenc Nádasdy. In 1585–1610, she ordered over 600 young girls to be murdered in the castle, allegedly to obtain their blood, which she used to maintain her

Čachtice Castle, dominating a rocky peak

youth. The investigations confirmed the charges and Elizabeth was imprisoned for the rest of her life within the walls of her residence. In 1708, the castle was captured and from then on it began to fall into ruin.

⓭ Beckov Castle

Road map B5. 20 km (12 miles) SW of Trenčín. 🚌 **Open** May–Oct: 9am–6pm Tue–Sun.

The castle ruins, looming on top of the 70-m (230-ft) rock above the small town of Beckov, provide a truly unforgettable sight. The structure was built at the turn of the 12th and 13th centuries as a link in the chain of Hungarian fortifications stretching along the Váh river valley. In the 14th century, the owner of Beckov was a powerful warlord, Matúš Čák. Later, the castle – converted into a Gothic and Renaissance residence – was owned by the Stibor and Bánffy families. In 1729, the fortress burned down and was never rebuilt. Now the most impressive part is the upper castle with its grand rectangular tower. There are also ruins of two palaces and a chapel.

⓮ Trenčín

Road map B5. 80 km (50 miles) NE of Trnava. 🚶 60,000. 🚆 🚌 Železničná. ℹ️ Mierové námestie 9. **Tel** (032) 650 47 09. 🖥 trencin.sk

Straddling the Váh river, the town of Trenčín has a well-preserved historic centre. In ancient times, the site was occupied by a Roman military camp, Laugaricio. It is still possible to see an inscription carved into the rock face below the castle concerning the victorious battle fought here in AD 179 with the German tribe the Quadi.
  Trenčín's huge Gothic **Castle** has undergone a thorough restoration. Built in the 11th century, it became, two centuries later, the property of Matúš Čák, one of Hungary's most powerful magnates, the

Beckov Castle, perched above a breathtaking drop

"Lord of the Váh and the Tatras". The dominant feature of the castle's silhouette is its tower, Matúšova veža, erected during the times of Čák. Adjoining it are the stately Gothic palaces built by Sigismund of Luxemburg and Louis of Hungary. Now they are occupied by the **Trenčín Museum** (Trenčinaske múzeum) as an exhibition venue, with reconstructed interiors of 11th-century feudal houses; a gallery of paintings from the Illésházy family estate; and an exhibition of historic arms. In the courtyard is Omar's well, 80 m (260 ft) deep, which was dug between 1557 and 1570.
  The town itself centres on the main square, Mierové námestie. The Baroque **Piarist Church**

Bathhouse in the Sina sanatorium, in Trenčianske Teplice

(Piaristický kostol) here, from the mid-17th century, has attractive *trompe l'oeil* paintings. The yellow Parish Church (Farský kostol), at the base of the lane to the castle, was rebuilt after a fire in 1528.

🏰 **Trenčín Castle**
Tel (032) 743 56 57. **Open** daily. 🖼

🏛 **Trenčín Museum**
Mierové námestie 46. **Tel** (032) 743 44 31. **Open** Tue–Sun. 🖥 muzeumtn.sk

⓯ Trenčianske Teplice

Road map B5. 14 km (9 miles) E of Trenčín. 🚶 5,000. 🚆 🚌 🎬 ArtFilm Festival: late Jun. 🖥 teplice.sk

The spa town of Trenčianske Teplice has a beautiful location on a site rich in mineral waters, which from the 14th century were known throughout the Hungarian kingdom for their therapeutic properties. From 1582, the town belonged to the aristocratic Hungarian Illésházy family. The most famous building is the Turkish bathhouse (1888), in which Moorish arches surround the central courtyard with spa waters spouting from stone fountains; women are not allowed in. There is also an exotic bathhouse in the 19th-century Sina sanitorium.

Fountain in the magnificent Europe Square, Komárno ▶

⑯ Továrniky Castle

Road map B5. 6 km (4 miles) NW
of Topoľčany. 🚍 to Topoľčany.
Closed to the public.

The small town of Továrniky
boasts a large castle. This
fortified structure, surrounded
by a moat, was built during the
time of the Turkish threat. In
the late 18th century, it was
remodelled to form a com-
fortable Baroque residence.
The extensive rebuilding turned
the former closed quadrangle
of the walls into a three-wing
palace with attractive two-
colour façade decorations and
mouldings, and a courtyard
open on one side.

Inhabited until 1945, the
castle later fell into disrepair.
In recent years, both castle and
grounds have been undergoing
a complete reconstruction. The
works, carried out by private
owners, are still not finished,
but it is already possible to see
from the outside the restored
buildings, which are set in a
beautiful English-style garden.

Továrniky Castle and gardens

Romanesque rotunda at St Emeram's
Cathedral in Nitra

⑰ Nitra

Road map B6. 90 km (56 miles) E of
Bratislava. 🚶 90,000. 🚐 🚍 Stanična.
🛈 Štefánikova 1. **Tel** (037) 741 09 06.
🌐 nitra.sk

As early as the 7th century, Nitra
was already a political and
commercial centre of the Slav
tribes north of the Danube.
At the turn of the 8th century,
this area was an independent
principality, ruled by Prince

Pribina, the first known ruler of
the Slavs. The Turks caused great
destruction here in the 16th and
17th centuries. Since the 19th
century, Nitra has grown into a
sprawling modern city.

The old town's dominant
feature is the **Castle**, on a
rocky ledge in the crook of
the Nitra river. It is surrounded
by 17th-century walls whose
one gate is accessed via
a stone bridge. The main
building of the castle complex
is **St Emeram's Cathedral**
(Katedrálny Biskupský Chram
sv. Emerama), consisting of
three churches that were
joined in the 18th century.
They comprise the
11th-century Romanesque
rotunda of St Emeram, the
Gothic upper church, and
the lower church built in the
17th century.

At the foot of the castle is
the Upper Town. Its centre,
Pribinovo námestie, is flanked
by Baroque and Neo-
Classical buildings. On the
south side is the **Grand
Seminary**, now housing the
Diocesan Library (Diecézna
knižnica) with its valuable
collection of books and
incunabula. Situated
outside the walls is the
Lower Town with
a twin-towered
Piarist Church (kostol
Piaristov), containing
magnificent frescoes.

The striking 1991
Andrej Bagar Theatre
(Divadlo Andrej Bagara)
overshadows the Neo-
Renaissance town hall,
which houses the **Nitra
Museum** (Nitranske
múzeum). In the
museum are displays

on archaeology, history and
the natural world.

Just east of the Nitra river
is the **Slovak Agricultural
Museum** (Slovenské
poľnohospodárske múzeum),
a fascinating collection of
reconstructed traditional farm
buildings, shops and houses,
with original machinery.

🏛 **Nitra Museum**
Štefánikova trieda 1. **Tel** (037) 651
00 00. **Open** daily. 🔲 🔲 🔲

🏛 **Slovak Agricultural Museum**
Dlhá 92. **Tel** (037) 657 25 53.
Open Mon–Thu (Fri–Sun by request).

⑱ Galanta

Road map B6. 35 km (22 miles) E
of Bratislava. 🚶 16,000. 🚐 🚍

Founded in the 13th century,
Galanta is in the Danube
Lowland. It has two Esterházy
palaces. The **Renaissance
Palace** (Renesaníný
kástiel) houses exhibits
on the town's history,
the Esterházy family,
and the Hungarian
composer Zoltán Kodály.
The other palace, not
open to the public, was
built in 1860 in English
Neo-Gothic style.

🏠 **Renaissance Palace**
Esterházyovcov.
Open Tue–Sun. 🔲

⑲ Mojmírovce Palace

Road map B6. 15 km
(9 miles) S of Nitra. 🚍 🔲
Tel (037) 779 82 01. 🌐 vic.sk

The history of
Mojmírovce Palace

Statue of St Urban in
Mojmírovice Park

View of Lomnický štít (peak) from the resort of Tatranská Lomnica

8 DUNAJEC GORGE

abča

↑ Kraków

○ Trstená

○ Zuberec

ORAVSKÝ CASTLE

Orava

59

Červený Kláštor

Zakopane

Ždiar

Podolínec

543

67

77

TATRAS MOUNTAINS

7 ⚹ Gerlachovský štít 2654m

Lomnický štít 2632m

○ Starý Smokovec

537

67

Liptovský Mikuláš

Štrbské Pleso

KRAJ

D1

18

Važec

D1

Poprad →

VÄTÝ KRÍŽ

10

Liptovský Hrádok

Vyšná Boca

Dumbier 2043m

Nízke Tatry

Závadka nad Hronom

72

66

Podbrezova

Brezno

Hron

Čierny Balog

Slovenské Rudohorie

Kokava n. Rimavicou

BANSKOBYSTRICKÝ KRAJ

531

Ipeľ

Rimava

ivaň

50

Mýtna

Veľké Teriakovce

Košice →

50

Rimavská Sobota

Halič

16 **LUČENEC**

571

75

Fiľakovo

71

Veľký Krtíš

Ipeľ

Getting Around

The southern part of Central Slovakia is easiest to get to by car or train from Bratislava or Budapest; the northern region from the Czech Republic (via Žilina) or Poland. The region's topography means that its transport network is limited. The main route is the west-east D1 motorway and, running parallel and to the south of it, the scenic Košice-Banská Bystrica railway line. The south-north 66/59 highway is twisting and can be congested. Buses serve most destinations in the region.

0 kilometres	20
0 miles	10

Key

═══ Motorway

┈┈┈ Motorway under construction

═══ Dual carriageway

─── Main road

┈┈┈ Minor road

═══ Scenic route

╍╍╍ Main railway

─── Minor railway

▰▰▰ International border

▭▭▭ Regional border

△ Summit

For keys to symbols *see back flap*

❶ Banská Bystrica

Banská Bystrica (Neusohl) is one of Slovakia's oldest towns. In 1255, it was granted royal privileges associated with the mining of gold, silver and copper, which brought wealth to the town and its inhabitants from medieval times. The town's prosperity is evident in many fine examples of religious and secular architecture. Banská Bystrica's main contribution to modern history is that in 1944 it became the centre of the Slovak National Uprising (Slovenské národné povstanie, or SNP).

The house at the end of Národna, with a passage to the market square

Exploring the town

The historic sights are concentrated on the route that runs along the pedestrianized Dolná, the large market square Námestie SNP, and Horná. The middle section of this area is occupied by Námestie Štefana Moyzesa – the central square, flanked by buildings of the old castle complex. Built in the 12th and 13th centuries, it consists of both religious and secular buildings. All that remains of the original town walls and the castle's 18 bastions are three bastions and one long section of the wall within the castle area. The castle complex also includes the parish Church of Our Lady (*see pp316–17*); the Church of the Holy Cross; the Matthias House; the barbican with a tower; and the town hall.

⛪ Church of the Holy Cross
🕙 9am Sun.

This aisleless, late Gothic church (Kostol Svätého Kríža), dating from 1492, was once known as the "Slovak church", since the majority of its congregation consisted of Slovaks. In 1782, a new entrance was added on the south side, with a carved date

1452, instead of 1492, on the portal. The interesting features of the interior include the 1652 stone font and the main altarpiece with statues of the Virgin Mary and Mary Magdalene, the work of Vavrinec Dunajský in 1834.

🏛 Matthias House

The astonishingly tall, six-storey Matthias House (Matejov dom) was built in 1479 for Beatrice, wife of the Hungarian King Matthias Corvinus. The south façade sports a Gothic portal, a stone balcony and the coats of arms of Matthias

The Old Town Hall (1500)

Corvinus and of the town, the latter dated 1479. Behind the Matthias House is the old cemetery.

🏛 Barbican and Town Walls

In the 16th century, the town was surrounded by mighty walls intended to protect it against Turkish invasion. Only some of the old fortifications have survived. Still standing are the Pisárska, Banicka and Farská bastions. The former defence tower with a draw-bridge and barbican is in Námestie Štefana Moyzesa. Hanging inside the tower are three bells; the heaviest weighs nearly 10 tonnes.

⛪ Church of Our Lady
See pp316–17.

🏛 Old Town Hall

Municipal Gallery Námestie Štefana Moyzesa 25. **Tel** (048) 412 48 64. **Open** 10am–5pm Tue–Fri, 10am–4pm Sat & Sun. 🆆 **ssgbb.sk**

Adjacent to the Church of Our Lady is the Old Town Hall (Stará radnica), a plain white building with a small tower and an arcaded loggia. Built in about 1500, it was remodelled in Renaissance style, in the second half of the 16th century. Now it is the home of Banská Bystrica's Municipal Gallery (Štátna galéria).

🏛 Námestie SNP

Central Slovak Museum **Tel** (048) 412 58 97. **Open** 9am–5pm Mon–Fri, 1–4pm Sun (also Jul–Aug: 9am–1pm Sat). 🆆 **stredoslovenskemuzeum.sk**

Thurzo House (Thurzov dom) is the most beautiful building in the market square. Its core consists of two Gothic houses, which at the turn of the 15th and 16th centuries became the property of the Thurzo family. The building was given its present appearance in the second half of the 16th century, when its façade was decorated with

Renaissance *sgraffito*. Since 1958, the palace has been the home of the **Central Slovak Museum** (Stredoslovenské múzeum). Its collections illustrate the region's history, from prehistoric times to the early 20th century.

The Renaissance **clock tower** was built in 1552. In the past it served as an observation post, a prison and torture chamber. During reconstruction works carried out in 1762 and 1784, it was found that the tower was not vertical. Now its top is out of line by 68 cm (27 in). In the 19th century, brass bands used to give concerts from the top-floor gallery. The place offers a magnificent view of the entire town and environs.

The 18th-century Jesuit church standing at the corner of the square, designed in early Baroque style, was modelled on the Il Gesú church in Rome. The resemblance is, however, far from obvious, particularly since in 1844 the church was given two square towers without cupolas.

The Baroque Marian column at one corner of the square dates from 1719. In the late 1960s, it was decided to remove this from Námestie SNP and

Detail of the house at No. 9 Dolná

replace it with a granite obelisk honouring the Red Army. The column was moved to a position in front of the Church of Our Lady. It was returned to its original site in 1993.

🏛 Dolná

At the extension of Námestie SNP are two streets with historic houses: Horná (Upper) and Dolná (Lower). **Bethlenov dom** at No. 8 Dolná is where in 1620 the Hungarian parliament elected Gábor Bethlen, prince of Transylvania, as the king of Hungary. The Latin inscription on the façade reads: "The Lord's blessing enriches the common people". The tower at the side of the courtyard is an original medieval structure.

The striking silhouette of the SNP Museum

🏛 SNP Museum

Kapitulská 23. **Tel** (048) 412 32 58. **Open** 9am–6pm Tue–Sun (to 4pm Oct–Apr). 🆆 muzeumsnp.sk

The Museum of the Slovak National Uprising is housed in a concrete building in two sections linked by a bridge. The building was erected in 1965, to a design by Dušan Kuzma. The extensive exhibits focus on the history of Slovakia in 1938–1945, with particular emphasis on the 1944 uprising against the Nazis, and on the fate of Slovak Jews. The surrounding park contains an exhibition of the weapons used by the insurgents, including tanks. Among its most interesting exhibits is an original Li-2 aircraft with full interior equipment, with visitor access.

Banská Bystrica Town Centre

① Church of the Holy Cross
② Matthias House
③ Barbican and Town Walls
④ Church of Our Lady
⑤ Old Town Hall
⑥ Námestie SNP
⑦ Dolná
⑧ SNP Museum

0 metres   200
0 yards   200

Banská Bystrica: The Parish Church of the Ascension of the Virgin Mary

Construction of the church (Nanebovzatia Panny Márie) began in 1255. In the early 14th century, it was widened and given a Gothic sacristy. Two centuries later, it acquired the presbytery, the oratory and the side chapels, and its famous altar of St Barbara. Following a great fire in 1761, it was rebuilt in Baroque style; in 1770, its interior was given new, magnificent furnishings.

★ Altar of St Barbara
The ornate Gothic altarpiece of St Barbara (patron saint of miners), in the north side chapel, is the church's greatest treasure. Made by Master Pavol of Levoča, it depicts the Madonna and Child, St Barbara and St Jerome.

View of the Church
The church's tower – grey with red decorations – is a town landmark. The simple arches of the tower windows indicate their Romanesque origin.

Interior
The most striking features of the beautiful interior are the pulpit and the organ loft. The bronze font, by Master Jodok, is a masterpiece of medieval metalwork.

Christ on the Mount of Olives
The vivid Baroque sculpture outside the church depicting Christ and saints was renovated in 1995.

Vault Paintings
The imposing Baroque paintings covering the barrel-vault are by Anton Schmidt. They were made during the renovation of the church, which followed the 1761 town fire.

Main Altarpiece
Paintings in the main altarpiece (1774) are by Jan Lukas Kracker. They portray the Assumption of the Virgin Mary and the Holy Trinity.

★ Side Altar
The south chapel, to the right of the nave, contains a 15th-century Gothic triptych of St Mary Magdalene, one of the most treasured items of the church's original furnishings.

Porch
The "new" main entrance in the porch, with a stellar vault and an attractive portal, was added in 1473–1516.

Zvolen Castle, a superbly preserved example of Gothic-Renaissance architecture

❷ Zvolen

Road map C5. 20 km (12 miles) S of Banská Bystrica. ⚄ 42,000. 🚃 🚌
ℹ Námestie Svobody 22. **Tel** (045) 530 32 19. **Open** 9am–5pm Mon–Fri.
🅦 **zvolen.net**

A settlement was established here by Bela IV in the mid-13th century. In 1326, Zvolen, known at the time in German as Altsohl, and in Hungarian as Zólyom, was granted town privileges. It soon became a trading centre and in the 19th century also a centre of the timber industry.

Zvolen Castle is in the town centre. Construction began in the reign of King Louis of Hungary, before 1382. At the start of the 15th century, it became the property of the Thurzos, one of Hungary's richest families. The new owners rebuilt the castle in Renaissance style and reinforced its system of fortifications. Now, carefully restored, it is one of Slovakia's best-preserved examples of 16th-century architecture. The castle chapel has a Gothic portal. In the 18th-century Baroque hall is a magnificent coffered ceiling divided into 78 fields filled with portraits of Habsburg kings and emperors. The castle houses permanent exhibitions of Gothic stonework and 16th–18th-century European art from the Slovak National Museum.

In the market square is the late 14th-century Catholic **Church of St Elizabeth** (sv. Alžbety). Inside is the chapel of Our Lady of Sorrows, dating from 1650. Amid the Gothic and Renaissance houses on the square is the Protestant **Church of the Holy Trinity** (sv. Trojice), built in 1921–3. It includes a Neo-Gothic altarpiece with a huge figure of Christ.

On the southwestern outskirts of the town are the ruins of **Pusty Fortress**. Scattered over a vast area in the middle of a forest are fragments of walls, bastions and gates of one of the biggest fortresses in medieval Europe.

🏰 **Zvolen Castle**
Open Tue–Sun. **Closed** Tue (Oct–Apr). 🗲

The Hall of Mirrors in the Palace of St Anton near Banská Štiavnica

❸ Banská Štiavnica

Road map C5. 40 km (25 miles) S of Banská Bystrica. ⚄ 10,000. 🚃 🚌
ℹ Námestie sv. Trojice 6. **Tel** (045) 692 05 35. 🅦 **banskastiavnica.sk**

Between the 13th and 18th centuries, Banská Štiavnica was one of Europe's main mining centres, and grew into the third-largest town in the Hungarian Kingdom. At the centre is Holy Trinity square (Námestie sv. Trojice), lined with Gothic and Renaissance houses. It has a sandstone Baroque Holy Trinity monument. On the south side is the 15th-century **Church of St Catherine** (sv. Katerína), with lovely net vaulting.

The **Old Castle** (Starý zámok) is a complex of buildings that bring together Roman, Gothic, Renaissance and Baroque styles. The whitewashed **New Castle** (Nový zámok), on a hillock to the south of the centre, was also built against the Turks. The town has a magnificent **Mining Museum** (Banské múzeum), with several sites, including an open-air area outside the centre.

🏰 **Old Castle**
Starozámocká 11. **Tel** (045) 694 94 74.
Open May–Sep: daily; Jan, Mar, Apr & Dec: Tue–Sun; Feb, Oct & Nov: Tue–Fri. 🗲

🏰 **New Castle**
Novozámocká 22. **Tel** (045) 691 15 43.
Open May–Sep: daily; Feb & Mar: Tue–Sun; Jan & Apr: Tue–Fri. 🗲

🏛 **Mining Museum**
Kammerhofská 2. **Tel** (045) 692 05 35.
Open May–Sep: daily; Jan & Feb: Tue–Fri; Mar, Apr & Oct–Dec: Mon–Fri. 🗲
🅦 **muzeumbs.sk**

Environs

In the village of Antol, 5 km (3 miles) southeast of Banská Štiavnica, is the Baroque **Palace of St Anton**, with beautiful interiors. It houses a museum.

🏰 **Palace of St Anton**
Tel (045) 691 39 32. **Open** May–Sep: Tue–Sun; Oct–Apr: Tue–Sat.
🗲 🎫 2 routes. 🅦 **msa.sk**

❹ Kremnica

Road map C5. 20 km (12 miles) W of Banská Bystrica. 🚗 6,000. 🚆 🚌 ℹ️ Štefánikovo námestie 35/44. **Tel** (045) 678 27 80.

This little mountain town was one of the richest in the Hungarian Kingdom from the 14th to the 19th centuries. Its source of wealth was the nearby gold mines. The history of gold mining and of the mint, which minted the highly valued "Kremnica ducats", and which still operates, are traced in the interesting **Museum of Coins and Medals** (Múzeum mincí a medailí) in the main square. Also in the square is a gold-covered Baroque Marian column. In the 15th-century **Castle** is the Gothic **Church of St Catherine** (sv. Katerína).

Statue of St Stephen, Church of St Catherine

🏛 **Museum of Coins and Medals**
Štefánikovo námestie 10/19. **Tel** (045) 674 26 96. **Open** Tue–Sun. 🚸

❺ Martin

Road map C4. 68 km (42 miles) NW of Banská Bystrica. 🚗 61,000. 🚆 Bitánkova. 🚌 ℹ️ M.R. Štefánika 9/A. **Tel** (043) 423 87 76. **Open** 9am–5pm Mon–Fri (Jul, Aug: also Sat).

A symbol of the Slovaks' struggle for a place among the nation states of Europe, Martin was where the famous Martin

Memorandum was announced in 1861 proclaiming the Slovak national rebirth programme. In 1918, the Slovak National Council approved the Martin Declaration expressing the wish to form, with the Czechs, the state of Czechoslovakia.

The town is rich in historic sites, such as the 13th-century **Church of St Martin** (sv. Martin). The **Slovak National Museum in Martin** (Slovenské národné múzeum) has many collections, both in the main building and in branches, mainly focusing on Slovak folk exhibits. One of the most spectacular is the **Slovak Village Museum** (Múzeum slovenskej dediny). This open-air museum 2 km (1 mile) south of the town is a huge collection of traditional wooden buildings principally from the Orava region in the north of Slovakia.

🏛 **Slovak National Museum in Martin**
Malá Hora 2. **Tel** (043) 413 10 11. **Open** Tue–Sun. 🚸 🌐 snm.sk

🏛 **Slovak Village Museum**
Jahodnícke Háje. **Tel** (043) 413 26 86. **Open** Nov–Apr: Tue–Fri & Sun; May–Jun: Tue–Sun; Jul–Aug: daily; Sep & Oct: Tue–Sun. 🚸 🌐 snm.sk

❻ Oravský Castle

Road map D4. 80 km (50 miles) N of Banská Bystrica. 🚆 🚌 to Oravský Podzámok. **Tel** (043) 581 61 11. **Open** May–Mar: daily. 🚸

Resembling an eagle's nest clinging to a mighty 120-m (400-ft) cliff, Oravský Castle is first mentioned in historical records of 1267. New parts of the castle were added gradually to the original citadel up until the 17th century. In 1800, the castle burned down, and restoration began only in 1953. Some of the castle's quarters are now used by the Orava Museum to display its archaeological, historical and ethnographic collections.

Viewing terrace on the walls of the Oravský Castle

Slovak Traditional Architecture

Historic wooden buildings are among Slovakia's greatest attractions. In almost every village it is still possible to see buildings erected centuries ago, using traditional methods, often without the use of nails. Many regions feature conservation sites of traditional architecture. The best known are Vlkolínec and Čičmany (*see p326*), both in Central Slovakia. Many treasures of traditional architecture have been gathered in open-air museums (skansen). The largest of them, the Slovak Village Museum in Martin, features 100 houses from northern Slovakia. In East Slovakia, in Bardejov (*see p337*), is one of the oldest open-air museums. In the same region are the Unitarian churches in the area around Svidník (*see p337*).

A timber house (1792) in the Slovak Village Museum

Gothic Church of St Martin in historic Martin

❼ Tatras Mountains

Slovakia's Northern Tatras mountains consist of three ranges: the Western Tatras (Západné Tatry), the High Tatras (Vysoké Tatry) and the small area of Belianske Tatry, a protected reserve with only one path open to the public. All are within the Tatra National Park. The most spectacular range, the High Tatras, is a magnet for walkers.

View from Around Zuberec
Zuberec, a village at the mouth of the Roháčska Dolina (valley), affords magnificent views of Roháče, the start of the Western Tatras.

Roháčsky Waterfall
This is one of the most scenic attractions of the 5-km (3-mile) long post-glacial valley, Roháčska Dolina.

Liptovský Mikuláš
The town, in a valley surrounded by peaks, is an interesting and convenient base for the Liptov region.

Liptovský Hrádok
Liptovský Hrádok is famous for the ruins of its 14th-century castle, later extended into a Renaissance palace and now housing an Ethnography Museum.

Habovka

Ospbitá
1687 m
(5535 ft)

1663 m
(5456 ft)

Zuberec

Grześ
1653 m
(5423 ft)

Červené Vrch

Krzesanica
2122 m
(6962 ft)

Salatín

584

1806 m
(5925 ft)

2050 m
(6726 ft)

Volovec
2064 m
(6772 ft)

2176 m
(7139 ft)

2158 m
(7080 ft)

Kamienista
2121 m
(6959 ft)

Baranec
2184 m
(7165 ft)

2194 m
(7198 ft)

Bystrá
2248 m
(7375 ft)

Liptovské   Tatry

Western   Tatras

Brobrovec

Smerčianka

537

Liptovský Mikuláš

Belá

Pribylina

Hybica

9

D1

Váh

18

D1

Východná

Prouba

Hybe

Liptovský Hrádok

72

Banská
Bystrica

0 kilometres   5
0 miles   3

Key
- ▨ Motorway
- ▤ Minor road
- ▤ Other road
- ≋ River
- –·– National border
- △ Peak

Ždiar

Founded in the 17th century, the village of Ždiar features many restored wooden highland houses with a variety of decorations.

❽ Dunajec Gorge

Road map E4. Rafting: Apr–Oct: 8am–7pm daily, various operators. 🚣
W **pieniny.sk**

The Dunajec river flows from west to east, dividing Slovakia and Poland, through Pieniny National Park. This is combined with a park in Poland to form the first international nature reserve in Europe, in 1932. Through this picturesque mountain scenery, the river has cut a magnificent 9-km (6-mile) long canyon, whose white limestone walls rise vertically, in some places to the height of 500 m (1,640 ft) above the water level. From April to October, it is possible to experience an unusual thrill: floating through the Dunajec Gorge on a wooden raft steered by the local highlanders.

The route, which runs along the most beautiful section of this mountain river, starts in Červený Kláštor and ends in Lesnica. Červený Kláštor, a former Carthusian monastery, is now the **Červený Kláštor Museum** with displays on the monks and the region's history. The **Monastery Church** has an interesting Gothic vault with Baroque polychrome paintings; its refectory is decorated with medieval frescoes depicting scenes from the Passion.

🏛 **Červený Kláštor Museum**
Tel (52) 482 20 57. **Open** daily.
🚣 W **muzeumcervenyklastor.sk**

Lomnický štít
Lomnický štít, the second-highest peak in the Tatras, is accessible by cable car.

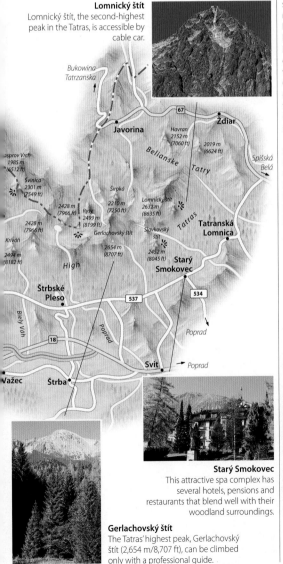

Bukowina Tatrzanska

Javorina

67

Ždiar

Havran 2152 m (7060 ft)

2019 m (6624 ft)

Spišská Belá

asprov Vrch 1985 m (6512 ft)

Belianske

Tatry

Svinica 2301 m (7549 ft)

Široká

2428 m (7966 ft)

Rysy 2499 m (8199 ft)

2210 m (7250 ft)

Lomnický štít 2632 m (8635 ft)

Tatras

Tatranská Lomnica

Gerlachovský štít

Slavkovský štít

2428 m (7966 ft)

Kriváň

2654 m (8707 ft)

2452 m (8045 ft)

Starý Smokovec

2494 m (8182 ft)

High

Štrbské Pleso

537

534

Biely Váh

Poprad

Poprad

18

Svit

Poprad

Važec

Štrba

Starý Smokovec
This attractive spa complex has several hotels, pensions and restaurants that blend well with their woodland surroundings.

Gerlachovský štít
The Tatras' highest peak, Gerlachovský štít (2,654 m/8,707 ft), can be climbed only with a professional guide.

Wooden rafts navigating the Dunajec Gorge

⑨ Bojnice Castle

The romantic, turreted Bojnice Castle is one of Slovakia's greatest tourist attractions. Rising high above the town, it was originally built in the 12th century. In the 13th century, it passed into the hands of the most powerful Hungarian warlord of the time, Matúš Čák. In 1527, the Thurzo family converted the castle into a comfortable Renaissance residence, and in the 19th century, its last owner, Count Ján František Pálffy, remodelled it into a stately residence resembling the Gothic castles of France's Loire valley.

Chapel
The chapel with its magnificent stuccoed and painted vault was built in the 17th century, in a former bastion.

Pálffy's Tomb
From the castle crypt, containing the magnificent marble tomb of Ján Pálffy, a passage leads to a cave inside the hill.

★ Golden Hall
The magnificent vault, made of pine and covered with gold leaf, was modelled on the interior of the Venetian Academy of Fine Arts.

Music Room
The present Music Room was once Ján Pálffy's bedroom. The piano pictured was made in Vienna in 1884.

Castle Grounds
Bojnice is in a large park with many rare species of trees, including what is claimed to be the oldest lime tree in Slovakia. In summer, events are staged in the grounds.

VISITORS' CHECKLIST

Practical Information
Road map C5.
5 km (3 miles) from Prievidza.
Tel (046) 543 06 33.
Open May: 9am–5pm Tue–Sun;
Jun–Sep: 9am–5pm daily; Oct–
Apr: 10am–3pm daily.
W bojnicecastle.sk

Transport
from Bratislava.

Central Castle
The rooms of the central castle are furnished in Gothic style. The top floor features the Knights' Hall.

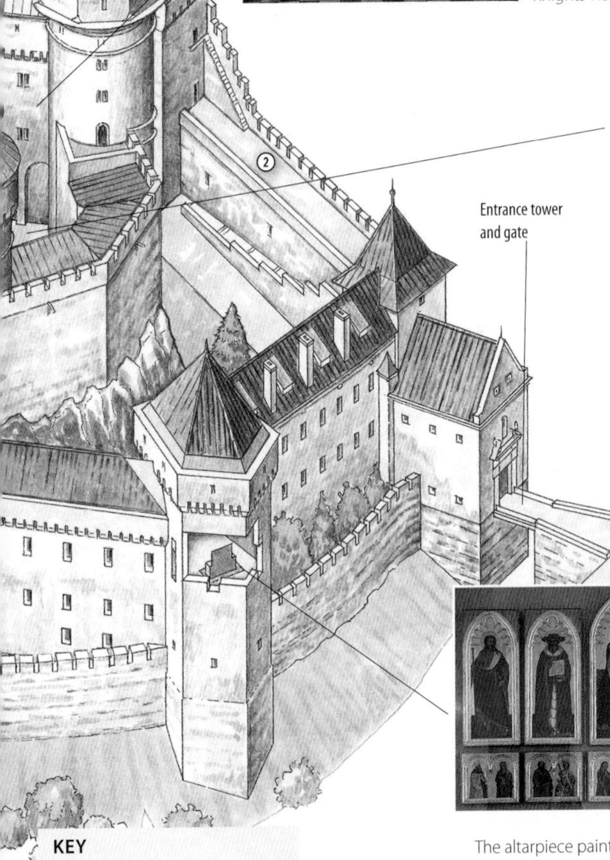

Entrance tower and gate

Well in the Fourth Courtyard
The well standing in the smallest of the castle's courtyards was once linked to an old thermal spring. Its decorative grille was made in 1895.

★ Bojnice Altarpiece
The altarpiece painted by Nardo di Cione – the only complete surviving work by the artist – is the most important piece from Ján Pálffy's collection. It was painted in the mid-14th century, using tempera paint on a wooden panel.

KEY

① Castle courtyards

② Neo-Gothic gallery

Traditional timber church, Svätý Kríž

❿ Svätý Kríž

Road map D4. 20 km (12 miles) E of Ružomberok. 🚍 680. 🚌 from Ružomberok.

The Protestant Evangelic Lutheran Church in the village of Svätý Kríž is one of the largest timber churches in Europe. This vast building has an area of 659 sq m (7,090 sq ft). It was transported to its present site from the village of Palúdza, which in 1982 was flooded to form the artificial lake of Liptovská Mara.

The church was built in 1774, when Emperor Leopold let Protestants put up churches, on condition that they were built of timber and outside town boundaries. It was constructed by a local carpenter, Jozef Lang, with 40 helpers, without the use of a single nail and without help from any architect. It took them eight months and 22 days. The church can accommodate 6,000 people.

🏠 **Evangelic Lutheran Church**
Tel (044) 559 26 22. **Open** daily. 🅿️
🚌 Sun 9am. 🖥 drevenykostol.sk

Environs
Vlkolínec, near the large, industrial town of Ružomberok, was in 1993 named a UNESCO World Cultural Heritage Site as a unique example of a well-preserved complex of 45 timber houses in a typical village of the Liptov region. Interesting features include the old well, which still supplies the village with water, and the 1770 belfry of the Baroque Church of the Virgin Mary.

⓫ Žilina

Road map C4. 29 km (18 miles) NW of Martin. 🚍 90,000. 🚌 🚌
ℹ️ Burianova medzierka 4.
Tel (041) 562 07 89. 🖥 zilina.sk

A good base for the nearby Malá Fatra mountains, the town of Žilina has a particularly striking main square, Marianské námestie. Arcades run along all four sides of the square market place at the centre of the old town. The most conspicuous of its colourful restored buildings are the Old Town Hall, the Baroque Church of St Paul (sv. Pavel) and the Jesuit monastery in the south-western corner of the square. Standing at the centre is the 1738 Marian Column.

Interesting sites along Farska include the **Holy Trinity Church** (Najsvätejšie Trojice) dating from around 1400, and the nearby **Burian Tower**, a 46-m (150-ft) tall Renaissance structure topped with a cupola identical to that of the adjacent church tower. In Námestie A Hlinku is the **Museum of Art** (Považská galéria) with a collection by modern Slovak artists. On a hillside at the west end of the town, in Závodská sesta, stands the **Church of St Stephen** (sv. Štefana), one of the oldest in Slovakia, containing 14th-century wall paintings.

⓬ Čičmany

Road map C5. 40 km (25 miles) S of Žilina. 🚍 200. 🚌 from Žilina.

This village in the Rajčanka valley resembles a set of gingerbread houses. For the last 200 years, the wooden walls of its buildings have been decorated with white geometric patterns painted with lime. In 1921, a fire consumed a large portion of Čičmany, but the village was rebuilt by its inhabitants in its original form. In the two-storey Raden's house (No. 42) is the **Považské Museum** with photographs, embroidered costumes, and furniture illustrating village life. There is an interesting section on tinkers.

🏛 **Považské Museum**
Tel (041) 500 15 11. **Open** Sep–Jun: Tue–Sun; Jul & Aug: daily. 📷 August.
📷 📷 🖥 pmza.sk

Traditional white painted decoration on a house in Čičmany

⓭ Vel'ké Uherce Palace

Road map C5. 48 km (30 miles) N of Levice. 🚌 🚌 **Closed** to the public.

Enjoying a lovely location on mountain slopes, the village of Vel'ké Uherce is known for its huge palace surrounded by an English-style park. The original Renaissance castle was built in 1622 by Michal Bossanyi. Remodelled in the 18th century in Gothic style, it was given the appearance of a Neo-Gothic residence in the spirit of English Romanticism in the second half of the 19th century. Until 1945, the palace was owned by the Thonet family, one of the world's

Coat of arms, Vel'ké Uherce Palace

Getting Around

Košice – the main town of the region – has an airport with domestic flights to Bratislava, and several international flights. Košice is also the major hub of bus transport. The main road running through East Slovakia is the 18 (international E50) leading from Žilina in Central Slovakia through Prešov, to Košice. East Slovakia is also crossed by the main Slovak railway line, which runs from Bratislava via Žilina to Košice, with an extension to Humenné.

The restored Košice Gate in the eastern district of Levoča

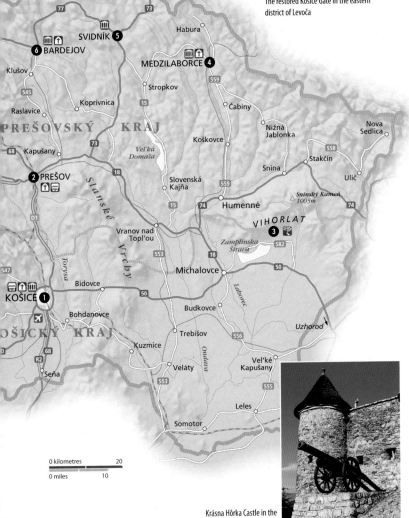

Krásna Hôrka Castle in the Slovenský kras

For keys to symbols *see back flap*

❶ Košice

Slovakia's second-largest city has roots reaching back to the 12th century. At the crossroads of major trade routes, it was granted in 1347 the same town privileges as the then capital of Hungary, Buda. In 1369, King Louis the Great gave the town its coat of arms, making it the first town in Europe to receive this by royal decree. Due to its proximity to the Hungarian border, the city has always had a large Hungarian population. Its historic old town now superbly restored, Košice is a lively, interesting city.

The Plague Column and beautiful houses in Hlavná

Exploring the town
The most interesting sights in Košice are clustered within its large historic centre. The main street, Hlavná, whose spindle shape is typical of the eastern region's towns, runs north–south, with the main squares, Hlavné námestie and Námestie slobody, and the cathedral in the centre *(see also pp334–5).*

🏛 Hlavná
This lovely avenue, full of shops and cafés, makes for an enjoyable evening stroll. The most striking of its buildings are the Gothic Levoča House (Levočský dom) and the old town hall, its façade decorated with sculptures of ancient heroes by Anton Kraus. The Plague Column (1722–3) is Košice's most beautiful piece of Baroque sculpture.

⬆ St Michael's Chapel
Hlavná 26.
The chapel (sv. Michal) was built in the 14th century, on the site of a cemetery south of St Elizabeth's Cathedral. The lower section of the building served as an ossuary. The upper section was used for celebrating masses for the souls of the dead. In the early 20th century, 17 old tombstones from the cemetery were built into the chapel walls. Highlights include the altarpiece depicting St Michael the Archangel; the lovely stone tabernacle; and, above the sacristy door, the oldest coat of arms of Košice.

🏛 St Elizabeth's Cathedral
Hlavná 28. **Tel** (255) 622 15 55. **Open** daily.
W dom.rimkat.sk 📷

Detail from St Elizabeth's Cathedral

Dominating the main square, and of great interest inside and out, St Elizabeth's Cathedral (Dóm sv. Alžbety) is the largest church in Slovakia, and a supreme achievement of the European Gothic. Its construction began in 1378. The main, western façade of this five-aisled church was originally meant to have two towers, but by 1477 only one was built. In 1508, works were completed on the vaulted presbytery. In 1775, the second tower of the cathedral was built, topped with a Rococo copper cupola. The present form of the church is the result of reconstruction that began in the late 19th century and restored the cathedral to its former appearance, close to the original design. Inside, the spectacular main altarpiece has 48 panels. Take time also to see the relief work over the north and west doors.

🏛 Urban Tower
Hlavná.
The Urban Tower (Urbanova veža) stands to the north of St Elizabeth's Cathedral. Built in the 14th century, it was remodelled in Renaissance style in 1628. St Urban's bell was cast in 1557 and installed inside the tower. Dedicating it to St Urban was intended to honour the patron saint of viniculture: wine production has always been a source of Košice's wealth.

🏛 Singing Fountain
Hlavné námestie.
In the square between the cathedral and the theatre is the Singing Fountain (Spievajúca fontána), which spouts water to recorded music. At night, the pearly jets are lit up by coloured lights that change with the rhythm of the music. The fountain is at the centre of a narrow water channel that runs the length of the square.

🎭 State Theatre
Hlavná 58. **Tel** (055) 622 12 31.
Open performances only. **W** sdke.sk
The imposing building of the State Theatre (Štátne divadlo) was built in 1897–99, to a design by Adolf Lang. Its lofty dome is topped with the torch-

Singing Fountain in Hlavné namestie, a well-known square in Bratislava

bearing figure of Dawn. The interior, with its beautiful auditorium and lyre-shape floor plan, features a magnificent ceiling with paintings of scenes from Shakespeare. The foyer and the rest of the theatre are richly decorated with stuccoes.

Jesuit Church

Junction of Hlavná and Univerzitna.

The church (Univerzitný kostol sv. Trojice), one of the finest remaining Baroque structures in Košice, was built in 1681 by the Jesuit order. Its austere, Early-Baroque façade bearing traces of the Renaissance style hides a lavishly furnished interior, which includes a 17th-century pulpit and stalls and a 19th-century main altar. The central nave and all the side chapels are beautifully decorated with magnificent *trompe l'oeil* paintings.

Bas-relief from the Jesuit Church's façade

Executioner's Bastion

Hrnčiarska 7. **Open** 9am–5pm Tue–Sat.

The bastion (Katova bašta) takes its name from the nearby house, which was once the home of the town's hangman. This semi-circular structure was built in about 1500 and served defensive purposes, housing eight guns. The lower section of the bastion is reinforced with slanting buttresses.

East Slovak Museum

Hviezdoslavova 3. **Tel** (055) 622 03 09. **Open** 9am–5pm Tue–Sat, 9am–1pm Sun. **vsmuzeum.sk**

One of Slovakia's oldest museums, the East Slovak Museum (Východoslovenské múzeum) was established in 1872 as the Upper Hungary Museum. Its vast collections, numbering half a million exhibits, are displayed in an early 20th-century Neo-Renaissance building. The impressive façade is decorated with the town's coat of arms and the carved figures of Perseus and Vulcan. The museum's greatest attraction is the "golden treasure of Košice" – a huge find of nearly 3,000 gold coins dating from the 15th to the 17th centuries.

Former Synagogue

Puškinova.

The former synagogue was built in 1926–7. In 1992, a bronze memorial plaque was added to the front of the building to commemorate over 12,000 Jews who were taken from Košice to concentration camps in 1944.

VISITORS' CHECKLIST

Practical Information

Road map F5.

240,000. Hlavná 59.

Tel (055) 625 88 88. **Open** 9am–6pm Mon–Fri, 9am–1pm Sat (also Jun–Sep: 1–5pm Sun).

kosice.sk

Transport

6 km (4 miles) from city centre. Staničné námestie Staničné námestie.

The Neo-Renaissance building housing the East Slovak Museum

Košice Centre

1. Hlavná
2. St Michael's Chapel
3. St Elizabeth's Cathedral
4. Urban Tower
5. Singing Fountain
6. State Theatre
7. Jesuit Church
8. Executioner's Bastion
9. East Slovak Museum
10. Former Synagogue

NÁMESTIE MARATÓNU MIERU
9 East Slovak Museum
HVIEZDOSLAVOVA
BACIKOVA
HLAVNÁ
KASÁRENSKÉ NÁMESTIE
ŠTEFÁNIKOVA
ZBROJNIČNÁ
MAISIARSKA
KOVÁČSKA
VODNÁ
MOYZESOVA
BIELA
Mestsky park
POŠTOVA
HRNČIARSKA
8 Executioner's Bastion
Jesuit Church 7
HRADBOVÁ
ORLIA
State Theatre 6
Singing Fountain 5
MLYNSKÁ
CYRILMETODEJSKÁ
HLAVNÉ NÁMESTIE
4 Urban Tower
10 Former Synagogue
St Elizabeth's Cathedral 3
ALŽBETINA
St Michael's Chapel 2
Train and bus stations 300 m (330 yards)
ZVONÁRSKA
PUŠKINOVA
NÁMESTIE SLOBODY
VRÁTNA
TIMONOVA
ROOSEVELTOVA
PRIBINOVA
0 metres 300
0 yards 300

Key

Street-by-Street *See pp334–5*

Street-by-Street: Around St Elizabeth's Cathedral

The long main street, Hlavná, the loveliest avenue in Slovakia, follows the old trade route through the town. It widens in its middle section where it is crosscut by Alžbetina and Mlýnská streets. This is the town's central point, marked by the lofty spire of St Elizabeth's Cathedral and the pointed, angular cap of the Urban Tower. The area is awash with stately Baroque and Neo-Classical buildings set amid greenery.

Singing Fountain
Built in 1986 by Russian experts, this huge fountain was the first attraction of its kind in Czechoslovakia.

Urban Tower
Following the Great Fire of Košice in 1556, the once Gothic tower was rebuilt in Renaissance style. It was then that it acquired the Urban Bell.

Urban Bell
The 5-tonne (some say 7-tonne) bell was removed from the tower and placed in the square in the 1960s.

HLAVNÉ NÁMESTIE

ALŽBETINA

Archbishop's Palace
The palace is one of the newest buildings in Hlavná. It was constructed in 1804, on the site of two older houses.

0 metres		20
0 yards		20

★ St Elizabeth's Cathedral

The resplendent Gothic main altarpiece (1474–7), with 48 panel pictures in its side-wings, depicts various scenes. Some parts include sculpture and illustrate the life of St Elizabeth, a Hungarian princess and patron saint of the town and the church.

Hlavná 39
Built for the Smidegh family in 1593, this house is one of many magnificent buildings on Hlavná.

★ St Michael's Chapel

The Archangel Michael is the patron saint of the 14th-century chapel in the cemetery by St Elizabeth's Cathedral. He is depicted in a doorway relief weighing the souls of the dead.

MLÝNSKÁ

NÁMESTIE SLOBODY

Hlavná 26
This 1901–2 Art Nouveau house is one of several notable Art Nouveau façades in the street.

Key

— Suggested route

The late 16th-century Rakoczy Palace (Regional Museum) in Prešov

❷ Prešov

Road map F4. 38 km (24 miles) N of Košice. ⚐ 91,000. ⚐ 🚌
ℹ️ Hlavná 67. **Tel** (051) 773 11 13.
Ⓦ presov.sk

Slovakia's third-largest town was first heard of in 1247. It was a thriving centre of salt mining from the 13th century, and mining ceased only in the 19th century. During the 16th and 17th centuries, it became a Reformation stronghold. One of the major events in the town's history was the 1687 Prešov massacre, when 24 Protestants were publicly executed on the town square for allegedly supporting an anti-Habsburg insurrection.

Dominating the town's historic district is the 1347 Gothic **Church of St Nicholas** (sv. Mikuláš), on the main street, Hlavná. It has magnificent Gothic paintings and Baroque furnishings, particularly its 17th-century high altar with figures of saints carved by Josef Hartmann. In front of the church is a Baroque Plague Column and

the 19th-century Neptune's Fountain. Opposite is the late 16th-century Renaissance **Rakoczy Palace**, now a **Regional Museum** (Šarišské múzeum). The suburb of **Solivar** features an interesting complex of historic buildings associated with salt mining.

🏛️ **Regional Museum**
Hlavná 86. **Tel** (051) 773 47 08.
Open Tue–Fri, Sun. 🖼️ 📷 🖥️
Ⓦ muzeumpresov.sk

❸ Vihorlat

Road map F5. E of Košice. 🚌

A small range of volcanic mountains, Vihorlat runs near the border with Ukraine. This is one of the quietest, least populated corners of Slovakia. The local attractions include the lovely reservoir, Zamplínská Šírava (Slovak Sea), surrounded by camp sites. In the Vihorlat Nature Reserve is **Sninský Crag** (Sninský Kameň), a steep climb to 1,005 m (3,300 ft), the final section ascended by steel

ladders. From the top, it is possible to see the emerald lake of **Morské oko** (Sea Eye) sparkling in the crater of an extinct volcano.

❹ Medzilaborce

Road map F4. 43 km (27 miles) E of Svidník. ⚐ 6,000. ⚐ 🚌

This small town, close to the border with Poland, owes its fame to the American painter Andy Warhol, leading creator of pop art. His parents, Ruthenian immigrants, came from the neighbouring village of Miková. The **Warhol Family Museum of Modern Art** (Múzeum moderného umenia) in Medzilaborce is in a chunky concrete building. On display are 18 of Warhol's original screen prints, including his iconic paintings of Campbell's soup cans, the blue cat and Ingrid Bergman as a nun. There are also mementos associated with his family.

The town was severely damaged during the two World Wars, but its attractive 18th-century Greek Orthodox **Church of the Holy Spirit** (sv. Ducha) has survived.

🏛️ **Warhol Family Museum of Modern Art**
A Warhola 749/26. **Tel** (09) 393 12 07.
Open Tue–Sun. 🖼️ 📷

Screen of icons in the Church of the Holy Spirit in Medzilaborce

Andy Warhol (1928–1987)

The real name of the king of pop art was Andrej Varchola. Born in the USA to Ruthenian parents, he studied painting and design. In 1942, he began to sign his works "Andy Warhol". Six years later, he had his first one-man show in New York. In about 1960, he started to paint pictures of everyday objects, banknotes, metro tickets and cigarettes. He executed his works with the precision of an illustrator, often choosing advertising motifs for his topics. His most famous works include the widely copied series of portraits of Marilyn Monroe.

Statue of Andy Warhol in Medzilaborce

Czechoslovak Army Monument at the Dukla Pass near Svidník

❺ Svidník

Road map F4. 53 km (33 miles) NE of Prešov. 🚇 13,000. 🚌

In the autumn of 1944, the Battle of Dukla Pass was fought against the Nazis near Svidník. Many thousands of Red Army soldiers were killed here. The **Battle of Dukla Museum** (Vojenské múzeum) is dedicated to this event. The modern building in the shape of an anti-tank mine houses thousands of exhibits associated with the battle. Some tanks and vehicles used in the battle are on display outside and en route to the Dukla Pass.

The **Museum of Ukraine-Ruthenian Culture** (Múzeum ukrajinsko-rusínskej kultúry) has artifacts of the Greek-Catholic Ruthenian minority. Part of the museum, on a separate site, is an open-air skansen of traditional Ruthenian wooden buildings.

🏛 **Battle of Dukla Museum**
Bardejovska 14. **Tel** (054) 752 13 98.
Open Tue–Sun. 🅿 ☑ 🆆 vhu.sk

🏛 **Museum of Ruthenian Culture**
Centrálna 258. **Tel** (051) 773 15 26.
Open Tue–Sun. 🅿 🆆 snm.sk

🏛 **Skansen**
Nad Svídníckym Amfiteátrom.
Tel (054) 752 29 52. **Open** May–Oct: daily. 🅿 🆆 muzeum.sk

Environs
At the Dukla Pass (20 km/12 miles north of Svidník) is the **Czechoslovak Army Monument**.

❻ Bardejov

Road map E4. 42 km (26 miles) N of Prešov. 🚇 32,000. 🚊 🚌 from Prešov. 🛈 Radničné námestie 21.
Tel (054) 541 61 86. 🆆 e-bardejov.sk

Mentioned by chroniclers as early as 1241, this large town has retained its medieval character. The superbly preserved old town's long market square, Radničné námestie, is flanked on three sides by over 40 houses built on typically narrow plots, with street-facing gables. The finest is No. 13, originally a Gothic structure remodelled in Renaissance style, now part of the **Šariš Museum**. The early 16th-century **town hall** at the centre of the square has Renaissance windows, an oriel and stone portals. The top façade bears a statue of the Knight Roland. Another branch of the Šariš Museum is here. The fourth side of the square is occupied by the **Basilica of St Giles** (sv. Egídius), a magnificent church with 11 medieval side altars. The town, on the UNESCO World Cultural Heritage list, also has very well-preserved medieval defensive walls.

Madonna in the Bardejov town hall

🏛 **Šariš Muzeum**
Radničné námestie 13.
Tel (054) 472 49 66.
Open Tue–Sun. 🅿 ☑ 🆆 muzeumbardejov.sk

❼ Kežmarok

Road map E4. 74 km (46 miles) W of Prešov. 🚇 17,000. 🚊 🚌 🛈 Hlavné námestie 46.
Tel (052) 449 21 35. 🆆 kezmarok.net

Kežmarok's most imposing historic sight is the vast, Neo-Byzantine **Lutheran Church** (Nový evanjelický kostol), work of the Viennese architect Theophil von Hansen. It contains the mausoleum of Count Imre Thököly, hero of Hungarian anti-Habsburg insurrections (see p267). In contrast, the old **Protestant Church** (Drevený kostol) nearby, built in 1717 of red spruce and

yew, has a richly decorated main altar, a carved pulpit and a stone font dating from 1690 that is older than the church itself. To the north of the town square with its Neo-Classical town hall stands a 15th-century **castle** built by Imre Zápolya, and remodelled by the Thököly family into a Renaissance residence; today, it is the **Kežmarok Museum**.

🏛 **Kežmarok Museum**
Hradné námestie 42. **Tel** (052) 452 26 19. **Open** May–Sep: daily; Oct–Apr: Mon–Fri. 🅿 ☑ 🖥

Main altar in the Protestant Church in Kežmarok

❽ Podolínec

Road map E4. 16 km (10 miles) N of Kežmarok. 🚇 3,000. 🚌 🛈 Námestie Mariánske 29. **Tel** (052) 439 12 05.

This small town in the Poprad river valley has a history going back to 1292. At the centre of its main square, flanked by Renaissance houses, is the late 13th-century **Church of the Ascension of the Virgin Mary** (Nanebovzatia Panny Marie), its presbytery decorated with Gothic wall paintings. The beautiful Renaissance belfry in front of the church, with a lavishly decorated attic, is from 1659.

The nearby mid-17th-century **Piarist Church and Monastery** have an interesting history. For three centuries, the monastery was home to the Piarist college founded by the bailiff of Spiš. In 1950–51, the Communists turned it briefly into a concentration camp for Slovak monks.

The Renaissance Thurzo House in the old centre of Levoča

❾ Levoča

Road map E3. 56 km (35 miles) W of Prešov. 🏠 14,600. 🚌 🚉 ℹ️ Námestie Majstra Pavla 58. **Tel** (053) 451 37 63.
🌐 **levoca.sk**

The former capital of the affluent region of Spiš, Levoča lies between the High Tatras and Slovenské Rudohorie mountains. The well-preserved historic centre is full of Gothic, Renaissance, Baroque and Neo-Classical buildings. Its main square, Námestie Majstra Pavla, features the Gothic **Church of St James** (sv. Jakub). This houses a set of 18 altarpieces, a collection of medieval and Renaissance sacred art. The 18.6-m- (61-ft-) high main altarpiece is the world's tallest Gothic altar. The over 2-m- (6-ft-) high statues of the Madonna, St James and St John the Evangelist are all by Master Pavol of Levoča, a sculptor of the Late Gothic, who also carved other altarpieces in the church. Just south of the church is the former **Town Hall** *(see right)*. The historical centre and the works of Master Pavol of Levoča are listed as UNESCO World Heritage Sites, as is the nearby Spiš Castle *(see p342)*.

Among nearly 60 historic houses around the main square are the striking **Thurzo House** (Thurzov dom) crowned with a Renaissance attic, and the **House of Master Pavol of Levoča**, now a museum of his life and work. At the edge of the historic district is the 14th-century **Old Minorites' Church** (Starý kláštor minoritov) that has a dazzling Baroque interior.

🏛️ **House of Master Pavol**
Námestie Majstra Pavla 20.
Tel (053) 451 34 96. **Open** 9am–5pm daily. 📷 🌐 **snm.sk**

Levoča: Town Hall

One of the town's most distinguished buildings, the town hall (radnica) was erected in 1550 in Gothic style, replacing an earlier building that had been destroyed by fire. In the early 17th century, it was remodelled along Renaissance lines. The bell tower dates from 1656–61, which, in the 18th century, was decorated with Baroque elements. The Neo-Classical pediments were added in the 19th century. The town hall is still used for civic functions, and it also houses the main branch of the Spiš Museum on the first floor, with exhibits on regional history.

★ **Arcades**
The original town hall did not have any galleries. The two-tier arcades were added to the central part of the building in 1615.

Cage of Disgrace

The wrought-iron contraption by the south wall of the town hall is the 16th-century "Cage of Disgrace", in which women who had committed minor crimes were locked up and put on public display. It used to stand in the park belonging to the Probstner family, who gave it to the town in 1933.

Town's Coat of Arms
This consists of a red shield with a double cross supported by two lions.

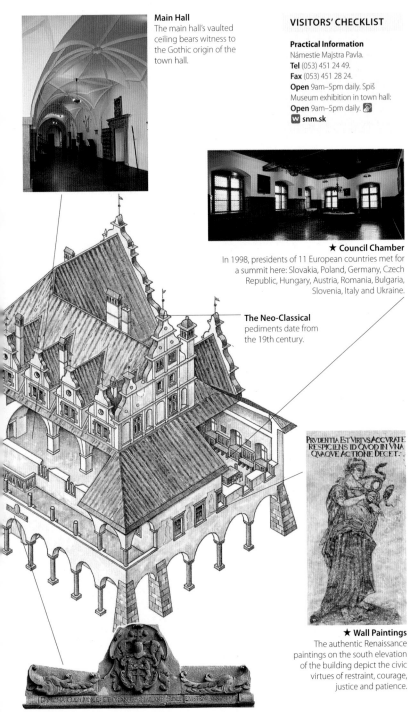

Main Hall
The main hall's vaulted ceiling bears witness to the Gothic origin of the town hall.

VISITORS' CHECKLIST

Practical Information
Námestie Majstra Pavla.
Tel (053) 451 24 49.
Fax (053) 451 28 24.
Open 9am–5pm daily. Spiš Museum exhibition in town hall:
Open 9am–5pm daily.
w snm.sk

★ Council Chamber
In 1998, presidents of 11 European countries met for a summit here: Slovakia, Poland, Germany, Czech Republic, Hungary, Austria, Romania, Bulgaria, Slovenia, Italy and Ukraine.

The Neo-Classical pediments date from the 19th century.

PRVDENTIA EST VIRTVS ACCVRATE RESPICIENS ID QVOD IN VNA QVAQVE ACTIONE DECET.

★ Wall Paintings
The authentic Renaissance paintings on the south elevation of the building depict the civic virtues of restraint, courage, justice and patience.

Coat of Arms
The town's coat of arms can be found above the central arch of the ground-floor arcades, on the west side of the building.

⑩ A Tour of the Slovenský kras

Limestone caves characterize the Slovak Karst, which runs in a wide arc along the Slovak-Hungarian border. Most of the country's karst phenomena occur here, including the vast majority of its 4,450 caves. Four of them – Domica, Gombasecká, Ochtinská aragonitová and Jasovská – are partly open to the public. A fifth cave, Dobšiná ice cave, is in the Slovenský raj (Slovak Paradise), another karst area about 40 km (25 miles) to the northwest (warm clothes are recommended for this cave). In 1995, all five were listed as UNESCO Sites.

④ **Úhorná**
Under the village of Úhorná, 14 km (9 miles) from Rožňava, is a reservoir, which was built in 1768 to prevent flooding. It supplied water to mines and iron mills.

③ **Krásna Hôrka**
One of Slovakia's finest castles, full of gorgeous furnishings. (Temporarily closed due to a fire in 2012.) Nearby is the mausoleum of the Andrássy family, who once owned the castle.

② **Betliar**
The Andrássy family owned this whimsical hunting lodge, which houses a large collection of trophies and is decorated in a variety of styles. One of its most interesting rooms is the magnificent library.

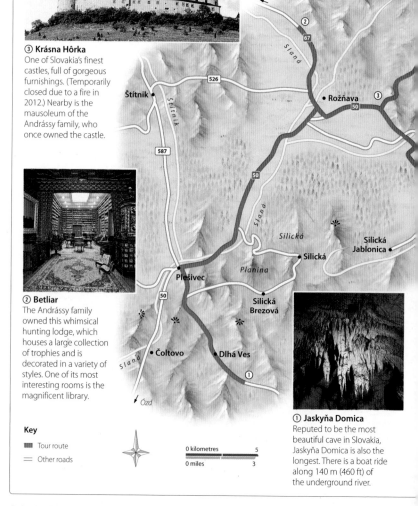

Key
▬▬ Tour route
═ Other roads

0 kilometres — 5
0 miles — 3

① **Jaskyňa Domica**
Reputed to be the most beautiful cave in Slovakia, Jaskyňa Domica is also the longest. There is a boat ride along 140 m (460 ft) of the underground river.

⑤ Zádielska Valley
The valley is an impressive 3-km (2-mile) long canyon cut in white limestone rocks, with walls rising to 300 m (985 ft). Flowing along its floor is the small stream, Zádielski Potok.

Tips for Drivers

Length: About 75 km (45 miles).
Stopping off points: Rožňava is a good base; other towns also have places for refreshments.
ℹ️ Rožňava, námestie Baníkov 32.
Tel (058) 732 81 01; 788 44 20.
W **slovenskyraj.sk**
W **ssj.sk** (cave information)

⑥ Jasov
Jasov features Slovakia's biggest monastery complex. Its interior contains fine examples of Baroque art.

Hačava

Lúčka

Bôrka

Moldava nad Bodvou

Jablonov nad Turňou

Turňa nad Bodvou

Košice

Miskolc

⑧ Medzev
A landmark in this small town, which was founded in the 13th century by German settlers, is the tower of the Church of Mary the Queen of Angels.

⑦ Jasovská Jaskyňa
It is claimed that this cave was discovered by monks from the nearby monastery in Jasov. Its underground corridors feature numerous old writings and drawings, the oldest dating from 1452. Within the cave, archaeologists have discovered traces of prehistoric habitation.

⓫ Spiš Castle

These forbidding castle ruins (Spišský hrad) are part of a historic complex, along with the small town of Spišské Podhradie (*podhradie* means "below the castle"), which lies between the castle and Spišská Kapitula *(see opposite)*, a settlement on a ridge 6 km (4 miles) to the northwest. Spiš Castle was the administrative capital of the Spiš region, a historic province populated by Saxon settlers. The oldest parts of the castle date from the 11th–12th centuries. After its 15th-century enlargement, it contained five courtyards. In 1780, it burned down. It is gradually being restored. Most impressive from a distance, it is nonetheless worth a visit for its spectacular views.

Walls
The defensive walls were rebuilt, reinforced and equipped with new gun positions by the Zápolya family, who owned the castle in the 15th and 16th centuries.

Vast Fortress
Occupying an area of 4 ha (10 acres), Spiš Castle is the remains of the largest fortress complex in Central Europe. In the 17th century, it had 2,000 inhabitants.

Gate
The entrance gate leads to a vast lower courtyard, nearly 300 m (985 ft) long and 115 m (380 ft) wide.

KEY

① **Round tower**, dating from the first half of the 12th century, was used as a residence and an observation point.

★ Upper Castle
Situated at the highest point, the now-ruined upper castle, with its tower and Romanesque palace, was built in the 13th century.

VISITORS' CHECKLIST

Practical Information
Road map E4.
🏔 3,500 (Spišské Podhradie).
Tel (090) 456 42 90.
Castle & Museum: **Open** daily, May–Sep: 9am–6pm; Apr & Oct: 10am–6pm; Nov: 10am–3pm. 🅿 🅲
ⓦ spisskyhrad.com

Transport
🚆 🚌 Spišské Podhradie, 3 km (2 miles) NW.

★ Tournaments
During the summer season, colourful historic pageants and knights' tournaments are held in the castle courtyards.

★ Museum
The museum allows visitors to view the castle kitchen, the bedrooms, the bathrooms, the castle armoury and the torture room.

★ Castle Chapel
Six wooden statues of saints adorn the interior of the 15th-century Gothic chapel of the Zápolya family. In 2003, the chapel underwent a complete renovation.

⓬ Spišská Kapitula

Road map E4. 35 km (22 miles) W of Prešov. 🚌

A small walled town on a ridge west of Spišské Podhradie, Spišská Kapitula has been, since 1776, the seat of the Spiš bishopric, the ecclesiastical capital of the Spiš region. Its dominant sight is the late Romanesque, twin-towered **St Martin's Cathedral**, dating from 1245–75 (see also p255). It has two Romanesque portals, an unusual statue of a white lion by the entrance, and unique medieval frescoes in the central nave. The interesting burial chapel of the Zápolya family, by the south wall, dates from the 15th century. Also on the town's one street is the imposing Baroque **Bishop's Palace** with a clock tower, and a row of Gothic canons' houses. Since 1993, Spišská Kapitula has been on the UNESCO World Cultural Heritage listing, with Spišské Podhradie and Spiš Castle.

🏛 **St Martin's Cathedral**
Tel (090) 456 42 90. **Open** May–Oct: 10am–4:30pm Mon–Sat, 1–4:30pm Sun. 🅿 🅲 ⓦ spisskyhrad.com

Environs
Žehra, a village 6 km (4 miles) southeast of Spišská Kapitula, features a 13th-century Romanesque Church of the Holy Spirit (sv. Duch), a white building with a tower and a bell, topped with onion-shaped wooden cupolas. Inside the church are magnificent 13th–15th-century frescoes covering the presbytery and one wall of the nave, and a 13th-century stone font.

St Martin's Cathedral at Spišská Kapitula with Spiš Castle in the background

TRAVELLERS' NEEDS

WHERE TO STAY

The Czech and Slovak Republics have a well-developed network of comfortable hotels, pensions and backpacker hostels, as well as rooms to let in private homes. Finding a bed for the night should never be a problem, even in a small town or a village, although some places in mountain areas may be closed outside the peak summer and winter seasons. In large cities, particularly Prague, it may be hard to find inexpensive accommodation, although there are plenty of budget choices in or near the centre, and some small pensions on the outskirts. The list of places to stay on the following pages gives the most attractive establishments in all price categories, including options such as backpacker hostels and B&Bs. The listings for the Czech Republic are on pages 348–53; those for Slovakia are on 354–7.

How to Book

Almost all hotels and hostels in the Czech Republic and Slovakia are featured on international booking sites such as **Booking**, **Airbnb** and **Hostelworld**. Reservations can also be made by contacting the establishment by phone or email. Early booking is advisable in major cities and mountain areas, especially during peak periods (New Year, Easter, May Day and high summer), when it can be quite a challenge to find vacancies. In Prague, the tourist and conference season lasts all year round, and finding a hotel on arrival may prove to be difficult at any time. Visitors can also book accommodation on **hotel-line.cz**, **limba.com** and **bookings.sk**.

Chain Hotels

Most hotels in the Czech Republic and Slovakia offer en-suite rooms with cable television and free Wi-Fi access. Rooms in more expensive hotels may have a mini-bar, 24-hour room service and laundry service. Fitness facilities are common, and hotels in the luxury bracket offer spa facilities or swimming pools. Apart from modern chain hotels such as Radisson and Hilton, visitors will also find plenty of grand historic hotels famous for their *fin-de-siècle* atmosphere. Recent years have seen the emergence of a new breed of boutique and design hotels that aim to make best use of local artistic traditions; alongside a good number of B&Bs, offering characterful accommodation.

Hostels and Lodges

There is a growing number of backpacker hostels in the Czech and Slovak republics, offering cheap, simple dorm accommodation in informal surroundings. Beds in hostels can be booked via the hostels' own websites or on specialist websites such as **Hostelworld** or **Czech Hostels Association**. Many offer doubles, triples, quads and dorms, and are becoming increasingly

Lovely yellow façade of the Grand Hotel Zvon in České Budějovice *(see p351)*

popular with tourists who enjoy the social aspects of backpacker culture but who want their own room. Hostels vary a great deal in terms of character – some have a bar on site and encourage late-night socializing, while others offer a bit more peace and quiet. The description on each hostel's website will make it clear what kind of atmosphere they offer. Breakfast is not available at all hostels – check while booking.

Pensions

There are a large number of pensions (*penzion* in Czech; *penzión* in Slovak) in both countries, particularly in the Czech Republic. These are usually cosy, inexpensive places offering rooms of a reasonable standard (with en-suite bathrooms), mostly with breakfast included. There's also an increasing number of B&Bs in both countries, usually

Grand Hotel Pupp in Karlovy Vary *(see p351)*

◀ Stylish interior of an upscale restaurant in Bratislava, Slovakia

Warmly decorated public area at Penzion Nostalgia, a pension in Central Slovakia *(see p356)*

family-run affairs in small towns and villages, although there's a growing handful of stylish urban B&Bs in major cities too.

Private Homes

Rooms in private homes for visitors are widely available in the Czech Republic. In Slovakia, their numbers are growing fast. Some local tourist offices can help with advance bookings.

Camp Sites

There are over 200 camp sites in the Czech Republic. In Slovakia, there are about 100 in the summer season, some also offering lodging in chalets and bungalows. Most have kitchens, washrooms and bathrooms available; some also have a shop and a bar. They tend to be crowded in the high season. Visit **camp.cz** for more information.

Agritourism

Slovakia is experiencing a growth in agritourism, or accommodation in farmhouse B&Bs.

Luxuriously appointed room at Radisson Blu Carlton, Bratislava *(see p354)*

In the Czech Republic, many farms offer accommodation in historic farmsteads, mills or cottages, where organic food is served. Guests can go hiking, cycling or horse riding. Check **Prázdniny na venkově** (Holidays in the countryside) for more information on farmhouse B&Bs.

Hidden Extras

While staying in a hotel, it is worth checking whether parking and breakfast are included. Also check the cost of extras such as mini-bars and telephone calls, as both can be expensive. Slovak resorts may charge visitors a "climate tax", a small environmental tourist tax.

Travelling with Children

Finding a place to stay with children does not present any major problems in both republics, and families are welcomed. In Slovakia, many pensions, agritourism farms and private homes encourage families with children and try to provide entertainment and play areas for their youngest guests. Some hotels, particularly in the Czech Republic, will supply a cot and maybe even a baby-sitting service.

Disabled Travellers

Many Slovak hotels and better-class pensions can accommodate disabled guests; almost all new facilities are built with their requirements in mind. In the Czech Republic, the needs of wheelchair users are taken into account generally only by the

top-class hotels, although this is slowly changing as new facilities are opened and are obliged to offer wheelchair access.

Recommended Hotels

The hotels listed in this guide have been chosen for a wide range of reasons and criteria, such as excellent facilities, outstanding location and good value. Listings cover a vast variety of accommodations, from family-run **pensions** to designer **boutique** hotels, from **historic** landmark hotels to comfortable **modern** options, and from affordable **budget** places to opulent **luxury** and **spa hotels**.

The "DK Choice" label is used for hotels that are the best of the best – remarkably outstanding options that may be known for their beautiful surroundings, have spectacular views, be housed in a historical landmark, have exceptional service, or a great atmosphere. Whatever be the reason, a "DK Choice" guarantees an especially memorable stay.

DIRECTORY

Agritourism

Prázdniny na venkově (Holidays in the countryside)
Tel 777 191 323.
W prazdninynavenkove.cz

Hostels

Czech Hostels Association
Sokolská 11, 120 00 Praha 2.
Tel 224 914 062. **Fax** 224 914 067.
W czechhostels.com

Reservations

W **bookings.sk** W **camp.cz** (camping in Czech and Slovak Republics) W **hotel-line.cz** (hotels in Czech Republic) W **limba.com** (Slovak travel agent)

Internet Booking Sites

Airbnb
W airbnb.com

Booking
W booking.com

Hostelworld
W hostelworld.com

Where to Stay in the Czech Republic

Prague

Hradčany & Malá Strana

Dům u Velké Boty Ⓚ
Budget **Map** 2 D3
Vlašská 30/333, Praha 1
Tel *257 532 088*
Ⓦ dumuvelkeboty.cz
In a handsome old town house,
the charming 'House of the Big
Boots' offers a personalized stay.

Hostel Little Quarter Ⓚ
Budget **Map** 2 D3
Nerudova 21, Praha 1
Tel *257 212 029*
Ⓦ littlequarter.com
A mixture of dorms and private
doubles on one of Malá Strana's
most animated streets.

Hotel Kampa Ⓚ
Budget **Map** 2 E5
Všehrdova 16, Praha 1
Tel *257 404 444*
Ⓦ praguekampahotel.com
Close to both Kampa Park and
Charles Bridge, this functional
hotel is an ideal sightseeing base.

Pension Dientzenhofer Ⓚ
Budget **Map** 2 E4
Nosticova 2
Tel *257 311 319*
Ⓦ dientzenhofer.cz
This shabby-but-chic pension in
a Baroque house offers comfort-
able rooms on a quiet street.

Domus Henrici ⓀⓀ
Boutique **Map** 1 C3
Loretánská 11, Praha 1
Tel *220 511 369*
Ⓦ domus-henrici.cz
Situated beside the Castle and
Strahov Monastery, this quiet
hotel has tasteful rooms.

Cheerful, arty decor at the Sax Hotel
in Prague

Hotel Hoffmeister ⓀⓀ
Boutique **Map** 2 F2
Pod Bruskou 7, Praha 1
Tel *251 017 111*
Ⓦ hoffmeister.cz
The imposing Hoffmeister has
flamboyantly furnished rooms,
lovely outdoor spaces and great
views across the river.

DK Choice

Sax ⓀⓀ
Boutique **Map** 2 D3
Jánsky vršek 328/3, Praha 1
Tel *257 531 268*
Ⓦ hotelsax.cz
Superbly positioned midway
between Malá Strana and the
Castle, Sax offers spacious
rooms, each decked out in the
style of a vintage era. Most of
the furnishings are original
collectors' items. Guests enjoy
breakfast and afternoon tea,
with delicious cakes, in the
spectacular glass-roofed
inner atrium.

Three Storks ⓀⓀ
Historic **Map** 2 E3
Valdštejnské náměstí 8, Praha 1
Tel *257 210 779*
Ⓦ hotelthreestorks.cz
Smart contemporary rooms in
a restored Neo-Classical town
house, right in the centre of
Malá Strana.

Alchymist ⓀⓀⓀ
Luxury **Map** 2 E3
Tržiště 19, Praha 1
Tel *257 286 011*
Ⓦ alchymisthotel.com
A Baroque former palace with
sumptuous, individually styled
rooms. Facilities include a
relaxing spa.

Aria ⓀⓀⓀ
Luxury **Map** 2 D3
Tržiště 9, Praha 1
Tel *225 334 111*
Ⓦ ariahotel.net
Rooms in this plush hotel are
themed around styles of
music and famous composers.
Guests have access to the
Castle's garden.

Golden Well Hotel ⓀⓀⓀ
Historic **Map** 2 E2
U Zlaté Studně 166/4, Praha 1
Tel *257 011 213*
Ⓦ goldenwell.cz
Lovely hotel on four floors of a
venerable old building, offering
well-furnished rooms with
comfortable bathrooms.

Price Guide
Prices are based on one night's stay in
high season for a standard double room,
Iinclusive of service charges and taxes.

Ⓚ   under 2000Kč
ⓀⓀ   2000–3500Kč
ⓀⓀⓀ   over 3500Kč

Staré Město and Josefov

Travellers' Hostel Ⓚ
Budget **Map** 3 C2
Dlouhá 33, Praha 1
Tel *224 826 662*
Ⓦ travellers.cz
This contemporary backpacker's
hostel is a popular place offering
both dorms and doubles.

Betlem Club ⓀⓀ
Boutique **Map** 3 B4
Betlémské náměstí 9, Praha 1
Tel *222 221 574*
Ⓦ betlemclub.cz
Beautiful medieval building
in a quiet Old Town square, the
atmospheric Betlem Club
has small but smart rooms.

U Zlatého Stromu ⓀⓀ
Historic **Map** 3 B4
Karlova 6, Praha 1
Tel *222 220 441*
Ⓦ zlatystrom.com
Handsome 19th-century house
with plush rooms and a music
pub on the ground floor.

Emblem ⓀⓀⓀ
Boutique **Map** 3 B3
Platnéřská 19, Praha 1
Tel *226 202 500*
Ⓦ emblemprague.com
Minimalist design, muted colours
and excellent facilities at this
contemporary hotel with a
superb Old Town location.

**Grand Hotel
Bohemia** ⓀⓀⓀ
Luxury **Map** 4 D3
Králodvorská 4, Praha 1
Tel *234 608 111*
Ⓦ grandhotelbohemia.cz
An opulent Art-Nouveau
hotel boasting vast rooms,
attentive staff, and a famously
genteel café.

Grand Hotel Praha ⓀⓀⓀ
Luxury **Map** 3 C3
Staroměstské náměstí 22, Praha 1
Tel *221 632 556*
Ⓦ grandhotelpraha.cz
Very popular due to its position
right on the Old Town square.
Large rooms have a mixture
of vintage furnishings and
modern conveniences.

Sleek interior of a room at the Josef, Prague

DK Choice

Josef ⓦⓦⓦ
Boutique **Map** 3 C3
Rybná 20, Praha 1
Tel *221 700 111*
ⓦ hoteljosef.com
Styled by Czech-born architect
Eva Jiřičná, Josef is a beautifully
executed exercise in modern
design, with lots of white surfaces
and lovely colour-coordinated
rooms. There is an outstanding
breakfast spread, a well-equipped
gym and multi-lingual staff.

Liberty ⓦⓦⓦ
Historic **Map** 3 C4
28. října 11, Praha 1
Tel *221 181 149*
ⓦ hotelliberty.cz
Understated elegance and
contemporary comforts at this
hotel housed in an original Art
Nouveau building. Spacious
rooms and a wellness centre.

Maximilian ⓦⓦⓦ
Modern **Map** 3 C2
Haštalská 14, Praha 1
Tel *225 303 118*
ⓦ maximilianhotel.com
Comfortable place known as the
'Goldfish Hotel' due to the optional
pets offered to guests on arrival.

Pariž ⓦⓦⓦ
Luxury **Map** 4 D3
U Obecního domu 1, Praha 1
Tel *222 195 195*
ⓦ hotel-pariz.cz
Fin-de-siècle decor make for an
evocative stay in a building full
of Art Nouveau touches.

Ventana ⓦⓦⓦ
Luxury **Map** 3 C3
Celetná 7, Praha 1
Tel *221 776 600*
ⓦ ventana-hotel.net
Classic Prague hotel featuring
Art Nouveau interiors and four-
poster beds.

Nové Město

Alton ⓦ
Budget **Map** 6 D2
Legerova 62, Praha 1
Tel *222 524 066*
ⓦ altonhotel.cz
Neat, friendly hotel next to
Pavlova metro station, and a short
walk from Václavské náměstí.

U Medvídku ⓦ
Pension **Map** 3 B5
Na Perštyne 7, Praha 1
Tel *224 211 916*
ⓦ umedvidku.cz
Czech pub and pension, 'The
Little Bears' has wood-beamed
rooms and a beer museum.

Majestic Plaza ⓦⓦ
Boutique **Map** 5 C1
Štepánská 33, Praha 1
Tel *221 486 100*
ⓦ hotel-majestic.cz
Both Art Deco and Biedermeier-
style rooms, and great castle
views from the seventh floor.

Metropol ⓦⓦ
Boutique **Map** 3 B5
Národní 33, Praha 1
Tel *246 022 100*
ⓦ metropolhotel.cz
Sleek hotel with nine floors of
glass-walled design. Small but
crisply decked-out rooms.

DK Choice

Mosaic House ⓦⓦ
Budget **Map** 5 B1
Odborů 4, Praha 2
Tel *221 595 350*
ⓦ mosaichouse.com
An eco-conscious hotel
with trendy rooms ranging
from four-star en-suite
doubles to hostel-style
dorms. A bustling bar
and restaurant with friendly,
attentive staff make this
a welcoming place for
travellers of all ages.

Opera ⓦⓦ
Boutique **Map** 4 F2
Tešnov 13, Praha 1
Tel *222 315 609*
ⓦ hotel-opera.cz
In a Neo-Renaissance building
that resembles a cake. Classic
furniture and vast windows.

Boscolo Carlo IV ⓦⓦⓦ
Luxury **Map** 4 E4
Senovážné náměstí 13, Praha 1
Tel *224 593 111*
ⓦ boscolohotels.com
Close to the main train station,
this hotel boasts Italian opulence
and an impressive spa centre.

Fusion ⓦⓦⓦ
Boutique **Map** 4 D4
Panská 9, Praha 1
Tel *226 222 800*
ⓦ fusionhotels.com
Characterful hotel with stripped-
down, industrial-style rooms, mod-
ern decor and a rooftop terrace.

Hotel Yasmin ⓦⓦⓦ
Modern **Map** 4 D5
Politických vězňů 12, Praha 1
Tel *234 100 100*
ⓦ hotel-yasmin.cz
Located close to Wenceslas
Square, Yasmin offers
comfortable rooms with
fresh, contemporary decor.

**Kempinski Hotel
Hybernska** ⓦⓦⓦ
Luxury **Map** 4 E3
Hybernská 12, Praha 1
Tel *22 62 26 111*
ⓦ kempinski-prague.com
In a beautifully reconstructed
19th-century building with great
amenities and a lovely garden.

Prague Inn ⓦⓦⓦ
Modern **Map** 3 C4
28. října 378/15, Praha 1
Tel *226 014 444*
ⓦ hotelpragueinn.cz
Well situated on the corner of
Wenceslas Square; offers chic
rooms in warm colours.

Radisson Blu Alcron ⓦⓦⓦ
Luxury **Map** 6 D1
Štěpanská 40, Praha 1
Tel *222 820 000*
ⓦ radissonblu.com
This Art Deco hotel has great
amenities, personal service
and an award-winning chef.

Seven Days ⓦⓦⓦ
Luxury **Map** 6 D1
Žitná 46, Praha 2
Tel *222 923 111*
ⓦ hotelsevendays.cz
Opulent hotel in a grand
19th-century building, with
large, comfortable rooms.

For more information on types of hotels *see page 347*

Further Afield

Anna Ⓚ
Budget
Budečská 17, Praha 2
Tel *222 513 111*
Ⓦ hotelanna.cz
Art Nouveau interiors and a lovely
breakfast room at this great-value
hotel in a quiet spot.

Ariston Ⓚ
Budget
Seifertova 65, Praha 3
Tel *222 782 517*
Ⓦ hotelaristonprague.cz
Three-star near the city centre
offering functional but spacious
rooms with wooden furniture.

DK Choice

Art Hotel Praha Ⓚ
Boutique
*Nad královskou oborou 53,
Praha 7*
Tel *233 101 331*
Ⓦ arthotel.cz
Family-run hotel located in the
peaceful embassy district. Each
room is different, with stylish
furnishings and atmospheric
lighting. Helpful staff and a
lovely garden terrace where
breakfast is served. The hotel
also hosts a private collection
of modern Czech art.

Hotel Trevi Ⓚ
Budget
Uruguayská 540/20, Praha 2
Tel *722 811 097*
Ⓦ praguehoteltrevi.com
In a quiet residential district with
modern rooms and a generous
buffet breakfast.

Ametyst ⓀⓀ
Modern **Map** 6 F3
Jana Masaryka 11, Praha 2
Tel *222 921 921*
Ⓦ hotelametyst.cz
Chic contemporary-style hotel
with sauna and solarium. The attic
rooms feature exposed beams.

NH Prague ⓀⓀ
Modern
Mozartova 1, Praha 5
Tel *257 153 430*
Ⓦ nhprague.com
Occupies two buildings linked
by a cable car. Smart rooms, two
restaurants and a lobby bar.

U Blaženky ⓀⓀ
Luxury
U Blaženky 1, Praha 5
Tel *251 564 532*
Ⓦ ublazenky.cz
A grand villa in Prague's best
residential district with elegantly
furnished rooms.

Angelo ⓀⓀⓀ
Boutique
Radlická 1, Praha 5
Tel *234 801 111*
Ⓦ angelohotel.com
Rich fabrics and bright colours
characterize the rooms. Among the
many facilities is an on-site sauna.

Le Palais ⓀⓀⓀ
Luxury
U Zvonarky 1, Praha 2
Tel *234 634 111*
Ⓦ palaishotel.cz
Belle époque hotel with plush
rooms, attentive staff and a great
wellness centre.

Mamaison Riverside Praha ⓀⓀⓀ
Boutique
Janáčkovo nábřeží 15, Praha 5
Tel *225 994 611*
Ⓦ mamaison.com
A splendid hotel with unparal-
leled attention to detail. Rooms
have Czech art on the walls.

Moods ⓀⓀⓀ
Boutique
Klimentská 28, Praha 1
Tel *222 330 100*
Ⓦ hotelmoods.com
A Czech children's story painted
on the walls, a moss wall in the
lobby and all-day breakfasts.

Central Bohemia

DK Choice

KOLÍN: Chateau Kotera ⓀⓀ
Boutique **Map** D2
*Komenského 40, Ratboř u
Kolína 281 41*
Tel *321 613 111*
Ⓦ hotelkotera.cz
Housed in a palace designed
in Neo-Classical style by Czech
architect Jan Kotěra, this hotel
has luxurious rooms and eager-
to-please staff. There is a
Mediterranean restaurant, plus
sauna and tennis courts.

KUTNÁ HORA: U Růže Ⓚ
Budget **Map** D2
Zámecká 52, 284 03
Tel *327 314 692*
Ⓦ ruzehotel.com
Family-friendly despite the
vintage-furnished interiors. Offers
tennis, squash, bowling and paintball
on site. Close to the famous ossuary.

**KUTNÁ HORA: U Vlašského
Dvora** Ⓚ
Historic **Map** D2
28. října 511, 284 01
Tel *327 514 618*
Ⓦ vlasskydvur.cz
Snug hotel in a 15th-century
building with well-appointed
rooms and Old Town views.

MĚLNÍK: Hotel Ludmila Ⓚ
Budget **Map** C1
Pražská 2639/2, 276 01
Tel *315 622 419*
Ⓦ ludmila.cz
Modern block with functional
but bright rooms. Bowling alley
and tennis courts nearby.

MĚLNÍK: U Rytířů Ⓚ
Budget **Map** C1
Svatováclavská 17, 276 01
Tel *603 556 333*
Ⓦ urytiru.cz
A charming little hotel near the
centre with appealing rooms
and a well-regarded restaurant.

MLADÁ BOLESLAV: U Hradu Ⓚ
Budget **Map** D1
Staroměstské náměstí 108, 293 01
Tel *326 721 049*
Ⓦ uhradu.cz
At the foot of the castle with
stylish rooms, two restaurants
and a garden terrace.

SÁZAVA: Sázava Ⓚ
Boutique **Map** D2
Benešovská 44, 285 06
Tel *773 570 007*
Ⓦ hotelsazava.cz
A bijou hotel in a Baroque
building with well-appointed
rooms, helpful staff and a
haute-cuisine restaurant.

A simple, neat room at the hotel Anna, Prague

Key to Price Guide *see page 348*

South Bohemia

ČESKÉ BUDĚJOVICE: Hotel Zatkuv Dum ®
Historic   Map C3
Krajinská 41, 370 01
Tel *387 001 710*
W zatkuvdum.cz
Occupying two Renaissance houses, this friendly place has modern furnishings.

ČESKÉ BUDĚJOVICE: U Solné Brány ®
Budget   Map C3
Radniční 11, 370 01
Tel *386 354 121*
W hotelusolnebrany.cz
Old-fashioned hotel offering simply furnished en-suites with small balconies or terraces.

DK Choice

ČESKÉ BUDĚJOVICE: Grand Hotel Zvon ®®®
Historic
Nám. Přemysla Otakara II 90/28, 370 01
Tel *381 601 601*
W hotel-zvon.cz
Occupying a trio of historic buildings on the main square, 'The Bell' boasts 16th-century architectural traditions. The reception area features stunning artworks and a 17th-century hand-carved ceiling. The rooms, of various sizes, are all of individual character. The hotel also has three restaurants.

ČESKÝ KRUMLOV: Krumlov House Hostel ®
Budget   Map C3
Rooseveltova 68, 381 01
Tel *380 711 935*
W krumlovhostel.com
Krumlov is full of hostels and this is one of the best, with a choice of dorms, doubles and apartments, plus social areas.

ČESKÝ KRUMLOV: Pension Rosa ®
Pension   Map C3
Linecká 54, 381 01
Tel *723 854 195*
W pension-rosa.cz
Congenial pension in a Baroque house on the edge of town. Offers smart rooms with modern facilities.

ČESKÝ KRUMLOV: Leonardo ®®
Historic   Map C3
Soukenická 33, 381 01
Tel *380 725 911*
W hotel-leonardo.cz
Housed in a 16th-century building with lovely wooden ceilings and a Baroque staircase.

Stately room at the Grand Hotel Pupp, Karlovy Vary

HLUBOKÁ NAD VLTAVOU: Štekl ®®®
Luxury   Map C3
Bezručova 141, 373 41
Tel *387 967 491*
W hotelstekl.cz
Romantic hotel in a Neo-Gothic building with rooms remniscent of castle interiors.

JINDŘICHŮV HRADEC: Vajgar ®
Budget   Map D3
Náměstí Míru 162/1, 377 01
Tel *384 361 271*
W hotel-vajgar.cz
Decent, standard hotel set in former merchants' dwellings.

ROŽMBERK NAD VLTAVOU: Ruže ®
Historic   Map C3
Rožmberk nad Vltavou 78
Tel *775 661 067*
W hotel-ruze.cz
Located in a 17th-century Renaissance house beneath the castle. Romantic rooms.

SLAVONICE: Arkáda ®
Historic   Map D3
Náměstí Míru 466, 378 81
Tel *384 408 408*
W hotelarkada.cz
In a Renaissance house in the town square offering atmospheric rooms with mod cons.

TÁBOR: Nautilus ®®
Historic   Map C2
Žižkovo náměstí 20, 390 01
Tel *380 900 900*
W hotelnautilus.cz
Attractive, airy, high-ceilinged rooms with classy furnishings and artworks. Set in a historic building.

TŘEBOŇ: Zlata Hvezda ®®
Historic   Map D3
Masarykovo náměstí 107, 379 01
Tel *384 757 111*
W zlatahvezda.cz
Well-appointed, modern rooms in an arcaded Renaissance building,

with a small wellness centre and a handful of romantic, opulent apartments.

West Bohemia

DOMAŽLICE: Konšelský Šenk ®
Historic   Map B2
Vodní 33, 334 01
Tel *379 720 200*
W konselskysenk.cz
A medieval house with views of the castle. Spacious, atmospheric rooms.

DOMAŽLICE: Pension Family ®
Pension   Map B2
Školní 107, 334 01
Tel *379 725 962*
W pensionfamily.cz
Convenient location near the main square; functional but bright en-suites.

FRANTIŠKOVY LÁZNĚ: Spa Hotel Centrum ®
Spa hotel   Map B2
Anglická 392/5A, 351 01
Tel *354 543 156*
W spahotelcentrum.cz
Stylish hotel with a wellness centre next to the main spa park.

KARLOVY VARY: Kavalerie ®
Budget   Map B1
T G Masaryka 43, 360 01
Tel *353 229 613*
W kavalerie.cz
In the quiet pedestrian zone, with bright rooms and relaxing decor.

KARLOVY VARY: Hotel Čajkovskij ®®
Spa hotel   Map B1
Sadová 44, 360 01
Tel *353 402 111*
W cajkovskij.com
A four-star hotel in a historic building with grand rooms, a spa and a restaurant catering for special diets.

DK Choice

KARLOVY VARY: Grand Hotel Pupp ®®®
Spa hotel   Map B1
Mírové náměstí 2, 360 91
Tel *353 109 111*
W pupp.cz
One of the Czech Republic's most celebrated hotels dating back to the early 18th century. The richly furnished rooms come with dazzling bathrooms. Amenities include a casino, an impressive concert hall with Neo-Baroque interiors, and a fabulous spa and beauty centre.

For more information on types of hotels *see page 347*

LOKET: Bílý Kůň ⓦ
Historic **Map** B1
T G Masaryka 109, 357 33
Tel *352 661 809*
Ⓦ hotel-bilykun.cz
In a Neo-Renaissance house
often visited by J W Goethe, the
'White Horse' has classy rooms.

**MARIÁNSKÉ LÁZNĚ: Hotel
Maxim** ⓦⓦ
Spa hotel **Map** B2
Nehrova 141/1, 353 01
Tel *354 603 301*
Ⓦ hotelmaxim.cz
Neo-Classical building with a mix
of contemporary and vintage
furnishings. The spa offers an
extensive range of treatments.

PLZEŇ: Irida ⓦ
Historic **Map** C2
Na Poříčí 398/3, 301 00
Tel *725 479 418*
Ⓦ irida.cz
Interesting 19th-century hotel
with good views, modern rooms
and on-site sauna facilities.

**PLZEŇ: Hotel
Continental** ⓦⓦ
Boutique **Map** C2
Zbrojnická 8, 305 34
Tel *377 235 292*
Ⓦ hotelcontinental.cz
Handsome building near the
harbour with high-ceilinged,
individually themed rooms –
such as "Casablanca" and "Paris".

PLZEŇ: Hotel Rous ⓦⓦ
Historic **Map** C2
Zbrojnická 7, 301 15
Tel *377 320 260*
Ⓦ hotelrous.cz
An old burgher's house that
was once the city's first brothel,
Rous has atmospheric en-suites
with mod cons.

The restaurant at hotel U Jezirka in
Liberec, North Bohemia

North Bohemia

DĚČÍN: Hotel Faust ⓦ
Budget **Map** C1
U Plovárny 43, 405 01
Tel *412 518 859*
Ⓦ hotelfaust.cz
Well-appointed en-suite rooms
at this intimate spot next to a
fishpond near the town square.

HŘENSKO: Hotel Praha ⓦ
Boutique **Map** C1
Hrensko 37, 407 17
Tel *412 554 006*
Ⓦ hotel-hrensko.cz
Stylish hotel on the edge of
České Švýcarsko National Park,
with great service and facilities.

LIBEREC: Hotel Praha ⓦ
Historic **Map** D1
Železná 2/1, 460 01
Tel *485 102 655*
Ⓦ hotelpraha.net
Modern rooms and apartments
with some original fittings in a
lovely Art Nouveau building.

LIBEREC: U Jezirka ⓦ
Budget **Map** D1
Masarykova 44, 460 01
Tel *482 710 407*
Ⓦ hotelujezirka.cz
Charming hotel in a leafy area
next to the zoo, botanical
gardens and aqua park.

DK Choice

LIBEREC: Hotel Ještěd ⓦⓦ
Boutique **Map** D1
Horní Hanychov 153, 460 08
Tel *485 104 291*
Ⓦ jested.cz
Perched on the 1012-m (3320-ft)
summit of Ještěd hill, this hotel
occupies the futuristic TV and
observation tower designed
by Karel Hubáček in 1966. The
furnishings and curving walls
are reminiscent of a sci-fi
movie. Access is via cable car.

LITOMĚŘICE: Dejmalík ⓦ
Budget **Map** C1
Sovova 3, 412 01
Tel *416 533 660*
Ⓦ hoteldejmalik.cz
Pleasant hotel in an old
townhouse offering en-suite
rooms with whirlpool bathtubs.

TEPLICE: Hotel Payer ⓦⓦ
Historic **Map** C1
U Hadích lázní 1153/44, 415 01
Tel *417 531 446*
Ⓦ hotelpayer.cz
Well-appointed rooms and many
facilities in a Neo-Classical
building with spa park views.

East Bohemia

DVŮR KRÁLOVÉ: Safari ⓦⓦ
Boutique **Map** D1
Štefánikova 1029, 544 01
Tel *499 628 255*
Ⓦ hotelsafari.cz
Ranch-style hotel with rooms
around a courtyard, with pool
and bowling; zoo next door.

**HRADEC KRÁLOVÉ: Nové
Adalbertinum** ⓦ
Pension **Map** D2
Velké náměstí 32, 500 03
Tel *495 063 111*
Ⓦ noveadalbertinum.cz
A lovely Baroque building on
the main square, with simple
but smart en-suites with TVs.

DK Choice

**HRADEC KRÁLOVÉ: U
Královny Elišky** ⓦⓦ
Historic **Map** D2
Malé náměstí 117, 500 03
Tel *495 518 052*
Ⓦ hotelukralovnyelisky.cz
Nicely converted pair of
burghers' houses dating from
the 14th century in the historic
town centre. Look out for the
original cellars and vaulted
ceilings. The spa centre and
wine bar are a definite bonus.

JIČÍN: Jičín ⓦ
Budget **Map** D1
Havlíčkova 21, 506 01
Tel *493 544 250*
Ⓦ hoteljicin.cz
Neat welcoming en-suites
decked out in restful pastels.
Located near the Valdice Gate.

LITOMYŠL: Petra ⓦ
Budget **Map** E2
B. Němcové 166, 570 01
Tel *777 613 061*
Ⓦ pension-petra.cz
Friendly pension in an arcaded
building with en-suites, some
with original vaulted ceilings.

PARDUBICE: Hotel Zlatá Štika ⓦⓦ
Modern **Map** D2
Štrossova 127, 530 03
Tel *466 052 100*
Ⓦ zlatastika.cz
Stylish, contemporary hotel that
offers sunny rooms and a good
restaurant and beer hall.

TRUTNOV: Hotel Adam ⓦⓦ
Historic **Map** D1
Havlíčkova 10, 541 01
Tel *499 811 955*
Ⓦ hotel-adam.cz
In an old building near the main
square with snug rooms.

Aerial view of the splendid Jurkovičův Dům, Luhačovice

North Moravia & Silesia

DK Choice

ČELADNÁ: Hotel Miura ⓦⓦ
Boutique **Map** F2
Čeladná 887, 739 12
Tel *558 761 100*
🅦 miura.cz
Unique rural spa retreat located amid the rolling meadows of the green Beskydy hills. Angular steel-and-glass buildings on stilts house the 39 designer rooms and suites. Miura has state-of-the-art fitness and wellness facilities, an 18-hole golf course and a gourmet restaurant serving creative Czech cuisine.

JESENÍK: Hotel Nodus ⓦ
Budget **Map** E2
K vodě 430, 790 01
Tel *731 526 686*
🅦 nodus.hotel-cz.com
Views across Jeseníky mountains. Sauna and massage on site.

OLOMOUC: Pension U Jakuba ⓦ
Pension **Map** E2
Ulice 8. května 9, 772 00
Tel *585 209 995*
🅦 pensionujakuba.com
Friendly pension in the city centre offering spacious doubles and self-catering apartments.

OLOMOUC: Arigone ⓦⓦ
Boutique **Map** E2
Univerzitní 20, 779 00
Tel *585 232 350*
🅦 arigone.cz
Stylish hotel with exposed Romanesque stonework and fully-equipped rooms.

OLOMOUC: Trinity ⓦⓦ
Luxury **Map** E2
Pavelčákova 22, 772 00
Tel *581 830 811*
🅦 hotel-trinity.cz
Beautifully renovated 13th-century building with retro furniture, modern art and a restaurant.

OPAVA: Iberia ⓦⓦ
Boutique **Map** F2
Pekařská 11, 74 601
Tel *553 776 700*
🅦 hoteliberia.cz
A 19th-century town house with Spanish-influenced decor and contemporary amenities.

OSTRAVA: Brioni ⓦⓦ
Boutique **Map** F2
Stodolní 8, 702 00
Tel *599 500 000*
🅦 hotelbrioni.cz
In the nightlife district, Brioni integrates chic style with pre-World War I elegance. Conference facilities and sauna on site.

South Moravia

BRNO: Grandezza ⓦⓦ
Boutique **Map** E3
Zelný trh 374/2, 602 00
Tel *542 106 010*
🅦 grandezzahotel.cz
Art Deco-styled rooms and a central arcaded courtyard in a palatial building.

BRNO: Premier Hotel International ⓦⓦⓦ
Luxury **Map** E3
Husova 16, 659 21
Tel *542 122 111*
🅦 hotelinternational.cz
Contemporary business hotel providing smart, well-equipped rooms plus two restaurants.

KROMĚŘÍŽ: Bouček ⓦⓦ
Historic **Map** F3
Velké náměstí 108, 767 01
Tel *573 342 777*
🅦 hotelboucek.cz
Welcoming hotel in a Baroque building with tastefully appointed rooms, some with lovely views.

DK Choice

LUHAČOVICE: Jurkovičův Dům ⓦⓦ
Historic **Map** F3
Lázeňské náměstí 109, 763 26
Tel *577 682 100*
🅦 lazneluhacovice.cz
Designed in 1902 by Slovak arcitect Dušan Jurkovič, this hotel in Luhačovice spa park is a fanciful combination of Art Nouveau and Carpathian folk styles. It boasts well-preserved period decor, luxury rooms and extensive wellness facilities.

MIKULOV: Réva ⓦ
Budget **Map** E3
Česká 2, 692 01
Tel *519 512 076*
🅦 hotelreva.cz
In the centre of the wine-making town with intimate rooms and a pretty summer terrace.

TELČ: Penzion Steidler ⓦ
Budget **Map** D3
Náměstí Zachariáše z Hradce 52, 588 56
Tel *721 316 390*
🅦 telc-accommodation.eu
Housed in an arcaded building next to main square. Simple rooms, some with lake views.

TŘEBÍČ: Grand Hotel ⓦⓦ
Modern **Map** D3
Karlovo náměstí 5, 674 01
Tel *568 848 560*
🅦 grand-hotel.cz
Chic hotel with warm, wood-floored rooms, sauna, bowling alley and fitness club.

VRANOV NAD DYJÍ: Hotel pod Zamkem ⓦ
Historic **Map** D3
Náměstí 45, 671 03
Tel *607 742 270*
🅦 pod-zamkem.cz
In a 16th-century edifice, 'Below the Castle' offers bright rooms, including triples and quads.

ZNOJMO: Morava ⓦ
Budget **Map** D3
Horní náměstí 16, 669 01
Tel *515 224 147*
🅦 hotel-morava-znojmo.cz
On an old town square with comfortabe rooms and a cellar bar specializing in local wines.

For more information on types of hotels *see page 347*

Where to Stay in Slovakia

Bratislava

Botel Marina €
Boutique **Map** A6
Nábrežie arm. Gen. L. Svobodu, 811 02
Tel *(02) 54 64 18 04*
W botelmarina.sk
Cabins and suites in a boat moored at the foot of the castle with mod cons such as Internet.

Hostel Possonium €
Hostel **Map** A6
Šancová 3996/20
Tel *(02) 20 72 00 07*
W possonium.sk
Doubles and dorms decorated with comic-strip-style murals. Atmospheric brick-lined bar and garden café.

Hotel Bratislava €
Luxury **Map** A6
Seberíniho 9, 821 03
Tel *(02) 20 60 61 50*
W hotelbratislava.sk
One of the city's biggest hotels, with smart rooms, sports facilities and good public transport links. Near the airport.

Hotel Set €
Budget **Map** A6
Kalinčiakova 29A, 831 03
Tel *(02) 49 10 96 00*
W hotelset.sk
Utilitarian good-value hotel with quiet rooms in a sunny location. Wheelchair access and gym.

Hradna Brana Devin €
Pension **Map** A6
Slovanské nábrežie 15, Devin, 841 10
Tel *(02) 60 10 25 11*
W hotelhb.sk
Small, congenial hotel next to Devin castle. Restaurant, café and lobby bar on site.

Tilia €
Pension **Map** A6
Kollárova 20, Pezinok, 902 01
Tel *(033) 641 24 02*
W hoteltilia.sk
Set in the shadow of the Small Carpathians in a village famous for its wine. Rooms in warm hues.

Arcadia €€
Luxury **Map** A6
Františkánska 3, 811 01
Tel *(02) 59 49 05 00*
W arcadia-hotel.sk
High ceilings, rich textiles and old-school furnishings in this plush pied-à-terre in Old Town.

Loft €€
Boutique **Map** A6
Štefánikova 864/4, 811 05
Tel *(02) 57 51 10 00*
W lofthotel.sk
Modern and historic buildings connected by an atrium. Wooden-floored rooms with sleek furnishings.

Mamaison Sulekova €€
Luxury **Map** A6
Šulekova 20, 811 06
Tel *(02) 59 10 02 00*
W mamaison.com
Modern apartments near the castle with swish bathrooms and kitchen.

Park Inn €€
Luxury **Map** A6
Rybné námestie 1, 811 02
Tel *(02) 59 34 00 00*
W parkinn.com
In the pedestrianized zone with plush rooms and an indoor pool.

Radisson Blu Carlton €€
Luxury **Map** A6
Hviezdoslavovo nám. 3, 811 02
Tel *(02) 59 39 00 00*
W radissonblu.com
Occupying a fine 19th-century building in the Old Town. Fantastic cocktails at Mirror Bar.

Tatra €€
Historic **Map** A6
Námestie 1 Mája, 811 06
Tel *(02) 59 27 21 11*
W hoteltatra.sk
A 1930s-vintage building with neat rooms, many with views of the presidential palace.

Tulip House €€
Boutique **Map** A6
Štúrova 15/10, 811 02
Tel *(02) 32 17 18 19*
W tuliphousehotel.com
Interesting, Art Nouveau building named for the tulip

Parking area outside Hotel Bratislava in the Slovak capital

design on the façade and retro furnishings.

Areal Zoska €€€
Pension **Map** A6
Piesok, Modra, 900 01
Tel *0905 769 866*
W zoska.sk
A 30-minute drive from the city, this alpine-style cottage has charming rooms, a garden and an outdoor pool.

DK Choice

Marrol's €€€
Boutique **Map** A6
Tobrucká 4, 811 02
Tel *(02) 57 78 46 00*
W hotelmarrols.sk
The rooms and apartments at the exclusive Marrol's come in a range of sizes. The furnishings are retro-styled, but conveniences ultra-modern. Excellent service with great attention to detail. Also offers a fine restaurant, well-equipped gym and business facilities on site.

Sheraton Bratislava €€€
Luxury **Map** A6
Pribinova 12, 811 09
Tel *(02) 35 35 00 00*
W sheratonbratislava.com
Riverside location, plus an impressive range of facilities including a pool and café-bars.

West Slovakia

KOMÁRNO: Bow Garden . €
Boutique **Map** B6
Štúrova 1017, 945 01
Tel *(035) 773 22 37*
W hotelbowgarden.sk
Housed in a former synagogue and winery with squash courts, bowling alley and gym.

LEVICE: Levi Dom €
Pension **Map** C6
Tyršova 10, 934 01
Tel *(036) 634 55 14*
W levidom.sk
A functional building with warm interiors that boast a distinct Mediterranean flavour.

The impressive façade of Hotel Thermia Palace, Piešťany

MALACKY: Hotel Atrium €
Pension   Map A5
Zámocká 1, 901 01
Tel *(034) 772 31 63*
w hotel-malacky.sk
Snug rooms in a quiet location,
plus a restaurant and café.

NITRA: Capital €
Modern   Map B6
Farská 16, 949 01
Tel *(037) 692 52 01*
w hotelcapital.sk
Stylish rooms and slick
service. Handful of wheelchair-
accessible rooms.

NITRA: Park Hotel Tartuf €
Historic   Map B6
Pusty Chotár 495, Beladice, 951 75
Tel *(037) 633 02 35*
w tartuf.sk
Beautifully designed interiors
and a music room in a wonderful
Neo-Classical manor house.

NITRA: Hotel Zlaty Kľ'učik €€
Modern   Map B6
Svätourbánska 27, 949 01
Tel *(037) 655 02 89*
w zlatyklucik.sk
Contemporary building on
the slopes of Mt Zobor, with
elegantly furnished rooms,
some offering sweeping views.

NOVÉ ZÁMKY: Hubert €
Pension   Map B6
Budovateľská 2, 940 60
Tel *915 77 82 38*
w hubertnz.sk
An intimate hotel just outside
town, with comfortable rooms,
professional service and a
renowned game restaurant.

NOVÉ ZÁMKY: Hotel Grand €€
Modern   Map B6
Pribinova 19, 940 01
Tel *(035) 640 44 24*
w hotelgrandnz.sk
Well-appointed three-star with
spacious rooms, many with
atmospheric attic ceilings.

**PIEŠŤANY: Balnea Esplanade
Palace** €
Spa hotel   Map B5
Kúpelny ostrov, 921 29
Tel *(033) 775 51 11*
w danubiushotels.com
Set amid lush parkland with spa,
massage and beauty treatments.

**PIEŠŤANY: Hotel Thermia
Palace** €€
Spa hotel   Map B5
Kúpelny ostrov, 921 29
Tel *(033) 775 61 11*
w danubiushotels.com
Elegant hotel in an Art Nouveau
edifice linked to the main spa
building next to Water World.

SENEC: Senec €€
Modern   Map B6
Slnečné jazerá-Sever, 903 01
Tel *(02) 45 92 72 55*
w hotelsenec.sk
Close to the Sunny Lakes
recreational zone with swimming,
sports and conference facilities.

ŠTÚROVO: Hotel Thermal €
Spa hotel   Map C6
Pri Vadáši 2, 943 01
Tel *(036) 756 01 11*
w vadas.sk
Utilitarian building next to the
Vadaš thermal baths complex,
offering rooms and apartments.

SVÄTY JUR: Maxim €
Budget   Map B6
Bratislavská 52/11
Tel *(02) 44 97 07 42*
w hotelmaxim.sk
Small hotel in a wine producing
village with neat rooms, restaurant
and cellar.

TRENČIANSKE TEPLICE: Flora €
Spa hotel   Map B5
17 novembra 14, 914 51
Tel *(032) 655 45 55*
w hotelflora.sk
Set in leafy grounds in the heart
of the spa resort, with simple but
comfortable rooms.

**TRENČIANSKE TEPLICE: Hotel
Margit** €
Historic   Map B5
T G Masaryka 2, 914 51
Tel *(032) 655 10 28*
w hotel-margit.webnode.sk
Well-equipped spa hotel with
a wellness centre and fine
dining housed in an imposing
old building.

TRENČÍN: Penzion Evergreen €
Pension   Map B5
Kubranská 8, 911 01
Tel *(032) 444 16 71*
w penzionevergreen.sk
A pleasant place to stay on the
outskirts of town with modern
furnishings and its own
restaurant and bar.

TRENČÍN: Hotel Elizabeth €€
Boutique   Map B5
M R Štefanika 2, 911 01
Tel *(032) 650 61 11*
w hotelelizabeth.sk
Named after the ill-fated
Habsburg Empress Elizabeth,
this grand Art Nouveau building
offers neat modernized rooms
and an appealing café.

TRNAVA: Penzion u MaMi €
Pension   Map B5
Jeruzalemská 3, 917 01
Tel *(033) 535 42 16*
w penzionumami.sk
On a quiet street near the
cathedral with 11 comfortable
rooms and a few apartments.

DK Choice

TRNAVA: Hotel Prestige €€
Boutique   Map B5
Sladovnicka 1523, 917 01
Tel *(033) 591 79 11*
w hotelprestige.sk
Designed by an award-
winning firm of architects,
Prestige is situated in a former
industrial zone which is
being revived as a business
park. Rooms are stylishly
decorated in a sensual range
of bronze and amber tones,
with fittings that are both
chic and practical. Trnava's
historic centre is within easy
walking distance.

Central Slovakia

BANSKÁ BYSTRICA: Dixon €
Family-friendly   Map C5
Švermova 32, 974 01
Tel *(048) 471 78 00*
w dixon.sk
A sports hotel and congress
centre with smart rooms, plus
tennis, squash and bowling.

For more information on types of hotels *see page 347*

BANSKÁ BYSTRICA: Hotel Lux €
Budget   Map C5
Námestie Slobody 2, 974 00
Tel *(048) 414 41 41*
W hotellux.sk
Pleasant rooms and efficient
service in a modern, concrete
70s-era hotel in the town centre.

**BANSKÁ ŠTIAVNICA: Penzion
Nostalgia** €
Pension   Map C5
Višnovského 3, 969 01
Tel *(090) 536 03 07*
W nostalgia.stiavnica.sk
This small inn, in a 16th-century
building, mixes traditional with
modern and quirky design.

**BANSKÁ ŠTIAVNICA:
Salamander** €
Historic   Map C5
J. Palárika 1, 969 01
Tel *(045) 691 39 92*
W hotelsalamander.sk
Centrally located in a pre-World
War I building with plain, neat
rooms and apartments.

BOJNICE: Kaskada €
Family-friendly   Map C5
Jánošikova 1301/24
Tel *(046) 518 30 10*
W kaskada.sk
Modern hotel with its own aqua
park and fully-equipped rooms.

BREZNO: Partizan €€€
Spa hotel   Map D5
Tále 108, Bystrá, 977 65
Tel *(048) 630 88 13*
W partizan.sk
On the fir-clad slopes of the Low
Tatras, this well-equipped resort
offers wellness facilities.

**DEMÄNOVSKA DOLINA: Hotel
Sorea SNP** €
Budget   Map D4
Jasná pod Chopkom 032 51
Tel *(044) 559 16 61*
W sorea.sk
Functional yet comfortable resort
hotel in a beautiful valley near
Jasná skiing region.

**DEMÄNOVSKA DOLINA: Hotel
Chopok** €€
Family-friendly   Map D4
Demänovská Dolina 20, 031 01
Tel *(044) 559 14 88*
W hotelchopok.sk
Smart rooms in a chalet-style
building with indoor pools, spa
and facilities for young children.

GERLACHOV: Hotel Hubert €
Family-friendly   Map D4
Gerlachov 302
Tel *(052) 478 08 11*
W hotel-hubert.sk
Opposite High Tatras' peaks with
horse-riding, baby-sitting and
other facilities.

LIPTOVSKÝ JÁN: Penzion Una €
Pension   Map D4
Starojánska 25, 032 03
Tel *(044) 526 33 29*
W penzionuna.sk
Family-run place with its own
wellness centre and a lovely
mountain-village location.

**LIPTOVSKÝ JÁN: Liptovsky
Dvor** €€
Family-friendly   Map D4
Jánska Dolina 438, 032 03
Tel *918 683 123*
W liptovskydvor.com
A holiday village of timber
chalets with access to ski slopes.

**LIPTOVSKÝ MIKULAŠ: Holiday
Village Tatralandia** €€
Family-friendly   Map D4
Ráztocká 21, 031 05
Tel *(044) 566 10 11*
W tatralandia.sk
Well-equipped family-sized cottages
next to Tatralandia aqua park.

MARTIN: Hotel Turiec €
Boutique   Map C4
A. Sokolika 2, 036 01
Tel *(043) 401 20 77*
W hotelturiec.sk
Renovated town-centre block
offering designer rooms with
contemporary facilities.

**PRIBYLINA: Grand Hotel
Permon** €€
Spa hotel   Map D4
Pribylina 1486, 032 42
Tel *(052) 471 01 11*
W hotelpermon.sk
Large rooms in a traditional
resort with steam baths, sports
facilities and mountain views.

RUŽOMBEROK: Kultura €
Historic   Map C4
Antona Bernoláka 1, 034 01
Tel *(044) 431 31 11*
W hotelkultura.sk
A characterful 1920s building
retaining many original features.
Convenient location.

STARÉ HORY: Altenberg €
Spa hotel   Map C5
Staré Hory 976 02
Tel *(048) 419 92 00*
W altenberg.sk
Chalet-style hotel that has
rooms with great views. Sauna
and massage facilities.

**STARÝ SMOKOVEC: Hotel
Smokovec** €
Modern   Map D4
Stary Smokovec 25, 062 01
Tel *(052) 442 51 91*
W hotelsmokovec.sk
Pleasant balconied rooms in a
hotel that makes a perfect base
for exploring the High Tatras.

The rustic Penzion Nostalgia, Banská Štiavnica

View of the courtyard at Bankov
Hotel, Košice

ŠTRBSKÉ PLESO: Hotel Patria €€
Modern   Map D4
Štrbské Pleso 059 85
Tel *(052) 449 25 91*
W hotelpatria.sk
Surrounded by high-altitude
scenery. Pleasant rooms, lots of
facilities and top-notch service.

TATRANSKÁ LOMNICA:
Tatranec   €
Family-friendly   Map E4
Tatranská Lomnica 202
Tel *(052) 446 70 92*
W hoteltatranec.com
A hotel and camp site in a scenic
mountain setting with a range of
activities on offer.

ŽDIAR: Ginger Monkey Hostel €
Budget   Map E4
Ždiar 294, 059 55
Tel *(052) 449 80 84*
W gingermonkey.eu
A cult backpacking destination
with dorms and doubles in a
traditional cottage.

ŽILINA: Dubná Skala €€
Boutique   Map C4
Hurbanova 345/8, 010 01
Tel *(041) 507 91 00*
W hoteldubnaskala.sk
Housed in a 19th-century building
with swish doubles and design-
conscious apartments.

East Slovakia

BARDEJOV: Bellevue €
Budget   Map E4
Mihálov 2503, 085 01
Tel *(054) 472 84 04*
W bellevuehotel.sk
Situated on a hillock in a green
suburban area, the family-
oriented Bellevue offers neat
en-suites, some with views.

KEŽMAROK: Hotel Club €
Historic   Map E4
Dr Alexandra 24, 060 01
Tel *(052) 452 40 51*
W hotelclubkezmarok.sk
An intimate hotel in a historic
building with bright interiors and
a restaurant specializing in game.

KOŠICE: Ambassador €
Modern   Map F5
Hlavná 101, 040 01
Tel *(055) 720 37 20*
W ambassador.sk
Traditional structure with
modernized rooms, including
some cosy en-suites in the attic.

KOŠICE: Bankov €€
Luxury   Map F5
Dolný Bankov 2, 040 01
Tel *(055) 632 45 22*
W hotelbankov.sk
Romantic retreat just beside a
quiet woodland, with plush rooms,
a stylish restaurant and a spa.

KOŠICE: Dalia €€
Pension   Map F5
Löfflerova 1, 040 01
Tel *(055) 799 43 21*
W hoteldalia.sk
Small family hotel with attractive
rooms, some featuring exposed
brick walls.

KOŠICE: Yasmin €€
Boutique   Map F5
Tyršovo nábrežie 1, 040 01
Tel *(055) 795 11 00*
W hotel-yasmin.sk
A 10-storey building packed with
thoughtful design and offering
suave, well-equipped rooms and
a wellness centre.

LEVOČA: Arkada €
Pension   Map E4
Námestie Majstra Pavla 26, 054 01
Tel *(053) 451 23 72*
W arkada.sk
Airy ensuites in a building from
the late middle ages, in Levoča's
evocative town square.

LEVOČA: Hotel Stela Levoča €
Historic   Map E4
Námestie Majstra Pavla 55, 054 01
Tel *(053) 451 29 43*
W hotelstela.sk
This landmark hotel in a
14th-century building offers smart
ensuites and modern comforts.

MEDZILABORCE: Eurohotel
Laborec €
Historic   Map F4
Andyho Warhola 195/28
Tel *(057) 732 13 07*
W eurohotel.sk
Renovated 1970s-era hotel;
a smart, well-located option
near the Andy Warhol Museum.

POPRAD: Hotel Seasons €€
Spa hotel   Map E4
Športová 1397/1, 058 01
Tel *(052) 785 12 22*
W aquacityhotel.sk
Stylish hotel that is part of an
aquapark fed by thermal waters.
Spa treatments and sports.

DK Choice

PREŠOV: Kaštieľ Fričovce €
Boutique   Map F4
Fričovce 4
Tel *(051) 791 10 67*
W kastielfricovce.sk
Situated in the beautiful
countryside of the Upper Šariš
region, this small hotel offers
romantic apartments in
Fričovce's Renaissance castle
and double rooms in one of the
outbuildings. Rustic furnishings,
but up-to-date facilities such
as free Wi-Fi.

PREŠOV: Šariš Park €
Spa hotel   Map F4
Železničná 1900, Veľký Šariš, 082 21
Tel *(051) 747 04 22*
W sarispark.sk
Spa and swimming centre
offering accommodation in
Carpathian log cabins.

PREŠOV: Dukla €€
Modern   Map F4
Námestie Legionárov 2, 080 01
Tel *(051) 772 27 41*
W hotelduklapresov.sk
A 50s-era concrete block,
transformed into a modern
business hotel in the town centre.

ROŽŇAVA: Čierny Orol €
Pension   Map E5
Námestie baníkov 17, 048 01
Tel *(058) 732 81 86*
W ciernyorol.sk
Simply-furnished but charming
accommodation in a old,
merchant's house.

SPIŠSKÁ NOVÁ VES: Hotel
Metropol €
Spa hotel   Map E5
Štefánikovo námestie 2, 052 01
Tel *(053) 417 47 00*
W hotel-metropol.sk
Smart, high-rise hotel based
around spa and wellness
facilities. Free Wi-Fi.

SPIŠSKÉ PODHRADIE: Hotel
Kapitula €€
Historic   Map E4
Spišská Kapitula 15, 053 04
Tel *(053) 454 25 81*
W hotelkapitula.eu
Spacious en-suites in a restored
canonry with a nice mix of old
and new furnishings.

For more information on types of hotels *see page 347*

WHERE TO EAT AND DRINK

The cuisines of both republics are typical of Central Europe, with hearty portions of meat, poultry and dumplings accompanied by fine beers and wines. In the Czech Republic, most restaurants serve the classic Czech culinary repertoire *(see pp360–61)*, although the number of establishments offering a fusion of Czech, modern European and global styles is on the increase, especially in the cities. Czech beer is world famous *(see p362)*, and beer halls are among the best places to eat in many towns. Similarly in Slovakia, restaurants serve classic Slovak cheese-and-dumplings dishes or modern, experimental variations on traditional themes. International cuisine is available in both countries, with Italian, Chinese, Mexican and Japanese food being most popular. Czechs and Slovaks enjoy eating out at any time, and you will find that traditional eateries and pubs are usually busy and also welcoming.

Art Deco interiors of Café Savoy, a Prague eatery popular for its schnitzels *(see p364)*

Eating Places

In the Czech Republic, the word *restaurace* (restaurant) is a very broad term – it can apply to a luxurious establishment serving expensive and sophisticated gourmet meals, or a popular local inn offering simple food, beer and spirits. Other types of eating places include *občerstvení*, a type of buffet bar with a limited selection of fast food, such as stews, soups or frankfurters. *Vinárna* (wine bars) usually serve food, as do some *kavárna* (cafés). Pubs known as *hospoda* or *hostinec* serve good-value, basic Czech food. There are many bistros serving modern-European cuisine, salads and sandwiches. Ice-cream kiosks, pizzerias and burger chains are all popular.

In Slovakia, you will find plenty of *reštaurácia* (restaurants) clustered within large towns and main tourist regions. A *koliba* or *salaš* is a good choice if you want to taste traditional Slovak cuisine – especially the ubiquitous *bryndzové halušky* or noodles with sheep's cheese. A *vináreň* or wine cellar usually offers tasty food. A Slovak *pivnica* or *piváreň* (pub) also serves meals, but at cheaper rates. *Občerstvenie* (Slovak buffets) serve simple hot dishes as well as a large selection of hearty potato salads, mixed with sausage, eggs and sometimes fish. In bigger towns, a range of fast-food restaurants and pizzerias can be found.

Opening Hours

Czech and Slovak restaurants usually open at 10am (sometimes at noon in Slovakia) and close at 10pm, or later. In small towns, eating places might close at 9pm and may have one or two days off per week – usually Monday and Tuesday. In mountain areas such as the Krkonoše in the Czech Republic or the Tatras in Slovakia, restaurants may open only during the summer and winter tourist seasons. Buffet bars in both countries are usually open all day from about 6am.

Prices and Tips

Prices of meals in Czech restaurants vary considerably. In small towns, a meal with beer usually costs 120–150Kč, or less, per person. Smart restaurants in bigger towns, particularly in Prague, are likely to charge up to several hundred crowns for a similar meal.

In Slovakia, you can have a two-course meal with dessert, in a reasonable restaurant, for €10–€25, and in the best establishments in Bratislava for about €50.

In both republics, service is not included in the price. It is customary, particularly in smart restaurants, to leave a tip of a dozen or so crowns, or 10 per cent of the bill. Credit cards are accepted by an increasing number of restaurants in both countries, but may be refused in small towns or rural regions.

International Menu

Menus written in Czech, English, German and Russian can be found at most restaurants in Prague. Elsewhere, English-language menus are fairly

Alfresco dining on the terrace of Krumlovsky Mlyn, Český Krumlov *(see p370)*

Restaurant Le Monde, opposite the Opera in Bratislava *(see p377)*

common, except in the provinces where the menu will be available only in Czech or Slovak. Daily specials are generally chalked on a blackboard placed outside the restaurant. For assistance with understanding a Czech menu, *see p431*; for a Slovak menu *see p432*.

When to Eat

Breakfast in the Czech and Slovak republics does not differ much from those in other Central European countries, usually consisting of tea, coffee, rolls, cheese and cold meat. Upmarket hotels offer a wider breakfast choice. Lunch is often hearty but is served and eaten quickly. Restaurants fill up in the evening, mainly with beer drinkers. Snacks are popular at any time, with plenty of sweet and savoury options available *(see p360)*.

Reservations

Tables can be reserved by telephone. Some restaurants can be booked via their website. There is no need to book for lunchtimes, but if you are planning a dinner on a Friday or Saturday evening, particularly in one of Prague's or Bratislava's better-known eating places, it is advisable to contact them and make a reservation in advance.

Dress Code

Czechs and Slovaks tend to dress casually and are not too set on formality, so it is generally not necessary to dress up when going to a restaurant.

Children

A number of restaurants in both republics offer high chairs for children, children's menus, and many will provide half-portions of the main-course dishes on request. Menus often include some children's favourites: pancakes (*palačinky* in Czech; *palacinky* in Slovak) with a variety of fillings, usually accompanied by fruit and topped with cream; and chips (*hranolky* in Czech; *hranolčeky* in Slovak).

Vegetarians

Meat is central to Czech and Slovak cuisine and it is hard to find dedicated vegetarian restaurants outside the capitals. In the main cities, some upmarket places offer menus with a section called "meatless dishes" (*bezmasá jídla* in Czech, *bezmäsité jedlá* in Slovak), although these often consist of cheese fried in breadcrumbs and very little else.

Disabled Guests

Restaurants providing good, level access are few and far between in both countries. The situation is slightly better in summer, when many restaurants have outdoor seating accessible from the pavement.

Smoking

In the Czech Republic, some restaurants permit smoking while others ban it completely; most have a separate room for smokers. However, smoking is totally prohibited in all other public places and is illegal for those under the age of 18. In Slovakia, a wall must separate smoking and non-smoking areas.

Recommended Restaurants

The restaurants listed in this guidebook have been chosen for a wide range of reasons and criteria. They are all representative of their setting, be that Prague, Bratislava, the historic towns of southern Bohemia or the mountain villages of Slovakia. Each stands out and has earned a noteworthy reputation.

Listings cover a vast variety of eateries, from simple, family-run taverns to contemporary bistros, formal white-tablecloth restaurants, and designer gourmet destinations. Particular attention is given to regional specialities, from the pork-and-dumplings of Bohemia to the roast fowl and fish stews of Slovakia.

The "DK Choice" label means the restaurant is highly recommended as it may serve especially outstanding preparations of local specialities, offer excellent value for money, be located in beautiful surrounds, a historically important building, a romantic atmosphere or be particularly charming. Whatever the reason, "DK Choice" guarantees a memorable meal.

Elegant dining area of La Degustation, an upscale restaurant in Prague *(see p366)*

The Flavours of the Czech and Slovak Republics

There is only a small difference between the cuisines of the Czech and Slovak Republics. Both base their cooking around Central European staples such as potatoes, rice and cabbage, along with meat such as pork or beef, or fish such as carp or trout, which are almost always roasted or grilled, and accompanied by light sauces and vegetables. The national food in the Czech Republic is *vepřo knedlo zelo*, a combination of pork, bread dumplings and sauerkraut. The Slovakian national food is called *bryndzové halušky*, consisting of special gnocchi noodles with original sheep cheese and bacon.

Blueberries

Atmospheric U Pinkasů cellar bar and restaurant, Prague *(see p367)*

Meat

In both the Czech Republic and Slovakia, the favourite is pork *(vepřové/bravčové)*. It is served as steaks, chops or stuffed. It also appears in goulash, hams and sausages. Dumplings, frequently in slices, may be served on the plate with pork. Don't miss the celebrated Prague ham *(Pražská šunka)*, a succulent, lightly smoked meat usually eaten with bread at breakfast or with horseradish as a starter in the evening. Veal, usually served as Wiener schnitzel *(smažený řízek/vyprážaný syr)*, is popular and good. In Slovakia, try the local goulash, *segedínsky guláš*, a combination of stewed pork, sauerkraut, spices and cream.

Beef in the region is not up to international standards, and needs to be prepared well to be edible. Most beef in top restaurants is likely to be imported. The Czech favourite is *Pražská hovězí pečeně*, roast beef stuffed with bacon, ham, cheese, onion and eggs. When it is cooked long and slow, it can be tender

Apple strudel   Eclair

Fruit buns   Chocolate cake

Plum jam bun

Apple crumble tart

Selection of typical Czech and Slovak cakes and pastries

Regional Dishes and Specialities

Stuffed eggs

Knedlíky (dumplings), either savoury *(špekové)* in soups or sweet *(ovocné)* with fruits and berries, are perhaps the Czech Republic's best-known delicacy. Once a mere side dish, they have now become a central feature of the nation's cuisine as chefs rediscover their charms and experiment with new and different ways of cooking and serving them. In Slovakia, crêpes *(palacinky)* play a similar role, and are eaten savoury as an appetizer or sweet as a dessert. The Slovaks do have a famous dumpling dish, however: *bryndzové pirohy* are stuffed with sheep's cheese and topped with bacon. Other specialities of the region include *drštková polévka/držková polievka*, a remarkably good tripe soup which, although an acquired taste, has seen a revival in recent years as better restaurants add it to their menus.

Rybacia polievka Halászlé
In southern Slovakia, try this spicy fish soup, made with carp, trout and mackerel.

Wild chanterelle mushrooms from the forests across the region

and delicious. In Slovakia, you will find *viedenská roštenka*, a sirloin steak fried with onions. Czech or Slovak lamb *(jehněčí/ jahňacie)* is not the best, either, though from mid-March to mid-May, good lamb is available in markets. Lambs are usually sold whole, with the head, which is used to make soup.

Game and Poultry

A wide variety of game is found in the forests around Prague as well as the Slovak mountains. In autumn, you will find duck, pheasant, goose, boar, rabbit, venison and hare on many menus. Duck is perhaps the most popular game dish, usually roasted with fruit or sometimes chestnuts, and served with red cabbage. Small pheasants, roasted whole with juniper and blueberries or cranberries, are also popular; venison is served grilled with mushrooms. Hare and rabbit are usually served in rich, peppery sauces.

Chicken is also very popular and many restaurants roast them on a spit, known as *grilované kurča*.

Fish

Fish is more popular in Slovakia than in the Czech Republic but, in both, fresh carp *(kapr/kapor)* is the traditional Christmas meal, usually baked and served with potato salad. Trout is often stuffed with almonds, and grilled.

Fresh vegetables on display at a Prague market stall

Vegetables

Vegetables in both countries are excellent, if strictly seasonal. However, they can be overcooked. Although more imported, out-of-season vegetables are appearing in supermarkets; they command high prices. As a result, the cabbage is both countries' top vegetable, especially in winter, used raw as a salad or boiled and served with meats. Sauerkraut is ubiquitous.

BEST LOCAL SNACKS

Sausages Street stalls and snack bars in cities and towns sell traditional sausages *(klobásy* and *utopenci)*, frankfurters *(párky)* or bratwurst, served in a soft roll with mustard.

Chlebíčky Open sandwiches on sliced baguettes are found in Czech city delicatessens or snack bars. Toppings are usually ham, salami or cheese, always accompanied by a gherkin *(okurkou)*.

Oštiepok Delicate sheep cheese sold in most food shops, some markets and sheep farms throughout Slovakia.

Syrečky These tasty cheese rounds from Olomouc have a pungent aroma and are served with beer and onions.

Palačinky Pancakes are filled with sweet cheese, fruits or jam, and are topped with hot chocolate or lashings of sugar.

Plněná paprika
Peppers stuffed with mince and rice, in a spicy tomato sauce, are very popular.

Vepřové s křenem/ Bravčové s chrenom
Roasted pork with red cabbage and sauerkraut or horseradish.

Ovocné knedlíky/knedle
Sweet dumplings are filled with fruit, usually blueberries or plums.

What to Drink

Beer is the most celebrated drink in both the Czech and Slovak Republics. But perhaps nowhere else in Europe is alcohol so freely available and in so many forms. In both countries, you can buy it not only in late-night shops and in almost all eating places, but even, for example, in railway station kiosks and buffets; these often serve wine and spirits alongside beer. Yet the best way to enjoy a drink is to join the locals for a glass or a tankard of beer in one of the many inns known as *hospoda* in Czech and *hostinec* in Slovak. You could also step into a beer hall or a wine bar where you can sample a wider range of drinks, and these are often accompanied by food.

Vinotéka sv. Urbana – a famous wine shop in Bratislava

Beer garden by the Vltava river in Prague

Beer (Pivo)

Both countries have many breweries. Normally served by the half-litre, beer is classed using the Balling scale, which measures the amount of sugar before fermentation. The most common types are *dvanáctka* (12 degrees) and *desítka* (10 degrees), *dvanáctka* being the stronger.

Favourite Beers

The best Czech beers are considered by many to be Pilsner Urquell (Plzeňský Prazroj) and Gambrinus, both made in Plzeň, Budvar from České Budějovice, Staropramen from Prague, Kozel from Velké Popovice and Zubr from Přerov.

In Slovakia, the most popular beers are Zlatý Bažant (Golden Pheasant), Corgoň, Topvar, Šariš and Kelt.

Czech Velkopopovický Kozel Beer Label
In the Czech Republic and Slovakia, the word *světlé* describes light beer. In both countries, you can also get a dark lager (*tmavé*).

Gambrinus (Czech)

Pilsner Urquell (Czech)

Kelt (Slovak)

Zlatý Bažant (Slovak)

Regent (Czech)

Budvar (Czech)

Wines

Although they are not big players in the international wine market, the Czech and Slovak Republics have a strong wine culture. Most Czech wine is grown in South Moravia, bordering Austria, but the Elbe Valley also produces fine wines including the Mělník variety.

The main region for wine in Slovakia is on the southern slopes of the Carpathian Mountains, but there are other wine producing towns closer to Bratislava including Pezinok, Modra, Nitra and Levice. In the east of Slovakia lies the world-famous Tokaj wine district (shared with Hungary), which produces sweet wines.

Rulandské Biele, a white wine from Slovakia

White wine from Moravia (Czech Republic)

Czech wines in boxes decorated with Art Nouveau paintings by Alfons Mucha

Spirits and Liqueurs

Those who like to sample stronger drinks in the Czech Republic can choose from a number of spirits, clear and flavoured. A flavoured spirit particularly worth recommending is *meruňkovice*, which has a delicate apricot flavour. Also popular is *slivovice*, a plum brandy. The best-known of the herb-flavoured spirits is Becherovka from the spa town of Karlovy Vary. Also worth trying is the slightly bitter *fernet*.

In Slovakia, there are several interesting spirits, including the juniper-flavoured *borovička*, produced from local berries and slightly resembling gin. There are two types of *demänovka* liqueur, the herbal (*bylinná*) and the dry (*horká*).

Becherovka (Czech Republic)

Borovička Spiš (Slovakia)

Trenčianske Hradné (Slovakia)

Soft Drinks

Popular Czech and Slovak soft drinks (*nealko*) include Vinea and Kofola. Vinea is a drink produced from grape juice, and there are white (Vinea biela) and red (Vinea červená) varieties. Kofola is a cola-type drink. Slovaks drink a lot of mineral water. The country has 1,657 registered sources of mineral water, 106 of them commercially exploited. The most popular Slovak mineral waters include Budiš (a source regularly utilized since 1573), Fatra, Kláštorná, Baldovská and Ľubovnianka. Mineral water is also very popular in the Czech Republic. The best-known local brands include Mattoni, a fizzy water from Karlovy Vary, and Dobrá Voda. In both countries, mineral water is relatively inexpensive.

The most popular Slovak mineral waters

Becher, a Mineral Water Cup
Traditionally used in spas to take the waters, this cup is named after Dr Jan Becher, the first person to conduct scientific analysis of the mineral waters in Karlovy Vary.

Where to Eat and Drink in the Czech Republic

Prague

Hradčany and Malá Strana

Bohemia Bagel Ⓚ
International **Map** 2 E3
Lázeňská 19, Praha 1
Tel *257 218 192*
Busy café offering a bumper choice of freshly baked bagels plus soups, sandwiches and healthy salads. Mains include vegetable chili and chicken burgers.

DK Choice

Café Lounge Ⓚ Ⓚ
International **Map** 2 E5
Plaská 615/8, Praha 1
Tel *257 404 020*
A go-to place from morning till night with beautiful interiors, including a secret courtyard. Serves great coffee, tasty breakfast, sandwiches and delicious fresh soup. The creative one- or two-course daily menus offer imaginative, filling fare with plenty of vegetarian options. Good selection of pastries and desserts.

Gitanes Ⓚ Ⓚ
International **Map** 2 E3
Tržiště 7, Praha 1
Tel *257 530 163*
Offers a well-chosen menu of Italian, French and Spanish cuisine featuring plenty of seafood and vegetarian options. The wine list is first class.

Kočár z Vidne Ⓚ Ⓚ
Central European **Map** 2 F4
Saská 520/3, Praha 1
Tel *777 043 793*
The 'Vienna Coachman' serves traditional Austrian cuisine in friendly intimacy. The Wiener schnitzel is among the best in the city; *Zwiebelrostbraten* (roast beef with onions) also comes recommended.

Konírna Ⓚ Ⓚ
Czech **Map** 2 E4
Maltézské náměstí 10, Praha 1
Tel *257 534 121*
Traditional Czech cooking with a modern twist. Konírna's chefs take their inspiration from old recipe books but add their own unique touch to produce some of Malá Strana's most imaginative cuisine.

Malostranská Beseda Ⓚ Ⓚ
Czech **Map** 2 E3
Malostranské náměstí 21, Praha 1
Tel *257 409 112*
Classic Czech food and beer served in an elegant building in the heart of Malá Strana. This buzzing lunch spot is known for its daily specials.

Nebozízek Ⓚ Ⓚ
International **Map** 2 D5
Petřínské sady 411, Praha 1
Tel *257 315 329*
One of the city's best park restaurants, offering indoor and outdoor dining with great views. Standard, reasonable fare.

Alchymist Ⓚ Ⓚ Ⓚ
International **Map** 2 D3
Nosticova 1, Praha 1
Tel *257 312 518* **Closed** *Sun & Mon*
In an interior that looks like a medieval alchemist's laboratory, this popular restaurant offers French and Lebanese cuisine. Delightful summer garden.

Café de Paris Ⓚ Ⓚ Ⓚ
French **Map** 2 E4
Maltézské náměstí 4, Praha 1
Tel *603 160 718*
Considered one of the best French brasseries in Prague – a family-run café with a small dining room, an excellent menu and a handsome selection of French wines.

Café Savoy Ⓚ Ⓚ Ⓚ
Café **Map** 2 F5
Vitezná 5, Praha 1
Tel *257 311 562*
Charming bustling spot with original Art Deco interiors, that

Welcoming interior of Prague's Café Lounge with leather and wood furnishings

---

Price Guide

Prices are based on a three-course meal for one, including half a bottle of wine, tax and service.

Ⓚ	under 500Kč
Ⓚ Ⓚ	500–800Kč
Ⓚ Ⓚ Ⓚ	over 800Kč

---

serves lovely coffee, good breakfasts, light lunches, filling soups and the famously crisp and succulent Wiener schnitzels.

Coda Ⓚ Ⓚ Ⓚ
International **Map** 2 E3
Tržiště 9, Praha 1
Tel *225 334 761*
Elegant, music-themed interiors and a rich menu featuring unique flavours from both Bohemia and across the globe. The rooftop terrace is ideal for an early evening drink.

Essensia Ⓚ Ⓚ Ⓚ
International **Map** 2 E4
Nebovidská 459/1, Praha 1
Tel *233 088 888*
An oriental-themed interior with an interesting mix of traditional Czech staples and classy modern cuisine, plus a broad-based selection of Asian dishes.

Kampa Park Ⓚ Ⓚ Ⓚ
Fusion **Map** 2 F3
Na Kampe 8b, Praha 1
Tel *296 826 102*
Modern fusion cuisine with a heavy accent on fish and seafood, served in stylishly decorated rooms beside the Vltava river on Kampa island. Impressive wine list.

U Malířů Ⓚ Ⓚ Ⓚ
International **Map** 2 E4
Maltézské náměstí 11, Praha 1
Tel *257 530 318*
Established in 1543, the restaurant features gorgeous period interiors and a fascinating menu with Czech classics, modern European and Mediterranean fare.

Staré Město and Josefov

Country Life Ⓚ
Vegetarian **Map** 3 B4
Melantrichova 15, Praha 1
Tel *224 213 366*
With a self-service buffet offering freshly-made hot and cold vegetarian dishes priced by weight, this is among the best bargain lunches in town. Also try the excellent sandwiches and desserts.

Kabul
Afghan   Map 3 A5
Karolíny Svetlé 14, Praha 1
Tel *224 235 452*
An eclectic menu, welcoming
staff and a local feel – Kabul
offers large portions of Afghan
fare and good pizzas. Very
crowded at lunchtime.

Las Adelitas
Mexican   Map 3 B4
Malé náměstí 13, Praha 1
Tel *222 233 247*
Neighbourhood eatery that
serves authentic Mexican food.
Bite into freshly prepared burritos,
enchiladas and quesadillas. There
is an interesting array of Mexican
beers and tequilas.

Lokál
Czech   Map 3 C2
Dlouhá 33, Praha 1
Tel *222 316 265*
Fun, old-style pub serving Czech
classics and lots of refreshing
Pilsner Urquell beer. Modern
lighting and wooden tables
create a warm friendly vibe.

Sisters
Fusion   Map 3 C2
Dlouhá 39, Praha 1
Tel *775 991 975*   **Closed** *Sat & Sun*
Lively, trendy café, the place to
go for *chlebíčky* – open sand-
wiches topped with a variety
of ingredients, that come in
an imaginative mix of Czech,
Mediterranean and Asian flavours.

Století
Czech   Map 3 A5
Karolíny Svetlé 21, Praha 1
Tel *222 220 008*
Prompt service and delicious
food are the key characteristics of
this centrally located, but often
overlooked, restaurant. The Czech
dishes on the menu come with a
creative modern-European twist.

U Provaznice
Czech   Map 3 C4
Provaznická 3, Praha 1
Tel *224 232 528*
Cheerful pub-restaurant in an
excellent location offering Czech
meat-and-dumplings staples at
reasonable prices. Frequently
packed with locals at lunch.

Kolkovna
Czech   Map 3 B3
V kolkovne 8, Praha 1
Tel *224 819 701*
Authentic Czech dishes
combined with excellent beer
make this brewery restaurant a
must-visit. Roast meats, goulash,
grill-steaks and game provide
plenty of choice.

Seating amid vibrant, eclectic wall designs at Lehká Hlava, Prague

DK Choice

Lehká Hlava
Vegetarian   Map 3 A4
Boršov 2/280, Praha 1
Tel *222 220 665*
One of the best vegetarian
restaurants in Prague does
a creative take on inter-
national cuisine, served in
trippy, cool interiors. The
extensive menu ranges from
Asian to Mexican to Lebanese.
The Thai red curry with tofu
is a real treat, as is the hearty
burrito. There are plenty of
vegan offerings too.

Maitrea
Vegetarian   Map 3 C3
Tynská ulička 6, Praha 1
Tel *221 711 631*
A beautiful restaurant with a
well-balanced menu that includes
Mediterranean, Asian and Mexican
dishes. Good-value lunch specials
are chalked up daily.

Mistral Café
European   Map 3 B3
Valentinská 56/11, Praha 1
Tel *222 317 737*
A casual place near the
Staroměstské metro station,
Mistral offers zippy European
dishes in a bright, bistro setting.

U Tří růží
Pub   Map 3 B4
Husova 232/10, Praha 1
Tel *601 588 281*
This brew house makes its own
beers and serves classic Czech
pub food, from pork ribs and
grilled chicken to rabbit and duck.

Barock
Asian   Map 3 B2
Parižská 24, Praha 1
Tel *222 329 221*
Casual but contemporary
interiors provide the backdrop

for an inventive menu of Far
Eastern culinary fusion, with a
focus on Thai and Japanese fare.

Chagalls
Central European   Map 3 C2
Kozí 5, Praha 1
Tel *739 002 347*
A well-regarded, contemporary
take on Central European cuisine.
Attentive service, welcoming
interiors and a convenient location.

Cotto Crudo
Italian   Map 3 A3
Veleslavínova 2a, Praha 1
Tel *221 426 880*
Sample the savoury nibbles or
feast on the excellent Italian fare,
which features beautifully presented classics. Follow up with some
dangerously delicious desserts.

Dinitz
Jewish   Map 3 B2
Bílkova 12, Praha 1
Tel *222 244 000*
Located behind the Spanish
Synagogue, Dinitz offers some of
the best kosher food in Prague. The
menu ranges from steak and pasta
to Middle Eastern specialities, including a selection of salads and
sandwiches. Takeaway available.

Divinis
Italian   Map 3 C3
Tynská 21, Praha 1
Tel *222 325 440*   **Closed** *Sun*
This wine bar-restaurant serves
refined Italian food, including
some exquisite pasta dishes, in an
intimate, elegant space. Extensive
selection of international wines.

Grosseto Marina
Italian   Map 3 A3
Alšovo nábřeží, Praha 1
Tel *605 454 020*
Enjoy beautiful river views,
excellent Italian food and superb
service, all on a boat. The top deck
is a great place to enjoy a drink.

For more information on types of restaurants *see page 359*

King Solomon
Jewish   Ⓚ Ⓚ Ⓚ   **Map** 3 B3
Široká 8, Praha 1
Tel 224 818 752
Traditional Kosher Jewish cooking with a Central European touch. Favourites include locally sourced game, poultry and freshwater fish.

Kogo
Italian   Ⓚ Ⓚ Ⓚ   **Map** 3 C4
Havelská 499/27, Praha 1
Tel 224 210 259
One of the most versatile Italian restaurants in town, with a choice of pizzas alongside seafood and veal-cutlet dishes.

La Bottega di Finestra
Italian   Ⓚ Ⓚ Ⓚ   **Map** 3 A3
Platnérská 89/11, Praha 1
Tel 222 233 094
Italian delicatessen and bistro serving a small but delectable selection of hams, cheeses, pasta dishes and main courses. The lamb and seafood dishes are outstanding.

La Casa Argentina
International   Ⓚ Ⓚ Ⓚ   **Map** 3 C2
Dlouhá 35, Praha 1
Tel 222 311 512
The swinging seats at the bar are one of the winning features of this restaurant, which serves the enduringly popular, huge juicy steaks.

DK Choice

La Degustation
Czech   Ⓚ Ⓚ Ⓚ   **Map** 3 C2
Haštalská 18, Praha 1
Tel 222 311 234
The ultimate Prague dining experience. Expect imaginative multiple-course fusion cuisine prepared with skill and verve. Six- to eleven-course tasting menus, each accompanied by perfect wine pairings to provide the ultimate gourmet experience. Friendly, well-informed staff.

La Finestra in Cucina
Italian   Ⓚ Ⓚ Ⓚ   **Map** 3 B3
Platnérská 90/13, Praha 1
Tel 222 325 325
Gorgeous surroundings, delicious food, exemplary service and an impressive wine list. The small, seasonal menu offers Italian favourites cooked to perfection.

La Veranda
Italian   Ⓚ Ⓚ Ⓚ   **Map** 3 B2
Elišky Krásnohorské 10/2, Praha 1
Tel 224 814 733   **Closed** *Sun*
Bright, homey interiors and a familiar menu of quality Italian fare – creative pasta combinations and a good choice of seafood. Locally sourced, organic ingredients are used.

Mlynec
Czech   Ⓚ Ⓚ Ⓚ   **Map** 3 A4
Novotného lávka 9, Praha 1
Tel 277 000 777
Set in an elegant pavilion beside the river, Mlynec focuses on locally sourced meat and fish. Roast lunches on Saturdays and Sundays; occasional live jazz.

Parnas
Czech   Ⓚ Ⓚ Ⓚ   **Map** 3 A5
Smetanovo nábřeží 1012/2, Praha 1
Tel 224 239 604
Art Deco restaurant on the Vltava river, close to Charles Bridge. Serves a fresh take on Czech cuisine. Expect hearty meat and poultry dishes mixed with innovative flavours.

Pizza Nuova
Italian   Ⓚ Ⓚ Ⓚ   **Map** 4 D3
Revoluční 1/655, Praha 1
Tel 221 803 308
One of the highest-rated pizzerias in the city, offering authentic thin-crust pies with a wide range of traditional Italian toppings, plus a few local combinations too.

Platina
Czech   Ⓚ Ⓚ Ⓚ   **Map** 3 A5
Karolíny Svetlé 27, Praha 1
Tel 239 009 244
Inventive Czech cuisine is served here. The regularly updated menu focuses on seasonal and locally sourced ingredients.

Red Pif
French   Ⓚ Ⓚ Ⓚ   **Map** 3 A4
Betlémská 9, Praha 1
Tel 222 232 086   **Closed** *Sun*
Minimalist, industrial-chic restaurant and wine shop that offers delicious French bistro fare – from freshly made snacks to full meals.

School Restaurant
Czech   Ⓚ Ⓚ Ⓚ   **Map** 3 A4
Smetanovo nábřeží 22, Praha 1
Tel 222 222 173
Well-prepared, creative cuisine based on traditional Czech recipes, served in a large modern dining space with views across the Vltava.

V Zátiší
International   Ⓚ Ⓚ Ⓚ   **Map** 3 B4
Liliová 1, Praha 1
Tel 222 221 155
A combination of high-quality Czech, French and Indian dishes to be enjoyed at this upscale, fine-dining venue located close to the Bethlehem Chapel.

Nové Město

Fama
Czech   Ⓚ Ⓚ   **Map** 3 C5
Vladislavova 18 Praha 1
Tel 224 949 305   **Closed** *Sun*
A large choice of Czech staples served with a contemporary twist. This pub-restaurant is also popular with Pilsner Urquell drinkers.

Home Kitchen
International   Ⓚ Ⓚ   **Map** 5 C1
Jungmannova 8, Praha 1
Tel 734 714 227   **Closed** *Sun*
Casual bistro-style restaurant that is great for a quick bite. The menu changes seasonally and includes soups, salads and sandwiches.

DK Choice

Nota Bene
Czech   Ⓚ Ⓚ   **Map** 6 D2
Mikovcova 4, Praha 2
Tel 721 299 131   **Closed** *Sun*
A rotating beer list and locally sourced Czech specialities make Nota Bene one of the hottest places around. Exposed brick walls, minimalist furniture and photos of old Prague set the tone in this youthful bar-bistro. For beer and snacks, head to the beer hall in the basement.

Neatly arranged tables in La Degustation, a popular dining destination in Prague

Stylish bare-brick walls with modern furniture and subtle lighting at Nota Bene, Prague

Novoměstský Pivovar   ⓀⓀ
Czech   **Map** 5 C1
Vodičkova 20, Praha 1
Tel *222 232 448*
Classic Czech meat-and-dumpling dishes served in a working brewery, with a great choice of beers. Large copper brewing vats loom behind the restaurant tables.

Pivovarský Dům   ⓀⓀ
Pub   **Map** 5 C2
Ječná 14, Praha 2
Tel *296 216 666*
Classic Czech pork and chicken dishes served in this lively brewery-pub that produces an exciting range of beers, from unfiltered pilsner to banana- and nettle-flavoured varieties.

Plzeňská restaurace   ⓀⓀ
Czech   **Map** 4 D3
Náměstí republiky 5, Praha 1
Tel *222 002 770*
An enjoyable evening awaits at this charming restaurant with its fabulous Art Nouveau interiors, wide-ranging menu of Czech dishes and friendly staff.

Radost FX   ⓀⓀ
Vegetarian   **Map** 6 E2
Bělehradská 120, Praha 2
Tel *603 193 711*
Attached to a well-known nightclub, Radost FX is a long-standing favourite among vegetarians. Sample filling soups, focaccia sandwiches and Mexican dishes here.

U Pinkasů   ⓀⓀ
Czech   **Map** 3 C5
Jungmannovo náměstí 15/16, Praha 1
Tel *221 111 150*
Much loved beer hall with typical wood-panelled interiors, serving generous portions of food and unpasteurized Pilsner

Urquell straight from the tank. A tourist hotspot, but attracts the locals as well.

Universal   ⓀⓀ
International   **Map** 5 B1
V Jirchárich 6, Praha 1
Tel *224 934 416*
Casual French-Mediterranean bistro with a creative menu spanning everything from freshly made pasta with imaginative sauces to classic steaks.

Čestr   ⓀⓀⓀ
International   **Map** 6 E1
Legerova 75/57, Praha 1
Tel *222 727 851*
The speciality here is beef cooked in a variety of ways. The meat is locally sourced and the menu features over 20 different cuts. Extensive wine and beer list.

El Emir   ⓀⓀⓀ
International   **Map** 3 C4
Václavské náměstí 1, Praha 1
Tel *224 281 099*
Lebanese place with oriental decor and an extensive menu featuring Middle Eastern meat dishes as well as lots of Mediterranean seafood. Ample choice for vegetarians.

Ginger & Fred   ⓀⓀⓀ
International   **Map** 5 A2
Jiráskovo náměstí 6, Praha 2
Tel *221 984 160*
Located atop Frank Gehry's famed 'Dancing House', the restaurant dishes up everything from gourmet fish-and-chips to braised lamb. Delectable desserts follow the mains.

Miyabi   ⓀⓀⓀ
Japanese   **Map** 5 C1
Navrátilova 10, Praha 1
Tel *296 233 102*   **Closed** *Sun*
One of the oldest and best Japanese restaurants in the city,

Miyabi offers superb sushi and an extensive menu of authentic main courses.

Pagana   ⓀⓀⓀ
Italian   **Map** 3 B5
Spálená 14, Praha 1
Tel *224 056 300*   **Closed** *Sat & Sun*
Classic Italian cuisine complemented by an exclusive list of Italian wines. The home-made pasta and Mediterranean seafood are particularly well-known. Hand-painted images grace the fabulous interiors.

Suterén   ⓀⓀⓀ
International   **Map** 5 A1
Masarykovo nábřeží 26, Praha 1
Tel *224 933 657*   **Closed** *Sun*
Housed in an Art Nouveau building, this restaurant offers an exciting menu of Mediterranean seafood, French classics and traditional Czech specialities with a touch of the contemporary.

U Emy Destinnové   ⓀⓀⓀ
International   **Map** 5 C2
Kateřinská 7, Praha 2
Tel *224 918 425*   **Closed** *Sun*
Creative international cuisine is what U Emy Destinnové is famous for, with Black Angus beef and seafood, including fresh lobster among the leading favourites.

Zvonice   ⓀⓀⓀ
Czech   **Map** 4 D4
Jindřišská věž, Jindřišská ulice, Praha 1
Tel *224 220 009*
Located on the upper floors of a 14th-century tower, this stylish eatery offers lavish traditional Czech and European dishes, including plenty of pork, poultry and freshwater fish. The Gothic interiors create a great ambience.

Further Afield

Kofein   Ⓚ
Czech
Nitranská 9, Praha 3
Tel *273 132 145*
Czech-inspired tapas, a good wine list and a range of inter-national mains are the main draws here. The daily specials ensure a regular stream of locals at lunch.

Hybernia   ⓀⓀ
Czech
Hybernská 1033/7, Praha 1
Tel *224 226 004*
Large bar-restaurant with a popular outdoor terrace. Serves Czech dishes with a creative modern twist. Well-priced daily specials make it a lunchtime favourite.

For more information on types of restaurants *see page 359*

Kastrol
Czech
Ohradské náměstí 1625/2, Praha 5
Tel *607 048 992*
Out in the southwestern suburbs, Kastrol is worth visitng for the flair and attention to detail with which the locally-sourced produce is cooked. Mains include classic pork and duck dishes Delicious desserts.

Kidó Ⓚ Ⓚ
Vegetarian
Šmeralova 22, Praha 7
Tel *233 320 426*
Hip café-bistro serving healthy breakfasts, vegan lunches, pasta and fish dishes. The cakes and tarts are outstanding. Groovy boho interiors.

Krystal Mozaika Bistro Ⓚ Ⓚ
International
Sokolovská 101/99, Praha 8
Tel *222 318 152*
A stylish café-restaurant that is good for a quick bite or a full meal. Krystal serves delectable quiche, gourmet burgers and French- or Mediterranean-influenced meals.

Sansho Ⓚ Ⓚ
Fusion
Petrská 25, Praha 1
Tel *222 317 425* **Closed** *Sun & Mon*
Quality Asian-inspired fusion cuisine in a casual, family-style dining space. The daily changing menu is prepared according to what is fresh in local markets.

U Buínů Ⓚ Ⓚ
Traditional Czech
Budečská 803/2, Praha 2
Tel *224 254 676*
Corner pub in the Vinohrady district with an atmospheric interior of wood-panelling and tiles. Pork, goulash and roast duck anchor the menu. Distinct Mediterranean accent to some salads and starters.

La Terrassa Ⓚ Ⓚ Ⓚ
Mediterranean
Janáčkovo nábřeží - Detský ostrov, Praha 5
Tel *725 161 616*
Enjoy tapas and other Spanish fare on a lovely renovated boat on the Vltava. Attentive staff and a good wine list ensure a steady stream of patrons.

DK Choice

SaSaZu Ⓚ Ⓚ Ⓚ
Asian
Bubenské nábřeží 306, Praha 7
Tel *284 097 455*
Classy Indonesian, Thai and Vietnamese cuisine prepared and served with passion, creativity and flair in oriental palace-like surroundings. The desserts are just as exotic as the mains at this award-winning restaurant. SaSaZu's popular nightclub is situated in the same building.

Central Bohemia

BEROUN: Na Ostrově Ⓚ
International **Map** C2
Na Ostrově 816, 266 01
Tel *311 713 100*
This hotel-restaurant serves a quality selection of Czech and European dishes. Freshwater fish and roast poultry play a prominent role on the menu. Handful of vegetarian choices.

DOBŘÍŠ: Zámecká Restaurace Ⓚ
Czech **Map** C2
Náměstí Svobody 1, 263 01
Tel *318 520 525*
Situated in Dobříš Castle, this atmospheric spot serves huge platters of pork, beef and poultry

along with Staropramen beer to wash it all down. Good value set menus.

KARLŠTEJN: Restaurace u Karla IV Ⓚ
Czech **Map** C2
Karlštejn 173, 267 18
Tel *773 600 181* **Closed** *Mon*
Three different dining rooms and a beer garden located right beside Karlštejn Castle. Offers traditional Bohemian cuisine. The restaurant also stages knights' tournaments and folk evenings.

KARLŠTEJN: Koruna Ⓚ Ⓚ
Czech **Map** C2
Karlštejn 13, 267 18
Tel *311 681 465*
Furnished in traditional style, this hotel-restaurant offers hearty Czech pork-and-dumplings staples alongside grilled meats, steaks and freshwater fish. The summer terrace has good views of Karlštejn Castle.

KOLÍN: U Rabína Ⓚ
Czech/Italian **Map** D2
Karolíny Světlé 151
Tel *321 724 463*
Freshwater fish and grilled steaks, lighter pasta dishes and some substantial salads are served in a simple comfortable setting.

DK Choice

KONOPIŠTĚ: Stará Myslivna Ⓚ Ⓚ
Czech **Map** C2
Konopiště 2, 256 01 Benešov
Tel *317 700 280*
This former gamekeeper's lodge, attached to the country seat of the Austrian Archduke Franz Ferdinand, is now an atmospheric restaurant. The menu is dedicated to locally sourced game dishes, with special emphasis on rabbit, venison and boar. Forest berries feature in many of the accompanying sauces. The locally brewed Ferdinand 7 Bullets beer makes an excellent accompaniment.

KUTNÁ HORA: Pivnice Dačický Ⓚ Ⓚ
Central European **Map** D2
Rakova 8, 284 01
Tel *327 512 248*
A large, traditional beer hall-style restaurant with folksy decor, good draught beer and frequent live music. The menu concentrates on Austrian and Czech classics such as wild boar goulash and Moravian smoked pork.

Chic, oriental decoration at SaSaZu, award-wining Asian cuisine restaurant in Prague

Key to Price Guide *see page 364*

Elegantly laid out tables at the opulent Chateau Mčely, Mladá Boleslav

KUTNÁ HORA: U Vlašského Dvora
Czech   ⓀⓀ
Map D2
28.října 521, 284 01
Tel 327 514 618
Pleasant hotel-restaurant serving excellent Czech cuisine in big portions, backed by a strong list of Moravian wines. Garden with an open grill during summer.

KUTNÁ HORA: U Zvonu
Czech   ⓀⓀ
Map D2
Zvonařská 286, 284 01
Tel 777 680 992
This small and cosy hotel-restaurant with a rustic feel offers traditional Czech fare and an international wine list. The set lunch menus are popular with local patrons.

MĚLNÍK: U Šatlavy
International   ⓀⓀ
Map C1
Náměstí Míru 30, 276 01
Tel 776 368 128
Stylish restaurant in the city centre offering a good selection of local standards and European classics including seafood. Pizzas and the daily set menus are excellent value.

MLADÁ BOLESLAV: Chateau Mčely
Gourmet   ⓀⓀⓀ
Map D1
Mčely 61, 289 36
Tel 325 600 000
In an out-of-town spa hotel, this bright restaurant excels in French-Italian haute cuisine, offering lavish set dinners and multiple-course tasting menus.

MLADÁ BOLESLAV: La Romantica
Mediterranean   ⓀⓀⓀ
Map D1
Viničná 1343, 293 01
Tel 326 734 054
Set partly in the rock under the town church, La Romantica serves a broad range of seafood, pastas and salads, with plenty of Italian- and Greek-influenced appetizers.

MNICHOVO HRADIŠTĚ: Podzámecká Restaurace
Czech   ⓀⓀ
Map D1
Arnoldova 91, 295 01
Tel 326 773 091   Closed Sun & Mon
Close to Karlštejn Castle and with castle-themed interiors, this restaurant has an extensive menu covering just about everything in the Czech culinary repertoire.

NELAHOZEVES: Zámek Nelahozeves
Central European   ⓀⓀ
Map C1
Zámek Nelahozeves
Tel 315 709 111
Closed Mon & Nov–Mar
Set in an impressive Renaissance castle, Zámek Nelahozeves focuses on a few Czech staples and executes them very well – goulash, fish and breaded chicken are among the standouts.

PŘÍBRAM: Zlatý Soudek
Czech   ⓀⓀ
Map C2
Náměstí T G Masaryka 98, 261 01
Tel 318 623 245
Lively place popular with local families. Has a wide-ranging menu that is particularly good with fish and game. Pleasant terrace dining in summer.

South Bohemia

ČERVENÁ LHOTA: Červená Lhota
Czech   ⓀⓀ
Map D3
Červená Lhota 6, 378 21
Kardašova Řečice
Tel 384 384 305
Located directly opposite Červená Lhota castle, this restaurant concentrates on

Czech pork-and-dumpling basics. Also prepares fish dishes and a handful of vegetarian choices.

ČESKÉ BUDĚJOVICE: Pizzeria Regina
Italian   Ⓚ
Map C3
Krajinská 41, 370 01
Tel 386 350 999
Relish substantial Mediterranean salads, excellent pizzas and pastas in a stylish town-centre pizzeria. Steaks and fish are also on the menu.

ČESKÉ BUDĚJOVICE: Masné Krámy
Czech   ⓀⓀ
Map C3
Krajinská 13, 370 01
Tel 387 201 301
Large, lively restaurant run by the Budvar brewery, serving hearty portions of dishes such as pork tail, roast duck and mixed-meat skewer-kebab. Wash it all down with the city's famous beer.

ČESKÉ BUDĚJOVICE: Olivier
International   ⓀⓀ
Map C3
Husova 21, 370 01
Tel 386 350 038
Pleasant bistro-restaurant with a grassy terrace and kids' corner. Serves a delicious range of pastas, risottos and Italian-style cuts of veal and steak. Wine shop and delicatessen on site.

ČESKÉ BUDĚJOVICE: Potrefená Husa
Czech   ⓀⓀ
Map C3
Česká 66, 370 01
Tel 387 420 560
A large and popular pub-restaurant with traditional pub food – lots of pork, chicken and steak, including some excellent grill options.

ČESKÉ BUDĚJOVICE: Gourmet Symphony
Central European   ⓀⓀⓀ
Map C3
Náměstí Přemysla Otakara II 28, 370 01
Tel 381 601 601
Traditional meat roasts, schnitzels and poultry dishes cooked and presented with imagination and finesse. Stylish interior with good views of the main square.

ČESKÉ BUDĚJOVICE: Hotel u Solné Brány
International   ⓀⓀⓀ
Map C3
Radniční 11, 370 01
Tel 386 354 121
Modern hotel-restaurant offering an extravagant selection of meat, fish and game dishes. The interiors are artfully decorated with tapestries and paintings.

For more information on types of restaurants see page 359

ČESKÉ BUDĚJOVICE: Life is Dream
International   Ⓚ Ⓚ Ⓚ
     Map C3
Kněžská 330/31, 370 01
Tel *733 609 225*
Intimate eatery in a medieval burgher's house that cooks up a creative range of modern European dishes fused with hints of Asian and Mexican flavours. Offers vegetarian choices, a big wine list and a children's menu.

ČESKÝ KRUMLOV: Krumlovsky Mlyn
Czech   Ⓚ Ⓚ
     Map C3
Široká 80, 381 01
Tel *736 634 461*
Set in a Gothic-Renaissance mill with folksy wooden benches, this is a good place for local meat dishes, freshwater fish and delicious traditional desserts.

ČESKÝ KRUMLOV: Laibon
Vegetarian   Ⓚ Ⓚ
     Map C3
Parkán 105, 381 01
Tel *775 676 654*
Bare stone, natural woods and ethnic textiles set the tone at this charming café-restaurant. Flavoursome fusion menu rich in beans, pulses, tofu and Mediterranean vegetables.

ČESKÝ KRUMLOV: Don Julius
Czech/Italian   Ⓚ Ⓚ Ⓚ
     Map C3
Náměstí Svornosti 11, 381 01
Tel *380 712 310*
One of the best places in town for quality Czech cuisine, plus good pizzas. Unconventional interiors with an open hearth and walls featuring a relief of the town square.

ČESKÝ KRUMLOV: Le Jardin
French   Ⓚ Ⓚ Ⓚ
     Map C3
Latrán 77, 381 01
Tel *380 720 109*
Formal, starched-tablecloth restaurant under the vaulted roof of a former monastery. Serves creative French fare with a menu that changes according to produce available. Multi-course tasting menus are available for gourmands.

JINDŘICHŮV HRADEC: Frankův Dvůr
Czech   Ⓚ
     Map D3
Jemčinská 125/4, 377 01
Tel *777 996 666*
A modern place decked out in the style of a traditional inn. Frankův Dvůr is known largely for its grilled meat dishes, but also offers a cross-section of Czech staples and the odd Asian-inspired dish.

JINDŘICHŮV HRADEC: Grand Hotel Černy Orel
Czech/Italian   Ⓚ Ⓚ
     Map D3
Náměstí Míru 165, 377 01
Tel *384 361 252*
Italian-themed decor and a largely Mediterranean menu characterize this hotel-restaurant. A lot of Wiener schnitzels and quality fish on the menu. Local beer and a good wine list.

JINDŘICHŮV HRADEC: Zlatá Husa
Czech   Ⓚ Ⓚ Ⓚ
     Map D3
Náměstí Míru 141, 377 01
Tel *384 362 320*
Top-class Czech cuisine and freshwater fish characterize the 'Golden Goose'. All dishes are impeccably prepared and presented. Dining rooms have an old-school elegance. Smooth service.

PRACHATICE: Bocelli
Italian   Ⓚ
     Map C3
Velké náměstí 39, 383 01
Tel *604 613 502*
A cosy, centrally-located restaurant that has a big choice of reasonably authentic pizzas, plus a few pasta, risotto and Mediterranean-salad choices.

PRACHATICE: Indian Restaurant Tandoor
Indian   Ⓚ Ⓚ
     Map C3
Horní 165, 383 01
Tel *388 310 618*   **Closed** *Sun*
Intimate two-room restaurant with a wide-ranging menu, including a good tandoori selection such as chicken tikka and shish kebab. There are plenty of options for vegetarians.

Wooden seating and retro memorabilia at Krumlovsky Mlyn, Český Krumlov

TÁBOR: Dobromila
International   Ⓚ
     Map C2
Školní náměstí 213
Tel *777 610 008*   **Closed** *Mon*
A restaurant that offers home-style local fare in a creative way – beautifully presented goulash, steaks, pastas and gourmet burgers. Delicious Dobromila beer to go with the food.

TÁBOR: Skochův Dům
Czech   Ⓚ Ⓚ
     Map C2
Žižkovo náměstí 22
Tel *381 251 221*
A lovely terrace on main square and an atmospheric medieval cellar for indoor dining; serves up Czech pork and poultry favourites alongside good steak. Well-priced daily specials pull in the locals.

TÁBOR: Goldie
Gourmet   Ⓚ Ⓚ Ⓚ
     Map C2
Žižkovo náměstí 20, 390 02
Tel *380 900 900*
High ceilings, large windows and works by Czech artists make for a special dining experience here. The menu is mostly modern European-meets-contemporary Czech. Lists a range of international wines.

TŘEBOŇ: Šupina
Seafood   Ⓚ Ⓚ Ⓚ
     Map D3
Valy 155, 379 01
Tel *384 721 149*
Surrounded by ponds, Třeboň is a famous fish-rearing area and this is reflected in the menu at the fish-themed Šupina. All the local freshwater varieties are prepared in imaginative ways.

DK Choice

TŘEBOŇ: Zlatá Hvězda
Czech   Ⓚ Ⓚ Ⓚ
     Map D3
Masarykovo náměstí 107, 379 01
Tel *384 757 111*
Set in the Zlatá Hvězda hotel on Třeboň's delightful town square, this elegant but homely restaurant takes local recipes and elevates them to haute-cuisine. Roast poultry and game dishes are served with exquisite fruit sauces; locally farmed carp is served baked, stewed or fried. There is plenty for vegetarians, including a unique hemp-leaf salad. The restaurant also brews hemp-leaf tea.

Key to Price Guide *see page 364*

West Bohemia

DOMAŽLICE: Konšelsky Šenk
Italian   Map B2
Vodní 33, 334 01
Tel *379 720 222*   **Closed** *Sun*
Located in a Baroque building close to the main square. The menu features a wide range of Italian fare, from pizzas through pastas to succulent *saltimbocca* (delicacy made of veal and ham).

FRANTIŠKOVY LÁZNĚ: Tri Lilie
Czech   Map B2
Národní 3/10, 351 01
Tel *353 825 756*
Luxurious restaurant attached to the hotel of the same name, offering lovingly prepared Czech food. Special focus on game and roast meats, as well as poultry. Opt for the good-value daily set menus.

HORŠOVSKÝ TÝN: Zámecká Restaurace
Seafood   Map B2
Náměstí Republiky 66, 346 01
Tel *379 423 483*
Quiet and intimate restaurant serving delectable Czech food and a good range of beers. The speciality is freshwater fish, with locally caught zander prepared in various ways.

KARLOVY VARY: Charleston Restaurant Club
English   Map B1
Bulharská 1, 360 01
Tel *353 230 797*
Situated in the business part of the city, Charleston tables original English recipes such as beef steaks as well as pork, poultry and fish dishes, appetizers and fresh salads.

DK Choice

KARLOVY VARY: Grandrestaurant Pupp
Gourmet   Map B1
Mírové náměstí 2, 360 01
Tel *353 109 646*
This grand hotel-restaurant is famous for its beautifully prepared European and Czech cuisine and old-school standards of service. The dining room looks like a charming relic of pre-World War I Europe. The food is mostly French and a trained sommelier will offer advice on the best wine to order with it. Desserts are opulent.

The palatial Grandrestaurant Pupp in Karlovy Vary with Neo-Classical interiors

KARLOVY VARY: Lázně V
International   Map B1
Smetanovy sady 1145/1, 360 01
Tel *602 266 088*   **Closed** *Sun*
Located in a historic spa building, Lázně V offers traditional Czech as well as Mediterranean cuisine in refined surroundings. The steaks here are particularly renowned.

KLATOVY: Strelnice
Central European   Map B2
Pražská 22, 339 01
Tel *376 709 888*
Filled with beer-making memorabilia, this pub-restaurant serves quality Czech food and pilsner beer. Grilled meats and pan-fried schnitzels are the specialities. Frequent live music.

LOKET: Bilý Kůň
European   Map B1
T G Masaryka 10, 357 33
Tel *352 661 809*
This elegant restaurant in the eponymous hotel serves classy Czech and European cuisine. Its spacious, leafy terrace has great views over the Ohře valley.

MARIÁNSKÉ LÁZNĚ: U Zlaté Koule
Czech   Map B2
Nehrova 26, 353 01
Tel *354 624 455*
A romantic inn serving quality local food. Try the roast goose, game and fish. It also offers daily set menus and a good selection of wines.

PLZEŇ: pi.jez.pi
Pub   Map C2
Americká 38, 301 00
Tel *608 182 478*
Contemporary, youthful bar and restaurant that brews its own pilsner and serves a range of food, from sandwiches and salads to heavy meat dishes and juicy steaks.

PLZEŇ: Stará Sladovna
Pub   Map C2
Malá 3, 301 00
Tel *377 225 151*
A roomy beer cellar packed with wooden pews, serving several local beers. Food ranges from snacks to roast duck and pork with walnuts and apples.

PLZEŇ: U Mansfelda
Czech   Map C2
Dřevěná 9, 301 00
Tel *377 333 844*
Popular pub-restaurant with rustic, exposed-stone interiors. Quality selection of game dishes, goulash and steaks. Also offers a children's menu.

PLZEŇ: Žumbera
International   Map C2
Bezručova 14, 301 00
Tel *377 322 436*
Enduringly popular pub-restaurant that serves well-kept locally brewed beer with Czech staples, a handful of vegetarian dishes and South American-styled grilled meats.

PLZEŇ: El Cid
Spanish   Map C2
Křižíkovy sady 1, 301 00
Tel *377 224 595*
Serves traditional Spanish dishes including plenty of seafood, in a formal restaurant upstairs and lively tapas bar downstairs. Also stocks a wide range of wines.

North Bohemia

DĚČÍN: U Přístavu
Seafood   Map C1
Lábské nábřeží 669/2, 405 02
Tel *412 532 557*
Scenically located on the shores of the Labe and decorated on a fishing theme, this is a great place to sample local fish – pan-fried or grilled.

For more information on types of restaurants *see page 359*

DK Choice

DOLNÍ CHŘIBSKÁ: Na Stodolci
Czech   Ⓚ   **Map** C1
Dolní Chřibská 40
Tel *412 381 028*
A rural pension and riding stable with a lovely restaurant in raw timber and red brick. Has a small but superbly balanced menu of meat and poultry reared by local suppliers. Roast duck with red cabbage is one obvious highlight; look out also for the great-value daily specials and try the home-made lemonade. The traditional desserts are heavy but irresistible.

LIBEREC: Ananda
Vegetarian   Ⓚ   **Map** D1
Frýdlantská 210/12, 460 01
Tel *485 103 741*   **Closed** *Sun*
Super café-bistro serving breakfasts, soups, sandwiches plus more substantial meals, mostly on vegan principles. There is a good-value salad bar, daily set lunches and delicious cakes on offer as well.

LIBEREC: Benada
Gourmet   ⓀⓀ   **Map** D1
Gutenbergova 3, 460 01
Tel *485 256 761*
Part of a chain but still deserving of a place in the gastronomic big league, Benada presents Mediterranean-Central European fusion cooking with a good balance of hearty dishes and light lunches.

LIBEREC: Bílý Mlýn
International   ⓀⓀ   **Map** D1
Tr. Svobody 295/30, 460 01
Tel *482 750 863*
Set on the shores of a lake on the outskirts of town, the 'White Mill' serves local lamb

and freshwater fish together with pasta dishes, piri piri and Argentinian steaks.

LIBEREC: Domov
International   ⓀⓀⓀ   **Map** D1
Ještědská 149, 460 08
Tel *482 771 251*
Rustic-looking gastro-pub on the western outskirts of town. Domov serves creative fare, mixing Czech meat-and-poultry staples with lighter, Mediterranean-influenced pastas and salads.

LITOMĚŘICE: U Zlatého Bažanta
Czech/Italian   ⓀⓀ   **Map** C1
Mírové náměstí 13/21, 412 01
Tel *732 517 090*
The 'Golden Pheasant' occupies a charming historic house with atmospheric vaulted interiors. The menu opts for a balance of Czech and Italian dishes. Good-value daily specials make this a popular place for lunch.

OSEK: Černy Orel
International   ⓀⓀ   **Map** C1
Vilová 18, 417 05
Tel *417 837 082*
A family restaurant that does everything from succulent grill-steaks and seafood to pastas and thin-crust pizzas, all served in dining rooms with a rustic semi-alpine feel. Vegetarian choices available.

RYNOLTICE: Jítrava
Traditional Czech   ⓀⓀⓀ   **Map** D1
Jítrava 70, Rynoltice, 463 53
Tel *485 172 105*
Classy inn decorated in rustic style, specializing in locally sourced game, organic meats and freshwater fish. The menu changes seasonally, but rabbit, venison and delicious roast lamb are usually featured.

ÚSTÍ NAD LABEM: Restaurace ve Střední Evropě
Central European   Ⓚ   **Map** C1
Lidické náměstí 7, 400 01
Tel *732 327 233*
The 'Restaurant in the Centre of Europe' opts for appropriately mid-European cuisine, with schnitzels, goulashes and chicken dominating a menu of hearty dishes.

ŽATEC: U Hada
European   ⓀⓀ   **Map** C1
Náměstí Svobody 155, 438 01
Tel *415 711 000*   **Closed** *Sun*
A small hotel restaurant with minimalist interior, offering a mixture of Czech and classical European cuisine. The steaks and fish dishes deserve a special mention.

East Bohemia

DVŮR KRÁLOVÉ: U Hlavačků
Czech   Ⓚ   **Map** D1
Riegrova 346, 544 01
Tel *499 329 206*
This simple eatery, which goes back to 1913, has a long and respected tradition of serving delicious Czech cusine. The set menus are a real bargain, and unpasteurized pilsner beer is served from the tank.

HAVLÍČKŮV BROD: Rusticana
Central Europe   Ⓚ   **Map** D2
Na Výsluní 1814, 580 01
Tel *569 425 932*
Quality Czech food is available but the real treat is the Balkan grill menu, with *pljeskavica* (gourmet burgers) and *ćevapi* (minced-meat kebabs) among the favourites. Garden seating in summer.

HRADEC KRÁLOVÉ: Na Hradě
Czech   Ⓚ   **Map** D2
Špitálská 5/175, 500 02
Tel *603 873 667*
Classic Czech pub-restaurant with long wooden benches and rustic artifacts on the walls. Sample traditional Czech cuisine including some great-value daily specials.

HRADEC KRÁLOVÉ: Šatlava
European   Ⓚ   **Map** D2
Dlouhá 101, 500 02
Tel *776 817 856*
Stylish bar-restaurant with fashionably adorned interiors, a winter garden and outdoor patio. The wide-ranging menu covers classic European meat and poultry dishes.

Homey dining area with wood and brick finish at Na Stodolci, Dolní Chřibská

Classic old-world vibe and unpretentious furnishings at Zelena Žaba, Pardubice

HRADEC KRÁLOVÉ: Localis
International   ⓚⓚ   **Map** D2
Velké náměstí 145/14, 500 03
Tel *495 588 153*
Chic café-bistro with minimalist interiors offering European mains, filling salads and Mediterranean light bites. The daily menus are chalked up in the window.

HRADEC KRÁLOVÉ: U Královny Elišky
European   ⓚⓚ   **Map** D2
Malé náměstí 117, 500 03
Tel *495 518 052*
Hotel-restaurant with an idiosyncratic but cosy interior. Choose from a broad range of European fare alongside the established Czech staples.

DK Choice

JIČÍN: U dělové koule
Czech   ⓚⓚ   **Map** D1
Havlíčkova 21, 506 01
Tel *493 544 250*
This smart but not over-formal restaurant in Hotel Jičín is renowned for its game dishes and roast meats. A range of lighter salads and pastas is also available. The two-course daily menus are a bargain, and there is a long list of good but not too pricey Moravian wines. Themed around the Austro-Prussian War of 1866, the interior is a veritable museum, packed with period weaponry and uniforms.

LIPNICE NAD SÁZAVOU: U České Koruny
Czech   ⓚ   **Map** D2
Lipnice nad Sázavou 55, 582 32
Tel *569 486 126*   **Closed** *Mon*
Old-fashioned place near Lipnice Castle featuring wood-panelled interiors and home-style Bohemian fare such as roasted duck or smoked knuckle. It was here that Jaroslav Hašek, author of *The Good Soldier Švejk* (1923), used to eat, drink and write.

LITOMYŠL: Bohém
European   ⓚⓚ   **Map** E2
Šantovo náměstí 181, 570 01
Tel *461 614 900*
Smart and sleek Bohém is housed in the centrally located Aplaus Hotel. It serves a refined and inventive selection of quality European cuisine, with predominant Austrian and Mediterranean accents.

PARDUBICE: Zelena Žaba
International   ⓚ   **Map** D2
Hronovická 929, 532 02
Tel *466 616 016*
The pub-restaurant of the Zelena Žaba pension offers good beer, big-screen sports and a moderately priced menu that ranges from pork and dumplings to Kung Pao chicken.

PARDUBICE: U Lva Bratranců
Czech   ⓚⓚ   **Map** D2
Veverkových 2707, 532 01
Tel *466 611 117*
Comfortable, mildly folky place with a lovely garden and an extensive menu featuring Czech meat-and-dumplings staples, game and fish. Try the tasty salmon steaks.

ŠPINDLERŮV MLÝN: Orange LeMoon
Gourmet   ⓚⓚⓚ   **Map** D1
Lesní 50, 543 51
Tel *499 433 103*
This stylish restaurant has a modern lounge-bar feel and serves Czech, Mediterranean and Japanese fusion cuisine.

Locally sourced meats and vegetables are innovatively integrated with herbs and spices from around the world. Garden dining with lava grill during summer.

SRCH: Na Výsluní
International   ⓚⓚ   **Map** D2
Na Výsluní 236, 532 52
Tel *466 414 459*
Smart dining in a delightful rustic location. The sophisticated menu includes seafood, steaks and vegetarian choices as well as traditional Czech lunches.

TRUTNOV: Restaurace u Kostela
European   ⓚ   **Map** D1
Bulharská 62, 541 01
Tel *777 605 150*
This café-restaurant has appealing chic interiors and a pleasant garden. The Central-European menu is strong on chicken dishes and roast meats. The daily specials are inexpensive.

North Moravia and Silesia

JESENÍK: Pizzeria Tosca
Italian   ⓚ   **Map** E2
Dukelská 203, 790 01
Tel *774 786 223*
More than just a good pizzeria, Tosca also serves up a satisfying range of pastas, salads and Mediterranean main courses. Vegetarians can go for the couscous-based dishes.

JESENÍK: Křížový Vrch
Czech   ⓚⓚ   **Map** E2
Za Pilou 6, 790 01
Tel *584 402 063*
This hunters' lodge-style restaurant is located in the district's oldest building and is well known for mouthwatering local classics, based on plenty of duck and game. House-specialities include venison and saddle of boar with cream sauce and cranberries.

NOVY JIČÍN: Restaurace Hotel Praha
Central European   ⓚⓚ   **Map** F2
Lidická 6, 741 01
Tel *730 821 490*
An elegant restaurant with stylish Art Nouveau decor, Restaurace Hotel Praha whips up delicious Central-European classics and local specialities with flair and an eye for quality.

For more information on types of restaurants *see page 359*

DK Choice

OLOMOUC: U Kohuta
Steak **Map** E2
Lafayettová 50/3, 779 00
Tel *585 222 192*
Closed *Sat & Sun*
Simple decor enlivened by the odd piece of domestic bric-a-brac provides the unlikely setting for one of Olomouc's most renowned restaurants, with a reputation for top-notch steaks. The rest of the menu changes frequently, although guests will usually find quality chicken and fish, and a widely-admired secret-recipe goulash. Children's portions are gladly served.

OLOMOUC: Moritz
Pub **Map** E2
Nešverova 2, 779 00
Tel *585 205 560*
Basement bar-restaurant and microbrewery serving its own unfiltered beer straight from the tank, accompanied by pub-favourites such as grilled sausage, pork hock and steak.

OLOMOUC: Svatováclavský Pivovar
Pub **Map** E2
Mariánská 4, 779 00
Tel *585 207 517*
Conveniently located at the centre of the town, this pub-restaurant has a huge range of home-brewed beers, daily specials and a long menu of Czech meat-and-dumplings standards.

OLOMOUC: Caesar
Italian **Map** E2
Horní náměstí - radnice, 779 00
Tel *585 229 287*
Café-restaurant and art gallery beneath the Gothic arches of the town hall. Choose from a refined selection of pasta dishes and Mediterranean salads. This is also a popular venue for coffee and cakes anytime of the day.

OLOMOUC: Hotel Trinity
European **Map** E2
Pavelčákova 22, 772 00
Tel *581 830 811*
Modern hotel-restaurant providing a subtle blend of Czech and Mediterranean cuisine, along with pasta, seafood, poultry and veal dishes. Generous portions.

OLOMOUC: Nepál
Asian **Map** E2
Mlýnská 4, 779 00
Tel *585 208 428* **Closed** *Sun*
Sharing a brick-vaulted building with an Irish pub, Nepál prepares

genuinely spicy main-course curries. The popular lunchtime buffet usually has plenty of choices for vegetarians.

OPAVA: U Krbu
European **Map** F2
Masařská 3, 746 01
Tel *553 613 488*
Located in the town centre, U Krbu offers a large selection of Czech and European dishes. Fish, pasta and steaks are particularly well represented. Pleasant summer terrace.

OSTRAVA: U Dvořáčků
Central European **Map** F2
Hladnovská 19, 710 00
Tel *596 245 454*
This game lodge-style restaurant displays hunting trophies and other rustic touches. The menu features game such as rabbit, venison and pheasant. Duck, pork knuckle and steak also feature.

OSTRAVA: Comedor Mexicana
Mexican **Map** F2
Zámecká 20, 702 00
Tel *596 208 515*
A Mexican restaurant that has broken out of its genre to become an Ostrava society favourite, the Comedor is both fun and refined. Features superb Mexican cuisine, steaks and an excellent wine list.

South Moravia

BRNO: Pivnice Pegas
Pub **Map** E3
Jakubská 4, 602 00
Tel *542 210 104*
Large and pleasant pub brewing its own light and dark beers on the premises. Serves Czech favourites including excellent

Delicious chicken and pasta gratin served in ramekins

goulash with dumplings. There is outdoor seating in the back courtyard during summer.

BRNO: Tři Ocásci
International **Map** E3
Gorkého 82/37, 602 00
Tel *775 702 778*
Mildly bohemian café with an artfully decorated interior. Serves great coffee and pastries alongside a Mediterranean-influenced menu of open sandwiches and hot meals.

BRNO: U Dobrého Pastýře
Slovak **Map** E3
Veveří 16, 602 00
Tel *777 094 110*
Complete with log-lined walls and sheepskin seat covers, the Carpathian highland-style 'Good Sheperd' is a great place to try *bryndzové halušky* (Slovak cheesy noodles) alongside pork and poultry staples.

BRNO: Bistro Franz
International **Map** E3
Veveří 461/14, 602 00
Tel *720 113 502*
This cool designer bistro is a great spot to enjoy budget international fare. The daily menus always feature creative vegetarian options. Packed with students from north of the Old Town.

BRNO: Borgo Agnese
Mediterranean **Map** E3
Kopečná 43, 602 00
Tel *515 537 500*
Smart modern eatery with views over the city. The great menu of Mediterranean-inspired fare features some imaginative pasta sauces. Extensive wine list.

BRNO: Hansen
International **Map** E3
Komenského náměstí 8, 602 00
Tel *737 364 000*
Housed in the Besedni Dum and named after the architect who designed it, Hansen serves refined Moravian-international food in a superb stucco-and-chandelier setting. Veal cutlets and pan-fried trout come recommended.

BRNO: Havana
Caribbean **Map** E3
Masarova 9, 628 00
Tel *544 238 380*
Cuban restaurant with high quality Caribbean cuisine. The decor is spectacular, and the building appears to be a crumbling Havana mansion, complete with tropical plants.

Smart and modish Koishi restaurant with vibrant interiors, Brno

BRNO: Il Mercato
Italian **Map** E3
Zelný trh 2, 602 00
Tel *542 212 156*
Sister restaurant to La Finestra in Prague, Il Mercato sits opposite Brno's daily food market and serves upscale Italian cuisine, with an accent on quality seafood, lamb and good wine.

DK Choice

BRNO: Koishi
Fusion **Map** E3
Údolní 326/11, 602 00
Tel *777 564 744*
Authentic Japanese sushi and a small but fascinating menu of other mains are served in this stylish restaurant in the shadow of Špilberk hill. The outdoor terrace is landscaped like a hillside Japanese garden. Combining classic European fare with exotic flavours has become a Koishi trademark. Sample lamb marinaded in miso sauce, or Mediterranean seafood with ginger.

BRNO: Valoria
Czech **Map** E3
Bohunická 292/2, 619 00
Tel *543 250 462*
Chic and modern restaurant in a suburban setting with a lovely garden that serves the finest Czech food with haute-cuisine panache. Diners can order á la carte or opt for a multi-course tasting menu.

JIHLAVA: Tři knížata
Fusion **Map** D2
Masarykovo náměstí 1189/44, 586 01
Tel *567 210 933* **Closed** Sun
Imaginative fusion cuisine that takes the best of locally

sourced ingredients while borrowing freely from Mediterranean and Far Eastern cuisines. The interiors are attractively presented with modern furnishings set under medieval arches.

KLENTICE: Café Fara
International **Map** E3
Klentice 166, 692 02
Tel *720 611 161*
Located in a former village parsonage midway between Mikulov and Dolní Vestonice, Fara serves up great coffee, cakes, salads and simple mains. It also has a good wine cellar. The barrel-vaulted interior is stuffed with homely furnishings and wall-hugging benches. Also features a summer terrace.

KROMĚŘÍŽ: Bouček Hotel Restaurant
International **Map** F3
Velké náměstí 108, 767 01
Tel *573 342 777*
Superbly plated Czech staples and European classics served on an arcaded terrace with wonderful views of the town square. Well-chosen wine list and live music at weekends.

TELČ: U Zachariáše
Czech **Map** D3
Náměstí Zachariáše z Hradce 33, 588 56
Tel *567 243 672*
Elegant restaurant with outdoor seating on the main square that serves large, quality portions of pork, beef and poultry, as well as locally farmed carp and other fishes. The high-ceilinged, airy interiors have a traditional decor.

TŘEBÍČ: U Jelínků
International **Map** D3
Žerotínovo náměstí 17
Tel *568 422 541*
Squeezed into the arched entrance to a backpacker's hostel, this Czech take on the gastro-pub idea mixes locally brewed beer with a food menu of Mediterranean-inspired salads, pastas and fish. Look out for the very well priced daily specials.

TŘEBÍČ: Elipso
Czech **Map** D3
Karlovo náměstí 5, 674 01
Tel *568 848 560*
The town-centre restaurant of the Grand Hotel presents Czech home cooking in refined, attention-to-detail style. It also has a long list of Moravian wines. The restaurant often organizes Moravian evenings with wine tasting and sampling of local, traditional dishes.

ZLÍN: Spirit
Fusion **Map** F3
Náměstí T G Masaryka 5556, 760 01
Tel *577 008 907*
Set in the Eva Jiřičná-designed Kongresové Centrum, Spirit is nestled beneath a ribbed glass dome. Seating circles around a central kitchen, which cooks up local cuisine with a touch of Modern-European finesse. The set lunches are a positive steal.

ZNOJMO: Na Věčnosti
Vegetarian **Map** D3
Velká Mikulášská 11, 669 02
Tel *776 856 650*
Housed in a Renaissance building together with a pub and an art gallery. The menu is predominantly vegetarian offering *bryndzové halušky*, pasta and some fish dishes. The desserts are famously delicious.

For more information on types of restaurants *see page 359*

Where to Eat and Drink in Slovakia

Bratislava

Bistro St Germain   €
International   **Map** A6
Rajská 7
Tel *911 331 999*
Popular both as a daytime bistro
and a night-time café; offers
sandwiches, burgers and salads
in a cosy setting of wooden
furniture and bookshelves. Live
music on weekends.

Bratislava Flag Ship   €
European   **Map** A6
Námestie SNP 8, 811 02
Tel *917 927 673*
In a fun-pub atmosphere
crammed with nautical bric-a-
brac, this is a popular night out
for young diners. The menu runs
a gamut of European fare from
salads to pastas and stews to
steaks along with Slovak dishes.

**Bratislavsky Mestiansky
Pivovar**   €
Slovak   **Map** A6
Dunajska 21
Tel *948 710 888*
A large beer hall and spacious
garden that serves meaty
standards such as goulash,
steaks and grilled sausages. Wash
them down with home-brewed
Bratislavsky ležiak pilsener beer.

Al Faro   €€
Italian   **Map** A6
Eurovea, Pribinova 81A
Tel *917 344 444*
Popular Italian restaurant serving
classic veal and seafood dishes as
well as pastas and pizzas. Located
in the Eurovea shopping mall, it
comes with good views of Danube.

Divná Muza   €€
International   **Map** A6
Radnicná 1
Tel *911 435 661*   **Closed** *Mon*
With tables spread across the
courtyard of the Apponyi Palace,
this is one of the most popular
restaurants in the Old Town.
Steaks, poultry and freshwater
fish provide plenty of choice.
Live music on summer weekends.

Elesko Wine Park   €€
Contemporary Slovak   **Map** A6
Modra 2275, 900 01
Tel *(02) 20 92 26 49*
Closed *Mon & Tue*
A blend of Slovak tradition and
haute cuisine in a modern dining
room in Modra, a wine-producing
village east of the city. Fresh lamb
and game is locally sourced.

Green Buddha   €€
Asian   **Map** A6
Zelená 4
Tel *944 044 048*
A stylish interior with oriental
touches provides the backdrop
to a menu that features authentic
Southeast Asian dishes, with
plenty of seafood and vegetarian
choices. The exotic desserts are
well worth trying.

Modra hviezda   €€
Slovak   **Map** A6
Behlavého 14
Tel *948 703 070*
Traditional poultry, rabbit
and game dishes, backed
with local wines, served
in homely surroundings.
Seating is in a bare brick cellar
or beside the cobbles of
Behlavého lane.

Parcafé   €€
Mediterranean   **Map** A6
Búdková 39
Tel *911 902 992*
An agreeable Spanish café-
restaurant beside Horský
Park serving a range of tapas
and some appetizing mains,
including lots of seafood. Try
the *paella* (Spanish rice dish)
or baked sea bass.

DK Choice

Pivnica u Zlatej Husy   €€
Slovak   **Map** A6
*Pezinská 2, Slovensky Grob,
900 26*
Tel *0905 525 417*
Just outside Bratislava, the
village of Slovensky Grob is
famous for its roast goose.
Translated as the 'Golden
Goose Tavern', this is the
most famous of many wel-
coming rustic inns serving
the local speciality. The
goose is usually served
whole (sufficient for a family),
although individual cuts
can also be ordered. *Lokša*
(potato pancakes) is the
traditional side order.

Sladovna House of Beer   €€
Brewery   **Map** A6
Ventúrska 5, 811 01
Tel *(02) 20 79 17 38*
A typical Slovak beer hall
serving meaty mains such
as steaks and pork knuckle.
Big-screen sport and beer
from the local Zlaty Bazant
brewery make this a popular
social venue for locals.

Zyllinder   €€
Central European   **Map** A6
*Hviezdoslavovo
námestie 19*
Tel *(02) 20 86 36 86*
With a superb main-square
location, 'Top Hat' serves up
dishes from the Habsburg
era, notably Wiener schnitzel
and Tafelspitz boiled beef,
in a spacious, retro-meets-
minimalist setting.

Albrecht Hotel   €€€
Gourmet   **Map** A6
Mudronova 82
Tel *902 333 888*
European haute-cuisine
with game and seafood is
well represented here. For
the full gourmet experience,
try Albrecht's multi-course
tasting menus. Stylish modern
rooms combine bare wood
and matt black surfaces.

Au Café   €€€
International   **Map** A6
*Tyršovo nábrežie 12
(entry via Viedenská cesta)*
Tel *(02) 62 52 03 55*
A long-time local favourite
on the south bank of the
Danube. It has fantastic views
of the castle and offers an
extensive menu of exquisite
spaghettis, risottos and hearty
grilled steaks.

Parisian-style atmosphere and vintage
decor at Bistro St Germain, Bratislava

FouZoo €€€
Japanese **Map** A6
Ševčenkova 34
Tel *901 747 474*
Japanese fusion restaurant
serving top-class sushi and
an appetizing variety of steak
or seafood mains. The decor
is an arty combination of
contemporary and retro science-
fiction influences.

Le Monde €€€
Gourmet **Map** A6
Rybárska Brána 8, 811 01
Tel *(02) 54 41 54 11*
Closed *Sat & Sun*
Situated in a historic house in
Old Town, Le Monde excels in
sophisticated French cuisine with
a modern slant. Many dishes have
a Mediterranean or oriental twist.
Fantastic views from the terrace.

Massimo Ristorante €€€
Italian **Map** A6
River Park, Dvorákovo
nábrežie 4, 811 03
Tel *0905 119 381*
Just a 10-minute walk from
the banks of the Danube, this
authentic and classy Italian
eatery serves satisfying meat
and seafood mains and delicious
home-made pasta.

Messina €€€
International **Map** A6
Tobrucká 4
Tel *(02) 57 78 46 00*
Located in the Marrol's boutique
hotel, warm colours and chandeliers set the tone for a seasonally
changing menu of creative
cuisine. Expect the best cuts of
meat and poultry, served with
inventive combinations of spices
and vegetables.

Tarpan €€€
Fusion **Map** A6
Májová 23, 851 01
Tel *(02) 44 25 02 16*
This cult restaurant near the
University of Economics in
Petržalka, south of river Danube,
mixes Czech standards such
as Wiener schnitzel with an
innovative array of modern-
European dishes, marrying local
ingredients with exotic spices.

UFO €€€
Fusion **Map** A6
Novy Most
Tel *(02) 62 52 03 00*
Located in the circular space
at the top of the pylon on
Novy Most bridge, stylish UFO
offers Mediterranean-Asian
fusion cuisine, cocktails and
delicious desserts. Breathtaking
views of the city.

Pleasant street views from the Massimo Ristorante in Bratislava

West Slovakia

KOMÁRNO: Banderium €€
Central European **Map** B6
Námestie M R Štefánika 11, 945 01
Tel *(035) 773 19 30*
Housed in an 18th-century
building, this is a great place to
sample paprika-rich Hungarian
fish dishes such as carp goulash
and *halászlé* (spicy fish soup).
Pasta dishes and local game
feature on the menu as well.

DK Choice

KOŠARISKÁ: U Juhasa €€
Contemporary Slovak **Map** B5
Košariská 89, 906 15
Tel *(034) 624 28 07*
Set in a lovely green valley
of the Small Carpathians, this
village farmstead has built a
reputation of serving exquisite
dishes made from home-reared
poultry and pork, locally hunted
game and garden vegetables.
Local wines and plum brandies
fill out an exciting drinks menu.
The home-made ice cream,
lemonade and fruit juices are
a welcome extra.

NITRA: Mikado Rouge €€€
Gourmet **Map** B6
Hollého 11, 949 01
Tel *(037) 321 03 58*
This modern-European restaurant
has people driving out from
Bratislava to enjoy the seasonal
menu of local game and fish.
Multi-course tasting menus are
paired with appropriate wines.

NITRA: Zlaty Klúčik €€€
Gourmet **Map** B6
Svätourbanská 27, 949 01
Tel *(037) 655 02 89*
Located on the slopes of
Mt Zobor, Zlaty Klúčik provides
excellent views from the terrace.
The menu focuses on contemporary

European cuisine with local
organic ingredients. Splendid
desserts and a good wine list.

NOVÉ ZÁMKY: Berek €
Slovak **Map** B6
Tatranská 177
Tel *(035) 644 61 21*
This old-fashioned, folk-style pavilion
in the Berek forest park offers local
staples, grilled chicken, freshwater
fish and an unlimited lunch buffet.

NOVÉ ZÁMKY: Hubert €€
Slovak **Map** B6
Budovateľská 2, 940 60
Tel *918 270 344*
Game and freshwater fish are the
specialities offered. Bargain daily
specials are a major attraction,
as are the summer terrace and
Japanese garden.

PIEŠŤANY: Le Griffon €€
International **Map** B5
Winterova 29, 921 01
Tel *(033) 774 19 03*
A smart café-restaurant with
a street-corner terrace serving
outstanding French and Italian
cuisine. Perfect for a light lunch
or a feast of steak or roast fowl.

TRENČIANSKE TEPLICE:
Kursalon €€
Central European **Map** B5
ul. 17 Novembra 32, 914 51
Tel *(032) 381 01 43*
Chandelier-illuminated place
in the spa park serving classic
Central European fare as well as
vegetarian dishes. A good wine
list and live music.

TRENČÍN: Elizabeth €€
Steakhouse **Map** B5
Gen. M R Štefánika, 911 01
Tel *(032) 650 61 11*
This hotel-restaurant is attractively
situated at the foot of Trenčín
Castle. Creatively prepared
classic European meat and
poultry dishes. The house spe-
ciality is the expertly grilled steak.

For more information on types of restaurants *see page 359*

TRNAVA: Patriot €€
International Map B5
Jeruzalemska 12, 917 01
Tel *(033) 551 25 11*
Globe-trotting bistro fare in
a homely bar-restaurant. Italian
pastas and risottos, juicy steaks,
roast fowl and Slovak dumpling
dishes compete for attention.

Central Slovakia

**BANSKÁ BYSTRICA: Hotel
Šachtička** €
Slovak Map C5
Šachtičky 34, 974 01
Tel *(048) 414 19 11*
Looking out onto mountain
slopes, this hotel-restaurant is a
great place to enjoy freshwater
fish, lamb, game, dumplings and
other Slovak staples.

**BANSKÁ BYSTRICA: Hotel
Dixon** €€
International Map C5
Švermová 32, 974 04
Tel *(048) 470 78 00*
Stylish hotel-restaurant offering
Slovak and classic European
dishes. Outdoor terrace with
an open grill in summer.

**BANSKÁ BYSTRICA:
Hotel Lux** €€
International Map C5
Námestie Slobody 2, 974 00
Tel *(048) 414 41 41*
Attractive views of the Old Town
and a broad Central European-
Mediterranean menu, including
plenty of vegetarian options. The
desserts alone merit a visit.

**BANSKÁ BYSTRICA:
Angels** €€€
International Map C5
Horná 25, 974 01
Tel *(048) 415 28 45*
Creative Central European-
meets-Mediterranean cuisine

Beautifully presented sweet delicacy at
Pivovar ERB, Banská Štiavnica

in an interior decorated with
angel symbols and dolls. Ivy-
and plant-lined outdoor
patio seating.

**BANSKÁ ŠTIAVNICA:
Pivovar ERB** €€
Pub Map C5
Novozámocká 2, 969 01
Tel *917 755 235*
Feast on pork hock, lamb
chops, goulash or fried breaded
cheese while quaffing some
of Slovakia's finest beer in
this modern pub. Furnished
with wooden tables overlooked
by copper brewing vats.

DK Choice

BREZNO: Tálska Bašta €€€
Slovak Map D5
Bystrá 108, Tále, 977 65
Tel *(048) 630 88 17*
Closed *Wed & Sun*
When it comes to turning
Carpathian mountain cuisine
into culinary gold, few places
come close. Housed in a sleek,
modern building inspired by
traditional shepherds' huts,
Tálska Bašta serves Slovak
dumpling-heavy cuisine
with finesse and imagination,
together with roast meats,
game and old-style desserts.
Try *šúľance* (potato dumplings
with poppy seeds or jam).

**CERVENÝ KLÁŠTOR: Gorlaská
reštaurácia u Petrika** €€€
Slovak Map E4
Červeny Kláštor 61, 059 06
Tel *0905 314 282*
Themed around Carpathian
folklore, this restaurant features
typical highland dishes of lamb,
poultry and game. Charming
setting with wood furnishings
and traditional music.

GERLACHOV: Hotel Hubert €€
International Map D4
Gerlachov 302, 059 42
Tel *(052) 478 08 11*
A café-restaurant complex,
offering local and international
cuisine, set amid the romantic
scenery of the High Tatras.
The menu includes plenty of
freshwater fish, pork and game.

JASNÁ: Tri Studničky €€€
Gourmet Map E5
Demänovská Dolina 5
Tel *(044) 547 80 00*
Known across Slovakia for
its outstanding haute cuisine,
'Three Wells' prepares everything
from French classics to grilled
steaks and pizzas with style
and creativity.

MARTIN: Martinka €€€
International Map C4
A. Sokolika 2, 036 01
Tel *(043) 401 20 77*
A stylish setting in a downtown
hotel. The menu features lamb,
poultry and freshwater fish,
alongside lighter Mediterranean
salads, pastas and risottos.

PARTIZÁNSKE: Afrodita €€€
Gourmet Map C5
Prievidzská 30, 972 46
Tel *0905 354 538*
Imaginative French-influenced
cuisine in a gorgeous castle setting.
The menu is strong on seafood,
game (including local mountain
goat) and exquisite desserts.

**STARÝ SMOKOVEC:
Lefevre** €€€
International Map D4
Starý Smokovec 25, 062 01
Tel *(052) 478 00 00*
Classy restaurant in the Grand
Hotel serving traditional Slovak
dishes and European-Asian
fusion cuisine. Refreshing
outdoor terrace in summer.

**ŠTRBSKÉ PLESO: Koliba na
Janovej Polianke** €
Slovak Map D4
Cesta k vodopádom 17, 059 85
Tel *(052) 449 21 30*
Stylish restaurant, café and pub
within the Tatra National Park.
Enjoy Slovak highland dishes
on wooden tables with folk
music in the background.

**TATRANSKÁ LOMNICA:
Zbojnicka Koliba** €€
Slovak Map E4
Tatranská Lomnica 192, 059 60
Tel *(052) 446 76 30*
The "Robbers' Cottage" presents
tasty Slovak mountain cuisine
in a folksy environment, with
wooden tables, traditional
ceramics and staff in
embroidered smocks.

**TATRANSKÁ LOMNICA: Grand
Hotel Praha** €€€
French Map E4
Tatranská Lomnica 8, 059 60
Tel *(052) 446 79 41*
Chandelier-lit dining at this
sophisticated restaurant, on
a choice of classic French
cooking. Plenty of fish and
options for vegetarians.

ŽDIAR: Goralska Krčma €€
Slovak Map E4
Ždiar 460, 059 55
Tel *(052) 449 81 38*
Traditional cheesy dumplings,
freshwater fish and roast meats
at this rustic restaurant with
splendid mountain views.

Key to Price Guide *see page 376*

ŽILINA: Gold Wing €€
International Map C4
Mariánske námestie 30/5, 010 01
Tel *918 628 913*
Imaginative modern European cuisine presented with panache at this elegant restaurant in the centre of town. Venison, fish and seafood are house specialities. Strong international wine list.

East Slovakia

KEŽMAROK: Hotel Club €€
Slovak Map E4
MUDr. Alexandra 24, 060 01
Tel *(052) 452 40 51*
A wide selection of Slovak and Central European dishes, with specialities including venison, boar and roast suckling pig. The interior flaunts hunting trophies. There is also a summer outdoor terrace.

KOŠICE: Golem €
Slovak Map F5
Dominikánske námestie 15, 040 01
Tel *(055) 728 91 02*
Traditional Slovak pub food, from smoked beef tongue to grilled pork and chicken, complemented with locally brewed ales. Choose between the wooden-floorboard beer hall or the summer garden.

KOŠICE: Hotel Bankov €€
International Map F5
Dolny Bankov 2
Tel *(055) 632 45 22*
A chandelier-illuminated dining room, a garden terrace and live piano music characterize this elegant spot in the suburbs. Central European veal, chicken and freshwater fish dishes are prepared and served with flair.

DK Choice

KOŠICE: Med Malina €€
Slovak Map F5
Hlavná 81, 040 01
Tel *(055) 622 03 97*
The dining room at Med Malina recalls granny's kitchen, complete with wooden sideboards and hanging clumps of garlic. Sample a spread of East Slovak specialities. The *pirohy* (pastry parcels stuffed with meat, potato, cabbage or cottage cheese) are well worth trying. Dishes such as *bigos* (meat and cabbage stew) and *zurek* (rye soup) betray the influence of nearby Poland.

Lavish dining room of Hotel Bankov with crystal chandeliers and coffered ceiling, Košice

KOŠICE: Villa Regia €€
Slovak Map F5
Dominikánske námestie 3, 040 01
Tel *(055) 625 65 10*
Atmospheric restaurant decorated with sepia photographs and vintage bric-a-brac. Serves generous grilled steaks, Slovak cheesy noodle staples and an unusually varied list of wines.

KOŠICE: Olive Tree €€€
Mediterranean Map F5
Hlavná 1, 040 01
Tel *(055) 325 11 00*
This DoubleTree hotel-restaurant offers a seasonal menu of pastas, salads, seafood and classic grilled steaks. Good for Sunday family brunch.

LEVOČA: Reštaurácia u 3 Apoštolov €
Slovak Map E4
Námestie Majstra Pavla 11, 054 01
Tel *(053) 451 43 52*
An elegant restaurant in the historic town centre offering traditional Slovak cuisine and a large selection of freshwater fish, including mountain trout. A choice of vegetarian dishes.

LEVOČA: U Leva €
International Map E4
Námestie Majstra Pavla 25, 054 01
Tel *(053) 450 23 11*
Attractive dining spot in a Baroque building. The Mediterranean-influenced menu includes pastas and risottos alongside Slovakian folk staples.

POPRAD: Forum Sabbathae €€
Slovak Map E4
Sobotské námestie 43, 058 01
Tel *(052) 776 96 02*
Restaurant, café and wine bar in an atmospheric Renaissance building. Specializes in game, steaks and rustic dumpling dishes. A good list of Slovak and international wines.

POPRAD: Sabato €€
Slovak Map E4
Sobotské námestie 6, 058 01
Tel *(052) 776 95 80*
Located in a 17th-century building in the historic heart of Poprad, Sabato serves typical Slovak comfort food such as baked pirohy dumplings plus lamb, poultry and fish dishes.

PREŠOV: Ludwig €€
International Map F4
Požiarnická 2
Tel *(051) 748 19 58*
Modern European cuisine with a Mediterranean flavour in a castle-style building close to the town centre. Elegant, period decor inside; pleasant garden seating outside.

SPIŠSKÁ NOVA VES: Hotel Metropol €€
International Map E5
Stefanikovo námestie 2, 052 01
Tel *(053) 417 47 00*
Chic hotel-restaurant with a broad choice of European dishes. Good selection of fish and some excellent desserts. Guests can dine outdoors on the patio in summer.

SPIŠSKÁ NOVA VES: Nostalgie €€
International Map E5
Letná 49, 052 01
Tel *(053) 441 41 44*
A historic restaurant with a contemporary-global menu. Offers Mexican, Italian and Creole options a well as local freshwater fish and poultry. Be sure to save room for dessert.

For more information on types of restaurants *see page 359*

SHOPPING IN THE CZECH REPUBLIC

In many ways, shopping is undergoing great changes in the Czech Republic, with shopping malls springing up in large and medium-sized towns, and international chains opening branches. This means that many standard essentials can be easily bought here. For a choice of goods with more of a Czech flavour, Prague cannot be beaten, particularly around Wenceslas Square and in the Staré Město. Elsewhere, you can still pick up good quality and sometimes quirky regional items in individual specialized shops – and browsing is an essential part of the pleasure. Typical Czech products include crystal glassware, craft items, wooden toys and antiques. Lovely Czech gems are also worth investigating, particularly garnets. There are some excellent book and music shops in Prague and around the country.

One of Prague's numerous antique shops

Opening Hours

Most shops open from 10am to 6pm, Monday to Friday; shopping centres and supermarkets usually stay open for longer, both earlier and later. Small shops may close for an hour at lunchtime. On Saturdays, shops close at 1 or 2pm, with large shopping centres remaining open until 8pm. On Sundays, only large shopping centres and selected food stores open for business, and in small towns and villages, all shops may remain closed, or some may open for just a few hours in the morning.

Sales

From time to time, some Czech shops offer seasonal price reductions, especially at the end of a season and after Christmas.

How to Pay

Larger shops accept major credit and debit cards, but smaller outlets prefer cash. Visitors from non-EU countries can claim a VAT refund of up to 14 per cent of the purchase price of some goods on leaving the country.

Markets

Prague has several famous markets. During its Christmas and Easter markets, the Old Town Square and Wenceslas Square fill with festive and traditional goods. There are two permanent markets. The central, open-air **Havel Market** sells fruit and vegetables as well as some toys and ceramics; it is open all year round from 7am to 6pm. The huge, mainly indoor **Prague Market** sells all sorts of consumer goods.

Outside Prague, local markets in most towns and cities sell produce and other everyday items, and sometimes crafts. In large cities, you can find markets where Vietnamese vendors sell Asian clothes. Along the border with the former East Germany, Vietnamese sellers also trade in cigarettes, alcohol, and even Czech glass and crystal. The biggest concentration of such trade is the Hřensko border crossing, along the road from Děčín to Dresden. A large market selling mainly alcohol has developed near the border with Poland, at the Kudowa-Náchod crossing.

Glass and Ceramics

Bohemia is famous for its high-quality lead crystal and ornamental glass. The main glass-producing regions are Krušné hory and the Šumava. In every town, it is possible to find a shop specializing in glass and crystal artifacts, and in the Staré Město in Prague there are literally scores of them; some of the best known are **Český porcelán, Dana-Bohemia, Moser** and **Artěl**. One large crystal wine glass, gilded and hand-painted with decorations, can cost in excess of 1,000Kč,

A decorative lamp from Harrachov

but truly beautiful products are worth their price.

Another interesting souvenir from the Czech Republic is a traditional earthenware beer tankard decorated with a Czech brewery logo.

Handicrafts and Folk Crafts

Fruit and vegetable market in Brno

Traditional crafts are alive and well in the Czech Republic. The range of original souvenirs includes ceramics, wooden vessels and wooden toys. The largest selection of such goods can be found at local markets, but gift and souvenir shops may also have some interesting items on offer.

Antiques

The Czech Republic is a country rich in antiques. During the 1990s, many shops opened specializing in antiques and now you can find them (called *Starožitnosti*) in almost every town. They are, of course, most numerous in Prague's Old Town. Well-known examples in the Old Town include **Bazar Nábytku, Dorotheum** and **Pražské Starožitnosti**. Their

The famous Czech "spa wafers"

range of goods includes mostly antique furniture, paintings, porcelain and a variety of old bric-a-brac. Prices are often more reasonable than in western Europe.

Food

Czech chocolates are particularly good. The great variety of types includes boxed chocolates, bars *(tyčinky)* and wafers. Spa wafers are traditionally taken with spa water; spa hotels and speciality shops often sell these. The Czech Republic is also a country producing excellent cheeses. In some delicatessens, you can buy long strings of smoked cheese. *Olomoucke tvarůžky*, oval cheeses with a distinct flavour, are also excellent.

Department stores, found in almost every large town, are a good bet for food shopping. Their food sections are usually on the ground floor.

Alcoholic Drinks

Famous Czech beers Pilsner Urquell (Prazdroj) and Budvar, which make excellent presents, can be bought in practically every food store. It is also worth boosting your own stock with a supply of local, lesser-known brands. When it comes to liquors, virtually all Czech brands, including the famous Becherovka, are available throughout the country. Absinthe and *slivovice* (plum brandy) are other popular Czech spirits.

Wines from South Moravia and the Mělník area are the finest and well worth taking back home. In Prague, a good selection of alcoholic drinks can be found in **Jan Paukert** delicatessen *(lahůdky)*. If you are in the wine-producing areas, you can usually visit the vineyards to taste and buy.

DIRECTORY

Markets

Havel Market
Havelská, Prague 1.
Map 3 B4.

Prague Market
Holešovice, Prague 7.
W holesovickatrznice.cz

Glass and Ceramics

Artěl
Celetná 29, Prague 1.
Map 3 C3.
Tel 224 815 085.
W artelshop.com

Český porcelán
Perlová 1, Prague 1.
Map 3 C5.
Tel 224 210 955.

Dana-Bohemia
Národní 43, Prague.
Map 3 A5.
Tel 224 214 655.

Hračky
Loretánské náměstí 3,
Prague. **Map** 1 B3.
Tel 603 515 745.

**Jan Cidrych –
Porcelán**
Jablonecká 1270, Liberec.
Tel 602 648 206.

Moser
Na Příkopě 12, Prague.
Map 3 C4.
Tel 224 211 293.

Sklárny Bohemia
Náměstí T G Masaryka
1130, Poděbrady.
Tel 325 611 618.

**Zdeněk Kleprlík –
Veste Glass**
Dědinova 2011, Prague 4.
Tel 272 934 117.
W vesteglass.com

Antiques

Antik Bazar
Pobrezni 42, Prague 8.
Tel 603 480 904.
W antik-bazar.cz

Bazar Nábytku
U Svobodárny 5a, Prague 9.
Tel 776 343 953.

Dorotheum
Ovocný trh 2, Prague.
Map 3 C3. **Tel** 224 216 676.

Galerie Art
Staroměstské náměstí 20,
Prague 1. **Map** 3 C3.
Tel 257 530 722.

Pražské Starožitnosti
Mikulandská 8, Prague.
Map 3 B5.
Tel 224 930 572.

**Starožitnosti
pod Kinskou**
Náměstí Kinských 7,
Tel 257 311 245.
W antique-shop.cz

Food and Alcoholic Drinks

**Jan Paukert
Delicatessen
and Wine Bar**
Národní 17, Prague.
Map 3 A5.
Tel 224 222 615.
W janpaukert.cz

SHOPPING IN SLOVAKIA

The souvenirs and presents most often brought back from Slovakia are handcrafted goods, such as traditional clothing, tablecloths, lace, wooden or china figurines, sculptures, ceramics and paintings – on glass, wood or ceramic. An original, although somewhat bulky, souvenir would be a *fujara*, a vast mountain horn up to 4 m (13 ft) in length! Visitors to the Tatras mountains can bring back a *valaška* – a highlander's walking stick.

The local cheeses are varied and delicious, and Slovak wines, beers and spirits are good value.

Shops in Slovakia range from small local outlets and bazaars and markets to department stores and supermarkets belonging to large international chains. The best places to buy Slovak handcrafted goods are at the numerous folk festivals, but you can also get them in specialist shops, which you will generally find in any of the larger towns.

A souvenir stall

Opening Hours

Shops in Slovakia are generally open from 9am to 6pm, although some food stores open as early as 6am and do not close until 8 or 9pm. Some shops open on Saturdays and Sundays, usually until 1pm.

Shops belonging to large chains, like Carrefour, Billa or Hypernova, are usually open every day of the week until late at night (Saturdays and Sundays until 5pm). Out-of-town hypermarkets such as Tesco are open 24 hrs. These are not to be confused with Tesco town centre department stores, which are open the same hours as smaller shops.

How to Pay

As in the Czech Republic, larger shops will accept major credit and debit cards, but smaller outlets will accept only cash.

Sales Tax

In the Slovak Republic, sales tax is known as DPH *(daň z pridanej hodnoty)*. It is charged on most goods at a flat rate of 19 per cent.

When they leave the country, visitors from non-EU countries can claim a refund of sales tax of up to 14 per cent of the purchase price of goods over €165.

Department Stores

Over the last decade, Slovakia, particularly Bratislava, has experienced a boom of large, modern, trendy shopping malls and galleries. Some of these are within walking distance of the city centre, and open seven days a week from 10am to 9pm. Most large department stores in town centres date from the Communist era, but their interiors have been adapted to modern trade requirements.

Some have been taken over by the Tesco group. The range of goods on offer is practically the same as that found on the shelves of all large stores in Europe.

Markets

In many Slovak towns and villages, the traditional market day is Saturday. This is when locals come out to buy the best locally grown and farmed fruit, vegetables and meat. The most famous weekly produce market takes place in the Miletičova market place in Bratislava (Miletičova 9).

At Slovak markets, besides buying all sorts of goods, you can also taste local delicacies, such as potato pancake *(lokša)* and fried garlic cakes *(langoš)*, as well as local wines.

Ceramics

Slovakia has some interesting ceramics. Majolica from Modra is particularly popular;

Goods on sale inside an UĽUV shop, Bratislava

Europe Place square and shopping mall in Komárno, West Slovakia

the factory shop in Modra, **Slovenská ľudová majolika**, has a superb selection, but its china is sold all over Slovakia.

Antiques

Antique shops (*starožitnosti*) are not as prevalent as in the Czech Republic, but are still found in most towns, and there are many interesting items and sometimes bargains to be snapped up.

Handicrafts and Traditional Art

The agricultural character of most of Slovakia's regions has helped to preserve a great many traditions and customs throughout the country.

An excellent present from Slovakia might be a doll dressed in traditional costume. Other interesting traditional Slovak items include embroidery, tablecloths, wood carvings, painted Easter eggs, dolls made of dried corn leaves or wire, and secular or religious paintings on glass, wood or ceramics. Slovak traditional artists are also renowned for their wood carvings, mostly depicting saints and Nativity figures. Complete Nativity scenes are quite pricey but make superb and unique presents or mementos that last for decades. Models of traditional Slovak wooden buildings are also beautiful items to bring home.

Traditional crafts and art products can be bought relatively easily in larger towns and tourist resorts. Try **U Žofky** in Bratislava, **Krausko a syn** in Bojnice, or **U Kráľa Mateja** in Spišská Sobota). **UĽUV** (Centre for Folk Art Production) is a chain of stores specializing in selling Slovak handicrafts.

Food and Drink

Slovak shops sell a variety of traditional local food products, such as sheep cheeses, including *bryndza*, smoked *oštiepky* and steamed *parenica*. The culinary speciality of the Malá Fatra region are *korbáčiky* – strings of plaited smoked and steamed cheeses.

Those who enjoy a tipple might like to bring home from Slovakia a few bottles of a local wine, liqueurs, the famous plum brandy *slivovica*, or cognac. They are all relatively inexpensive. Slovak Zlatý bažant bottled beer is excellent.

DIRECTORY

Ceramics

Detvianske ľudové umenie
Partizánska St, Detva.
Tel 0903 969 967.
🔲 dlu.sk

Folk – Folk
Rybárska Brána 2,
Bratislava.
Tel (02) 54 43 48 74.

I.N.A Business
Obchodná 60, Bratislava.
Keramika Hand Made
Vajanskeho 10, 934 01
Levice.
Tel 0903 219 544.

Ľudové umenie Kramaričová
Alžbetina 32/34, Košice.

Slovenská ľudová majolika
Dolná 138, 900 01 Modra.
Tel (033) 647 29 41.
🔲 majolika.sk

Antiques and Handicrafts

Antique Erika
Dolný Val, 010 01, Žilina.
Tel 0905 906 668.

Kora
Hurbanovo námestie
46, Bojnice.
Tel (046) 541 24 95.

Staro Žitnosti
Pavel Haluška, Ul. 1. mája
19, Liptovský Mikuláš.
🔲 antikliptov.com

U Kráľa Mateja
Sobotké námestie
1774/31, Poprad – Spišská
Sobota. **Tel** 0907 564 312.
🔲 antiq.sk

U Žofky
Michalska 5, Bratislava.
Tel (02) 54 43 19 94.

UĽUV Stores
🔲 uluv.sk
Main store:
Obchodná 64, 816 11
Bratislava.
Tel 0915 987 299.

Other branches:
Dolná 14, 974 01 Banská
Bystrica.
Tel (048) 412 36 57.

Radniené námestie 42,
085 67 Bardejov.
Tel (054) 472 29 84.

Námestie SNP 12, 811
06 Bratislava.
Tel (102) 52 92 38 02.

Hlavná 137 – kolégium,
080 01 Prešov.
Tel (051) 773 22 66.

Tatranská Lomnica 36.
Tel (524) 467 322.

CZECH ENTERTAINMENT

The Czech Republic offers a wide variety of entertainment for its visitors, with something for every taste and interest. Those who enjoy nightlife will get the most from Prague, with its scores of nightclubs, theatres, cinemas and music venues. Outside Prague, the options are more limited, but most other large towns and cities have a lively cultural scene, though it may be mostly for Czech speakers. During the main holiday period, numerous Czech castles stage knights' tournaments with brilliant displays of fencing or swordsmanship. In the evenings, dramatic episodes associated with the site's history are performed. Concerts of early and Baroque music and organ recitals take place in castles and churches. Many towns and tourist resorts organize club nights and rock concerts featuring local and international artists.

An outdoor performance of a play in Český Krumlov, South Bohemia

Information

Information on what is on and where in Prague can be found in the listings of the weekly English-language *Prague Post*, sold in the city and available on the Internet (*www.praguepost. com*). Here and elsewhere, tourist offices are also a good source of information, and look out for free leaflets and posters in the local area.

Booking and Prices

Tickets for cultural events in the Czech Republic are not excessively expensive: they range from around 100Kč (for one of the smaller theatres in Prague) up to 3,000Kč (for a concert by a major orchestra).

Concert and theatre tickets can be booked by telephone or by letter. Tickets to Prague's National Opera or National Theatre can also be purchased on the Internet. Group tickets to the most popular performances can be booked well in advance. If you are visiting in the summer, it makes sense to book ahead for performances you

particularly want to see and they will deliver the tickets to your hotel.

Cinema

There are cinemas throughout the country, even in small towns. They show the latest foreign releases (often Hollywood blockbusters), as well as Czech productions. Most foreign films are shown in their original language with Czech subtitles. One of the biggest multi-screen cinemas in Prague is the

Classical music concert in Prague's State Opera

Cinema City Flora complex. The largest Czech cinema event is the annual **International Film Festival** held in late June and early July in Karlovy Vary.

Theatre

Most large towns have a theatre, often a historic building with a beautiful interior. Czech theatre has a long tradition. Prague's **National Theatre** (*see pp96–7*) is the city's main theatre, but there are many mainstream and fringe theatres, such as the **Laterna Magika** and the **Komedie**, both of which stage more avant-garde productions.

As a rule, theatres display the plays that are currently in repertoire on the front of the building, but posters advertising current productions can also be seen locally. Few productions outside Prague are in English.

Classical Music and Opera

Classical music has a long tradition in the Czech Republic. The country has produced some great composers, including Bedřich Smetana, Antonín Dvořák, Leoš Janáček, and Bohuslav Martinů. Works by Czech composers figure in the repertoires of local orchestras all year round. Although most orchestras and concert halls close for the holiday season, that is when numerous classical music concerts are staged in churches, castles and palaces. Many churches, in Prague and several other large cities, organize concerts of Baroque music.

The **Rudolfinum** *(see p84)* is the home of the Czech Philharmonic Orchestra. The Prague Symphony Orchestra is based at the **Municipal House** *(see pp86–7)*. The **State Opera** and the **Estates Theatre** in Prague stage first-class operas and ballets.

Brno has a very active classical music scene; the **National Theatre** is a superb concert venue.

Imposing façade of the Mahenovo Theatre in Brno

Music Festivals

Another great attraction for music lovers are the Czech music festivals (for specific festivals, *see pp30–33*). The most famous is **Prague Spring International Music Festival**. Prague also stages an **International Jazz Festival** in October.

One of the best ways to sample Czech folk music is at one of its many folk festivals; enquire at tourist offices for details of events, which can be very crowded.

Nightlife

There are large numbers of music and dance clubs that specialize in different kinds of music, so that most music fans will be able to find something to their liking. Every large Czech town has a music club, although their greatest numbers are in Prague.

The best-known cultural centre in Prague is **Palace Akropolis**. This complex includes a theatre, concert hall, exhibition space, café and restaurant. It hosts many world music artists. **Agharta Jazz Centrum** is perhaps Prague's best jazz club; it is very popular so if you want to see a particular performer it is vital to book. **Malostranská Beseda** puts on rock, jazz, blues, country and folk music.

Outside Prague, check the flyposters for the current information on gigs and clubs. Most cities and larger towns have venues with live music nightly, mainly from Czech bands and musicians. Techno and dance is very popular throughout the country. Top Czech and some foreign DJs can be seen; again, check flyposters for details.

For gay and lesbian visitors, Prague has the most nightlife to offer. The magazine *Amigo* has listings. **Friends** is one of the most popular gay bars. Outside Prague and Brno, gay venues are much scarcer.

DIRECTORY

Tickets

☒ **ticketpro.cz**

Cinema

Cinema City Flora
Vinohradská 151, Prague 3.
Tel 255 742 021.
☒ **cinemacity.cz**

Theatres

Komedie Theatre
Jungmannova 1,
Prague 1. Map 3 C5.
Tel 224 222 734.
☒ **divadlokomedie.cz**

Laterna Magika
Národní 4, Prague 1.
Map 3 A5.
Tel 224 901 448.

National Theatre
Národní 2, Prague 1.

Map 3 A5.
Tel 224 901 448.
☒ **nationaltheatre.cz**

Classical Music and Opera

Estates Theatre
Ovocný trh/Železná,
Prague 1. Map 3 C4.
Tel 224 901 448.
☒ **narodni-divadlo.cz**

Municipal House
Náměstí Republiky 5,
Prague 1. Map 4 D3.
Tel 222 002 101.
☒ **obecnidum.cz**

National Theatre, Brno
Dvořákova 11, Brno.
Tel 542 158 111.
☒ **ndbrno.cz**

Rudolfinum
Alšovo nábřeži 12, Prague.
Map 3 A3.
Tel 227 059 227.
☒ **rudolfinum.cz**

State Opera
Wilsonova 4, Prague 1.
Map 4 E5. Tel 224 227
266. ☒ **opera.cz**

Music Festivals

International Jazz Festival
☒ **jazzfestivalpraha.cz**

Prague Spring
☒ **praguespring.cz**

Nightlife

Agharta Jazz Centrum
Železná 16, Prague 1.

Map 3 C4. Tel 222 211 275.
☒ **agharta.cz**

Friends
Bartolomějská 11.
Map 3 B5.
Tel 226 211 920.
☒ **friendsprague.cz**

Malostranská Beseda
Malostranské nám. 21,
Prague 1.
Map 3 C4.
Tel 774 277 060.

Palace Akropolis
Kubelíkova 27, Prague 1.
Tel 296 330 911.
☒ **palacakropolis.cz**

Rock Café
Národní 20, Prague 1.
Map 3 B5.
Tel 224 933 947.
☒ **rockcafe.cz**

SLOVAK ENTERTAINMENT

In Slovakia, the wide-ranging cultural entertainment on offer should satisfy most visitors. There are scores of theatres, cinemas, discotheques, dance clubs, concert halls, art galleries and museums. Visitors can see performances given by world-class artistes (mainly in large towns), as well as attend numerous folk festivals (more likely in the provinces). The best-known Slovak cultural event is the Bratislava Cultural Summer, which runs from June to September and includes classical, jazz and folk music performances as well as theatre and cinema shows. Similar festivals take place in other larger towns in the summer, as well as in some smaller tourist centres and spa resorts. Summer and autumn are the liveliest times to visit in terms of cultural events, but there is a great deal of interest all year round, particularly in Bratislava and the other major cities.

Performers at a pop concert in Bratislava

Information

The free English-language weekly *The Slovak Spectator* is a good source of information about what's on in the capital and around the country. The official tourist website www.slovakia.travel is also very informative and comprehensive. On the ground, try tourist offices for up-to-date local information.

Ticket Prices

It is hard to generalize about prices but a ticket to a Slovak Philharmonic concert or to the Slovak National Theatre will cost about €10–€20, a cinema ticket may cost as much as €5.

Cinema

Slovakia has a relatively large number of cinemas, particularly in Bratislava, but also in small towns and villages. The country has film clubs and alternative cinemas, which show non-commercial films. Most films are subtitled.

Modern multiplex cinemas such as **Cinema City** can be found in Bratislava. Most cinemas in Bratislava show 3D films.

Theatre

The beginnings of Slovak theatre go back to the Middle Ages. Out of the 24 national theatres that exist in Slovakia, a few give performances in foreign languages. These include Hungarian theatres in Košice and Komárno; Romany in Košice; and Ukrainian-Ruthenian in Prešov. Few performances are in English. Particularly outstanding is the contemporary theatre in Bratislava, **Astorka**.

Other theatres that enjoy spectacular successes include **Nová Scéna**, which is popular for musicals, **Radošín Naive Theatre** (Radošinské naivné divadlo), the avant-garde **GUnaGU** and **Aréna Theatre**, or **Theatre LOĎ**, which performs on a ship on the Danube. All are based in Bratislava, but productions may go on tour.

Slovakia also plays host to several international theatre festivals, including the Bábkarska Bystrica (festival of puppet theatres) in Banská Bystrica. The musicals, mime and puppet events enable non-Slovak speakers to enjoy Slovakia's rich traditions.

Classical Music, Opera and Ballet

The main establishments associated with classical music, opera and ballet have their homes in the capital. The **Slovak Philharmonic Orchestra** has been housed in the Neo-Baroque **Reduta** building *(see p286)* since 1949. In 1960 it gave birth to the Slovak Chamber Orchestra. The country's best opera

Foyer with bar in a Bratislava cinema

and ballet theatre is the **Slovak National Theatre** *(see p286)*.

Music Festivals

Each year, numerous music events and festivals take place throughout Slovakia *(see also pp260–63)*. The most prominent are the **Bratislava Music Festival** and **Bratislava Jazz Days**, both in the autumn.

The best-known Slovak festival of popular music is Bratislava Lyre, which used to be one of the flagship national entertainment events under Communist rule, and now is a nationwide song festival. The most important and the biggest folk festivals take place in Východná, Myjava, Detva, Zuberec, and Červený Kláštor.

Nightlife

Bratislava pulsates with life round the clock. From April until early October, countless outdoor areas for beer, wine and music spring up around the town. In the evenings, the focus of social life is in bars and pubs on the outskirts of the Old Town, in Korzo. Late at

Performance by the Slovak Philharmonic Orchestra

night, you may choose to venture into a fashionable discotheque or visit one of the capital's music clubs housed, for example, in the post-Communist nuclear shelters. The flourishing nightlife is encouraged by the relatively low prices of drinks.

The best-known and most popular clubs and discos in Bratislava include: **17's Bar** (rock), **Café Kút** (reggae), **Le Club** (live DJs), **Trafo Music Bar** (contemporary beats), **Casey** (disco), **Malecon** (Latino) and **Harley Davidson** (rock).

Club life is not limited to the country's capital city – those who enjoy spending their time this way can also find something to their liking in Košice, Trnava, Martin, Lučenec and in the foothills of the Tatras, although the entertainment on offer will be rather modest compared with that of Bratislava.

Inevitably, Bratislava is the place with the most nightlife to offer gay men and lesbians. Two established gay clubs are **D4** and **Apollon**.

DIRECTORY

Cinema

Cinema City
Shopping Centre Eurovea.
Tel (02) 68 20 22 22.
w cinemacity.sk

Theatres

Aréna Theatre
Viedenská cesta 10,
Bratislava. **Tel** (02) 67 20
25 57. w divadloarena.sk

Astorka Theatre
Námestie SNP 33.
w astorka.sk

GUnaGU
Františkánske námestie 7,
Bratislava. **Tel** (02) 54 43
33 35. w gunagu.sk

Nová Scéna
Živnostenská 1, Bratislava.
w nova-scena.sk

**Pressburger
Klezmer Band**
w klezmer.sk

Theatre LOĎ
Tyršovo nábrežie,
Bratislava.
Tel 0903 449 650.

Classical Music,
Opera and Ballet

**Slovak
National Theatre**
Pribinova 17, Bratislava
Historical Building
(Opera) Hviezdoslavovo
námestie Bratislava.
w snd.sk

**Slovak Philharmonic
Orchestra**
Palackého 2, Bratislava.
Tel (02) 59 20 82 33.
w filharm.sk

Music Festivals

Bratislava Jazz Days
w bjd.sk

Nightlife

17's Bar
Hviezdoslavovo námestie
17, Bratislava.
Tel 0903 259 429.

Apollon Gay Club
Panenská 24,
Bratislava.
Tel 0948 900 093.
w apollon-gay-club.sk

Café Kút
Zámočnícka 11,
Bratislava.
Tel (02) 54 43 49 57.

Casey
Botanická 35, Bratislava.
Tel 0907 290 111.

Harley Davidson
Rebarborová 1, Bratislava.
w harley-davidson.sk

Le Club
Hviezdoslavovo námestie
25, Bratislava.
Tel (02) 54 41 03 42.

Malecon
Námestie L. Štúra 4,
Bratislava.
Tel 0910 274 583.

Rock OK
Šafárikovo námestie 4,
Bratislava. w rockok.sk

Trafo Music Bar
Ventúrska 1 (Erdödy
Palace), Bratislava.
Tel 0907 704 849.
w trafo.sk

SPORT AND LEISURE IN THE CZECH REPUBLIC

Visitors to the Czech Republic can find plenty of opportunities for all kinds of leisure pursuits, and it is possible to plan a whole trip here around a particular activity. The mountains provide ideal areas for hiking and rock-climbing in summer, as well as being a paradise for snow enthusiasts in winter. An interesting way to explore the country is by bicycle; although the climbs can be steep, the surroundings are spectacular. Natural mineral spas have attracted visitors for centuries, and many resorts, especially in the west, are based around these spas. Canoeing along Czech rivers is becoming increasingly popular, while numerous reservoirs are suitable for sailing. There are also many opportunities for running, horse riding, golf and tennis. Tourist information offices have information on what is available.

Hiking and walking trails are a common sight in the mountains of the Czech Republic

Hiking

The mountains and foothills offer many opportunities for hiking. Almost every region has a dense network of marked trails, which makes it easy to reach destinations by following the most interesting routes. The many excellent hiking areas include the Šumava (see pp150–51), Krkonoše (see pp210–11) and the Český ráj (see pp208–9). A great help to hikers are the **Czech Hiking Club** (Klub Českých turistů) hiking maps, at a scale of 1:50,000, which include the marked trails and are available from most Czech bookshops.

The most convenient and cheapest form of overnight accommodation, particularly in the mountains, are hostels and shelters (see p346). Some bus and train routes link with points along the trails, making it easy to do a linear hike.

Cycling

Bicycles are plentiful in the Czech Republic. Numerous hotels and tourist resorts offer bicycles for hire, and many regions provide special marked trails for cyclists. These are in addition to international routes that run through the country. Special maps for cyclists can be

Cyclists on a quiet rural road in the Czech Republic

obtained from bookshops. There are no problems with transporting a bicycle (kolo) on a train.

Skiing and Snowboarding

The most popular skiing region is the Krkonoše mountains, with its famous ski jump in Harrachov. There are also well-maintained ski runs and lifts in the Jeseníky mountains in North Moravia, the Šumava (see pp150–51) in South Bohemia and other areas. Cross-country skiing is also widely enjoyed in the Czech Republic, with many regions providing marked routes for its enthusiasts. Snowboarding is growing in popularity and there are facilities in major winter sports resorts.

Rock Climbing

The country abounds in areas suitable for rock climbing. The best known among them is the Český ráj (see pp208–9), north of Prague, where keen climbers will find numerous weathered sandstone rocks, with marked climbing trails representing various degrees of difficulty. Another region popular with climbers is the Adršpach and Teplice Rocks (see p212) in East Bohemia, close to the Polish border. The tourist offices in these regions can provide excellent information, including details of mountaineering clubs.

Canoeists on the Vltava, near Nova Pec, South Bohemia

offer, which differ from spa to spa. The Czech Republic's most famous spas are in West Bohemia and include Karlovy Vary (*see pp176–7*), Mariánské Lázně (*p171*), and Františkovy Lázně (*p174*). There is also Luhačovice in South Moravia (*p241*), Teplice in North Bohemia (*p193*), and Jeseník in North Moravia (*p223*).

Water Activities

Many Czechs are water sports enthusiasts, enjoying windsurfing, sailing, canoeing, swimming and angling. This landlocked country has numerous lakes and reservoirs offering excellent conditions for these sports, as well as many rivers. Canoeing along turbulent mountain rivers is a relatively new sport here, with a particularly good stretch on the Labe (Elbe) in Krkonoše. Equipment can be hired from the many sport centres beside every lake.

Fishing is highly regulated so needs some planning. Contact the **Czech Fishing Union** (Český Rybářský Svaz) for detailed information, including times of seasons.

Spas

Spas have been popular for several hundred years (*see p176*) and still have thousands of visitors annually. Visitors drink the often foul-tasting spa water, traditionally using a special vessel called a *becher* (*see p363*). They also bathe in the warm waters, and undergo some of the medicinal treatments on

Golf and Tennis

Golf is gaining in popularity here. Currently there are over 100 golf clubs affiliated to the **Czech Golf Federation** (Česká Golfová Federace) and their total membership is over 20,000. Tennis courts can be used, for a fee, in any town that has a sports centre. Many hotels have tennis facilities, some open to non-residents.

Anglers on the shore of Lake Lipno in the Šumava, South Bohemia

DIRECTORY

Hiking

Czech Hiking Club
Revoluční 1056/8a,
Prague 1.
Tel 251 610 181.
W kct.cz

Skiing

Czech Skiing Association
Zátopkova 2, 160 17
Prague 6.
Tel 242 429 256.

Jeseníky Tourist Information Centre
Palackého 2/1341,
790 01 Jeseník.
Tel 584 459 514.

Železná Ruda Information Centre
Klostermannovo námesti 295 (town hall), 340 04 Železná Ruda, Šumava.
Tel 376 397 033.

Rock Climbing

Český ráj Information Centre
Náměstí Českého ráje 26,
511 01 Turnov.
Tel 481 366 255.
Fax 481 366 256.
W infocentrum-turnov.cz

Czech Climbing Organization
W czechclimbing.com

Fishing

Czech Fishing Union
Nad Olšinami 31, 100 00
Prague 10.
Tel 274 811 751.
W rybsvaz.cz

Spas

Czech Spa Information
Palackého nám 46/11,
379 01 Třeboň.
Tel 606 063 145.
W jedemedolazni.cz

Františkovy Lázně
W frantiskovylazne.cz

Karlovy Vary
W karlovyvary.cz

Luhačovice
W luhacovice.cz

Mariánské Lázně
W marianskelazne.cz

Teplice
W lazneteplice.cz

Golf and Tennis

Czech Golf Federation
Strakonická 2860, 150 00
Prague 5.
Tel 296 373 111.

Czech Tennis Association
Ostrov Štvanice 38, 170 00
Prague 7.
Tel 222 333 444.

Spectator Sports in the Czech Republic

The most popular spectator sport in the Czech Republic is undoubtedly football. Matches played by the national team as well as club matches are followed with great interest. Since some individual Czech players have been reasonably successful internationally, the Czechs also like following foreign games. Attending a match or watching live in a Czech pub is a memorable event. Czechs are truly world class in ice hockey, and matches often generate an emotional reaction from spectators. Another sport with an enthusiastic following is motorcycle racing; the Grand Prix competitions held in Brno are major international events.

Motocross, a sport with many keen spectators

Czech tennis player Jiří Novák during a match

Tennis

Although some of the major international Czech stars of tennis, such as Martina Navrátilová, Ivan Lendl and Jana Novotná perhaps now have their greatest successes behind them, the sport still enjoys considerable popularity in the Czech Republic. As well as watching matches, many people like to play tennis, as can be seen by the large numbers of tennis courts in towns and cities around the country.

Football

The Czechs have always been great fans of soccer, and in recent years, following the successes of their national team in European Championships in Holland and Portugal, their interest has grown even further. The local clubs, such as AC Sparta Praha, and Viktoria Plzeň, are well known in Europe. Some Czech players, such as Petr Čech or Milan Baroš, who play for European clubs, are also famous. The season is from September to December and March to June.

Ice Hockey

Czech ice hockey players can be seen on the winners' rostrum of virtually every world championship held in this sport. The national team won gold in the 1998 Winter Olympics. The Czech Tipsport Extraliga is one of the best leagues in Europe and Prague's youngest club, Lev Praha, is part of the world's second best Kontinental Hockey League (KHL) The ice hockey season is from September to April.

Motorcycle Sports

The Czech Republic has been a manufacturer of quality motorcyles for many decades, and motorcycle sports such as motocross and cinder-track racing are both avidly followed here. The Czechs have some high-class competitors and enjoy watching them battling. Brno Grand Prix cinder-track races attract thousands of spectators from all over Europe.

DIRECTORY

Football

Football Association of the Czech Republic
Diskařská 100, 160 17 Prague 6.
Tel 233 029 111.
W fotbal.cz

Ice Hockey

Czech Ice Hockey Association
Harfa Office Park, Českomoravská 2420/15, 190 00 Prague 9.
Tel 211 158 000.
W cslh.cz

KHL
W khl.ru

Motorcycle Sports

Czech Autoclub
Na Strži, 1837/9 Prague 4.
Tel 261 104 279.
W uamk-cr.cz

The Ice Hockey World Championships in Prague, 2004

SPORT AND LEISURE IN SLOVAKIA

Slovaks love all types of outdoor activities and fresh-air pursuits and their country is full of areas and facilities devoted to amateur sports. The favourite game year round is football, and athletics is also popular. In winter, ice hockey is enthusiastically pursued. In mountain sports, skiing and ice climbing are the Slovaks' speciality. The country has a well-developed infrastructure for hiking and bicycle touring, both excellent ways to explore the landscape. It is also possible to take to the water on one of the many lakes and rivers, which offer an exciting variety of conditions. People wishing to pamper themselves could visit one of the Slovak health resorts and spas. Tourist offices are the best places for information about local leisure facilities.

Cross-country skiing, as popular as downhill

Skiing and Snowboarding

Slovakia has ideal conditions and facilities for many winter sports. The Slovak Carpathians feature numerous downhill runs and ski lifts. The best-known ski resorts are Jasná, which is south of Liptovský Mikuláš, and Ružomberok, both in the Tatras mountains. In East Slovakia, there is Kojšovská Hol'a near Košice. The lower mountain ranges offer ideal conditions for cross-country skiing. Snowboarding can be practised at all ski resorts.

Horse Riding

The popularity of equestrian sports in Slovakia is on the rise. New studs and riding centres are springing up all over the country, mainly near large towns and in tourist regions. The area that is the most ideally suited for horse riding is the sparsely populated border region of Lower Beskydy (Bukovské vrchy). One of the best-known riding events in Slovakia is the annual Mengusovské Rodeo, held in the village of Mengusovce, in the foothills of the Tatras mountains.

Hiking

A dense network of clearly signposted walking trails makes hiking relatively straightforward, particularly in the mountain regions. The trails are marked with their degree of difficulty, which is helpful when organizing an excursion. Maps at various scales with the trails marked are widely available, as are English (and German) walking guides to the country. The most rewarding areas include the High Tatras *(see pp320–21)* and the gentler Vihorlat range *(see p336)*. Wear several layers of warm clothing at all times in the High Tatras.

Rock and Ice Climbing

The best mountaineering area in Slovakia is the High Tatras *(see pp320–21)*. The local hostels make excellent bases for expeditions into the upper regions of the mountains. You can also practise rock climbing in the Malá Fatra, Slovenský raj and Pieniny National Park *(see p311)*. For ice climbing, a popular destination is the frozen waterfalls of the Slovenský raj.

Cave Exploration

Around 3,900 caves have been found in Slovakia, mainly in the regions of the Slovenský raj, Slovenský kras *(see pp340–41)*, Low Tatras, and Tatras. Twelve are open to visitors. The biggest known cave system in Slovakia, which is over 30 km (18 miles) long, is in the Demänovská valley, near Liptovský Mikuláš.

Pony trekking in the region of Spiš Castle, East Slovakia

Cycling

Cycling holidays are rapidly gaining popularity with the Slovaks. As part of the European cycle network, Slovakia has marked cycling routes that cover about 3,500 km (2,175 miles) and this network is being constantly extended. Mountainous areas offer strenuous but rewarding cycling, while the going is easier along the Danube, or following the Váh river valley, and in the East Slovakian Lowlands.

Cycling in Slovakia

Water Activities

Although Slovakia is a landlocked country with no large lakes, watersports enthusiasts can enjoy themselves on dammed reservoirs, many of which have jetties and equipment hire facilities. The most popular Slovak artificial lakes include Liptovská Mara and Slňava on the Váh, near Piešťany.

White-water rafting can be experienced on the Belá river, and also on stretches of the Váh. The longest artificial rafting run in Central Europe is situated in Čuňovo, near Bratislava. Mountain canoeing enthusiasts can certainly enjoy trips down the Danube, Hornad and Váh rivers, as well as on the artificial canoe course in Liptovský Mikuláš. The Dunajec Gorge in Pieniny National Park is a beautiful and popular spot for both rafting and canoeing (see p321).

Spas

Slovakia is famed for its mineral and medicinal springs, boasting numerous modern resorts with a range of effective treatments and therapies on offer to a local and international clientele.

The best-known Slovak resorts include Piešťany (see p304), Trenčianske Teplice (see p305) and Bardejovské kúpele in East Slovakia. Some of them have relatively small bathing facilities in the form of single pools (often in historic buildings); others have large complexes or even vast aquaparks.

Golf and Tennis

Golf has become very popular in Slovakia over the past few years. There are beautiful courses in the High Tatras (Black Stork), in Central Slovakia (Gray Bear) and around Bratislava (Black River, Welten and Skalica).

Tennis is a fairly popular sport in Slovakia. You can find tennis courts at sports centres in larger towns, also at hotels and recreation centres in tourist resorts and spas. Many are open to visitors and non-residents.

Messing about in a boat on a lagoon near Košice, East Slovakia

DIRECTORY

Skiing and Snowboarding

Jasná
Nízke Tatry (Low Tatras).
Tel 0907 886 644.
W jasna.sk

Skipark Kojšovská Hoľa
Letná 42, 040 01 Košice.
Tel (055) 799 55 78.

Skipark Ružomberok
Hrabovská cesta 1679/31,
Ružomberok.
Tel/Fax (044) 432 26 06.
W skipark.sk

Ski Park Vyšné Ružbachy
Vyšné Ružbachy 333.
Tel 0903 616 003.
W skiparkvruzbachy.sk

Hiking

High Tatras
W tatry.sk

Rock Climbing

Climbing Routes
W tatry.nfo.sk

International Mountaineering & Climbing Federation
W theuiaa.org

Mountain Rescue
Tel 527 877 711. **In an emergency call** 18300.
W hzs.sk

Cave Exploration

Cave Locations
W ssj.sk

Cycling

Slovak Cycling Association
Tel (02) 44 45 67 52.
W cyklistikaszc.sk

Spas

Bardejovské Kúpele
086-31 Bardejovské Kúpele.
Tel (054) 472 42 45.
Fax (054) 472 35 49.
W kupele-bj.sk

Kúpele Rajecké Teplice
Tel (041) 549 42 56.
Fax (041) 549 36 74.
W spa.sk

Slovak Health Spa Piešťany, Inc.
Winterova 29, 921 29

Piešťany. **Tel** 0903 664 164.
Fax (033) 775 77 39.
W piestany.kupele.org

Slovak Spas
W kupeleslovenska.sk

Slovenské Liečebné Kúpele Trenčianske Teplice
914 51 Trenčianske-Teplice.
Tel (032) 651 40 00.
Fax (032) 651 47 59.
W slktn.sk

Golf

Slovak Golf Union
W skga.sk
Tel (02) 44 45 07 27.
W international.sk
W tale.sk
W golfskalica.sk
W golf.sk

Spectator Sports in Slovakia

Sport is a very important part of life for the Slovaks. This can be clearly seen in the impressive numbers of sports centres and facilities. The expansion of the sports infrastructure has resulted in a substantial increase in the successes achieved by Slovaks in the highest ranking international events, including world championships and Olympic Games. The disciplines in which they excel, and which are most closely followed by spectators, are ice hockey, soccer and tennis. Canoeing and kayaking also draw the crowds.

Michal Martikán in the Olympic slalom canoeing race, Athens

Miroslav Šatan, captain of the Slovak national ice hockey team

Football

This is the second most popular sport in Slovakia. The greatest achievements of Slovak players in the international arena has been when FC Artmedia Petržalka (from near Bratislava) reached the UEFA Champions' League in 2005, and the national team progressed to the last 16 in the 2010 FIFA World Cup.

Skiing and Snowboarding

Slovaks are very proud of their prowess in snow sports. Slovak skiers are starting to score international successes in Alpine and Classic skiing. The most recent star is the young Alpine skier Veronika Zuzulova, hailed as the future of Slovak skiing. The top cross-country skier is Alena Procházková. Snowboarders have done well in the past, with Radoslav Zidek winning silver in the snowboard cross event at the 2006 Winter Olympics.

Ice Hockey

The national sport of the Slovaks is ice hockey. In fact, the professional players who won the ice hockey world championship in 2002 for their country are regarded as real heroes. The legends of Slovak ice hockey are: Stan Mikita, Peter Šťastny, Vladimir Dzurila and Miroslav Šatan. In 2012, Slovakia's most popular club, HC Slovan Bratislava, became a part of the Kontinental Hockey League (KHL).

Other Sports

Slovak competitors are also successful in sports such as swimming, shooting and mountain canoeing. Michal Martikán has won four Olympic medals in slalom canoeing.

Tennis is another popular game. The most successful current players are Lukáš Lacko, Martin Kližan, Daniela Hantuchová, Dominika Cibulková and Magdaléna Rybáriková. Major tournaments are held at the National Tennis Centre in Bratislava.

DIRECTORY

Ice Hockey

KHL
🅦 khl.ru

Slovenský zväz ľadového hokeja
Trnavská cesta 27/B, 831 04 Bratislava.
Tel (02) 32 34 09 01.
Fax (02) 32 34 09 21.
🅦 szlh.sk

Football

Slovak Football Association
Trnavská cesta 100, 821 01 Bratislava.
Tel (02) 48 20 60 00.
Fax (02) 48 20 60 99.
🅦 futbalsfz.sk

Skiing

Slovak Ski Association
Karpatská 15, Poprad.
Tel 0918 249 159.
🅦 slovak-ski.sk

Veronika Velez Zuzulova, successful Slovak skier

PRACTICAL INFORMATION

The Czech and Slovak Republics are both very friendly destinations for visitors, attracted by the architecture as well as the natural beauty of the High Tatras. Numerous historic sights and attractions, good roads, efficient internal transport, tasty local food and a wide choice of accommodation result in the steadily growing numbers of visitors to these countries. Once you have arrived, a well-developed network of tourist information offices, which in both countries can be found in even quite small places, provides invaluable help to travellers. The practical information below and opposite concerns the Czech Republic; pages 398–9 give practical information on visiting Slovakia.

When to Visit the Czech Republic

The best time of year for visiting the country is between May and September. During these months, the warm weather makes for pleasant camping, mountain trekking and relaxing by or swimming in lakes and rivers. Some castles, museums and other historic sights, particularly in small towns and villages, open their doors to visitors only during this high season.

During school holidays (July and August), camp sites and some resorts tend to fill up, so it is better to visit in May, June or September if you want to avoid the crowds. Prague in particular is inundated with visitors in July and August and can be unbearably crowded.

Late September is an interesting time to visit Moravia for its grape harvest season. In winter, many regions of the Czech Republic offer good snow conditions.

Visa and Customs Regulations

Citizens of EU countries do not need a visa when entering the Czech Republic; it is enough to carry a passport (valid for at least 6 months beyond your return date) or an ID card. New Zealand, Australian, US and Canadian citizens can stay for up to 90 days without a visa. For up-to-date information, consult your nearest Czech Embassy (or visit www.mfa.cz).

Customs regulations do not apply to visitors from within the EU as long as they stay within the EU guidelines for personal use.

Embassies

For selected embassies in the Czech Republic, see the directory opposite.

A tourist information office, Tábor

Tourist Information

The Czech Republic has a very efficient network of tourist information offices, which can be found in almost every town, village and resort. In large cities, they are usually in railway stations; otherwise they are often in the town square. They are open from 9am to 5pm (7pm in Prague) and provide information on accommodation, eating places, museums, art galleries and historic sights; they also offer free booklets and sell maps, guidebooks and postcards. Staff can usually speak fluent German and good English.

It is worthwhile contacting a Czech tourist office where you live before leaving to help plan your trip.

Visit their excellent websites (www.czechtourism.com, www.czech.cz or www.prague welcome.cz) for the latest happenings and events that may coincide with your visit.

Business Hours

Most banks and offices are open from 9am to 5pm; some have a lunch break. (For shop opening hours, see p380.)

Charles Bridge in Prague – a popular destination all year round

◄ View of the trams at Little Quarter Square, Prague

Horse-drawn transport in Karlovy Vary, West Bohemia

Museums and Historic Sights

Between May and September, museums in most large Czech towns are open Tuesday to Sunday from 9am to 6pm. From October to April, many open from 9am to 5pm, sometimes changing to Monday to Friday. In smaller towns, many museums are open only from May to October, 9am–4pm, or 5pm; some open only at weekends.

Other sights, such as castles, churches, convents and monasteries, are open to visitors from May to September, Tuesday to Sunday 9am–4pm, or 5pm. Many close for lunch between noon and 1pm. In April and October, some provincial sights are open only at weekends; from November to April, many are closed, though a few can be visited by appointment. Many historic sights can be visited only by guided tours (at least five people). In smaller places, the keys to buildings may be with a custodian (often a private individual); a notice on the door says who to contact.

Tickets to some of the main tourist sights in Prague

Admission Prices

Admission to museums and historic sights outside the capital is not expensive, costing around 40–60Kč. Children over six and students are generally given a discount of 30–50 per cent, while under sixes are often free. Expect higher ticket prices in Prague.

Travelling With Children

Children are welcomed, although there are few facilities (such as play areas) specifically for them. There are, however, plenty of open spaces in which children can let off steam. (For eating with children, *see p359*.)

Disabled Travellers

Despite some improvements, the Czech Republic is still not that easy to negotiate for disabled travellers. In some places, particularly in Prague, there are hotels, restaurants, bars, museums and historic sights that have been adapted to the needs of the disabled. However, in many towns and cities, the prevalence of cobbles means that wheelchair users will find getting about uncomfortable, but possible.

Accessible public transport is patchy. A number of railway stations and trains, and some of the capital's metro stations and newer buses, do have wheelchair access. The Prague Public Transport Offices have a list of wheelchair-accessible transport *(www.dpp.cz)*.

Language

While many people in Prague speak English, knowledge of English in the provinces is less common, and so it is useful to know some Czech basics. The most popular greeting is *dobrý den* (good day), or in the morning *dobré ráno* (good morning). When parting you can say *ahoj* (cheers), or *na shledanou* (goodbye) or *nashle*. (*see also* Phrasebook, *pp431–2*.)

Measures and Electrical Appliances

The Czech Republic uses the metric system. The mains voltage is 220–230 volts. Standard Continental European two-pin plugs are used.

DIRECTORY

Embassies and Consulates in the Czech Republic

Australian Consulate
Klimentská 10, 110 00
Prague 1.
Tel 221 729 260.

British Embassy
Thunovská 14, 118 00
Prague 1.
Tel 257 402 370.

Canadian Embassy
Muchova 6, 160 00
Prague 6.
Tel 272 101 800.

New Zealand Consulate
Malé náměstí 1, Prague 1.
Tel 234 784 777.

US Embassy
Tržiště 15, 118 01 Prague 1.
Tel 257 022 000.

In the Slovak Republic

British Embassy
Panská 16, 811 01 Bratislava.
Tel (02) 59 98 20 00.

Embassy office of Canada
Hotel Carlton, Mostová 2,
Bratislava.
Tel (02) 59 20 40 31.

US Embassy
Hviezdoslavovo námestie 4,
811 02 Bratislava.
Tel (02) 54 43 08 61.

Tourist bus in Bratislava's Old Town

When to Visit Slovakia

Slovakia is an attractive destination for visitors throughout the year. Spring and autumn are good times for mountain hikes, bike tours and cave exploration. Summertime is excellent for swimming in the numerous pools and bathing centres (ordinary and thermal) and for enjoying water sports on its artificial lakes. In winter, Slovakia tempts visitors with its excellent ski slopes, and more unusual attractions such as swimming in outdoor thermal pools.

Those interested in visiting museums, open-air museums (skansens) and castles should bear in mind that from October to May many of them are closed, particularly those situated in the provinces. However, sights in Bratislava and other large towns generally remain open throughout the year.

Visa and Customs Regulations

Nationals of EU countries are admitted to Slovakia on presenting a valid passport or an ID Card, but if they intend to remain in the country for more than 90 days, they are required to report to the police and apply for a resident's permit.

Foreigners entering the Slovak Republic have to carry €56.40, or the equivalent in any convertible currency, in the form of travellers' cheques, cash or credit cards, for each day of their intended stay (children up to the age of 16 need half this amount). This rule is, however, applied to EU citizens only in exceptional circumstances. The sum may be reduced on the presentation of documents confirming advance payment for some services, such as hotel bookings or car hire.

At customs, as in the Czech Republic, EU nationals can bring into Slovakia the maximum allowed within the EU guidelines for personal use.

Embassies

For selected embassies in the Slovak Republic, see the directory (p397). There are British and US embassies in Bratislava. Visitors from Australia and New Zealand to the Slovak Republic are covered by their respective embassies in Vienna, Austria.

Tourist Information

Local tourist information centres provide details on accommodation, the region's natural attractions, also its cultural and sporting events. The most reliable information can be obtained from any of the 49 AICES affiliated offices (Asociácia informačných centier Slovenska), with their head office in Liptovský Mikuláš (www.infoslovak.sk or www.aices.sk). In addition, many places have their own information centres providing the same type of services. These may sell parking permits and local discount cards for tourists; they may also exchange foreign currencies. In some of these centres (although still very few), it is possible to book hotel accommodation. Unfortunately, almost none of the maps, guidebooks and information brochures that can be obtained from tourist information offices are free; the best you can hope to be given for free are a few pamphlets.

Tourist information offices are usually open 9am to 5pm, occasionally until 4pm or 6pm. Some of them close for an hour at lunchtime. On Saturdays, many such offices close at 1pm, and on Sundays, many remain closed all day. Their staff usually speak English and German.

Slovak tourist offices outside Slovakia are few and far between, but it is worth consulting websites such as www.slovakia.travel or www.infoslovak.sk for information when planning your trip.

A branch of the Prague Information Service in Staroměstské náměstí

Museums and Historic Sights

Slovakia has numerous interesting historic sites from various eras: from the Neolithic and Bronze Ages to relatively recent times. In most towns, you can find regional, historic or local museums. These often open all year from 9am to 5pm, though they may open Tuesday to Sunday in summer and Monday to Friday in winter. The most interesting open-air museums (skansens) exhibiting

Waiting to get started at a ski school

traditional rural buildings, can be found in the country's northern regions, in Martin-Jahodníky (from all over Slovakia), Zuberec (Orava), Stara Ľubovňa (Spiš), Svidník (Ukrainian-Ruthenian) and Humenné (Zemplín). The historic villages of Čičmany and Vlkolínec enjoy the status of "living skansens". Opening hours vary, with some staying open all year and others only during the summer months.

Many Slovak castles and historic buildings are open from May to September, Tuesday to Sunday from 9am to 5pm, closing for an hour for lunch. They open at weekends in April and October. Some close completely from November to March. Opening hours of major sights are listed in this guide. Many can be seen only on a guided tour; ask if there is an English guide as tours are usually in Slovak.

Some large churches and cathedrals open on the same basis as museums. Others are open only during services. At other times, seek admission from the local caretaker or priest, whose address is often given on the door.

Admission Prices

Museum entrance fees are not high in Slovakia– they vary from €2 to €4, with concession tickets for children and students at around €1. A few major castles charge more. At Bojnice, for instance, a standard ticket costs €8, and concessions are €3.50. At Orava a standard ticket is €6, while a concession is €3.

Travelling With Children

Slovakia is a child-friendly country. Public parks feature many playgrounds; there are also children's play areas in some supermarkets. The most attractive places are the numerous swimming pools, with ordinary and thermal pools. The country's best-known aquapark is Tatralandia, near Liptovský Mikuláš. Its competitor is the ever-expanding Aquacity park in Poprad. Children are also sure to enjoy the zoos in Bratislava, Bojnice, Košice and Spišská Nová Ves.

The youngest travellers can expect generous discounts in hotels, as well as on public transport; for example, a child up to the age of six travels free on Slovak railways.

Disabled Travellers

Facilities for disabled visitors are limited in Slovakia. Many of the trains have wheelchair access to at least one carriage, but it is often difficult to negotiate the station itself in order to reach the train. Many older buildings are gradually being adapted to

the needs of disabled users. (For access in hotels, *see p347*; for restaurants, *see p359*.)

Language

Slovakia's official language is Slovak, commonly spoken by about 86 per cent of the population. In the country's southern region, with its Hungarian minority (about 10 per cent of the population), the signs and names of places are given in both Slovak and Hungarian. Bilingual signs can also be seen in northeastern regions inhabited by, amongst others, the Ruthenian (Ukrainian) minority. You can also communicate in Czech anywhere in Slovakia without any problem. In towns and tourist resorts, a knowledge of English and German is reasonably widespread.

Measures and Electrical Appliances

Slovakia uses the metric system. The mains voltage is 220–230 volts. Standard Continental European two-pin plugs are used.

Local Time

Slovakia's clocks are set to Central-European time (GMT + 1), that is, the same as most of the countries of Continental Europe. As in neighbouring countries, the clocks are put forward by one hour on the last Sunday in March (summer time) and back again by one hour on the last Sunday in October (winter time).

Children playing in front of Grassalkovich Palace, Bratislava

Personal Security and Health in the Czech Republic

The Czech Republic is a relatively safe country. Outside the capital, thefts and muggings are rare, and therefore it is safe to walk the streets even late at night. However, in Prague it is wise to be more safety conscious as pickpockets often target visitors, but even here the situation is better than in many other large European urban areas.

A historic pharmacy in the town of Klatovy, West Bohemia

A "black sheriff"   A police officer

Police

The Czech police (policie) wear black uniforms with the silver police emblem displayed on the chest. Like everywhere, they attend to safety on the streets and roads and pursue criminals. They drive grey cars with blue and yellow stripes and the word "Policie" along the side.

Large towns also have municipal police (městská policie), who deal with illegal parking. A special police branch is responsible for border control. "Black sheriffs" are private security guards.

If you have a crime to report, the municipal police should be your first point of contact. Ask for a translator if no English is spoken.

Guarding Against Theft

In large towns, and particularly in Prague, in crowded places (such as Prague Castle or the metro) you should be on the alert for pickpockets. Always keep your money and documents in a safe place and out of view, and be extra vigilant if anyone seems to be crowding you. At night it is best not to carry large amounts of money on you. If a hotel safe is available, keep valuables locked away. Make a photocopy of your passport and write down credit card numbers. Cars parked in the street are generally safe, but you should not leave luggage or valuable objects in view.

Health Care

There is a fair standard of health care in the Czech Republic, and medical help can be obtained anywhere in the country without any problems. In emergencies and in life-threatening situations, EU nationals with an EHIC card are entitled to receive free medical treatment, but in all other cases, hospitalization or medical help has to be paid for. It is advisable to take out travel insurance to cover any medical costs incurred

abroad. The water is safe to drink, but mineral water is more palatable.

Pharmacies

For minor ailments and accidents, you can turn for advice to the nearest pharmacy (lékárna). Pharmacies may be found in large towns. They are generally open on weekdays from 8am until 6pm, and on Saturdays until 2pm. You will find 24-hour pharmacies only in major cities.

DIRECTORY

Emergency Numbers

Ambulance Tel 155.
Police Tel 158.
Municipal Police
Tel 156.
Fire Brigade
Tel 150.
Roadside Assistance
Tel 154.
Emergency Operator (English)
Tel 112.

Medical Help

Adults' Emergencies
Městská Poliklinika
Spálená 12.
Tel 222 924 295.

Children's Emergencies
Všeobecná FN Ke Karlovu 2.
Map 6 D4.
Tel 224 967 777.

Dental Emergencies
Městská Poliklinika Spálená 12.
Tel 222 924 200.

24-Hour Pharmacy
Pohotovostní Lékárna Palackého 5.
Tel 224 946 982.

Police patrol car in the Czech Republic

Personal Security and Health in Slovakia

In Slovakia, crime that is directed at tourists remains relatively rare, and Slovaks are peaceful people, who try to solve any disagreements by way of negotiation rather than open confrontation. Nevertheless, as in other countries it is always advisable to follow a few basic rules of safety, particularly if you are in a large city.

Slovak policeman   Slovak municipal police officer

Police

The police patrol the streets on foot (in large town centres) or travel in marked radio-cars. Some towns also have a municipal police *(mestská polícia)*.

In a threatening situation, contact the police (Policajný zbor Slovenskej republiky, PZ SR) by calling the emergency numbers, or by going immediately to a local police station (Obvodné oddelenie PZ SR), to the district command (Okresné riaditel'stvo PZ SR) or to the regional command (Krajské riaditel'stvo PZ SR).

Guarding Against Theft

The best way to protect yourself against losing documents, cash or other valuables is to take a few basic precautions, particularly in crowded places. Keep your money in a safe place, out of view. On public transport, you should pay attention to any unexpected and unforced contacts or collisions with other passengers. It is also unwise to sleep on the train if you are travelling alone. In a parked car, do not leave money,

cameras, or any other valuables in view.

Make a photocopy of your passport and write down credit card numbers, and keep valuables that you don't need on a daily basis locked away in the safe if you are staying in a hotel.

Health Care

In emergencies and in life-threatening situations, EU nationals with an EHIC card are entitled to receive free medical treatment, but in all other cases, hospital-ization or medical help has to be paid for. The cost of a visit to a doctor is about €13. A one-day stay in hospital costs about €40, to which you have to add the cost of examinations, tests, medicines and transport.

Slovak pharmacy sign

It is best to take out travel insurance providing good cover, and if you do need to claim, keep all documentation. Foreigners travelling to Slovakia do not require any immunizations or vaccinations. The water is safe to drink, but mineral water, which is more pleasant to drink, is widely available.

Pharmacies

Pharmacies *(lekáreň)* can be found in all towns and larger villages. In minor emergencies, their staff will recommend suitable medication. They are generally open 8am–6pm. In larger towns, there is usually a pharmacy open 24 hours.

DIRECTORY

Emergency Numbers

Emergency Operator
Tel 112.
Ambulance
Tel 112, 155.
Police
Tel 112, 158.
Fire Brigade
Tel 112, 150.
Municipal Police
Tel 159.
Mountain Rescue
Tel 18 300.

Medical Help

Dental Emergencies
Drieňová 38, Bratislava.
Tel (02) 43 42 34 33.

Adults' Emergencies
Strečnianska 13, Bratislava.
Tel (02) 63 83 31 30.

Children's Emergencies
Limbová 1, Bratislava.
Tel (02) 59 37 11 11.

24-hour Pharmacy
Ružinovská 12, Bratislava.
Tel (02) 48 21 10 11.

Typical red-and-white Slovak ambulance

Banks and Currency in the Czech Republic

The Czech currency is the Czech crown. Although the republic is part of the EU, the euro is not generally accepted, particularly outside Prague. The best way to take money with you is in the form of a debit card, and to draw out the money you need as you go along. In this way, you can avoid carrying large sums with you, and, by using ATMs, you can withdraw money outside banking hours. Banks and bureaus de change also change money.

ATMs

There is a wide network of ATMs, which can be found even in small towns. Most of them accept foreign cards, such as MasterCard, VisaPlus, Visa Electron or Cirrus/Maestro. You can use these to withdraw cash as you need it.

Banks and Bureaus de Change

Every town has a branch of the major banks such as **Komerční Banka** or **Česká Spořitelna**, where you can exchange money. The rate used is the exchange rate labelled *valuty nákup* ("we buy"). Banks are generally open Monday to Friday, from 9am until 5pm. The commission on exchanging money is usually 2 per cent. Money

ATM in Louny

can also be changed at Čedok travel agents, who also charge 2 per cent commission. Private bureaus de change sometimes add higher commission charges, and the rate of exchange is often much less favourable than that offered by banks. It is not worth changing money in hotels, which offer the worst rate of exchange. You should also not change money with street touts. They generally do not offer better rates than the banks, and often try to cheat visitors by handing them forged banknotes.

Credit Cards

Credit cards can be used to pay in upmarket hotels and

DIRECTORY

Main Branches of Banks

Česká Národní Banka (Czech National Bank)
Na příkopě 28, Prague.
Map 3 C4.
Tel 224 411 111.
W **cnb.cz**
Rooseveltova 18, 601 10 Brno.
Tel 542 137 111.

Česká spořitelna
Rytířská 29, Prague.
Map 3 C4.
Tel 800 207 207.
W **csas.cz**

Československá Obchodní Banka
Na příkopě 18, Prague.
Map 3 C4.
Tel 800 300 300.
W **csob.cz**

GE Money Bank
Hybernská 20, Prague.
Map 4 D3. **Tel** 844 111 145.
W **gemoney.cz**

Komerční Banka
Václavské náměstí 42, Prague.
Map 4 D5.
Tel 955 545 111.
W **kb.cz**

UniCredit Bank
Náměstí Republiky 3A, Prague.
Map 4 D2.
Tel 800 140 014.
W **unicreditbank.cz**

Main Branches of Bureaus De Change

American Express Business Travel Centre
Na Příkopě 19, Prague.
Map 3 C4. **Tel** 222 800 100.
W **americanexpress.com**

Eurochange
Opletalova 30, Prague.
Map 3 C4. **Tel** 224 243 614.

InterCHANGE
Mostecká 5, Prague.
Map 3 C4.
Tel 257 531 580.
W **interchange.cz**

Modern building of the Czech National Bank, in Ústí nad Labem

restaurants, and in large shops. In the provinces, many small shops do not accept credit cards, so it is always advisable to carry some cash.

Travellers' Cheques

If you wish to avoid carrying large sums of money with you, you can buy travellers'

cheques before leaving home, and then cash them on arrival or as you travel. The most popular cheques in the Czech Republic are American Express and Citicorp, but larger banks will accept any type. Some major hotels in large towns will also accept payment by travellers' cheque.

Currency

The country's monetary unit is the Czech crown (Kč), which is divided into 100 hellers. When you are touring small towns and villages, it is always preferable to carry lower denominations of Czech banknotes because many smaller establishments may find it difficult to give change for a 1,000, 2,000 or 5,000Kč note.

Banknotes
Czech banknotes are in denominations of 100, 200, 500, 1,000, 2,000 and 5,000Kč.

100Kč note

200Kč note

500Kč note

1,000Kč note

2,000Kč note

5,000Kč note

50 crowns (50Kč)

20 crowns (20Kč)

10 crowns (10Kč)

5 crowns (5Kč)

2 crowns (2Kč)

1 crown (1Kč)

Coins

Czech coins come in the following denominations: 1, 2, 5, 10, 20 and 50 crowns (Kč). All coins have the Czech emblem (a lion rampant) on the reverse.

Banks and Currency in Slovakia

The national currency of Slovakia is the euro, which replaced the Slovak Koruna in 2009. The largest of the Slovak banks accept travellers' cheques, which can also be cashed in the bureaus de change found in tourist areas and cities. ATMs can be found everywhere. Also, increasing numbers of services and retail outlets accept credit card payments. Most Slovak banks also change money. In large shopping malls, particularly in the bigger cities, you will find branches of banks open until 8 or 9pm.

ATMs

Credit- or debit-card holders will find ATMs installed outside virtually every bank and operating 24 hours; they accept Maestro, MasterCard, Visa, Diners Club, American Express, and other cards. Before withdrawing money from an ATM, find out the rate of commission charged by the bank for the service.

ATM in Skalica

Banks

In towns and large tourist resorts, there are no problems with finding a bank for changing or withdrawing money. The most frequently encountered are branches of large banks: **Sberbank**, **Slovenská sporiteľňa**, **VÚB**, **Tatra Banka** and **OTP**. Slovak banks are generally open from 8am to 5pm (the smaller the town, the earlier the closing time). Sometimes they close for an hour for lunch.

Travellers' Cheques

Travellers' cheques issued by Thomas Cook, American Express and Visa are accepted at branches of VÚB, Tatra Banka, Slovenská sporiteľňa, and in selected bureaus de change. Their commission is usually about 1 per cent of the cheque's face value and the lowest commissions are charged on US dollar and pound sterling cheques.

Credit Cards

Credit cards are accepted at petrol stations, larger shops and most hotels. The number of places in Slovakia that accept "plastic money" is growing all the time, however, as with the Czech Republic, in the provinces many small shops do not accept credit cards, so it is always advisable to carry some cash.

DIRECTORY

Main Branches of Selected Banks

Slovenská sporiteľňa
Central Office Tomášikova 48, Bratislava.
Tel (02) 58 26 81 11.
Ⓦ slsp.sk

Branches
Námestie SNP 18, Bratislava.
Tel 0850 111 888.
Fax (02) 58 26 86 70.

Suché Mýto 1, Bratislava.
Tel 0850 111 888.
Fax (02) 58 26 86 70.

Pribinova 4, Košice.
Tel 0850 111 888.
Fax (02) 58 26 86 70.

Tatra Banka
Central Office Hodžovo námestie 3, Bratislava.
Tel (02) 59 19 11 11.
Ⓦ tatrabanka.sk

Branches
Zámocká 6, Bratislava.
Františkánske námestie 3, Bratislava. Vysoká 1, Bratislava.
Hlavná 1, Košice. Dolná 2, Banská Bystrica. Hlavná 108, Košice. Hlavná 9, Trnava.
Námestie SV Egídia 95, Poprad.

Selected Branches of Bureaus de Change

Jager
Námestie Osloboditeľov, Liptovský Mikuláš.
Tel (044) 551 40 09.

Safe Change
Hlavná 5, Košice.
Tel 0905 392 487.

Zmenáreň Aurika
Námestie sv. Egídia 22, Poprad.
Tel 0908 844 818.

Bank façade in Banská Bystrica

The Euro

Sixteen member states of the EU have now replaced their traditional currencies with a single European currency, the euro. Austria, Belgium, Cyprus, Finland, France, Germany, Greece, Ireland, Italy, Luxembourg, Malta, the Netherlands, Portugal, Slovakia, Slovenia and Spain have all chosen to join the new currency; the UK, Denmark and Sweden have stayed out. The euro was introduced in Slovakia on 1 January 2009, with notes and coins coming into circulation. A very short transition period of only two weeks allowed euros and the Slovak koruna to be used simultaneously. All euro notes and coins can be used anywhere inside the participating member states.

Bank Notes

Euro bank notes have seven denominations. The €5 note (grey in colour) is the smallest, followed by the €10 note (pink), €20 note (blue), €50 note (orange), €100 note (green), €200 note (yellow) and €500 note (purple). All notes show the stars of the European Union.

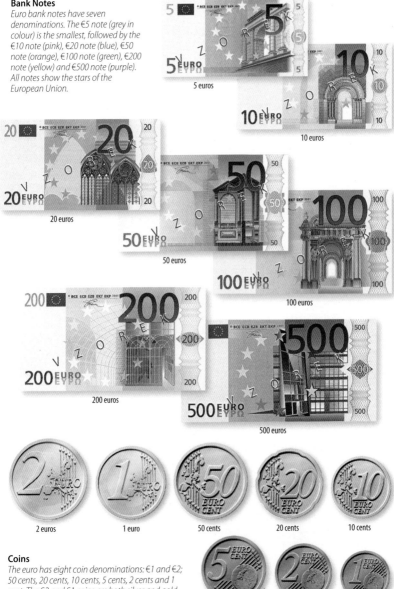

5 euros

10 euros

20 euros

50 euros

100 euros

200 euros

500 euros

2 euros

1 euro

50 cents

20 cents

10 cents

5 cents

2 cents

1 cent

Coins

The euro has eight coin denominations: €1 and €2; 50 cents, 20 cents, 10 cents, 5 cents, 2 cents and 1 cent. The €2 and €1 coins are both silver and gold in colour. The 50-, 20- and 10-cent coins are gold. The 5-, 2- and 1-cent coins are bronze.

Telephone and Mail Services in the Czech Republic

Telephone and mail services in the Czech Republic are very efficient. Every town and large village has a post office and public telephones can be found even in small villages and are usually in good order. Post offices are similarly widespread and efficient, delivering international mail reliably. Internet access is springing up in many locations so should not be a problem.

A man uses a public telephone booth in Prague

Using Public Telephones

The landline telephone network in the Czech Republic is run by O2 (Telefónica). Blue kiosks marked with the company's logo contain card-operated telephones; the cards can be bought at post offices and newsstands. If you are travelling to remote villages, take a phonecard with you as they may be hard to find. O2 Trick cards cost 180Kč. With over 15,000 telephone kiosks, the Czech Republic is one of the few remaining countries with such a high density of public telephones. The coin-operated booths accept euros as well. The call tariffs from public telephones vary depending on the distance (local or long-distance calls) and the time of day. One minute of an international call costs between 10 and 20Kč. Calls can also be made from hotel rooms but charges are often much higher. For a map of the phone booths in your area, check www.o2.cz.

Mobile Phones

If you wish to use your own mobile phone, you need to arrange for a roaming service with your operator before leaving home. Mobile phone operators in the Czech Republic include Vodafone, O2 (Telefónica) and T-Com.

Czech Numbers

All numbers consist of nine digits and the area code is an integral part of the telephone number. Even when making a call from within a town, it is necessary to dial the area code.

If you experience problems with getting through, it is likely that the number has changed.

Mail Services

At a post office you can send a letter or parcel, make a telephone call and buy postage stamps (*známky*). The latter are also sold at news kiosks. A postage stamp for a postcard to any EU country costs 25Kč. It is best to send international parcels from main offices. Czech letter boxes are painted orange. At the main post office in every large town (marked Pošta 1), you can use the poste restante service for receiving mail; you need to present your passport to collect any letters. Post offices also offer a money exchange service. Their opening hours are 7am to 7pm on weekdays, and 7am to noon on Saturdays.

The orange-and-blue logo of the Czech Post Office, a post horn

Internet and E-Mail

All towns have Internet cafés, along with public places that provide Internet access. Ask at the local tourist office for the nearest if you cannot find one. Many hotels also offer Internet access, sometimes free and, in larger business hotels, wireless. Prices for access are generally reasonable; the connections are fast, so that fans of web surfing can indulge in their favourite pastime without any problems.

Useful Numbers

- Dial these prefixes before the Czech number when calling from abroad: from the UK and Ireland 00420; from USA and Canada 011420; from Australia and New Zealand 0011420.
- Directory enquiries: 1180.
- International info: 1181.

Using a Phonecard Telephone in the Czech Republic

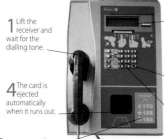

1 Lift the receiver and wait for the dialling tone.

2 The message *Vložte telefonní kartu* tells you to insert the card into the slot. The display shows you the credit left on your card.

3 When the words *Volte číslo* appear, dial and wait to be connected.

4 The card is ejected automatically when it runs out.

Emergency numbers

By pressing this red button, you can hear instructions in English.

Telephone and Mail Services in Slovakia

Slovak telephone and mail services are widely available and efficient. Public phones are mostly in good working order, and there are generally no problems with making a call, local or international. Post offices can be found in all towns and larger villages. The number of Internet cafés is steadily increasing; they are mostly situated in the centres of large towns.

Slovak news kiosk, one of many that sells telephone cards

Using Telephones

The payphones in Slovakia, operated by T-Com, are accessible by both coin and card. However, the service is quickly diminishing due to a massive reduction in the country's use of payphones. There are only 200 remaining booths, of which not all are properly functional. If you are in doubt, seek advice at a post office. Cheap, single-use SIM cards can be purchased at news kiosks and grocery stores, such as Tesco and Billa. These are easier to use for international calls, and are sold for less than €10.

Some major towns have telephone exchanges in which you can make a phone call and pay the total cost at the end. Calls from hotel telephones tend to be expensive; it is advisable to check the rates before making an outward call. There are currently three mobile phone operators in Slovakia: T-Com, O2 (Telefónica) and Orange.

Slovak post box

Slovak Numbers

Except the Bratislava region, Slovakia has three-digit area codes (the first digit is always 0), and when making a long-distance call, you should dial the area code of the town or the region, followed by the subscriber's number. Local calls do not need the area code. Area codes for Slovak telephone numbers are included in this guide.

Mail Services

Post offices can be found in all towns and larger villages. They generally open from 8am until 6pm, Monday to Friday, and 8am until 1pm on Saturday. In large towns, you can find some post offices that open on Sundays. A postage stamp *(známky)* for an ordinary letter costs €1; a parcel up to 2 kg (4.4 lb) costs €4; an international package up to 1 kg (2.2 lb) in weight costs €25. As in the Czech Republic, a poste restante service is available in the main post office (Pošta 1)

in each major town. You will need your passport in order to collect your mail.

Internet and E-Mail

Many cafés, shops, hotels and public places offer free wireless Internet services. For visitors without smartphones or laptops, there are several Internet cafés and shops, so finding them should not present too many difficulties. Sometimes a sign may be hung along the main street, but the actual entrance may lead through gates, corridors and backyards. These kinds of establishments are often located in cellars. They charge about €1.50–€2 per hour, with the total charges being calculated by the minute. Many hotels offer Internet access to guests.

Using a Phonecard Telephone in Slovakia

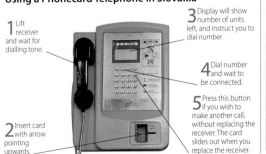

1 Lift receiver and wait for dialling tone.

2 Insert card with arrow pointing upwards.

3 Display will show number of units left, and instruct you to dial number.

4 Dial number and wait to be connected.

5 Press this button if you wish to make another call, without replacing the receiver. The card slides out when you replace the receiver.

Useful Numbers

- Dial these prefixes before the Slovak number (including area code) when calling from abroad: from the UK and Ireland 00421; from USA and Canada 011421; from Australia and New Zealand 0011421.
- International directory enquiries: 12 149.
- Directory enquiries within Slovakia: 12 111.

GETTING TO THE CZECH AND SLOVAK REPUBLICS

The easiest way to reach both the Czech and Slovak Republics is by air. Prague airport is served by many airlines, including several low-cost carriers. Bratislava has fewer flights, and one option is to fly to Vienna, just 50 km (31 miles) from Bratislava, which is better connected. Travelling by train or coach is also possible; it is often cheaper than air travel and enables you to see more of the country, though may take longer. Road and rail links are excellent from most of Europe.

Travelling by Air to the Czech Republic

The country's biggest air transport hub is Prague's Václav Havel Airport, for both international and domestic flights. You can fly there from almost any large European city in less than two-and-a-half hours. The main Czech carrier is **ČSA** (Czech Airlines), although Prague is also served by most major European airlines, and an increasing number of low-cost carriers, including **easyJet**, **Ryanair** or **Wizz Air** from the UK, Ireland and Hungary. Those travelling from Australia, New Zealand and Canada usually have to fly to another European capital and take a connecting flight to Prague. For a list of airlines, see the directory.

From Václav Havel Airport to Prague

Prague's Václav Havel airport is located about 20 km (12 miles) northwest of the city centre. A regular public bus service runs from the airport to Nádraží Veleslavín metro (bus 119) and to Zličín metro (bus 100). The journey takes about 30 minutes. The airport is also linked to the city centre by a regular shuttle mini-bus service run by CEDAZ. Buses leave every 30 minutes from 7:30am to 7pm, and tickets cost Kč150 per person. CEDAZ also offers an on-demand mini-bus service to and from the airport.

There are taxis in front of the terminal. Book the taxi in advance at the information booth by the exit doors to ensure a fair price.

Other Czech Airports

The other main airports in the Czech Republic are in Ostrava, Brno and Karlovy Vary. Domestic flights are served by ČSA between Prague and Ostrava. Specialist airlines operate small aircraft fleets which can be chartered for private clients and offer pleasure flights for tourists.

Travelling by Air to Slovakia

Bratislava's M R Štefánika Airport is served by airlines from all over Europe, including an increasing number of low-cost carriers. A further option for visitors to western Slovakia is to fly to Vienna's Schwechat International Airport, less than 50 km (30 miles) from the border (see below). Vienna may also be the most convenient gateway for travellers from North America and Australasia. Visitors heading for the mountain region of northern Slovakia might consider taking

DIRECTORY

Airlines Serving the Czech and Slovak Republics

Austrian Airlines
W austrian.com

British Airways
Tel 239 000 299.
W ba.com

ČSA
V Celnici 5, Prague.
Tel 239 007 007.
W csa.cz

easyJet
W easyjet.com

Lot Polskie Linie Lotnicze S.A.
W lot.com

Lufthansa
W lufthansa.co.uk

Ryanair
W ryanair.com

Smart Wings
W smartwings.com

Wizz Air
W wizzair.com

The Prague Václav Havel airport forecourt

a flight to Krakow in Poland, which is nearer than Bratislava, and heading south from there.

Transport from the Airport to Bratislava

Bratislava's airport is 12 km (7 miles) from the city centre; the bus journey (on bus no. 61) takes 30 minutes and a taxi takes 15 minutes. Vienna's airport, 50 km (31 miles) from Bratislava, operates a regular bus service to the Slovak capital.

Other Slovak Airports

Slovakia's internal airports are in Bratislava, Žilina, Košice, Piešťany, Sliač and Poprad-Tatry (5 km/3 miles from Poprad). Both Czech Airlines and Air Slovakia serve these airports.

Ticket Prices

Prices of air tickets vary tremendously: they depend on the airline, the time of year, the type of ticket ("open" or with a fixed return date), the validity period, and many other factors, as well as where you purchase the ticket. Most airlines offer special concessions for children; some also offer reductions to families and group travellers. It is also worth looking for special promotions that are, from time to time, offered by various airlines, for selected routes. Usually, it is

Glazed interior at Bratislava Štefánika airport

worth booking the ticket well in advance. The Internet is a good starting point for shopping around for a good deal.

Low-Cost Airlines

Low-cost airlines offer a good range of deals on flights to Prague, Brno, Bratislava and Krakow in Poland, and the number of routes is increasing all the time. For the lowest fares, you should book via the Internet as far in advance as possible. Flights generally do not include in-flight meals, although refreshments are usually sold on board. A useful website for checking the latest low-cost routes is *www. flycheapo.com*.

A welcome to visitors at Štefánika airport

By Coach

You can get to both the Czech and Slovak Republics by coach operated by one of the international carriers who run scheduled services between main European cities. Travelling by coach is generally less expensive than by air, but it may sometimes be less comfortable, and – above all – takes much longer. The coaches on international routes are generally well equipped with air conditioning and have reclining seats. Further details are available from the operator before you book. It is worth taking a blanket or a sleeping bag with you and, for a cold night, a flask filled with a hot drink.

By Train

Train travel offers more comfortable conditions than travel by coach (particularly if you travel in a sleeper/couchette), but it should be stressed that standard fares on international train routes are usually very high – the cost of such a journey may not be much lower than travelling by air, for example. The cost can be considerably reduced if you buy discounted international tickets well in advance, or with passes for travellers under 26 or for those over 60. Details and application forms for such passes can be obtained from ticket offices at international railway stations.

Bratislava Štefánika airport exterior

Travelling in the Czech Republic

Travelling by train is a great way to see the Czech Republic. They are inexpensive, run frequently and usually arrive on time, and they enable you to reach virtually any town. Taking a bus is somewhat more expensive but can be faster. The ČSAD buses (Czech Bus Transport Company) run services to every town and village in the country. Bus and train timetables can be found at the website address *www.jizdnirady.cz*. The republic has a network of well-maintained roads so using a car (whether hired or your own) is an ideal way to visit remote places.

Exterior of Praha Hlavní Nádraží, the main railway station in Prague

Travelling by Train

The rail network is run by Czech Railways (České dráhy/ **ČD**); it is most developed in the northern and western regions of the country; in the south and east, there are fewer train services. The route between Prague and Ostrava is run by private trains, such as RegioJet and LEO Express. Detailed information on train and bus services is available at the website address *www.cd.cz*.

There are several kinds of train in the Czech Republic. The slowest and the cheapest is the local train *(osobní vlak)*, which runs on local routes and stops at every station. The Fast trains *(rychlík)* and Express trains operate on long-distance routes and do not stop at every station. They include first- and second-class carriages. On such trains, you may

reserve a seat *(místenka)*, although it is not compulsory.

Fast trains have several levels and prices. On express trains, it is best to reserve a seat if you want to guarantee one. On more upmarket express trains, such as InterCity and EuroCity, it is compulsory to make a seat reservation. The highest standard is offered by SC trains (SuperCity), which have first and second class carriages; you need to reserve a seat in advance. These trains run on the Prague to Ostrava route. For overnight travel, you can use the Euronight train, and opt to pay extra for a couchette *(lehátkový vůz)*.

Train Tickets

Tickets for all types of trains run by České dráhy can be booked in person, at railway station ticket desks or on the Internet

at *www.cd.cz*. For RegioJet and LEO Express trains between Prague and Ostrava, book tickets at the specific station desk, or on the Internet at *www.regiojet.cz* and *www.le.cz*.

Children up to the age of six travel free on Czech railways, and young travellers, up to the age of 15, are entitled to a 50 per cent reduction, but they must be able to prove their age with documentation. Note that a return ticket will cost you less than two singles.

The international InterRail tickets, which entitle holders to unlimited travel for select periods of time throughout Europe, are honoured in the Czech Republic. Also honoured are the Euro Domino tickets, entitling the holder to a certain number of travel days within one month.

Railway Stations

Czech railway stations, even those found in small towns, offer a full range of facilities necessary for travellers. All stations, from the largest to the smallest, are clean and well-kept; almost all of them have restaurants or a bar selling beer and other alcoholic drinks, and a ticket office. Many stations in small or middle-sized towns do not have traditional, raised platforms; instead they have a system of open tracks, and the station-master sets up boards giving details of the trains that are just about to arrive and depart. From April to October, bicycles are available to rent from Czech railway stations. You can rent a bicycle from one train station and return it at another.

Inside Masarykovo Railway Station in Prague

Luggage

At all larger railway stations, you can deposit your luggage at the left-luggage office, or leave it in a self-service locker. On large stations, there are also porters who help with the luggage.

Travelling by Bus

Czech bus transport functions very efficiently. Several local bus companies run a nationwide network of services that includes virtually all towns and villages, even the most remote ones. Travelling by bus is generally more expensive than by train, but it is also quicker. **Student Agency** buses provide comfortable travel from Prague to other cities. Bus stations are usually a short walk from the centre of a town, and often near the train station.

Tickets are available from ticket desks at bus stations in large towns, and it is worth buying in advance for weekends when services are less regular. On minor routes, tickets are usually bought from the driver. The country's largest bus transport hub is the Prague Florenc station. Prague and Brno also have regular bus links with many European cities.

Travelling by Car

Well-maintained roads and long sections of motorway make driving one of the best methods of exploring the country. A foreigner driving on

A typical Czech bus picking up passengers at a station

Czech roads must carry a valid international driver's licence, an ID card (visitors from outside the EU must also carry passports), the vehicle registration document and a third-party insurance policy ("Green card").

The car should be marked with letters identifying its country of origin (if not, you may incur an on-the-spot fine). The driver must carry inside the vehicle a warning sign in the form of a red triangle and a first-aid kit. Babies and children must always be strapped in appropriate seats.

An information sign about speed limits

Motorcyclists and their passengers must wear crash helmets in the Czech Republic. The maximum speed permitted for cars and buses is 50 km/h (30 mph) in built-up areas, 90 km/h (55 mph) on open roads and 130 km/h (80 mph) on

motorways. Drivers must use dipped headlights at all times.

Driving after consuming any alcohol at all is strictly prohibited and if discovered, the driver may have to pay a stiff fine, or risk being detained by the police.

Roads and Road Signs

Czech motorways are marked with the letter D followed by a number; the major roads are indicated by the letter E and a number. The Czech motorway network is not very extensive compared to that in many other European countries, but it is growing steadily. In order to be allowed to use it, you have to buy a disc, available at border crossings and larger petrol stations. The disc should be displayed on the windscreen. Not doing so could incur a very heavy fine. City roads tend to be busy, while outside these conurbations traffic is minimal.

Car Hire

It is possible to hire a car in advance via a major car hire firm. Local representatives, found at airports and in upmarket hotels, may offer cheaper deals. In order to hire a car, you must be at least 18 years of age, have a valid driver's licence and an identity document recognized in the Czech Republic, with a photo.

DIRECTORY

Train Travel

ČD (České dráhy)
Tel +420 840 112 113.
(Also in English.)
w cd.cz/eshop

Bus Travel

Student Agency
w jizdenky.studentagency.cz

Czech country road

Travelling in Slovakia

Slovak trains are clean and fast, and railway stations are often located in interesting historic buildings. There are fewer railway lines than in the Czech Republic, however, mainly due to the country's mountainous terrain. Travelling on inter-city buses is relatively cheap, fast and reliable but the service can be patchy in some areas. The most convenient way to travel around the country is by car, particularly the further east you go, as the public transport network becomes sparser.

Railway station building in Piešťany

Travelling by Train

Trains in Slovakia are run by **ŽSR** (Železnice Slovenskej republiky). They run frequently, are usually clean and punctual, and the quality of the track makes for a fast and smooth journey. Travelling on some of the routes that run through scenic mountain ranges (particularly the Banská Bystrica to Diviaky and Brezno to Margecany sections) is in itself a tourist attraction. Some of the local routes are served by railbuses that stop at every station.

Slow trains *(osobný vlak)* are indicated on timetables *(cestovný poriadok)* with the letters "Os", and, if the route is also served by a railbus, with "MOs". A slightly higher level of service is provided by limited-stop trains *(zrýchlený vlak)*, marked with the "Zr" symbol; tickets cost virtually the same as for the slow trains. These stop only at some stations, although more frequently than fast trains.

Fast trains *(rýchlik)*, marked with the symbol "R", operate on longer routes between larger towns. Even faster, but no more expensive, are express trains *(expresný vlak)*, marked with the symbol "Ex". These link all major towns in Slovakia, and some of

them go also to the Czech Republic and Austria. The top category of trains are the fast EuroCity (marked "EC") and InterCity (marked "IC"). They link Bratislava with Košice and Banská Bystrica; and Košice and Banská Bystrica with Prague, Berlin and Budapest. Tickets for these trains are not all that expensive – about €2.50 more (including a reserved seat) than for a slow train.

Train Tickets

Slovak railways are relatively inexpensive. The cost of a journey by slow train per kilometre works out at about 40 cents. Fare reductions of 20 to 60 per cent (depending on the age of the passengers) are

offered to groups. Children up to the age of six travel free. A family ticket for three to six people, including up to four children aged 15 and under, offers a 20 per cent fare reduction. Holders of the International Student Identity Card (ISIC) receive a 50 per cent reduction.

Reservations

Seat reservation may be compulsory *(povinné)* or optional *(nepovinné)* on fast, express, EuroCity and InterCity trains. This information is given in the timetables against each train. For some overnight trains, it is also possible to buy a couchette *(ležadlový lístok)* or a bed in a sleeping compartment *(lôžkový lístok)*. Places can be reserved at railway station ticket offices, at selected travel agents or on *www.slovakrail.sk*.

Railway Stations

Slovak railway stations *(železničná stanica)* in large towns are generally clean and well-maintained. They often occupy historic buildings dating from the days of the Austro-Hungarian empire. In smaller towns and villages, their standard is also fair, although often they do not have ticket offices *(pokladňa)*. If this is the case, you have to buy the ticket from a conductor on the train.

Luggage

At all larger railway stations, you can leave your luggage at the

Train travelling through a beautiful tract of Slovak countryside

People riding a bus in Bratislava

left-luggage office (úschovňa batožín), or deposit it in a self-service locker (úložné skrinky).

Travelling by Bus

Bus stations (autobusová stanica) are not the world's cleanest, but buses run quite frequently, and tickets are fairly cheap. Bus stations are often located near a town's railway station. You need, however, to be careful when consulting timetables, as they are often speckled with countless additional symbols, which indicate, for instance, that the bus in question runs only spasmodically (premáva), and at weekends does not run at all (nepremáva). Older buses tend to operate on local routes, but the situation is somewhat better on inter-city routes. Private bus companies run some routes. You can buy tickets at the bus station, or on local trips, directly from the driver.

Sign showing speed limits in Slovakia

Travelling by Car

Roads are reasonable and do not present any special problems to drivers, particularly since traffic is not very heavy. Visitors from the EU arriving in Slovakia by car are not required to have a "Green Card" or an international driving licence. It is necessary, however, to carry the vehicle registration document with you.

Slovak regulations require every car to be equipped with a first-aid kit, a warning triangle, a spare wheel and a reflective vest. Children up to the age of 12, or up to 150 cm (5 ft) tall, must travel strapped in appropriate seats in the back of the vehicle. Seat belts should be kept fastened throughout your journey. All year round, dipped headlights must be permanently switched on. Motorcyclists are obliged to wear crash helmets. It is not permitted to drive at all with any alcohol in your bloodstream.

The maximum permitted speed on Slovak motorways is 130 km/h (80 mph) for cars and 110 km/h (70 mph) for buses; elsewhere it is 90 km/h (55 mph) on open roads and 50 km/h (37 mph) within built-up areas. People under 18 are not permitted to drive vehicles on Slovak roads, even if they hold a valid driving licence from another country.

Roads and Road Signs

Signposting on trunk roads in Slovakia is clear; problems start only when entering large towns. The highest category of Slovak roads are the motorways (diaľnica), marked with a D followed by a number, set on a blue background. All motorways are toll roads. The toll is paid by buying a disc. This can be annual (€50); or valid for one month (€14); or valid for ten days (€7).

The disc should be placed in the upper corner of the windscreen. Discs can be purchased at border crossings, in petrol stations and at larger post offices. Dual carriageways are also toll roads.

Car Hire

The number of car hire companies (autopožičovňa) in Slovakia is on the increase. Most are found in Bratislava and Košice. The international companies, such as Hertz, Avis, Europcar and Budget, offer mainly Western makes of car. There are also local firms, such as **Auto Danubius**, which hire Škodas.

DIRECTORY

Train Travel

W slovakrail.sk

Car Hire

Auto Danubius
Ráztočná 60, Bratislava.
Tel 0903 788 205.
W autodanubius.sk

Scenic view of the Slovenské Národné Povstanie bridge across the Danube, Bratislava

Getting Around Prague

The historic centre of Prague is a relatively small area that is best explored on foot. There is also an efficient network of buses, trams and metro trains. This public transport system (*dopravní podnik* or DP) has offices in metro stations and at some major route junctions which have transport maps and timetables, and sell tickets and passes. Three- or seven-day passes can be used on trams, trains, boats and buses.

The Metro

The Czech capital is served by three metro lines: A (green), B (yellow) and C (red). They crisscross, making it easy to change trains and, as a result, travel around virtually the entire city quickly. The metro service operates from 5am until shortly after midnight. During morning and evening rush hours, the trains run every 3–5 minutes; early in the morning and late at night, and on weekends and public holidays, their frequency is every 8–12 minutes.

A tram stop in Prague, signalling the next arriving trams

Driving and Parking

Due to the volume of traffic and narrow streets, driving around Prague is difficult. There are also many pedestrianized areas and restrictions on cars. During the rush hour, the streets frequently get jammed. It is therefore not a good idea to try to see Prague by car. If you have a car and wish to make a one-day trip into the city, you can leave the car on the outskirts and use the Park and Ride car parks, intended for people who wish to travel in by metro. Central Prague has allocated areas for

paid parking, so if you are lucky enough to find a space (which is not easy), you will have to pay at the meter. Illegally parked cars get clamped or towed away to a special police compound.

Buses and Trams

The MHD (Městská Hromadná Doprava, Municipal Transport System) buses run according to the timetables displayed at every bus stop. Buses on some

of the routes are modern, low vehicles that are suitable for wheelchairs and pushchairs.

Prague and other large towns (Ostrava, Brno, Plzeň, Liberec, Olomouc and České Budějovice) also have trams. As they move along, the driver calls the stops through the microphone. Prague's tram network has 26 lines. During weekends from the end of March until November, there is also a historic tram line, no. 91 (*nostalgická linka*), from the Střešovice depot to the city centre. Tickets can be bought from attendants on board.

Night Transport

Night buses (no. 601 upwards) and trams (51 upwards) run in Prague after midnight.

Taxis

Taxis are the most comfortable, but also the most expensive method of getting around town. You can find them at taxi ranks, hail them on the street, or call them by telephone or via the Internet. Prague taxis do not come in any one colour, and their only distinctive mark is the illuminated TAXI sign on the roof. Prices vary: 40Kč for "slamming the door" and 20–30Kč for every kilometre, depending on the company.

Bicycles

Prague has many bicycle lanes, to which new ones are always being added. However, they run outside the historic centre. The traffic and cobbles mean that cycling in Prague is not particularly comfortable. Bicycles can be hired in special shops, as well as in many hotels and hostels.

Walking

If you wish to explore Prague on foot, you should equip yourself with a street map. Small maps can be obtained free of charge at tourist information offices.

The interior of Můstek metro station in Prague

Getting Around Bratislava

The best way to see the mostly pedestrianized historic centre of Slovakia's capital city is on foot. For longer journeys, or outside the centre, Bratislava has a well-developed network of bus, tram and trolleybus services, although some of the fleet have seen better days. Those who enjoy night-time entertainment can return home via the night services. Car drivers may find it difficult to get a parking space, and leaving a car illegally parked could incur a very heavy fine. Cycling is a good alternative.

Bratislava trolleybus

Buses, Trams and Trolleybuses

Bratislava has an excellent network of bus services. Some of the older vehicles are being replaced with modern ones. There are also trams (električka) running within Bratislava (and in Košice). The stops (zastávka) are marked with appropriate signs. Bratislava also has a trolleybus service, as do Košice, Prešov, Žilina and Banská Bystrica. In Bratislava, a standard ticket is valid on buses, trams and trolleybuses. You need to buy your ticket in advance and validate it on board the vehicle, or obtain a one-, two-, three- or seven-day pass if you are making several journeys.

Between the hours of 11:30pm to 4am, the capital city is served by 20 night-time lines, including trolleybuses and buses (marked with an 'N' before the numbers).

Driving and Parking

Driving is far from the best way to see Bratislava. Traffic packs the streets and there are many one-way and pedestrianized streets. Finding a place to park in Bratislava and other large towns (outside weekends and evenings) is virtually impossible.

If you do find a space, you need to pay for parking at the meters (ensure you have enough loose change), or use a ticket (parkovacia karta), on which you have to mark the time of leaving the vehicle. These tickets can be purchased at shops and kiosks. Parking charges vary from 30 cents to €2 per hour. A one-off payment for leaving a car (€1.50–€3.50 on average) is charged by car parks situated close to tourist attractions.

Non-payment or illegal parking is penalized by wheel-clamping or towing the vehicle to a police compound. Having your vehicle released in Bratislava will cost you €165.

Taxis

Taxis are available in Bratislava and other Slovak towns, and also in major tourist resorts. The average charge is €1 per kilometre. Before starting on a journey, you should ask the driver how much he will charge you for the trip, and, just to be sure, check the initial reading of the meter.

Bicycles

Bratislava and its environs have 60 marked bicycle routes; their total length is 942 km (585 miles). The number of routes are expanding, and Slovakia is currently connected to three EuroVelo routes – EV6, along the Danube; EV11, connecting Košice to Poland and Hungary; and EV13, popularly known as the Iron Curtain Trail. Bicycle lanes have also been provided in Košice, Banská Bystrica and Žilina, and their environs.

Walking

Exploring Bratislava and other major cities on foot is an excellent idea. Most of the historic attractions are clustered within a small area, and, besides, almost every town has a pedestrianized zone (pešia zóna). Tourist information offices provide a free street map of the centre of Bratislava.

One of Košice's old trams, which offer tours of the city

General Index

Page numbers in **bold** refer to main entries.

Acknowledgments

Hachette Livre Polska wishes to thank the following people at Dorling Kindersley:

Publisher
Douglas Amrine

Publishing Manager
Anna Streiffert

Managing Art Editor
Kate Poole

Project Manager
Jacky Jackson/Wordwise Associates Ltd

Consultant Editor
Ferdie McDonald

Cartography
Uma Bhattacharya, Mohammad Hassan, Stuart James, Jasneet Kaur, Casper Morris

DTP Designers
Vinod Harish, Vincent Kurien, Natasha Lu, Rakesh Pal, Alistair Richardson, Azeem Siddiqui

Factchecker
Dr Tomas Kleisner

Proofreader
Stewart Wild

Indexer
Helen Peters

Jacket Designer
Sonal Bhatt

Hachette Livre Polska also wishes to thank the following people and institutions who assisted in the preparation of this book:

Additional Text
Lucy Mallows, Beth Potter, Jakub Sito Barbara Studnik Wócikowska

Additional Illustrations
Dorota Jarymowicz

Additional Photography
Zora Groholová, Nigel Hudson, Oldřich Karasek, Ian O'Leary, Robert Pasieczny, Filip Polonský, Clive Streeter, Barbara Sudnik-Wójcikowska, Wendy Wrangham

Additional Picture Research
Marta Bescos Sanchez, Rhiannon Furbear, Ellen Root

Revisions and Relaunch Team
Ashwin Raju Adimari, Lydia Baillie, Subhashree Bharati, Jon Bousfield, Rajesh Chhibber, Louise Cleghorn, Vidushi Duggal, Zora Groholová, Amy Harrison, Integrated Publishing Solutions, Cincy Jose, Silvia Kuruczová, Maite Lantaron, Darren Longley, Nicola Malone, Bhavika Mathur, Sonal Modha, Marianne Petrou, Filip Polonský, Rada Radojicic, Erin Richards, Avijit Sengupta, Azeem Siddiqui, Deepika Verma, Tanveer Zaidi

Maps
Jarosław Talacha, Michał Zielkiewicz

The Publishers also thank the following individuals and institutions for permission to reproduce photographs or photograph their establishments; to take photographs inside their premises; and to use photographs from their archives:

Artothek (Susanne Vierthaler).
Chrám sv. Barbory, Kutná Hora, for permission to photograph inside the church.
Corbis (Bartłomiej Sych).
Kunsthistorisches Museum, Wien (Ilse Jung)
Muzeum Kroměříž (Jiři Stránský)
Muzeum Města Brna (Pavel Ciprian) for permission to photograph Špilberk.
Muzeum Jindřichohradecka (Jaroslav Pikal)
Národní památkový ústav (Jaromir Kubů) for permission to photograph inside Karlštejn Castle.
Národní památkový ústav, Brno (Zdeňka Dokoupilova) for permission to photograph inside Kroměříž Castle.
Národní Knihovna Česke Republiky v Praze (Renáta Sádlová).
Oblastní Galerie, Liberec (Zdenka Hušková).
Barbora Ondrejčáková of the International Film Festival in Karlovy Vary.
Országos Széchényi Könyvtar (Orsolya Karsay)
Obecni dům, Prague (Augustina Vaňková) for permission to photograph the interiors and for her kind help.
Náměstí na Hané Palace for permission to photograph their coach.
Jaroslav Pecha for permission to photograph inside Panna Mária church in Banská Bystrica.
Slovak National Tourism Centre (Ján Bošnovič) for materials, photographs and information, and for his extraordinary help and kindness.
Slovenská Narodná Galériá, Bratislava (Maria Čorejová).
Uměleckoprůmyslové museum v Praze (Alena Zapletalová)
Židovské Muzeum v Praze (Michael Dunayevsky).

Picture Credits
a-above; b-below/bottom; c-centre; f-far; l-left; r-right; t-top

Works of art on the pages detailed have been reproduced with the permission of the following copyright holders:

Aristide Maillol *Pomona* 1910 © ADAGP, Paris and DACS, London 2011 104bc; Alphonse Marie Mucha *The Arts: Dance* 1898 26cr, *The Arts: Music* 1898 27cl, *Poster for Sokol Movement* 1912 99bl; Marie Cernisova Toyen *The Dangerous Hour* 1942 © ADAGP, Paris and DACS, London 2011 27br.
123RF.com: Juliane Jacobs 96tr.
4Corners Images: Borchi Massimo 249br..
AKG-Images: 35bc, 36bl, 40clb, 80cla, 81bl; **Alamy Images:** Alan Copson City Pictures 33bc; Bon Appetit 374bc; CTK 93clb; Dennis Chang - CZ Prague 406cl; Radek Detinsky 394-5; Greg Balfour Evans 355tl; Peter Erik Forsberg 329b; Chris Fredriksson 361c; imageBROKER 196; isifa Image Service s.r.o. 130-1, 207b, 215b; 412br; B. O'Kane 400bl; Lubos Paukeje 343br; © Profimedia CZ s.r.o 95cl, 149tl; Robert Harding Picture Library Ltd 88; Aleksandr Ugorenkov 413br; ZUMA Press, Inc 271crb; **Anna:** 350br; **Archív Hlavniho Mesta, Prahy (Clam-Gallasuv Palác):** 41bl, 70clb, 76tr, Archiwum Zdjęć Karela Kryla: 25cr; **Art Archive** Janaček Museum Brno/ Dagli Orti 25tc; **Artothek:** 26cr, 27cl, 27br; **AV Studio:** 266tl, 267tl, 267crb; **AWL Images:** Walter Bibikow 152-3, 172-3, Gavin Hellier 226, Steve Outram 344-5, Ian Trower 252.
Bankov Hotel: 357tl, 379tr; **Bistro St Germain:** 376br;
Bridgeman Art Library: Jean-Loup Charmet Collection 45tl, 74cla; *The Meeting of Napoleon and Francis I,* by Jean

Antoine Gros. 42crb; Rosegarten Museum, Constance 38cla.
Café Savoy: 358cl; **Cafe Lounge**: 364bc; **České Švýcarsko o. p. s.**: 191crb; **Chateau Mčely**: 369tl; **Corbis**: 24br, 36clb, 43cb, 44cl, 44tr, 103tr; Alinari Archives 176bl; Paul Almasy 48crb, Archivo Iconografico, S.A. 42cl; Austrian Archives; Haus-, Hof- und Staatsarchiv, Vienna 36bc, 270crb; Bettmann 28c, 43br, 48tl, 48br, 133tr; Stefano Bianchetti 269tr; Eye Ubiquitous/John Dakers 410tr; FLPA/Philip Perry 257br; Marc Garanger 271tr; Hulton-Deutsch Collection 24tr, (Lancaster) 49tl; JAI /Ken Scicluna 214; George D. Lepp 19tc; Buddy Mays 32cra; Gail Mooney 361tl; Ali Meyer 42tr, 268cl; Nature Picture Library/Wild Wonders of Europe/Ruiz 181b; © Reuters 260c, 390cla; Reuters/Yannis Behrakis 393tr; Reuters/Mike Blake 393bl; Reuters/Petr Josek 390bl; D. Robert & Lorri Franz 257bl; Galen Rowell 191tl; Rykoff Collection 46br; Scheufler Collection 45cla, 45br, 46crb, 46bl, 270tl; SOPA/SOPA RF/ Pietro Canali 72; Liba Taylor 254bl; Roger Tidman 257bc; Peter Turnley 18b, 49cb, 49bl; Miroslav Zajic 48cr; Zefa 45cra; **Joe Cornish**: 99cr.
Roman Delikát: 268bl; **La Degustation**: 359br, 366bl;;
Dreamstime.com: Alessandro0770 13bl; Andrey Andronov 85br; Anyaivanova 74br; Ievgeniia Arkhipova 294; Jennifer Barrow 137b; Helena Bilková 257clb; Lukas Blazek 180; Czanner 328; Eduardo Gonzalez Diaz 85br; Dennis Dolkens 248bl; Inna Felker 77cr; Frenta 11tr; Marian Garai 276; Gary718 50-1; Nataliya Hora 12bl; Ispace 236tr; Boris Jaroscak 246bl; Johnnydevil 120; Pavel Kohout 136; Lerka555 11clb; Miroslav Liska 249tr; Peter Lovás 254t; Marina99 16; Mikhail Markovskiy 141tl; Jozef Mikat 306-7; Mirekdeml 12tc, 75ca; Olgacov 253b; Stanislav Říha 13tr; Rorem 249br, Sborisov 77tc; Scanrail 116-7; Richard Semik 213br, 248tc; Serrnovik 310; Spectral-design 10br; Tomas1111 2-3, 244-5, 272-3; Tupungato 413tl; Jiri Vaclavek 91c; Martin Valigursky 322-3; Vanessak 54; Voltan1 247t; Zoom-zoom 247bc.
ECB: 405 all.
Fotolia: mirvav 277b.
Getty Images: Samuel Kubani 409bl; Massimo Pizzotti 282tr; Stephen Saks 160.; **Glowimages**: LOOK-foto/Franz Marc Frei 158tr; **Grand Hotel Pupp**: 351tc, 371tr.
Hotel Bratislava: 354br.
International Film Festival, Karlovy Vary: 31cr; **Istockphoto.com**: narvikk 408bl.
Josef: Stefan Schuetz 349tl; **Jurkovičuv Dum**: 353tl.
Kancelář Prezidenta Republiky: 35br; **Oldřich Karasek**: 20cr, 22cl, 30cl, 33cra, 60tr, 61bl, 92bc, 210bl, 211crb, 211cra, 211tl, 341tl, 362cl; **Jaroslav Klenovsky**: 237cb; **Koishi**: 375t; **Krumlovsky Mlyn**: 358br, 370bc; ;
Jaroslav Klenovsky: 241cr; **Dalibor Kusák**: 106br; **Kunsthistorisches Museum**, Wien: portrait of *Emperor Sigismund*, by Pisanello 38cb.
Lebrecht Music and Arts Photo Library: RA 29bc; **Lehka hlava, Prague**: Dagmar Hájková 365tr; **Leonardo Media Ltd.**: 359br; **The Lobkowicz Collections**: 57clb.

Mary Evans Picture Library: 38tr, 39tc, 43tc, 46tl, 47tr, 47clb, 47bl; **Massimo Ristorante**: 377tr; **Mestske Muzeum, Bratislava**: 268–9c; **Müllerova vila**: 107br; **Museum of the History of Science**, Oxford: Samantha von Gerbig, 41tl; **Muzeum Hlavní ho Mésta Prahy**: 44-5; **Muzeum Kroměříž**: *Pink Portrait* by Max Švabinsky 27tr.
Na Stodolci: 372bl; **Národní Galerie v Praze**: Graficka sbirka 39br, 41crb, 69br, 97br; Klaster sv Anezky 79cl; Klaster sv. Jiri 26br, 34, Šternberský Palac 62–3 all; Veletrzni Palac 104–5 all; **Národní Knihovna České Republiky**: 40tl; **Narodni Museum v Praze**: Vlasta Dvorakova 37cr, 38bl, 38–9c, 39cb, 39cr, 40bc, 41bc, 67br, 76br; Muzeum Antonina Dvořáka Muzeum Bedricha Smetany 44bl; Tyrsovo Muzeum 99bl; **Národni Památkový Ústav**: *St Elizabeth*, by Master Teodoryk 26cl; **Nota Bene**: 367tl.
Oblastní Galerie, Liberec: *Manor House in Benatky*, by August Pettenkofen 185c; **Obrazárna Pražskeho Hradu**: 58tl; **Official Tourism and Travel Guide to Bratislava**: 281ca; **Országos Széchényi Könyvtar**: *Tartar's Raid* miniature 266crb.
Pawel Pasternak: 29tr; **Penzion Nostalgia**: 347tl, 356bl; **Photolibrary.com**: Jon Arnold Images: 8–9; **Pivovar ERB**: 378bl; **Bohumír Prokúpek**:28cla.
Regional Museum in Vysoké Mýto: Jiří Junek 28br; **Restaurant Le Monde**:359tl; **Robert Harding Picture Library**: Michael Jenner 66cla; Peter Scholey 67cra; **ROPID**: 411tl, 414ca.
SaSaZu, Prague: 368bl; **Slovak National Tourism Centre**: 31ca, 260b, 261cra, 262cra, 263bl, 316bl, 316cl, 316tr, 317tl, 317cra, 317crb, 321br, 326cr, 343bl, 343cb, 343ca, 347bl, 363bl, 382br, 386cla, 386bc, 387tr, 393cla, 409c, 409tr; **Slovenska Narodna Galeria**, Bratislava: *Jan Francisci, Captain of Slovak Insurgents*, painting by Peter Michal Buhúň: 264; **Státní Ústredni Archiv**: 36tc; **Státní Židovské Muzeum**: 53tr, 81br; **Lubomír Stiburek**: 91ca; **Barbara Sudnik-Wójcikowska**: 21clb; 256cl, 256cr, 256bc, 257tl, 257cr; **Svatovítský Pokland, Pražhý Hrad**: 37cl, 37bc.
U Jezirka: 352bl; **U Pinkasú Restaurant**: 360cl; **Uměleckoprümyslové Múzeum v Praze**: 42bc, 99br; **Gabriel Urbánek/UMP**: 27bl.
Courtesy of Vintage Design Hotel SAX Prague: 348bl.
Peter Wilson: 108br.
Zelena Žaba: 373tl.

Front Endpaper: **Alamy Images**: imageBROKER Rcr; **AWL Images**: Gavin Hellier Lbc; **Corbis**: JAI/Ken Scicluna Lclb; **Dreamstime.com**: Ievgeniia Arkhipova Rbl; Lukas Blazek Rc; Czanner Rbr; Marian Garai Lbr; Gary718 Ltr; Johnnydevil Rtl; Pavel Kohout Rtc; Serrnovik Rbc; **Getty Images**: Stephen Saks Rtr.

Jacket
Front and spine top: **Alamy Images**: Luis Dafos.
All other images © Dorling Kindersley
For further information see: www.dkimages.com

Special Editions of DK Travel Guides
DK Travel Guides can be purchased in bulk quantities at discounted prices for use in promotions or as premiums. We are also able to offer special editions and personalized jackets, corporate imprints, and excerpts from all of our books, tailored specifically to meet your own needs.

To find out more, please contact:
in the United States **SpecialSales@dk.com**
in the UK **travelspecialsales@uk.dk.com**
in Canada DK Special Sales at **general@ tourmaline.ca**
in Australia **business.development@pearson. com.au**

English–Czech Phrase Book

In an Emergency

Where is the telephone?	**Kde je telefon?**
the nearest hospital?	**nejbližší nemocnice?**
Help!	**Pomoc!**
Please call a doctor!	**Zavolejte doktora!**
Please call an ambulance!	**Zavolejte sanitku!**
Please call the police!	**Zavolejte policii!**

Communication Essentials

Yes/No	**Ano/Ne**
Please	**Prosím**
Thank you	**Děkuji vám**
Excuse me/forgive me	**Promiňte**
Hello/Good morning	**Dobrý den**
Goodbye	**Na shledanou**
Good evening	**Dobrý večer**
Goodnight	**Dobrou noc**
What is it?	**Co to je?**
Why?	**Proč**
Where?	**Kde?**
When?	**Kdy?**
today	**dnes**
tomorrow	**zítra**
yesterday	**včera**
morning	**ráno**
afternoon	**odpoledne**
evening	**večer**
there	**tam**
here	**tady, zde**
How are you?	**Jak se máte?**
Very well thank you	**Velmi dobře, děkuji**
Where is/are…?	**Kde je/jsou …?**
How far is it to …?	**Jak je to daleko?**
Do you speak English?	**Mluvíte anglicky?**
I don't understand	**Nerozumím**
Pardon?	**Prosím?**
big/large	**velký**
small	**malý**
hot	**horký**
cold	**studený**
open	**otevřeno**
closed	**zavřeno**
entrance	**vchod**
exit	**východ**
toilets	**toalety, záchod**
men/gentlemen	**muži, páni**
women/ladies	**ženy, dámy**
vacant	**volno**
engaged	**obsazeno**

Sightseeing

art gallery	**galerie**
castle	**hrad, zámek**
church	**kostel**
garden	**zahrada**
old town/city	**staré město**
palace	**palác / zámek**
railway station	**nádraží**
square	**náměstí**
street	**ulice**
stop (bus, tram)	**zastávka**
theatre	**divadlo**
ticket	**lístek**
tourist information	**turistické informace**

Shopping

I would like…	**Chtěl(a) bych …**
Do you have … ?	**Máte …?**
How much does it cost?	**Kolik to stojí?**
What time do you open/close?	**V kolik otevíráte/zavíráte?**
expensive	**drahý**
cheap	**levný**
size	**velikost**
number (size)	**číslo**
colour	**barva**

Shops

antiques	**starožitnictví**
bakery	**pekárna**
bank	**banka**
bazaar/market	**trh**
bookshop	**knihkupectví**
camera shop	**obchod s fotoaparáty**
clothes shop	**oděvy**
department store	**obchodní dům**
glass, china	**sklo, porcelán**
news kiosk	**novinový stánek**
pharmacy	**lékárna**
post office	**pošta**
shoe shop	**obuv**

In a Hotel

Do you have a vacant room?	**Máte volný pokoj?**
with a bathroom	**s koupelnou**
with a shower	**se sprchou**
I have a reservation	**Mám rezervaci**
key	**klíč**
porter	**vrátný**

Eating Out

Do you have a table free for .?	**Máte volný stůl pro …?**
I'd like to reserve a table	**Chtěl(a) bych rezervovat stůl**
I am a vegetarian	**Jsem vegetarián(ka)**
Waiter!	**Pane vrchní!**
The bill, please	**Prosím, účet**
breakfast	**snídaně**
lunch	**oběd**
dinner	**večeře**
fixed-price menu	**standardní menu**
starter/snack	**předkrm**
dish of the day	**nabídka dne**
main course	**hlavní jídlo**
dessert	**dezert**
wine list	**nápojový lístek**
tip	**spropitné**
bill	**účet**

Menu

bramborové hranolky	chips
brambory	potatoes
chléb	bread
citrón	lemon
cukr	sugar
čaj	tea
džus	juice
houby	mushrooms
houska	roll
hovězí	beef
husa	goose
jablko	apple
jahody	strawberries
jehněčí	lamb
kachna	duck
kapr	carp
káva	coffee
knedlíky	dumplings
krůta	turkey
kuře	chicken
máslo	butter
maso	meat
minerálka	mineral water
šumivá	fizzy
nešumivá	still
mléko	milk
ovoce	fruit
palačinky	pancakes
pečené	baked/roasted
pepř	pepper
polévka	soup
pivo	beer
ryba	fish
rýže	rice
salát	lettuce, salad
smažené	fried
sůl	salt
sýr	cheese
šunka	ham
uzeniny	cold meats, butchers
vejce	egg
vepřové	pork
víno	wine
voda	water
zákusky	cakes
zelenina	vegetables
zmrzlina	ice cream

English–Slovak Phrase Book

In an Emergency

Where is the telephone?	Kde je telefón?
the nearest hospital?	najbližšia nemocnica?
Help!	Pomoc!
Please call a doctor!	Prosím, zavolajte lekára!
Please call an ambulance!	Prosím, zavolajte sanitku!
Please call the police!	Prosím, zavolajte políciu!

Communication Essentials

Yes/No	Áno/nie
Please	Prosím
Thank you	Ďakujem
Excuse me/forgive me	Prepáčte
Hello/Good morning	Dobrý deň
Goodbye	Dovidenia
Good evening	Dobrý večer
Goodnight	Dobrú noc
What is it?	Čo to je?
Why?	Prečo?
Where?	Kde?
When?	Kedy?
today	dnes
tomorrow	zajtra
yesterday	včera
morning	ráno
afternoon	odpoludnia
evening	večer
there	tam
here	tu, sem
How are you?	Ako sa máš?
Very well thank you	Ďakujem, dobre!
Where is/are…?	Kde je/sú…?
How far is it to …?	Ako ďaleko je do…?
Do you speak English?	Hovoríte po anglicky?
I don't understand	Nerozumiem
Pardon?	Prosím?
big/large	veľký
small	malý
hot	horúci
cold	studený
open	otvorené
closed	zatvorené
entrance	vchod
exit	východ
toilets	toalety, WC
men/gentlemen	muži, páni
women/ladies	ženy, damy
vacant	voľné
engaged	obsadené

Sightseeing

art gallery	galéria
castle	hrad, zámok
church	kostol
garden	záhrada
old town/city	Staré Město
palace	palác, kaštieľ
railway station	železničná stanica
square	námestie
street	ulica
stop (bus, tram)	zastávka
theatre	divadlo
ticket	listok
tourist information	turistické informačné centrum

Shopping

I would like…	Chcel/a/ by som…
Do you have… ?	Máte…?
How much does it cost?	Koľko to stojí?
What time do you open/close?	O ktorej otvárate/zatvárate?
expensive	drahý
cheap	lacný
size	veľkosť
number (size)	číslo
colour	farba

Shops

antiques	antikvariát, starožitnosti
bakery	pekáreň
bank	banka
bazaar/market	tržnica
bookshop	kníhkupectvo
camera shop	fotoslužba
clothes shop	odevy
department store	obchodný dom
glass, china	sklo, porcelán
news kiosk	novinový stánok
pharmacy	lekáreň
post office	pošta
shoe shop	obuv

In a Hotel

Do you have a vacant room?	Máte voľnú izbu?
with a bathroom	s kúpeľňou
with a shower	so sprchou
I have a reservation	Mám reserváciu
key	Kľúč
porter	vrátnik

Eating Out

Do you have a table free for?	Máte voľný stôl pre…?
I'd like to reserve a table	Chcel/a/ by som zarezervovať stôl
I am a vegetarian	Som vegetarián /ka/
Waiter!	Čašník!
The bill, please	Prosím si účet
breakfast	raňajky
lunch	obed
dinner	večera
fixed-price menu	pevná / cena
dish of the day	ponuka dňa
starter/snack	predjedlo
main course	hlavné jedlo
dessert	dezert, múčnik
wine list	vínna karta
tip	tringelt
bill	účet

Menu

bravčové	pork
čaj	tea
chlieb	bread
čierne korenie mleté	pepper
citrón	lemon
cukor	sugar
džús	juice
hovädzie	beef
huby	mushrooms
hus	goose
koláč	roll
jablko	apple
jahňacie	lamb
jahody	strawberries
kačka	duck
kapor	carp
káva	coffee
knedle	dumplings
kuracina	chicken
maslo	butter
mäso	meat
minerálna voda	mineral water
sýtená	fizzy
nesýtená	still
mlieko	milk
morčacie	turkey
ovocie	fruit
palacinky	pancakes
pečené	baked/roasted
polievka	soup
pivo	beer
ryba	fish
ryža	rice
šalát	lettuce, salad
soľ	salt
syr	cheese
šunka	ham
údeniny	cold meats, butchers
vajíčka	eggs
víno	wine
voda	water
vyprážané	fried
zákusky	cakes
zelenina	vegetables
zemiakové hranolky	chips
zemiaky	potatoes
zmrzlina	ice cream

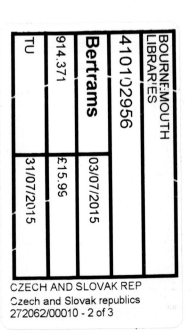

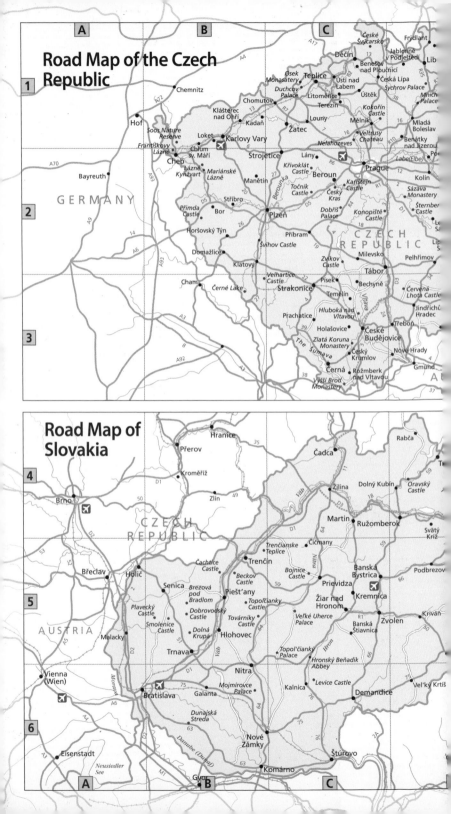

Road Map of the Czech Republic

GERMANY

Chemnitz

Hof

Bayreuth

Soos Nature Reserve
Františkovy Lázně
Cheb
Loket
Chlum sv. Máří
Lázně Kynžvart
Mariánské Lázně

Kláštěrec nad Ohří
Kadaň
Chomutov
Osek Monastery
Duchcov Palace
Teplice
Ústí nad Labem
Litoměřice
Terezín
Louny

Karlovy Vary
Žatec
Strojetice

Mělník
Veltrusy Chateau
Nelahozeves
Lány
Prague
Kokořín Castle
Úštěk

Děčín
České Švýcarsko
Frýdlant
Benešov nad Ploučnicí
Jablonné v Podještědí
Lib
Česká Lípa
Sychrov Palace
Mnich Palace
Mladá Boleslav
Benátky nad Jizerou
Labe (Elbe)

Přimda Castle
Bor
Stříbro
Manětín
Plzeň
Křivoklát Castle
Beroun
Točník Castle
Český Kras
Karlštejn Castle
Dobříš Palace
Konopiště Castle
Kolín
Sázava Monastery
Šternberg Castle

CZECH REPUBLIC

Horšovský Týn
Domažlice
Cham
Černé Lake
Klatovy
Švihov Castle
Příbram
Velhartice Castle
Zvíkov Castle
Milevsko
Tábor
Pelhřimov
Bechyně
Písek
Temelín
Strakonice
Prachatice
Hluboká nad Vltavou
Holašovice
Zlatá Koruna Monastery
Český Krumlov
České Budějovice
Třeboň
Červená Lhota Castle
Jindřichů Hradec
Nové Hrady
Gmünd
Černá
Rožmberk nad Vltavou
Vyšší Brod Monastery
The Šumava

Road Map of Slovakia

Hranice
Přerov
Kroměříž
Brno
Zlín

CZECH REPUBLIC

Rabča
Čadca
Žilina
Dolný Kubín
Oravský Castle
Svätý Kríž
Martin
Ružomberok
Čičmany
Trenčianske Teplice
Trenčín
Bojnice Castle
Banská Bystrica
Prievidza
Kremnica
Podbrezov
Žiar nad Hronom
Zvolen
Banská Štiavnica
Kriváň

Břeclav
Holíč
Senica
Čachtice Castle
Brezová pod Bradlom
Beckov Castle
Piešťany
Topolčianky Castle
Plavecký Castle
Dobrovodský Castle
Smolenice Castle
Dolná Krupá
Tovarníky Castle
Hlohovec
Trnava
Veľké Uherce Palace
Topolčianky Palace
Hronský Beňadik Abbey
Demandice
Veľký Krtíš

AUSTRIA

Malacky
Bratislava
Galanta
Mojmírovce Palace
Nitra
Kalnica
Levice Castle

Vienna (Wien)
Eisenstadt
Neusiedler See
Dunajská Streda
Nové Zámky
Győr
Komárno
Štúrovo
Danube (Dunaj)